WAR IN WORLD HISTORY

VOLUME **2** SINCE 1500

WAR IN WORLD HISTORY

Society, Technology, and War
from Ancient Times to the Present

Stephen Morillo
Wabash College

Jeremy Black
University of Exeter

Paul Lococo
Leeward Community College, Hawaii

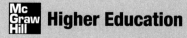
Mc Graw Hill **Higher Education**

Boston   Burr Ridge, IL   Dubuque, IA   New York   San Francisco   St. Louis
Bangkok   Bogotá   Caracas   Kuala Lumpur   Lisbon   London   Madrid   Mexico City
Milan   Montreal   New Delhi   Santiago   Seoul   Singapore   Sydney   Taipei   Toronto

Published by McGraw-Hill, an imprint of The McGraw-Hill Companies, Inc., 1221 Avenue of the Americas, New York, NY 10020. Copyright © 2009. All rights reserved. No part of this publication may be reproduced or distributed in any form or by any means, or stored in a database or retrieval system, without the prior written consent of The McGraw-Hill Companies, Inc., including, but not limited to, in any network or other electronic storage or transmission, or broadcast for distance learning.

This book is printed on acid-free paper.

1 2 3 4 5 6 7 8 9 0 QPD/QPD 0 9 8

ISBN: 978-0-07-052585-6
MHID: 0-07-052585-4

Editor in Chief: *Michael Ryan*
Publisher: *Frank Mortimer*
Sponsoring Editor: *Jon-David Hague*
Editorial Coordinator: *Sora Kim*
Marketing Manager: *Pamela Cooper*
Production Editor: *Holly Paulsen*
Manuscript Editor: *Thomas L. Briggs*
Design Manager: *Margarite Reynolds*
Text Designer: *Linda Robertson*
Cover Designer: *Margarite Reynolds, Asylum Studios, and Stephen Morillo*
Art Editors: *Sonia Brown and Robin Mouat*
Illustrators: *Mapping Specialists, Dartmouth Publishing, and Stephen Morillo*
Photo Research Coordinator: *Alexandra Ambrose*
Photo Research: *Emily Tietz, Editorial Image, LLC*
Production Supervisor: *Louis Swaim*
Composition: *10/12 Galliard by ICC Macmillan Inc.*
Printing: *45# New Era Matte Recycled, Quebecor World*

Cover: "Officer," painting of a modern soldier by author Stephen Morillo. Photo by Kim Milone Gleason.

Credits: The credits section for this book begins on page C-1 and is considered an extension of the copyright page.

Library of Congress Cataloging-in-Publication Data
Morillo, Stephen.
   War in world history : society, technology, and war from ancient times to the present. Volume 2, since 1500
Stephen Morillo, Jeremy Black, Paul Lococo.
      p.   cm.
   Includes index.
   ISBN-13: 978-0-07-052584-9 (v. 1 : alk. paper)
   ISBN-10: 0-07-052584-6 (v. 1 : alk. paper)
   ISBN-13: 978-0-07-052585-6 (v. 2 : alk. paper)
   ISBN-10: 0-07-052585-4 (v. 2 : alk. paper)   1. Military art and science—History.
2. Military history.   3. War.   I. Black, Jeremy.   II. Lococo, Paul.   III. Title.
   U27.M63 2008
   355.02—dc22   2008027488

www.mhhe.com

From SRM to Lynne, who has never known me without this project!

Contents

Preface

This book is a history of the world as viewed through the lens of war. It is designed for use at the college level as a textbook for military history courses or as a textbook or supplemental reading for world history courses. As a general introduction to and synthesis of this topic, we believe it will also interest general readers, especially those interested in military history. But while military history is undoubtedly a popular topic, popularity alone cannot justify a new textbook in intellectual terms. What can a world history textbook focused on warfare offer to students and teachers, in college or outside the curriculum?

WHY WAR?

Warfare has been one of humankind's most prevalent activities throughout history. Military preparations and organization have been central to the internal structures of many human communities. War itself is one of the major ways in which those human communities have interacted with each other, and it has often been intimately connected to other significant forms of contact and influence, whether as a vector for spreading disease, an accompaniment to or form of trade and economic exchange, or a partner of religious expansion.

Because making war has been such a central activity of so many human communities, it makes a good lens through which to view the rest of history, providing a thematic connection among many facets of human experience, as well as being a topic important in its own right. The stresses of war sometimes cast a particularly revealing light on social structures, exposing the strengths and weaknesses of institutions and testing the cultural cohesion of communities in ways that few other activities do.

Despite this, warfare has been largely unexplored up to now as a theme in world history. True world history textbooks are far more common now than they were even ten years ago. Many of the most recent, in attempting to organize the mountain of material world historians face, have begun structuring their narratives around themes such as technology or cultural contact. Some have even taken an almost entirely thematic approach, exploring various cross-cultural topics, such as the family, religion and the state, or frontiers, from a global perspective. War almost never shows up in these lists of themes except perhaps as an aspect of the conflicts of the twentieth century.

This neglect of military history is doubly odd given that the last twenty-five years has seen an explosion of specialist studies in the field, works that have fundamentally redefined military history as an arena of academic investigation. The nineteenth- and early-twentieth-century traditions of military historiography, dominated by ex-military men writing about decisive battles and the "Art of War" for other ex-military men and amateur war buffs, nearly killed the field for serious historians. But since the mid-1970s, the "new military history" has revitalized military studies. European medieval historians, examining a society organized for war, played a leading role in creating the new military history; more recently, fierce and productive controversies over the early modern period's Military Revolution and the modern age's "revolution in military affairs" have extended the new approaches to histories of war to many times and places.

Central to the new military history has been the process of placing warfare in context or, more accurately, in its many contexts—socioeconomic, institutional, and cultural. One of the aims of this book, therefore, is to synthesize and integrate the new military history from a global perspective. As a military history text, then, we attempt always to examine war and warriors as parts of functioning societies. The mutual relationships between war and its contexts—both the effects of war on society and the effects of society on war (including the development of new technologies as part of both)—are fundamental to understanding why wars have been fought in the many ways history has witnessed. Unlike many histories of warfare, we integrate naval warfare and maritime activity (as well as air war in the twentieth century) into this big picture of the development of armed force through the millennia. In general, the aims and methods of the new military history have shaped the focus of our text.

Focus

Thus, what we write about is war and its contexts. Students of military operations will find some campaign history here. The vast scope of chronology and geography entailed by a global history necessarily limits the amount of detailed narrative possible. The emphasis is on analysis rather than storytelling. Nevertheless, each chapter highlights battles and campaigns that demonstrate classic and sometimes unchanging aspects of the "Art of War," as well as illustrating changes in tactics and practices in response to new challenges, weapons, and environments.

But the larger emphasis, as noted above, is on contexts. Three broad areas stand out in this respect.

First, **political and institutional contexts:** The institutional organization of warfare in all societies has always had important connections to the powers of elites and states and to methods of rulership and government. The structures of power place important constraints on military organization and activity—for example, in influencing who can be recruited and how. The exercise of force has also been a consistent and often paramount factor in the distribution of political power within polities; politics and political institutions in turn affect the use of warfare as a tool of state policy. War not only is affected by but also affects its institutional context.

Second, **social and economic contexts:** This area includes the effects of class structure (closely related to political contexts) and the issue of economic support for military activity. Economic productivity and the technologies of transportation shape logistics in decisive ways, and logistics—the art of keeping military forces in being—has been perhaps the dominant constraint on methods and patterns of waging war throughout history. The economic sphere also includes technology generally. Changing weaponry springs to mind naturally when technology is mentioned in relation to warfare, but technologies that were either nonmilitary, such as the printing press, or only military tangentially or partially, such as the steam engine, have consistently played a major role in shaping how war has been waged. Finally, armed conflict has always had significant effects on societies and economies ("the effect of war on society" was an early rallying cry of the new military history), most often wreaking havoc and destruction, but in a significant minority of cases stimulating economic growth and inventiveness.

Third, **cultural contexts:** From the point of view of world history, war is not just an activity, it is a nexus of cultural production. Given the elite status of many warrior classes in world history, warrior values have shaped many cultures. War and religion have frequently been in alliance (holy or unholy depending on one's perspective). Many cultures have placed various ritual constraints on the practice of war, while reactions to warfare ranging from glorification to condemnation are probably rivaled only by love as a dominant theme in world literature, with war far outdistancing romance in popularity in many cultures.

War literature as a source for military history brings us to another aspect of the focus of this volume. The sources available from the world's many societies and the amount of secondary historical investigation published for different areas vary tremendously. A work of synthesis such as this one is dependent on the specialist work of many previous scholars and is inevitably shaped by these questions of availability. In our case, the result is an emphasis on the major Eurasian civilizations and, up to 1700, the central Asian nomads with whom those civilizations coexisted. Within that ecumene, the literature tends to place somewhat more emphasis on western Europe than some other areas of historical inquiry. This focus is almost inevitable for the last two centuries of European military dominance (with a few important exceptions). Before that time, the merits of such emphasis are more debatable but were for us less a matter of debate than of necessity. While we have tried always to keep our perspective global, we must await further research for a more even balance of details from across Eurasia.

We have undoubtedly shorted the military histories of sub-Saharan Africa, the pre-Columbian Americas, Australia, and Oceania. Partly, this is again a matter of the available secondary literature. But it is a matter partly of defining war and looking only at what rises over our own arbitrarily chosen "military horizon," one of two preliminary questions we must examine before proceeding.

TWO PRELIMINARY QUESTIONS

These two questions, to which there are no clear answers, are these: What counts as *war,* and what are the origins of war in human history?

With regard to the first question, there is clearly a vast range of human violence. But the boundaries separating one sort of violence from another—in particular, organized warfare from more individual and perhaps random acts of violence—are fuzzy in the extreme. Limiting a definition of warfare to "organized state activity" not only eliminates many violent tribal conflicts that probably should count as some form of warfare but also is too restrictive even if we don't consider tribes. Much of the armed conflict in early medieval Europe and most of the aggressive activity of nomadic peoples from the Asian steppes have been unproblematically treated as warfare despite the fact that "states" among some of those peoples existed only tenuously at best and had no monopoly on war making even where they did exist. Mere numbers cannot serve to distinguish true warfare from something less, for the violent application of armed force by states has often been carried out by remarkably small forces. Attempts to distinguish "real" warfare from more ritualized forms of violence in terms of seriousness of intent or casualty rates fail both for vagueness and because almost all forms of warfare have had a significant ritualistic element, which simply removes the question one step without resolving it. In short, there are no clear criteria for the ranking of human violent activity on a continuum from murder to melee to missile strike.

The very attempt to make such divisions, however, points up the near universality of warfare, at least under broader definitions, as a feature of human culture. This brings us to the question of the origins of war.

There is a vast and complex literature on this subject, and one that is changing rapidly. The investigations span the fields of evolutionary biology and evolutionary psychology, neuroscience and brain studies, anthropology, sociology, and history. As yet, however, no clear consensus has emerged. This is in part because any explanation for the origins of war depends on how war is defined: Organized warfare as a cultural invention of complex, hierarchical cultures clearly differs in origin, at least to some extent, from the sorts of conflicts hunter-gatherer tribes may have engaged in. The lack of consensus also derives from the politically charged nature of the topic. Explanations for the origins of war are taken, rightly or wrongly, to have implications for the issue of the inevitability of war versus possibilities for modern peace movements.

The topic is also politically charged, at least potentially, in terms of gender, because war has been and continues to be largely a male activity, even when recent gender integration of armed forces is taken into account. In the past, of course, females have had close connections to warfare as victims of rape, abduction, and killing; as producers in the economies that supported war; as camp followers, wives, and a key part of "home fronts"; as cementers of alliances through marriage; and as pretexts for going to war, even if there were never a Helen who saw a Troy. But females have participated in war only occasionally as leaders and even more rarely as fighters, a fact that complicates both the explanations for and the politics of explaining the origins of war.

In this text, we will answer the first question, of what counts as war, only by implication, and our answer is probably arbitrary at that. We will attempt to answer the second question, about the origins of war, briefly in Chapter 1. This introduction will lead us quickly to the established presence of war in the earliest civilizations of southwest Asia—ancient city walls speak eloquently to the necessities of communal defense even at that early stage of settled cultures—and simply trace its evolution since then. Does the near universal presence of war in history mean that war is an inevitable part of the human condition? Perhaps, but until very recently, slavery was a near universal feature of human societies. It is now much less common. Conditions change, and the organized responses of communities evolve accordingly. Our job as historians is to help understand the past. Predicting the future is far trickier.

ORGANIZATION: CHRONOLOGICAL SECTIONS

In tracing the evolution of warfare through the ages and around the globe, we have divided this study into six chronological parts of five chapters each. In the first five parts, four of the chapters cover warfare on land, divided along geographic and cultural lines. The fifth chapter examines naval warfare and maritime activity from a global and comparative perspective. By the sixth part, land, sea, and, increasingly, air warfare are woven together in chapters that are all global. The parts are as follows.

Part 1: The Ancient World, 2000 BCE–400 CE. This section moves from the rise of the earliest armies, built first around infantry and then the war chariot, perhaps the world's first complex weapons system, to the armies of the classical worlds of Greece, Persia, Rome, India, and China. The section examines the creation of the cultures of war among early civilizations, the rise and perfection of massed infantry armies, and the invention of galley warfare in the Mediterranean.

Part 2: The Age of Migration and Invasion, 400–1100. This section begins with an examination of nomadic life and warfare on the central Asian steppes, and the threat that nomadic peoples posed through several millennia to settled societies. From the Chinese frontiers to the Western Roman Empire, this was an age shaped by the forces of migration and nomadic invasion, including at sea, where nomadic peoples carried out one of the two major types of maritime activity.

Part 3: The Age of Traditions in Conflict, 1100–1500. Major nomadic conquests, culminating in the Mongol Empire, continued in this period as well, joined by religious crusades and merchant activity as forces of increasing cultural interchange. Growing merchant activity and improved technology began to transform the potentials of naval power, while interaction both spread ideas and techniques of warfare farther afield and threw the particular characteristics of separate military traditions into sharper relief.

Part 4: The Dawn of Global Warfare, 1500–1750. Gunpowder weaponry dominated this period. In Europe, an ongoing transformation reached revolutionary proportions, while cannon and musketry were implicated in military transformations in much of Asia and in the taming of the nomadic threat to settled societies. Above all, guns and ships launched the new age of global integration, beginning with the conquest of the Americas, and created a new age of naval power that was no longer simply an adjunct to land warfare.

Part 5: The Age of Revolutions and Imperialism, 1750–1914. Eighteenth-century linear tactics and the first attempts at raising mass armies in revolutionary and Napoleonic France initiated a period of rapid social, technological, and economic change, with direct and revolutionary implications for the practices of warfare. Industrialization, mass armies, and the beginnings of a firepower transformation launched European nations on the path to global dominance. At sea, the perfection of the age of sail gave way to ironclads and naval arms races.

Part 6: The Age of Global Conflict, 1914–Present. Rapid technological change continued to transform warfare as first firepower and then transportation and maneuver saw revolutionary advances. The results were played out on the battlefields of two world wars, as military doctrine struggled to keep up with the pace of change both before and after 1945. War in the air joined war on land and sea, and by the late twentieth century, the use of combined-armed forces in terrains and theaters around the world, often against unconventional opponents in unconventional wars, posed new problems for the planning and execution of military operations.

ORGANIZATION: VOLUME DIVISIONS

The standard edition of this text is available in a two-volume format split at roughly 1500: Volume 1 includes Parts 1–3 and Volume 2 includes Parts 4–6. This format follows the usual division of western and world civilization courses, for which this book can be used as a supplementary (or even main) text, and allows a standard semester split of military history survey courses.

But teachers using this text should note that a number of other options are readily and easily available through McGraw-Hill's Primus system for custom-published texts. Simply go to Primus on the McGraw-Hill Higher Education website at www.mhhe.com/primis, choose Social Sciences/Humanities and then History, and choose *War in World History* from the available texts. Then create your own splits. You can order single parts by themselves. Those on a quarter system can create three volumes: up to 1100 (Parts 1 and 2), from 1100 to 1750 (Parts 3 and 4), and since 1750 (Parts 5 and 6).

There is no limit to what Primus will let you do. Interested in teaching a naval history survey? Put together Chapters 5, 10, 15, 20, and 25, and you've got naval history from the dawn of boats to the beginning of the twentieth century. Focused on European land warfare? Chapters 7, 12, 16, 21, 22, and 23 cover the topic from 400 to 1900; add Chapters 3 and 4 for Greece and Rome and Part 6 for war since 1900. *War in World History* gives you comprehensive coverage. Primus gives you customizable flexibility. The combination lets you build the course you want to teach.

FEATURES

Within the chronological sections, *War in World History* offers a number of features designed to enhance the usefulness of the text. Each chapter includes, in addition to the main text, material set off in boxes that deals in more detail with some aspect of military history. We have included three types of boxed material, each aimed at illuminating a different aspect of the topic.

Sources boxes provide selections from primary source material, giving students a window into the past, a look at the writings professional historians use to draw their conclusions, and the opportunity to draw their own.

Highlights boxes focus on particular battles, sieges, or campaigns, providing the opportunity to examine operational details and aspects of specific strategies and tactics not possible in the course of the main text.

Issues boxes raise and explore historiographical controversies—how historians are currently arguing about important issues in military history—and examine historical topics of general or long-term relevance in a comparative perspective and in the framework of the content of the chapter.

In addition to the boxed material, each chapter concludes with a short list of **Suggested Readings** on the chapter's topics. **Maps and illustrations** act as visual guides to the geography of politics, campaigns, and battles, and show the appearance of warriors and warfare, including arms, weapons, and fortifications, in ways that words cannot convey. Finally, each five-chapter part concludes with a **Commentary** section that sums up the key themes of the five chapters and examines global and comparative developments outside the geographic framework of the chapters. We hope that these features help make this text a useful and engaging introduction to the world of military history.

ACKNOWLEDGEMENTS

The authors would like to acknowledge the helpful comments of many readers of the manuscript at various stages; their feedback, both formal and informal, helped improve the book significantly. They include:

Richard Abels, *US Naval Academy*

William Thomas Allison, *Weber State University*

David Bachrach, *University of New Hampshire*

Jonathan M. Beagle, Western *New England College*

Porter Blakemore, *Mary Washington College*

Theodore F Cook, *William Paterson University*

Phyllis Culham, *US Naval Academy*

Hugh Dubrulle, *Saint Anselm College*

William Hamblin, *Brigham Young University*

Steven Isaac, *Longwood University*

Wayne Lee, *The University of North Carolina at Chapel Hill*

Michael V. Leggiere, *LSU-Shreveport*

Timothy G. Lynch, *California Maritime Academy, CSU*

John Lynn, *University of Illinois*

Alex Roland, *Duke University*

Jonathan Roth, *San Jose State University*

Frederick Schneid, *High Point University*

Spencer Tucker, *VMI*

Everett L. Wheeler, *Duke University*

Our editor at McGraw-Hill, Jon-David Hague, helped immeasurably in moving the project forward. Special thanks go to Michael Pavkovic, United States Naval War College, who originally conceived the project but who was unable to be a part of its completion for personal reasons.

4

THE DAWN OF GLOBAL WARFARE, 1500–1750

CHAPTER 16

The European Transformation: Western Europe, 1450–1720

From about 1450, the European population and economy, set back by a century of crisis that included the Black Death, began to expand again. Governments started to reestablish order and to rebuild their financial and administrative structures, soon surpassing the levels of efficiency they had achieved prior to the age of crisis. This recovery spurred renewed expansion on the borders of western Europe, where a long-established combination of commercial interests, missionary zeal, and military aggression carried Europeans after 1490, in a new age of crusading, to new worlds and on new paths to old worlds.

Thus, building on trends woven into the fabric of western European society since its restructuring in the century around the year 1000, a general transformation of European life picked up steam, driven in large part by the increasingly pervasive influence of merchant capitalism. The three centuries after 1450 saw an influx of wealth and new ideas from around the world, the rise of a powerful merchant class, the creation of the early modern state, and successive intellectual upheavals: the Renaissance, the Reformation, and the Scientific Revolution. The cumulative effects of this ongoing evolution were eventually revolutionary in the realms of politics, economics, social life, and religion, as well as intellectual worldview, as western Europe followed a developmental path that increasingly distinguished it from the rest of the world. Yet western Europe for most of this period retained significant similarities to the rest of the world, similarities imposed by the universal limitations of slow communications and energy sources limited to wind, water, and malnourished muscle, whether human or animal. It would take the Industrial Revolution, built on foundations laid in this period but postdating it, to create both global European dominance and the modern world.

Ongoing transformations in European military practices were one aspect, one in a specific sphere, of this general transformation. And as, in other areas, the changes wrought in military practices were significant—perhaps even revolutionary by 1720—but not, in themselves, conclusive in setting Europe apart from the rest of the world.

Many historians have identified the military changes of this period of European history by the term "Military Revolution." Given the deep continuities of structure and evolution in the western European sociomilitary system since 1050, Military Revolution is a convenient but problematic and potentially misleading label for the military aspect of the general European transformation. As a result, the Military Revolution debate has become a centerpiece of European (and world) historiography in this period (see the Issues box "The 'Military Revolution'"). Whatever we call them, the military transformations of 1450–1720 in western Europe seem to occur in two major stages. From 1450 to 1660, there was a period of experimentation in which many new techniques and technologies were introduced, changes whose potential, for one reason or another, was not fully realized. Then, between 1660 and 1720, came a period of consolidation in which states finally harnessed the changes of the previous period and moved them forward decisively.

EXPERIMENTATION, 1450–1660

Administration

Armies and States   The relationship between political development and military change was a central aspect of the European transformation, one that acted normally as a positive feedback loop. That is, states that created more efficient administrations and more effective ways to raise money found that they could deploy those resources to create bigger, better-controlled armies. In turn, richer states could replace unpaid part-time soldiers with paid professionals; they could also retain already mercenary forces for longer periods and in greater numbers. Any state that managed to do so raised the stakes for its neighbors. And the cost and administrative problems associated with bigger, more expensive armies stimulated further measures to reform and improve government. The search for money led states into the business of promoting trade and commerce, as urban merchant wealth became an increasingly important source of finance through loans and taxation. Bigger and better armies also became more responsive tools of state power, as states moved toward a more complete monopoly over the use of armed force.

Yet there were limits to this mutual reinforcement. It was easy for European governments to seriously overreach their resources during times of war and, in a crisis of immediate need, to devolve power, rights, and control onto localities and regions in exchange for quick cash. There was no straight line from military effort to political centralization, and most of the state building stimulated by war actually had to occur in times of peace and recovery. Lacking these, a state could suffer as easily as strengthen: Spain's long run as the most active and powerful military player in Europe (funded by gold and silver from the Americas) left the relatively strong monarchy of 1500 relatively weak by 1660.

And war could work as a positive stimulus only on a united sociopolitical structure. The Wars of Religion, which pitted Catholics against Protestants for a century beginning in 1550, as often within states as between them, also disrupted the traditional bond between rulers and the aristocratic class, slowing states' ability to respond to military need. France especially saw military advances blunted by civil war. And throughout Europe, political development was uneven and diverse. States' constitutional paths were shaped as much by prior political structures, economic developments, and internal bargaining as by defensive necessity, and military innovation issued from not just strong central monarchies, as in Spain, but small Italian city-states of varying political persuasions and decentralized polities like the Dutch Republic.

Raising Armies   The advance and limitations of government power to 1660 are well illustrated by the history of standing armies: permanently maintained forces having continuity in units and administration.

In some ways, such units were not new. For example, the English had, in effect, maintained a standing army of occupation in Normandy in the 1420s and 1430s, and royal military households had existed throughout the Middle Ages. But such forces achieved new prominence and administrative form beginning with the establishment of the French *compagnies d'ordinnonce* near the end of the Hundred Years War in the 1450s. These companies were made up of standardized *lances,* with each lance built around a heavy cavalryman supported by several light horse and archers. Charles the Bold of Burgundy advanced the process in the next decade by creating standing units with numerical designations, unique banners, and common uniforms for the first time since the Roman Empire. Charles's innovations were precocious and were not sustained after his death, but they pointed the way to increasing administrative standardization (see below). The Spanish monarchy, especially once bullion from the Americas began to fill its coffers, supported a sizable standing military establishment, and some of the *tercios,* their standard infantry units, maintained substantial administrative continuity.

But money shortages kept the true standing cores of most states' armies quite small, so the effect of these early moves toward permanent establishments should not be exaggerated. No state could fight a war with its standing forces alone. Active campaigning required hiring reinforcements, so the total number of soldiers on any state's payroll fluctuated wildly throughout this era. There was a slow upward trend, with noticeable jumps around 1500 and 1580, though the size of individual armies in the field did not grow correspondingly because armies over roughly 30,000 men (and often less) were hard to maintain logistically. And even many forces that look more or less permanent were, in fact, contract troops rehired at the beginning of each campaign season.

Contract troops, or mercenaries, thus came to form the bulk of all European armies from 1450 to 1660. Mercenaries could be hired as individuals, but states did not have the administrative capacity to recruit large numbers of troops individually. They turned instead to private contractors (who might or might not be military men), who agreed to provide a certain number of men in exchange for a lump sum payment that was supposed to cover both the recruits' pay and the recruiter's profit. Similar forms of contracting had been in use for centuries, especially in England. Their spreading popularity, despite the obvious temptations to corruption they presented to

The "Military Revolution"

The term "Military Revolution" was coined by Michael Roberts in a 1956 article. Widely accepted for almost twenty years, Roberts' ideas came under renewed scrutiny in the mid-1970s, and debate exploded in the 1980s, highlighted by Geoffrey Parker's book *The Military Revolution*. The Military Revolution is now a staple of military, early modern European, and world historiography. Why has the idea been subject to such debate? For two paradoxically related reasons. First, whether there was a military revolution (and if so, what it consisted of) is open to debate. But, second, whatever it was (or wasn't), the topic has significance far beyond military history.

The broad elements of military change in early modern Europe are generally agreed on and include tactical changes, new strategic problems, growing army size, and the relationship of these changes to changes in European society and government and Europe's place in the world. These topics are examined in detail in this chapter. But extracting a single revolution, whether in terms of time period or cause, from these elements has proven extremely difficult—right down to arguments about what constitutes a revolution. Roberts' original formulation dated the revolution to the century 1560–1660 and focused on the tactical innovations of Maurice of Nassau in Holland and Gustavus Adolphus of Sweden as the driving force of change. Parker pushed the starting date back to 1530 and stressed the role of Italian breakthroughs in fortress design, in response to cannon, as the basic stimulus, putting technology at the center of the process. Other revolutionary moments have been identified in the mid-fifteenth century, with the introduction of cannon; in the century after 1660, with the emphasis on political change, especially in France, as the cause rather than the consequence of military change (and related to another revolutionary moment between 1789 and 1815); and even in the fourteenth century, in relation to infantry forces. Medieval military historians increasingly question whether there was a military revolution at all, as just about all the trends cited by early modern historians as "revolutionary changes" compared to earlier medieval practices turn out to have originated in the medieval period, with supposed change attributable to misconceptions of medieval warfare (see Chapter 12.) In short, every major assumption and many points of detail involved in defining a military revolution have been questioned, and the debate continues. We can probably say that western European warfare was revolutionarily different and effective, by world standards, by sometime in the eighteenth century, but no single revolutionary period or episode can be isolated as decisive. Rather, the revolutionary result was the end product of a seven-century evolution of a western European socio-military system whose major elements had been in play since the mid-eleventh century. "Military Revolution" is thus both an illusory concept and a misleading label.

Yet if we recognize its problems, the Military Revolution as a label is convenient shorthand for a vast topic whose significance is undeniable. While efforts to identify and define a military revolution have often degenerated into pedantic

recruiters, did not reflect simply the inability of states to do the job themselves. The emergence of regular markets for mercenary service and a recognized class of military entrepreneurs provided armies to states with some efficiency, as well as demonstrating the increasingly pervasive legalistic and capitalist structure of western European society. Market forces of a sort may also be seen at work in the way that certain regions specialized in certain kinds of troops: English longbowmen, Swiss and German pikemen, Spanish swordsmen and arquebusiers, French heavy cavalry. Social conditions and geography also played a role in this, as poorer, mountainous regions such as Switzerland were less likely to produce cavalry or gunners.

nit-picking over definitions, the debate over the causes and effects of the Military Revolution has remained not only voluminous but stimulating and important. This is because the debate ties military history to broader topics of social and political change, the "rise of the West," and the philosophical approaches historians use to view history—all of which are sources of contention in themselves. In doing so, it has been material to the resurrection of military history as a respectable academic field in the past twenty years.

Military development connects to social and political change not just in terms of the effect of warfare on society (whether directly through besieging and plundering cities or indirectly with armies serving as a vector for the spread of disease) but in terms of the relationship of military effort and technique to state building and the creation of the "modern European state." Here a central question involves the dominant direction of causation. That is, did changes in warfare shape state formation, or did political change facilitate military innovation? To oversimplify, there are two poles of this debate philosophically. First, technological determinism traces revolutionary consequences primarily to the introduction of new technology (and thus tends to see innovations in weaponry, for example, as the ultimate cause of political advance). Second, a school of social history emphasizes long-term continuities in social structure and economic development as the key factor in political development, and so tends to see technology as a dependent variable, crucially affected by the context into which it is introduced.

Between these positions lie a whole range of analyses combining differing inputs of "capitalization" and "coercion"—money and guns, commerce and war—in the creation of the wide range of early modern European political forms.

The debate becomes even more highly charged when the role of the Military Revolution in the "rise of the West" is discussed, because the "rise of the West" is itself a politically burdensome concept, hard to define (what is "the West"?), hard to pinpoint (at what point was "the West" "dominant"?), and easily subject to problems of Eurocentrism—problems that no work on the topic, including this one, can escape.

It is difficult to synthesize the Military Revolution debate because it is ongoing and no clear consensus has emerged among its specialists; this text has a perspective but does not presume to have the definitive answer. But there are lessons that the debate shows quite clearly. The very words "Military Revolution" demonstrate the power of a simple label attached to a clear explanation to shape historical debate, as well as the dangers that attach to such labels in terms of oversimplification and sterile arguments about terminology. But the richness of the debate also shows the interconnectedness of the many aspects of past human experience, warning against monocausal or monodirectional explanations for complex phenomena. And there is no clearer example to show that history is not just about discovering what happened but also about explaining why, and thus that history is a process—an ongoing discussion and constant reinterpretation—rather than a fixed set of truths about the past.

But the market demand for total numbers may also have contributed to the homogenization of weapons and tactics: The most numerous types of soldiers by the seventeenth century, musketeers and pikemen, also wielded the weapons that required the least training to use effectively. Market forces affected supply in another way: Many mercenaries were poor men who chose military service when civilian employment eluded them.

What states gained in administrative relief from the use of contract companies (and, at times, entire armies were hired en masse under a single mercenary captain), they lost in terms of control. No state fully solved this problem in this period, but two states took significant steps toward tying armies back to the government. In the Dutch Republic, Maurice of Nassau built his tactical innovations (see below) on a foundation of administrative reforms starting in the 1580s. Instead of dismissing mercenary units at the end of each campaign season and then rehiring them the next spring, he retained them year-round. And despite the fact that only a small minority of the soldiers in his army were actually Dutch, he provided long-serving veterans with state pensions as an inducement to loyalty and stability. Then in Sweden in the 1620s, Gustavus Adolphus created a state army that was built on a system of national service, with units drawn from particular regions and pensions provided to veterans. Administrative permanence and ties to the state thus underlay the tactical abilities of these armies. But again, while significant, the overall impact of these developments was limited in a number of ways. Both states were small. Maurice rarely used his army in open battle. And once the Swedish army entered the Thirty Years War, Swedish units quickly became a minority of Gustavus's forces. Maurice and Gustavus pointed the way to a potential for state armies that was not yet fully realized.

Organization and Discipline   Whether armies were standing forces or mercenaries, their organization centered on the leadership class. In most regions, the aristocracy continued to dominate the officer corps, especially at the top ranks, another way in which armies reflected the social structure from which they emerged. Indeed, to refer to an "officer corps" may imply a greater division of military and social hierarchy than existed in this period. Aristocrats were military leaders because they were social leaders, and they often raised units of troops for the government because they had the economic resources and regional connections to be able to do so.

And yet there was a movement toward a greater professionalization of warfare and leadership. This was stimulated in part by the printing press. There was an explosion of military publications, both classical treatises on war (part of the inspiration for Maurice's reinvention of drill came from his reading of printed editions of Vegetius, the late Roman writer on military affairs) and an increasing wave of contemporary books including numerous editions, many pirated, of Maurice's own infantry regulations. A number of these publications focused on the new technologies of war: Guides to ballistics and treatises laying out systems of fortification design proliferated with the spread of cannon and handguns. Armies therefore saw the rise of "scientific specialists" such as artillerists and engineers to new prominence as officers, as well as the emergence of career soldiers who made warfare their study as well as their livelihood. But since many such careerists were also aristocrats, professionalism did little to threaten the social structure.

The third type of leader was the mercenary entrepreneur. As a sort of warrior-capitalist practicing private enterprise, such men were also products of their society, though a different part than produced the established aristocracy. Some indeed had noble or knightly blood. But like many merchants of the age, who used their mercantile wealth to buy titles of nobility, mercenary captains often achieved title and prestige as a result of their financial and military success. In fact, the co-opting of mercenary captains into the aristocracy was simply the latest expression of a long-established aspect of western European culture: the ennobling effect of being a warrior. This extension of warrior values and the sense that "might makes right" from the medieval to the early modern period was far less revolutionary in the long run than the parallel upward movement of merchants, since their success was based not on war but on the highly nontraditional basis of wealth and commerce.

Despite the continuing personal (and thus eclectic) character of the leadership class, which tended toward diversity in unit strength and organization, there was also significant movement toward standardization in this period. One of the consequences of contracting troops for longer terms of service was the establishment of more permanent units and with them the ability to regularize drill, tactics, clothing, and weapons.

The retention of these troops in the pay of the developing nation-state meant that it was possible, and useful, for units of troops to serve together for extended periods. Such long-term service together led to the creation of a new type of esprit de corps that had been absent in Europe since the time of the Romans. These semipermanent units were often composed of men from a particular ethnic group now fighting under the banner of a foreign master. The Dutch army, for example, had separate companies of English, French, German, and Walloon troops in addition to Dutch ones. The same was true of the Swedes, who organized their German, Scottish, and Swedish troops into distinct companies and brigades.

In order to ensure that these companies possessed some military cohesion, the Dutch instituted uniform articles of drill and clothing. John of Nassau, a cousin and aide to Maurice, drew inspiration from the Hellenistic writer Aelian and wrote a military manual that defined the Dutch method of drill—or discipline—with the musket and pike. In the case of musket drill, John identified forty-two movements for loading and firing, and assigned each a word of command. Thus, all troops, regardless of ethnic origin (or previous military service), now had a single set of drill and commands. Moreover, lest these troops forget their new allegiance, and to help separate friend from foe, at first individual companies and later entire armies were outfitted with coats of the same color or other distinguishing features such as sashes.

Finally, these new units were also provided with particular pieces of equipment depending on their role in the army—the panoply of the pikeman, musketeer, and cuirassier (see the section on tactics for these terms) were all standardized. Now each type of soldier with his prescribed drill and equipment and in his established company could be easily deployed into model formations and battle lines.

But just as there were limitations on the creation of true state-run armies before 1660, there were similar limitations on the professionalization of officers and the standardization of armies. Cash shortages often limited the standardization of equipment and contributed significantly to poor standards of discipline. Unpaid mercenaries deserted or turned into a plundering mob at the first opportunity on campaign. Revolts by armies were almost nonexistent, but mutinies—essentially, strikes—were common. The Spanish army in the Netherlands mutinied almost annually in some periods of the war there. Some European observers contrasted European standards of discipline in the sixteenth century unfavorably with those of the Turks. Mercenary service also undermined standardization in terms of uniforms, as independent mercenary soldiers objected to the servile implications of uniform dress.

The fundamental limitation, however, was that the disruptions of the religious wars prevented the consolidation of state power. Schismatic aristocrats resisted central control and so diffused efforts at imposing discipline and standardization. As a result, the changes in European warfare up to 1660 were practical responses to new technologies and resources, but they did not arise out of a transformed social structure. The technologies and techniques of warfare thus remained readily exportable—and, as both the Ottomans and the Japanese showed in this period, could be wielded more effectively than by Europeans themselves. It would be the social transformations of the next period that would render not the technology but the technique of European warfare difficult to imitate.

Strategy

Strategic Aims   Experimentation dominates the history of military administration and tactics in this period. In contrast, strategically, there was little that was truly innovative.

There were, to be sure, attempts at bold strategic strokes on a grand scale. Many were initiated by Spain, not only the dominant power of the time but the one most Committed to offensive action in one form or another, both as defender of Hapsburg hegemony in the Netherlands and the empire and as leader of the Counter-Reformation (Figure 16.1). The Armada campaign of 1588, which attempted an ambitious coordination of a battle fleet with a transport fleet and an army, was the most spectacular of these in both planning and failure. It demonstrates the rising importance of sea power to strategy on a continental and global scale. Probably the most innovative strategies were pursued in overseas empire building, and ultimately, the policies with the biggest, most revolutionary effects were those that forged links between commerce, wealth, and empire on one hand and war (especially war finance) on the other. These links are explored in detail in Chapter 20.

Within Europe, the Spanish Road demonstrates the possibility for grand strategic conception and execution. A combination of grand strategic and political arrangements that Hapsburg Spain made for moving troops and supplies from Spain and Italy north along the Rhine to the Netherlands, it also served to hem in and threaten France, Spain's major rival for dominance. It shows that grand strategy was inseparable from the politics of the emerging early modern state system and dynastic competition. It also shows, however, that it was easy for the strategic reach of European states to exceed their grasp. All the resources of Spain could not ensure victory from the Spanish Road: In the end, France was not contained, nor was the Dutch Revolt subdued. And at no time could the Spanish Road be maintained by purely military means.

The majority of strategic ambitions were much more limited than this. Geography and politics concentrated much warfare in traditionally important and contentious areas such as northern Italy and the Low

Figure 16.1 Europe in 1580, at the Height of Hapsburg Hegemony
Note how the Hapsburg's possessions were able to politically and militarily isolate France and the rebellious Dutch colonies through the formation of alliances along the Rhine (the Spanish Road).

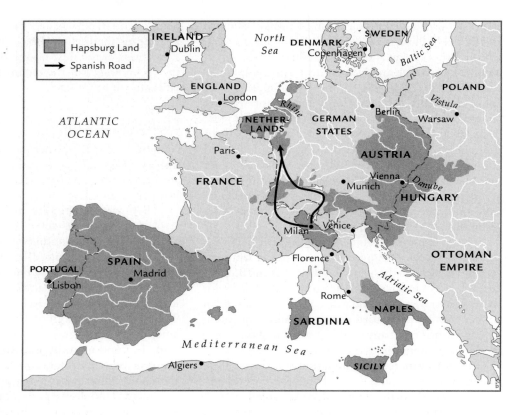

Countries (Netherlands, Belgium, Luxembourg) or in areas such as central Germany where no great power dominated. Within those theaters and elsewhere, generals found their strategic options limited by two major practical considerations: logistics and the dominance of siege warfare.

Logistics   The logistical constraints that had shaped strategy since ancient times continued in force in this period: Transport was slow, and no army could travel very far or survive for long just on carted supplies. Armies on campaign had to live off the land by pillage, plunder, and "contributions" from local populations. Armies of 20,000 were as populous as most cities and faced supply crises if forced to stay in one place very long unless waterborne transport were available. The growth of total military establishments thus exacerbated supply difficulties, as ambitions again tended to outstrip practical capabilities.

Gunpowder weaponry contributed to such difficulties. Cannon were heavy and slow to cart, and they bogged down completely on wet roads, and powder and ammunition had to be carried with an army as well, since they could not be foraged. Governments, straining simply to put troops in the field and to build and rebuild fortifications (see below), were slow to develop systems of central depots and assured cartage. And new industries for manufacturing weapons, ammunition, uniforms, and other necessities struggled to keep up with demand. It also took time and much experimentation for governments to arrive at satisfactory methods of purchasing or requisitioning supplies from manufacturers (including state-run industries).

Meanwhile, armies also lived off the land because plunder was still an essential element of attracting men to the military life. Not just the countryside but cities taken by siege suffered the consequences. Finally, fodder for all the animals an army needed—cavalry horses and pack animals—constituted the most pressing necessity and the least able to be supplied from depots. The availability of fodder virtually dictated the campaign season of late spring to late fall. (See the Sources box "Foraging.")

The results of this logistical nightmare were threefold. First, commanders faced a strategic dilemma. They could move rapidly, living off the land, at the cost of accomplishing little of strategic value, since permanent gains depended on taking fortresses. Or they

Soldiers Attacking Civilians This engraving illustrates typical relations between soldiers and civilians during the fifteenth to seventeenth centuries as described in the Sources box "Foraging." In this case, however, the peasants are resisting with their farm tools.

could try to organize supply lines at the cost of seeing their rate of march reduced to a crawl, compounded by the necessity to reduce every fortress on the line of march. Second, many fought-over areas suffered terrible devastation. For example, much of central Germany during the Thirty Years War was reduced to a wasteland, and whole towns disappeared. Third, armies themselves consistently suffered far more casualties from hunger, disease, and desertion than from combat. High rates of wastage complicate calculations of the effective size of military establishments in this period. The devastation of the Thirty Years War in particular brought about a movement toward more controlled supply arrangements. But only the more effective governments that emerged after 1660 would be able to begin to address these problems.

Siege Warfare Changes in siege warfare were central to the military developments of this period in Europe. The gradual appearance of effective siege guns beginning in the early fifteenth century initiated the transformation. By the middle of the century, siege cannon were rendering the old style of medieval fortifications extremely vulnerable. The high, relatively thin walls of medieval castles could be breached and toppled quickly by the direct, low-trajectory fire of cannon. Further, these walls provided a poor platform for the mounting of defensive guns: Blind spots were many, and the guns' blasts shook the walls dangerously. Suddenly, over a thousand years of accumulated

wisdom about fortification was rendered irrelevant. The potential for rapid reshaping of the political map that this ascendance of the offensive in siege warfare created was demonstrated in limited ways by France in the last decade of the Hundred Years War and by Charles the Bold's Burgundy. But it was Charles VIII of France's invasion of Italy in 1494 that brought these developments to the forefront of European warfare. Briefly, from 1494 to perhaps 1530, the new weapons almost eliminated sieges, as towns and forts capitulated at the first threat of cannonade. Gunpowder mines also added a new effectiveness to an old siege technique, as galleries (tunnels) filled with gunpowder could not just collapse walls but blow them to pieces. Battles therefore assumed a temporarily central role in war and were fought with unusual frequency. But by 1530, new principles of fortress design were being worked out in Italy that would restore familiar patterns to European warfare.

To counter the fire of siege guns and create a platform for counterfire, the walls of gunpowder forts were made much thicker and lower. The height necessary to resist escalade was created by the excavation of a broad ditch surrounding the wall that also helped prevent mining. A counterscarp leading up to the ditch further protected the walls from direct fire. These low, massive walls were punctuated by pointed bastions designed so as to provide mutually supporting fields of fire: Every part of the walls could be covered by cannon and muskets. (See the diagram in Chapter 18.)

SOURCES

Foraging

In the following passages, the German writer Grimmelshausen, who actually fought in the Thirty Years War, gives a vivid, harrowing account of the realities of campaigning.

■   ■   ■

I am not inclined to lead the peace-loving reader with these plunderers into my father's house and yard since what came to pass there is indeed terrible. The episode demands, however, that I leave the events for posterity in my tale . . .

[Soldiers arrive at the farm of Simplicius's family.] The first thing that the plunderers did was to put their horses in the stable, after which each had his own particular task to execute, and in which each showed pure destruction & ruin. While some began to slaughter, boil and roast as if a merry banquet were to be held, others in their turn stormed through the house, upstairs and downstairs. Even the private chamber was not safe from them. . . . Others assembled great packs from cloth, clothing and all sorts of household goods, as if they wanted to open a junk shop somewhere, and whatever they did not intend to take with them was destroyed. Some stabbed at hay & straw with their daggers as if they had not had enough sheep and swine to skewer; Others shook the feathers out of the quilts, which they instead filled with bacon, cured meats, and other things, as if it would be better to sleep on them that way; Still others smashed the oven and windows to pieces, just as if they had an eternal summer to proclaim. Others bashed copper- and tinware and then packed up the bent & ruined pieces; They burned beds, tables, chairs and benches, and this although many cords of firewood lay in the yard; And finally bowls and plates had to be broken into pieces, either because they just preferred to eat roasted food or because

they only planned to have one meal there. Our milkmaid had been treated so badly in the stable that she couldn't walk out, even to speak of which is a disgrace. They laid the hired man tied up on the ground, propped his mouth open with a piece of plywood and poured a milking bucket filled with water from manure-pile puddles into his body, and they called this a Swedish Brew. They then forced him to lead a party [of soldiers], and captured men and animals and brought them back to our yard. . . .

Then they started by taking the flints out of their pistols and instead screwed the peasants' thumbs into them, torturing the poor rascals. It seemed as though they wanted to burn witches, since they even put one of the captured peasants into the oven and set after him with fire, although he had not yet confessed to anything. They wrapped a rope around the head of another and twisted it tight with a stick so that blood spurted from his mouth, nose and ears. In short, each had his own innovative way to torture the peasants, and thus each peasant has his singular torment. . . . I do not have much to say about the women, maids and daughters they captured, because the soldiers would not let me see how they dealt with them, but I do know that now and again one heard piteous screams from the corners of the house.

SOURCE: Hans Jacob Christoph von Grimmelshausen, *Simplicissimus*, ed. Roef Tarot (Stuttgart: Niemeyer, 1967), trans. Lyne Miles-Morillo.

Building in stone or masonry was not even necessary. Bastions built of earthworks, perhaps faced in timber, could be thrown up quickly and relatively cheaply to great effect, since earth walls could absorb cannon shot almost endlessly without collapsing. But earthworks required constant upkeep, so masonry walls

appeared wherever finances and planning allowed. Earth and masonry construction continued to complement each other throughout this period.

Faced with such obstacles, besiegers had to dig in to avoid defensive fire; they also dug in to defend against relief armies. Standard siege techniques thus

Battle Outside Lunburg, 1578 This sixteenth-century engraving of a battle in the Netherlands shows the nature of operations during that time. This battle, with prominent use of firearms, is being fought on the outskirts of a town protected by modern fortifications. During this period, sieges and the attempts to relieve them dominated operational efforts.

came to include lines of circumvallation and contra-vallation and sets of trenches that approached the walls in a zigzag pattern to avoid enfilading fire. The approach trenches brought the siege battery up to where a breach could be methodically blasted in the walls while a section of the ditch was filled. This was a time-consuming process, however, and determined defenders could sometimes erect a new temporary earthwork wall behind the breach, necessitating further bombardment. In short, the new forts reimposed the traditional medieval patterns of positional, siege-based warfare.

For half a century, Italian engineers brought the new principles to building projects and sieges all across Europe. By the 1590s, Dutch engineers, under the constant stimulus of having to defend the republic against the Spanish, had taken the lead in fortress design, extending the bastion system (mostly in earthworks) with numerous outworks and making use of Dutch topography to flood ditches and create vast moats. By the mid-seventeenth century, French engineers were emerging as Europe's best. But it was not until after 1660 that state-run schools of engineering emerged to provide institutional and national continuity to the profession of military engineer.

The effects of the rise of the new gunpowder fortresses have been much debated (see the Issues box on page 306). Did they stimulate the growth of armies? Perhaps—larger armies were useful in besieging such strongholds. But the stimulus was unevenly spread and probably only a minor element in the process of army growth, a process determined mostly by the limits of logistics and state administrative development. What is certain is that guns made siege warfare more expensive in terms of both men and money. Both cannon and small arms extended the range of the defense from within a fortress far beyond that of crossbows. Further, the bastion design was intended to project the defenders' firepower, whereas the strength of the medieval castle was essentially passive. Casualties in both attack and defense thus rose dramatically. The rapid rise of entrenching as a vital element of siege work attests to the potentially devastating effectiveness of defensive fire. And combat casualties only added to the casualties caused by hunger and disease that siege warfare with its concentrations of people in one place had always fostered. Sieges were less dramatic than battles, but they undoubtedly cost far more lives. Good siege trains and the new-style forts needed to defend against them were also expensive in terms of money. The rapid rate of innovation and change throughout the sixteenth and into the seventeenth century meant that guns had to be constantly replaced and some forts had to be rebuilt.

The rise of gunpowder-based siege warfare thus furthered the growing dominance in warfare exerted by rich states at the expense of nobles and poor states. (Large states such as France were usually the richest as well, but the Dutch Republic and Venice both showed the capacity of small states with significant commercial wealth to take advantage of the new technologies.) It also promoted the professionalization of war through the prominence it gave to engineers and to publications on the science of fortification. But the effects of gunpowder-based siege warfare were mostly concentrated in a few highly strategic and rich, urbanized areas such as northern Italy and Flanders and along the northern borders of France. Elsewhere, fortification was less pervasive and influential. Cannon, forts, and sieges were therefore an important aspect of the European transformation, but they were not the driving force behind it.

Tactics and Drill

Pike and Shot   The period from 1450 through the end of the Thirty Years War around 1650 is characterized as the age of pike and shot, based on the two weapons that were the standard arms of the bodies of infantry who came to dominate the armies of early modern Europe. The first weapon, the pike (a long spear ranging from thirteen to eighteen feet in length and usually wielded with both hands), was of course an ancient weapon that became popular again as bodies of foot troops served together and developed the unit cohesion necessary to employ the pike effectively. When used by a body of well-disciplined and -trained soldiers, the pike was a formidable weapon. A unit of steady pikemen presented an almost solid wall of bristling spear points that could keep even the bravest and the most heavily armored horsemen at bay.

The second weapon was a new one: the hand-held firearm. Depending on the time period, it was called the arquebus or musket. Although the length of the barrel and the weight of the projectile could vary—the musket was the longer and heavier of the two—the basic technology was the same. Both were smoothbore weapons that employed the same firing mechanism, the matchlock. The matchlock used a burning wick, or match, that was applied to a pan filled with powder when the trigger was pulled. The match then ignited that powder and sent a flash through a touch hole; in turn, the flash detonated the main charge of powder in the barrel. While not very accurate, the matchlock firearm did have two considerable strengths. First, the weapon possessed extensive stopping power: At a range of 100 yards, the two-ounce ball fired from a musket could penetrate even the most modern, shot-proof, armor or bring down the largest destrier (warhorse). Second, unlike some of the missile weapons of the earlier period, the matchlock was a weapon whose use could be learned quickly even by raw troops, especially with the advent of training manuals. While the longbow and even the crossbow could be equally deadly and more accurate at longer ranges, the time needed to train troops in their use was dramatically longer.

Infantry Tactics   During the latter part of the fifteenth century, disciplined bodies of pike-armed infantry begin to appear in ever-increasing numbers in most European armies. Without doubt, the successes of the Swiss against the Austrians and Burgundians was a catalyst for the introduction of pike units in many armies (indeed, many armies recruited Swiss units en masse). While the early success of the Swiss was due to the use not of pikes but of halberds (a pole-arm that combined a heavy ax blade, beaked hook, and spear point), the key principle was the same: Well-disciplined and -trained infantry armed with a longish pole-arm could keep even the best aristocratic horsemen at bay and even defeat them. The cohesion of the Swiss, even those who became mercenaries, was based on communal ties. All of the troops from a particular canton fought together under officers who were elected by the rank and file.

By the beginning of the sixteenth century, the Swiss had established a structure and tactical model that would be emulated by most European armies. In Germany, for example, the emperor Maximilian founded the *Landsknechts* as a body of professional infantry in imitation of the Swiss. Indeed, the *Landsknechts* even copied the Swiss manner of dress and would become sought-after mercenaries in their own right.

The Swiss and *Landsknechts* formed in large columns of pikemen supported by other troops, some armed with halberds or large swords, others with firearms. Clearly, in this tactical model, pikemen were the dominant type of foot soldiers, with other troops serving in support roles. In the case of halberdiers and swordsmen, these troops were often formed into a *forlorn hope* whose task was to precede the pike column and to disrupt enemy pike units by literally hacking their way through the wall of enemy pikes. Arquebusiers, who at this time formed the *shot,* were either deployed as skirmishers in front of the column or interspersed between the files of pikemen.

Pikes generally outnumbered shots by a considerable proportion during this period, usually forming about 80 percent of the infantry forces. One reason for the large number of pikemen relative to arquebusiers was the slow rate of fire by the latter. The men with firearms needed the protection of the pike column while they reloaded their weapons; they were particularly vulnerable to enemy horsemen. At the same time, men with firearms showed that they, in turn, could disrupt the tightly packed bodies of pikemen with their firepower.

During the second decade of the sixteenth century, Swiss and *Landsknecht* formations faced stiff competition from the Spanish, who were innovative in a number of ways. First, the Spanish established the first large units of permanent infantry, the *tercios,* predecessors of the royal armies of the seventeenth century. The Spanish army of the period had emerged out of the *Reconquista* of Spain from the Moors and therefore had developed into almost a national force. The *tercios* were large regiments of soldiers, numbering as many as 3000 infantrymen, who had, at least originally, a regional identity and who served together for an extended time. Indeed, each *tercio* developed its own uniform, which provided its identity. For example, the "*tercio* of the dandies" was known for its colorful uniforms.

Second, the Spanish were innovators in that the *tercios* increased the ratio of firearms among their foot soldiers. By the 1520s, the ratio of pikemen to arquebusiers in Spanish units had been reduced to about three to one, and by the end of the century, it would reach one to one. This gave the Spanish a much greater quantity of firepower, which was to play a decisive role in a number of Spanish victories during the Italian wars. Moreover, the Spanish did not make extensive use of the halberd as did the Swiss and the *Landsknechts,* but rather deployed soldiers armed with sword and buckler to duck underneath the rows of spear points in order to disrupt enemy pikemen. This type of fighting with sword and shield was much imitated during the Renaissance: It was viewed as a classical revival, as it appeared to hearken back to the Roman style of fighting.

The Spanish also experimented with new formations to accommodate the increased number of arquebusiers and, by the 1560s, musketeers. In general, though, the arquebusiers and musketeers needed to remain close to the main body of pikemen since their relatively slow rate of fire made them vulnerable. Often, the *tercio* was deployed into a large square, with pikes in the center and arquebusiers and musketeers formed up on the corners of the pike column to provide all-around protective firepower for the pikemen.

Some of the important developments in infantry tactics were initiated at the end of the sixteenth century by three Dutch reformers from the house of Nassau: William Louis, John, and Maurice. It is interesting that these reforms were to find their genesis with the Dutch, since the military experience of the Dutch emphasized siege warfare rather than open battle. Maurice, for example, had not fought in a battle before the Dutch discipline had been introduced, and he fought only one major battle afterward. Instead, the impetus for reform seems to have been a desire to revive classical models.

The Dutch tactical reformers made three major contributions. The first centered on a new method of firing for musketeers called *countermarch firing.* In this mode of firing, the musketeers formed up in six (or sometimes twelve) ranks. After the men in the first rank had fired together in a volley, they retired to the back of the formation and began reloading according to a set sequence of motions defined in the Dutch drill manuals. The men of the second rank, now at the front of the formation, discharged a volley and then retired. This rotation continued until the original first rank had returned to its position, reloaded and ready to fire again. This method of countermarch fire made musketeers less vulnerable since they could keep up a steady volume of fire against the enemy. Countermarch fire also allowed for the ratio of musketeers to pikemen to increase. Dutch muster returns show that by the early seventeenth century Dutch units had approximately three musketeers for every two pikemen.

Countermarch fire, however, required well-trained and -disciplined troops. This was the second innovation of the Dutch reformers—in this case, as discussed earlier, by John of Nassau. John's drill and command were formalized in the *Wapenhandelinghe van Roers,* which was published in 1607 under his supervision. This volume described the Dutch methods for the use of both pike and musket.

The third Dutch reform altered the size and formation of infantry units. The Dutch broke with the tradition of large blocks of troops used by the Swiss, *Landsknechts,* and Spanish, instead using smaller battalions. The battalion contained 550 men, not coincidently the size of the Roman cohort recommended by Vegetius. The new method of countermarch fire allowed these battalions to be deployed in fewer ranks, generally six or twelve as opposed to the very deep column formations employed by other nations. These battalions thus at the same time were more flexible than the large, 3000-strong *tercios* and made better use of manpower by thinning out the formation.

Seventeenth-Century Drill Manual   This plate, from the time of James I of England (1603–1625), depicts a fully armed musketeer and is typical of the illustrations that appeared in the many drill manuals of the period. He carries a matchlock musket with rest and a bandolier of ammunition, often referred to as "the Twelve Apostles."

Cavalry and Cavalry Tactics   By 1500, the size of armies had grown dramatically, and virtually all of the growth, in terms of both numbers and tactical innovations, had taken place in the ranks of the infantry. At the beginning of this period, the heavily armored horsemen, now often styled as gendarmes rather than knights, were still the heart of the cavalry. But even as infantry forces increased in numbers, the quantity of gendarmes remained the same. Clearly, the main reason for this declining proportion was financial. The cost required to equip a fully armored and mounted man-at-arms was substantial. This was compounded by the fact that units of pike and shot were able to stand up to armored cavalry and inflict heavy casualties on the horsemen. Indeed, the loss of the expensive and difficult-to-obtain warhorse was a greater loss than the man-at-arms himself.

As a result, other types of less expensive cavalry begin to appear as part of European armies, first to supplement and later to replace the men-at-arms. The cavalryman who took the place of the gendarme as the main type of battlefield trooper was the *Reiter*, or cuirassier. These men wore lighter armor, sometimes called three-quarter armor, and were equipped with a sword and brace of pistols in lieu of the gendarme's heavy lance. This change in weapons and armor reflected the growing realization that the nature of battle was changing. The horseman faced growing numbers of disciplined infantry and so was no longer able to run roughshod over foot soldiers.

Cavalry tactics therefore underwent changes that reflected the changing battlefield. The adoption of sword and pistols was part of the increasing trend toward a reliance on firepower. Cavalry, no longer able to trample infantry, now sought to use firepower to disrupt the infantry and then turn to the charge. A new tactic was developed to implement this disruption—the *caracole*—in which *Reiter*, or cuirassier cavalry, would gallop up to infantry and, rather than charging home, discharge their pistols and wheel away to reload. Other troopers would then follow up, fire, and wheel off to reload. In some respects, this was a version of countermarch fire for horsemen. After enough casualties had been inflicted on the infantry, the horsemen would deliver a final volley and only then charge home.

Unfortunately, this tactic was never fully successful since infantry firearms outranged those of the cavalry and the tighter formations of men on foot allowed for a greater volume of fire. But if cavalry were no longer able to charge home, they did still have uses on the battlefield. For instance, they could engage enemy horsemen with the aim of driving them off and then attacking the vulnerable flanks of enemy foot troops or unsupported artillery. Likewise, cavalry were essential in pursuing a defeated enemy.

Artillery   While artillery was a key element of early modern armies, it was primarily in siege warfare that it was most useful, at least until the end of the seventeenth century. The reason for their lack of a major impact on the battlefield was that cannon were generally rather immobile: Once deployed, they could not be moved during the battle. Therefore, although the cannon might wreak some havoc in the enemy ranks as the battle opened, the battle might develop in such a way as to render the position of the guns less useful over time. Moreover, at the beginning of this period, the reloading process was quite time consuming, with cannon sometimes getting off only a few rounds during a battle. In fact, the Swiss were thought to be able to close the distance between themselves and enemy guns before the latter could reload even once. Further, artillery pieces were manned by civilian contractors. These men were generally not willing to defend their guns, and, so, as the action drew near, many decided simply to abandon their guns altogether.

The Swedish Synthesis

The age of pike and shot reached its apogee during the Thirty Years War in the Swedish army of Gustavus Adolphus. The Swedish army adapted and enhanced many of the developments of the first phase of the European transformation. Not only did the Swedish army draw on the various tactical and technological changes of the preceding two centuries, it was also composed of the new type of long-term soldier, both native Swedes and mercenaries, which made it one of the most veteran and thus steadfast forces of its day.

The Swedish Brigade   The core of Gustavus's army was his Swedish infantry, which included foreigners fighting under the Swedish Discipline. The origins of this infantry force lay in the national levy of the fifteenth and sixteenth centuries. Sweden, however, did not have a large population, and so Gustavus augmented the traditional levies with mercenaries, notably Germans and Scots. The army that he led into Germany during the early days of the Thirty Years War consisted of as many foreigners as Swedes.

The basic tactical unit of the Swedish army was the squadron, the Swedish equivalent of the Dutch battalion. In theory, this consisted of some 500 men divided between musketeers and pikemen—288 musketeers and 216 pikemen—although usually nearly 100 of the muskets were detached from the squadron for other duties. Several of these squadrons, usually three or four, were formed together into a brigade, which acted as the basic unit of maneuver. These brigades served together on a long-term basis and so developed a group identity. Each brigade had its own uniform, so that they came to be recognized by the color of their coats—for example the Yellow Brigade, Red Brigade, Green Brigade, and so on.

The formation employed by the Swedish squadrons featured a combination of firepower and shock. The squadron's firepower came from its musketeers, who were drawn up six deep. While the Swedes still made use of countermarch fire, they also developed an early form of volley fire, in which the files of musketeers were doubled, forming themselves shoulder to shoulder three ranks deep. The first rank knelt, the second crouched, and the third stood; on command, all three ranks fired simultaneously, delivering a devastating quantity of fire in a single instant. The musketeers' firepower was further enhanced by the use of battalion guns. These were light, three-pound artillery pieces, developed by a Scottish artillery officer in Swedish service, that could be manhandled to keep pace with the infantry. These artillery pieces, added considerable punch to the squadron's already formidable volley. This blast of fire was followed up with shock action: a charge delivered by the pikemen and the musketeers, who wielded their heavy muskets as clubs. The squadrons within a given brigade were deployed in a checkerboard fashion, usually drawn up in two lines. This arrangement, reminiscent of the Roman legions, allowed the units in the two lines to advance and withdraw without hindering one another.

Swedish Cavalry   The shock of the Swedish foot was magnified by the Swedish cavalry forces. Most of the Swedish horsemen were light horse, a more lightly armed version of the cuirassier wearing only half-armor (a cuirass without additional protection for upper arms and thighs). During his campaigns against the Poles, Gustavus came to realize that his cavalry were ill-suited to the caracole, since most carried only a single pistol, and reloading was cumbersome. Instead, he turned to the tactics of the Polish cavalry, which stressed the charge and relied on the speed of more lightly armored troopers. Gustavus was also able to thin the ranks of his cavalry formations, since the caracole required deeper formations than those of charging horsemen. Although the Swedish cavalry preferred swords, they still made use of the pistol, but only as they prepared to charge home. The emphasis on the charge, coupled with the iron discipline of the Swedish squadrons, allowed them to overrun enemy horsemen whose formations and inclination toward using pistols rather than swords put them at a disadvantage.

Artillery   In addition to attaching battalion guns to his infantry, Gustavus reformed the heavier Swedish artillery. For the first time, the artillery became a part of the regular army, crewed by soldiers rather than civilian contractors. Gustavus further organized his artillery into companies as permanent tactical units and, ultimately, as regiments. The creation of an artillery arm of the Swedish military also allowed for the standardization of the various pieces of ordinance. The cannon of the Swedish army were

Pike and Shot Battle, 1620 The illustration depicts the Battle of White Mountain, November 8, 1620, one of the early battles from the Thirty Years War fought in Bohemia. It clearly shows the deep formations that were still in use at that time. The thinner formations used by Gustavus Adolphus's Swedes would become more the norm by the end of the period.

lightened to make them more mobile and consisted of three calibers—6-, 12-, and 24-pounders—in addition to the 3-pound battalion guns. The Swedish guns were made even more effective by the development of prepared ammunition, transported in wooden cases. This early use of prepared rounds for the artillery allowed Swedish gunners to fire as quickly as their comrades in the infantry.

The Swedish army of the Thirty Years War was able to bring together all of the technological and tactical advances up to that time. It should be noted, however, that other armies were moving toward a similar pattern of warfare. What separated the Swedes from many of their contemporaries and made them so effective was not just their weapons and formations. Rather, it was that they were a long-term force that campaigned together over time, learned as an institution from those campaigns, and fought under a strict discipline forged as much by their Lutheran religion as by war.

Consolidation, 1660–1720

Before roughly 1660, tactical and technological innovations in both siege warfare and battle, including drill, were significant. But their potential, measured

in global terms, was to a great extent unrealized due to limitations of logistical and administrative support and a lack of consistent discipline and unit continuity. European armies had no clear advantage over other gunpowder armies such as the Ottomans, and the techniques of European warfare were still readily exportable with the technology. But the end of the Wars of Religion allowed a reconsolidation of political power around the traditional royal-aristocratic partnership. In the context of renewed political unity and reform, states could harness the changes of the previous period and move them forward decisively.

Royal Armies

It was the France of Louis XIV, the "Sun King," that would lead the way. France had long been the largest and richest kingdom in Europe, but it had been hard hit by civil war during the Wars of Religion. Cardinals Richelieu and Mazarin had begun reconstructing central authority under Louis XIII and during Louis XIV's minority. The Sun King and his chief ministers pushed royal absolutism to new heights, promoting economic development, improving royal finances, and extending the scope and efficiency of royal administration. On these foundations were built significant military reforms, which forced Louis' rivals to imitate him or risk conquest.

The main thrust of Louis' military reforms was to make the army into a responsive instrument of royal power. Mercenary companies were turned into official state regiments, with private contracts replaced by standardized terms of service. Many formerly independent mercenary captains ceased being private entrepreneurs and became officers of the state. Military rank and paths of promotion, though still subject to political influence, were regularized. The new permanent regiments with their professional, aristocratic officers were given names, numbers, insignia, and banners and began to develop their own regimental histories and culture.

The decline of mercenary service in favor of professional state service reduced the role of foreigners in such armies. Officers for the French army came from the aristocracy; the rank and file of enlisted men were recruited (indeed, often conscripted) from marginal elements of the population. The social divide between officers and men in such armies contributed to the need for brutal standards of discipline, though uniform drill and harsh discipline were also the key to the tactical effectiveness of royal armies (see below). But recruiting from the aristocracy and from society's margins also reduced the impact of recruiting on the productive elements of society, a conscious application of mercantilist policy. Nonetheless, royal armies were expensive instruments that made major demands on state finances. Every state stretched its newly developed resources to the limit, and the sizes of military establishments shot up dramatically after 1660. By 1700, France was maintaining over 400,000 soldiers on the rolls in wartime, numbers unprecedented since Roman times.

The financial demands were increased by the imposition of central control over all aspects of military administration. The state now assumed responsibility for supplying its soldiers with weapons (often, before, provided by the individual), uniforms, and regular rations. Housing, too, came to be part of the package, as billeting—the housing of troops in civilian homes—was phased out and barracks were built wherever permanent garrisons were stationed. Royal forts also became central supply depots connected to each other and to armies in the field by organized systems of cartage and shipping. Centralized control of many aspects of military administration also centralized costs.

Finance would, in fact, be the Achilles heel of absolutist armies, especially in France, a problem inseparable from the political and social structure of absolutist states. The more the formal mechanisms of power were concentrated in royal hands, the less incentive the aristocracy had to pay for a power they had little formal say over, despite their role as social leaders and military officers. France's inability to tax its aristocrats continued to prove a crippling handicap, one shared to some extent by all the emerging absolutist states. It was thus left to England, with its odd political system sheltered on its island, to create what would prove to be the most significant breakthrough in military administration and finance in the era. The aristocrats, great merchants, and landed gentry, who had a voice in royal government through Parliament, paid for the privilege by taxing themselves; the resources this provided to the government were harnessed and multiplied by the creation in the 1690s of the Bank of England and the Sinking Fund, an assured mechanism for paying off government borrowing. The invention of deficit financing and a secured national debt allowed England, with a population much smaller than that of France, to more than match its great rival's military expenditures and to exploit the increasing wealth of its overseas trade and empire (won largely during wars with France) for military purposes. In short, Britain implemented a thoroughly modern fusion of capitalism, government, and military power. Given the scale of the royal shipyards (see Chapter 20), we can even speak of a nascent military-industrial complex. In this set of developments, we see a true military revolution.

Strategy

Positional Warfare   The creation of royal armies and the imposition of effective central control affected strategy, mostly by further emphasizing cautious, positional warfare. Commanders were wary of committing their expensive forces to battle; attritional losses from a siege might be just as high but were easier to replace gradually than the sudden high losses risked in battle. And since control of fortifications was the goal of most campaigning, battles were at best a hazardous and indirect means to that end.

Unleashing armies to live off the land to increase mobility also became a less viable option. In part, this was a cultural reaction against the devastating excesses of the Thirty Years War, but practical considerations contributed. Foraging loosened commanders' control over individual soldiers significantly, and the risks of desertion and loss of discipline were thus high.

When foraging took place (and it was still a regular aspect of supply on campaign, crucial especially for fodder), it was more closely controlled and limited. Commanders attempted to regularize the collection of rations from the countryside through markets or compensated requisitioning. This reflected both conscious policy aimed at maintaining the productivity and goodwill of areas targeted for conquest, and the necessity for greater planning in supplying armies much larger than any seen since Classical times. Armies therefore became more closely tied to fortification-based depots and supply lines of carts and (where possible) shipping.

This does not mean that maneuver, especially at the operational level, was impossible. Skillful maneuver could drive an enemy force back by threatening its supply lines, or it could cut a fortress off from its supporting field army, rendering it vulnerable to a siege. And paradoxically, the slow average rate of march of armies placed a premium on administrative speed: An army that could get into the field even a few weeks before its foes could literally steal a march, often the difference between success and failure in taking a city or fortress.

Attack and defense of fortresses dominated strategy and campaigning. When battles did occur, they were almost always the result of a siege, as the besieging army faced off against a determined relief force. Generals' desire to cover sieges with an army that remained free to maneuver increased their demands for manpower, contributing to the growth of standing forces. Even more, the sheer number of forts requiring garrisons promoted such growth.

With fortress-depots more than ever the foci of campaign maneuvers in attack and defense, fortification and siege warfare shifted decisively from an art to a science. Vauban, Louis XIV's master of fortification, perfected systems of fortification design and siege technique, systematizing and rationalizing the practical wisdom accumulated over the prior 150 years. The founding of a royal engineering school ensured the continuity and development of the science, a crucial element of institutional continuity previously lacking.

Marlborough That positional warfare need not be static was shown by the campaigns of John Churchill, Duke of Marlborough. As the leader of the Allied coalition against Louis XIV in the War of Spanish Succession, he needed to be diplomat, general manager, staff officer, and general all in one, and he

usually succeeded at all. His careful logistical planning showed at its best in the Blenheim campaign. He managed to march his Anglo-German army from his base in the Netherlands up the Rhine to a rendezvous with his ally Prince Eugene in Bavaria along the Danube. Depots along the way provided food, clothing (including spare boots), and secure rest spots. Though the daily march was little over six miles, the cumulative result was a triumph of strategic mobility and Allied cooperation that turned the tide of the war. Marlborough's subsequent campaigns in Belgium were more restricted in scope but still provide examples of daring maneuver and the use of deception. In addition to maintaining mobility, Marlborough sought battle to an unusual degree. He recognized that, by shattering the aura of French invincibility, victories had a positive effect on the morale of the alliance and that clearing a theater of enemy field forces enabled Allied armies to divide up and prosecute several sieges at once.

Amphibious Operations Finally, the boldest and in many ways most successful strategic strokes of this period were amphibious operations that demonstrated the still-rising importance of naval power. England proved to be the master of this new domain. The Royal Navy supported English campaigns in Ireland, the seizing of Gibraltar, and operations against French outposts in Canada, the Caribbean, and southern Asia. Strategy was becoming globally oriented.

The Emergence of Linear Tactics

By the middle of the seventeenth century, most of western Europe had begun to adopt to some degree the innovations in tactics and drill that the Swedes used during the Thirty Years War. But the decades from 1660 through 1720 saw continued advances in weaponry, drill, and tactics. A new system of warfare emerged, driven partly by administrative and technological changes and partly by developments in warfare along Europe's frontiers, especially with the Turks.

Infantry Weapons and Formations The most profound changes in tactics affected the growing infantry forces of European states and were in general predicated on an ever-greater emphasis on firepower. One major factor that increased the firepower of infantrymen involved changes in the musket and its ammunition. During the later seventeenth century, the matchlock musket became lighter, easier to handle, and thus much quicker to load. Speed of loading was also enhanced by the widespread use of prepared cartridges.

As a result, by the 1690s, the ratio of musketeers to pikemen in a battalion had risen to four or five to one. While this clearly increased the firepower available to infantry units, it also created a problem: It left the musketeers vulnerable to shock tactics, especially by enemy horsemen, should their firepower not stop the enemy in his tracks. The pikemen, usually located in the battalion's center, could not protect the large number of musketeers and would themselves eventually succumb to concerted attacks by enemy cavalry to their flanks and rear. Novel approaches were taken to address the problem. One method attempted by the French army was to break the pikemen up into three groups, with one quarter deployed to each flank of the battalion's musketeers and one half massed in the center of the unit. Another approach involved *fraising* the battalion: forming the unit in five ranks—the first two of musketeers, followed by one of pikemen, and finally two more of musketeers. Neither of these solutions, however, proved acceptable. In the case of the first, it seems not to have been much employed, undoubtedly since it took an already insufficient number of pikemen and parceled them out into even less functional groups. Fraising also seems to have been little used; in fact, the French army forbade its use because it wasted the firepower of fully half the musket-armed infantry by putting them too far back in the formation to bring their weapons to bear.

The situation would not be successfully addressed until the adoption of a new weapon, the bayonet. The bayonet was first introduced in the 1640s, but only on a limited scale; it would not be in widespread use until the 1670s. The first such weapons were plug bayonets—in effect, little more than daggers fitted into the barrel of the musket. They had the undesirable side effect of keeping the musketeer from firing his weapon, a situation exacerbated by the difficulty of plugging the bayonet into the barrel while holding a lighted match. While plug bayonets did allow musketeers to defend themselves against enemy horsemen—the front rank, for example, could fix bayonets and act as pikemen of sorts while the rear ranks continued to fire—the plug bayonet hindered offensive operations by infantry. The volley followed by a charge, as performed by Gustavus's Swedes, was not possible with the plug bayonet, as it took too much time to affix the blade to the musket. The shortcomings of the plug bayonet in this respect were all too obvious (see the Highlights box "The Battle of Killikrankie").

Checkerboard to Line   By the late 1690s, two new weapons had become generally available that addressed the various problems relating to the vulnerability of musketeers and contributed to changing battlefield tactics. They were the flintlock musket and the socket bayonet. The flintlock was a marked improvement over the matchlock. Instead of requiring a lighted match to create the spark, the flintlock had a flint strike a frizzen, or hinged steel cover, that covered the priming pan, thus creating a spark. This allowed the flintlock to fire more quickly and reliably, increasing firepower even further. It also allowed units to close their ranks more tightly, since no one had to worry about having a lighted match too close to a neighbor who was pouring black powder into his musket. The socket bayonet featured a ring or tube that was fitted over the musket's barrel, thus allowing the musketeer to fire while his bayonet was fixed. This enabled the musketeer to deliver a volley and immediately follow up with shock tactics or defend against an enemy charge. Pikemen, rendered obsolete, disappeared.

The effect of these two technologies was to allow infantry formations to thin out even further. More rapid reloading and the elimination of pikemen made three-rank lines possible; fewer ranks made for more efficient delivery of firepower. But the opportunity did not compel change; an external stimulus contributed. The tactical system employed by the infantry at the end of the seventeenth and beginning of the eighteenth century was colored by wars fought on the European frontier against the Ottomans. While the Swedish checkerboard formations worked well against the large formed units of the Spanish school or even against other Europeans using the new, smaller Dutch/Swedish battalions, this formation was less effective against the more fluid Turkish form of warfare in which small, fast-moving groups penetrated intervals between units, thus leaving the flanks and rear of the first line vulnerable. To counter this, European armies began deploying in lines without gaps between battalions. A second, likewise unbroken, line was often positioned as a reserve. This was the beginning of the style of linear warfare that would dominate the battlefields of Europe for the next century and a half (see Chapter 21).

The Battle of Killikrankie, 1689

Killifrankie took place on July 27, 1689, during the Jacobite rebellion in Scotland that followed the expulsion of James II by William of Orange. The campaign began in April 1689 when John Graham, Viscount Dundee, raised the standard of revolt in favor of James II's claims. A government army led by General Hugh Mackay took the field. The government troops numbered some 4500 men, but most of the troops were inexperienced; indeed, one regiment had only recently been recruited for the campaign. Mackay spent the early summer campaigning with a small force in the north while the bulk of the government troops besieged strategically important Edinburgh Castle. After the castle fell on June 13, Mackay joined his troops there and decided to move against the Jacobite stronghold at Blair Atholl. Dundee, with a force of perhaps 2800 Highlanders, moved to reinforce Blair Atholl, reaching it before the advanced guard of the government army, which then retired to the defensible pass of Killikrankie in order to block further advances by the rebels. Mackay decided that it was not sufficient to block the Jacobite forces—they must be defeated. He thus advanced out of the pass to attack.

Dundee's Jacobite army occupied a piece of high ground. Most of the army consisted of Highland levies, the better off of whom were armed with matchlock muskets and, if aristocrats, a brace of pistols. The great majority, however, were armed with broadswords and axes. Their tactic was the devastating "Highland charge," a wild, undisciplined rush designed to unnerve and overwhelm the enemy.

The government forces drew up three ranks deep on a ridgeline within sight of Dundee's forces.

The government army consisted of six regiments of foot armed with matchlock muskets and plug bayonets, a small force of fusiliers armed with flintlocks, two small cavalry troops, and three light artillery pieces. Mackay's plan was to use his small artillery train to goad the enemy into charging his line, which would, in turn, devastate the Highlanders with volley fire.

Unfortunately, the artillery was not very effective, and the Highlanders were not to be drawn out at Mackay's convenience. Instead, they held their ground until dusk, at which time they quickly and unexpectedly charged the government troops. The regulars fired a volley at close range that inflicted heavy casualties on the Highlanders, but it did not stop them. At this point in the battle, the inexperience of the government troops proved fatal. The troops had waited to fire, but now the Highlanders had closed before they could either reload their muskets or fix their plug bayonets. The resulting melee was a disaster for Mackay's forces. Many broke and ran, sweeping away the cavalry attempting to relieve them. Fortunately, the Jacobites halted their pursuit to loot the regulars' baggage train.

The battle was a resounding victory for the Highlanders. They killed nearly 1000 government troops and captured 500 more, with the loss of only 200 of their own, although Dundee was among those slain. Killikrankie showed the inherent weakness of the plug bayonet, especially in the hands of inexperienced soldiers faced with a foe with good morale and motivated to join the battle hand to hand.

CONCLUSION

By the early eighteenth century, 700 years of evolution and development, decisively consolidated since about 1660, had produced in Europe a unique socioeconomic regime. The social structure was increasingly shaped by merchant capitalist dynamics, which also contributed to the economic growth and global aggressiveness of western Europe. Capitalism fit with and fostered a legalistic, contractually based, framework for social exchange that, in turn, shaped the political structure of European states, both absolutist and constitutional. At the same time, the Scientific Revolution was producing a new view of nature. In these ways, European kingdoms were increasingly different from most of the rest of the world.

This unique social formation supported armed forces that were effective tools of state policy and increasingly effective projectors of European political and economic ambition. Their reach was still limited, and European forces were by no means dominant everywhere. For instance, the interior of Africa was largely untouchable for nonmilitary reasons, mostly having to do with disease. And east Asia could still more than hold its own against European armies: Qing China met Tsarist Russia on equal terms, and Japan's closed-door policy went unchallenged. Likewise, European influence in south Asia was limited. Nonetheless, European techniques of war were becoming increasingly effective and went virtually unchallenged at sea.

In 1720, the European technology of war, with the important exception of the bayonet, was little different from sixty years earlier. But the techniques—the social control exercised within armies and navies, and the social implications of European-style armies—had been transformed. Not only were European armies more effective than many others, they were hard to copy because the political and social structures necessary to create them were inimical to traditional patterns of social organization and political hierarchy. The European transformation had reached a revolutionary threshold.

SUGGESTED READINGS

Black, Jeremy. *European Warfare, 1660–1815.* New Haven: Yale University Press, 1994. An important reexamination of the Military Revolution thesis; emphasizes reconsolidation of central authority as the key context for technological and military change. See also his *European Warfare, 1494–1660* (London: Routledge, 2002), for the earlier years of this period.

Brewer, John. *The Sinews of Power.* Cambridge: Harvard University Press, 1988. The fundamental work on the rise of the financial-administrative state and birth of a military-industrial complex in England as the key to military power.

Duffy, Christopher. *Siege Warfare.* New York: Routledge, 1985. A clear, detailed study of fortifications and siege techniques. See also his *Fortress Warfare in the Age of Vauban* (New York: Routledge, 1975).

Glete, Jan. *War and the State in Early Modern Europe.* London: Routledge, 2002. A thorough examination of the interdependence of finances and war, emphasizing the corporate nature of early fiscal-military states.

Hale, J. R. *War and Society in Renaissance Europe.* New York: St. Martin's Press, 1985. Looks at the social implications of warfare, especially in Italy and Germany.

Lynn, John, ed. *Tools of War.* Champaign: University of Illinois Press, 1990. A collection of articles critically examining the notion of technological determinism; important in the Military Revolution debate. For the period from 1610 onward, his *Giant of the Grand Siècle* is an excellent study of the French army as institution in this time of change.

Parker, Geoffrey. *The Military Revolution.* Cambridge: Cambridge University Press, 1988. The work that revitalized the study of early modern warfare by putting it in a global context and claiming primacy for technological and military innovation. Compare his *Army of Flanders and the Spanish Road,* 2nd ed. (Cambridge: Cambridge University Press, 2004).

Rogers, Clifford, ed. *The Military Revolution Debate.* Boulder: Westview Press, 1995. A collection of articles including Michael Roberts' seminal formulation of the Military Revolution thesis; uneven but still useful.

Tallett, Frank. *War and Society in Early Modern Europe.* New York: Routledge, 1992. An excellent synthesis of much recent work on early modern warfare.

Tilly, Charles. *Coercion, Capital and European States, 990–1990.* Oxford: Oxford University Press, 1992. An interesting conceptualization of the linked growth of political and military power.

Wood, James B. *The King's Army.* Cambridge: Cambridge University Press, 1996. A fine case study of the French army during the Wars of Religion, testing many Military Revolution theses against focused evidence.

CHAPTER 17

Cannon and Cavalry: Eurasian Expansion, 1500–1750

If the adoption of gunpowder weaponry in western Europe in the context of an ongoing evolution of the European sociomilitary system eventually produced revolutionary results, the spread of guns seems to have created an even larger and more immediate revolution in the rest of Eurasia. Various peoples of nomadic origins (or at least nomadic ethos and tactical tradition) added guns to their arsenals. The resulting military systems—syntheses of the mobile horse warriors of the steppes with the wall-blasting effects of cannon and, often, the defensive power of fortifications and infantry musketry—proved potent and fueled the expansion of the largest and most militarily powerful land empires of the age. The Ottomans, perhaps the most successful example of this pattern, had, in 1500, probably the greatest army in the world. But the Mughals in India, the Safavids in Persia, and the Muscovite princes in Russia—as well as the Qing dynasty in China, considered in Chapter 19—all followed this pattern.

The consequences of the rise of what some historians have called "gunpowder empires" (see the Issues box "Gunpowder Empires") were in fact revolutionary in at least one way. By drawing so heavily on the Central Asian cavalry tradition, the synthetic military systems of these expansionist powers drew the cycle of interaction between settled and nomadic peoples to a climax and a conclusion. The Ottomans and their like were the last great conquerors with nomadic origins, and by 1750 most of the steppe peoples had lost both their independence and their ability to threaten their settled neighbors in a serious way. Deep trends in demographics, economic development, and mechanisms of state power certainly played a role in finally shifting the balance of power away from the horse people. But it was their use of gunpowder and gunpowder fortifications, along with forces of steppe cavalry, that was central to the Eurasian empires' ability eventually to subordinate those same allies.

In another way, however, the revolution was illusory. The synthesis of cannon and cavalry was based in social and political structures that not only were traditional but remained largely untransformed by the military synthesis. As a result (and in contrast to western Europe, where social and economic transformation lay at the heart of changing military practice), the great Eurasian empires ended this period facing very traditional problems of fragmentation and conservatism. Though most in 1700 could still hold their own with European forces, especially away from European soil, and had for most of the period been as good as or better than the Europeans in their own ways, by 1750, the military consequences of these two divergent paths were beginning to tell in favor of European-style warfare. But in 1500, no one could possibly have predicted this outcome. Cannon and cavalry empires were the great powers of this age (Figure 17.1).

THE OTTOMAN EMPIRE, 1453–1699

Symbolically, the Ottoman state achieved imperial or great-power status with the capture of Constantinople in 1453. The sultans at that point inherited the Byzantine imperial mantle to reinforce Islamic and Turkish traditions dating back to the Great Seljuk Empire. But Ottoman military and administrative systems were already well developed by the time "The City" fell to them (see Chapter 11 for the rise of the early Ottomans). A combination of masses of cavalry, both horse-archers and heavy horse, with a disciplined, musket-bearing infantry corps of Janissaries and an impressive artillery train both reflected the structure of the Ottoman state and gave the sultans a potent, flexible weapon with which to pursue their aims.

Ottoman history after 1453 falls into three broad phases. Up to 1566, the Ottoman tide flowed

Gunpowder Empires

Some historians have claimed that there was an age of *gunpowder empires* in world history. The argument is that the introduction of gunpowder weapons—in particular, cannon that rendered medieval fortifications obsolete—made possible the creation of the major Eurasian empires in this period. Rulers who obtained a monopoly on the new weapons, so the argument goes, were able to run their opponents out of the game before technological diffusion could even the playing field. Only in Europe did such a monopoly fail to materialize, and therefore only in Europe was there no unified empire and consequent continued evolution of gunpowder weapons. This argument is clearly related to versions of the Military Revolution paradigm (see the Issues box on page 306).

A closer look reveals problems with this conception. For one, it ignores the continuing vital role of nomadic-style cavalry in the military systems of these empires, as this chapter will argue. It also tends to fall into a technological determinist trap of expecting the same results everywhere from the same technology. In fact, the histories of the empires considered in this chapter, as well as the histories of Japan and China in this age (see Chapter 19), demonstrate that the effect of new technology varies critically depending on the social, economic, political, and cultural contexts into which it is introduced.

Mostly, however, the concept of gunpowder empires exaggerates the role of gunpowder weapons in the dynamics of these empires' expansions. Safavid Persia grew out of Shiite religious enthusiasm and had reached its limits before it ever made much use of cannon. The Mughals used cannon in a few early victories, but their cavalry was the key to their military superiority on the battlefield; and, in sieges, their cannon were relatively ineffective against Indian forts already built to withstand good siege machinery and often possessing guns of their own. Bribery and numbers took forts for them more than cannon did. The Muscovite princes rarely had to besiege strong forts in building their empire, and even against other Russian princes, their artillery merely confirmed an already existing dominance. The Ottomans perhaps fit the model most closely, but even there it is a major oversimplification.

If gunpowder weapons played a role in these imperial histories, it was more as a factor in internal politics than in external expansion. Big guns formed part of the imperial panoply of splendor, balancing the factional tendencies of local aristocrats as much through their symbolic presence as through their effectiveness as weapons. This role was significant, and, certainly, both cannon and infantry small arms formed part of the military arsenals of these empires. But they were not revolutionary in their effect, and so the idea of gunpowder empires probably overemphasizes gunpowder technology.

---

powerfully, as expansionism and military success fed each other. But conquests gradually became more difficult, for reasons we will analyze below, and between 1566 and 1699, the empire entered a period of stasis. The eighteenth century then saw the slow emergence of problems that would become critical in the nineteenth century. This chapter will focus on the first two periods.

The Structure of the Ottoman State

Several characteristics of the Ottoman state and ideology shaped Ottoman military forces and how

they were used. The Ottoman Empire managed a paradoxical combination of expansionism with a fortress mentality, while the political character of the Sultanate also shaped military policy and was, in turn, influenced by military power.

Expansionism   Like many traditional empires, the Ottoman Empire was expansionist, at least in intent. In a world based on agricultural production, expansion made sense in part as the only way of increasing the wealth of the state. Two particular aspects of the Ottoman state further contributed to its expansionist impulse.

Figure 17.1 Cannon and Cavalry Empires This map shows the expansion of the major cannon and cavalry empires from the early sixteenth through the early eighteenth centuries. Note in particular the reduction of the Central Asian steppes as an independent area.

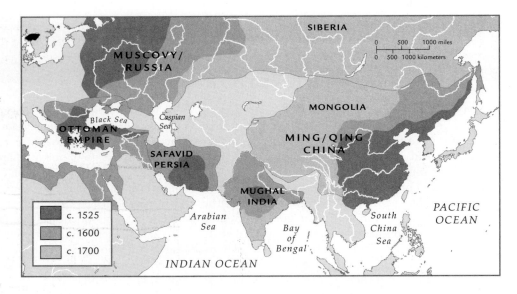

First, the origins of the Ottoman state as a *ghazi*, or frontier warrior, state built into Ottoman policy an Islamic-inspired drive to conquer infidel lands. Even after the expansion of the empire slowed and a more defensive-minded grand strategy came to dominate in practice, the continuing use of *ghazis* and the nomadic ethos of the *sipahi* cavalry (see below) reflected an offensive-minded, *jihad*-oriented ideology within elements of the army and state.

But internal politics was perhaps even more important in fostering expansionism. Offensive campaigns and the conquests they brought were essential to the sultan's ability to control the elites of the empire. Campaigning brought together the rural landholders who dominated local society and kept them under his watchful eye. The booty captured on campaign and the new lands brought under Ottoman rule, granted out as new *timars* (see below), served both as rewards for service and as an inducement to loyalty and further service. It is significant that the *sipahi* cavalry who formed the bulk of this class and whose *timar* landholdings obliged them to serve began to decline in effectiveness as the expansion of the empire slowed. Cause and effect are difficult to untangle—it could be that decreasing effectiveness of the cavalry led to fewer successful campaigns. But logistical difficulties and the limits imposed by the Ottoman pattern of mustering (itself partly a product of the dynamic of elite management; see below) seem to have had more to do with the end of expansion; the decline of the *sipahis* then followed.

A Fortress Mentality   Despite its expansionism, the Ottoman state also operated within a sort of fortress mentality that had implications for military organization and practice. Partly this reflected the empire's Byzantine heritage. Byzantium had pursued an essentially defensive grand strategy for nearly a millennium with effects on economic and cultural as well as military and diplomatic policies (see Chapters 8 and 11). Aspects of some of these policies carried over into Ottoman practice, especially as the Sultanate found itself, like Byzantium, surrounded by hostile powers. The empire consistently faced the problem of meeting its European foes with a hostile Shiite dynasty in Safavid Persia to its rear, or vice versa. Diplomatic contacts between Austria and Persia (and in reaction between the Sultanate and the French monarchy) reflected this problem.

This was especially true economically. The Sultanate viewed economic policy within the context of traditional military concerns. Thus, trade was managed more for security than income: Ottoman merchants were restricted in their ability to travel outside the empire, and incoming foreign merchants were channeled into foreign quarters in the major trade ports. The result was that tax revenues to support the military continued to come predominantly from agricultural levies, a limitation that would begin to tell in Ottoman competition with the smaller but ultimately more prosperous mercantilist states of western Europe. Further, the closed nature of the Ottoman economy created even more problems when inflation hit the

European economy with the influx of American precious metals. Higher prices in Europe drew Ottoman goods away from the less lucrative home market, where prices were more centrally controlled, but since such exports were not officially sanctioned, they spawned a black market that deprived the Sultanate of any tax benefits from the trade. And when inflation did spread to the east, it had the effect of raising the costs of maintaining the Ottoman military without raising tax receipts, which came mostly from fixed tax farms. Higher costs also reduced the ability of individual *timar* holders to equip and supply themselves properly, another factor in the decline of this arm of the Ottoman army.

Finally, the Ottoman fortress mentality showed up directly in the system of large and extensive fortifications that came to guard the European (and, to a lesser extent, the Persian) frontiers of the empire. These provided security and the backbone of a system of depots that supported the field army on campaign, but they also represented a large and increasing fixed cost in material, maintenance, and garrison troops.

Succession Problems   Succession problems also affected Ottoman military structure and practice. As in many Islamic states, strictly hereditary succession was problematic but crucial in an essentially absolutist polity. The Ottomans had managed to limit the old Turkish system whereby claims to rule passed to any member of the extended ruling clan, which led to much partition and strife. Sovereignty was held to descend strictly in the direct line of the sultans. But rivalry between brothers and half-brothers would prove a persistent source of infighting. It also tended to increase the influence of the harem on dynastic politics—especially of the sultan's favorites (and thus mothers of rival brothers) within it, who gained greater access to sultans who ceased campaigning regularly with the army after the mid-sixteenth century. The empire expanded under a line of capable rulers who emerged through good fortune from this system. But a larger, more secure empire increased the succession stakes, and sultans began to come to the throne after childhoods of seclusion that protected them from assassination by rivals but left them less than fully prepared for active rule, especially for military command.

The rivalries the system generated also created an opening for kingmaking, an opening exploited with increasing regularity (and at increasing cost to the state) by the Janissary Corps. As the elite armed force stationed in the capital and its environs, the Janissaries were ideally placed to throw their often decisive weight behind whichever rival to the throne promised them better terms. But not surprisingly, their military effectiveness declined as their political influence grew.

Organization of Ottoman Military Forces

The Janissaries arose out of the fundamental tension that shaped the organization of Ottoman military forces, the delicate balance between central and provincial forces. This tension was reminiscent of a similar Byzantine dynamic and tended to increase as the empire expanded. And, as noted above, it reflected the central role of elite management in shaping Ottoman military policy.

Local and familial loyalties had held together early Ottoman forces (see Chapter 11). But as Ottoman territory expanded, the warrior elites on *timar* lands who made up the *sipahi* cavalry came to have local and regional interests divergent from those of the sultan and his entourage in the capital. The sultans created the Janissary Corps and the artillery train that constituted the key central forces in part to balance the influence of the provincial *sipahis*. These central forces were dominant in the army from the time of their creation in the early fifteenth century until well into the sixteenth century. Gradually, however, the influence of the provincial forces increased, due to two major factors. First, the increasing costs of war began to outrun the ability of the Sultanate to pay. War costs thus led to decentralization as provincial commanders and their troops were granted greater autonomy and control over their land grants in exchange for bearing directly more of the costs of campaigning, a process that has parallels in the experience of Hapsburg Spain. Second, increasing corruption at the center reduced the effectiveness of central troops and therefore increased the importance of provincial levies.

Central Forces   The artillery and the Janissaries were the key elements of Ottoman central forces. The Ottomans adopted the use of artillery for siege warfare early in their history. Borrowing from Europeans, they created cannon that were technologically on a par with western guns well into the sixteenth century. Their proficiency with cannon became clear in 1453 when huge Turkish guns blasted holes in the walls of Constantinople. The sultans maintained a preference for really big guns: The largest Ottoman cannons were too heavy to move easily on campaign

Ottoman Janissaries   This engraving shows two members of the elite force of Janissaries, some of the best-disciplined and -equipped troops of the sixteenth and seventeenth centuries. The figure on the left is equipped with a matchlock musket.

and so were often forged on the spot by the experts who also acted as artillerists. Preference for size derived partly from shortages of the metals needed to cast large numbers of smaller pieces and even more from the psychological and internal political effect of conspicuously sized guns. But it meant that the Ottomans fell increasingly behind the Europeans in terms of mobile field artillery.

The Janissaries formed an even more famous element of Ottoman armies and symbolized their transition from frontier *ghazi* state to settled empire. After experiments with creating an infantry corps from sons of nobles, criminals, or prisoners of war, the sultans began taking Christian children from their Balkan provinces and turning them into slave soldiers. Isolated, trained in Islam and Turkish as well as the military arts, these recruits developed a strong esprit de corps and unit identity that was the basis of their discipline and effectiveness in battle. In addition to swords and axes, the corps early on adopted muskets and for a time in the fifteenth and sixteenth centuries were probably the most effective gunpowder infantry in the world.

Janissary numbers tended to increase over time, both because the sultans rewarded their early successes and because positions in the corps became hereditary.

Their pay also tended to increase as a result of their influence over the succession: The first Janissary revolt occurred in 1449, and thereafter, new sultans often made rewarding the corps their first act. The fiscal burden the corps placed on the state therefore also increased steadily. At the same time, their relative effectiveness in battle tended to decline. Heredity reduced the effectiveness of training, and once Janissary tactical traditions were established, institutional inertia and cultural inflexibility blocked attempts at change. The corps never adopted the technique of volley fire, for example. By 1700, the corps had become as much a problem for the state as an effective military tool.

Provincial Troops   In terms of numbers, the main force of Ottoman armies through the sixteenth century was the *sipahi* cavalry. *Sipahis* were heavily armed horse-archers capable of both missile and shock tactics. They were supported through the *timar* system, in which each trooper received the rights to income from designated estates. From the *timar* grant, the *sipahi* was expected to support himself and provide his own horse and equipment. Large *timars* obligated the holder to bring extra troopers proportional to the value of the *timar*. The *sipahis* in many ways represent the fusion of nomadic and settled elements within Ottoman culture and society. Fixed land grants supported warriors who maintained at least a symbolic connection to their nomadic ancestors and carried on a version of nomadic tactical traditions.

But the economic constraints mentioned above and the tendency of *timar* holders to become estate managers and thus reluctant soldiers gradually undermined *sipahi* effectiveness. Therefore, by 1600, the sultans were increasingly looking elsewhere for the numbers needed to fill out their field armies. The seventeenth century saw increased reliance on *ghazis*— frontier tribesmen marginalized from the mainstream of Ottoman society—and provincial levies for both infantry and cavalry. While providing significant numbers, often with high levels of enthusiasm, such troops lacked formal training. The central government was also extremely reluctant to give them firearms, as they feared arming local rebellions. Again, Ottoman forces increasingly diverged from the patterns developed in western Europe.

The final element of Ottoman armies came from nomadic allies such as the Tatars and Cossacks and from vassals of the sultans. While such sources continued to be able to provide tens of thousands of light cavalry well into the eighteenth century, the troops were hardly reliable or disciplined. They could be useful at times for scouting and harassing an enemy supply line; but, as their chief interest was booty, they often proved as dangerous to their Ottoman allies as to the enemy.

Patterns of Campaigning

Three fundamental features of the Ottoman state and army significantly influenced the patterns of Ottoman campaigning. The sultans' need to exercise central control was the first. Second, the key troops in the army, the *sipahi* cavalry and the Janissary Corps, demanded limits to campaigns. The *sipahis*, as estate holders, always wished to return home from campaign to oversee harvesting and winter management of their lands. Similarly, the Janissaries resisted wintering away from the comforts of their permanent barracks in Constantinople. Third, logistical constraints tended to reinforce the limits of the Ottoman campaigning season. The Ottoman army traveled as a vast, virtually self-sufficient mobile fortress, but one needing a steady stream of supplies and lots of fodder for the many cavalry and draft horses. The combination of these factors produced a stereotyped pattern of Ottoman campaigns.

Campaigns were carefully planned. When the sultan decided sometime in midwinter on the direction of the next year's campaign, usually toward either the Balkans or the Safavid frontier, he drew up orders for troop preparation and the dispatch of supplies. Funds were sent to the provincial governors and allied rulers to purchase necessities. Agents went to villages on the proposed route of march to organize supplies and ensure that the villagers were harassed as little as possible. Carts and draft animals, numbering in the hundreds of thousands for major campaigns, were also gathered.

In order to ensure central control, the sultan ordered most *timar* holders and allied rulers to gather with their followers near Constantinople, when possible just after the feast of Ramadan, which commemorated the first revelation of the Quran to Muhammad. (Those along the line of march joined the army as it marched through.) The muster ground rapidly became a well-organized military camp, constructed in advance by thousands of craftsmen and workers. Contingents had assigned places in the camp. The sultan's own tent, designed to echo the tents of the nomadic past, dominated the center, surrounded by the Janissaries and the artillery train. As the host marched off, the sultan or his representative brought along important symbols—the war banner of Muhammad and the sword of Umar—to raise morale and demonstrate that the campaign was a *jihad*, further reinforcing the central role of the sultan in the army and state.

The need for fodder and the agricultural demands of estate management meant that the standard campaigning season ran from early April until mid-to-late October. But mustering at Constantinople meant that the army usually did not get under way until perhaps June. Routes of march tended to follow rivers, which provided the only way to transport supplies to the equivalent of a moving city. Slow travel, especially if the artillery train was substantial, meant that campaigns into Hungary or deep into Persia saw the army arrive at the theater of operations late in the summer, with only a month or two to accomplish anything before fodder became scarce and the *sipahis* and Janissaries demanded to return home.

This dynamic first slowed and then stopped Ottoman expansion. Basically, the empire reached the physical limits sustainable by a field army of seasonal soldiers based in the capital. Fortresses and garrison troops could hold the established frontier with the help of periodic campaigns by the army, but they could not push the borders any farther out. The character of the two main frontiers differed somewhat. Logistical difficulties were more critical in the deserts of Persia, whereas the Austro-Hungarian frontier was better supplied but also much more heavily fortified. The time needed to conduct a siege prevented much Ottoman progress there after about 1560.

This pattern of campaigning had two other consequences. Need for central control meant that the sultans always had some difficulty fighting on two fronts at once, preferring to pacify one front with truces when the other demanded attention. And the self-reinforcing pattern of conquest that produced plunder that maintained the loyalty and effectiveness of the army was broken by the limits of expansion. The same system proved less capable of fighting defensive wars over the long run. The empire had the resources and the fortifications to hold its ground for decades after 1560, and even to launch the occasional offensive (see Highlights box on page 331), but the quality of the army slowly declined. By 1700, a slow and irregular retreat from the limits reached in the sixteenth century had begun. But not until the nineteenth century would the situation become serious enough to force the empire into substantial reforms (see Chapter 24).

Tactics

Battle Tactics   At least down to 1500, one of the hallmarks of Ottoman military success was tactical flexibility. The Ottomans proved willing to adapt to local conditions and adopt the useful tactics and weapons of their enemies. Victories over the Hungarians in the 1480s, for example, came from using Hungarian-style small arms and tactics learned in several previous defeats. Nevertheless, a somewhat stereotyped Ottoman battle plan gradually emerged that combined the various strengths of Ottoman troops.

Though less useful in battles than sieges because of their immobility, Ottoman cannon sometimes played an important a role in field combat, especially at the opening of an encounter. Placed at the center, cannon reinforced the firepower of the Janissaries, who formed the core of an infantry block anchoring the Ottoman line. The Janissaries themselves also came to follow a set routine. Once ordered to fire, they kept up a relentless hail of musketry and arrow fire—not in organized volleys, but with each man firing and reloading until ordered to stop. They then took up their swords and battle-axes and charged to the accompaniment of drums, horns, and fifes, terrifying their enemies with their apparent fearlessness. European observers noted Janissary steadiness in combat as late as the eighteenth century, when Janissary charges were often cut down by disciplined musket fire.

The infantry, especially the Janissaries, also acted as the fulcrum for attacks by the *sipahi* cavalry. The cavalry generally formed in a shallow crescent formation on either side of the infantry, with the wings inclined toward the enemy. The design was intended to facilitate flanking attacks. The charge of the *sipahis*, like that of the Janissaries, was renowned for its fierceness and shock value, though not for its discipline. Provincial levies and allied troops played the distinctly secondary role in this scheme of absorbing the brunt of enemy attacks—acting as cannon fodder—and lending mass to the Ottoman formation.

At its best, the Ottoman combination of light and heavy cavalry with disciplined infantry and some artillery fire proved potent and flexible. Against foes with substantial cavalry, such as the Mamluks and Safavids, the Ottoman advantage in firepower and infantry sta-

bility often carried the day, as at the battle of Chaldiran in Persia in 1515, where entrenched Janissaries and chained-together artillery repulsed Persian cavalry assaults. Against European foes who could deploy effective infantry, the mass and mobility of the cavalry could be effective. But after reaching maturity about 1500, there was little development of Ottoman tactical doctrine. Success, in part, bred complacency. The Janissaries became entrenched culturally and politically, and the social and economic factors outlined above undermined some of the bases of Ottoman effectiveness. The army could still be formidable, but it increasingly lost whatever edge it had over its foes at the height of its success.

Siege Tactics   Ottoman siege tactics achieved their greatest success, in many ways, at the siege of Constantinople in 1453. Mehmed II, "the Conqueror," began his preparations in 1451 by placing cannon in two fortresses on the straits of the Bosporus to control traffic into "The City." In 1453, he initiated the siege with roughly 100,000 men. The defenders had the massive and heretofore impregnable walls of the city on their side, but only about 8500 men, mostly Italians, to defend them. The key to Mehmed's success was the construction of massive cannon by a Hungarian in his employ. One had a barrel twenty-five feet long and fired a stone ball weighing nearly a quarter of a ton. In under two months, the great guns slowly but surely demolished the walls and towers of the city and battered a large enough breach for the Ottoman troops to break through. After three days of slaughtering and looting, Mehmed had a new capital city.

The assault confirmed several characteristics of Ottoman siege warfare that had already begun to develop. Massive but relatively immobile siege artillery would remain an Ottoman trademark, but with decreasing effectiveness as new fortification designs spread (see Chapter 16). That led to the extensive use of gunpowder mining to create breaches and assaults by massive numbers of troops with little regard for casualties. Though the Ottomans did use entrenching to approach fortress walls, they did not keep up with the scientific design of siege trenches developing in western Europe, and they never used lines of contravallation around their army to protect against relief forces. Another telling distinction between Ottoman and western European practice was that elite Ottoman troops such as the Janissaries and the *sipahis* never dug their own trenches as soldiers in the west did. Rather,

The Sieges of Vienna, 1529 and 1683

In May 1529, Sultan Suleyman the Magnificent led his army north toward Vienna, the capture of which would help ensure control of his recently acquired Hungarian territories. He was joined by several thousand Hungarian allies. Terrible weather and bad roads slowed the advance and forced him to leave behind most of his heavy artillery. Suleyman finally reached Vienna in late September, giving the defenders time to establish defenses, including demolishing buildings just outside the city walls.

The Ottomans began digging trenches, laying mines, and constructing earthworks. Thousands of common soldiers died digging a broad trench aimed directly at what spies reported was the weakest spot of the city walls. Ottoman light guns pounded the walls of the city but to limited effect. Still, the Ottoman assault was relentless, and the defenders lost thousands in sallies to delay the digging. On October 9, mines blew a gaping breach in the wall, but the Austrians patched it that night, before the Ottoman assault that began the next day, led by the Janissaries. The Ottomans did not disguise their tactics, which consisted of relentless pressure on one or two spots along the wall, and the Austrians massed defenders by the breach. Tightly packed small-arms and cannon fire repulsed several waves, causing massive casualties. Two more mines destroyed adjoining sections of the wall, but again, massed Ottoman attacks were repulsed by the small-arms and cannon fire of the defenders. Finally, on the night of October 14, the Ottomans struck their tents and withdrew.

The second Siege of Vienna, in 1683, was led by Grand Vizier Kara ("Black") Mustafa, commanding probably the largest Ottoman army ever assembled, assisted by allies and tributaries. Again, the army moved slowly once past Belgrade. This time, the Ottomans brought some heavy artillery, but they proved of little use except as antipersonnel weapons. Kara Mustafa reached Vienna in mid-July and began digging mines and trenches with little regard for the thousands killed in the process.

If the Ottomans conducted this siege much as they had the earlier one, their opponents were quite different. The Austrians had the assistance of other Christian powers in the region. Further, the city of Vienna itself was much better protected to resist a siege: Construction of the walls, moats, bastions, counterscarps, and trenches was influenced by a century and a half of European improvements in defensive fortification.

Ottoman assaults were relentless and, in typical Ottoman fashion, pressured one main location rather than spreading the defenders thin. There were breaches of the outer fortifications, including one of the main bastions, but the Ottoman could not penetrate the interior walls. Early in September, in a driving rain, the Ottomans launched several fierce assaults on the city, with mines providing openings into one of the main bastions. But disciplined Austrian infantry fire backed by a tremendous bombardment forced the Ottomans back from even this small advance.

Kara Mustafa's attention was directed at forcing his way into the city. In this, he followed standard Ottoman procedure, which exposed his rear to relief forces. On September 12, a combined force of Austrians, Poles, and various German princely armies, all nominally under the command of the Polish king John Sobieski, attacked the Ottomans from the rear. Not only had Kara Mustafa not provided defenses for this contingency, but once the attack came, the Ottomans had great difficulty in rearranging their artillery from assault on Vienna to defense against the relievers. Disciplined Christian cavalry attacks supported the steady advance of combined infantry and artillery: Artillery in front of the infantry pushed the enemy back, and the infantry then advanced, holding the position until the artillery could be brought forward to repeat the sequence. The result was an Ottoman rout and Kara Mustafa's execution in front of Sultan Mehmed IV.

The failures of the sieges of Vienna thus show both the limits of Ottoman expansion and the ossification of Ottoman tactics and weapons.

Turkish Siege Artillery
This print depicts a Turkish army besieging a town in Hungary at the end of the sixteenth century. Note the substantial artillery park, lower left and far right, as well as camels, used for supply transport, in the lower left.

conscripts and nonmilitary laborers were forced into doing the dirty work. This kept the soldiers safer for a while but reduced the effectiveness of the entrenching and mining.

Ottoman sieges were thus, like sieges by western armies, slow and expensive affairs. But unlike their European rivals, the Ottomans failed to advance their science of sieges significantly after 1600. While large numbers, a disregard for casualties, and effective use of mining could at times still carry the day, major Ottoman efforts became increasingly less likely to succeed over time, especially when they took place at the end of a long logistical rope (see the Highlights box "The Sieges of Vienna, 1529 and 1683"). In this respect, Ottoman siege warfare replicated the patterns of Ottoman warfare as a whole: great initial success, a long period of uninventive effectiveness, and a decline that is easy to exaggerate—Ottoman victories were still possible in the mid-eighteenth century, even against well-drilled European foes—but was nonetheless real and eventually telling.

MUGHAL INDIA, 1526–1720

At its height, the Mughal Empire extended throughout the Indian subcontinent and included much of present-day Afghanistan and parts of Central Asia. The founder of the Mughals, Babur, could trace his ancestry to both Chingiz Khan and Tamerlane, and

the military system he constructed bore a strong resemblance to those of his ancestors'. Yet, once the Mughals (which is a Turkish form of the word *Mongol*) had established themselves in northern India, they, like the Ottomans after their early conquests, discovered the necessity to adapt their military system to local patterns and to ruling a settled empire.

The Mughal State and Military System

Based originally in Afghanistan, the Mughals were the inheritors of a part of the former empire of Tamerlane. The organization and order imposed by Tamerlane mostly collapsed after his death, and fighting was endemic among his heirs. The Mughal army was composed of Turks, Mongols, and Afghans, predominantly mounted archers and lancers in the steppe tradition. The Mughals raided northern India for over 100 years after Tamerlane's devastation there, but only in the sixteenth century did they turn plundering into conquest.

Babur invaded in 1526, aiming for a permanent presence. At that time, much of northern India was under the tenuous rule of the Afghan Lodi dynasty. When the two forces met at Panipat, Babur found himself greatly outnumbered. However, Babur had in his army two large cannon and several hundred men armed with matchlocks. Babur chained his carts together and placed his artillery and matchlockmen behind this protective wall in emulation of Ottoman practice. With the cannon and artillery firing on successive waves of Lodi cavalry, Babur scored an impressive victory. Further victories came as a result of both superior technology and superior skill, for although Hindu rulers rapidly acquired their own cannon, they were defeated before they could learn to use them effectively. Babur established workshops in his capital at Agra where cannon were manufactured, while Mughal cavalry superiority continued to underpin their success.

By the middle of the emperor Akbar's reign (1556–1605), the Mughal military system had undergone reforms designed to stabilize rule of the large, heavily populated empire by accommodating the shifting alliances, inner frontiers, and ill-defined states of Indian society (see Chapter 14). The result was a system that in many respects resembled that of the Ottomans. The military factories that had been established by Babur were expanded and placed under closer control, and a bureaucracy was organized to ensure that funds and resources were available to support further conquest.

The key to the Mughal military system and rule of India was the emperor, who stood at the apex of a highly centralized system of control. Military commanders held all important civil posts, and the military came under increasingly centralized administration. The people and resources of the Mughal Empire were, in turn, militarized: All who staffed the expanded civil bureaucracy were given military ranks, including clerks, accountants, and even cooks. An imperial paymaster controlled the treasury and paid both the civil officials and the Mughal standing army. Even the bulk of the Mughal army, which was raised for particular campaigns by local commanders, was funded to a significant extent from the imperial treasury.

The key to Akbar's military organization was the *mansabdar* system. *Mansabdars* were local military commanders recruited by the emperor, to whom they were directly responsible. Each *mansabdar* owed a number of soldiers, always stated as a multiple of ten in emulation of the Mongol military system. Funds for the recruitment of soldiers, overwhelmingly cavalry, came from two sources: the imperial treasury and grants of land to the *mansabdars,* a system resembling the *timar* system of the Ottomans. In addition to men, *mansabdars* owed quotas of horses, elephants, and carts. When called to join a Mughal military campaign, the *mansabdar* brought his men to various muster areas. Just before the campaign, the emperor would pick commanders for groups of *mansabdars* and their men from among a cadre of generals. During the campaign, the *mansabdar* was responsible for the supply and discipline of his men. The *mansabdar* system helped accommodate the shifting alliances of Indian politics, as land grants and bribes could convert enemies into *mansabdars* during a campaign, avoiding the need for a fight.

The Mughal Army

The Mughal army consisted of two parts. The standing force was composed primarily of Turkish and Afghan tribesmen recruited from their homelands, as well as Persians, Hindu Rajputs, Arabs, and Ethiopians. Europeans served too, especially when the end of the Thirty Years War left many soldiers there unemployed. Surprisingly few Indian Muslims were recruited into the Mughal standing army. This fairly small standing force, consisting in part of *ghulams,* the slave soldiers of the emperor, was supplemented by soldiers recruited for particular campaigns. A large corps of bureaucrats managing logistics and personnel supported Mughal cavalry, artillery, and infantry on campaign.

Cavalry   The most important arm of the Mughal military was their cavalry. The Mughal army, in fact, was essentially an army of horsemen, reflecting Mughal origins as well as lessons learned by earlier Muslim conquerors of India. The horses themselves were almost all obtained from outside India, which was a key factor in the Mughal desire to control their Afghan and Central Asian lands. The horsemen were primarily archers, although a number in the standing army were also armed with lances and matchlocks. In several battles, these matchlock-armed cavalrymen proved key to Mughal victories over Rajput cavalry. Each horseman was also armed with a sword since standard Mughal tactics called for the soldiers to dismount after their cavalry charges and fight as infantry.

Artillery   By the late sixteenth century, Mughal factories were producing large numbers of cannon of various weights and sizes. The largest could hurl a ball weighing over 120 pounds, while the lightest were designed to be carried and set up by two-man teams. The Mughals probably learned about artillery from the Persians, as nearly all of the early Mughal artillerymen were Persian. But when the Mughals came into contact with the Portuguese, they began constructing cannon in the Portuguese style. Many Portuguese were hired to supervise this construction and even to man the artillery on the battlefield. Eventually, the ranks of the artillery force came to be filled almost solely by men of mixed Indo-European background, while the officer ranks were dominated by Europeans.

Two characteristics distinguished Mughal artillery. First, the Mughals loved big, heavy guns, useful for display but not so useful against many inaccessible Indian forts; in fact, some of the guns were so heavy that elephants were needed to haul them to the battlefield. Second, the Mughals relied on quantity rather than quality. Early Mughal cannon were comparable to those of the Ottomans and Europeans, but the Mughals did not keep up with advances elsewhere even though they had a number of Europeans in their employ. Unlike the Ottomans, however, the Mughals faced opponents who rarely were equipped with firearms in any quantity, and so they felt little pressure to improve their artillery.

Infantry We need not say much about Mughal infantry as it did not play a major role in the wars of the empire. Most infantry were raised by *mansabdars* outside their quota obligations. Infantry in the standing army were armed with matchlocks and formed part of the Imperial Guard. On campaign, they normally remained with the emperor, and when they fought, it was in support of the artillery. In some battles, the infantry were mounted on elephants and fired matchlocks in support of cavalry charges. However, most of the infantry served as guards for the baggage train or camp.

Strategy and Tactics

Strategy The Mughal emperors called themselves *caliph,* in competition with the Ottoman rulers, and saw their mission as holy war to spread the rule of Islam. Also like the Ottomans, Mughal expansionism held the empire together, as the emperors used the land and spoils of conquest to reward their followers and unify the Mughal elite. While early Mughal strategy had consisted of rapid raids by small cavalry armies, later Mughal strategy consisted essentially of overwhelming an enemy with numbers. Certainly, the element of surprise was discarded as enormous Mughal armies marched accompanied by many civil officials, merchants who sold supplies at traveling bazaars, entertainers, and prostitutes, with drums and horns

announcing to all their arrival. The intent was as much to awe potential enemies into joining the imperial side as it was to defeat them; the same processions also served to cement the allegiance of subordinates already allied to the empire. Such Mughal armies did not actively seek battle and aimed to end sieges with bribery rather than assault. As political display and for campaigning in southern India, Mughal armies worked well enough, overawing opponents with technological and numerical superiority. But against foreign foes such as the Safavids and Uzbeks, the ponderousness of the Mughal army was a great hindrance. Victory in these quarters usually resulted only from the hiring of whole tribes of Central Asians who utilized the tactics of the region.

Battle Tactics Early Mughal armies often fought battles in which they were greatly outnumbered, putting a premium on the tactical ingenuity of Mughal commanders. But as the empire expanded under Akbar and Mughal armies grew, the role of the commander was greatly reduced, and Mughal tactics became standardized. The Mughals preferred to fight in large, open spaces to take advantage of the numbers and mobility of their cavalry. In battle array, the artillery was placed in the front center, chained together in Ottoman fashion and protected by earthworks. Just behind the artillery were matchlockmen, whose function was to protect the artillery from assault. Cavalry occupied both wings. Farther behind the artillery was the emperor or the commander of the army, usually mounted high on an elephant, and a force of elite cavalry used to turn the enemy flanks. Finally, still farther back was a rear guard or reserve of both cavalry and infantry.

After beating drums and sounding horns announced Mughal intent, battles opened with an artillery barrage. Since the Mughals emphasized quantity of artillery, they did not develop the skill to fire their cannons in rapid succession—each gun usually fired only once. At some point during the artillery bombardment, the cavalry would advance; as it approached the enemy lines, the artillery would cease firing. After several cavalry charges that saw the firing of matchlocks and arrows, the cavalry would dismount and close with the enemy force. Mughal elite troops almost always aimed for the enemy center while the rest of the army attempted to turn the flanks. The sheer numbers of Mughals in an assault almost guaranteed success, but on those occasions when the Mughals were repulsed, the retreat was a rout, for

Mughal Army Conducting a Siege   Here we see a Mughal army laying siege to a fortified town. The sultan is surrounded by Mughal horsemen equipped with lances and bows, while in the background, a large number of cannon fire on the fortifications.

the Mughals had no plans for orderly withdrawal. The feigned retreat, a staple of their nomadic ancestors, was nonexistent by the mid-sixteenth century.

Sieges   The Mughals were forced to engage in a great number of sieges, in which they relied on bribery, numbers, and gunpowder. They followed a common strategy in sieges, with minor variations. First, using their superior numbers, they surrounded the fortress or fortified city. Gunpowder mines were dug to try to blow up the foundations of the walls. Next came bombardment of the gates and walls where possible, though the thick walls and inaccessible nature of many Indian forts rendered artillery less than useful in this role; artillery also fired into the interior of the fortress to cause fires and damage structures. For walls that were too high for artillery to fire over, wooden structures were constructed on which cannon were

placed. Sometimes elephants were also used to batter down the gates of the fortress. Once there had been a breach or the defenses had been greatly weakened, enormous numbers of soldiers were sent to storm the fortress, many carrying scaling ladders. There was no organization to this storming; large numbers were thought sufficient to overwhelm the enemy. The Mughals also built a large number of fortresses for defense and as arsenals and storehouses. These usually had exceptionally high, thick walls surrounded by a moat, designed to withstand artillery bombardment.

Decline

As the Mughal armies grew larger and larger, they became increasingly difficult to maintain. Akbar and his immediate successors strove mightily to keep from having to live off the land or, at least, to purchase supplies while on the march, but when discipline broke down, Mughal soldiers often ravaged local areas. This was happening with increasing frequency by the late seventeenth century, and the Mughals were unable to manage the internal resistance put forth by the Maratha Confederation and other Indian regional powers. Weak leadership only compounded these problems. At their height, the Mughals had been very successful at ruling such a large, heavily populated land. They were never really defeated, but they gradually decayed to the point at which India was again effectively divided into independent principalities.

SAFAVID PERSIA

Safavid Persia was born of Shiite religious fervor and shows another face of the interaction of gunpowder weaponry with nomadic warriors.

Persian Geography and Society

Two major factors shaped Persian military organization and practice in this period as in most of its history. First, Persia sat at a crossroads of southwest Asia, closer and more open on several sides to nomadic incursion than either the Ottomans or the Mughals—and, in fact, more so than Muscovite Russia. Persian rulers were therefore always balancing the incorporation of nomadic tribes and peoples into their armies with suppression of nomadic revolts and incursions. Any army a Persian shah raised had to be able to deal with traditional steppe horse-archer tactics. At the same time, Persia's central position put it in potential conflict with the Ottomans to the west, especially over the Iraqi regions centered on Baghdad, and with the Mughals to the east. In 1664, a third front opened (or took new form), when Cossacks under Russian direction invaded from the north for the first time. Geopolitics definitely dealt Persian rulers a bad hand.

Second, Persia was less urbanized than the Ottoman realm or Mughal India—indeed, less urbanized by 1700 than Russia. Persian society and government were thus dominated by a powerful rural aristocracy that headed the tribal divisions within the kingdom. This aristocracy provided the spearhead of heavy cavalry that had been characteristic of Persian armies for centuries. But the small number of cities in the kingdom meant that Persian shahs had fewer urban resources to draw on in constructing an army. This was reflected in the minuscule role played by any kind of infantry in most Persian armies, as well as the difficulty Persian rulers had in sustaining a native gun-casting industry (to which a lack of raw materials also contributed). As a result, the Persian use of gunpowder weapons owed more to outside intervention, mostly by Europeans, than did Ottoman or Mughal practices. Urban revenues from trade were also inconsequential, so that money for military expenditures came from traditional land taxes or direct exchanges of land for service.

The Persian Military

The Persian army that lost to the Ottomans at Chaldiran in 1515 was almost entirely cavalry, divided between lancers and horse-archers on the old Mongol model. It was fierce in attack but reflected the tribal divisions of the kingdom, reducing its responsiveness to central direction. It is easy to exaggerate the extent of its defeat at the hand of the mixed Ottoman force, however. This was a hard-fought battle; though the steadiness and firepower of the Ottoman infantry eventually carried the day, the Persians were able to retreat in good order, as all-cavalry forces are often able to do when facing infantry.

On the other hand, much of Mesopotamia including Baghdad fell to the Ottomans in the wake of the battle, and the rest of the century saw the Safavids engaged in inconclusive wars against Uzbek tribesmen and border wars with the Ottomans that failed to dent the sultan's conquests. It was not until the end of the century, during the reign of the greatest Safavid ruler, Shah Abbas I, that Persian forces were significantly reorganized. Taking advantage of a European delegation sent in 1598 to gain Persian aid against the Ottomans and led by the English artillery expert Robert Shirley, Abbas re-created the Persian army along Ottoman lines. An excellent artillery train and a disciplined, musket-bearing infantry corps of slave soldiers became the core of a central standing army that not only allowed the Persians to meet the Ottomans on equal tactical ground but, like the Ottoman central forces, allowed the shah to control the rural aristocracy more effectively. Abbas furthered this goal by creating a new tribe designed to give him the basis for a central cavalry force. It drew the elite warriors from the established tribes and so weakened both the tribal divisions and the aristocracy that benefited from them. The new army showed its value at the battle of Sis in 1606, where it routed a larger Ottoman force. Many of the lands lost in the wake of Chaldiran, including Baghdad, were recovered, and in 1612, favorable peace terms were signed.

Unfortunately for the Safavids, by heightening the role of central forces, the new military and state structure forged by Abbas also increased the dependence of the system on strong and effective central direction. After Abbas died in 1629, such direction was often lacking, and Abbas's gains slipped away. Baghdad fell to the Ottomans again in 1638, and though wars with the Moghuls were indecisive, by the end of the century, the Russians, using Cossack raiders, and the Dutch, coming from the sea, were both making inroads against Persian occupiers of their territory.

The Safavids thus reproduce, albeit on a smaller scale and for a less extended time, the dynamics of gunpowder-nomad synthesis visible in Ottoman and Mughal history. Under strong leadership, the combination of an artillery train, disciplined musket-bearing infantry, and a large cavalry contingent following a version of the steppe nomad tactical tradition proved potent and flexible and spearheaded the expansion of powerful empires. But these states were vulnerable to weak leadership and to the decentralizing tendencies that always plagued traditional empires; indeed, the added costs associated with the military systems that characterized these states often ended up contributing to decentralization. Trapped between new, expensive forms of military force and old forms of revenue raising and social structure, the Safavids, like the

Ottomans and Mughals, achieved a period of power but not a lasting transformation of their world.

MUSCOVITE RUSSIA, 1450–1720

The first mention of Moscow as a Russian principality is at the end of the twelfth century. At the time, Muscovy was little more than a minor state under the sway of the more powerful principality of Novgorod. The coming of the Mongols in the thirteenth century, however, initiated the rise of Muscovy to ultimate dominance over Russia. Thirteenth-century Russia was a patchwork of states that originated in the ninth century with the Kievan Rus, a mixture of Scandinavian, Slavic, and Finno-Ugaritic peoples ruled by a Scandinavian warrior elite. By the thirteenth century, the Kievan polity had grown to encompass a large area stretching from the White Sea in the northeast to the Carpathians in the southwest. The Rus state was not, however, strongly centralized; rather, it was a loose confederation of princes tied together by common culture and language. Moreover, in addition to the decentralization inherent in such a grouping of principalities, the Rus polity suffered internal divisions. Each prince had to contend for authority with rival princes from smaller towns within his state, with his *boyar* status (the top-tier aristocracy), and with the local *Veche,* the town council of his capital. By the early thirteenth century, these competing pressures had seriously weakened the power of the Kievan Rus and left them ripe for conquest.

The Mongol Conquest and Its Effects

After some initial probes, the Mongols launched a well-planned invasion of Rus territories in 1236. Over the next four years, the Mongols capitalized on the disunity of the Rus princes and in relatively short order conquered one principality after another. By the end of 1240, the principalities of the Rus were part of the Mongol Empire (see Chapter 13 for details).

Mongol Rule in Russia   The Mongols ruled the Russian principalities indirectly. By the mid-fourteenth century, the Mongols had established a capital at Sarai in southern Russia—a massive tent city that served as the center of Mongol authority. Over time, most of the Rus rulers were forced to make a trek to Sarai where they would seek a charter from the Khan of the Golden Horde (as the Russian Khanate was known). On occasion, the Rus princes were even required to travel to the heart of the Mongol Empire at Karakorum to received their charter. Once chartered, the princes, under the supervision of Mongol officials, were responsible for administering their own lands, including collecting tribute and taxes to be handed over to their Mongol overlords, raising troops to support Mongol military expeditions, and keeping their populations, especially the lesser nobility, in line. Even the great national hero of this period, Alexander Nevsky, famous for his victories over the Swedes and Teutonic Knights, ruthlessly suppressed several revolts by the nobility of Novgorod. The level of direct Mongol presence depended on the location of the principality: greater in the south, less intensely in the north. In this way, the Golden Horde ruled over the Russians for more than a century.

The Mongol Impact   The effects of Mongol rule have generally been viewed as extremely detrimental to the subsequent development of a Russian state. This is particularly true of Soviet historians, who traditionally have viewed the "Tatar yoke" as having retarded the political, social, and economic development of Russia, setting it back several centuries with no positive effects. While it is true that tribute flowed from Russia to the Mongols, the Russians gained corresponding economic advantages as part of the Mongol Empire in terms of interregional trade. Moreover, the Russian princes learned much of state and military organization from the Mongols, adopting Mongol institutions of administration and finance, including those for collecting taxes.

The Rise of the Muscovite State

The Mongols were the context for the rise of Muscovy. At the beginning of the fourteenth century, Moscow was one of many Russian statelets vying for power and the support of the Mongol Khans. By the end of that century, the Muscovites were on the rise, having handed the Mongols their first major military setback at Kulikovo Field in 1380. While it would take Moscow another century and a half to dominate the majority of Russian principalities, the institutions that made the Muscovite princes so successful date to the period of Mongol rule.

One important element of Moscow's success was the delicate balancing act that the princes of Moscow were able to achieve in their dealings with their Mongol overlord. On the one hand, the Muscovite princes became the chief tax collectors for the Golden

Horde, providing them with economic benefits including the ability to draw off money. It also provided them with Mongol support against neighboring principalities. This support allowed Moscow to overcome her nearby rival of Tver during the fourteenth century. On the other hand, the Muscovites were also able to portray themselves as champions against Mongol rule. Dmitri Donskoi played this game particularly well. In 1380, Dmitri was able to muster substantial support from other Russian princes for the battle at Kulikovo Field, where he fought Mamai, one of the two rivals to the throne of the Golden Horde. The Russians were victorious, which did much to undermine the myth of Mongol invincibility. Two years later, a Mongol army under the khan Tokhtamysh (who had defeated Mamai for control of the Golden Horde) laid waste to Muscovite territory. Dmitri was, however, able to find his way back into the good graces of the khan and resume his position as tax collector for the Golden Horde.

Another reason for the success of Moscow was the alliance between the prince and the Orthodox Church. Beginning in the second quarter of the fourteenth century, the Muscovite princes secured the continuing presence of the metropolitan, the head of the Orthodox Church in Moscow. This allowed the metropolitans in Moscow, who were in general supporters of the prince, to use their influence and religious powers, including that of excommunication, in pursuit of Muscovite political goals.

Finally, over the course of the fifteenth and sixteenth centuries, Muscovite rulers were able to bind the aristocracy to them. In particular, they gained the support not only of their own aristocracy but also of the nobility of other states, by converting traditional military obligations, whereby a boyar could leave the service of one lord to seek another, into more permanent service to the Muscovite princes. It became treason for a boyar to seek another lord. The growth of Moscow at the expense of neighboring states during the fifteenth and sixteenth centuries made this possible, as the Muscovite prince became the only ruler capable of financially supporting the nobles. Moreover, through a complex system of ranking, the Muscovites were able to incorporate the nobility from other states into their service hierarchy while maintaining the rank of both the traditional and the new nobility. The service hierarchy was also extended to the lesser provincial nobility through the awarding of *pomesti'a,* or land grants, that were given on the condition of continued service. This allowed for a

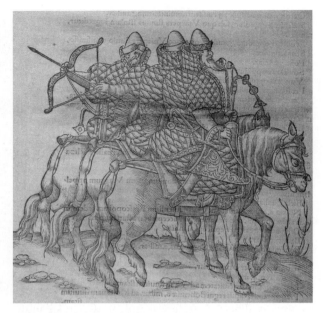

Muscovite Cavalryman   These men are typical of the service gentry who formed a significant portion of Muscovite armies. They are armed with a composite bow and protected by quilted armor. Their equipment reflects the nature of Muscovy's nomadic enemies.

substantial increase in the numbers of the lesser gentry who would come to form the armies of Muscovy. Both of these developments gave the Muscovite rulers a large and dependent aristocracy.

The Muscovite Military System

The Muscovite armed forces evolved from the fourteenth through the seventeenth centuries, embracing some of the new technologies, organizations, and tactics being used both in the west and by the Ottoman Empire (see the Sources box "Muscovite Military Forces").

Noble Cavalry   By transforming the Russian nobility into service aristocracy, the Muscovite princes were able to field large numbers of noble cavalry. These men formed the majority of Muscovy's armed forces throughout this period. They were traditionally expected to provide their horses, equipment, and provisions. As a result, most of Moscow's cavalry forces were equipped to suit local conditions. The great majority were armed with bows and light armor, and the wealthier among them also had sabers and

SOURCES

Muscovite Military Forces

The following passage is from the treatise on sixteenth-century Russia Of the Russe Common Wealth, *written by English diplomat Giles Fletcher, who visited Muscovy in 1591. These passages reflect his understanding of the two key components of the Muscovite military forces: the service nobility who formed the officer corps and a large portion of the cavalry, and the increasingly important foot soldiers carrying firearms. Fletcher was a well-educated man and an astute observer of the Muscovite state.*

■ ■ ■

The soldiers of Russia are called *synovia boiarskie,* or the sons of gentlemen, because they are all of that degree by virtue of their military profession. For every soldier in Russia is a gentleman, and none are gentlemen but only soldiers that take it by descent from their ancestors, so that the son of a gentleman and a soldier withal and professeth nothing else but military matters. When they are of years able to bear arms, they come to the office of *Rozriadnyi,* or great constable, and there present themselves, who entereth their names and allotteth them certain lands to maintain their charges, for the most part the same that their fathers enjoyed. For the lands assigned to maintain the army are never certain, annexed to this office without improving or detracting one foot. But that if the Emperor have sufficient in wages, the room being full so far as the lad doth extend already, they are many times deferred and have nothing allowed them except some one portion of the land be divided into two, which is a cause of great disorder within that country when a soldier that hath many children shall have sometimes but one entertained in the Emperor's pay. So that the rest, having nothing, are forced to live by unjust and wicked shifts that tend to the hurt and oppression of the *muzhiki,* or common sort of people. The inconvenience groweth by maintaining his forces in a continual succession. The whole number of his soldiers in continual pay is this: first, he hath of his *dvoriane,* that is, pensioners or guard of his person, to the

number of 15,000 horsemen, with their captains and other officers that are always in a readiness.

Of footmen that are in continual pay he hath to the number of 12,000, all gunners, called *streltsy,* whereof 5,000 are to attend about the city of Moscow or any other place where the Emperor shall abide. And 2,000, which are called *stremian-nye streltsy,* or gunners at the stirrup, are about his own person at the very court or house where himself lodgeth. The rest are placed in his garrison towns, till there be occasion to have them in the field, and receive for their salary or stipend every man seven rubles a year, besides twelve measures apiece of rye and oats. Of mercenary soldiers that are strangers, whom they call *nemtsy,* they have at this time 4,300 of Polonians; of Cherkasy, that are under the Polonians, about 4,000, whereof 3,500 are abroad in his garrisons; of Dutches and Scots, about 150; of Greeks, Turks, Danes, and Swedens, all in one band, 100 or thereabouts. But these they use only upon the Tartar side and against the Siberians, as they do the present, on the other side against the Siberians, as they do the Tartar soldiers, whom they hire sometimes, but only for the present, on the other side against the Polonian and Sweden, thinking it best policy so to use their service upon the contrary border.

SOURCE: Giles Fletcher, *Of the Russe Common Wealth* (Cambridge: Harvard University Press, 1966), pp. 54–56.

heavier cuirasses. By the mid-sixteenth century, it had become clear that in order to compete with the western Europeans and the Ottomans, it was preferable to have a better-armed force. As a result, *pomesti'a* holders were required to bring one fully armed horseman

(including an extra horse) for every 400 acres of land rather than a larger but less well equipped retinue.

Firearms   While firearms were known in Russia as early as 1380, they did not appear in large numbers until a century later, thanks in part to the marriage of Ivan III to a Byzantine princess who had connections to the papacy. As a result, Italians expert in the manufacture of firearms made their way to Moscow. By the end of the fifteenth century, the Muscovites were producing their own cannon and powder. And within a few decades, the Muscovite princes could muster as many as 2000 cannon for a siege, where such weapons were most useful.

By the mid-sixteenth century, handguns were appearing in ever-greater numbers. Initially, the Muscovite foot solders, usually town militia forces, were armed with more traditional weapons such as the bow. When firearms did appear, they were often in the hands of foreign mercenaries such as Lithuanians and Germans. But once again, in response to developments in Europe and among the Ottomans, the Muscovites began to develop home-grown infantry with firearms—the *strel'tsy*, or musketeers. The first were 3000 men who were part of the tsar's infantry guard raised in 1550. Shortly thereafter, larger numbers of *strel'tsy* began to appear in Muscovite armies; some 12,000 were in the army by 1563.

The *strel'tsy*, who were often based in towns, became increasingly unreliable both politically and militarily and were eventually disbanded by Peter the Great. In the interim, the Muscovites experimented with a new body of infantry called *soldati*. These were armed in the European fashion with a mixture of pikes and muskets, and they were organized into regiments drawn from a mix of foreign mercenaries, newly enfranchised members of the lesser gentry, and even conscripted peasants. However, they never proved to be a satisfactory military force and so were replaced by the more modern regiments of Peter the Great.

The Cossacks   During the sixteenth century, the Muscovites made increasing use of irregular cavalry forces, the famous Cossacks. The Cossacks were not really an ethnic group but rather a group of frontiersmen, often made up of those fleeing the increasing autocracy of the Muscovite state. These men organized themselves into warrior brotherhoods, and many became brigands and pirates or were hired by Moscow's enemies including the Poles. By the late sixteenth century, the Muscovite state was making efforts to bring the Cossacks into line by offering cash subsidies and land in exchange for military service. The Cossacks thus became a part of the service class, albeit amongst its lower ranks.

CONCLUSION

Eurasian cannon and cavalry armies were often more than a match for any European armies during the period up to 1700 or 1750. This reflects the fact that gunpowder technology could be and was put to good use in different ways by different states. Perhaps more than gunpowder technology, in fact, what united these Eurasian empires was the strength of their imperial institutions and traditions. State power made possible the union of steppe traditions with new weapons and sedentary infantry forces; military success and the combination of types of forces it was built on, in turn, helped maintain the state. In this, they resembled Japan and China in this same period, as we will see in Chapter 19. Regions with less well defined mechanisms of state power, as well as areas such as the Americas that were significantly behind Eurasia technologically, reacted to gunpowder weapons and military challenges in different (though not necessarily unsuccessful) ways, as we will see in Chapter 18.

But if state power lay at the heart of the success of cannon and cavalry armies, state power also lay at the heart of the problems emerging for many of them by late in this period. Large imperial armies were expensive to maintain, and none of these empires, bound to traditional agrarian patterns of economic organization, proved capable of sustained military success. Often, success depended on expansion, but there were limits to how large an empire could be before it became ungovernable given the communications technology of the time. And expansion itself often exacerbated problems with regionalism and factionalism that could also become acute if expansion stopped and the flow of plunder that kept factionalism at bay ceased. Of the great Eurasian empires considered in this chapter, only Russia, least tied to steppe nomadic traditions, was able to build on its success in this period and go on to even greater military power in the second half of the eighteenth century. The rest faced graver and graver problems.

SUGGESTED READINGS

Chase, Kenneth. *Firearms: A Global History to 1700*. Cambridge: Cambridge University Press, 2003. Argues that proximity to steppe nomads determined patterns of gunpowder development throughout Eurasia; strong on detailed history of gunpowder technology, but overall, a simplistic and unconvincing thesis.

Davies, Brian L. "The Development of Russian Military Power, 1453–1815." In *European Warfare, 1453–1815,* ed. Jeremy Black. New York: St. Martin's Press, 1999. A good survey of the institutional development of the Russian armed forces; also puts Russia into the context of the Military Revolution debate. This entire collection has other useful chapters on many areas of the world covered in this chapter (including the Ottomans) and in Chapter 18.

Gommans, Jos. "Warhorse and Gunpowder in India *c.* 1000–1850." In *War in the Early Modern World, 1450–1815,* ed. Jeremy Black. Boulder: Westview Press, 1999. A clear and accessible conceptualization of the parameters of Indian warfare in this period. This entire collection has valuable chapters on many areas of the world covered in this chapter (including the Ottomans) and in Chapter 18.

Hellie, Richard. *Enserfment and Military Change in Muscovy.* Chicago: University of Chicago Press, 1971. A useful study that puts the rise of serfdom into the context of the gunpowder revolution in Russia.

Jackson, Peter, and Lawrence Lockhart, eds. *The Cambridge History of Iran: Volume 6, The Timurid and Safavid Periods.* Cambridge: Cambridge University Press, 1986. A standard history of Persia during this period; not focused on military history, but traces political and military events.

Lord Kinross. *The Ottoman Centuries: The Rise and Fall of the Turkish Empire.* New York: Morrow, 1979. A narrative history of the Ottoman Empire that includes many details of Ottoman military life.

Keep, John L. H. *Soldiers of the Tsar: Army and Society in Russia, 1462–1874.* New York: Oxford University Press, 1985. An excellent narrative history of the interaction of war and society in the Muscovite era; also puts this period into a context of Russian military developments through the end of the nineteenth century.

Murphey, Rhoads. *Ottoman Warfare, 1500–1700.* New Brunswick: Rutgers University Press, 1999. A fundamental recent analysis of Ottoman military action in its political, fiscal, and social contexts.

Parry, V. J. "Materials of War in the Ottoman Empire." In *Studies in the Economic History of the Middle East,* ed. M. A. Cook. Oxford: Oxford University Press, 1996. Surveys both strengths and weaknesses of the materials available to the Ottomans, particularly for war making.

Richards, John F. *The Mughal Empire.* Cambridge: Cambridge University Press, 1993. A good overview of the Mughal Empire, including a section on the emperor Akbar as military commander.

Shaw, S. J. "The Origins of Ottoman Military Reform: The Nizam-i Cedid Army of Sultan Selim III." *Journal of Modern History* 37 (1965), 291–301. A dated but useful discussion of an Ottoman attempt to reform its military system.

CHAPTER 18

Conquests and Contacts: Europeans Abroad, 1500–1700

Gunpowder weaponry came to much of the world beyond western Europe and Eurasia through diffusion from these centers of power. Europeans, especially, brought guns with them around the world between 1500 and 1700, as often as items of trade as tools of conflict. Gunpowder weaponry produced different effects in areas whose central governments were often less powerful than the European states or the Eurasian cannon and cavalry empires, and whose climate and terrain were sometimes unsuitable for horse raising, but the impact of such weapons could still be significant. Nor was the impact necessarily negative or one-sided in favor of the European adventurers who came to Africa, Southeast Asia, and even parts of the Americas. Gunpowder technology was still simple and inexpensive enough during this period to diffuse rapidly, while climate, disease, and logistics all played at least as large a role as weaponry in shaping the outcomes of the age's encounters. Europeans for the most part were confined to small coastal enclaves established to facilitate trade rather than as launching points for large-scale territorial conquest. And defense of these enclaves often depended as much on skillful diplomacy and alliances with local powers as on military strength.

The Americas, of course, represent a large exception to the limited nature of European conquests between 1500 and 1800. In fact, for reasons explored below, the initial conquests of the Spanish conquistadors exceeded all expectations and laid the foundations for a vast and lucrative land-based Spanish Empire in the Americas. But apart from the Spanish takeover of the Aztec and Inca empires, the pattern of European impact in the Americas, on closer inspection, resembles that found elsewhere: coastal (that is, dependent on naval power and connections) and limited, despite advantages ranging from disease to technology, partly because similar patterns of technological diffusion took hold. More important, the initial

triumph of Spanish arms in Tenochtitlan and Cuzco should not color our picture of the entire period excessively. Here, as elsewhere, a Military Revolution, especially one confined to western Europe, is hard to find.

WARFARE IN AFRICA, 1415–1570

The Iberian–North African Frontier

The first efforts of European expansion beyond the continent were not the famous expeditions to the New World or to India, but much closer to home. A desire to drive Islam from Iberia led on to a counteroffensive in North Africa that aimed at European domination of the frontier between Christendom and Islam in the western Mediterranean (Figure 18.1). For several centuries, the Iberian peninsula and the Maghrib (that is, the North African coast) had formed a porous frontier across which people, trade, disease, and military technology and techniques regularly moved. Muslim states on the peninsula regularly received reinforcements of troops from the Maghrib. Christian states in Iberia likewise had adapted their tactics and operational methods to meet the challenges posed by the Muslims, employing, for example, a substantial number of light cavalry, called *jinetes*, to deal with their more lightly armed and equipped enemies and to engage in the constant "little war" along the frontiers of their kingdoms.

In the early fifteenth century, the Christian Iberian kingdoms renewed the *Reconquista*, the reconquest of Iberia from the Muslims. Granada finally fell to Spain in 1492, but Portugal was in a position to look toward North Africa as early as 1415, motivated by several factors to carry the war to the Maghrib. The first was primarily military: Control of the region would interdict the arrival of troops and supplies to

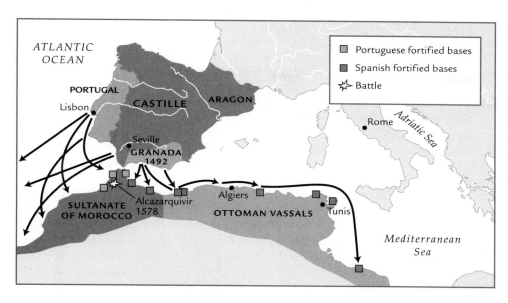

Figure 18.1 North Africa, 1415–1570 Portugal and Spain expanded into North Africa by means of fortified coastal bases. The Iberian advantages of gunpowder and fortifications proved short-lived: Many forts fell to the Ottomans after 1520, and the Moroccans defeated the Portuguese at Alcazarquivir in 1578.

Granada, and after 1492 would ensure that North Africa could not inspire or aid rebellion in the peninsula. Strategically, it would also hinder Ottoman efforts to control the western Mediterranean, efforts that materialized in the mid-sixteenth century. There were also commercial factors: Morocco was agriculturally wealthy and produced excellent horses. Moreover, control of North Africa would allow the Iberians access to the trade and precious metals of West Africa.

In their early campaigns, the Portuguese enjoyed some important advantages. These included early hand-held firearms and artillery and the strategic and operational mobility provided by their ships. Through the fifteenth century, developments in firearms, artillery, fortifications, and military organization widened the gap between the Iberians and their opponents. In the sixteenth century, however, the nature of the Hispano-Maghrib frontier, Ottoman aid, and competing strategic demands on the Iberian states led to equilibrium; eventually, the Iberians were forced to leave North Africa in Muslim hands.

Portugal and Morocco in the Fifteenth Century

The Portuguese came to Morocco in 1415 when they captured the coastal town of Ceuta. In addition to the factors noted above motivating the attack, King John I had come to the throne as the founder of a new dynasty with considerable support from the urban elements of Portugal. In order to appease the crusading

zeal of the landed warrior elites, including the influential Prince Henry the Navigator, John supported the crusade against the Marinid dynasty in Morocco. The army included a siege train equipped with mortars and cannon, but these went unused when Ceuta was taken by assault, and they figured in only a limited way in the defense of the newly won town, since its medieval curtain walls were not designed to support artillery.

The Portuguese success was thus the victory of a medieval crusading army over a traditional North African Muslim army. The Marinid army was like most Muslim forces of the time. Its strengths were tactical flexibility and large numbers of fine cavalry. Its weaknesses were structural: It was a composite of many different troops of varying quality. The heart of the army was the *hashm*, or royal retinue, a standing force of military slaves, distinguished soldiers, and specialist mercenaries (such as Christians from Spain armed with firearms). Supporting the *hashm* were state-supported regulars and unpaid irregulars, both drawn from tribes tied to the dynasty by special benefits such as tax exemptions. Finally, a variety of irregular forces ranging from urban garrisons to *mujahidin*, religiously motivated warriors, served in campaigns. Another problem for the Marinids was internecine power struggles. One rival group, the Wattasids, took advantage of increasing Portuguese pressure and their control of key positions to overthrow the dynasty in 1472. Tribal leaders called *sharifs*, alleging descent from Muhammad and claiming secular and religious authority, also increasingly undermined Marinid and later Wattasid authority. In Morocco, as in Europe, religious fragmentation hindered consolidation of state authority.

The Hundred Years War for Morocco   Exploiting their early victories proved difficult for the Portuguese, even against the weakening Marinids and with their own increasing use of firearms and cannon. For example, in 1437, King Duarte's army, including a strong artillery train, assaulted Tangiers but was unable to breach the fortifications. Poor placement of the guns and an audacious sally by the garrison led to the capture of a number of Portuguese cannon and an ignominious defeat. The rebuff at Tangiers and the lure of the lucrative Atlantic trade led to a two-decade hiatus in Portuguese attacks on Morocco. But the Portuguese resumed their efforts in the 1460s, responding to attacks on their outposts and the Wattasid revolt, with the addition of large numbers of bronze cannon and mercenary gunners. The assault began in earnest in 1471, when King Alfonso V launched an invasion with a force of 400 ships and 30,000 men. The campaign culminated in the capture of Arzila and ultimately led to the fall of the Marinids at the hands of the Wattasids. This was the beginning of a Hundred Years War for supremacy in Morocco that would not be decided until 1578.

The years 1471–1520 were the high-water mark of Portuguese fortunes. The Portuguese made extensive use of cannon ranging from small antipersonnel pieces to very large siege pieces. They also began to build more modern artillery fortifications to defend their new acquisitions. But continued internal strife that beset the ruling Wattasid dynasty was the crucial factor. By the early 1500s, a group of *sharifs* had established the Sa'dian state, which drew on religious zeal but also recognized the importance of western technology and tactics. The Sa'dians created an army that had one foot in traditional North African warfare but that also made use of mercenaries employing firearms, both on foot and on horse, as well as modern artillery. The Sa'dians defeated the Wattasids in 1536 (and during the course of this struggle refined their military forces) and finally defeated the Portuguese in 1578 at Alcazarquivir (Wadi-I-Makhazan) (see the Highlights box "The Battle of Alcazarquivir, 1578").

Spain and the Ottomans in North Africa   With the successful completion of the *Reconquista* in 1492, Spain was also poised to move against the Muslims in North Africa, and there was discussion of continuing the *Reconquista* across the Mediterranean. While this was attractive to some of the crusade-minded warrior elite, the monarchy seems to have had plans to open a new frontier across the Atlantic. In fact, as early as 1478, Spanish ships had sailed to secure bases in the Canary Islands, and in 1494, the crown agreed to support Columbus's second voyage. Moreover, the French invasion of Italy in 1494 drew Spanish attention to the dynastic struggle with the Valois kings of France.

In 1497, however, the Spanish crown did support a renewed crusade that returned possession of the town of Melilla to Spain. Beginning in 1505, more vigorous campaigns were launched at the instigation, with the financing, and partially under the leadership of the warrior-cleric Cardinal Cisneros of Toledo. Between 1505 and 1510, several key coastal ports were taken including Mers-el-Kebir, Oran, Bougie, and Tripoli, as well as an island fortress outside the harbor of Algiers. These fortified *presidios* were to act as a bulwark against Muslim incursions and a base from which the Spanish could exert control over allied African tribes, thereby using "the barbarian to fight the barbarian."

In the course of the 1510s and 1520s, the Spanish were distracted from the African frontier by the amazing gains made in the New World and continuing conflict with France. The Spanish were pressed first by a band of corsairs led by the brothers Barbarossa who, after some initial victories, were forced to seek help from the Ottomans in order to sustain their offensive against the Spanish. From the 1530s onward, the struggle in North Africa took on the character of an imperial conflict, with the Hapsburgs (both Spanish and Austrian) fighting the Ottomans and French on several fronts. The importance of maintaining European holdings weakened the Spanish in North Africa, and Ottoman squadrons raided the Spanish coastline. But with Ottoman defeats at Malta and Lepanto (and the growing exhaustion of all the combatants), the Ottomans ceased major operations in the western Mediterranean. Continuing attention away from the Hispano-Maghrib frontier left the few remaining Spanish possessions west of Algiers in a defensive posture.

Sub-Saharan Africa

The Portuguese experience in Africa south of the Sahara provides further evidence of the limits of European military power in this age, as well as of the

HIGHLIGHTS

The Battle of Alcazarquivir, 1578

In 1578, King Sebastian of Portugal led an invasion of Morocco with the intention of defeating the Sa'dian ruler, Abd al-Malik, who was supported by the Ottomans, and extending Portuguese influence in Morocco. He was aided in his crusade by other European monarchs including Philip II of Spain and William of Orange in France. He also had the support of Mutawakkil, a Sa'dian exile ousted by Abd al-Malik. In July, Sebastian landed in Morocco with a mixed force of 18,000–20,000 men, consisting mainly of infantry including five Portuguese *tercios,* one of which was composed of nobles unable to provide the funds for service as cavalry; various mercenaries including Castilians, Germans, Walloons, and a contingent of papal musketeers; and perhaps seventy cannon. Sebastian lacked the resources to raise a cavalry force sufficient in numbers to match the Sa'dians. Mutawakkil supplied about 1000 cavalrymen and 1000 arquebusiers.

Abd al-Malik led a force that was substantially stronger, numbering some 70,000 men, about one-third infantry and two-thirds cavalry, and perhaps thirty-six cannon. His forces were also mixed, including men from his *hashm,* regulars, Andulusians, tribal levies, and urban militias, some of dubious value. At its core, however, was a modern, well-armed force that may have included as many as 18,000 men with firearms, both on foot and on horse. He also had some fine *sipahi* heavy cavalry.

On August 4, Sebastian drew up his forces in the traditional three "battles" with *tercios* in each line, his baggage in the center, and his weak cavalry on the wings. Abd al-Malik deployed three lines of arquebusiers, backed by a large block of regular infantry and cavalry and with cavalry on the flanks, including units of mounted arquebusiers. Both sides set their artillery before their main battle lines.

The engagement began with an exchange of artillery fire. The Sa'dians advanced quickly, firing on the Portuguese artillery and attacking with cavalry. The cavalry eventually broke the Portuguese gunners, and Sa'dian arquebusiers overran the guns. Sa'dian cavalry and mounted arquebusiers then attacked the main Portuguese line, but the *tercios* stood their ground. The mounted arquebusiers, rather than launching suicidal attacks on the pike squares, used a kind of caracole tactic on the Portuguese. Unfortunately for the Sa'dians, some of their less reliable troops took the opportunity to desert the field. For the moment, the battle hung in the balance. When the Portuguese cavalry launched an attack that drove off some of the Sa'dian cavalry, Abd al-Malik personally led a countercharge that included the *sipahi* heavy cavalry. It pushed the crusader horse back into their own lines, disrupting them. Though Abd al-Malik was killed in the charge, Portuguese efforts to drive off the Sa'dian cavalry opened a gap in their lines. The Moroccan cavalry quickly exploited it, with the mounted arquebusiers pouring volley after volley into the Portuguese rear. Sebastian's troops broke and fled; Sebastian was killed in the rout. Some 15,000 Europeans were killed or captured while the Sa'dians lost 7000–8000. Abd al-Malik was replaced by his brother Ahmad, who commanded the right flank during the battle. The victory spelled the end of Portuguese ambitions in Morocco.

importance of context in shaping how newly introduced gunpowder weapons were used. Geography and biology played a part in limiting Portuguese influence. African rivers were mostly unsuited to navigation by sailing ships, confining the Portuguese trading presence to fortified coastal enclaves, while military incursions inland faced not just effective African opposition but debilitating tropical diseases (see the Issues box on page 348). But the military picture is dominated by African contexts and successes even beyond these factors.

After establishing a presence on the Gold Coast in the 1480s, Portuguese forces seized a number of trading cities on the east coast of Africa in the early

1500s, both to serve as stations on the route to India (see below) and to control the trade of East Africa itself. Their focus on gold, however, disrupted traditional patterns of trade in ivory and other goods, and inland tribes affected by the disruption fought back. In southern East Africa, in the area of the Zambezi River, attacks by the Mang'aja tribes were met by significant expeditions in the 1590s, for example. Several hundred Portuguese arquebusiers and pikemen, supported by African allies, invaded Mang'aja territory. But Manga'aja earthen fortifications proved immune to artillery fire, while Mang'aja ambushes and attacks that took advantage of densely forested terrain unsuited to firefights negated any tactical advantage Portuguese soldiers might have had in battle. Two separate Portuguese forces were slaughtered, and Mang'aja raids continued. But the coastal forts held, and the Mang'aja failed to reestablish their ivory trade, making losers of both parties in the long run.

In Angola, Portuguese forces became players from the 1570s in already established patterns of warfare in the area, while muskets, as a common item of trade, diffused rapidly even to Angolan forces not allied with the Portuguese. The Angolan climate, soil, and agriculture could not support populations as dense or urbanized as in Europe, with significant effects related to the use of gunpowder weapons. Lack of cities meant lack of forts, which reduced the usefulness of artillery that was in any case difficult to transport in largely roadless terrain. And muskets in this context—few forts, limited logistics, and no cavalry (horses survived African diseases at even worse rates than Europeans)—did not lead to the adoption of close ranks and mass fire as in Europe, but instead were adopted alongside native archery into a tradition of light infantry skirmishing. Such troops softened up the enemy line for attack by small, elite bodies of heavy infantry, whose flanks and rear the skirmishers also protected. Portuguese pikemen with their body armor proved useful as heavy infantry, but not decisively better than similar Angolan forces. Portuguese commanders who failed to adopt Angolan tactical traditions invariably lost their battles, and at times their lives, and so Portuguese influence in the area remained limited.

Assessment   In all, Iberian experiences in Africa involved some temporary successes early on but were mostly a tale of limitations and later retreats. But if they do not demonstrate much military advantage stemming from the early stages of the European transformation, they did extend the effects of the *Reconquista* as a training ground for the conquistadors who spearheaded the Iberian arrival in the Americas.

THE CONQUEST OF THE AMERICAS, 1492–1700

The European incursion into the Americas, which resulted in the rapid creation of a Spanish empire and more slowly in enclaves for other European powers, is often presented as the first overseas expression of the new European superiority in warfare created by the Military Revolution. But much of the story of European conquest in the Americas occurs too soon to have been affected by the truly unique features of the European military transformation. Many of the military advantages Europeans enjoyed against native armies in the Americas would have been there for any Eurasian power. Further, the European military advance in the Americas is far less determined and triumphant than it appears at first sight.

First Contacts: European Advantages

Europeans did, of course, enjoy a number of clear advantages when early contact with the natives turned into conflict. Technological, social, and biological factors all contributed to this initial edge.

Weapons and Technology   The most obvious advantage lay in weaponry. The isolated civilizations of the Americas were built on a narrow technological base that knew gold, silver, and a limited use of bronze but that were for practical military purposes still in the Stone Age. Against Indian clubs, slings, arrows, and obsidian swords, Europeans deployed a range of more effective tools. Most important was iron, forged into steel swords whose durability, flexibility, and ability to hold a sharp edge were unmatched by anything the Indians could deploy. Defensive use of iron armor in the form of helmets, chain mail or plate body armor, and reinforcements for shields was also important, though less so than the use of offensive weapons. In many areas, iron armor proved too hot, cumbersome, and rust-prone for regular use, and many Spaniards, in particular, adopted Aztec-style quilted cotton armor instead, retaining just the steel helmet. Finally, iron also made crossbows a powerful, if slow-firing, missile weapon.

Europeans also brought gunpowder with them, as well as arquebuses and cannon. Such weapons had a huge psychological impact especially in first encounters, as much because of their awesome noise and smoke as for their killing power. But gunpowder weapons, in fact, saw somewhat limited use in major combats: Their rate of fire was slow, and supplies of powder and shot were limited. Only in the siege of Tenochtitlan (see the Sources box on page 351) did gunpowder play a decisive role in the first century of European incursions. More important than gunpowder were horses, which provided Europeans with the advantages nomads had enjoyed against sedentary peoples for millennia in Eurasia: tactical mobility and superior height in combat. Again, the novelty value of cavalry heightened the effectiveness of horsed soldiers in initial encounters. Cavalry spearheaded European armies; the use of horses was limited only by their small numbers and by areas of unsuitable terrain.

Europeans' most decisive technological advantage was their ships. This was not a combat advantage (except again at the siege of the island city of Tenochtitlan): No native peoples had anything resembling warships. Rather, European ships linked European outposts in the Americas to the resources of other outposts and the home continent and carried the spoils of conquest back to Europe. Ships thus allowed Europeans, once they gained a foothold in the new lands, to deploy their massive demographic and economic advantages over native civilizations, an advantage obscured by the small size of the initial invading forces. Ships were also the key technology for Europeans' edge over other Eurasian peoples in exploiting the Americas, given Europe's geographical proximity to the new lands.

Further, ships were a *secure technology:* They could not be copied or adopted and used by Indian groups, unlike the other European technologies. Technological transfer played a significant role in the shape of European conflict in the Americas. Within 20–50 years of initial contact, Indian groups consistently made headway in adopting the most effective aspects of European technology: steel-bladed weapons, guns, and horses. The Spanish, lucky enough to gain an empire before this adoption took hold, also proved capable of limiting the transfer within their sphere. Effective central control imposed strict prohibitions on the sale, trade, or giving of guns, swords, and horses to Indians. The prohibitions were effective because they continued a policy initiated with respect to the Muslims of Spain during the *Reconquista* and because the Spanish conquistadors saw the possession of weapons in terms of class and status, and thus were inclined to maintain a monopoly. But in areas where other Europeans settled, decentralized political control and the dominance of commercial values over warrior-aristocratic values created a lively trade that ended up arming many tribes against the intruders.

Experience The second area of European advantage was in experience of other worlds. In addition to centuries of Spanish contact with and combat against Muslims during the *Reconquista*, Europeans in general had knowledge of other parts of the globe. The new worlds they encountered in the Americas might have been strange and terrible or exotic and wonderful, but such qualities were expected and perceived through the lens of a cultural history of alien contact going back to the Greeks. The Indians had no such experience. As a result, Europeans entered into contact driven by strong motives—the classic triad of gold, glory, and God—that gave them confidence in their mission and superiority and that extended a complex, deep-rooted crusading impulse (see Chapter 12). In contrast, their opponents were initially baffled and caught completely off guard. This advantage was heightened still further where Europeans met natives with less complex social organizations than the great American empires.

Disease The final European advantage was biological. Eurasian diseases to which Indians had no resistance contributed to both short-term disruptions—ravaging the defenders of Tenochtitlan, for example, and throwing the Inca succession into crisis—and long-term social and demographic disaster in the process of European expansion (see the Issues box "Disease in Warfare").

Assessment Together, these various advantages were certainly significant. But, particularly with regard to the great empires, the Aztecs and Incas, even the combination of these factors was not enough on its own to be decisive. The Spanish forces that conquered Mexico and Peru were logistically very vulnerable—no sword or gun can save one from starvation—as almost all their advantages were tactical, not operational. And

Disease in Warfare

The major role played in the conquest of the Americas by the Eurasian disease pool, which decimated Amerindian populations, makes acutely visible a constant in warfare from ancient times. The brute fact is that far more soldiers died of disease than from enemy action in every war until the Russo-Japanese War of 1904–5 on the Japanese side and until World War I in general terms. Adding in civilian casualties from diseases spread by armies and the conditions created by war, including famine, tilts the balance still farther: Counting the worldwide influenza epidemic of 1918–19 as an effect of World War I makes World War II the first in which total casualties from direct application of force outnumbered those from disease. Attrition on campaign, in camp, in winter quarters, and in the population as a whole was simply a universally accepted, unavoidable, and therefore largely invisible part of military experience until recently.

Major plagues do occasionally emerge to the fore in war accounts: Thucydides' account of the plague in Athens near the beginning of the Peloponnesian War is the classic example. Such epidemics undoubtedly affected the socioeconomic ability of the states they struck to maintain their military strength. English and French armies shrank in the wake of the Black Death in 1348, for example, while the same disease a decade earlier contributed seriously to destabilizing Mongol rule in China. And war efforts could be affected in more direct ways. Arguably, Athens' worst loss from the plague was the death of Pericles and his steadying hand on Athenian strategy, just as losses among the Aztec and Inca rulers compromised their responses to the Spanish.

But it was endemic rather than epidemic diseases that were more pervasive and so less visible.

Large concentrations of men and their camp followers created unavoidable problems of sanitation and breeding grounds for the spread of infections; dysentery may be the biggest killer of soldiers in history. Conditions that pertained to any army were exaggerated by prolonged concentrations of forces in one place and consequent shortages of fresh food and water. Sailing ships were one such environment: Early modern navies were constantly ravaged by nutrition-related diseases such as scurvy. But above all, sieges were always associated with outbreaks of disease both within the city and among the attackers. Attackers and defenders both made sporadic use of this fact by launching diseased corpses at each other with siege engines in a primitive attempt at germ warfare: The Mongols spread the Black Death to Caffa in the Crimea in this way, whence the plague spread via a Genoese trading galleys to Europe.

The lack of a scientific theory of disease propagation hindered such efforts, however, and account for a final characteristic of the effect of disease on war. Outside of the Americas, disease patterns tended to favor defenders over attackers. Local immunities and adaptations were generally more powerful than any premodern military technology. Most significantly, diseases that affected men and horses blunted the impact of armies from temperate regions and of horsed nomads on tropical and subtropical areas; the European inability to penetrate much of sub-Saharan Africa before the late nineteenth century reflects this general pattern. It would take the modern germ theory of disease to hold natural afflictions at bay within armies and turn designer germs into another weapon in the horrifying arsenal of modern war.

these forces were tiny. Despite their tactical advantages, they could have been overwhelmed by superior numbers, especially in Mexico, where the technological divide was not as great as in Peru. And, in fact,

outside the great empires, European forces had much less immediate military success, which says something about their limitations. A close look at the two imperial conquests shows that political structures, Indian

Figure 18.2 The Aztec Empire in 1500

assistance, and a big dose of luck all contributed to European success.

The Aztec Empire

Aztec Warfare The Aztecs had settled in the central valley of Mexico around 1300, founding their capital at Tenochtitlan in 1345. Initially tributaries of the Tepanecs, they overthrew their masters in 1428 and went on to create, in less than 100 years, the biggest Mesoamerican empire to that time (Figure 18.2).

The Aztec Empire, like earlier Mesoamerican polities, was hegemonic rather than territorial in structure. That is, areas conquered by the Aztecs retained their local rulers, laws, and religion, supplying the Aztecs with tribute and, at times, military assistance in the form of soldiers, porters, or supplies. The empire was held together not by armies of occupation and Aztec administrators, but by the perception of Aztec power—that is, the Aztec ability to punish noncooperation by reconquest and imposition of heavier tribute. The Aztecs' need to periodically renew the image of their power reinforced a tendency to expansionism that derived from the benefits in tribute, wider trade networks, and prisoners for ritual sacrifice that an expanding empire brought. The system was very cost effective, but periodic revolts by subject city-states were an inevitable aspect of the system as well.

The Aztec army that projected imperial power had at its core a military aristocracy that formed a professional standing force. Rank and status within this class were earned in battle, especially by the capture of prisoners. This elite was backed by commoner warriors in great numbers drawn from the urban and rural populations: One of the Aztec strengths was a large demographic base. The usual campaign season was December to April, the dry season after the harvest, when roads were passable, supplies were plentiful, and farmers were available for duty.

Aztec warriors were armed with bows with bronze-tipped arrows, slings, spear-throwers, and obsidian-bladed broadswords and spears. The missile weapons were quite effective, and an exchange of missiles usually opened battles. The bladed weapons were also effective, their chief disadvantages compared to steel swords being their weight and fragility; but as slashing weapons they quickly earned Spanish respect. The elites wore padded cotton armor that provided good protection at a light weight.

The chief limitation on Aztec armies was logistical. With no pack animals or wheeled transport, all supplies had to be carried by porters, generally one for every two soldiers. This meant that Aztec armies could march only about three days beyond friendly territory to fight a battle and that sieges were very rare. Conquests of polities larger than a city-state, such as alliances and rival empires, therefore had to be piecemeal, with Aztec forces chipping away at the edges of coalitions or surrounding the central city-state of an empire, cutting them off from allies, and wearing them down. The strategy against a powerful foe could also include a *xochiyaoyotl*, a "flower war." This was a form of ritual combat between elite soldiers that tied up the enemy army at small cost while conquests of encirclement were pursued. It could also escalate into a war of attrition and full conquest: The overall ritual nature of Mesoamerican war has been much exaggerated, and killing of foes was as much a part of Aztec war as capture of prisoners.

The Spanish Invasion The usual patterns of Mesoamerican warfare, including the political structure of the empire, created a number of advantages for the small Spanish army under Hernan Cortes that arrived on the coast of Mexico in 1521. As outsiders to the culture, the Spaniards were able to some extent to play outside the rules, increasing the surprise factor in their operations. They were unaware of the usual conventions of surrender, threat, and negotiation, for example, and so did not respond in expected ways to Aztec emissaries. This contributed to the indecisive response of the Aztec ruler Montezuma to the invasion, as Spanish intentions were often opaque. The timing of the invasion during the off-season further confused the issue—how could an army be seriously at war in the summer? Finally, it is likely that Montezuma completely misread the Spanish approach to Tenochtitlan as indicative of respect and submission, as it would have been for a rival Indian leader.

But even more important was the effect of the Spanish arrival on the hegemonic politics of the empire. Montezuma had only recently come to the throne and was still establishing himself as a hegemon to be respected by the subject tribes and states of the empire. And plenty of states were ready to resist or throw off Aztec rule. As a result, the Spaniards found themselves embraced by ready Indian allies and exploited as the shock troops of a perfectly normal revolt. As soon as they had some success against Aztec forces, perceptions of Aztec invincibility began to shift among their subjects, swelling the ranks of the revolt.

Indian allies provided Cortes with crucial intelligence, vital supplies, and logistical support, without which his small force would have starved, and with the numbers necessary to meet a formidable Aztec army on more equal terms. In effect, the Spaniards became the steel-shod spearhead of an Indian-based

The Siege of Tenochtitlan The various tactical advantages that the Spaniards possessed over the Aztecs are depicted in this drawing based on an Aztec original that shows the impact of steel-bladed weapon, horses, and Indian allies in combat.

deconstruction of Aztec rule. Thus, the political structure of the empire and Montezuma's hesitant leadership served to vastly magnify the effects of the Spanish technological advantage. Even so, the Spanish forces were close to defeat several times and suffered major losses in being expelled from Tenochtitlan. But a smallpox epidemic aborted an Aztec counterattack, and once Tenochtitlan fell a second time to a determined siege, in which Indian numbers and disease among the defenders combined with Spanish cannon to wear down a fierce and determined defense (see the Sources box "The Siege of Tenochtitlan"), the Aztec Empire ceased to exist.

New Hegemons The problem for the allies who overthrew the Aztec hegemony was that no Indian group could then assume their dominant position—indeed, the whole point for many was to assert their independence from a hegemon. But this left the Spaniards to continue to play off one group against another and, using their superior tactical force, to install themselves as the new hegemons of the system. The empire thus fell to the Spaniards almost from the top down: Once the center was taken, the rest followed from the established political dynamics of the system. Admittedly, Spanish control of the polity then

SOURCES

The Siege of Tenochtitlan

The following passages—one from an illustrated Aztec account preserved and translated by the Spaniards, the other from the memoirs of a member of Cortes' party—give two distinctly different accounts of the siege of the Aztec capital city.

■ ■ ■

[An Aztec account:] When the canal had been filled up, the Spaniards marched over it. They advanced cautiously, with their standard-bearer in the lead, and they beat their drums and played their chirimias as they came. The Tlaxcaltecas and the other allies followed close behind. The Tlaxcaltecas held their heads high and pounded their breasts with their hands, hoping to frighten us with their arrogance and courage. They sang songs as they marched, but the Aztecs were also singing. . . .

The Aztec warriors hid when the enemy reached solid ground. They crouched down to make themselves as small as possible and waited for the signal, the shout that told them it was the moment to stand up and attack. Suddenly they heard it: "Mexicanos, now is the time!"

The captain Hecatzin leaped up and raced toward the Spaniards, shouting "Warriors of Tlateloco, now is the time! Who are these barbarians? Let them come ahead!" He attacked one of the Spaniards and knocked him to the ground, but the Spaniard also managed to knock Hecatzin down. The captain got up and clubbed the Spaniard again, and other warriors rushed forward to drag him away.

Then all the Aztecs sprang up and charged into battle. The Spaniards were so astonished that they blundered here and there like drunkards; they ran through the streets with the warriors in pursuit. This was when the taking of captives began. . . .

Nothing can compare with the horrors of that siege and the agonies of the starving. We were so weakened by hunger that, little by little, the enemy forced us to retreat. Little by little they forced us to the wall.

On one occasion, four Spanish cavalrymen entered the market place. They rode through it in a great circle, stabbing and killing many of our warriors and trampling everything under their horses' hooves. This was the first time the Spaniards had entered the market place, and our warriors were taken by surprise. But when the horsemen withdrew, the warriors recovered their wits and ran in pursuit.

[A Spanish account:] At the entrance to the Plaza we placed a cannon and with it did great execution, for the enemy were so numerous that the Plaza would not hold them all. The Spaniards seeing that there was no water there (which was our greatest danger) determined to enter the Plaza, and when the enemy saw this carried into effect and observed the multitude of our allies (although they had no fear of them unless they were in our company) they fled with our allies after them until they were shut up in the court Temple, which was enclosed with a masonry wall.

This enclosure would be large enough to hold a town of four hundred houses. However, a breach was made and the Spaniards and allies captured it and remained there and on the Towers for a good while. When the people of the city saw that there were no horsemen with us they turned again on the Spaniards and drove them from the towers and courts, and as our men were in great danger, for it was worse than a retreat, they took refuge in the porticoes of the courts; however, the enemy had chastened them so severely that they abandoned these and retreated to the Plaza whence they were driven out into the street and were obliged to abandon the cannon which had been placed there.

The Spaniards, unable to withstand the onset of the enemy, retreated in great danger and would have suffered great loss had it not pleased God that at that moment three horsemen should arrive who entered the Plaza, and when the enemy beheld them they thought there were more of them and began to flee and the horsemen killed some of them and regained the courts and enclosure.

SOURCES: M. Leon-Portilla, ed., *The Broken Spears* (Boston: Beacon Press, 1962), pp. 105–9; Bernal Diaz del Castillo, *The Discovery and Conquest of Mexico, 1517–1521,* trans. A. P. Maudslay (New York: Da Capo Press, 1956), p. 408.

altered its shape: Spanish administration was more territorial than hegemonic. Nonetheless, the consolidation as much as the conquest itself fit the common Mesoamerican pattern.

Consolidation of Spanish rule was also assisted by the way Spanish ambitions fit into the Mesoamerican socioeconomic system. Once in control, the Spaniards, though often conflicted among themselves, aimed primarily at two goals. First, they wanted to extract precious metals, the search for which fell largely outside everyday patterns of Indian activity and occupations. Second, they wanted agricultural workers and miners, as the new rulers inevitably reshaped Mexican society in terms of the lord–peasant relations of their home country. Since the mass of Indian peasants within the areas ruled by the Aztecs were already used to toiling for military-aristocratic masters, the transition in that sense to Spanish rule was not huge. This congruence encouraged a transition from war to peace that was further facilitated by the influence of Spanish friars and missionaries aiming to convert the Indians to Christianity.

This is not to deny continued Spanish brutality, especially in coercing mine work and taking slaves from the peaceful sedentary population. But the lack of Indian resistance to European diseases militated against these practices in the long run (while spurring the trade in African slaves), at the same time that it put the seal of demographic decline on any Indian ambition to rise against the new rulers.

Assessment   The Spanish conquest of the Aztec Empire therefore appears not so much as a triumph of European arms as a story of Indian division. Head to head, the Aztecs had the military ability to defeat the invaders. But the political structure of the Aztec Empire made it vulnerable: Uprisings were built into the system, creating the openings and allies without which Cortes could not have succeeded. Better luck in the timing of the invasion, in terms of both the yearly cycle and the establishment of the new Aztec emperor's rule, and a more decisive response by Montezuma early on could have led to the defeat of the invasion (which ran against official Spanish policy and was justified only post hoc by its success) and the establishment of more "normal" diplomatic contacts between Spain and Mexico. But making such resistance work was always going to be a difficult management problem for the Aztecs, because their empire by its very nature harbored so many potential enemies.

Figure 18.3 The Inca Empire in 1500

The Inca Empire

Inca Warfare   Like the Aztecs, the Incas had risen to dominance in their world fairly recently before the Spanish invasion, initiating their expansion in the mid-fourteenth century. By 1530, they controlled a vast empire stretching down the Andes from present-day Colombia to Chile and including part or all of Bolivia, Peru, and Ecuador (Figure 18.3). Given the limited trade contacts the Peruvian world had even with Mesoamerica, the Incas had come to dominate most of civilization as they knew it.

Despite their isolation, the Incas developed an amazingly sophisticated political and military apparatus. Unlike the Aztec Empire, the Inca Empire was territorial, not hegemonic. Each newly conquered area was fully incorporated into the existing hierarchical administrative structure of the state, headed by Inca local and regional administrators. Inca rulers did not hesitate to reorganize the territorial administrative divisions to suit their policies or to force the human geography into conformance with their plans. Conquered tribes were sometimes resettled, in whole or in part, to distant parts of the empire to reduce their ability to foment discord. The local elites who survived Inca conquest were usually separated from their people by being "invited" to the Inca capital, essentially as hostages. Once there, they were gradually integrated into the Inca ruling elite; offspring of local elites were given an Inca education and instructed in the Inca religion, which was imposed on top of or in place of local religions throughout the empire. The ruling family was integral to the religion, as, like the Japanese royal house, they claimed descent from the sun god. Providing landed support for a growing number of royal mummies, cult objects themselves, was one spur to continued expansion of the empire. In short, rule of the empire was highly centralized and focused on a dominant and ideologically awesome royal house. The only weakness in Inca administration was their lack of a true written language, though a sophisticated mnemonic system of colored ropes and knots and a class of official historians and record keepers mitigated the deficiency.

The geographic range of the Inca Empire was stunning, including as it did not just a vast horizontal expanse of land but a wide variety of vertical divisions, from the low coastal and tropical jungle lands, through the temperate midlevel elevations, to the high peaks and valleys of the upper Andes. Economic exchange among these various climate zones gave economic vitality and unity to the empire and created wealth for the state. Tying the whole empire together and facilitating economic exchange was a system of royal roads. Though made only for foot traffic, they were as well built as Roman roads: The engineering involved just in the suspension bridges that spanned great gorges is testament to Inca skills. The roads also served similar functions: first, the movement of Inca armies, and second, the movement of goods. These functions came together in the form of royal supply depots maintained along the roads. The combination of roads and depots allowed for the rapid movement of messages via a system of runners and gave Inca armies, many tens of thousands strong, tremendous mobility.

The Inca army reflected the territorial divisions of the administration. Universal conscription produced a mass of soldiers wielding a variety of regional weapons, led by a professional officer corps. Spearheading Inca forces was a full-time professional army of military aristocrats tens of thousands strong that included an imperial guard of several thousand. The Incas' effective military mobilization of their population certainly exceeded that of the Aztecs and rivaled any state's in the world. In the 1500s, the Incas could maintain three independently operating armies of over 30,000 men at the same time. And the terrain itself was an ally of the Incas. Not only were the steep mountains and narrow passes easily defensible, but the sheer altitude of much of the empire could be debilitating to lowlanders, who lacked the greater lung capacity highland peoples had acquired through evolution. Finally, Inca warfare was deadly in intent and execution, with no culture of taking prisoners as in Mesoamerica.

The great Inca weakness in the face of the Spaniards, however, was their weaponry. Though they knew the use of bronze, almost all their weapons were of stone, wood, and bone and were designed for crushing blows, delivered by club or sling. They lacked slashing and cutting weapons such as the Aztec obsidian swords, and they underutilized the archery skills of jungle peoples on the fringes of the empire. Shortages of good wood, another consequence of high elevation, also kept the length of Inca spears down. The result was that Inca armies were far more vulnerable to Spanish weaponry, especially cavalry charges, and less able to penetrate Spanish armor than were the Aztecs, and so were at a severe disadvantage in head-on fights on open ground.

The Spanish Invasion

Francisco Pizarro came on this unknown civilization in 1532, and, once again, the timing of his expedition proved fortuitous for Spanish fortunes. The empire was near the end of a civil war, brought on by a succession crisis that arose when the heir to the throne died in an epidemic probably passed via Indian tribes from Spanish settlements in the Caribbean. Already, European diseases were opening the way for European weapons. The new Inca emperor, Atahualpa, was as yet insecurely established on the throne and still preoccupied with his rival when Pizarro's small force began its march into the heart of the empire. As a result, Pizarro's progress was unopposed when his force was at its most vulnerable. Atahualpa also seems to have severely underestimated the danger the newcomers posed, as to Inca spies the Spaniards appeared to be a poorly disciplined rabble. Conversely, Pizarro was aware of the political situation from local accounts. He had Cortes' experience in Mexico as a guide to exploiting Indian political divisions. These would include the resentments of recently conquered tribes within the empire, though to a somewhat lesser extent than in Mexico: Civil war rivalries were crucial in the centralized Inca state. And he and his men were familiar with fighting Indians in Central America and the Caribbean.

All these factors came together in Pizarro's capture of Atahualpa at Cajamarca, in what was less a battle than a diplomatic ambush and slaughter. Atahualpa's ignorance of the foreigners led him needlessly into the trap. The extreme centralization of Inca government and the semidivine nature of Inca kingship now became a major handicap to further resistance. Atahualpa's forces were paralyzed by his captivity, compounded by his orders not to attack or risk a rescue operation. Adherents of his rival for the throne welcomed the Spaniards as liberators and provided them with supplies and guides. Again, the Spanish march from Cajamarca to the capital at Cuzco was largely unopposed, with the Incas ignoring all the potential advantages of terrain and ambush along the way. Divisions among the Incas became even more serious after Pizarro had Atahualpa executed in a moment of panic, as the Spaniards were able to put weak or willing collaborators on the throne who continued to legitimize, at least partly, the actions of the invaders. Only in 1536 did Manco Inca succeed to the throne and unite the opposition.

Still, despite all the handicaps imposed by the political situation, Inca armies did oppose the Spanish force. Gunpowder played little role in such encounters. Missile fire was not central to the outcome of the battles for the empire, and Inca fortresses were virtually impervious to cannon: Even when the terrain did not make them inaccessible, Inca stonework was massive enough to resist cannonades. Instead, battles on open ground proved disastrous for the Incas because steel and horses gave the Spanish cavalry a huge edge against Inca troops. But the Incas were neither stupid nor suicidal, and they soon developed countertactics. Spaniards were ambushed in narrow passes and crushed by boulders rolled down on them. Small groups were isolated and attacked, as the natives took advantage of their vast numerical superiority. And to the limited extent that they could, the Incas made use of captured Spanish

arms and horses. Manco Inca more than once entered battle riding a horse, wearing helmet and breastplate, and wielding lance and sword. But the technological divide was too vast for such adoptions to be made widely or effectively, and the political defeat at the outset of the war rendered Inca tactical adaptation too little and too late.

But only just. After the initial Spanish success in capturing the major cities of the empire and installing a puppet emperor, two major uprisings led by Manco Inca nearly succeeded in expelling the invaders. Turning the tables, the Incas took advantage of rivalries between Spanish factions. Their new tactics were effective in the right terrain, but three things in the end doomed the revolts. First, enough Indians adhered to the Spaniards and their puppet to give vital support in several key battles. Second, the full weight of the Spanish Empire was brought to bear as reinforcements poured in on the Spanish side. And, third, Spanish technology and tactical cohesion proved too overwhelming in battle. The Spaniards lost far fewer men in seven years of Inca warfare than in the single disastrous expulsion from Tenochtitlan. Still, with all their advantages, it took seven years of hard fighting to complete the conquest of Peru—far longer than the conquest of Mexico had taken—and the resistance ultimately ceased only when Manco Inca was assassinated by Spanish renegades he had rescued and taken into his camp for a year.

New Central Rulers As in Mexico, the established political structure of the Inca Empire facilitated Spanish rule once the fighting was over. The centralized state administration was taken over by the newcomers. Their position was legitimized by the cooperation of the puppet emperor: Technically, the empire continued to exist, overseen by a Spanish governor, though Spanish policies rapidly transformed the social and economic landscape, eroding the Inca character of Peru.

And again, as in Mexico, to the mass of native peasants used to toiling for a military aristocracy, the shift to Spanish rule, especially at first, must not have been earth shattering. The Spaniards sought the same things they did in Mexico—precious metals and the profits of landlordism—and they found both. The Potosí silver mines alone would finance Spanish power in Europe for a century. And the potato, an Inca staple, would in the end be more valuable to the world's population than all the Americas' gold and silver combined. Finally, again as in Mexico, the ravages of disease, compounded by brutal Spanish labor systems in the mines, sealed native fortunes demographically.

Assessment　If the political structure of their empire was always going to be the central problem for Aztec resistance to the Spaniards, no matter when they came, military technology was the key problem for the Incas. In different circumstances, this might have been a more solvable problem—and different political circumstances are imaginable, for in many ways, the fortuitous timing of the invasion seems to have been a key factor in Spanish success.

Given even just another 1 or 2 years before Pizarro's arrival, the Incas would have presented a much more united and focused front to the invaders. Given another 5 to 10 years, the empire would likely have become a tougher nut to crack even with Spanish advantages in weaponry, especially if intelligence of the Spanish presence farther north had made it to the Inca court, as it may well have. Given another 50 years—unlikely but not inconceivable, since the existence of the empire was unknown to Europeans even by rumor before Pizarro came on it, and if Pizarro's expedition had disappeared no follow-up was guaranteed—a European conquest could have become very difficult. Another 50 years to consolidate and organize a state lacking the inherent structural weaknesses of the Aztec Empire; another 50 years to adjust to the European presence farther north, learn from other Indians' experiences, and, most important, close the gap in weapons technology somewhat—the possibilities are intriguing.

The Incas didn't have any extra time, though, and alternate outcomes must remain purely speculative. But they arise from a close reading of the actual course of Spanish conquest. The technology gap made European success in Peru in 1532 likely, but luck and contingency played a role as well, and a longer history for the Inca Empire still tantalizes us as a great might-have-been.

Beyond the Frontiers of the Great Empires

The limitations of Spanish military superiority and the dependence of the conquests of Mexico and Peru on native political factors is further demonstrated by Spanish and other Europeans' experience beyond the frontiers of the great empires. Here, expansion was slow, outright military triumph hard to come by, and European influence was spread as much or more by economic and religious inroads as by warfare.

The Gran Chichimeca and Spanish North America　The first frontier the Spaniards had to deal with was the Gran Chichimeca, the northern Mexican plateau that was home to fierce nomadic warriors. This had been a long-standing frontier for the sedentary states of central Mexico. The Spaniards inherited it, and it soon became a more acute military problem. This was because early silver finds in the area led to the rapid establishment of mining settlements at a considerable distance from the heart of Spanish control. Spanish cattle ranches also began to encroach on the traditional lands of the nomads. Supply wagons and cattle made tempting targets for plundering raids by the nomads, who also attacked in defense of their lands.

Although they did not have horses, in other respects, these native peoples posed problems for their sedentary foes similar to those that Central Asian nomads had created for millennia. They were tough, mobile, elusive foes; excellent archers; and fierce, terrifying fighters. They had little respect for the Spaniards or their sedentary Indian allies, whom they considered soft and effeminate. The terrain they inhabited was often too rough for cavalry pursuit. Further, in the face of Spanish initiatives, they proved capable of large-scale tribal alliance and cooperation.

For fifty years, from 1550 to 1600, the Spaniards tried repeatedly to tame this frontier militarily. Spanish soldiers were attracted to the frontier by the promise that they could enslave whatever nomads they captured, though they often simply turned this privilege against the peaceful sedentary natives they were supposed to protect. Allied Indian armies were recruited for the fight. But little progress was made, despite expenditures that ate up the profits of the silver mines being protected. And in one frightening way, after decades of conflict, the problem threatened to get far worse, as the nomads began capturing Spanish horses and learning to ride. The vastly increased mobility this gave the native warriors could have made the frontier uninhabitable.

New Spanish leadership, following the advice of friars and missionaries on the frontier, abandoned the attempt to crush the nomads "by fire and sword" and instead pacified them through largely nonmilitary means. With gifts of food, nomad groups were bribed into joining sedentary settlements. Peaceful attempts at conversion were substituted for Spanish raiding and slave making, with dramatic results. And with the demographic weight of steadily encroaching settlements of sedentary Indians and Spanish cattle ranchers, the bulk of the nomadic population was slowly absorbed. The gains were consolidated by the construction of small fortified outposts that became the centers of new settlements. This pattern of mostly peaceful conversion to and absorption into the Spanish economic system, forged in the heat of the Gran Chichimeca, became the model for the continued expansion of the Spanish frontier in western North America.

Central and South America Spanish and Portuguese progress elsewhere in Central and South America was even less impressive. The Yucatan, on the other side of the Aztec Empire, was subdued only slowly and incompletely. Its terrain was inaccessible, it lacked a strong draw for European adventurers—no big gold or silver finds turned up there—and the extremely decentralized politics of the area made takeover both difficult and unprofitable. The slowness of European advance also allowed the natives time to acquire some of the technology of the invaders, especially steel blades of various sorts, despite prohibitions on such trade.

The same story repeated itself on a larger scale throughout much of South America outside of Peru and the Portuguese settlements in coastal Brazil, connected to the homeland by ship. Progress in extending European control over inland areas by 1700 was minimal. Even in the Caribbean, where the European advantages came earliest and were most overwhelming, Caribs held on to some islands—partly by playing one European power off against another—well into the seventeenth century and executed effective raids on European settlements using canoes. It was only with the arrival of fully professional regiments from newly effective royal armies after 1680 (see Chapter 16), in the context of heightened regional conflict between England and France for control of the developing lucrative sugar trade, that spelled the end of this resistance. The date is significant as evidence for developments in Europe: Again, only sometime in the second half of the seventeenth century did the ongoing military transformation of Europe truly set it apart from many other areas of the world in terms of military effectiveness.

Other Europeans in North America The character of English, French, and Dutch settlement in North America was quite different from the aristocratic Spanish model. Colonies tended to be "fragment" societies, drawn from the middle and lower strata of the home country. Occupying little-used coastal areas, they looked to an ideal of agricultural self-sufficiency and had little use for Indian labor or souls. Indian relations were an uneasy mix of necessary cooperation and intermittent conflict.

In this context, technological transfer was far more significant than in Spanish lands: Indians gained knives, guns, and horses in significant numbers, making them far more formidable opponents in battle. At times, Indians were even armed deliberately by their European allies, especially the French, as much to fight against other Indians as against Europeans. The slow progress of European settlement depended mostly on demographics, a trend benefiting the English settlements above all. They had the biggest flow of immigrants, and agricultural success in the temperate climate of their colonies created a rapidly growing class of American-born Englishmen. Population growth in the intensive farming and commercial culture of the English colonies contrasted with Indian populations that were less concentrated to begin with and were in decline from the spread of European diseases. But this long-term trend was slow to be decisive in the context of other factors, and again, progress prior to 1700 was limited.

Intra-European Conflict

A final, very significant aspect of warfare in the Americas between 1500 and 1700 was intra-European conflict. Just as Indians fought other Indians with and without European intervention, Europeans fought each other with as much ferocity as they showed the natives. It is in intra-European warfare that the ongoing results of the military transformation of Europe show up most clearly. Most of the warfare was focused on sea power, in terms of both ship-to-ship battles (see Chapter 20) and battles for control of ports and harbors. Modern gunpowder fortresses soon guarded these strategic sites, putting their strongest face to the sea to resist bombardment by hostile fleets. At stake in this warfare were the vast treasures of precious metals and other goods and resources—the colonial riches that fueled Europe's economic growth in this age were the prize to be claimed by the winner. By 1720, Britain was emerging as that winner.

Spanish Gunpowder Fortress   Castillo de San Marcos, St. Augustine, Florida, a Spanish bastioned gunpowder fort of the type that protected European trade outposts in the Americas and Southeast Asia during the sixteenth and seventeenth centuries.

SOUTHEAST ASIA

European efforts to create empires in India and Southeast Asia began soon after the first Portuguese ships found their way around Africa. Throughout the sixteenth and seventeenth centuries, first Portugal and then the Netherlands worked to dominate Indian Ocean trade with Europe, especially trade in spices from the East Indies. Portugal built on its experiences in eastern Africa, constructing a series of fortified outposts at strategic spots along the Indian Ocean periphery, such as Goa, Hormuz, and Melaka. Their purpose was to force merchants to call at one of these outposts and pay duties on their goods—in effect, an elaborate protection scheme. However, as Portugal became more adept in managing this system, their military advantages shrank. The relatively small Portuguese military forces could not cope with the increasing ability of local powers to resist them, as well as more serious challenges by other European powers.

When the Dutch arrived in the East Indies in the sixteenth century, they aimed not only to oust the Portuguese but to replace and control the whole trading system. They sought, unlike the Portuguese, to control the sources of the spices, as well as to monopolize as much as possible the transport of products from the East Indies. In both cases, military power was utilized to support merchant trade policies. But European military power was balanced by local adoption of European military technology and by the limited forces, especially on land, that Europeans could bring to bear in the region.

The Portuguese Empire

India and the Acquisition of Goa   Portugal came to dominate, if not actually control, much of the Indian Ocean trade with Europe, especially in spices, though they remained minor players in the overall Asian spice trade (the majority of which was local or intra-Asian). The architect of the successful strategy was the admiral Afonso de Albuquerque. The Malabar coast of India was an important entrepôt (intermediate trading) region as well as trading center for goods from the Indian interior. Albuquerque's small but powerful fleet allowed him to take the island of Goa in 1510, from which the Malabar coast could be monitored. Goa became the capital of Portugal's Asian empire, eventually including a foundry to produce many of the cannons on which Portuguese dominance depended.

The choice of Goa proved wise. Other forts were constructed along the Indian mainland, sometimes to be retaken by local Indian powers. Goa and its fortifications, however, proved resilient, falling to Indian power only in 1691. Indeed, Portugal's primary problem in maintaining control of Goa was not strictly military: Diseases killed off thousands over the years and were especially deadly to the few European women who traveled out east. Intermarriage with Indians and Africans, and employment of them (and their offspring) as bureaucrats, soldiers, and sailors, was the only way the Portuguese could maintain their control.

Portugal in the East Indies   As at Goa, naval artillery was important to Albuquerque's conquest of Melaka, strategically located along the Malay coast, across from the Indonesian island of Sumatra. In 1509, a Portuguese mission to the Sultan of Melaka was met violently, and many of the Portuguese were taken hostage. The following year, Albuquerque led a force of about fourteen ships and over 1200 men, including 200 Indian recruits, to Melaka. The sultan had 20,000 men at his disposal, as well as gunpowder weapons, though their effectiveness did not match that of the Portuguese: After the battle, the Portuguese reported having seized nearly 3000 firearms. Several Chinese merchants in the city defected to the Portuguese, providing a Chinese junk that allowed the Portuguese to get closer to the city center. During the subsequent bombardment, the sultan fled and the city surrendered. Albuquerque stayed a few more months, building defensive fortifications and sending out scouts to survey the Moluccas, the spice islands that were the main object of European interest in Asia in the sixteenth century. Melaka had been the preeminent trading port of Asia, and the Portuguese had no intention of changing that; proclamations made clear their interest in protecting and managing trade relations, not in acquiring more territory.

Fortification and Opposition   Several forts rose in the spice islands, especially on Ambon and Ternate, but these were never very secure; the Portuguese gained more through alliances and treaties with local rulers than by direct military action. Local Muslim rulers tried unsuccessfully to retake Melaka. The Portuguese continued to be the dominant player at sea,

especially after defeating a large Javanese fleet in 1521, yet their local opponents were rapidly acquiring firearms technology. Although Melaka held out against repeated attacks, many of the other Portuguese forts fell or were only held at great expense. Despite Portuguese efforts, Melaka declined as a trading port as merchants began utilizing others such as Aceh and Johor. Melaka's decline strained the Portuguese financial ability to sustain their military presence in the area.

The Dutch in the East Indies

At the dawn of the seventeenth century, opponents of the Portuguese found an ally who could challenge Portuguese naval domination: the Dutch. At the time, the Netherlands was involved in a desperate struggle for independence from the Spanish crown that took on a global dimension in the late sixteenth century when the Dutch acquired knowledge of Portuguese sailing routes to the East. Whereas early Portuguese involvement in the East Indies had been almost solely concerned with commerce, the Dutch also had strategic interests that led them to engage in larger-scale conquest of the islands of the East Indies.

Early Actions in the East Indies   The first few Dutch voyages to the East Indies in the late sixteenth century made a poor impression. Several Dutch companies competed with each other as well as the Portuguese for the spice trade, and their heavy-handed actions led at times to hostilities. Finally, in 1602, the various Dutch enterprises merged into the Dutch East India Company, also known by its Dutch initials, VOC. Dutch interests and actions became more focused, and the VOC was able to take advantage of its superior organization, financing, and military power. That very year, the Dutch unsuccessfully besieged Portuguese Melaka. While preparing for future assaults, the Dutch worked to oust the Portuguese from the Spice Islands. Treaties were concluded with local rulers allowing the Dutch to trade and to establish fortifications. The lesson of the Portuguese involvement was that these forts were essential if European powers were to operate safely and securely in the region. The VOC also allied itself with local opponents of the Portuguese, especially the kingdom of Johor. The two allies jointly besieged Melaka in 1607, with the VOC supplying the sea power and Johor the manpower. Only timely reinforcements from Goa preserved the Portuguese position.

Establishment of VOC Headquarters at Batavia

Controlling trade remained the primary interest of the VOC. By 1605, the Dutch had chased the Portuguese out of Ambon, with local opponents of the Portuguese supplying the essential land forces. However, the Dutch position on Ambon, as on other spice islands, required constant military vigilance and often action, as the Ambonese accepted Dutch dominance no more readily than they had Portuguese rule.

By the 1620s, the VOC was monopolizing the spice trade far more completely than had the Portuguese, based on control of production centers as well as sea-lanes. Naval supremacy remained essential: During these early decades, the Dutch never had more than about 2000 regular troops, relying on local allies for soldiers, but at sea they rarely maintained fewer than ninety effective ships. Islands were isolated one by one; faced with serious resistance, the Dutch destroyed cities, towns, and crops, and even relocated local populations.

Dutch involvement on the island of Java demonstrates clearly the difficulties caused by their military advantages at sea not being duplicated on land. Desiring a better headquarters to locate warehouses and manage operations in the East Indies, the VOC determined in 1619 to take the port of Jakarta on the island of Java. The VOC had established a small fortified trading post in the city in 1615 and had renamed it Batavia (the Roman name for Holland). In May 1619, a Dutch fleet sailed into the harbor and devastated the city with an artillery bombardment. Occupying an almost vacant city, the Dutch fortified further to resist inevitable attempts at reconquest by local rulers. To get the manpower needed for a successful defense, the VOC recruited Chinese (and some Japanese), and soon a large majority of the population of the city were Chinese. The VOC came gradually to control most of the lands surrounding Batavia. Holding this territory, let alone expanding it, required more alliances with local leaders, as well as sponsoring revolts and coups against some of their most powerful opponents.

The Conquest of Melaka

While the Portuguese continued to hold Melaka, Dutch supremacy at sea could not be taken for granted. Indeed, even on land, the Dutch had reason to be concerned; in the 1620s and 1630s, Portuguese assistance to opponents of the Dutch in Java was a serious problem. In June 1640, the VOC again allied with Johor, the leading local antagonist of the Portuguese, to besiege Melaka. The VOC supplied twelve warships and about 1500 men, while Johor contributed forty ships and over 20,000 men, but the Dutch role was crucial. In addition to erecting a complete naval blockade, the Dutch instructed their Johor allies in the latest European siege techniques. During five months of constructing siege trenches and mines, the Dutch and their allies lost thousands to disease and exhaustion. In early 1641, with the defenders nearly out of gunpowder and starvation claiming many, the Dutch successfully stormed the fortifications guarding the city. The Dutch then reneged on a promise to give Melaka to Johor, instead taking over and strengthening the Portuguese fortifications so well that, until many years later, they never kept more than 500 or so regulars in the city.

VOC Dominance of the East Indies

With the conquest of Melaka, the VOC became the key power in the region. It had chased the Portuguese out of the East Indies and gained almost complete control of the spice trade. It soon added control of the tin trade and a monopoly in the Japanese silver trade to its portfolio. Profits fueled further VOC involvement in Javanese affairs, leading to increasingly direct control over Java. But in addition to ongoing struggles with local powers, the Dutch shortly faced new competition in the area from European rivals (Figure 18.4). Shifts in naval power (chronicled in Chapter 20) and the growing British and French presence in India (traced in Chapter 21) challenged Dutch maritime and trade power, while the narrow economic and manpower bases of their ground forces kept Dutch control stretched and precarious. We will return to these topics in Chapter 24.

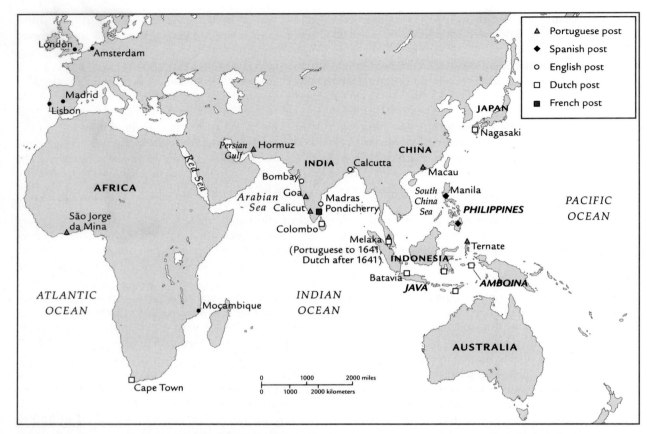

Figure 18.4 European Trade Empires c. 1700   This map shows the major trade posts and colonies established in Asia and Africa by the five major European colonial powers by 1700. Some had changed hands: Melaka, for example, was Portuguese until 1641, when the Dutch took it over.

CONCLUSION

By 1700, the European presence around the globe was growing gradually. European powers would take decisive steps in the eighteenth century, based on the emerging advances in European military technique and on the growing prosperity the far-flung European commercial empires were generating. But for the most part, European gains before 1700 were limited in scope and nature. Even where they appeared most impressive—Spanish America and parts of Southeast Asia—the European presence was built more on cooperation with local powers than on military might. This was reflected culturally in the Americas, where the apparent dominance of Catholicism hid a vital and thriving syncretism with indigenous religion; militarily in Southeast Asia, where not just alliances with local powers but the use of native but European-trained troops was gaining in importance (see Chapter 21 for British sepoys in India, for example); and economically in Africa, where the slave trade found willing participants on both sides of the exchange. In short, this was an age not of European dominance, but of European participation on a global scale. That participation was itself new and significant, but it was not a sign that a military revolution had transformed Europe's place in the global power structure. European limitations were even clearer in East Asia, which we take up in the next chapter.

SUGGESTED READINGS

Boucher, Philip P. *Cannibal Encounters: Europeans and Island Caribs, 1492–1763*. Baltimore: Johns Hopkins University Press, 1999. Traces the military and cultural interactions on the Caribbean islands, including the effectiveness of Carib resistance.

Cook, Weston. *The Hundred Years War for Morocco: Gunpowder and the Military Revolution in the Early Modern Muslim World*. Boulder: Westview Press, 1994. Examines the century-long struggle between Portugal and the Moroccan dynasties, with attention to the impact and adoption of firearms and attendant military organization and tactics in the region.

Guilmartin, John. "The Cutting Edge: An Analysis of the Spanish Invasion and Overthrow of the Inca Empire, 1532–1539." In K. Andrien and R. Adorno, *Transatlantic Encounters*. Berkeley: University of California Press, 1992. An important military analysis of the impact of the technological gap between the Spanish and the Incas.

Hassig, Ross. *Aztec Warfare. Imperial Expansion and Political Control*. Norman: University of Oklahoma Press, 1995. An excellent functional analysis of Aztec warfare, challenging many myths of "ritualism" and nonseriousness in Meso-American war.

Hemming, John. *The Conquest of the Incas*. New York: Penguin Books, 1983. A detailed narrative of Pizarro's expedition, told with understanding of the Inca side of the conflict.

Hess, Andrew. *The Forgotten Frontier: A History of the Sixteenth-Century Ibero-African Frontier*. Chicago: University of Chicago Press, 1978. An excellent review of the role played by the Maghrib as a frontier battleground between Christendom and Islam in the sixteenth century.

McNeill, William. *Plagues and Peoples*. New York: Anchor Press, 1976. A classic account of the impact of disease in world history.

Powell, Philip Wayne. *Soldiers, Indians and Silver: The Northward Advance of New Spain, 1550–1600*. Tempe: Arizona State University Press, 1975. Demonstrates the limits of Spanish military conquest in the struggle against nomadic tribes in north Mexico.

Prescott, William H. *The Art of War in Spain: The Conquest of Granada 1481–1492*, ed. Albert D. McJoynt. London: Routledge, 1995. An updated edition of Prescott's study from 1837; includes a useful introduction to armies and warfare in late fifteenth-century Spain.

Ricklefs, Merle. *A History of Modern Indonesia Since 1300*. Stanford: Stanford University Press, 1993. The standard introduction to Indonesian history, with attention to the give and take involved in the growth of Dutch colonialism in the area.

Russell-Wood, A. J. R. *The Portuguese Empire, 1415–1808*. Baltimore: Johns Hopkins University Press, 1998. A comprehensive account of the dynamics of the Portuguese imperial project, stressing the interconnections between Asia, Europe, and the Americas.

Thornton, John. "The Art of War in Angola, 1575–1680." *Comparative Studies in Society and History* 30:2 (1988), 360–378. An excellent examination of how the use of gunpowder weapons in sub-Saharan Africa was shaped by environmental and demographic constraints.

Vogt, John. "Saint Barbara's Legion: Portuguese Artillery in the Struggle for Morocco 1415–1578." *Military Affairs* LXI (1977), 176–182. A useful survey of the type and number of artillery pieces as well as their employment by the Portuguese in Morocco.

CHAPTER 19

East Asian Transformations: Japan and China, 1500–1750

The coming of European-style gunpowder weapons and warfare to East Asia highlights the limitations and contingencies of European penetration and success elsewhere, for the Japanese and Chinese virtually dictated the terms of their contact with Europeans. This was a result, not just of the distance between East Asia and Europe, but of the strength of East Asian governmental and military traditions. Both Japan and China—the latter the original home of gunpowder—adopted gunpowder weapons readily, because their military and political structures were evolving or had already evolved in directions compatible with the use of guns. Their experience cautions against interpretations of early modern military transformation based too heavily on new technology: Social technology mattered as much or more in changing patterns of warfare. This was true even where guns made a clearer difference to an old pattern: By the end of this period, as China's history shows, civilizations armed with guns had decisively and permanently shifted the balance of military power away from steppe nomads.

JAPAN

By the time Japan faced European contact in 1543, it was already well into a dramatic transformation of its own ways of war, one that closely paralleled that going on in western Europe. As a result, Japanese armies of the *sengoku-jidai*, the "age of the country at war," adopted gunpowder technology easily and effectively, and were able to dictate the terms of their continuing contact with Europe. By the mid-seventeenth century, this meant a virtual prohibition of Japanese contact with the outside world and a politically imposed freeze on further military evolution.

Sengoku Japan, 1477–1615

New Politics: The **Daimyo** *Domains*   The results of the Onin War (1467–77; see Chapter 14) fundamentally altered the political and military environment of Japan. The war effectively destroyed the *shugo,* the military governors who tied the provinces to a national political structure, and reduced the Ashikaga shoguns to a minor power around Kyoto.

In place of the old *shogun-shugo* system, the *daimyo* emerged. The daimyo, a group with mixed origins in the warrior social scale, were the local and regional warlords who had often been the subordinates of the *shugo*. Residing in the provinces while the *shugo* stayed in the capital, the daimyo built up their local influence and followings, and when the *shugo* self-destructed, the daimyo converted their local influence into control of independent domains whose geography differed significantly from any polities seen before in Japan. Geographically, daimyo domains were small, compact, and contiguous, unlike the scattered lands and income rights of earlier warrior leaders. They often centered on a castle and increasingly were protected at their borders by a system of forts. Politically, daimyo domains were independent states. There was no national system of authority or control over the domains—the emperors and the shoguns continued to exist, but for nearly a century, they were little more than cultural figureheads. The daimyo were highly competitive, engaging in nearly constant warfare to protect and expand their holdings. But because of the lack of a national political stage to jump onto, this warfare was, until the 1560s, fairly localized. (See the Issues box "Comparative History and Japanese 'Feudalism,'" which places the daimyo system in broader historical context.)

Many daimyo began in the decades after 1477 to make their rule over their domains more effective. First, they exercised closer control and more consistent

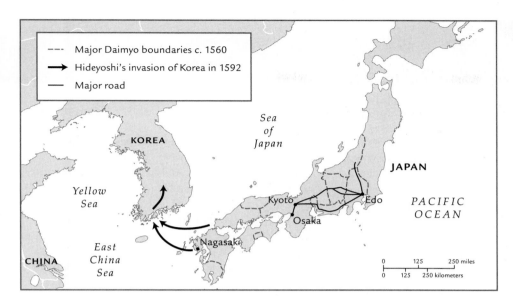

Figure 19.1 Japan in the Sixteenth Century

discipline over their vassals and subordinates. In this they were aided by changes that had already taken place in the structure of the warrior class. The move from assigning income rights from scattered estates (the *shoen* system) to the granting of land from the local warlord's estates had tied warbands more closely to particular locales and leaders. This practice continued, and as the economy developed and daimyo financial resources increased, the grants were increasingly issued in terms of cash rather than actual land. In short, samurai became tied to their lords through a direct, revocable cash nexus. Such relationships were established contractually, though the relationship was more one-sided in favor of the lord than in European social contracts. This form of relationship arose to replace the kinship ties of earlier times, and while lacking the apparent moral force of kinship, it proved more practical as long as the lord was successful. Daimyo further increased their control over their followers by gathering them as much as possible in the castle-towns that served as their capitals.

Closer control over followers went hand in hand with better government. The financial resources that aided daimyo control over their followers came from their development of better taxation methods. The daimyo began making detailed land surveys of their domains and adjusting agricultural taxes more closely to actual output. They also encouraged commerce and the income it brought by gathering merchants and artisans to their castle-towns. Better taxation

was, in turn, only part of a general move to more effective administration. Written laws were developed, often arising initially out of codes of conduct aimed at the daimyo's military men. The literacy of the warrior class meant that they could be used as both fighters and administrators. The internal security that the daimyo could bring to their domains encouraged the spread of daimyo justice into lower levels of society as villagers and merchants, previously self-governing, looked to the daimyo for order. This, in turn, reestablished within the domains a sense of public duties and prerogatives, legitimizing daimyo rule. In short, authority and legitimacy came to coincide with real power for the first time at the local and regional level: These were small but intensively ruled polities (Figure 19.1).

Daimyo control was further enhanced by widespread social changes during this age. Villages, threatened by the uncertainties of the age and the loss of national political restraint on local warrior activity, asserted themselves more actively. They formed their own armed associations, financed in part by the growing market success of at least some farmers in the expanding economy. Greater stratification of the peasant class encouraged the emergence of an armed leadership among them, who then looked to the daimyo for support against aggressive local warriors. In exchange, the villages provided the daimyo with growing resources of money and soldiers recruited for daimyo armies. Greater village assertiveness squeezed

Comparative History and Japanese "Feudalism"

The dominance in Japan since Kamakura times of a rural warrior aristocracy in the context of somewhat weak central government has long invited comparison of Japan with medieval Europe, where similar conditions prevailed. Such comparisons have almost always been cast in terms of feudalism: Archibald Lewis's *Knights and Samurai: Feudalism in Northern France and Japan* is perhaps the most prominent example of a widespread historiographical phenomenon. A closer look at the comparisons, however, reveals a number of difficulties with this equation and casts light on both the pitfalls and the potential of comparative history.

The first difficulty is that the concept of feudalism has become problematic even in European history (see the Issues box on feudalism in Chapter 7). Second, even if feudalism were an uncontested idea, its application to Japanese history could be misleading. Since historians' model of feudalism arose from the study of western Europe, looking for feudalism elsewhere risks shoehorning non-European histories into a European mold. Some assume, for example, that European feudalism followed a natural trajectory of development and then look for that trajectory elsewhere. This raises the danger of misreading the evidence to find what "should" be there or, if a different trajectory is seen, of explaining what went "wrong" in the non-European case (a danger that is even more acute with the concept of capitalism).

Such dangers have afflicted western views of Sengoku Japan. The feudal model has led many historians to see the Sengoku age as the epitome of feudal breakdown and anarchy. Daimyo domains are equated with the small castellanies and lordships of northern France, with the feudal kingdom (France and Japan) taken as the unit of comparison because of the prominence of weak central authority in the feudal model. But by emphasizing the division of the larger political unit, this view obscures important forces of unity and political cohesion developing within the daimyo domains (see below). Without the feudal preconception, daimyo domains appear more readily as independent polities within a "Japan" that is more akin to "Europe" than to any one kingdom within Europe.

At a lower level of the feudal model, the European norm has inspired numerous comparisons of the structures of warrior society—of landholding and military service, for example—that often obscure the important differences between the two societies more than they illuminate their

local warriors from below just as the daimyo were exerting greater pressure from above. Caught between these two forces, local warriors became more dependent on daimyo support and as a result more amenable to daimyo control.

Both the growing economy and daimyo military competition created opportunities for talented and ambitious men to improve their fortunes, and the century or so from 1477 to the 1580s was a time of unprecedented mobility in the Japanese social structure. The character of the age is expressed in the Japanese term *gekokujo*—"the high overcome by the low." Poor merchants became rich, peasants rose through the ranks to attain important military postings, and

ambitious subordinates overthrew their leaders. The best road to security, though not guaranteed, lay in military success. But in the changed political context of the times, with new administrative, fiscal, and disciplinary resources available to leaders and the talent unleashed by social flux, military success no longer consisted of individual and family glory as it had in earlier times. Political, governmental, and social change stimulated and, in turn, was influenced by new ways of warfare.

New Warfare: The Japanese Military Transformation   In the new political context, the goals and aims of warfare changed. Honor within a countrywide commonalities. This problem, too, is most critical in the Sengoku age, when massive daimyo armies must be explained, in the context of the feudal model, as a more "impersonal and bureaucratic feudalism" than existed in Europe. "Bureaucratic feudalism" is a self-contradictory concept that dissolves on close inspection.

Application of the feudal model also invites the equating of terms that occupy apparently similar places in the model, but that may not, in fact, be at all equivalent. The linking of "knights" and "samurai" exemplified in Lewis's title is the best example of this. "Knight" and "samurai" do not designate highly similar phenomena: The class connotations of the former make it closer to *bushi* in pre-Tokugawa Japan. Equating samurai and knights inevitably equates the fighting techniques of the two regions' warriors when, in fact, their tactics were significantly different—especially, again, in the Sengoku age with its samurai armies of disciplined massed infantry formations. The word "emperor" provides another example. Both Japan and the Holy Roman Empire had officers who are commonly identified in English as emperors. But functionally, the two officers played very different roles, and it might be more useful to compare the Japanese emperor's role with that of the pope in Europe as a symbol of cultural and religious unity, a source of legitimacy, and a political actor in some conflict with military authorities.

None of this means that abstract or idealized models of social, political, and economic organization are useless. Comparative history could not be done without them. The case of feudalism in Japan, however, warns us to beware of facile comparisons of terms and of models derived too narrowly from one culture. Still, generalizations derived from functional descriptions and comparisons of different areas can be useful. While Sengoku Japan may not have been feudal, it has interesting similarities to sixteenth-century Europe functionally. Both areas were politically divided and consumed with wars that became increasingly serious in terms of the survival of small states. Both areas were undergoing economic expansion that contributed new material and manpower resources to the arsenals of prospective state builders. And both areas were ruled by elites who were essentially military in background, outlook, and training. Against such a background of functional similarity, key differences—such as the date of the introduction of gunpowder weapons—can illuminate developments in both areas.

hierarchy was no longer worth aiming at. Instead, conquest of neighboring domains became the goal of ambitious daimyo, as conquest now legitimated itself rather than working against a system of central assignment of lands. This meant that the seizure of forts and the ability to guard and administer captured territory increasingly guided strategy. Siege warfare took on new importance. One result was that the number of forts increased as networks of strongholds provided mutual support for one another and dominated districts more securely. The size and strength of forts also increased. This was especially true after Oda Nobunaga, the most innovative of the Sengoku daimyo, rebuilt Azuchi Castle massively in stone in the early 1570s: Azuchi established a new standard of construction, and impressive stone fortifications thereafter anchored the most powerful domains.

With conquest now the primary goal, as the level of competition rose, the number of domains steadily decreased in the century after 1477. Stronger states, whether through more skillful leadership, deployment of greater resources, or accidents of geography and circumstance, gradually swallowed up smaller, weaker, and unluckier states. There were over a hundred independent domains in 1477; by the 1570s, the number of significant political powers was little more than a score.

The economic development that characterized this era loosened somewhat the logistical constraints on strategy. Better administration and a more developed transportation system allowed larger armies to find and transport supplies more reliably. But logistics were still central to strategy. Especially when more extensive struggles for dominance among the largest domains emerged in the 1560s, control of the two major roadways connecting eastern to western Japan, the Tokaido and the Nakasendo, became crucial, and a number of important campaigns were fought along stretches of either road. Some of the most important castles also arose on or near both roads, further focusing strategy around the control of communications and supply routes.

The new emphasis on territorial control and siege warfare notwithstanding, generals in Sengoku Japan still sought battle fairly frequently. Several factors explain this. Despite economic growth, increasing army size kept logistical constraints tight, leading generals to seek swift, decisive conclusions to campaigns. The continuing culture of direct conflict and honor, while no longer as applicable to individual actions, still guided the daimyo, partly because battlefield success cemented the loyalty of followers and attracted new recruits. And daring generals could risk battle to avoid a positional war of attrition against superior forces, as Oda Nobunaga did at Okehazama in 1560, defeating an army of 20,000 with his force of only 2000 in a surprise attack. Finally, the importance of a limited number of castles in the tight geographic confines of domain warfare brought sieges and battles together: A significant siege would often bring a major relief effort leading to combat, as at Nagashino in 1575 (see the Highlights box).

Changes in strategy required changes in armies, and Sengoku armies changed in ways made possible by the prior governmental and social transformations within daimyo domains. First, army size went up steadily after 1477 as the daimyo drew on their improved fiscal and administrative resources. Armies at first numbered in the hundreds and low thousands—apparently no increase from earlier eras. But there were more such forces, and they were drawn from smaller geographic areas; political division disguised for decades the overall increase in military manpower. But by the mid-sixteenth century, many armies numbered in the tens of thousands, and the large coalition armies at the end of the century approached and sometimes exceeded 100,000 men.

Second, the basis of service continued to evolve, affecting not just the *bushi* who had formerly served out of loyalty and kinship bonds and for land rewards, but also the *ashigaru*—the lowborn village foot soldiers—who had earlier served when called into the field by the local lord. Increasingly, all the troops under a daimyo served for cash as paid, professional contract troops. The terms might have been dressed up in the old language of personal dependence to add a moral element to the bond of leader and follower in an age rife with betrayal and ambition, but, functionally, these were professional standing armies, not feudal forces as they have often been portrayed (see the Issues box).

Third, the increase in army size affected the social composition of armies. The old warrior elites no longer formed the bulk of a general's useful troops. Instead, much like the knightly class in Europe under similar circumstances, they became subordinate commanders in the larger forces of the time. Elite groups of *bushi* also continued to act as heavy cavalry strike forces on the battlefield. Well-armed mounted troops from the warrior elite thus still played a key role in Sengoku warfare, but they formed a much smaller proportion of armies as a whole.

In their place, massed infantry rose to the fore. Whereas in earlier eras there was little glory to be gained from employing bodies of *ashigaru,* now the shift to territorial warfare made large blocks of trained infantry useful for taking and garrisoning forts. Their new prominence was reinforced because well-trained infantry, as opposed to the ad hoc peasant levies of earlier times, were also useful for winning battles, in which role they were cost effective. As Asakura Toshiage advised his heirs in 1481, "Even if one has a sword valued at 10,000 cash, he will not overcome 100 men carrying spears valued at 100 cash. Therefore, if one has 10,000 cash and buys 100 spears, having 100 men to carry them he should be able to protect an entire flank." Given the fiscal and administrative resources to raise and train 100 men, the logic was unassailable. The daimyo drew such soldiers from the expanding population, especially the armed village associations. The changing composition of armies was thus both a cause and an effect of the growth in army size, and both depended on the social and governmental transformations taking place within daimyo domains.

New armies fought in new ways, and it is at the tactical level that the metamorphosis of Japanese warfare is clearest. The infantry were armed not just with

Sengoku Soldiers   This plate shows a mounted *bushi* equipped with traditional lance, bow, and sword and a foot soldier armed with a matchlock musket and swords. Both were probably samurai, as was the spearman in the rear.

spears but with bows, and they effectively combined defensive staying power with missile cover. The Portuguese introduced guns to Japan in 1543 (see below), and from the 1560s, arquebusiers increasingly joined the ranks of Japanese infantry as well. Sixteenth-century Japanese infantry seems to have been capable of mass maneuver, of adopting a variety of formations, and of coordinating their efforts not just with different arms of the infantry but with cavalry forces as well. The discipline and level of training achieved by Japanese infantry is indicated by the probable use of volley fire by Oda Nobunaga's arquebusiers at Nagashino in 1575 (see the Highlights box below), several decades before Maurice of Nassau invented it in Europe.

New tactics also prevailed among the elite warriors, whether fighting as infantry or cavalry. The individualistic tendencies of the *bushi* were subordinated to mass tactics: Breaking ranks to engage in individual combat, previously a way to earn honor and glory, was now a breach of discipline punishable by death. Units of heavy cavalry could still provide an offensive strike force on the battlefield, and, like the infantry, they were capable of operating in a number of different formations and in concert with other units of the army.

Not just individual units but whole armies were trained to take up a variety of formations, depending on the terrain and whether they were attacking or defending. Chronicles colorfully described such formations with names such as "crane's wing"; they may have exaggerated the number and intricacy of the different formations, but drill and practice made them possible among sixteenth-century armies. For instance, Takeda Shingen's army at Kawanakajima in 1561 was able to form up at night after secretly exiting a fortress and crossing a river. Generals directed their armies from field headquarters served by messengers, who delivered orders to the units and reports back to the commander. In short, the tactics of Sengoku armies reflected their professionalism.

Siege techniques also changed, but less radically than battlefield tactics. Against weaker strongholds, rapid mass assault was often still the first choice. Older wooden fortresses were vulnerable to fire arrows, as were the roofs and some inner buildings of the newer stone fortresses. Mining was also used, though, unlike in Europe, Japanese mines were intended to provide a route for assault as often as to undermine the walls, as were attacks on a fort's water supply. But the stronger stone fortifications of the 1570s and after could resist almost anything except extended blockade or treachery. With their low, massive walls—those at Osaka Castle are almost nineteen yards thick—fronted by ditches, they could even resist the bronze artillery that became part of besiegers' arsenals late in the century, though Japanese siege and field artillery never got bigger than about nine-pounders and so did not play a decisive role in siege warfare during this period. But the new styles in fortress design did represent a response to the threat of cannon, at least in part.

Changes in the size, composition, and tactics of Japanese armies, ongoing since 1477, explain the ease with which gunpowder weapons entered Japanese warfare after their introduction by the Portuguese in 1543. Nearly a century of military transformations preceded the widespread use of the arquebus in the 1570s, transformations that reconfigured the patterns of Japanese warfare and rendered Sengoku armies, in effect, gunpowder ready. They were integrated into already existing units of disciplined mass infantry by the order of innovative daimyo such as Oda Nobunaga, rather than filtering into tactical practice from the bottom up. Top-down imposition of a new weapon reflected the control the daimyo exercised over their followers and the discipline of the forces they commanded. The vast bulk of arquebuses in use by the end of the century were not European weapons. Working with just a handful of Portuguese prototypes,

Japanese smiths quickly mastered the techniques of manufacturing guns. The rapid growth of a Japanese gun industry also indicates the preexistence of a number of necessary social and economic structures. Japanese metallurgy was among the best in the world: Compared to a samurai sword, an arquebus was a simple piece of smithing. The smiths were set to work by political leaders with the will and incentives to adopt a new weapon that held potential social dangers, given the ease with which it could be used. And a developed economy with extensive market mechanisms made acquisition of raw materials and distribution of the finished product relatively easy. It was not just Japanese armies that proved ready for the gunpowder age.

As in Europe, economics probably played as large a role as purely tactical considerations in the adoption of the arquebus. Guns and bullets were not much more expensive to make than bows and arrows, and the manpower costs could be considerably less: Arquebuses were easier to learn to use effectively than were bows, which required long training. Arquebusiers could thus be raised quickly in significant numbers to supplement an army's bowmen and increase its firepower. The rapid growth in the overall numbers of Sengoku armies clearly put a premium on affordable, effective manpower, encouraging the spread of the new technology. Handgunners were never numerically dominant in sixteenth-century armies, but their relative numbers were still increasing in the early seventeenth century when the political context again changed dramatically, with momentous consequences for the Japanese use of the gun (see below).

As noted above with siege warfare, cannon played a smaller role in the tactical history of gunpowder in Japan than in western Europe. Small, high-quality artillery pieces were manufactured along with handguns, but they seem to have had only a minor effect on the battlefield. Japan's mountainous terrain and resulting limitations on wheeled transport probably constrained the mobility of artillery and made large guns particularly unwieldy and so impractical.

The overall effect of the introduction of gunpowder weapons into Japan was thus to reinforce trends already underway in Japanese warfare. A complex set of economic, social, administrative, and political changes created both the incentives and the means for Sengoku daimyo to transform their military forces into instruments that could easily adopt guns. From this perspective, the introduction of guns themselves was not revolutionary.

A broader structural and functional comparison of developments in sixteenth-century Japan and sixteenth-century western Europe shows striking similarities politically, economically, socially, and administratively. But in this comparison, Japan acts as a sort of control, with a key variable, gunpowder, missing until late in the process of change. The history of Japan's military revolution therefore sheds some comparative light on western Europe's military transformation during this period, suggesting that the long-term evolution of western Europe's social, economic, and administrative resources played a larger role in its military development, and gunpowder a less causal role, than technology-centered accounts sometimes indicate.

Toward Unification

The main difference between Japan and Europe was geographic: Japan's military transformation took place on a smaller, more restricted, stage whose isolation made it less subject to outside competition. As a result, by the 1560s, the stakes of Sengoku warfare were rising: The increasing scale of warfare was bringing into conflict the major daimyo powers. They began vying for greater regional dominance that might set the stage for the reunification of Japan under one government. Three daimyo—Oda Nobunaga, Toyotomi Hideyoshi, and Tokugawa Ieyasu—led the way toward unification and eventually a stable political settlement.

Oda Nobunaga A ruthless campaigner and an insightful innovator, Oda was one of the great captains of the age (see the Highlights box "The Battle of Nagashino, 1575"). From his small but strategically positioned domain on the Tokaido Road east of Kyoto, he rose from relative obscurity to dominate the central third of Japan and lay the foundations of a new political order. He laid those foundations after first clearing out the rubble of a previous age. He ended the Ashikaga shogunate. Systematic campaigning around Kyoto destroyed the power of the great Buddhist warrior temples. His conquests also eliminated many daimyo houses, and his economic reforms began to erode the independence of merchant and village associations, even as he exploited the resources they provided.

In place of the old, he invented the new. He led the way in perfecting the more effective administrative and taxation mechanisms of the Sengoku age,

HIGHLIGHTS

The Battle of Nagashino, 1575

The rising fortunes of Oda and his chief ally, Tokugawa Ieyasu, heightened their rivalry with other powerful *daimyo* domains. One of the strongest, just north of the Tokugawa domain, belonged to the Takeda clan, long led by the great warrior Takeda Shingen. Shingen died in 1573 and was succeeded by his son Katsuyori, who inherited his father's lands and the powerful Takeda army, perhaps the best in Japan at the time. It was built for shock attacks: units of disciplined infantry spearmen, like Swiss phalanxes, supported by elite cavalry and some arquebusiers and bowmen. Takeda forces under Shingen had inflicted a major defeat on Ieyasu at Mikata-ga-Hara in 1572 and were well positioned to make a bid for national hegemony.

Katsuyori invaded the Tokugawa domain in 1575, initially aiming at the major town of Okazaki, which a traitor had promised to open to him. But the plot was discovered, and Katsuyori instead turned his army of 15,000–20,000 to the key border fortress of Nagashino, held by a bitter enemy of his with 500 men. As Katsuyori established his siege headquarters, the garrison managed to get a message out to Ieyasu that they had only enough food for three or four days. The reply that relief was on the way reached both the defenders and the besiegers. Ieyasu had secured the support of Oda, and their combined forces numbered about 38,000. Many of Katsuyori's senior advisors counseled a cautious retreat, but he was determined to offer battle.

The area west of Nagashino across one of the rivers that guarded the fortress on two sides was a hilly plain broken by several small streams. Oda designed his deployment to blunt the impact of the Takeda shock tactics. He had a mile-long staggered set of palisades made of poles, nets, and screens erected in front of his army. Immediately behind the palisades, he stationed 3000 of his best arquebusiers, trained to fire 1000 at a time in continuous volleys. A small force was stationed in front of the palisades to lure the Takeda forces into a charge. Katsuyori obliged. The Takeda units charged in dense formations that Oda's arquebusiers blasted away at with a greater effect than even Oda had anticipated. Not only were the Takeda attacks slowed and disrupted, some were stopped in their tracks. Countercharges through the gaps in the palisade by the heavy infantry and cavalry in Oda's army finished the job. Katsuyori lost over 10,000 men—almost two-thirds of his army. Almost as devastating was the death of seven of the remaining Twenty-Four Generals who had been Takeda Shingen's trusted military advisors. The allied army lost just over 6000 men.

Takeda power never recovered from the devastating defeat at Nagashino. Combined Oda and Tokugawa forces completed the subjugation of the Takeda domain seven years later, reflecting their rise to dominance in the wake of their victory. Oda's tactics brought new prominence to disciplined ranks of ashigaru arquebusiers as significant elements of daimyo armies. Nagashino was thus influential politically, militarily, and symbolically, and constitutes the pinnacle of Oda Nobunaga's career as a general.

and, from there, he built a model of the new military system. His castle at Azuchi initiated a new age in Japanese fortification, and he was the first daimyo to make extensive and effective use of arquebuses. But he was also a victim of the age, as he died when one of his vassals, in a bid for power, ambushed him in Kyoto in 1582 while most of his armies were out

campaigning. The completion of his work was left to his lieutenants.

Toyotomi Hideyoshi   The lieutenant who emerged from the subsequent confusion was the son of a peasant who had risen through the ranks of Oda's army on the basis of his military skill. Hideyoshi defeated the rebel who had ambushed Oda, and by avenging his lord, he managed to assume control of his coalition. A series of campaigns and alliances brought the rest of Japan under his domination by 1590, though it was the political domination of a federation of the most powerful daimyo, not an outright military conquest. But his power was sufficient to allow him to redistribute provinces to different daimyo to the benefit of his allies and supporters.

Hideyoshi now turned his sights to bigger prey, aiming at no less than the conquest of Ming China by way of Korea. Japanese forces invaded in 1592; their superior discipline, tactics, and firepower overcame the initial Korean resistance and brought the southern half of the peninsula under Japanese control. But Korean victory at sea, led by Admiral Yi Sung Sin and his ironclad tortoise ships (see Chapter 20), cut off Japanese reinforcements and supplies, while Korean land forces turned to guerrilla tactics rather than head-to-head confrontation. When Chinese forces intervened in October, Hideyoshi's army retreated to a fortified perimeter around the port city of Pusan. A renewed offensive in 1598 inflicted a number of defeats on the allied Chinese and Korean armies, but Hideyoshi's death in August was followed closely by another crushing naval defeat, and Japanese forces evacuated Korea.

While Hideyoshi's goal was unrealistic, the effort did serve to unify and redirect the vast daimyo military forces built up over the previous century, and Japanese success in conventional ground warfare demonstrated the extent of the military transformation wrought in the Sengoku age. What Hideyoshi failed to accomplish was a stable political settlement in Japan, for when he died his heir was still an infant.

The Tokugawa Settlement, 1615–1800

Tokugawa Ieyasu   Hideyoshi had provided for a council of regency composed of the most substantial daimyo to rule until his son Hideyori came of age. Tokugawa Ieyasu, for decades the most important ally of Oda and Hideyoshi and now the single most powerful member of the council, engineered a conflict. In 1600, the struggle erupted into open war between the Tokugawa and their close supporters, and a loose and fractious coalition of daimyo headed by the Ishida, Uesugi, and Mori clans. In a brief and decisive campaign in the late summer, Ieyasu outmaneuvered his opponents, seizing control of the

Tokaido and Nakasendo roads. On October 21 at Sekigahara, his 70,000 troops defeated an allied army of 120,000, a significant number of whom switched sides as the battle was being contested, deciding the outcome.

Ieyasu now dominated the country, though Hideyori still presented a threat from his stronghold at Osaka Castle, where disaffected warriors gathered. But Ieyasu bided his time and gathered his strength. A descendant of the Minamoto, he had himself declared shogun in 1603, establishing his capital at Edo (modern Tokyo). Finally, he manufactured a crisis in December 1614. Edo forces besieged Osaka, and in June 1615, the castle fell; Hideyori and thousands of his supporters died. Through skill mixed with luck and longevity, Ieyasu had won out: he died a year after Osaka fell, but his descendants ruled as shoguns until the mid-nineteenth century.

A Revolution Reversed   Building on the work of his predecessors, Ieyasu and his heirs constructed a political system designed to minimize conflict. Tokugawa Japan was, as under Hideyoshi, a federation of nominally separate daimyo domains dominated by the Tokugawa house and the houses most closely bound to them. The daimyo of the various domains were made to reside every other year in Edo and to leave members of their family in Edo, essentially as hostages, when they weren't there themselves. This not only kept potential rivals under close watch but also drained the resources they might have used on armies into maintaining two separate domestic establishments in their accustomed style. The number of daimyo military retainers was regulated, and the building or repair of castles, many of which had been taken over by Edo troops, was tightly controlled.

The outside world, too, was made to bend to the demands of internal security. Foreign access to Japan was increasingly restricted, as was Japanese access to foreigners. In 1624, travel abroad was prohibited and the Spaniards were expelled, the English having already withdrawn voluntarily. Much of this had to do with Christianity, which had made significant inroads among the Japanese since the 1540s. But the Edo authorities saw Catholicism, especially, as a threat because it encouraged allegiance to the pope in addition to (or instead of) the shogun and emperor, and persecution of Japanese Christians intensified after 1615. After a major Christian uprising in 1638 on the Shimabara peninsula, the Portuguese, suspected of fomenting the rebellion, were expelled, and the country was closed to all foreign contact save for one Chinese and one Dutch ship a year (the Dutch having sent a warship to support the Edo troops suppressing the rebels).

To further secure their hold on power, the authorities systematically demilitarized the country. Sword hunts, aimed at removing weaponry from the peasants, had been initiated by Hideyoshi; it was now illegal for anyone but retained samurai to carry weapons, and the warrior profession rapidly became a closed social caste. Further, the longer peace was maintained, the more the samurai themselves were transformed from real warriors to the inheritors of a warrior ethos who, in fact, acted as administrators and as the trendsetting elite of a growing consumer culture. With the suppression of two attempted coups in 1651 and 1652, Japan settled into 200 years of an internal peace broken only by sporadic, localized, and easily defeated peasant uprisings.

It is in this context that the Japanese abandonment of gunpowder technology must be viewed. Edo controlled the manufacture and distribution of guns, and after the 1638 revolt, orders virtually ceased. The Japanese gun industry soon disappeared, and by 1700, only scattered antique arquebuses remained of the vast sixteenth-century arsenals. This reflected not a cultural decision against a destructive technology—though it was cloaked in a revival of the Cult of the Sword that fit well with the emergence of the samurai as a closed social class—but a clear political decision to control all forms of potentially disruptive social and political activity. This decision was made possible by the end of political competition within Japan and the ability of the Shogunate to eliminate foreign intervention. Politics, not culture, reversed the gunpowder revolution in Japan, to the benefit of the country's ruling elite.

CHINA

The debacle the Mongols inflicted on the Ming dynasty at the battle of Tumu in 1449 (see Chapter 14) pushed the Ming into a defensive stance toward its northern neighbors. With a century of wall building, China attempted to seal itself off from the Mongols and other nomadic forces, while civilian (especially eunuch) control of the Ming army increased. The only innovations in Ming military strategies and tactics came during the mid-sixteenth century in response to

increasingly destructive raids by the Wako, Japanese pirates, along the eastern coast of China. War with the more technologically advanced and disciplined Japanese army in Korea in the late sixteenth century highlighted the debilitated state of the Ming army.

The Manchu conquest of China in the mid-seventeeth century had tremendous consequences for China's military history. The late Ming dynasty had taken fledgling steps in the use of Western-style gunpowder weapons. The Manchu Qing dynasty vastly expanded the use of these weapons until by 1700 they had become fully integrated into the Qing military system. As in Japan, their adoption came easily to a military system already built around massed infantry. The Chinese version of the early modern military transformation allowed the Qing dynasty to accomplish two goals only temporarily realized by earlier Chinese dynasties: successfully balancing an effective military force with civilian control, and the permanent subjugation of the Mongols.

The Late Ming Dynasty, 1500–1644

A Changing System   The early Ming dynasty followed the Song in stressing civilian control, even at times at the expense of an effective military with its threat of overly powerful separatist generals (see Chapter 14). Civilian governors wielded significant control over the military forces of the provinces, and the garrisons near the capital at Beijing were normally commanded by either civil officials or eunuchs. But by the mid-fifteenth century, the soldiers themselves were in sorry shape, the landed support system having broken down. Soldiers were expected to come from hereditary families, but by the 1450s, the desertion rate was so high that serious recruiting efforts were conducted for the first time. Many of these new recruits were criminals, thugs, or other rootless people, sent to the dangerously understaffed frontier garrisons. This lowered the prestige of the military, not high to begin with, even further among the common people. But garrisons continued to lack men; by the mid-sixteenth century, armies were being sent out into the countryside to engage in mass recruiting, which consisted mainly of press-ganging any male who could not escape. As a result, the average age of Ming soldiers increased tremendously, since old men found it harder to outrun the press-gangs.

The defeat at Tumu in 1449 left China dangerously vulnerable. The Ming court realized that it could not count on its army and so decided to engage in massive wall building to close China off from Mongol attacks. China's vast wealth allowed this, but it still involved the transport of tens of thousands of workers and untold thousands of tons of building materials, food, and other supplies to often sparsely settled areas of the frontier. Utilizing the natural topography as much as possible, the Ming built a barrier, mostly of stone, complete with guard posts, watchtowers, barracks, and other defensive features. In some areas, there were actually lines of overlapping walls that served as fallback positions where soldiers could retreat if overwhelmed. This massive barrier is what has come to be called the "Great Wall of China." Many people mistakenly believe that this is the same wall constructed by the Qin dynasty in the third century BCE. But the Ming wall that we see today is much larger and more strongly constructed than the earlier Qin wall was. Ming commanders believed that even if the wall could not prevent a serious Mongol invasion, it would hold it up until Ming forces could be brought up to the line. The wall, then, was meant to neutralize the Mongols' advantage in mobility.

The Ming reformed their armies several times in the sixteenth century. While significant problems remained, particularly among the frontier armies, the reforms allowed the Ming to more effectively counter the external threats to China. The armies near the capital, now collectively called the Palace Army, were replenished by taking almost all the fittest soldiers from the territorial garrisons, dealing a final crushing blow to that system's usefulness to the defense of China. Additionally, many thousands of families were forcibly relocated to lands along the frontiers and expected to provide soldiers for the Great Wall defenses and the garrisons.

The Ming in the sixteenth and seventeenth centuries also came to rely more on gunpowder weapons, adopting European-style weapons to replace older Chinese designs dating from Song times. In 1523, two Portuguese ships were captured and their store of firearms studied. Soon, Chinese weapons makers were constructing handguns and, especially, cannon in the European style. More cannon were bought from the Portuguese, and by the late 1500s, a factory had been established in the Imperial City in which Portuguese Jesuit fathers supervised the construction of large cannons of brass or bronze. These were then mounted on wooden swivels at strategic spots along the Great Wall and the walls of cities near the northern frontier.

There is some debate among scholars as to the means by which the Chinese began extensive use of a modified version of the Portuguese matchlock handgun, which the Chinese called the *Niao-Chong* or *Niao-Qiang* (both meaning "Bird Gun"). The sources seem to indicate that the Chinese first acquired Japanese modifications of Portuguese handguns from the Wako (Japanese pirates). However originally acquired, once they had these models, the Ming military established facilities for the production of thousands of the matchlocks. The largest factories were in Beijing and Nanjing, but by the 1560s, factories for the production of matchlocks could be found in nearly all the larger military garrisons. Gunpowder weapons thus fit into an already established pattern of government distribution of weaponry to centrally controlled infantry forces, necessitating little change in military administration. But the quality of the guns was uneven, and the actual production figures were almost certainly much lower than official reports stated.

An elaborate set of sturdy defensive walls, a million-man army along the frontier, and the increasing use of gunpowder weapons should have given the Ming army the capability of defending against northern attacks. But in reality, the defensive arrangement failed to prevent the Mongols from raiding almost at will for many years. Beginning in 1550, the Mongols, under their leader Altan Khan, launched annual raids into the interior regions of northern China. Several times, the Mongol armies reached the very gates of Beijing before being either chased or bribed away. The raids on the capital areas became so destructive that the Ming court debated whether to relocate the capital to Nanjing. Instead, peace was obtained only after the Ming agreed to provide subsidies and border markets to the Mongols. Ironically, these subsidies were much less expensive than the elaborate defenses the Ming had tried to maintain.

The Military Response to the Wako Raids   The eastern coast of China had often been a tempting target for pirates based on the myriad islands off the coast. Pirates were a nuisance but usually not of much consequence to the empire as a whole. However, in the mid-sixteenth century, a new and much larger pirate threat challenged China. In the early years, most of these pirates came from Japan, and their bases were located on Japanese islands. Thus, they acquired the Chinese name "Wokou," though most often they are called by the Japanese pronunciation, "Wako." Eventually, the Japanese pirates allied with local Chinese pirate gangs to form large criminal organizations numbering hundreds of vessels and thousands of men.

Whole sections of the Chinese coast were stripped of valuables, including locals taken as slaves, and the Wako established bases on the islands off of China and, in some cases, on the mainland.

The Ming government was at a loss as to how to stop these attacks. The Wako could choose their point of attack, strike, and flee before imperial forces arrived. The Ming court could not afford to garrison hundreds of miles of coast with armies that were in bad shape anyway. The arrival of a Ming army chasing the Wako frequently led to further destruction by Ming soldiers, and many local fishermen had their fishing boats confiscated after accusations of assisting the Wako. The emperor sent edicts to Japan demanding that the Japanese government do something to stamp out the Wako lairs in Japan, but the chaotic situation in Japan after the Onin War meant that there was nothing resembling a centralized government that might have cracked down on these pirates (see above).

In 1556, the Ming general Qi Jiguang was appointed to defend the province of Zhejiang against Wako attacks. To do so, Qi basically redesigned the Ming military system. Recruiting local men from good families, he paid and supplied them regularly from a new head tax. Trusted subordinates, often family members, commanded in the field and coordinated with the civil bureaucracy, leading to the force being called the "Qi Family Army." Qi organized militia forces in the villages, built watchtowers on the coast, and garrisoned offshore islands. Fierce discipline earned the trust of the local population. Qi used the winter months, free of raids, for training, much as Maurice of Nassau did (see Chapter 16): Qi's detailed descriptions of training drills became the basis of military manuals studied in China for centuries afterward. Qi's system was so successful that by 1562 he had been given full charge of the overall campaign against the pirates. The Qi Family Army thus became a national army, though one personally loyal to Qi.

In 1567, Qi was called on to manage the national defense against the Mongols. He instituted a system similar to his coastal defenses—small local militias, hundreds of small watchtowers, gunpowder weapons, and constant drill for the field forces—designed to slow the mobile Mongol forces enough to overwhelm them with massed infantry. There were even a few Ming cavalry raids into the steppe lands, as Qi's plans called for the army to not merely remain on the defensive. The system showed signs of success, but the Qi Family Army alarmed many at the Ming court.

Thus, in 1582, once the danger had passed with Ming capitulation to Mongol demands for subsidies and trade, Qi was relieved of command and personally denounced by the emperor (see the Sources box "Maintaining the Civil-Military Balance"). He had never used his army except in defense of China and was always limited by the need for funding from the central government, but the civilian authorities were still under the influence of Tang dynasty precedents and distrusted powerful military figures. Qi was permanently removed from office, and some of the Ming armies reverted to their former sorry state, while some units continued to utilize Qi's system and manuals. All generals understood the meaning of Qi's removal, and the suspicions that any successful military commander would raise among the civilian officials. Ironically, independent generals did eventually threaten the safety of the Ming dynasty during the Manchu invasions of the seventeenth century.

The Collapse of the Ming and the Manchu Conquest

The defeat of the Wako and the reduction of the Mongol threat were misleading indicators of the state of the full Ming military. For many units, nonexistent training and discipline made much of the army indistinguishable from bandit gangs. Often, many of the best troops guarded grain and tax transports to the capital, and not the frontiers. Too many of the officers, whether recruited by heredity, military exam, sale of commissions to rich merchants, or imperial appointment (usually of eunuchs), were incompetent and corrupt.

Late in the century, the Japanese invasion of Korea posed a serious threat to Ming stability. Eventually, China sent nearly 200,000 soldiers into Korea. Ming military officials scoured the Chinese countryside to press-gang new recruits, and many millions of ounces of silver were expended on weapons and supplies. Some generals were conscientious and performed their duties well, fighting the Japanese to a standstill. But others saw the war as merely another chance at graft, and there were reports of thousands of Chinese soldiers starving and freezing to death in Korea. Even with the corruption and incompetence of many military and civil officials, Ming logistical efforts were still quite impressive. Clearly, the dynasty was not yet on its last legs.

The war with Japan was a tremendous drain on Ming finances and increased military corruption, but the truly impressive Chinese economy, mainly in the south, made this manageable—at least for a few more

SOURCES

Maintaining Civil-Military Balance

The irony of Qi Jiguang's dismissal from office by jealous and fearful civil officials is highlighted by his own writings on civil-military relations, which are excerpted here.

■ ■ ■

In the Ming dynasty, Heaven and Earth are protected only through the operation of Yin and Yang; peace is only maintained through the use of civil ["wen"] and military ["wu"] authority. The terms "civil" and "military" have comparable meaning to "yin" and "yang." Therefore, in quelling disturbances it is also necessary to use a balance of Yin and Yang. Both civil and military authorities must be utilized in order to be successful.

Qi goes on to explain how ancient times saw constant war because there was a failure to balance civil and military. Even later dynasties—such as the Han and Tang—had difficulty managing this balance.

During the early years of the Ming dynasty there were many military affairs [battles]. Because the [soldiers] strove mightily for success, they believed they deserved greater rewards [than they had received]. This caused them to lead many disturbances. Therefore, gaining a country is not sufficient; the military must be attended to as well as civil affairs if the country's ability to have long-term peace is not to be hindered.

Over the past 200 hundred years [since the founding of the Ming dynasty in 1368], as the civil laws and regulations have become perfected, [civil] conflicts and factions have been controlled. It is the responsibility of the generals and other officers to lead the masses in battle. Decisions concerning supplies, salaries, reward and punishments [for the military] are all the responsibility of the civil officials. The high government officials should establish the regulations concerning equipment and training of the ranks. All of these [duties] are very important, and so the power of the civil and military authorities is divided. However, when we look at Yin and Yang, we find they may appear to be separated, but in actual fact they are complementary. [At the present time] we do not have this sort of complementary situation [regarding the relationship between civil and military authority].

Therefore, I propose that the imperial court in addition to establishing a division among the officials. . . . His Majesty should broadly announce to all his officials, both high and low [military and civil] that their enthusiasm should be solely directed toward protecting the people.

SOURCE: Qi Jiguang, *Lian-Bing Shi-Ji,* trans. Paul Lococo.

decades. By the 1620s, much of the Ming army existed only in name. Imperial subsidies for military affairs were raised, yet less and less reached the troops in the garrisons, especially along the northern frontier. There were numerous reports of starvation among the soldiers, and whole units mutinied. At the same time, raids from Manchuria became more frequent and severe. Whole new armies, following the example set during the war with Japan, had to be recruited. The foundries in the capital worked overtime to produce enough cannon to defend Chinese cities inside and outside the Great Wall (it had been found that the mounted Manchus had great difficulty overcoming the firepower of these weapons). But by the 1640s, the Ming had to deal not only with Manchu raiders but also large rebel armies often composed of Ming deserters. Generals were given enormous autonomy to deal with these twin threats, and a situation not unlike that of the late Tang dynasty arose. Just as China appeared on the verge of succumbing to regional warlords, the Manchus changed from raiders to invaders and, through a brilliant combination of military and political strategies, conquered and reunified China.

The Early Qing Dynasty, 1644–1757

Formation of the Eight-Banner System The Manchus were tribal peoples descended from the Jurchens who had conquered north China in the twelfth century (see Chapters 9 and 14). These tribes recognized the sovereignty of the Ming court but were not directly administered by the Ming. Ming policy was to see that the Manchus remained divided, but as the dynasty weakened, the Manchu tribes became progressively more united under a dynamic tribal chieftain named Nurhachi (1559–1626).

As new tribes became part of Nurhachi's domain, they were incorporated into the system called the "Eight Banners." Although conceived primarily as a military instrument, Banner designations determined their members' lives, from economic well-being to social status. Each adult Manchu male, along with his family and any slaves, was assigned to a unit of 200–300 called a *Niru*. Five *Niru* made up a *Jalan*, and five *Jalan* formed a Banner designated by a colored flag. At first, there were four Banners: Yellow, White, Blue, and Red; later, four more were added, using the same colors fringed in gold or red. Each Manchu male was expected to be an expert horse-archer, and each *Niru* was required to supply a certain number of soldiers from its members, with the rest engaging in agriculture or other economic activities. Active-duty soldiers wore uniforms and, for the heavy cavalry, suits of armor of the same color as their Banner. Nearly all Manchu soldiers were light or heavy cavalry; infantry units were composed of Chinese or Korean war prisoners.

At the head of each Banner, Nurhachi placed one of his sons, and he appointed other relatives as hereditary heads of most of the *Jalan*. However, much like Chingiz Khan, Nurhachi demanded military competence; sons who failed this test were replaced, though for political reasons Nurhachi sometimes assigned a deputy who exercised field command instead of directly replacing an incompetent Banner or *Jalan* commander. The Banners trained constantly when not on campaign, with several Banners often engaging in great hunts together, again in emulation of the Mongols of Chingiz Khan.

It was Nurhachi's son and successor Hung Taiji who modified the Eight-Banner System into an instrument capable of conquering China. As relentless as his father, Hung Taiji expanded and bureaucratized the Banners and introduced new weapons. Mongol tribes that had been brought under Manchu control through alliance or conquest were organized into four (later eight) Mongol Banners commanded by Manchu nobles and organized like Manchu Banners. Eight Chinese Banners were added in the 1640s from Ming armies that had defected to the Manchus. The significance of these Chinese Banners was much greater than simple numbers. Almost all of the Chinese in these Banners were from Chinese-settled regions of Manchuria. They usually spoke Manchu as well as Chinese and, as the Manchus conquered territories in China proper, served as intermediaries.

The Chinese Banners also usually served as the infantry and artillery arms of the Manchus. The artillery role of the Chinese Banners proved crucial to Manchu success in the early stages of the conquest of China. We noted earlier that the Ming had come to rely heavily on cannon for defense against Manchu raids, and the Manchus had often been frustrated by the effectiveness of cannon in repulsing their attacks. Nurhachi himself died from wounds suffered as a result of cannon fire. Hung Taiji became convinced that gunpowder weapons were essential for Manchu success and succeeded in obtaining a number of weapons in raids on Ming strongpoints known to have large firearms stores. He also obtained the services of Portuguese who agreed to organize cannon factories in the Manchu capital of Mukden. Units in the Chinese Banners were subsequently trained in the use of artillery for offensive action, resulting in much greater success in capturing Ming walled cities, as well as in the field.

In 1636, Hung Taiji proclaimed the establishment of the Qing ("Pure," in contrast to the corrupt Ming) dynasty, and stated his intention to conquer all of China. After subduing the Chahar Mongols to secure his right flank, he launched a series of invasions to subjugate Korea. The new Chinese Banner artillery proved invaluable in taking Korean fortresses, and the Korean king soon accepted the Qing ruler as his sovereign, securing Hung's left flank. In 1644, a year after Hung Taiji's death, the Ming dynasty collapsed when one of the large rebel bands devastating the land captured the capital of Beijing. The Qing Eight Banners invaded less than two months later and seized Beijing.

The Qing Military System Postconquest Once established in Beijing, the Qing dynasty worked to ensure the final destruction of the Ming. Various members of the Ming imperial house continued to raise armies in southern China to oppose the invaders. If

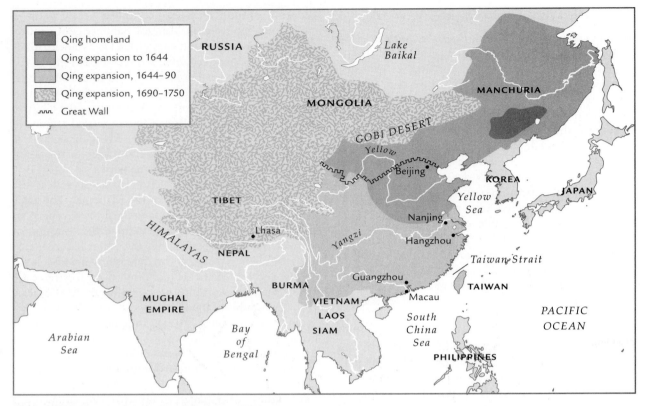

Figure 19.2 Expansion of the Qing Dynasty to 1750

Qing armies had been composed only of the Eight Banners, China might have seen a situation reminiscent of the Song, when the Jurchens had proved incapable of conquering the south. However, the Qing armies that invaded the south were composed overwhelmingly of surrendered Ming armies under Chinese generals. The combined Qing armies were successful, and by 1662, the only area of China not under Qing control was the island of Taiwan, to which the last desperate Ming remnants had fled.

Chinese generals who aided the Qing were rewarded with provinces to rule; the Eight Banners primarily guarded the capital. But a revolt by these generals in 1673, suppressed only with help from loyal Chinese armies, led to a reorganization. The military system established after the revolt was suppressed in 1682 resolved the age-old Chinese concern about maintaining an effective military yet keeping it from being used against the ruling dynasty. This system remained in force until the mid-nineteenth century. Not only was the imperial court not threatened by

military uprisings until the very end of the dynasty in the twentieth century, but through the eighteenth century, Qing armies engaged in large-scale military expeditions that added immense lands to the Qing Empire and permanently ended the Mongol threat to China (Figure 19.2).

The Qing military was divided into two systems: the Eight Banners and the Green Standard Army. The Eight Banners continued to be the main military prop of the dynasty, with their own officer corps and administrative organization located next to the Forbidden City. The bulk of the Eight Banners continued to garrison the capital region and Manchuria. The rest of the Bannermen were posted in garrisons located at strategic cities throughout China or along strategic waterways, especially the Yangzi River and the Grand Canal in southern China. Banner garrisons were kept strictly segregated from the general population, with those in cities having their own walled compounds. Banner units were often rotated from garrisons in the capital or Manchuria to the

Qing Military Outpost   This painting, from the time of the British mission to China in 1796, shows the fortification of a Qing military outpost. The troops under review are elite Bannermen, armed much as they would have been during their conquest of China a century and a half earlier.

provincial garrisons, and only the officers were allowed to bring their families along with them on these moves. Membership in the Banners continued to be hereditary, but when the total Banner population grew too great, it was common for units from the Chinese and Mongol Banners to be reclassified as civilians. Thus, while Chinese Bannermen in 1700 made up a majority of the Banner population, by 1800, so many Chinese Bannermen had been reclassified that a large majority of the Banner population was Manchu.

While officers in all the Banners gained their status through inheritance, actual appointment of Banner officers and all promotions were strictly controlled by the emperor through the Banner office in the capital. It was not unusual for a commoner Bannerman who had distinguished himself in combat to be promoted to officer rank, rising sometimes as high as Banner commander. Each Banner compound included a large training field, and while in garrison, officers were expected to lead their men in training. By the mid-eighteenth century, most of the Manchu Bannermen were infantrymen, and only a few elite Manchu cavalry units existed, all of them kept in the capital region.

In contrast, nearly all of the Mongol Bannermen were cavalry, often posted to the provincial garrisons. In 1757, there were over 250,000 active-duty Bannermen and tens of thousands of supernumeraries.

The Green Standard Army was composed of Han Chinese and was primarily conceived as a constabulary force, designed to maintain local order and suppress small-scale disturbances at the local or provincial level. Their numbers reached over 600,000 by the mid-eighteenth century, though rapid population growth makes this figure less impressive than it may seem. But command of Green Standard units was very fragmented. No single officer was allowed to command more than 5000 men except in wartime, and throughout China, there were hundreds of small outposts, some manned by as few as 12 men, who patrolled their areas of responsibility, provided local security, escorted prisoners to exile, guarded tax shipments, and performed other security duties. Each province had a Green Standard general in administrative charge of all the Green Standard forces in his province with the exception of the provincial governor's personal brigade, which never totaled more than 5000 men.

Recruitment for the Green Standard Army was not officially hereditary, but the vast majority of recruits came from sons or brothers of serving soldiers. Green Standard military service was generally a lifetime occupation, though it was easy to be reassigned to civilian status if one desired. When serving soldiers had no sons or brothers, nephews or other relatives might be recruited, and the Qing sometimes even recruited from families with no military background. Pay, equipment, rations, and training in the Green Standard Army were all centrally controlled by the Board of War. Pay and benefits in the Green Standard Army were much lower than in the Eight Banners, but, at least until the nineteenth century, the soldiers usually received their pay on a regular basis. While each province had a Green Standard cavalry component, this was never very important, and the great majority of soldiers were infantry or artillerists.

Officers in the Green Standard Army usually came from one of two sources. First, all Eight Banner officers were eligible for appointment to the Green Standard Army. This typically happened only temporarily when units of the Green Standard Army were on active campaign. Such officers did not lose their Banner status, which meant that they continued to receive higher pay and benefits than their counterparts. Also, rewards for and evaluation and promotion of Banner officers in the Green Standard Army were handled by the Banner office, not the Board of War, which normally administered the Green Standard Army. Second, officers were acquired through the military examination system. Success meant passing a series of exams that tested knowledge of the traditional Chinese military classics, such as the *Sun Zi*, and tests of physical strength and endurance. Horseback riding, archery, and the lugging of heavy rocks were some of the components of these physical tests. Technically, the officer ranks were open to anyone who could pass the exams, but most of the candidates came from families that traditionally supplied officers to the Green Standard Army. In some cases, it was also possible, as in the Eight Banners, for a soldier who had distinguished himself in battle to be promoted to officer rank. It was even possible for a Green Standard soldier to get enrolled in the Banners for feats of exceptional skill and bravery in combat.

Various types of firearms became standard weapons in all the Qing armies by 1700. Both the Banners and the Green Standard Army relied on the matchlock

musket as their standard weapon. There were two basic types of matchlock, both similar in design to those used in the late Ming dynasty. In addition to large weapons factories in Beijing and other major cities, each of the larger garrisons had production facilities for manufacturing matchlocks, gingals (a heavy, two-man musket), and various-sized cannon. The largest cannon were manufactured in Beijing under the supervision of Jesuit fathers, as under the Ming dynasty, and were called "Red Barbarian Cannon" in recognition of their origins. It was also common for Jesuit cannon makers to be sent to battlefields on the frontiers to construct especially large cannons on the spot. Private production and ownership of firearms was prohibited by the Qing court, but this prohibition was only laxly enforced. Thus, there were thousands of firearms in the hands of local people, weapons that were often used in criminal ventures.

Why did the Qing military continue using matchlocks instead of the more reliable flintlocks that by the eighteenth century had become the main handguns of European armies (see Chapter 16)? Qing military commanders were aware of these weapons, even encountering their use in a war against Burma in the 1770s. Qing officers wrote often of the superior weapons the Burmese had purchased from the French, yet no steps were taken to acquire, let alone adopt, these weapons. For whatever reason—perhaps lack of effective opposition—the Qing armies did not begin using flintlocks until well into the nineteenth century, after the Opium Wars with Great Britain.

It is also notable that, as in Japan, the introduction of gunpowder weapons into China was not in itself revolutionary. The Chinese state had the mechanisms to incorporate the use of firearms into its already very large infantry armies, so European-style firearms did not transform the Chinese system. Gunpowder weapons did have some impact on the structure of Manchu society, which originally had been led by a tribal elite of mounted archers. Yet firearms were only one factor—and a small one at that—in the transformation of the Eight Banners into a bureaucratic, centrally controlled military force.

While little affecting traditional Chinese society, the expanding use of gunpowder weapons exerted powerful influences on China's relations with the northern nomadic peoples, changing the shape of geopolitics in the region. In siege warfare, both defensively and offensively, the Ming ability to withstand Mongol and Manchu sieges had been greatly enhanced by the use of these weapons. The Qing also learned to utilize gunpowder artillery for offensive purposes in siege warfare, enabling them to secure the interior of China and their western frontiers. Thus, the use of firearms gave China a final decisive advantage over the steppe nomads of Mongolia. In the eighteenth century, the Qing fought two wars in the Jinchuan area, encompassing western Sichuan and eastern Tibet, a mountainous region where native peoples had constructed hundreds of small stone fortresses. To subdue the area, the Qing military had to overcome each of these fortresses, an immense task that took years to accomplish, since taking each fortress required hundreds of men. Jinchuan would not have been subdued without gunpowder weapons, which bombarded the defenders with a variety of explosive and flame projectiles. For the larger stone fortresses, the Qing army constructed enormous cannon on the spot.

Military Campaigns of the Eighteenth Century

The eighteenth century saw China more secure within its borders than at almost any time in its long history. From the late seventeenth century, in a series of sometimes massive expeditions, the Qing secured control of Taiwan; subdued Tibet, western Sichuan, and Xinjiang; forced Burma, Nepal, and Vietnam to accept or resume tributary status with China; and, possibly most important, pacified Mongolia, ensuring that it would never again threaten Chinese stability. While diplomacy and economic inducements played a role, these were overwhelmingly military accomplishments.

These campaigns were coordinated through an institution established by the emperor Yongzheng (1723–35) called the Grand Council. Most members of the Grand Council were Manchu noblemen who were given broad powers by the emperor to conduct the military affairs of the dynasty. The Grand Council, with the approval of the emperor, chose commanders and units to be sent, as well as arranging all aspects of logistics. Relay stations were established throughout the empire, allowing the emperor and his Grand Council to dispatch messengers quickly and provide directions to civilian authorities regarding supply and transport. Commanders of expeditions were given a commission granting them broad authority over conduct of the army in the field. These commanders

received their commissions in solemn ceremonies presided over by the emperor, and their communications and requests went directly to the emperor, often bypassing even the Grand Council. Imperial granaries and weapons depots were established along the major transportation routes, allowing armies to take to the field and be supplied without burdening local areas.

Commanders for these campaigns were usually Manchus or Chinese Bannermen with extensive prior experience in Qing military operations. Green Standard officers who had distinguished themselves in earlier expeditions might also be tapped for high command positions. Soldiers for these expeditions came from both the Eight Banner and Green Standard Army garrisons. Often, commanding officers of Green Standard units sent on such expeditions were appointed from the Banner garrisons around the capital. In any case, units, whether Banner or Green Standard, could come from any part of the empire. Banner units from Manchurian or frontier garrisons came to be regarded as the most reliable in combat, while those from interior garrisons were considered less worthy. For example, the Banner garrison at Nanjing was believed to be almost unfit for combat duty. This was borne out when an investigation revealed that the Bannermen of the garrison, rather than training in mounted archery, had taken their complement of horses and set up a chain of horse soup restaurants in the city. For Green Standard units, those from Guizhou and Hunan gained a respectable reputation, while those from the Zhejiang garrisons earned imperial contempt.

The most momentous of the eighteenth-century expeditions was the one that finally subdued the Zunghar Mongols in the 1750s. The Qing, like the early Ming, had no difficulty in supplying the large armies necessary to march into the vast Mongolian steppe lands. The strategy used by the Qing commanders was to have their cavalry and that of their Mongol allies track down and hold Mongol concentrations of forces until the main infantry and artillery units could catch up. The mobile Mongol cavalry were no match for the large formations of Qing infantrymen armed with matchlocks and the destructive Qing artillery. Surviving Zunghars were ruthlessly exterminated, putting an exclamation point on the Qing efforts to end the threat to China from the northern nomads.

CONCLUSION

The military transformations going on in East Asia between 1500 and 1800, though associated as elsewhere with the introduction of gunpowder weaponry, demonstrate the dominance of political and socio-economic arrangements in the adoption and influence of new technology. China's vast and sophisticated (though not always effective) military administration adopted guns with little trouble and few revolutionary results in social terms. The Japanese experience is even clearer on this point, since Japan, uniquely, "derevolutionized" its military system after initially adopting guns very effectively. Under the Tokugawa, Japan's ruling elite valued stability more than progress. Thus, the new military technology had no necessary revolutionary effect unless the environment it entered was in some way already ripe for radical transformation.

The history of East Asia in this period also highlights the limited reach of any European "superiority" in this age. Only after the Industrial Revolution would China and Japan fall significantly behind the West militarily, and Japan, in fact, fell behind only briefly before joining the industrial military powers in the nineteenth century. On the other hand, China's experience with the Mongols under the Qing shows that in at least one sphere the gunpowder age had wrought a decisive change in the global balance of military power: not (yet) toward Europe, but toward all settled civilizations and away from the horsed nomads of Central Asia. Given the latter's millennia of dominance, that development surely does qualify as revolutionary.

SUGGESTED READINGS

The Cambridge History of Japan, Vol. 4: Early Modern Japan. Cambridge: Cambridge University Press, 1991. A standard introduction that provides the broad context for the military developments of the period.

Chan, Albert. The Glory and Fall of the Ming Dynasty. Norman: University of Oklahoma Press, 1982. Contains several interesting chapters discussing the late Ming military.

Chase, Kenneth. Firearms: A Global History to 1700. Cambridge: Cambridge University Press, 2003. Has some serious analytical flaws in parts, and should be read carefully; still, contains a wealth of information on East Asian military systems, weapons, tactics, and battles.

Hall, John W. Government and Local Power in Japan, 500 to 1700. Princeton: Princeton University Press, 1966. A seminal study of the province of Bizen; examines the links between central institutions and local landholding and administration.

Huang, Ray. "The Liao-tung Campaign of 1619." Oriens Extremus, 1981. One of the very few detailed descriptions of a Chinese military campaign.

Morillo, Stephen. "Guns and Government: A Comparative Study of Europe and Japan." Journal of World History 6 (1995), 75–106. Reassesses the Sengoku age (and the European Military Revolution) in comparative perspective; stresses socioeconomic causation over technological stimuli.

Perrin, Noel. Giving Up the Gun. Boston: D. R. Godine, 1980. A clear, readable account of the rise and fall of guns in Japan; good on what happened, but compare Morillo for causation, as Perrin seriously underestimates political motivation.

Totman, Conrad. Politics in the Tokugawa Bakufu. Cambridge: Harvard University Press, 1967. A classic study of the workings of Japanese government after unification.

Turnbull, Stephen. Battles of the Samurai. Arms and Armour Press, 1987; Samurai Armies, 1550–1600. Osprey, 1979. Provide a wealth of detail about the composition and tactics of Sengoku armies.

Waldron, Arthur. The Great Wall of China: From History to Myth. Cambridge: Cambridge University Press, 1990. An extensive discussion of the construction of the Great Wall during the Ming dynasty as a security/military matter.

Wakeman, Frederic, Jr. The Great Enterprise. Berkeley: University of California Press, 1985. Contains a wealth of information concerning late Ming–early Qing military affairs, including the early Qing Banners and their social origins, and descriptions of particular military actions.

Waley-Cohen, Joanna. "China and Western Technology in the Late Eighteenth Century." American Historical Review 98 (1993), 1525–1544. Discusses the important role of Western-style artillery in some of the campaigns of the late eighteenth century.

CHAPTER 20

The Age of Sail: Naval Warfare, 1500–1750

As the previous chapters in this part have shown, a Military Revolution is hard to find in land warfare in this period, with gunpowder-related transformations affecting a number of areas of the world in various ways that gave no clear advantage to any one area. Only with the consolidation of western European advances in military technique in the first half of the eighteenth century did that region start to move ahead of the rest of the world. As yet, however, that advantage was limited in scope and global impact.

The same is not true of naval warfare. Here, unequivocally, is a military revolution of the greatest magnitude, one that fundamentally altered the nature of naval warfare in ways that had a tremendous global impact. It is not an exaggeration to say that changes in naval warfare and maritime activity generally were the most important developments of this age.

Heretofore, military commanders engaged in naval warfare only as an adjunct of land warfare. Ships generally had to stay close to shore, tied to ports by limits of logistics, navigation, and ship strength. A warship was usually little more than a merchant ship loaded with soldiers—not marines—untrained for fighting onboard ship. They needed little training, because naval battles usually involved the convergence of two fleets for a melee of boarding actions—essentially, infantry warfare on floating platforms. While the specialized fighting ship had a long history in the Mediterranean, galleys were little more than purpose-built troop transports. Their restricted cargo spaces and large crews, not to mention limited sea-keeping abilities, kept them more closely tied to ports and shores than most other ships. In short, naval warfare up to this point had scarcely existed outside the context of land warfare, and it exerted a similarly low impact on the global stage, where the horse-riding nomads of the steppes linked Europe and Asia while most of the rest of the globe developed in isolation.

As we saw in Chapter 15, by the fifteenth century, two areas had begun to develop naval technologies that had the potential to break these limitations: China and western Europe. For a variety of reasons, only Europe pursued the possibilities. By 1500, a combination of social and economic structures and new technologies had created along Europe's Atlantic seaboard not only the means but also the motive to begin exploiting the world's oceans in new ways. China's decision to opt out, among other factors, helped open the opportunity.

Over the next two and a half centuries, these new structures and technologies would allow Europeans to forge an economic and military revolution at sea. The world's oceans became highways instead of barriers, drawing whole new continents into an emerging global economy. European navies, capable of cruising for months with only minimal contact ashore, became the first in world history to exercise control of the seas, at least in some sense—control that they used to seize much of the world's carrying trade and to fight each other for access to colonies. Naval power was suddenly as important as land power. This chapter traces that revolution.

THE TOOLS OF REVOLUTION

European ability to exploit the seas in new and revolutionary ways were a product not just of new technology—the cannon-bearing, full-rigged ship—but of unusual forms of social and economic organization. In fact, these socioeconomic structures preceded and gave rise to the technologies that were their instruments. Before examining the key naval technologies of this age, therefore, we must set the stage for their invention and use.

Structures: Crusaders and Capitalists

The combination of cannon and ships symbolizes perfectly the synthesis of mercantile and military interests, and thus the mix of private and public motives and structures, that launched the naval revolution.

Motives for European Expansion   The trio "gold, God, and glory" often sums up the variety of motives behind European exploration and expansion. This phrase does, in fact, capture neatly the major cultural elements that lay behind expansion: greed for material gain generally, but specifically the rise of capitalism, a predatory economic system based on the acquisition of private property and exploitation of its possibilities for wealth creation, which enjoyed increasing influence within the structure of western European society; a missionary religious impulse; and military competition.

In naval terms, the city-states of northern Italy had pioneered a capitalist, or at least a proto-capitalist, model of maritime activity starting as early as the twelfth century (see Chapter 15). Though at first economic concerns were subordinated to political ones in these polities, success brought about a reversal so that Italian naval warfare was increasingly waged for the sake of commerce. Italian galleys protected merchant shipping, secured ports and favorable trade treaties, and even carried valuable cargo. This model was already becoming influential in the rest of western Europe when, starting about 1450, Portuguese success in opening routes to lucrative sources of gold, salt, and slaves in West Africa suggested its potential value. When Vasco da Gama sailed round the southern tip of Africa and reached India in 1498, six years after Columbus (who sailed for Spain) had discovered a new route to something (at first, it wasn't clear what), the material benefits of maritime expansion became obvious. Although royal control continued to characterize Portuguese and Spanish imperial structures, Asian trade goods and, most important, the riches of the Americas thenceforth fueled an ongoing transformation of the western European economy and society that saw an increasing role for private firms.

The three major cultural elements often intermingled. For example, even so clear an economic triumph as cutting out the Mediterranean middlemen from the Indian spice trade had other equally important attractions. Because the key middlemen were the Muslim Ottoman Turks, the Portuguese certainly envisioned their economic end run on the Turks as a strategic move in the ongoing religious struggle between Christianity and Islam. Portugal and Spain both transported the crusading impulse that had become an integral part of western European culture since the eleventh century (see Chapter 12) overseas. When the Reformation split Europe religiously, religious competition continued to be a motive for competitive European activity overseas, whether crusading or missionary.

Finally, the crusading impulse itself fused religious zeal to the militaristic culture of Europe's ruling aristocrats. The search for individual glory (and its concomitant wealth and status) drove many a conquistador to adventure, to be followed by privateers such as Francis Drake, Queen Elizabeth's corsair, who mixed commerce and profitable warfare. If over the course of two centuries competition between kingdoms and states gained in importance, this simply altered the framework for seeking fame and fortune, not the motive itself, while state competition was often little more than the glory seeking of kings writ large.

Institutions: Public, Private, and In Between
The mix of economic, religious, and military motives that drove Europeans abroad is reflected in the institutions and practices of maritime activity and naval warfare during this period. Navies, as instruments of state possessing their own institutional foundation, were a relatively late product of this synthesis. We should be careful not to draw anachronistic boundaries between state navies and private merchantmen or corsairs, or between mercantile and military goals in naval warfare.

No state in 1500 could afford to maintain a standing navy of more than minimal size, and most had none at all. Temporary needs for ships in wartime were met by requisitioning or hiring merchant vessels complete with their crews and captains. Royally owned vessels were a minority in the squadron Drake used to raid Cadiz in 1587, for example. Private ships continued to contribute to state naval squadrons in times of war well into the seventeenth century, despite the increasing distinction between purpose-built warships and merchant ships. The rise of chartered trading companies such as the English and Dutch East India Companies created another source of private fleets, as well as providing pools of experienced sailors and captains. That these companies were privately held but state-sanctioned monopolies is itself another example of the cooperation of public and private interests in the creation of maritime enterprises. In general, trade and war were two sides of the same coin, whose profits flowed to both the state and merchant capitalists, and whose activities were not easily separated. Piracy could shade into legitimate trade and could gain enough state support (or at least tacit acquiescence) to become a weapon of warfare little different from official attacks on merchant shipping.

Over the course of this period, however, clearer lines emerged separating the use of force at sea, which governments attempted to monopolize, and trade, which fell to private merchants. This separation coincided with the rise of standing, bureaucratic navies beginning in the late seventeenth century. This development did little, however, to untangle the mix of economic and political motives inspiring naval conflict, whose stakes if anything increased through this period. And ultimately, the bond between state and private interests reached its greatest strength near the end of this period in the complex of state and private manufacturing, financial, and political institutions and concerns that built and sustained the Royal Navy after 1688 (see below). Given that warships were probably the most complex, sophisticated, and expensive technology of the age, it is not surprising that their creation stimulated the most advanced expressions of institutional organization known to that time in Europe.

Technologies: The Full-Rigged Ship

The centerpiece of naval warfare in this age was the technologically complex, cannon-bearing, full-rigged ship. The two main components of this complex were the ship itself, with its sailing and navigational instruments, and the technologies for delivering firepower from the base the ship provided.

Ships, Sailing, and Navigation

There had been two European shipbuilding traditions before the fifteenth century, the Mediterranean and the North Sea–Baltic sea. The two crossbred over the course of the fifteenth century, both contributing to the final result. Mediterranean frame-first construction replaced northern shell-first construction, but using the lines of the heavier, rounder northern trading ships, such as the cog, that used stern rudders for steering. Frame construction allowed for larger hulls, so that the single square-rigged mast of the northern tradition required supplementing. A square-rigged foremast was added, then a mizzenmast aft that was fore-and-aft rigged on Mediterranean lines. The three-masted plan became standard, eventually with square rigging added even on the mizzen topmast and fore-and-aft rigging added between the masts. The result, even in its early form, was a ship with adaptable sailing qualities. A further Mediterranean element—longer, leaner lines reminiscent of a galley, came to distinguish full-rigged warships—in early form called galleons—from their tubbier mercantile kin.

Complementing the basic hull and sail plan of the ship was a set of navigational technologies and techniques that had been gradually adopted or invented over the previous couple of centuries and that made sailing far from shore more and more feasible. The magnetic compass indicated direction, the astrolabe could determine latitude (degrees north or south of the equator), and systems such as playing out ropes with knots tied in them at regular intervals gave a way to measure speed (in knots), at least roughly. There was no direct method to determine longitude (east-west position) until the invention of accurate shipboard chronometers in the late eighteenth century, but from a known starting point, direction, speed, and latitude could provide a rough estimate of longitude through geometry. The tools were in place to chart the world's sea-lanes comprehensively.

The full-rigged ship was a labor-efficient merchant vessel, requiring a relatively small crew while providing ample cargo space. And the same characteristics made it a labor-efficient warship, especially when cannon replaced masses of infantry as its chief armament. One result was a ship that could stay at sea for far longer periods than any previous vessel because it could carry plenty of supplies relative to its crew size. Barring accidents or damage in battle, a stout wooden ship could sail for several years before its hull required cleaning and repair. The limits on its endurance were human. Supplies of food and especially water would only keep for so long, making stops for watering and provisions periodically necessary; and lack of fresh food added vitamin-deficiency diseases such as scurvy to the epidemics that were likely to attack crews living in crowded, unsanitary conditions. All that full-rigged ships needed to become revolutionary warships were offensive firepower. Cannon would provide that.

Cannon and Firepower

Ships had begun carrying guns almost as soon as guns appeared in European warfare. At first, however, these were small arms wielded by infantrymen. It was not that the ships were too fragile to absorb the recoil of large cannon mounted perpendicular to the beam without being shaken apart, as was the case with ships in some other parts of the world (including Mediterranean galleys, which mounted their big guns at the bow). The ships were sturdy enough. But even guns permanently mounted on ships had to be relatively small because they sat on the open top deck: thus, if they were too heavy, they would make the ship top-heavy and subject to capsizing (as several major fifteenth- and early-sixteenth-century warships did). Open gun ports cut in the side of the ship could only be placed so far down; otherwise, when the ship heeled over in a crosswind, it would flood through the ports. The breakthrough came in 1501 when a Frenchman invented the hinged gun port. Now large cannon could be mounted on the sturdy lower decks of the ship, creating the possibility of broadside volleys. No longer would a ship have to ram an opponent or, more likely, grapple and board it, to attack it. Now it could sail past and deliver a concerted blast of solid shot at the enemy's hull, rigging, and crew, disabling and perhaps even sinking it.

At least in theory. Widespread use of effective broadside gunnery was still decades, perhaps a century, away in 1520. Large naval cannon were unreliable. Built from bars of iron fused together, they were as apt to explode as to deliver a shot to the foe. Cast-bronze guns were much safer and, by holding greater charges, could deliver significantly larger weights of shot. But bronze was many times more expensive than iron, making the arming of one ship, never mind a fleet, with an extensive broadside battery extremely costly. But even with these limits, the potential of sailing ships carrying broadside-mounted cannon was evident by the mid-sixteenth century.

In fact, the basic formula of naval military technology in place by 1520 or so would not change in major ways until the coming of steam and iron in the nineteenth century. There would be constant incremental improvements in hull design, sail plans and sailing qualities, food storage and sanitation, and firepower (see below). The size of warships would also increase slowly but steadily from an average of 500 tons in the mid-1500s, to 2000 tons in 1700, to 3000 tons in 1800, with corresponding increases in the number, size, and caliber of cannon. But the ships Nelson fought with at Trafalgar in 1805 (see Chapter 25) were clearly of a type with their ancestors of 300 years earlier.

HMS *Sovereign of the Seas*   A 232-foot-long, 102-gun ship of the line built for Charles I of England in 1637, the *Sovereign* was rebuilt to 90 guns under Cromwell, fought in all three Dutch Wars, and continued in service in the Royal Navy until it was accidentally burnt in 1696.

THE ELEMENTS OF NAVAL POWER

The Evolution of Tactics

As we have just seen, the invention of gun ports led naturally to broadside gunnery by individual ships. Broadside gunnery, in turn, would seem to have led naturally to the classic tactic of such ships—the battle in line-ahead formation, meaning that each ship followed the ship ahead of it in a line, with the entire line sailing past (or parallel to) the enemy fleet, delivering its shot as it went. The inevitability of this tactic was confirmed by the fact that its first use came as early as 1502, when a squadron of Portuguese ships used it to destroy a fleet of Arab dhows off the Malabar coast of India.

Yet a second use of the tactic in a major battle would have to wait almost fifty years, and it came into regular use only slowly after that. The limitations of cannon quality and number mentioned above, combined with long-ingrained traditions of melee tactics aimed at boarding, inhibited change. And in some ways, boarding continued to make perfect sense: If successful, it gave the victor possession of the enemy ship, a valuable prize in its own right and perhaps an improvement on the victor's original vessel. Changing tactical traditions had their own logic and momentum, which we will consider below, but they were made possible in the first place by improvements in the technology of firepower.

Technological Developments English smiths made the first successful cast-iron cannon in the 1540s, taking advantage of luck. Iron deposits in southern England were naturally alloyed in ways that kept the molten iron from crystallizing and becoming brittle as it cooled; the castings therefore did not burst on firing. It took another century for iron cannon to become completely reliable and replace bronze cannon in the largest calibers, but the spread of iron guns made it cheaper to equip ships with large numbers of cannon. It is no coincidence that broadside ships from England made their first significant inroads into the previously galley-dominated world of the Mediterranean in the 1570s; prior to that date, northern round ships had deployed little more firepower than the best-armed galleys.

An even bigger limitation on the effectiveness of broadside firepower was that the muzzle-loading barrels of large naval guns, mounted on inadequately mobile carriages, could not be hauled inboard far enough for reloading during battle. Thus, after the first round of shot, members of the gun crew had to crawl outside the hull on the barrel to reload, hanging over the water and exposed to enemy shot and small-arms fire. Even when this worked, ships so armed could get off a round only every five minutes or so. Not surprisingly, many ships probably fired only one round in battle, using a point-blank broadside as an antipersonnel prelude to boarding—this seems to have been what most of the ships of the Spanish Armada of 1588 did.

The solution came in the 1620s or 1630s—the origin of the invention is unclear—with a block-and-tackle system rigged to the wheeled gun carriage. The gun's recoil would send it inboard where the tackle would bring it to a controlled stop and allow the gun to be reloaded inboard and hauled back out for the next shot. A shot a minute was now possible with much improved crew safety, producing a vast increase in firepower. The increased importance of firepower is reflected in the standardization of gun sizes and of ship types based on firepower. Starting in England in 1618,

ships were rated in four and eventually six classes according to the number of gun decks they had and the number of guns they carried. The top three ratings came to be known as ships of the line, as they were heavily enough gunned to ensure that a small, outgunned ship did not end up opposite a larger enemy ship and create a weak link in a line of battle. The bottom three ratings, which came to known collectively as frigates, performed workaday tasks such as commerce raiding and protection, battle fleet screening, and scouting or message carrying. Standardization probably also stimulated the gradual increase in ship size mentioned above, as did steady improvements in the skills and knowledge of European shipwrights.

The other major technological refinements that made line-ahead tactics possible involved improvements in the sailing qualities of the ships, improvements that made the maneuvers necessary to form and maintain a line ahead in battle easier. The main improvement came in sail plans. Sixteenth-century ships were seriously underpowered, with far too little sail area for their displacement. The gradual addition of two additional sails above the mainsail on each mast helped both to increase canvas area and to divide the area into smaller pieces that held the wind more efficiently. Fore-and-aft sails rigged from the bowsprit to the foremast and then between the three masts added to ships' ability to tack, sail close-hauled to the wind (perpendicular or even somewhat into the direction of the wind), and maneuver in and out of port. Ships' rigging also got better—easier to use, safer, and stronger—and hull shapes gradually improved. By 1670, the effects of the Scientific Revolution were being felt in advanced English shipyards, where mathematical analysis and hydrodynamic testing honed the knowledge of shipwrights accustomed to relying on tradition and intuition, though the value of these tests was not huge. A final improvement came only in the latter half of the eighteenth century. Accumulations of barnacles and seaweed steadily fouled wooden hulls, reducing speed, while marine worms could do serious damage. Copper sheathing much reduced both problems, extending the active life of ships between refits and overhaul.

The slow but steady improvement of naval technology over this period speaks not just to demands on the part of navies in the face of fierce competition but to the widespread network of private entrepreneurs and craftsmen who competed to supply better materials to governments and to the emerging scientific culture of this civilization. The instruments of naval warfare are among the best indicators of the transformation of

European society under the linked pressures of merchant capitalism and military competition.

Tactics: Firepower and the Melee

Still, all the technological improvements outlined above only made line-ahead tactics possible; they did not compel them. For example, the English planned for and fought a standoff gunnery battle with the Spanish Armada (see the Highlights box on page 394) less from tactical conviction than to avoid closing with Spanish ships that had massive superiority in manpower. Despite the victory, the limited effects of English gunnery could hardly have forced a preference for standoff gunnery over the melee, and the lack of major naval battles between the time of the Armada and the First Anglo-Dutch War (1652–54) hindered further development of naval tactics.

Nevertheless, improvements in ships' firepower affected conceptions of melee combat. Before cannon, melee tactics almost always involved closing with enemy ships so as to grapple and board them. This was still a possible goal, and a necessary one when capturing the opposing ship was the goal, as in much piracy. But broadside gunnery now offered a second use for melee tactics. By closing but not grappling, ships could deliver point-blank salvos aimed at disabling or destroying an enemy ship. The advantage a melee offered was the chance to bring several friendly ships to bear on a single enemy, not only attacking from both sides but delivering raking fire to the bow or stern as well. A broadside into an enemy's stern, where glass and windows instead of heavy planking made the ship vulnerable, could be particularly effective, sending shot through the length of the ship, killing crew, damaging internal structures, and with luck igniting the powder magazine with explosive results fatal to the ship as a whole.

In other words, closing for a melee offered a way to increase the effects of firepower. For stoutly built wooden ships were not easy pickings for smoothbore cannon firing round solid shot. As with any smoothbore weapon, accuracy was poor at almost any range. Round shot was a blunt, smashing weapon that lacked penetrating power and had no explosive charge. Because almost every hit would strike a ship above its waterline, a ship's natural buoyancy usually prevented it from being sunk outright. To send a major warship to the bottom, one needed either to score a rare lucky hit that might trigger a magazine explosion or inflict a massive cumulative amount of damage. The effects of firepower came in three forms. First, a ship's hull could be sufficiently damaged to threaten its seaworthiness or even to prevent it from sailing with its fleet. English gunnery from the First Anglo-Dutch War on aimed at this sort of ship-disabling fire, as did Dutch gunnery, though the lighter weight of Dutch shot reduced its effectiveness compared to the English. Second, shot could be aimed high at masts, sails, and rigging, as a more direct way of stopping a ship's progress. Damaged rigging could also leave a ship stranded but was less likely to force it to strike its colors (surrender) than was hull damage. At close range, the effectiveness of high shot could be increased by using chain shot, two balls connected by a chain, or bar shot, two balls connected by a solid bar. Finally, both types of antiship fire could produce casualties among the crew so severe as to cripple the ship as a fighting unit or to force its surrender. In addition, when fighting at close range, cannon could be loaded with bags of nails and other iron scraps, producing a deadly blast of metal shards explicitly intended to kill opposing crewmen, often as an immediate prelude to boarding. Battles during the age of sail were, in fact, among the bloodiest in naval history in relative and even absolute terms, with casualties sometimes numbering in the thousands.

The risk of fighting in such a way was, of course, that while one engaged the enemy at close range in an attempt to disable his vessel, one's own ship might be similarly disabled. Thus, not only the weight of shot but also a ship's rate of fire—hence the importance of training—could provide significant advantages in combat. The French navy after 1680, for example, was usually tasked with protecting merchantmen from British depredations and sought only to slow its attackers through disabling fire, rather than engage them in decisive battle for control of the sea, and so to escape with its own fleet and convoy intact.

Nonetheless, because all three types of disabling fire, as well as the prospect of ganging up on enemy ships, all depended on closing the range in naval combat, melee tactics offered commanders an inducement to close with the enemy. Both the English and Dutch fleets entered the First Anglo-Dutch War seeking melees, and the early actions of the war off Dover in May 1652, at Kentish Knock in September (both English victories), and at Dungeness (a Dutch victory) in November, were confused general actions. The limitations of melee action, however, quickly revealed themselves to the leading commanders on each side, Englishman Robert Blake and Dutchman Maarten Tromp, two of the most innovative tacticians of the

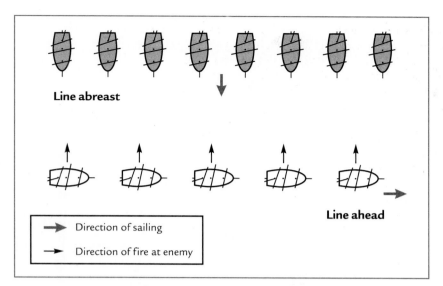

Line abreast

Line ahead

→ Direction of sailing

→ Direction of fire at enemy

Line-Abreast Versus Line-Ahead Naval Tactics Line-abreast tactics, the standard formation for galleys, whose striking power was in their bows, was also used by sailing ships closing for melee action. But it limited firepower until the melee. Line-ahead tactics maximized firepower and facilitated central control of fleet movements at the expense of closing for potentially decisive actions.

age. First, melees exposed one's own ships to closer-range enemy fire, while the confusion they fostered often prevented a fleet from bringing its maximum firepower to bear. Second, and even more important, fleet commanders discovered that they could not control the course of a melee once it started. In response, Blake and Tromp had begun organizing their fleets for line-ahead action, although Tromp at first could not persuade Dutch provincial authorities of the need to fight the fleet apart from the large convoys they were tasked to escort. The next action, the running Three Days Battle (February 28 to March 2, 1653), resulted in a victory for Blake, who was seriously wounded. In March, he and his fellow Generals at Sea (changed to "admiral" shortly thereafter) in the Commonwealth navy issued a set of "Instructions for the better ordering of the Fleet in Fighting," the first official directions for maintaining line-ahead formation in battle. Tromp also gained permission to fight the fleet first, then to escort convoys.

Tactics: The Development of the Line Ahead

The "Fighting Instructions," as they came to be called in the British navy through numerous reissues over the next century, paid immediate dividends in June when the Englishman George Monck used line-ahead tactics to defeat Tromp in the Battle of Gabbard Bank. Soon, most major European navies had copied the "Fighting Instructions," because their prescription for the line-ahead procedure—each ship to follow the one ahead of it at 100-yard intervals, with the

line as a whole following the admiral's lead—seemed to solve the two major problems of melee action. Significantly, a successful line formation brought the entire fleet's broadside gunnery to bear on the enemy while protecting the vulnerable bows and sterns of all the ships in line except the first and last. Even more crucially, it gave the admiral some semblance of control over his fleet during the course of the battle, for as long as the line stayed intact, it would continue to mimic the actions of the flagship. However, the command and control this gave an admiral was crude in the extreme. The tendency of individual captains to improvise required authorities to enforce adherence to the "Fighting Instructions" more rigidly than was ideal. Responses to unexpected situations had to be simplified and stereotyped (in other words, they had often to be inadequate responses to the threat or opportunity presented) because means of communication between ships were so limited. Navies developed flag systems that could transmit a prearranged set of orders, but again, these were limited in number and flexibility, and fog, darkness, the smoke of battle, and any number of other factors could easily obscure such signals. Until the introduction of reliable wireless telegraphy and radio in the mid-twentieth century, ship-to-ship communication would remain a critical problem in battle. A line-ahead formation did, however, allow a commander to keep his fleet together and to direct its course once a battle began. Subdivision of the fleet into three divisions (called in the Royal Navy the Red, White, and Blue),

Line of Battle Tactics   At the Battle of the Nile in 1798, Admiral Nelson's British fleet gained a decisive advantage over the French fleet, moored near the coast in line of battle, by sending a squadron inshore of the moored line while the rest attacked from seaward, "doubling" the French ships.

forming the van, center, and rear of the fleet in line, added another layer of predictable control.

Because signaling was so crude, the "Fighting Instructions" and their kin attempted to prescribe the proper course of action for the captain of each ship as well as for each division and the fleet as a whole, so that captains could anticipate what they needed to do. The grand tactics of naval battles in line-ahead formation therefore tended to fall into regular patterns, with the two fleets either sailing parallel courses, van to van and so on down the line, or on opposite courses past each other. Prebattle maneuvering often focused on attempting to gain the *weather gauge*, that is to form one's line upwind of the enemy. This gave the fleet with the weather gauge the option of closing to attack, and it also kept the smoke of battle in the enemy's face. The French navy in the latter part of this period again formed an exception to this rule, preferring the downwind position from which they could attempt to draw away from the action while still protecting their convoy. Of course, throughout the age of sail, the vagaries of wind shifts often wreaked havoc with plans; sudden changes in the strength and direction of the wind played a significant part in the outcome of a number of battles.

So line-ahead tactics made the most of the limited control a commander had over his fleet and attempted

to ensure a continuous volume of fire from the entire fleet (the process of closing against an enemy line would often leave the rear lagging at greater range at the start of battle). The cost, especially when commanders maintained formation mechanically, was a lack of initiative, which translated into lost opportunities to achieve decisive victories. Matching one's line ship-to-ship against the other offered few chances to create a decisive advantage somewhere along the line and prevented the really close gunnery that a melee allowed. Furthermore, signaling difficulties and the rigidity of subordinates sticking to the "Fighting Instructions" could hinder a winning side's exploitation of whatever advantage it gained. Finally, a fleet that maintained its line could usually withdraw mostly intact even if it got the worst of the battle. The "Fighting Instructions" took these limitations into account and attempted to provide remedies. Recognized tactical variations on the strict line ahead, available especially to fleets with some numerical advantage over their foes, included doubling the van or (more often) rear of the enemy line—that is, sending a squadron or division to the far side of the line so as to subject the doubled ships to fire from both directions—and breaking the enemy line by sailing a squadron or division through it. The former, however, was difficult to pull off unless one's fleet had a clear sailing advantage, and the latter risked dissolving one's formation

ISSUES

Line Ahead as Orthodoxy

Historians have debated whether the stultifying effects of the "Fighting Instructions" were increased or exposed by two battles at the end of this period and the resulting courts-martial of the admirals and captains involved. The cases certainly show the difficulties of making rigid instructions work in the everchanging world of wind and waves.

In February 1744, a British fleet of twenty-eight ships of the line under the command of Vice-Admiral Thomas Mathews stood off Toulon in southeastern France in a blockade of twelve Spanish ships of the line. On February 8, sixteen French ships of the line led the Spanish out, but for two days, contrary winds prevented an engagement and kept Mathews from even forming his fleet into line. When the enemy line finally began to sail off on February 11, Mathews ordered an attack, although his fleet, including a lagging rear squadron under Vice-Admiral Richard Lestock, was not properly formed. In an inconclusive fight, the allies got the better of Mathews.

As a result, the British Admiralty court-martialed Mathews, Lestock, and eleven captains. Mathews received convictions for a number of violations of the "Fighting Instructions," including initiating the fight without his whole squadron and without bringing his line abreast of the allies, and he was sacked. Lestock, who argued that his superior officer's two signals—to engage and to maintain line ahead—were mutually exclusive, was acquitted. Though politics probably outweighed logic in Lestock's case, the result as some historians see it was to turn line-ahead doctrine into dogma.

The results of the Battle of Minorca in May 1756 complicated the verdict on Mathews. The action began when Admiral John Byng with twelve ships of the line attacked an equal number of French ships supporting a French siege of Port Mahon on Minorca. The fleets approached in lines on opposite courses. When Byng tacked to come onto the same course as the French, mistakes in the movement separated his two divisions, leaving Byng's division behind and his van to fight alone against the French line. In response, Byng attempted to bring his whole division around together, rather than break formation and rush alone in his flagship to a controlling position in the van. Unfortunately for Byng, the French mauled the British van before the admiral could rescue it, forcing his withdrawal. Subsequently, Port Mahon fell.

Byng, too, faced a court-martial, but on this occasion, following the line-ahead strictures of the "Fighting Instructions" proved an inadequate defense. Instead, the court convicted Byng of failing to do his utmost to defeat the French and relieve Minorca, both capital offenses. The court recommended leniency, but as Voltaire, who witnessed the event, later wrote, Byng was executed by firing squad on his own ship "to encourage the others."

To encourage them to do what? The channel between adherence to the "Fighting Instructions" and adequate aggressiveness must have seemed mighty narrow to "the others," and the waters on either side treacherous. The effect of the two cases together was probably to stifle initiative but also to stimulate the search for ways to again free it. But that search would take some time before resulting in the pinnacle of naval tactical genius fifty years later (see Chapter 25).

and having the battle degenerate into a melee. The weight of the "Fighting Instructions" inclined toward forcing admirals into engagements between two coterminous lines, in fact making no explicit provision for breaking an opposing line.

Some circumstances still called for a melee—for example, when one force significantly outnumbered the other or when an enemy's line had given way and

tried to run from a line-ahead duel. In either case, the admiral could raise the flag for a general chase, in which each ship took off after enemy targets of opportunity, although usually this was a decision that a commander didn't take lightly. Indeed, the leeway afforded an admiral in combat proved a matter of serious debate within the Royal Navy (see the Issues box "Line Ahead as Orthodoxy"), so that the "Fighting

Instructions" more often than not stifled initiative. While the formalists—advocates of strict adherence to the line ahead until the enemy had been routed—held the upper hand in the debate for most of this period, Admiral Edward Hawke's daring and successful use of the general chase in the Second Battle of Finisterre (1747) heralded a more creative approach to naval tactics within the Royal Navy, culminating in Horatio Nelson's triumph at Trafalgar (see Chapter 25).

Tactics: Winners and Losers   British fleets were not uniformly successful in combat in the 100 years after the advent of line-ahead fighting in the 1650s, but they won more than they lost. Their success was a result not of superior tactics—all navies used roughly the same precepts for engaging in battle—nor of superior technology: If anything, the French had consistently better ships. Good leadership played an intermittent role, but above all, it was experience that told. British seamen had more practice and training, and more real experience, than any of their rivals, and this factor told consistently in the heat of action. Their sailing was more practiced, and their gunnery was more consistent, accurate, and effective.

This greater level of experience was largely a result of the differences in strategic doctrine between the British and their main rivals, especially the French, though tactical success first made possible and then helped maintain that doctrinal difference. It is therefore to naval strategy in the age of sail that we now turn.

The Emergence of Strategy

Unlike tactics, where the potential of the new technology took some time to be fully realized in practice, strategy witnessed immediate transformations. As soon as they reached the Indian Ocean in 1498, the Portuguese under Afonso de Albuquerque began trying to use the long-distance capacities of their ships to seize control of trade and establish an empire bound together by naval power. While some of the elements of Portuguese strategy had appeared before, the sheer geographic scale of this enterprise made it new. The Spaniards, too, began using naval power in support of imperial enterprises, though not as creatively as the Portuguese. It took the other European naval powers another 100 years to catch up to Portuguese conceptions and practice, while the rest of the world was rapidly left behind. The basic components of naval strategy included control of merchant shipping, empire building of various types, and a broad set of activities related to control of the seas. The impact of naval strategy is reflected in the creation during this period of the first self-conscious theory linking economic and military activity: mercantilism.

Winning the Carrying Trade   The fundamental importance of merchant activity to naval strategy was obvious from the start to Albuquerque, who set out to monopolize not just the shipment of Asian luxury goods back to Europe but the intra-Asian carrying trade as well. The first line-ahead action in 1502 was fought to enforce this aim, and the superiority of European ship-building traditions and cannon to anything in the Indian Ocean made success possible. Only the Red Sea, where galley warfare on the Mediterranean model held sway, escaped Portuguese domination in the sixteenth century, and that was but a minor setback. Thereafter, only other European powers rivaled Portuguese control: The arrival after 1600 of English and, above all, Dutch fleets, backed by the greater resources those nations could bring to bear, rapidly overwhelmed the overstretched Portuguese. These interventions, organized and funded by the English and Dutch East India Companies, illustrate the power of public-private cooperation to generate resources and action well beyond what any government could accomplish on its own. The profits generated by the carrying trade were, in fact, vital to funding the importation of Asian luxury goods to Europe, which produced little that Asia wanted. American precious metals, available to Europeans because of naval power, were the other source of the cash paid for Asian imports. And it was not just in Asia that the carrying trade became a point of conflict. The First Anglo-Dutch War began when England passed its Navigation Acts, designed to break up a virtual Dutch monopoly on the intra-European carrying trade.

The tactical ability of European ships to force their way into local trade routes played a vital role, especially at first, in the expansion of European maritime activity in Asia. But some aspects of European naval technology diffused fairly rapidly around Asian waters. That this resulted in no serious challenges to European dominance at sea shows that technology was only one factor: European naval activity, unlike its land warfare in the sixteenth and seventeenth centuries, was already a product of a complex socioeconomic formation and set of practices that were foreign to the structures of most other civilizations. As a result, potential competitors found it difficult to reproduce the range of activities and materials needed to sustain competition at sea. Further, almost none had any interest in doing so. At least in theory, both China and Japan had the ability at every level to match European efforts; however, both followed an isolationist policy for much of this period that actively kept their ships and merchants off the seas. In short, the seas were a new world foreign to most traditional agrarian-oriented societies. The Europeans dominated the seas in large part because no one else cared about them.

Empire Building   Japan further demonstrated the limits of European naval power by successfully excluding all European trade into Japan (save for one Dutch and one Chinese ship a year) after 1640. The carrying trade was still dependent on local cooperation by the land powers whose goods were shipped. Moreover, ships needed friendly way stations where they could take on fresh water and provisions. Albuquerque again immediately recognized this problem in naval strategy, and even as he set about seizing the carrying trade, he also began establishing fortified bases around the perimeter of the Indian Ocean and into Southeast Asia. These coastal "factories" served both as support points for the ships and as the focal points of trade with the various Asian producers. Goa, on the west coast of India, became the most important of these Portuguese outposts.

What emerged is what can be called a *coastal entrepôt empire.* The idea was not entirely new, but the difference between a series of outposts connecting, say, Venice to Constantinople and one connecting Lisbon to Goa and the rest of the Indian Ocean basin is vast enough to form a new type in practical terms. Given the limited abilities of European land forces in this period, this remained the dominant model for European ambitions in Eurasia and Africa, and characterized much European activity in the Americas as well. It involved linking chains of outposts by sea, the entire operation being (it was hoped) self-funding through the trade profits it generated. Closely related was the naval role in the creation and maintenance of more extensive colonial outposts, at first in the Spanish Americas and later by England and France in North America. Here, however, the self-sufficiency of colonies with significant hinterlands made for a different emphasis in the structure of the imperial project, with the imperial power involved in producing the products for trade (for example, silver, tobacco, and sugar) as well as shipping them. Eventually, by the eighteenth century, this sort of empire was even more valuable than those built on the Asian luxury trade: The value of Britain's sugar trade from the Caribbean alone came to exceed the total value of its Asian trade by the mid-eighteenth century. Sea links were vital to the maintenance and exploitation of both types of empires. Attempts to protect those links from attacks, especially by European rivals, meant the expansion to a global stage of two characteristic forms of naval activity: the *guerre de course,* or "war against commerce," that could shade into privateering and piracy, and the convoys and defense of fortified posts this entailed.

Control of the Seas?   Beyond the carrying trade and the creation of empires linked by sea routes, both of which had existed before albeit on a smaller scale, the new naval technology created an entirely new possibility for naval strategy. Specifically, the endurance of sailing ships—their ability to cruise for months with only minimal contact ashore—meant that navies could finally aim at controlling the actual sea-lanes, rather than monopolizing the shores where fleets were based, which is all that control of the seas had ever meant before this time. Of course, for much of this period, the actual ability of navies to execute this strategy was severely limited because the endurance of the men aboard the ships was considerably less than that of the ships. Inadequate logistical support from home in terms of pay and, more crucially, supplies subjected the crews to shortages that only increased their vulnerability to diseases and fostered insubordination and mutiny. Only gradually in the eighteenth century, with advances in state administration (see below) and knowledge of nutrition and sanitation, would control of the seas become a practical reality in European waters, and even then, navies remained too small and slow to enforce complete control everywhere (Figure 20.1).

Control of the sea-lanes was the direct route to protecting friendly merchant shipping (sailing in convoys was safer than sailing alone, but convoys were difficult to coordinate and were still vulnerable), hindering enemy merchant shipping, attacking and defending colonies, and either making possible amphibious invasions or preventing them. How was control to be achieved? An invasion could always be met as it arrived, or its fleet could be attacked even after it landed,

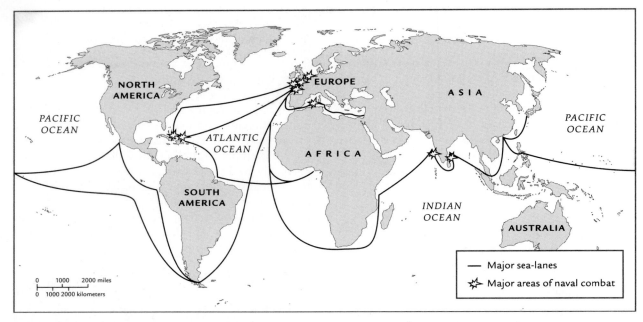

Figure 20.1 The World of Naval Strategy, 1500–1750   Although sea-lanes came to connect most of the world during this period, naval combat was concentrated in only a few areas: the English Channel, the western Mediterranean, the Caribbean, and the coasts of India.

disrupting its communications and logistics (see the Highlights box "The Spanish Armada and the Korean Turtle Ships"). But the direct route to control of the seas was to defeat the enemy fleet in battle. This is, in fact, exactly what both the English and Dutch aimed at in the Anglo-Dutch Wars, especially the First and Second (the Third was a Dutch fight for survival), and so these wars featured a dense concentration of major fleet actions. Neither side proved capable of maintaining a decisive advantage for long, but for periods in each war, one side or the other would emerge from a successful battle in position to sit off the enemy coast and bottle up the defeated fleet. Thus, in the First War, the English under Blake blockaded Holland after the Battle of Gabbard in 1653, and Michael de Ruyter, perhaps the greatest Dutch admiral, followed up his victory in the Four Days Battle in June 1666 during the Second War by blockading the English fleet in the Thames, though a refitted English fleet quickly broke that blockade and, in turn, raided the Dutch coast.

The strategic pattern between England and France, with one exception, was somewhat different. The exception came first: With the end of the Anglo-Dutch Wars in 1674, the former enemies became allies against the

rising power of Louis XIV's France. Louis' minister Colbert built up the French navy to the point that, at the outbreak of the War of the League of Augsburg in 1688, it deployed more and better ships than the allies. On July 10, 1690, the French inflicted a serious defeat on a combined Anglo-Dutch fleet at Beachy Head, and control of the seas lay within French grasp, with which they could have sent an army to Ireland, perhaps even invaded England, and seriously threatened British merchant shipping. But Louis refused to seize the opportunity, and the allies desperately rebuilt their strength in the interim. Two years later, when he was ready to invade England, the French Channel fleet, unsupported by their Toulon fleet due to unfavorable winds, went down to decisive defeat at allied hands at the Battle of La Hogue, May 29 to June 3, 1692. France never again seriously threatened English control of the Channel.

Why did Louis not seize the strategic chance he had? It is hard to say. France was primarily a land power, and Louis' focus was on expanding his frontiers on the continent. Further, Colbert, a finance minister and architect of French mercantilism (see below), conceived of naval power in economic terms, which meant that he favored war against merchant shipping rather than direct fleet confrontations. Both views underestimated the importance of naval power. French intervention at least in Ireland could have tied up English resources and prevented their orchestrating and funding the coalitions that frustrated Louis' continental ambitions, and *guerre de course* without control of the seas proved no more than an expensive irritant to England, contrary to Colbert's expectations of economic ruin for the island nation.

But defeat at La Hogue left the French little choice. Often unable and otherwise unwilling to challenge English naval supremacy, *guerre de course* (and protection of their shipping with convoys) became their standard naval strategy for the rest of the eighteenth century. England reinforced the pattern by developing a strategy of blockading the French fleets in their ports at the outbreak of war, preventing their getting much open-water training. The result was that even though French ships continued to be, as a rule, better than their English counterparts, their crews lacked the training and confidence of English sailors and gunners. Thus, when naval combat did occur, the French were more often than not on the losing end: A defeatist strategy bred defeat in battle.

Mercantilism: The Emergence of Theory   It is easy when writing about naval strategy to assume the importance of maritime activity and immediately move to analysis of how it was used. But—to return to the point we made earlier about European domination of the world carrying trade resulting from lack of competition—from a global perspective, it was the European interest in sea power that was unusual, especially in the way it connected sea power explicitly to economic gain. By the seventeenth century, that connection had produced the first self-conscious theory of mercantile and naval activity in its relation to state power, a set of ideas that go under the label of mercantilism. Mercantilism had two basic premises: First, a country should try to obtain a favorable balance of payments from its external trade (maximizing exports and minimizing imports) so that the difference, which would come in the form of specie, could be used to pay for armies and navies; and second, the total volume of world trade was constant (the premise exploded by economist Adam Smith). The logical conclusion was that, to improve its balance of trade, a country had to aggressively seize a bigger slice of a static pie. The tools for accomplishing this turned out to be a combination of chartered merchant trading companies backed by well-armed navies. The Anglo-Dutch Wars were about control of trade routes; Colbert's support for a *guerre de course* strategy stemmed from the same principles. So theory (even if, as Smith later showed, flawed theory) encouraged the activities that came to characterize European naval warfare.

The Growth of Administration

Probably the most significant change that navies underwent between 1500 and 1750 was administrative. Naval technology changed incrementally; tactics followed on a steady course visible early on; and strategy emerged in outline as early as Albuquerque. On the other hand, the middle decades of the seventeenth century saw a rapid evolution, away from the ad hoc organization and heterogeneous collections of ships that characterized navies up to that point, and toward standing navies of royally owned ships backed by a permanent bureaucratic infrastructure. This paralleled a similar process among armies, though the naval advance actually happened somewhat earlier. It reflected the strengthening of state power as the Wars of Religion subsided and the traditional partnership between monarch and nobility was reestablished (see Chapter 16), as well as the continuing advance in resources available to governments—especially money from increasing trade.

Shipbuilding and Logistics   One reason organization came somewhat earlier to naval administration than to land warfare is that warships were the biggest, most complex technology of the time. The mechanisms needed to bring large numbers of them on line therefore had to be correspondingly sophisticated. Private shipyards continued to build smaller craft for navies throughout this period, but royal shipyards increasingly monopolized the construction of ships of the line. Both royal and private yards had to employ armies of workmen and draw materials from great distances. The best shipbuilding timber, for instance, came from the Baltic. Naval powers worked to ensure their access to raw materials, but southern European powers were inevitably at a disadvantage in obtaining northern forest products. Shipbuilding was not yet a science, however, so industrial espionage and the diffusion of naval technology involved on-the-spot study and the hiring of skilled shipwrights from established yards, as Peter the Great

The Spanish Armada and the Korean Turtle Ships

In 1588, King Philip II of Spain dispatched a massive invasion force against his nemesis Queen Elizabeth I of the island kingdom of England (Figure 20.2). Four years later, Toyotomi Hideyoshi, ruler of a newly united Japan, launched a massive seaborne invasion against the peninsular kingdom of Korea. On conventional grounds, both had good reason to expect success. Philip and Hideyoshi each deployed one of the largest and best-trained armies in the world at the time, with disciplined formations of musketeers, pikemen, and swordsmen featured in both. Their opponents, in contrast, possessed only small, poorly equipped, and inadequately trained armies. What neither invader anticipated was the creative and ultimately decisive use of naval power by their enemies—one providing a foreshadowing of the dominant tactics of the age, the other supplying a futuristic view into the days of ironclads—and as a result, both invasions failed.

The Armada His plans for a 1587 invasion having been disrupted by Francis Drake's raid on Cadiz, in July 1588, Philip sent 130 ships including 20 large galleons, 8500 seamen, and 19,000 troops under the Duke of Medina Sidonia toward the English Channel, to rendezvous with the Duke of Parma's army in the Netherlands before landing in England. On July 19, English scout ships sighted the Armada off Cornwall, and the next day an English fleet of about 120 royal, London, and private ships under Lord Howard of Effingham, with Drake second in command, sailed out of Plymouth to meet it. Though outnumbered in total guns, the English had a nearly two-to-one advantage in long-range cannon, could resupply their fleet from friendly shores, and boasted faster and more maneuverable ships than those of the Spaniards.

A running fight up the Channel began on July 21 off Plymouth. English gunnery caused considerable damage at first, sinking one ship and preventing

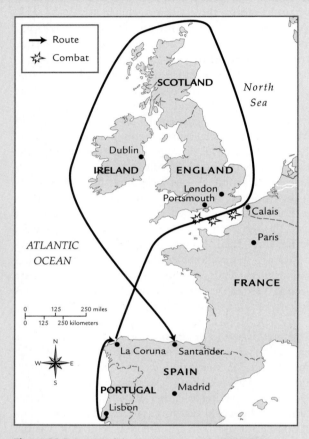

Figure 20.2 Route of the Spanish Armada, 1588

the Spaniards from landing on the Isle of Wight. Short of ammunition but still basically intact, the Armada anchored off Calais on July 26, hoping to resupply and meet Parma, but the latter was blockaded in the Belgian port city of Bruges by a Dutch fleet. Before dawn on July 28, the English sent several fireships into the anchorage. Sidonia ordered the Armada to cut their anchors, intending to return, but disorganization and unfavorable winds sent the fleet straggling up the Flemish coast pursued by the English, who would concentrate several ships against one target and pound away with alternating broadsides.

Unable to make any Netherlands port, Sidonia decided to sail home by going around the British Isles. Storms and starvation finished the work begun by English cannon: Only 63 of 130 ships returned to Spain in September, with an even higher percentage of men lost. The English sank or captured roughly 15, another 19 were wrecked on the Scottish and Irish coasts, and the rest were lost at sea.

Tactically, the defeat of the Armada gave a small foretaste of the standoff broadside gunnery tactics that came to dominate naval warfare. Superior sailing and better firepower played their role, but much English gunnery was ineffective at ranges great enough to avoid boarding, while bad luck and weather contributed greatly to the Spanish catastrophe. Strategically, however, the defeat of the Armada was a testament to naval power. A superior army and a navy equipped for troop transport and boarding had been foiled by a fleet built for sail and gunnery. The repulse of Philip's great expedition marked the beginning of the decline of Spanish power.

The Turtle Ships   Having united Japan, Hideyoshi gathered an army of 130,000 to conquer Ming China (and keep a mass of potentially restive samurai busy). A veteran force honed in the wars of unification, it had never fought overseas, and the navy that ferried it to Korea (the path to China) was a hastily put-together collection of transports and merchant ships. Korea, on the other hand, had a fairly pathetic army lacking any muskets, but a set of provincial navies that featured purpose-built warships that carried up to forty midsized cannon. Some of them, designed by the admiral of the Chulla navy, Yi Sung Sin, were oar propelled and covered over completely in planking

designed to resist boarding. These shells certainly had metal spikes as further defense and probably (the sources are not completely clear) were covered over in metal plates. Thus, armed with iron-clad gunboats and led by an admiral of genius and bravery much like his contemporary Francis Drake, the Korean navy set out to change the course of the war.

The first wave of invaders reached Pusan in southern Korea unmolested at sea and proceeded to execute a lightning conquest of much of Korea. But guerilla resistance made them even more dependent on supplies from home, and the reserves were needed for the invasion of China, which had come to the aid of its ally. Meanwhile, Admiral Yi first destroyed many of the transports still sitting in Korean harbors, then met the large fleet bringing the second wave of invaders. Making devastating use of broadside gunnery and fire arrows from line-ahead formations, he destroyed a large portion of the Japanese fleet at the Battle of Han-San in July 1592. Pursuing the remainder to An-Kol, he finished the job. All told, Yi's fleet sank fifty-nine Japanese ships, halted the invasion of China, and helped force the Japanese back to a small perimeter around Pusan by cutting off their supplies and reinforcements.

After five years of desultory fighting and negotiating, Hideyoshi launched a second invasion from the Pusan perimeter in 1597. The invading fleet arrived unmolested because Yi had lost his command through the scheming of political rivals. But after the Japanese defeated a Korean fleet and again advanced against Chinese and Korean resistance as far as Seoul, Yi returned and again cut communications between the invaders and Japan. Yi died inflicting one final massive defeat on the Japanese evacuation fleet at Chinhae Bay in November 1598. With Hideyoshi also now dead, the Japanese retreated to an isolation that would last 250 years.

SOURCES

Peter the Great and the Creation of the Russian Navy

Tsar Peter I (ruled 1682–1725) is credited with creating, in 1696, the modern Russian navy. Though warships had existed in Russia in reigns prior to his, Peter rigorously applied himself to founding a permanent western European–style naval establishment. The task proved exceptionally complicated, as building, maintaining, and deploying a modern navy involves coordinating the efforts of an elaborate infrastructure of harbors and ports, arsenals, shipyards, training institutions, and so on, which simply did not exist in Russia. In this "Preface to the Maritime Regulations," issued in 1700, Peter (referring to himself in the third person) describes how he pursued this goal.

■   ■   ■

A suitable place for shipbuilding was found on the river Voronezh, close to the town of that name, skilful ship-wrights were called from England and Holland, and in 1696 there began a new work in Russia—the construction of great war-ships, galleys, and other vessels; and so that this might be for ever secured in Russia, and that he might introduce among his people the art of this business, he sent many people of noble families to Holland and other states to learn the building and management of ships; and that the monarch might not be shamefully behind his subjects in that trade, he himself undertook a journey to Holland; and in Amsterdam, at the East India wharf, giving himself up, with the other volunteers, to the learning of naval architecture, he got what was necessary for a good carpenter to know, and, by his own work and skill, constructed and launched a new ship.

The following "Instruction to Russian Students Abroad Studying Navigation," issued by Peter in 1714, illustrates the sorts of concerns and needs facing the founder of an early modern navy.

1. Learn [how to draw] plans and charts and how to use the compass and other naval indicators.
2. [Learn] how to navigate a vessel in battle as well as in a simple maneuver, and learn how to use all appropriate tools and instruments; namely, sails, ropes, and oars, and the like matters, on row boats and other vessels.
3. Discover as much as possible how to put ships to sea during a naval battle. Those who cannot succeed in this effort must diligently ascertain what action should be taken by the vessels that do and those that do not put to sea during such a situation [naval battle]. Obtain from [foreign] naval officers written statements, bearing their signatures and seals, of how adequately you [Russian students] are prepared for [naval] duties.
4. If, upon his return, anyone wishes to receive [from the Tsar] greater favors for himself, he should learn, in addition to the above enumerated instructions, how to construct those vessels aboard which he would like to demonstrate his skills.
5. Upon his return to Moscow, every [foreign-trained Russian] should bring with him at his own expense, for which he will later be reimbursed, at least two experienced masters of naval science. They [the returnees] will be assigned soldiers, one soldier per returnee, to teach them what they have learned abroad. . . . And if anyone other than soldiers learns [the art of navigation] the treasury will pay 100 rubles for the maintenance of every such individual. . . .

SOURCE: L. Jay Oliva, ed., *Peter the Great* (Englewood Cliffs: Prentice-Hall, 1970), pp. 43–44, 50.

did in creating a Russian navy (see the Sources box "Peter the Great and the Creation of the Russian Navy"). Logistical considerations affected not just the building of fleets but their maintenance as well. Here,

the establishment of regular bureaucracies with steady supplies of money was crucial to improving fleet support, for while home ports could provide food and ammunition if a fleet operated in friendly waters, beyond friendly bases, supplies had to be purchased—one reason powers with increasingly global commitments, such as England, worked to establish or capture bases in the key theaters. Gibraltar, for example, the gateway to the Mediterranean, fell to the British around 1700 and has remained in their possession since.

Manpower   Perhaps the most consistent problem for navies in the age of sail was getting and keeping full crews. Conditions aboard ship were often less than attractive (though no worse generally than aboard merchant ships), and for much of the period, pay was not always forthcoming on time. Enlistment was usually voluntary, but governments often had to resort to bounties in times of emergency to induce enough sailors to join up, and they occasionally resorted to impressment. The social composition of navies reproduced that of the armies of the age: The officer class was overwhelmingly aristocratic, and the enlisted men overwhelmingly from the lower rungs of society, though perhaps, given the close connection between manpower pools for merchant marines and navies, a slightly more productive lower rung than that which manned armies.

This social divide necessitated, in part, the same harsh discipline as in armies. If anything, the confined quarters and minimal chances for desertion for crews at sea raised the pressure level and the severity of discipline in navies: Floggings and executions were run-of-the-mill occurrences, and captains exercised dictatorial powers on their ships. The alternative to desertion among seamen was mutiny, which was also not uncommon. Drill and training contributed to discipline, though as the disparity between French and British efficiency levels in the eighteenth century shows, there was no substitute for extensive experience in making for good sailing and gunnery in combat.

The harshness of discipline exacerbated the problem of maintaining crews at full strength after they had been recruited. Many sailors deserted when they could, while far more died regularly of disease. The beginning of a cruise was critical, for lots of men from different areas carrying different germs were suddenly thrown together in cramped quarters, making them breeding grounds for epidemics, including bubonic plague, which continued to strike navies as well as cities well into the seventeenth century: Plague prevented the Dutch from blockading London in 1673, for example. Expeditions to the tropics could be deadly as well, as crews encountered tropical diseases for the first time and often died in droves. Moreover, long cruises always brought on vitamin deficiency diseases such as scurvy because fresh food, especially fruits and vegetables, became scarce, leaving crews malnourished on hardtack biscuit and dried meat. Combat casualties periodically took a heavy toll, though disease was a bigger killer in the long run, as in armies.

Remedies for these various ills were slow in coming. The relationship between diet and disease was established only gradually: It was not until well into the eighteenth century that British ships began carrying stores of limes to prevent scurvy outbreaks. Military medicine aboard ship was probably even worse than ashore, where it was marginally useful at best. And it was the rare captain or admiral who recognized that humane treatment of his crew, including regular pay and generous distribution of prize money for enemy ships captured or sunk in battle, did more than the lash and the yardarm to encourage efficiency and reenlistment.

The British Synthesis   For various reasons, England (Great Britain after the Act of Union with Scotland of 1707) tended to lead the way in European naval affairs. Its island geography, of course, was the major factor (though Japanese isolationism in this period warns against simple geographic determinism). The defensive moat provided by the English Channel made it possible for the English government to focus its resources on the navy instead of a standing army and at the same time made a marine orientation through trade necessary. An active merchant community, in turn, provided resources for the navy, a partnership extending back into the Middle Ages. Politically, again in part because of the isolation of the island kingdom, Parliament had emerged by 1600 as a near-equal partner to the king in central government, in contrast to the royal absolutism that was becoming the norm on the Continent. This, too, weighed against maintenance of a large standing army, which parliamentary interests rightly saw as a potential tool of royal tyranny; a navy posed no such threat and, in fact, served the interests of the increasingly important merchant capitalist element in the polity. Victory over the Spanish Armada in 1588 formed the cornerstone of a growing glorification of naval might within the kingdom. The beginnings of English colonialism in North America reinforced the maritime orientation of the nation and initiated the flow of wealth that would allow continued naval build-up.

Ironically, the Civil War in 1642–48 between king and Parliament ended up reinforcing naval interests.

Oliver Cromwell's government, though dependent as a virtual military dictatorship on its army, took a general interest in military organization that extended to the navy, while mercantile interests had greater weight in a government shorn temporarily of the influence of great aristocrats. The Commonwealth undertook a massive naval building program in 1649–52, instituted bureaucratic reorganization resulting in an Admiralty Commission, and reformed conditions on shipboard, improving food, regularizing pay, and instituting prize money. It was this reformed navy that fought the First Anglo-Dutch War. The organization and construction programs carried over into the Royal Navy of the Restoration of 1660, when the monarchy returned to power.

It was then the results of the Glorious Revolution of 1688 and the establishment of the constitutional monarchy in 1689 that allowed the final pieces of a truly modern fiscal-military organization to be put in place. Having in effect established the sovereignty of Parliament within the central government—no taxes could be raised nor any army maintained without parliamentary consent—the landed and mercantile interests who controlled Parliament proved willing to pay for the state they now controlled. Thus, unlike almost everywhere on the Continent, every class in England contributed to paying taxes, including those who could afford it most. In times of emergency, of course, even this generous tax base could not pay for major wars out of current income. Shortly after the revolution, therefore, the government established the Bank of England, on the model of the Dutch central bank, as a holder of government and private deposits and as the clearinghouse for government borrowing. The invention of the Sinking Fund, a section of the government budget set aside for the repayment of loans guaranteed against future tax receipts, made it possible for the government to issue debt in the form of bonds, as well as to borrow through conventional channels, to an almost unlimited extent. The result was that Britain could regularly outspend France despite a much smaller population base, maintaining rock-solid fiscal solvency while France defaulted on its debts three times in the eighteenth century.

This spending ability was applied in large part to the Royal Navy, as maintenance of British superiority at sea became a central tenet of government policy (the army remained relatively small, as subsidies to allies provided the bulk of the ground forces British continental interests required). The main government dockyards at Portsmouth, Deptford, and Chatham became major proto-industrial centers employing thousands of workmen. But the influence of the fiscal-military state was more pervasive than its direct role indicates and not as consistently benign as this account might imply so far. In an economy that was already highly commercialized, the state played a central role when it pursued its main business, war. War could create financial crises by putting pressure on credit. It interfered with trade, and while some merchants benefited from higher prices, others lost ships to enemy action and money to slumps in whole sectors of the economy. In other words, the state, through its fiscal and military policies and mechanisms, affected—and was assumed to affect—the lives of everyday British subjects.

The modernity of this pervasive fiscal-military structure is indicated by the concerns some contemporaries had about it. One worry was that the new nexus of mercantile, bureaucratic, and fiscal interests were undermining the influence in government of the aristocracy, the great landed families who in traditional terms should have been the natural leaders of society. In other words, capitalism was already breaking down old class structures through the mechanisms of state power, pointing toward a shape of the modern state very different from that of traditional kingdoms. Another worry was that the levels of taxation necessary to sustain great-power military commitments would have a harmful impact on the economy and society, a familiar complaint from modern times. There were also worries that the very combination of mercantile and military interests created by the state would be self-perpetuating, to the benefit of a narrow interest group. That is, the same sectors of society tended to receive government contracts for construction and supply and to hold the government debt that funded such projects. That those sectors could then form a powerful lobby for keeping the country at war, or at least preparing heavily for war (and so guaranteeing the continuation of their investment and contracting incomes), is echoed precisely in President Eisenhower's farewell address in 1961, in which he famously warned of the baleful effects a military-industrial complex could have on United States democracy. The emergence around 1700 of a modern military-industrial complex in England is a sure sign that naval warfare was the cutting edge of military and political modernity in Europe and the world.

CONCLUSION

Within Europe, the emergence of the British system had already begun to put Britannia on the road to ruling the waves by 1750. What remained to cement that position was for a series of tactical developments, fostered by admirals of daring and genius, to break the indecisiveness of line-ahead tactics and add British dominance in battle to dominance in strategy, administration, and economics. These developments are traced in Chapter 25.

Globally, domination of the sea-lanes by Europeans in general and Britain in particular was the key factor in fueling new forms of economic activity, allowing massive accumulation of wealth and eventually, in Britain, spurring the decisive transformation from a preindustrial to an industrial economy. It was that transformation that would carry Europeans to domination of the world on land and sea in the nineteenth century.

Thus, the new forms of maritime activity and naval warfare that Europeans forged in the period 1500–1750 proved revolutionary both in themselves and for what they caused: The sailors on the decks of the full-rigged, broadside-bearing wooden ships of the age were both the true military revolutionaries of the time and the midwives of the industrial age.

SUGGESTED READINGS

Brewer, John. *The Sinews of Power: War, Money and the English State, 1688–1783*. Cambridge: Harvard University Press, 1988. A fundamentally important account of the rise of the fiscal-military state in England and the central place of the Royal Navy in this process.

Brummett, Palmira. *Ottoman Seapower and Levantine Diplomacy in the Age of Discovery*. Albany: SUNY Press, 1994. Challenges Eurocentric accounts of the rise of European sea power by attempting to reconceptualize the Ottoman role in the early sixteenth century.

Cipolla, Carlo. *Guns, Sails and Empires: Technological Innovation and the Early Phases of European Expansion, 1400–1700*. New York: Minerva Press, 1967. An old but classic and still useful account of the rise of European maritime power.

Glete, Jan. "Warfare at Sea 1450–1815." In Jeremy Black, ed., *War in the Early Modern World, 1450–1815*. London: Routledge, 1999. A brief but clear overview of the developments of the period at sea; balanced strategic, tactical, and administrative coverage. For an extended treatment, see his *Warfare at Sea, 1500–1650* (London: Routledge, 2000), which looks at technological, financial, and social dimensions of the development of naval warfare for the first half of the period covered by this chapter.

Guilmartin, John. *Gunpowder and Galleys*. (See Chapter 15.)

Harding, Richard. *The Evolution of the Sailing Navy, 1509–1815*. New York: St. Martin's Press, 1995. A thorough account of the history of the Royal Navy, tracing organization in the context of policy and administration.

Landstrom, Bjorn. *The Ship*. See Chapter 10.

Mahan, A. T. *The Influence of Sea Power upon History, 1660–1789*. Boston: Little, Brown, 1890. Reprinted in numerous editions. Lays down a theory of naval warfare and provides extensive narratives of major actions. (See the Sources box in Chapter 25 and attendant discussion.)

Perez-Mallaina, Pablo. *Spain's Men of the Sea: Daily Life on the Indies Fleets in the Sixteenth Century*. Trans. Carla Rahn Phillips. Baltimore: Johns Hopkins University Press, 1994. An excellent social history of maritime life in Spain's naval forces; full of vivid detail, and the best starting point for understanding what life was like on wooden ships.

Rasor, E. L. *The Spanish Armada of 1588: Historiography and Annotated Bibliography*. Westport: Greenwich Press, 1993. An excellent entry point into the vast literature surrounding the Grand Armada.

Russell-Wood, A. J. R. *The Portuguese Empire, 1415–1808*. Baltimore: Johns Hopkins University Press, 1998. A classic study of naval power and maritime activity in the context of the first seaborne empire of global proportions.

Sweetman, Jack, ed. *The Great Admirals: Command at Sea, 1587–1945*. Annapolis: Naval Institute Press, 1997. A set of detailed examinations of some of the most important naval commanders of the age, who did much to shape strategy and tactics at sea; good general summaries of naval developments frame the individual studies.

Turnbull, Stephen. *The Samurai: A Military History*. London: Routledge, 1977. Contains a fairly detailed narrative of Hideyoshi's invasions of Korea and the victories of the Korean turtle ships.

COMMENTARY: PART 4, 1500–1750

In global terms, two themes stand out in the military history of 1500–1750. First, this period witnessed the reversal of the military superiority of nomads that had lasted for two millenia. Now, for the first time, settled civilizations gained a decisive edge against their steppe rivals. Second, the world's oceans saw the rise of new forms of naval power linked to the emergence of truly global trade networks, with a consequent globalization of warfare (as well as other forms of cultural contact). Both of these developments were related to the development of gunpowder weaponry, though neither trend was directly caused by changing technology.

NOMADS AND SETTLED PEOPLES

There was a steady advance of settled states at the expense of nomadic peoples after 1500. While groups such as the Mughals and Manchus, who were seminomadic or looked back to nomadic heritages, still had a significant impact in this period, their successes rarely came as purely nomadic cavalry forces, and they proved to be the last flarings of nomadic power against the tide of civilization. Chronically unsafe borderlands connecting the steppes to Persia and the Ottoman realm were at last stabilized. The Mughal conquest was the last one India would have to face from the northwest. The Russian frontier in Central Asia was pushed forward, and by 1750, this European state had Pacific outposts. Perhaps most significantly, China, which had fallen to Mongol conquest in the 1270s and had faced serious Mongol threats in subsequent centuries, turned the tables in the late seventeenth century and brought Mongolia under its rule. The Dragon Throne then proceeded to dominate much of Central Asia at the expense of nomads and Russians alike. The process was even repeated in miniature in northern Mexico with the taming of the nomadic (but not horse-riding) Chichimecas by Spanish settlers and their native allies.

The causes of this shift in the Eurasian balance of power are manifold. From one perspective, it was simply the culmination of a long and cyclical process in which nomadic conquerors revitalized and connected areas of civilization, which, in turn, expanded as the nomadic tide inevitably receded. Fundamental to the direction of this trend was the growing population and resource base of settled civilizations. Ever-more farmers and the merchants, bureaucrats, priests, and soldiers they supported meant ever-more land brought under cultivation and an increasing disparity in the numbers of people and goods of all types that civilizations could bring to bear against their nomadic neighbors. Constrained by the environment that shaped their military skills, there could be no such growth among the horse people. After 1500, this general trend was magnified by a specific type of good available only to settled armies: guns. In conjunction with systems of fortification being extended around and into the steppes, gunpowder made sedentary infantry much more formidable against nomadic cavalry forces. The combination of secure bases and improved firepower was one for which the nomads had no real answer. But too much emphasis should not be placed on guns alone, for steppe horse-archers retained considerable military utility throughout this period. This is demonstrated by the fact that the most effective military systems of the age were, in fact, syntheses of settled and nomadic elements. The last waves of nomadic success, in particular in India, China, and the Near East, created hybrid states that had nomadic roots, and often retained a nomadic ethos, but that could also draw on the resources of vast settled empires. The Mughals, the Manchus, the

Safavids, and above all the Ottomans could raise armies consisting of traditional horse-archers supported by infantry—some of it, such as the Ottoman janissaries, disciplined and armed with muskets—and trains of siege artillery. The combination made for powerful expansionist states that helped seal the fate of the steppe lands. Even the Russians with their Cossack allies used this form of military syncretism.

This epochal shift was beneficial to the civilizations around the steppes in terms of removing a long-standing threat to their security. But the consequences of success were complex. It is possible that the removal of the nomadic threat led to complacency in the big, land-based empires surrounding the steppes. With the nomads tamed, the engine of renewal and deadly competition was stilled, and a major incentive for military inventiveness was removed. In the event, none of the major Eurasian empires were fully prepared to meet a new form of competition coming from the Eurasian periphery, though small shiploads of Europeans posed little threat to any of them militarily during this period. Further, the general success of settled civilizations meant that by 1700 the steppes, long a highway of trade and cultural interaction, had been fragmented and divided among the great empires. While it is unclear exactly what the effect of this was on trade, it coincided with the rise of a new form of highway for the world's commerce: the oceans. The growing importance of maritime trade, though not new to this period, reached a critical new level economically and militarily just as the steppes went into decline.

THE WORLD AT SEA

Several trends characterize the use of naval power in this era. First, at least at sea, Europe moved from being a fairly marginal player in the world's economy and military affairs to being a central force in both. The reasons for Europe's creation of navies and merchant marines that could exploit the world's oceans fully are complex. But once launched, they were propelled not just by wind but by a combination of state and private interests that proved self-perpetuating. These navies created a revolution in war at sea that had global significance. This is partly because the second trend was for European maritime expeditions to move from voyages of discovery (from the European point of view) to domination of the world's network of maritime trade. This involved the creation of new forms of empire. The Portuguese, following in many ways a model pioneered by the Italian city-states of Venice and Genoa, established trade outposts around the Indian Ocean. These small, fortified enclaves acted as bases for fleets and as exchange points with the mainland economies that supplied the goods shipped to Europe. The Spanish pioneered the exploitation of colonies in the New World that drew on native and slave manpower as well as settlers, while some later northern European colonization of the Americas created settler enclaves. The role of private interests is indicated by British penetration of India, which derived from the activities of the British East India Company.

Why did Europeans become so dominant at sea after 1500? Part of the answer lies in the powerful technological combination of full-rigged ships carrying large, effective cannon. This technological package could ship cargo and men almost anywhere relatively cheaply, as small crews could handle large payloads. The ships were stoutly built—stronger than the ships produced by any other area at the time. And even a few cannon not only secured a merchantman against many pirate attacks but made it into a potential pirate craft itself. Purpose-built warships with broadside armament were truly formidable weapons systems. It was here, at sea, that a Military Revolution undoubtedly took place between 1500 and 1750. As a result of this package, European ships came to carry both trade to and from Europe and local Asian trade commandeered from Asian carriers, with the profits from both and from American precious metals funding further purchases of Asian goods. Thus, while European entry into the world system of trade was in some ways parasitical on the major productive areas of Asia, it was a successful parasitism that lifted Europe closer to the prominence of the major Asian states. But the second reason for European dominance of the seas was that they faced little if any organized or determined opposition. The major states outside of Europe had little interest in the seas or maritime trade. Such trade was important in their economies, especially to certain classes within their population, but official doctrines and attitudes paid little attention to it (as in India) or were actively hostile to it (as in China and, after 1600, Japan). They were land-based empires. The significant threats to their security, such as the nomads discussed above, and the political and economic interests of their elite classes, were in landholding and agriculture, as they had always been. With the partial exception of the Ottomans in the Mediterranean, no state navies emerged to challenge the European monopoly of the sea. In effect, the Europeans were playing a new game, and they had the field to themselves.

The consequences of this new mode of naval activity were momentous. It made possible the first truly global age, as the Americas were brought within the Eurasian sphere of activity. The Columbian exchange of diseases, plants, and animals had huge long-term effects on both Old and New Worlds. This naval activity also, as noted, moved Europeans closer to the center of the world stage. By 1750, Britain was probably the world's second-greatest power behind China, with France a close third. But European power should not be exaggerated: Their influence beyond the seas and immediate coastal areas, even in the Americas, was limited. European navies were far ahead of the rest of the world's; their armies, despite significant transformation, still were not, at least not decisively.

Assessing Gunpowder

Both the shift in power away from nomads and the shift in power toward Europe at sea were connected to the emergence of gunpowder weaponry, and this age is in many ways an age of gunpowder. But it is important in assessing the role of gunpowder in the military history of this period not to assign too great a causal weight to its appearance. The deep, structural causes of both shifts were complex and rooted in long-term demographic, economic, and social trends that predated gunpowder by centuries. Gunpowder became an important mechanism in the progress of both trends, but it was not a cause of either.

It is also important to bear in mind that the use and impact of gunpowder weapons varied greatly across Eurasia, Africa, and the Americas. Effective use of guns was not a European monopoly—the Ottomans and Japan both arguably made better use of guns at times, and others such as the Mughals made good use of them in contexts different from those in Europe—nor were guns revolutionary wherever they were used. This is because guns were still a simple enough technology that their use was largely shaped by the political, military, and social contexts in which they were employed. Nor were these different uses noticeably different in effectiveness until the very end of this period, when evolving European techniques for employing guns, rather than any major technological breakthroughs, began gradually to create a small advantage for European armies. It is therefore difficult to argue that a Military Revolution had taken place in European land warfare that was even remotely comparable to what had transpired at sea. European dominance in land warfare was a product partly of the eighteenth but mostly of the nineteenth century.

In other words, the real age of revolutions was yet to come. It is the subject of the next part of this book.

PART 5

THE AGE OF REVOLUTIONS
AND IMPERIALISM, 1700–1914

CHAPTER 21

Bullion and Bayonets: Linear Tactics on a Global Stage, 1680–1789

The eighteenth century in Europe saw the consolidation and perfection of the advances in military technique, technology, and institutions that had appeared in the last decades of the seventeenth century. Those advances, in turn, were the end result of seven centuries of slow transformation of Europe's sociomilitary system (see Chapters 12 and 16). Military developments of the eighteenth century in Europe were part of (and drew on) a larger set of transformations in European life that included demographic and economic growth; the spread of a rationalist, scientific worldview with the Enlightenment; and new forms of government and cultural expression. And they began at last to make European ways of war not just different from but noticeably more effective than those in most of the rest of the world, although the difference was still limited in important ways.

The foundation for this period of consolidation and perfection was more effective central authority—stronger governments—which could draw on an increasing range of institutions in support of their war efforts. More effective governments, in turn, could impose on their armies ever-more-effective discipline and drill. Better drill, especially in the use of infantry small arms, allowed a steady increase in the firepower of European armies. Steadily improving technology, itself a result of an increasingly scientific culture, added to the effects of drill, discipline, and institutions.

The combination of better techniques and better technology resulted in increasingly professionalized armies capable of flexible responses on the battlefield and, most famously, of the linear tactics that characterized major battles in Europe in this age. It was such armies that began to increase the still-limited European impact on the global stage.

Europeans and Turks   This drawing shows European drill masters attempting, largely without success, to teach modern European techniques to the Turks. It was technique, tied to socioeconomic change, rather than technology that began to give European armies some advantage over their Turkish foes in the eighteenth century.

INSTITUTIONS

Governments, Economies, and Armies

The foundation for the increasing military power of many European countries was an increasingly systematized and rational connection between governments and their war machines, on the one hand, and the economy, on the other. This link was clearly recognized at the time and had found expression, as part of the seventeenth-century movement toward rational analysis, in the first coherent theory of governmental management of economics: mercantilism (see Chapter 20). It is significant that mercantilism was an economic theory with a military rationale at its core. Mercantilists argued that since the total volume of world trade was constant (an assumption Adam Smith exploded in 1776), a country maximized its profits from that trade by expanding its exports (by, for example, supporting trading companies) and limiting its imports (through tariffs and encouraging local industry). Why maximize the import-export differential? Because the difference would then flow to the country in gold and silver, which could be used to finance armies and navies.

Economic Resources

Though flawed as theory, mercantilism probably did encourage economic development, especially in terms of economic resources that affected military might. The most crucial of these were manufacturing capacity and the proceeds of global mercantile empires.

The eighteenth century saw a steady expansion of Europe's manufacturing base. This was most evident in Britain, where the early stages of the Industrial Revolution began to transform production of cloth and machinery from the middle of the century, but was true to a lesser extent across the Continent. Many of the growing industries had direct military connections: European output of muskets, cannon, gunpowder, and ammunition rose steadily, as did production of boots, cloth made into uniforms and sails, and the other varied equipment needed to outfit an army or navy. The manufacturers were mostly private firms, but they benefited from the steady and assured stream of government contracts. Competition among them encouraged innovation in manufacturing techniques, resulting most importantly in increasing standardization of weapons and other equipment, and pointing the way toward mass production of weapons assembled from interchangeable parts. Even if most of this production stayed within Europe for use in its internal wars, the steady increase in the quality and quantity of arms Europe could produce had global implications. At the apex of this set of developments stood the royal shipyards and allied manufacturers that built and supplied the British navy, the clearest example of the emergence of proto-military-industrial complexes.

Closely linked to the expansion of European manufacturing, again most strongly in Britain, were the resources of global mercantile empires. Colonies and trading posts fed tax revenues, direct income, colonial raw materials, and "ghost" manpower (the slave and colonial labor, especially that devoted to food production, that freed European laborers to work in industry) into European economies and, in turn, provided markets for manufactured goods. The massive wealth generated by the Caribbean sugar trade with Britain, greater in value in 1750 than all its Far Eastern trade combined, cannot be underestimated as a basis for both British economic development and the military strength the nation deployed in the century.

Finance

The governmental connection to manufacturing was by 1700 much more direct than it had been previously because states increasingly undertook to provide everything—weapons, clothing, housing, training, and even medical care—directly to their soldiers, who themselves increasingly were directly paid by the state rather than obtained through independent contractors. This drove up the direct costs of war tremendously and emphasized the role of money as the sinews of war, in the common phrase of the time. Therefore, the ability of states to tap their economies directly became a key measure of military potential.

Britain again led the way in finance. This was partly a result of the peculiar political arrangements the island kingdom had constructed over the centuries, focused on a Parliament with considerable financial control. The Glorious Revolution of 1688 made Parliament the sovereign power in England, with control over taxation and the raising of armed forces. Since this was a Parliament drawn from the greater and lesser landowners, merchants, and aristocrats of the realm, Britain found itself with a government run by, and thus more or less willingly paid for by, the richest members of the polity. To this solid tax base was added in the 1690s a national Bank of England modeled on and soon surpassing the Dutch central bank, capable of channeling significant loans to the government. Repayment of such loans was guaranteed by the invention of the Sinking Fund, whereby government loan repayments were secured against future taxes. The creation of these flexible financial institutions and a national debt, tapping the wealth of the British global economy, allowed Britain to borrow cheaply and in almost unlimited amounts and so to finance war efforts far beyond the scale of her population. Britain's position as one of the two preeminent military powers of the century (with China) was built on this financial base, which not only funded Britain's army and navy but subsidized her continental allies in major land wars.

Continental powers under absolutist monarchs imitated British developments as best they could, but

Pandours and Hussars
Pandours and Hussars were light irregular cavalry forces, usually from the Balkans, who raided enemy territory, terrorizing the population and burning whatever supplies they could not carry away.

they were consistently crippled by the tax-exempt status of most continental aristocrats. Attempts at reform usually ran into resistance, for aristocracies would not buy into a government they could not control more directly, a control precluded by royal absolutism. Thus, although continental powers deployed increasing resources throughout the century, their finances were consistently more precarious than Britain's. In fact, France, the largest continental power and Britain's direct rival, defaulted on its obligations more than once, most disastrously in 1789, under the burden of war debts.

Nevertheless, all the European powers raised more money and maintained more centrally controlled military establishments in the eighteenth century. Some of their greater monetary resources went to creating or improving institutions that supported military establishments. The focus here was on those branches of government that conducted recruiting and provided logistical support. This stimulated the emergence of and drew on the capabilities of ever-more-professional bureaucracies. Though every European state's bureaucracy fell far short of the ideal, state service was increasingly seen as the domain of impersonal professionals serving on the basis of merit and devoted to the interests of the state. Efficiency in government contributed to military efficiency, and both were key elements of a growing culture of rationalism and calculated efficiency.

Military Institutions and Society

All societies were militarized, in the sense that armies and navies were a significant government preoccupation, and their financing, direct or indirect, was a major issue for both state and citizenry. As a consequence, war had an impact on many civilians. The military acted and interacted as part of a complex social pattern; it was not separate from society but, instead, part of it. The multifaceted links between troops and civilians encompassed recruitment, billeting, logistics, and sexual relations. For example, the presence of a garrison led to an increase in the rate of illegitimate births in the area. This was disruptive and also put pressure on social welfare, as extended families, charitable organizations, and orphanages had to cope with the bastard offspring, even as large numbers of the women who had had relationships with soldiers were convicted of infanticide. In part, such relationships reflected the extent to which the housing of troops was less segregated than is the case today. Troops were particularly important in garrison towns, which included all capital cities. In Paris in 1789, a key role in the French Revolution was played by troops permanently based there, who lived and worked among the populace, who pursued civilian trades when not on duty, and who were thus subject to all the economic and ideological pressures affecting the people. The sporadic but growing use of barracks in preference to billeting soldiers directly among the populace, an attempt to segregate military personnel from the surrounding civilian world, was only partially successful, tending especially to break down where units were stationed in one place for long periods.

The military and society each shaped the other; in fact, the military was more shaped by civil society than is often appreciated—indeed, more than most contemporaries wanted. The influence of social pressures and class assumptions and the play of personality, on the part of both officers and men, acted to weaken the structures of military hierarchy and to compromise formal discipline. On the other hand, vertical alignments existed in the military, alongside horizontal status or class-based ones, just as in civil society. These often fostered informal consensual practices that compensated for weaker formal discipline.

There was also a feedback mechanism, with several aspects of the war-society relationship proving of particular importance for military capability and effectiveness. This was especially true of recruitment practices and their underlying ethos, which were key elements in the interaction of the military and civilians.

In pointed contrast to the modern West, there was broad acceptance of both war and killing. In this, the military reflected the nature of society, and its actions exemplified contemporary attitudes toward human life. Killing was generally accepted as appropriate, both for civil society—as a response to crime, heresy, and disorder—and in international relations. War itself seemed necessary. In modern functional terms, it was the inevitable product of an international system that lacked a hegemonic power. To contemporaries, in contrast, war was the best means by which to defend interests and achieve goals. Throughout society, violence was a legitimate means to defend personal worth, in the form of honor, and thus seemed more acceptable than it does today.

By modern Western standards, a large percentage of males served in the military, in part because the high rate of casualties ensured the need for a constant flow of replacements. This increased the percentage of civilians affected by having husbands, fathers, brothers, and sons in the military, and the attendant disruption and sense of loss. War therefore affected, at least indirectly, a large percentage of the female population.

Rulers and the Military Armies were generally seen as an essential attribute of sovereignty. This was also linked to military aesthetics. A good-looking army was valued by rulers, and that was a key reason why rulers preferred tall recruits to shorter ones. For the same reason, rulers frequently designed the uniforms for their troops. Red and white, the colors of the British and French, looked good even if they made soldiers more conspicuous to sharpshooters. Armies were also of value for their part in enabling rulers and, to a lesser extent, aristocrats to fulfill the roles attributed to them and that they were generally willing to discharge. Military leadership was an important role, one sanctioned by history, dynastic tradition, and biblical examples. Many rulers indeed saw war, in which they often served in person, as their function and justification as defenders of their subjects and inheritance—a source of personal glory, dynastic aggrandizement, and national fortune. The celebration of the royal hero as victor was part of a long European tradition in its most impressive function, the display of power. War was not the sole sphere in which such display could occur, but it was the one that best served the aggressive dynastic purpose that illuminated so many of the states of the period. Emulation of ancestors, former monarchs, and contemporaries, and also sheer excitement—all played a role in the royal desire to fight. (For further discussion of the nature of warfare in this period, see the Issues box "Limited Warfare?")

As a result, the military was a section of the community that governments needed and cared for, albeit at a basic level. Their sustenance was provided during peacetime, although wartime campaigns posed serious problems. Further, although pay was generally low and frequently delayed, troops were the largest group paid by governments. Moreover, despite the presentation of drill as a harsh system for segregation and control, discipline in general was not always as savage in practice as it was in theory. Indeed, this was a common feature of the law enforcement of the period, which was often, in practice, tempered by mercy (and, at times, by spreading Enlightenment attitudes mitigating against torture and other forms of excessive—or cruel and unusual, as the new American Constitution put it—punishment) and episodic due to understaffed enforcement institutions and lack of resources. A small number of hard cases received a disproportionate number of the most severe punishments.

There were also signs of improvement in the treatment of soldiers. A growing emphasis on the morale of individual soldiers motivated disciplinary reforms, as well as improvements in medical and hospital care

ISSUES

Limited Warfare?

The warfare of the late seventeenth and much of the eighteenth centuries is frequently presented in military historiography as limited and indecisive. Two contrasts contribute to this picture.

First is the contrast presented by the savagery visited on civilians by the armies of the mid-seventeenth century, especially the Thirty Years War in Germany, when large areas suffered repeated rounds of foraging, deliberate devastation, and consequent depopulation. Intractable ideological conflict between Protestant and Catholic forces, as well as the depradations of mercenary units that got out of state control, seemingly heightened the destructiveness of war and made it difficult to end. In contrast, eighteenth-century warfare was characterized by more tightly controlled royal armies pursuing more limited political aims and fighting from a logistical platform of royal depot-fortresses that reduced the need to forage. The "enlightened despots" of the eighteenth century, furthermore, are said to have recognized the economic costs of war on their populations and to have contributed to more humane and circumscribed military practices. Thus, limited war.

Second, the contrast between the vast scope and decisive battle-oriented character of the French Revolutionary and Napoleonic Wars of 1792–1815, on the one hand, and the apparently limited scope, emphasis on maneuver and sieges, and minor political consequences of much eighteenth-century warfare, on the other, contributes to the impression of indecisiveness. Scholars keen to stress the role of change in the revolutionary period generally do so by emphasizing the apparent stability and conservatism of earlier practices. Moreover, it is difficult for many to accept that warfare was "for real" in an eighteenth-century world in which artifice, convention, and style played such a major role.

The impression created by these contrasts, however, is certainly overdrawn and can be viewed from different perspectives. There was nothing limited about eighteenth-century warfare to those engaged in it. Battles occurred more frequently than the usual picture allows, and massed, close-range firepower contributed to very high death rates. Siege warfare spread the casualties out over a longer period than battles, but it often also caused more total deaths. High death rates in warfare habituated soldiers to killing at close quarters, so the treatment of civilians cannot be said to have improved much, as any reader of Voltaire's novel *Candide* would recognize. The harsh treatment of civilians across Europe in part reflected that which soldiers could mete out to each other. And plenty of opportunities still existed for harsh treatment, for while a defending force might rely more on depots for supply, any offensive campaign into enemy territory still lived off the land both by policy and by necessity. Further, while individual wars might have been ended diplomatically more easily than during the seventeenth century, they could also be started with relative ease, and many were.

Moreover, rulers, ministers, generals, and admirals were determined to achieve victory, and they were frequently able to do so. There was nothing inherently indecisive about seventeenth- and eighteenth-century strategy and tactics, except perhaps at sea, although even then the intention of naval tactics was to ensure a decisive result (see Chapters 20 and 25). Indecision was, if anything, a product of political rather than military factors, especially the inability of states to exploit fully their military potential. The ability of Western states to operate outside Europe, and their success, both within and outside Europe, in defeating non-European powers, was also notable. Indeed, the impression of indecisiveness conveyed by eighteenth-century warfare is largely an illusion of a Eurocentric focus. The global and colonial gains made by Britain as a result of the War of Spanish Succession (1701–14), the Seven Years War (1756–63), and various wars in India, never mind the decisive consequences of Britain's lone defeat in the American Revolution, arguably outweigh any ephemeral result gained by Napoleon during his wars (see Chapter 22), wars from which only Britain (again) emerged with lasting gains. The "decisiveness" of Napoleonic warfare is undeniable in operational terms—terms enshrined in military mentalities by post-Napoleonic theorists led by Clausewitz. Through a different lens, eighteenth-century warfare was often at least as decisive on global and strategic scales.

from the late seventeenth century. Reforms also undermine arguments that the position of troops was uniform or that their treatment was always bleak. Indeed, the fighting qualities of the armies and navies that confronted the forces of revolutionary France in the 1790s did not stem simply from discipline or belief in their cause. They also reflected a professionalism born of training and responsible treatment.

TECHNOLOGY

Technological changes in the tools of warfare were usually dependent on and called into being by the economic and institutional context detailed above. Technological changes, in turn, had their own impact: Linear tactics grew out of the combination of drill and new weapons such as the socket bayonet.

Patterns in Weapons Innovation

There were two main patterns in weapons innovation that we may note before examining specific developments. First, the eighteenth century was a period of constant incremental improvement of a basic set of weapons. Gunpowder weaponry, both infantry small arms and artillery, dominated the process. The steady refinement of firing mechanisms, ammunition, and manufacturing processes reflected several influences. The newly emerging methods of experimental science and more sophisticated mathematics led weapons designers and their users to test, tinker with, and improve their designs, while mathematics contributed directly to making ballistics more accurate, thus improving the accuracy of cannon fire. Europe's market economy and network of private arms manufacturers competing for lucrative government contracts provided the economic incentive for improving both weapon designs and the volume, reliability, and cost of manufacture.

But the second main pattern was that major changes were in reality very limited. Expense and still significant technological limitations were the key brakes on the creation and adoption of significantly different weaponry. The large royal armies that had emerged by the beginning of the eighteenth century strained their states' resources just in terms of manpower and basic equipment. Once they were armed to a certain level, with the standard kit of smoothbore muskets and artillery, most states could not afford to reequip them in any major way. Thus, even significant improvements such as the flintlock firing mechanism (see below)

took several decades to diffuse through all Europe's armies; states with the weakest manufacturing base, such as Russia, took longest to complete such conversions. Further, the weapons of the day fit so tightly into an established system of training, drill, and social structure that significant changes would have been difficult to implement without completely reconstructing an army's routine, something no state could contemplate. The weight of prior investment and institutional inertia only grew heavier as armies became more systematized and established. Finally, despite its growth, Europe's manufacturing sector, not yet industrialized, did not have the capacity to retool and refit an entire military establishment with any rapidity. Most arms makers were small firms with limited ability to invest in new machinery, and most manufacturing techniques were still based more on traditional knowledge than scientific process. The age of rapid technological development had not yet arrived.

Developments in Weaponry

The new weapons developed included the socket bayonet and the flintlock musket in the late seventeenth century, the elevating screw for cannon in the eighteenth, and paper cartridges. A series of innovations offered incremental improvements in effectiveness. For example, the introduction of conic ramrods, employed to push the shot down the barrel, allowed for a reduction in the difference between the muzzle caliber and the ammunition caliber, and thereby promoted more precise targeting.

Bayonets Toward the close of the seventeenth century, the development of the bayonet altered warfare in Europe by transforming infantry capability and combat. The early plug bayonet (see Chapter 16), introduced in the early 1640s, was inserted in the musket barrel and therefore prevented firing. This bayonet, based on a weapon used by hunters, was named after Bayonne in southwest France. These bayonets were daggers that, if necessary, could be inserted into muskets, making them a useful weapon against boars.

It has been claimed that the French army was using the bayonet by 1642. Use rapidly spread, and by the 1670s, specialized units such as dragoons and fusiliers were being issued bayonets. At the siege of Valenciennes in 1677, the first French bayonet attack occurred. By the 1680s, bayonets had become far more common. These bayonets were essentially double-edged dagger blades, about one foot long, attached to a handle that was also about a foot long and that was the same diameter as the musket's bore. The handle was fixed in position by working it into the musket. In 1672, bayonets were issued to a unit in the English army, Prince Rupert's dragoons.

As an example of the incremental nature of military change, the plug bayonet was replaced by ring-and-socket bayonets, developed in the 1680s. These allowed firing with the blade in place. The bayonet was turned and locked in place, providing firmness in combat; this led to the phasing out of the pike, which was now redundant. Bayonets were a better complement to firearms in fulfilling the pike's defensive role against attacking infantry and cavalry, and they also had an offensive capability against infantry and, on occasion, cavalry. Firepower was greatly enhanced as a result of the replacement of pikemen.

This change was largely carried out in the 1680s and early 1700s. The Württemberg troops sent to campaign against the Turks in Greece in 1687–88 had no pikes, and the Saxon and Württemberg armies converted to bayonets between the late 1680s and the mid-1690s. In 1687, the Marquis de Louvois, the French army minister, instructed Vauban to make a prototype bayonet. Given Vauban's skills in fortress design, this was a testimony to his general ability.

Brandenburg-Prussia adopted the bayonet in 1689, and Denmark followed suit in 1690. At the Battle of Fleurus (1690), in the Nine Years War, or War of the League of Augsburg (1688–97), some German units attracted attention by repulsing French cavalry attacks despite being armed only with muskets and unsupported by pikes. Russia adopted the bayonet in the early 1700s. In contrast, the Turks were slow to do so: They were used, and then only in relatively small numbers, from the 1730s.

Flintlocks   The replacement of matchlocks by flintlocks was a major shift in firing mechanism that increased the speed and reliability of musket fire, with major consequences for effectiveness both in Europe and farther afield. Flintlocks made musket fire less dependent on the weather. Matchlocks had been affected by wind, rain, and general humidity, with the latter a particular problem in the Tropics. The flintlock musket, in which power was ignited by a spark produced through striking flint against steel, was more expensive but lighter (not requiring a rest), more reliable, easier to fire, and more rapid-firing than the matchlock. The rate of fire, aided by the spread of prepackaged paper cartridges

that provided the correct amount of powder, almost doubled. Without the hazard of the burning matches previously used to ignite powder, musketeers were also able to stand closer together, which increased the firepower per length of unit frontage.

The first form of flintlock ignition system was the snaphaunce lock, which appeared in the mid-sixteenth century. The more classic flintlock was developed from this in the early seventeenth century. These flintlocks were used for hunting and for pistols, but it took time to introduce the flintlock as a major military weapon because of the cost.

The Austrians adopted the flintlock in about 1689, the Swedes from 1696, and the Dutch and English by 1700. In England, all the new regiments raised from 1689 on were equipped with flintlocks. The new land pattern musket could be fired at least twice a minute and weighed one pound less than the matchlock previously used. Like the earlier adoption of the arquebus, the spread of the flintlock was not instantaneous, however—unsurprisingly so, as the cost of one flintlock was equal to the annual wages of an agricultural laborer. Nevertheless, as an indication of competitive pressures and the clear advantages of the flintlock, its adoption was quicker than that of the arquebus. Although French regulations permitted the use of flintlocks by some soldiers from 1670, matchlocks were not completely phased out until 1704. This delay probably owed much to cost, but the Nine Years War (1688–97) led the French to decide to change over; this shift was decreed by an ordinance of December 1699. Many Swedish units continued to use older forms of firearms. The impact of the flintlock was magnified by the replacement of the pike by the bayonet.

Low muzzle velocity led to dreadful wounds, because the more slowly a projectile travels, the more damage it does as it bounces off bones and internal organs. Soldiers fired by volley rather than employing individually aimed shot. It was difficult in any case to aim in the noise and smoke of a battlefield; further, the heavy weight of muskets led to musket droop and thus to a tendency to fire short. Soldiers also suffered bruising as a result of the weapons' strong recoil.

Even in perfect conditions, effective range for an individually aimed shot was only about fifty yards, although this has been the subject of much debate, and some certainly claimed to have shot accurately at greater range. In any event, it was unusual to exceed three shots a minute. Accuracy was compromised by the nature of the barrel (unrifled, or ungrooved, and, in order to avoid fouling by powder and recoil, generally a loose fit for the shot that left much windage, or space between bore and shot); the shot, often elliptical and thus unlikely to travel as designed; the slow lock time; the need for rapid firing; and the absence of accurate sights. The shot, as a result of the significant windage, bounded down the bore and might leave the barrel in any direction, a process known as balloting. Worn flints and blocked touch-holes caused misfiring, while reloading became more difficult as the bore fouled. The development of iron, instead of wooden, ramrods was believed to increase the rate of musket fire. However, these ramrods often bent and jammed in the musket, or broke, or rusted, and frequent use of the ramrod distorted the barrel into an oval shape.

There were also production problems with the musket, in part a consequence of the limited capabilities of eighteenth-century industry, not least the absence of standardized mass production. The caliber of individual Prussian muskets ranged between 18 and 20.4 millimeters, while their length varied by up to 8 centimeters. The French 1754-model flintlock was largely handmade, the parts were not interchangeable, and the lock was intricate and difficult to standardize. Further, in 1757, it was estimated that many French muskets could not fire six times without danger of breaking. The situation was little better in the early 1790s, as parts still had very limited interchangeability.

Nevertheless, despite their limitations, flintlocks offered large-scale battlefield firepower, and as a result, many were made. Between 1701 and mid-1704, the British Ordnance Office issued 56,000 muskets. The main Russian state arsenal at Tula produced an annual average of nearly 14,000 muskets between 1737 and 1778. In the 1760s, the French produced 23,000 muskets annually at Charleville and Saint-Etienne, and in 1777, France supplied 23,000 muskets to the American revolutionaries. And by 1814, the British had 743,000 serviceable muskets in store. European armies were not to experience a comparable change in weaponry until the introduction of rifled guns in the nineteenth century.

Artillery Artillery was a sphere in which governments welcomed the opportunities presented by technological progress. Improved boring techniques during the eighteenth century enabled a reduction in the weight of cannon, allowing for more mobile deployment on the battlefield. In the early eighteenth century, a Swiss gunmaker, Johann Maritz, developed a new system of manufacturing cannon. Previously, guns had been cast around a core—which was very difficult to align accurately with the exterior—in a unique mold. In 1715, Maritz and his sons introduced a technique for casting cannon in the solid with the cascabel (a projection behind the breech) facing down, resulting in greater density at the breech, where the shock of the discharge was greatest. The bore was then drilled out horizontally, producing a smoother and more accurate bore. This system spread throughout Europe. Improved casting was crucial to the effectiveness of artillery: Poorly cast guns might crack and had to be allowed to cool between rounds. The new guns were safer, more predictable, more uniform, and lighter, as the Maritz system permitted thinner barrels and a closer fit (windage) between shot and barrel, so that smaller powder charges were possible. This made it safer to reduce the thickness of the chamber in which the explosion occurred. The new casting method helped make artillery more mobile, and this ensured that it came to play a bigger role on the battlefield.

LINEAR TACTICS

Infantry, Cavalry, and Artillery

Infantry It had been very complicated to coordinate pikemen and musketeers in order to ensure the necessary balance of defensive protection and firepower. The new technologies of bayonet and flintlock, in contrast, led to the longer and thinner linear formations and the shoulder-to-shoulder drill in order to maximize firepower that were to characterize European infantry in the eighteenth century, both within Europe and overseas. The use of the bayonet and of flintlocks encouraged the development of offensive tactics, not least because more effective infantry weaponry led European forces to phase out body armor, thus increasing the mobility of their troops. Initially, however, bayonet drills were based on pike drills, with an emphasis on receiving advances. It was not until the 1750s that a new bayonet drill made it easier to mount attacks.

Despite the bayonets, hand-to-hand fighting on the eighteenth-century battlefield was relatively uncommon, and most casualties were caused by gunshot. At the Battle of Malplaquet in 1709, the bloodiest battle of the War of the Spanish Succession, about 2 percent of the wounds suffered by French troops

The Battle of Minden
This painting of the Battle of Minden, fought in 1759 between British and German forces (left) and the French (right), clearly shows both the long linear formations typical of the day and the multiple lines that gave linear armies depth and tactical reserves.

were the result of bayonets. Nevertheless, bayonets were seen as important and were increasingly part of armaments. In 1786, Sir William Fawcett, the British adjutant general, returned to George III two guns the king had sent him, "the bayonet of that which is intended for the use of the Light Infantry having been made to fix, agreeably to your Majesty's directions."

A bayonet charge, preceded by a volley, became a standard British tactic from the late 1750s. At the Battle of Minden in 1759, a key engagement in the Seven Years War, the courage and fire discipline of the British infantry won the battle. They misunderstood orders, advanced across an open plain, and then repulsed two charges by French cavalry. Most of the cavalry casualties were caused by musket fire, but those who reached the British lines were bayoneted. These charges were followed first by a French infantry advance and then by another cavalry attack, which again was stopped by musketry and bayonets. This victory greatly lessened the possibility of French pressure on Britain's ally, Frederick the Great of Prussia.

There were variations in the method of volley fire in which either ranks (lines) or platoons fired, with the Dutch system of platoon fire becoming common during the War of Spanish Succession (1701–14), except among the French. In the 1740s, the Prussians used the Dutch system, with each platoon firing separately, producing a rolling fire, although the French continued to fire by ranks. The French commander Marshal Saxe, the victor over the British at the Battle of Fontenoy in 1745, noted that "the present method of firing by word of command, as it detains the soldier in a constrained position, prevents his leveling with any exactness . . . according to the present method of loading, the soldiers, in the tumult and hurry of an engagement, very seldom ram down their charge, and are also very apt to put the cartridges into the barrel without biting off the caps, by neglecting to do which, many of the arms are of course rendered useless." But similar problems affected all infantry forces of the day. Therefore, while some infantry (especially, from the 1740s, the Prussians) gained some advantage, man for man, in firepower, maneuverability, and discipline over their foes, battles were likely to be won not by superior individual skill but by numbers, chance, and superior generalship, especially in maneuvering and combining infantry with other arms.

Artillery   The technical improvements in artillery noted above made artillery steadily more useful on eighteenth-century battlefields. Above all, lighter, more mobile, guns allowed for the repositioning of batteries on the fly—something that had been impossible in most seventeenth-century battles. Guns could thus be brought to bolster key defensive positions and, more crucially, moved forward to support an attack, as Frederick the Great did at Leuthen (see the Highlights box "The Battle of Leuthen, 1757"). Generals began to create larger concentrations of guns, a trend that would culminate in the grand batteries of Napoleonic practice. But the limited range of smoothbore, muzzle-loaded cannon still required that guns be brought forward of their infantry to open a bombardment, exposing guns and gunners to rapid cavalry strikes. Coordination of infantry, artillery, and cavalry thus required careful timing and experience. Above all, it required artillery officers with daring, initiative, and skill, and the artillery became fully incorporated into regular chains of command. Gone were the civilian specialist engineers who often manned seventeenth-century guns.

Cavalry   Though firepower, from both massed infantry and more mobile artillery, steadily increased in importance through the century, cavalry remained a vital part of every European army. In addition to performing crucial operational duties including scouting and screening, cavalry continued to have significant battlefield uses. The limited range and slow rate of fire of musketry left space for massed cavalry charges that could decide a battle, as when the British cavalry at Blenheim in 1704 cut through the stretched middle of the French line at the end of the day. Artillery unsupported by infantry was quite vulnerable to cavalry attack. But cavalry success against infantry usually depended on catching the infantry tired, disordered, or exposed on flank or rear. Thus, cavalry was also needed to dispute possession of exposed positions against enemy cavalry and to counter enemy cavalry threats generally—again, the performance of Frederick's cavalry at Leuthen provides an excellent example. Finally, cavalry was indispensable in pursuit of a retreating foe.

Mobility was the key to cavalry effectiveness, so like their infantry counterparts, European cavalry steadily shed armor, especially after bayonets completely replaced pikes, reducing the reach of infantry cutting and stabbing weapons. Service in the cavalry also tended to remain the preserve of better-off recruits: It was still the most prestigious part of every army.

Battlefield Patterns

Though eighteenth-century battles were never universally the cautious and stereotyped conflicts they are sometimes presented as, some general patterns of tactical practice are discernible.

We have noted already the impact of bayonet and matchlock technology on tactical formations, leading to longer, thinner lines of infantry designed to maximize the firepower each unit could bring to bear. A second impetus toward more linear formations came from Austrian and Hungarian experiences against the Turks, whose masses of light cavalry consistently threatened to envelop Austrian lines. More extended formations effectively countered this threat and emphasized the growing disparity in firepower between European and Turkish forces.

Yet in another way, "linear" tactics is something of a misnomer for eighteenth-century combat at the grand tactical level. For one of the most significant changes from mid-seventeenth-century warfare was the greater size of individual field armies that the states and economies of the eighteenth century could support. Field forces usually numbered around 20,000 and almost never exceeded 50,000 in the Thirty Years War; by the War of Spanish Succession, armies of 50,000–80,000 were the norm. Larger forces meant that, while individual units formed up in longer, thinner lines than had musket-and-pike formations, armies as a whole could deploy in ways that made greater use of second lines and reserves. A comparison of the deployments at Breitenfeld in 1632—essentially, one line of infantry with artillery in the center and cavalry on the flanks facing a similar formation—with the deeper, more mixed and flexible orders of battle both sides employed at, for example, Blenheim in 1704 or in many of Frederick the Great's battles shows this clearly. Such deployments placed a premium on pre-battle maneuvering in order to maximize any possible positional advantage for either the attacker—the basis of Frederick's so-called oblique attacks—or the defender. In the latter case, generals tried to protect their flanks by basing them on defensible or impassable ground, forcing attackers into costly frontal assaults. Strong defensive positions and the inherent defensive staying power of massed infantry necessitated staged attacks designed to draw in the enemy's reserves before a decisive assault on some weakened part of the line could be launched. The high casualty rates that characterized such battles were no accident.

Larger armies and more extended formations created new problems of command and control, not least in the use of reserves, which could well be crucial. Nevertheless, armies even of 80,000 troops could be deployed on a battlefield that a single commander could have some chance of keeping track of, despite clouds of smoke and variations in terrain. Certainly,

HIGHLIGHTS

The Battle of Leuthen, 1757

Fought on December 5, 1757, this was one of the most important battles in the Austro-Prussian part of the Seven Years War (1756–63). Frederick II, the Great, of Prussia, with a first-rate army of 35,000 troops, advanced to attack a 54,000-strong Austrian army under Prince Charles of Lorraine. Frederick, critically, took and retained the initiative by using a fine example of what is sometimes called an oblique attack (Figure 21.1). This was an important variation on the customary linear tactics of the age: Frederick devised a series of methods for strengthening one end of his line and attacking with it, while minimizing the exposure of the weaker end. This tactic depended on the speedy execution of prebattle operational maneuvers designed to bring Frederick's army to the flank of the enemy line, avoiding a frontal assault. This required well-drilled and well-disciplined troops and risked exposing his army to attack during the flanking march.

Approaching from the west, Frederick used the cover of a ridge to swing the bulk of his army south, turning the Austrian left flank, while a feint led the Austrians to commit their reserves to bolster their right. The Prussians were helped greatly by the use of mobile artillery. Charles, in response, wheeled his army around, creating a south-facing front stretching through the village of Leuthen.

The second phase of the battle centered on repeated Prussian attacks on this new front,

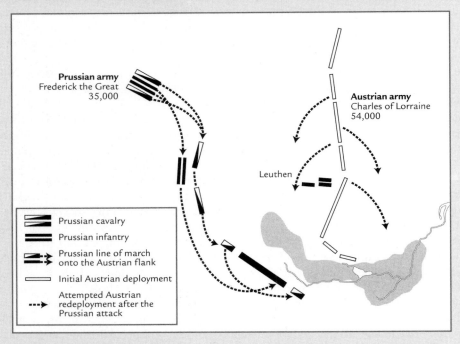

Figure 21.1 The Battle of Leuthen

especially on Leuthen, which was finally carried after bitter fighting. But the Prussian infantry became exposed to the Austrian cavalry. An Austrian cavalry counterattack was prevented from reaching the open flank of the Prussian infantry by the prompt action of the Prussian cavalry, and the battered Austrian infantry finally fled. As so often occurred in the period, nightfall brought the battle to an end.

The Prussians lost 6,380 killed and wounded, the Austrians 10,000 killed and wounded and 12,000 prisoners. After their defeat, the Austrians abandoned most of Silesia, possession of which province had been the focus of the war. Leuthen was a hard-fought victory by a well-honed army. It reflected Prussian firepower, Frederick's skilled exploitation of the terrain, the quality of the Prussian cavalry, and the ability of Prussian commanders to take initiatives.

Figure 21.2 Europe in 1763

the psychological struggle between opposing generals played a significant role in the outcome of many battles. Frederick the Great held a particular advantage over some of his more cautious Austrian opponents in this respect, although, as king as well as general, he also benefited from the concentration of authority. But a professional officer corps became, in fact, more vital than ever as armies grew, and the intelligence and initiative of subordinate commanders played a large role in the success of armies in combat. The development of military academies reflected a conscious embrace of the need for a professionalized military education.

Strategic Settings

The strategic settings for linear tactics differed significantly within and beyond Europe, with extra-European strategy providing a much wider stage for bold moves and unconventional approaches.

Strategy Within Europe The close balance of military ability among the major European powers, reinforced by the consistent formation of large coalitions, did much to limit both strategic ambitions and options for much of the century (Figure 21.2). Also, as in previous centuries, the most contested areas were heavily fortified, which tended to result in careful positional warfare, as did the reliance of large armies on depots and slow cartage for supplies of ammunition and even, to some extent, food. Logistics, particularly in the context of notions of limited war (see the Issues box on page 408) thus remained a major constraint on the rapid overland movement of armies. It was not that generals did not seek bold, decisive strokes, but that such strokes were hard to find in Europe. Continental wars tended to end in mutual exhaustion and a truce.

As a result, once Louis XIV's expansionism had been thwarted at the beginning of the century, the map of European territories changed little. Poland, having failed to develop an effective government or army, disappeared almost without a fight, partitioned by Prussia, Russia, and Austria. Austria also made gains at the expense of the Ottomans (see below). But among the major European powers, only Frederick II's rapid seizure of Silesia from Austria was significant, and almost all the fighting caused by that move was Frederick's defense of his new territory.

Strategy Beyond Europe   On the less confined global stage, however, strategies became vast and ambitious, belying the notion that eighteenth-century warfare was inherently unimaginative and limited. Much of this strategy was focused on European colonial outposts and was thus necessarily amphibious (see also Chapter 25). Britain, the leading naval and colonial power in the world, was the leading practitioner and beneficiary of this sort of strategy, tying down French armies in Europe by financing coalitions of continental allies, blockading French fleets in port, and using command of the seas to isolate and pick off French colonial possessions in North America, India, and the Caribbean. But perhaps the most spectacular success among amphibious strategic moves was the Franco-American convergence on Yorktown in 1781 (see below). The virtually unimaginable and highly fortuitous coordination of a New Jersey–based American army with a Caribbean-based French fleet succeeded in ending the American Revolution. Still, Britain's steady exploitation of its usual maritime supremacy made it the big winner in the century-long colonial competition with France and other European powers.

The scope of these global strategies brought European armies into conflict with a variety of foes in different terrains. Again, far from being inflexible and brittle, royal armies showed themselves capable of adapting to different tactics and opponents, bringing the lessons of frontier warfare back to Europe in the form of increased use of skirmishers, scouts, and light cavalry forces while imposing their own style on areas under their control (see below). Strategy and tactics worked together, and neither was as static as the eighteenth century is sometimes portrayed.

Global Impact

The European presence on the global stage definitely increased in the eighteenth century, in particular in its past twenty-five years. Explaining this growing impact involves distinguishing between the technologies of war and the techniques used to employ those technologies, examining the characteristics of the areas where European influence was greatest, and recognizing the still significant limitation of European power.

Technique and Technology

What increasingly set the European way of war apart from that of other areas of the world in this period was not, fundamentally, technology. Rather, it was the whole range of techniques used to employ armed force, techniques extending from battlefield tactics to the institutional and bureaucratic structures necessary to raise, train, and command European-style armies. These techniques were linked organically to European social structure, governmental practices, and economic activity: Technique was a product of an entire sociomilitary system. While in a broad sense this had always been true of every military system, the general similarities between most preindustrial civilizations had meant that large disparities in the effectiveness of ways of war had heretofore been difficult to achieve. The great disparity prior to the age of gunpowder had been between civilizations and nomadic societies, with the nomads enjoying a general superiority based on an entire way of life foreign to settled peoples (see Chapters 6 and 13). What European developments produced by the middle of the eighteenth century was a similar disparity based on an entire way of life. But this time, it was a difference between settled peoples.

In brief, the effective independent use of European weaponry required the ability to produce such weapons. Some non-Europeans bought significant quantities of arms from Europeans, especially in theaters such as India where Europeans competed; and some, including some Indian states, produced their own muskets and cannon, some of very high quality. But such production tended to come in short bursts sponsored by an ambitious ruler; sustained production and internally generated improvements depended on competitive political and market economic structures rarely found outside Europe. The mass infantry armies that employed the weapons could only be created by strong central governments with professional bureaucracies and secure tax bases. Such armies and governments threatened the roles and privileges of traditional elites, so that the political will to create such forces was rarely uncontested even where it existed. As a result, the European way of war became increasingly more difficult to copy because its set of practices required the support of a social system that was steadily becoming more foreign to traditional modes of organization. In other words, non-Europeans who wished to defend themselves against European intrusion now faced the problem of having to "become European"—adopting European ways at odds with their own traditions—in order to develop European-style armies. This problem, already evident in some regions in the late eighteenth century, would become critical across the globe in the nineteenth century (see Chapter 24).

A few non-European powers did succeed in importing a good deal of the European model. The Marathas in India, in particular, created a fairly effective force that combined European-style infantry and artillery with their traditional cavalry. But it is revealing that the most successful European-style armies outside Europe were either in "new Europes" (the British American colonies) or in Indian states under or competing directly with European rule (see below). In contrast, the gunpowder technologies of 1500, amenable to simpler techniques, had been readily imported by many powers in the sixteenth century, including the Ottomans and the Japanese, both of whom arguably made better use of them than did Europeans (see Chapter 17).

The end result of this development was a growing advantage for European forces. Technological innovation, though slow and incremental, was steady in Europe by now because it was a product of a socioeconomic system with a capitalist core. Institutional and economic support for warfare was steadily becoming more impersonal and therefore reliable: Logistics and leadership were also products now of a system rather than of personalities. Perhaps the best comparison is with the Ottomans. Turkish tactical traditions were still, through much of the eighteenth century, not a bad match for European incursions, as their influence on European tactics, noted above, shows. Though they lost more battles than in earlier centuries, they still won their share. But their main problem against direct European competition involved maintaining armies in the field year-round and over the course of a long war. This was a problem of political will (or lack thereof), administrative corruption, and economic difficulties. Europe's bureaucrats and merchants pushed back the Ottoman frontier as much as its generals and soldiers did. Similarly, British success in India resulted as much or more from the advantage that the institutional immortality and memory

of the East India Company gave it over all-too-mortal Indian rulers who might, individually, create armies that were a match for company forces but who could not guarantee the skill or interest of their dynastic successors.

War and Mercantile Empires

The basis of European success is indicated by the fact that most extra-European conflict between European powers centered on already extant mercantile empires and colonies, and often resulted from the private initiatives of trading companies that raised their own military forces, rather than from official government policy. The British presence in India, for example, was the creation of the British East India Company. But political rivalries played an important role: The century-long economic and military contest between England and France that started with the War of Spanish Succession became global in scope, affecting the Americas and India most of all. The two most significant developments to arise out of this mercantile-military nexus were the spread of European-style drill to the local allies of competing European powers under European leadership and, most important, the American Revolution.

Local Allies and Tactical Traditions   Western forces operating overseas faced novel challenges, and this led to tactical and organizational initiatives. These had only a limited impact on conflict back in Europe, but they reflected the extent to which Western warfare involved a range of tasks and, therefore, challenges. The most important was the development in India of forces that fought on the European model. This fusion of European training and Indian manpower created an opportunity for the European imperial powers, as well as a threat to their position. Indeed, such a fusion was to be a basis of British military power in the nineteenth century, helping in the creation of an imperial state of hitherto unprecedented size and scope. The first Indian troops raised by the East India Company appear to have been two companies of Rajputs enlisted at Bombay in 1684. The mostly native East India Company army was 18,200 strong in 1763, 115,000 in 1782, and 154,000 in 1805. Its officer class remained almost exclusively British, however (as, in fact, the bulk of officers in the armies of its rivals remained European), reflecting and modeling the growing organization of the British-controlled state of India.

A New Europe: The American Revolution   The War of American Independence tends to overshadow other events that occurred between the Seven Years War and the French Revolutionary Wars in the standard Western approach. It was not the sole conflict in the period, but it was important in the global context, and not only because it led to the birth of the United States, the modern military (and academic history) superpower. The war was the first major revolutionary conflict; the first large-scale, transoceanic conflict between a European colonial power and subjects of European descent; and, from 1778, a significant episode in the longstanding struggle between Britain and France. In North America, the war was both revolutionary, in that it was one of the first important modern instances of the "nation in arms," and traditional, in that it was essentially fought on terms that would have been familiar to those who had been engaged in recent conflicts in Europe and North America. The American response to battle, adopting the lines of musketeers of European warfare, was scarcely surprising, as numerous Americans had served in the midcentury British wars against the Bourbons, over 10,000 of them as regulars, while many others were familiar with the methods of European armies, especially the British, through reading, observation, or discussion.

Infantry dominated the battlefields in the middle colonies. However, the potential impact of the trained British musketeers with bayonets that initially inspired fear among the Americans was lessened by the ability of the latter to entrench themselves in strong positions. The value of this tactic was amply demonstrated by the heavy casualties among the British attackers at the Battle of Bunker Hill (June 17, 1775) as they sought to overawe their opponents in the first battle of the war. The terrain of much of America was appropriate for such defenses. In place of the open farmland of much of the northern European plains, where the Seven Years War had been waged in Europe, there were narrow valley routes flanked by dense woodland, deep rivers with few crossing points, and, in New England, the omnipresent stone walls that created ready-made defensive positions. British generals such as Howe and Clinton responded with flanking maneuvers. However, heavily encumbered British regular units, maneuvering and fighting in their accustomed formations, were not only vulnerable in the face of entrenched positions and unsuited to the heavily wooded and hilly terrain of the Canadian frontier, they were also not ideal for the vast expanses of the South. In that relatively sparsely populated region, supplies were harder to obtain. Further, aside from the ports, there were fewer places that it was crucial to hold, and therefore less opportunity for positional warfare, which the British sought to force on the Americans. The hot and humid climate of the South also posed problems for the troops.

In addition to geography, the political dimension helped ensure that the American war and western European *ancien régime* warfare seemed sufficiently different that the practitioners of the former appeared to have little to teach those of the latter. The greater geographic scope and smaller army sizes of American compared to European warfare meant that there were major contrasts in staff-work logistics and operational concepts, while British strategy was fundamentally affected by the politics of widespread commitment to independence on the part of many Americans. This was also true operationally, in the case of the major contributions made by American militias, not least in partisan warfare. This undermined the southern strategy adopted by the British in 1780–81, as it proved impossible to consolidate the British position in the Carolinas. Frederick the Great did not have to face such opponents in Europe.

American generals often used skirmish lines, night marches, and hit-and-run attacks. However, George Washington not only commanded, in the Continental Army, a force that matched many of the socio-professional assumptions of the British army but also chose to fight essentially in a manner to which the British were accustomed; they were not obliged to rethink totally their way of fighting. This was in marked contrast to the unfamiliar logistical and political problems that the British faced in North America. Nevertheless, translated to America, European tactics and fighting quality brought success, strikingly so in 1776, and at the Battle of Camden in 1780, where the British fired accurately as they advanced. Further, British regulars were better at night fighting than the Americans. The Hessian troops hired by the British were also flexible in their tactics, as at the Battle of Long Island in 1776 where they advanced first in skirmishing order.

The British fought to win, but generally cautious generalship and the absence of cavalry to exploit victories made it difficult to translate success in the field into overwhelming American losses, and these occurred only when the revolutionaries held a position whence there was no route for retreat, as at Fort Washington in 1776 and Charleston in 1780. As the revolutionaries became more accustomed to battlefield conditions,

SOURCES

The Battle of Guilford Courthouse

General Nathaniel Greene's account of the March 1781 battle in North Carolina that, though a tactical defeat for the Americans, induced General Cornwallis through high casualties to abandon the Carolinas, contributing substantially to American victory.

■ ■ ■

. . . Finding that our force was much more respectable than it had been, and that there was a much greater probability of its declining than increasing, and that there would be the greatest difficulty in subsisting it long in the field in this exhausted Country, I took the resolution of attacking the Enemy without loss of time, and made the necessary disposition accordingly; being persuaded that if we were successful it would prove ruinous to the Enemy, and if otherwise, it would only prove a partial evil to us. . . .

The greater part of this Country is a Wilderness, with a few cleared fields interspersed here and there. The Army was drawn up upon a large Hill of ground surrounded by other Hills, the greater part of which was covered with Timber and thick under brush. The front line was posted with two field pieces just in the edge of the Woods. . . . The second line was in the Woods about 300 yards in the rear of the first, and the continental Troops about 300 yards in the rear of the second. . . .

The action commenced by a cannonade which lasted about twenty minutes, when the Enemy advanced in three Columns, the Hessians on the right, the Guards in the center and Lieut. Col. Webster's Brigade on the left. The whole moved through the fields to attack the North Carolina Brigades who waited the attack until the Enemy got within about 140 yards, when a part of them began a fire, but a considerable part left the ground without firing at all; some fired once, some twice, and none more. . . . The General and field Officers

did all they could to induce the Men to stand their Ground, but neither the advantages of the position nor any other consideration could induce them to stay. . . . The Virginia Militia gave the Enemy a warm reception and kept up a heavy fire for a long time, but being beaten back, the action became general almost every where. . . . In a word the conflict was long and severe, and the Enemy only gained their point by superior discipline. They having broken the 2d Maryland Regiment, and turned our left flank, and got into the rear of the Virginia Brigade and appeared to be gaining our right, which would have encircled the whole of the Continental Troops, I thought it most advisable to order a retreat. . . . We lost our Artillery and two Ammunition Wagons, the greater part of the Horses being killed before the retreat began, and it being impossible to move the pieces but along the great road. After collecting our Stragglers we retired to this Camp 10 miles distant from Gilford.

[The British lost 532 men out of about 1900; the Americans 326 out of about 4500.] Most of the [missing] have gone home, as is but too customary with Militia after an Action. . . . Our Men are in good spirits and in perfect readiness for another field Day.

SOURCE: Richard K. Showman, Dennis Michael Lonrad, et al., eds., *The Papers of General Nathaniel Greene* (Chapel Hill: University of North Carolina Press, 1976).

their ability to repel British attacks, as at Saratoga in 1776, or to inflict serious casualties, as was shown by the heavy British losses in their victory at Guilford Courthouse in 1781, increased (see the Sources box "The Battle of Guilford Courthouse").

Without reliable popular support in the Thirteen Colonies, the British were obliged both to obtain the bulk of their supplies from Britain and to employ much of their army in garrison duty, an obligation made more necessary by the need to protect supply

The Surrender of Cornwallis   Lord Cornwallis's surrender to General Washington's army at Yorktown effectively ended the Revolutionary War. Cooperation between American ground forces and the French fleet was decisive in the Yorktown campaign.

bases and the crucial transshipment points. Thus, only a part of the army was available for operations, while the seizure of new positions, especially New York and Newport in 1776, forced the British to deploy still more of the troops as garrison units. This helps account for the British emphasis on decisive battles, because it was only by destroying the American field armies that troops could be freed from garrison duty in order to extend the range of British control. American skill and determination in avoiding such defeat was therefore crucial.

From 1778, France, which earlier had provided crucial military supplies to the revolutionaries, formally entered the war, in an attempt to reverse the hegemony Britain had established in the Seven Years War. French intervention added to the range of urgent British military commitments elsewhere in the world. It also threatened British naval control of North American waters and thereby challenged the application of its resources and the articulation of its imperial system. This was followed in 1780 by the dispatch to North America of an expeditionary force under Count Jean de Rochambeau, a veteran of

French campaigns in Germany in the War of Austrian Succession and the Seven Years War. The arrival of this force meant that the French threat was not only a naval one. Already, in 1778, French entry had led the British to abandon Philadelphia.

In 1779, France's ally Spain (which had provided the Americans with gunpowder and bullion via Havana) joined her, and in 1780, the Dutch followed. The result was a major challenge to British power that both helped distract attention and resources from the war in North America and contributed directly to the British defeat at Yorktown in 1781: A large French fleet at the mouth of Chesapeake Bay blocked the attempt to relieve the army besieged there, and General Cornwallis was forced to surrender. This led directly to a crisis of confidence among British parliamentarians, the fall of the government, and peace negotiations.

Lessons and Parallels   Elsewhere, despite losses in the West Indies, West Africa, and the Mediterranean, and the Gulf Coast of North America, most of the British Empire survived attack, including Gibraltar and Jamaica, which had been Spanish targets. British success in retaining most of its empire in part reflected the problems its opponents faced with coalition warfare and, as such, mirrored Prussia's survival in the Seven Years War when attacked by Austria, France, Russia, and Sweden. Coalition warfare posed particular problems for command and control. The War of American Independence also reflected the extent to which much Western warfare did not take place in Europe, although exceptionally so for this conflict.

Moreover, the war indicated the narrow margin between success and failure, as can be seen by contrasting the results of Yorktown in 1781 and the Saintes in 1782. British victory over the French fleet in the latter can be seen as an achievement for a tried naval system, but British failure at Yorktown, as well as at the hands of the Marathas at Wadgaon in India in 1779, indicated that the success of the British military system depended on contingencies. So, too, did the contrast between the success of French military intervention in North America and its failure in India, where the dispatch of troops and warships did not help France's ally, the Sultan of Mysore, overthrow the British in southern India. Had the French general Bussy reached India without delay, with healthy troops and with all his artillery, he would have been more likely to achieve his objectives, not least because Suffren, the French admiral there, was a better naval commander than de Grasse, his counterpart off North America. However, Bussy had far fewer troops than the 10,000 men he had requested, in part because of the ships that were prevented from sailing or were intercepted by the British navy. Losses from scurvy also affected the French.

Land-sea coordination was a matter of both planning and contingencies. British positions, such as Québec in 1776 and Gibraltar in 1779, could be relieved by sea, but those that were not relieved, such as Pensacola and Yorktown in 1781, and Minorca in 1782, were lost. Conversely, British initiatives, such as the plan to capture Cape Town from the Dutch in 1781, were thwarted by the arrival of French warships. The war also indicated Spain's continued military effectiveness. The Spaniards captured Baton Rouge, Manchac, and Natchez in 1779, and Pensacola in 1781; in the last, a Spanish grenade ignited a gunpowder magazine. The world of Spanish commitments, which extended to Algiers in 1775 and the English Channel in 1779 (both unsuccessful expeditions), was very different from that of Prussia, another reminder of the diversity of the period.

Britain as World Power   The War of American Independence ended with the Peace of Versailles in 1783. France received Tobago and Senegal, while Spain received Minorca and Florida. Yet the major British territorial loss was to the Americans, not the French, and Britain remained the leading European power in India. Britain, despite the loss of her American colonies (or even because of that loss, as it clarified her responsibilities and objectives), was by the end of the century the winner in the competition with France. This victory raised her to a position of one of the two great world powers. A brief consideration of the other highlights the continuing limits of European power.

Limits of European Power

China was the other great power of the eighteenth century. The Manchu conquest produced a military system that combined the best features of nomadic cavalry and gunpowder-wielding, fortress-based infantry (see Chapter 19). Internally stable from the 1680s and, like Europe, benefiting from demographic growth and a booming economy, Qing China witnessed a century of imperial expansion that brought it by the 1760s to its greatest territorial extent ever. Tibet, Nepal, and vast areas of Central Asia, including the once-threatening Mongol heartland, came under Chinese control. Qing armies drove the Russians from the Amur River region in the 1680s and had nothing to fear from any European power throughout the century. China was a successful example of a large, traditional, land-based empire. Furthermore, even in 1780, there was little to choose between the efficiency of Chinese and European bureaucracies, the dynamism and standard of living of the core Chinese and European economies, and the richness of Chinese and European intellectual traditions. The dramatic shift in the balance of power toward Europe by 1830 is explicable, however. For the thing, the European (especially British) economy tended to concentrate colonial wealth in England, stimulating industrialization, whereas Chinese policy tended to distribute wealth more equally, so that population growth eventually outran economic growth. For another, economic and military competition in Europe drove technological progress and expansionism faster than in unified China. But the shift was not necessarily predictable nor even inevitable in 1780.

Nor was China the only roadblock to European power in the Far East. Burma successfully played off one European power against another and expanded its sphere of influence. In general, large land-based powers' independence was not threatened by European contact in this period. European influence was still mostly confined to coastal and near-coastal areas, even in the Americas. This emphasizes again that naval warfare and the connection of that warfare to trade and mercantile colonies and empires was the crucial aspect of European advantage—and that advantage came in part because no one else cared to contest the Europeans in that realm. European land warfare, though gaining an edge on other styles, was still not a decisive factor against most foes. The armies that could be sent overseas were too small, supported by too-limited resources, and (at times) too ravaged by tropical diseases to impose European wills freely. Further, most European military effort was expended within Europe. The global ambitions of Europe's monarchical polities, including Britain, were quite limited. They did not want larger empires, and such expansion as did take place was, again, often a result of private, not official, initiatives.

In sum, the eighteenth century was not an age of attempted or achieved European dominance, and we should not read the imperialism of the nineteenth century teleologically into the eighteenth. European armies were by 1789 professional, drilled forces with standardized arms and equipment. But two vital factors were still missing from the equation that would make Europe dominant: First, the expansion of politics beyond a monarchical scope by the creation of national armies motivated by nationalist ideology; and, second, industry, and the range of technological breakthroughs (including medicine), economic muscle, and impetus to expansionism it would bring.

CONCLUSION

By the late eighteenth century, the consolidation of eight centuries of European social, economic, and military evolution was reaching its limits. The social and political structures of absolutism could not raise the size of military establishments significantly, nor could the traditionally organized and powered European manufacturing base equip and supply significantly larger armies for extended periods.

But that very evolution had laid the foundations for truly revolutionary developments in the next century, developments that were closely linked to each other. Mass popular armies, motivated by nationalist ideology, would shatter the social and institutional limits on military manpower (see Chapter 22). And even more fundamentally, the rise of industrial capitalism would provide the wherewithal to feed, equip, and transport these new armies with an ever-expanding range of new military technologies and economic might. These developments would have a massive global impact (see Chapters 23 and 24). An age of revolution was at hand.

SUGGESTED READINGS

Anderson, Matthew. *War and Society in Europe of the Old Regime, 1618–1789*. New York: St. Martin's Press, 1988. An effective guide to the main elements of war in this period.

Black, Jeremy. *European Warfare in a Global Context, 1660–1815*. London: Routledge, 2007. Brings his *European Warfare 1660–1815* (London: UCL Press, 1994) up to date; a comprehensive and authoritative account distinguished by its global perspective.

Duffy, Christopher. *The Military Experience in the Age of Reason*, 2nd ed. Ware, Hertfordshire: Wordsworth Editions, 1998. Good for the social and intellectual contexts of warfare in the eighteenth century.

Frost, Robert. *The Northern Wars, 1558–1721*. Harlow: Longman, 2000. The best introduction to warfare in northern Europe.

Hill, J. Michael. *Celtic Warfare 1595–1763*. Edinburgh: J. Donald, 1986. An account of a type of conflict very different from the European norm.

Starkey, Armstrong. *War in the Age of Enlightenment, 1700–1789*. Westport: Greenwich Press, 2003. Focuses more on the role of ideas than other works of this type.

Ward, Harry. *The War for Independence and the Transformation of American Society*. London: Routledge, 1999. Locates the American War of Independence in its wider context.

Wilson, Peter. *German Armies: War and German Politics, 1648–1806*. London: Routledge, 1998. Important for the connection of armed force to politics both within and between German states.

CHAPTER 22

From Bastille to Blockade: Revolution and the Napoleonic Wars, 1792–1815

The series of conflicts that began with the outbreak of war between Austria and revolutionary France in the spring of 1792 and lasted until the defeat of France's dictatorial ruler Napoleon Bonaparte by British and Prussian forces at Waterloo in 1815 was the most sustained in Europe since the Thirty Years War of 1618–48. Further, it was more far-flung than the latter because it directly involved Britain and Russia and also spanned the world of the European colonies. As a result, these wars were waged in the Caribbean and the Indian Ocean as much as in such traditional European battlegrounds as the Rhineland and northern Italy.

The Revolutionary and, especially, Napoleonic Wars have played such a central role in traditional military historiography that the question of how revolutionary the warfare of the period actually was becomes central. And as we will see, the answer is mixed. In some ways, the warfare of this period simply represented the culmination (some might say perfection) of trends visible in the eighteenth century that we examined in the previous chapter. Above all, this was true of the technological means of waging war, where major changes would not be seen until after 1830. But in other ways, including army numbers and organization, there were advances that would later be multiplied by new technology, and the period saw developments in the ideology of war, especially in the rise of modern nationalism, that would have increasing importance globally. For wars such as these had global implications and must be assessed at least in part from a global perspective. Such a perspective casts a different light on the strategic shape and overall significance of wars viewed too often simply as paradigms of excellence in the "Art of War."

CONTEXTS FOR WAR

The Revolutionary and Napoleonic Wars took place in a Europe that was on the cusp of revolutionary developments in politics—of which the French Revolution itself was the first and most crucial episode—social structure and class conflict, and economics. Such contexts complicate the task of assessing the nature of the wars themselves, for disentangling cause and effect can be difficult. Further, the real impact of change even in these areas would often come after the wars were over, so that revolutionary transformation should definitely not be overstressed as the context for these wars.

The Political Context

Geopolitics This is especially true of the political context in terms of the geopolitics and strategic interests of the major powers of Europe in 1789, which existed in a diplomatically mediated state system that had been in development for a century and half when the wars broke out.

The geopolitical map of Europe can be analyzed in terms of three main categories of powers and places (Figure 22.1). First, there were what might be called the continental powers—the countries whose outlook and major concerns were, first and foremost, focused within Europe and on the other continental powers: France, Austria, and Prussia. Prussia was the most confined to a purely European perspective, and despite a reputation for military effectiveness built during the wars of Frederick the Great, it was in the most precarious position. Austria looked outward a bit more thanks to a shared border with the Ottomans, but since its relations with the latter were confined to the Balkans, it was hardly less Europe-centered than Prussia. France, on the other hand, had considerable overseas possessions in the Americas and the Indian ocean, and had the potential, at least, to be among those powers with significant enough extra-European interests to transcend the continental category. But in practice, French focus and effort remained European during the wars of this period.

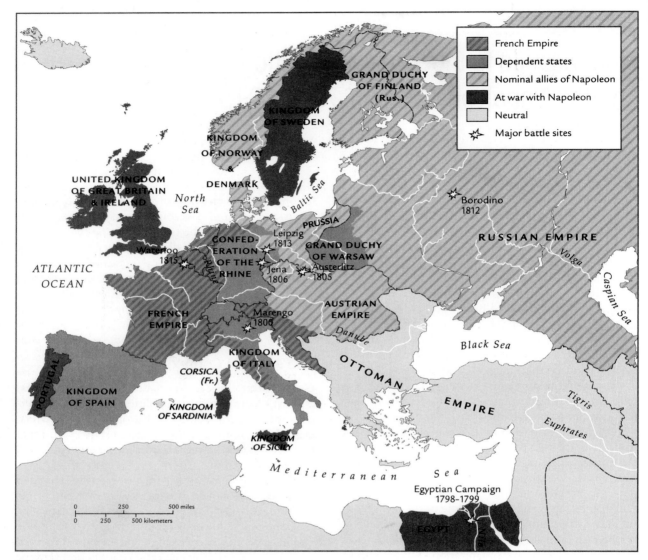

Figure 22.1 Europe Around 1808

A second category consisted of what might be called battle zones: the Low Countries (Belgium, Holland, and Luxembourg), the Rhineland, northern Italy, and Poland. These were characterized by weak or fragmented polities (despite usually rich economies) that occupied geographic passageways between great powers and thus saw a disproportionate share of warfare.

Third, there were the extra-continental powers. The two most important were Britain and its network of colonies concentrated in the Americas (even after the loss of the Thirteen Colonies) and in India, and Russia, whose interests looked not just to eastern Europe but south toward the Black Sea and the Ottomans, and

east to Siberia and its border with the Asian superpower China. In the second rank, Spain and its American colonial empire was also to play a role in the wars.

The varied interests and outlooks of these different powers played a major role in causing participation in the conflicts of the period and help explain why there were not solely two clear-cut sides at conflict—revolutionary and counterrevolutionary—from 1792 to 1815. Continuity of interests from before 1792 account for the Austrian, Prussian, and Russian partition of Poland in 1795, which extinguished its independence until 1918. Long-standing territorial interests also reflected Russian involvement in the Baltic and the Balkans, Prussian expansionism in north Germany, and Spanish aspirations in Italy and Portugal. Of course, Britain had colonial ambitions, and it was not only the French who were predatory. Such concerns could take precedence over ideological issues and encourage alliances of mutual profit and benefit that might be at odds with ideology. Thus, having fought revolutionary France from 1793, Spain allied with it from 1796, undermining the position of its recent ally Britain. Similarly, in Germany, the electors (princes) of Bavaria, Saxony, and Württemberg each allied with Napoleon, in turn receiving territories and promotion to kingships. The pursuit of territorial expansion was driven by the sense of flux and opportunity created by the disruptions of the French Revolutionary and Napoleonic period. Further, concern about expansionism by others helped spur powers forward. This was particularly so in the case of Poland, where Austrian and Prussian expansionism owed much to concern about each other and about the apparently inexorable westward advance of Russia. Indeed, for all three powers, especially Russia, the Polish question was at times as important as, if not more important than, the fate of western Europe. This can be underplayed because of the influence of labels such as "the French Revolutionary and Napoleonic Wars."

Such factors created serious problems for states trying to construct coalitions against France and also produced tensions within them. Britain, which used the profits of its global trade network to finance these coalitions, frequently complained about the failure of its allies to focus on France. Thus, in 1795, Prussia left the First Coalition and did not fight France again until 1806, in the War of the Third Coalition. Badly defeated that year, Prussia became a French client state and was unwilling to support Austria against France in 1809, in the War of the Fourth Coalition. Prussia also assisted in the French invasion of Russia in 1812; indeed, it did not turn against Napoleon until 1813, after the total failure of that invasion, although it then pressed hard for the overthrow of Napoleon. Thus, ideology frequently provides little guidance to the policies of particular states.

The Politics of Absolutism Nevertheless, the internal politics of the major European powers and the relationship of those politics to the French Revolution were a critical aspect of the political context of the wars. We will examine the ideological issues further below. What is important here is a recognition of the limits and contradictions of ancien régime (the old

European order) absolutist polities, limits and contradictions that had in large part led to the French Revolution and threatened the ability of French opponents to respond effectively to the threat posed by revolutionary armies.

These had to do with the dynamics of royal absolutism, which was in reality far from absolute. The political monopoly exercised by monarchs to the formal exclusion of nobility, bourgeoisie, and commoners was bought from the nobility with the granting of legal privileges, including tax exemptions and power over their peasant tenants, and social privileges that included, for example, Prussian noble expectation not just of a command position in the army but of relative freedom of action in that position. Royal power could not exist without noble consent (as rulers of both Prussia and Austria discovered when they tried to abolish serfdom on noble estates). However, the cost of noble consent was a system that created a target for discontented bourgeois interests and threatened the bases of popular support. Such limits constrained the ability of French opponents to adopt the French *levée en masse* (a general conscription), for example, because of its implications for the absolutist order of politics.

These contradictions and constraints were avoided to some extent and in different ways by Britain and Russia. The peculiar British constitutional settlement that emerged after the Glorious Revolution of 1688 meant that aristocratic power was real and institutionalized. And both the openness of British nobility to newcomers by wealth and the mechanisms of parliamentary influence, which allowed for the purchasing of representation by mercantile and manufacturing interests, assured broad support among all the politically powerful classes (with the vital side effect that the British fiscal system was both solid and apparently bottomless, unlike those of many absolutist states—the French Revolution had begun, after all, with a French bankruptcy crisis). Russian absolutism, in contrast, was more firmly rooted in a subservient nobility tied to state service and the lack of much of a troublesome bourgeoisie—protected, in a sense, by its economic backwardness as Britain was by its advanced economy. It is not coincidental that these two powers formed France's most persistent and dangerous foes.

Social Contexts

The limits and contradictions of absolutism with respect to the rising power of the bourgeoisie is clearly also a social context of the wars. Threats to aristocratic legal and social power, again defused in the British system and less pressing in Russia, formed the social backdrop of revolutionary ideology and the justification for French-created regime change in a number of places. The reordering of society by the revolution released a great deal of human and material resources, contributing to the effectiveness of French military efforts throughout the period.

Social complexity—or, more bluntly, class conflict—also contributed to the uses of military force in this period as in most others. The French revolutionaries fielded forces against domestic opponents. The various struggles against counterrevolutionaries, especially in the Vendée in western France in 1793–94, were antecedent to the bitter civil conflict and counterinsurgency warfare of the nineteenth, twentieth, and twenty-first centuries, not least with the difficulties of distinguishing between fighters and civilians, and with atrocities against the latter. Napoleon's rise to power dates to 1795, when he came to the aid of the French government using artillery firing at point-blank range, the "whiff of grapeshot," to put down a rebellion in Paris. As a result, he was given command of the Army of Italy, which provided a springboard via military success to political power.

Economic Contexts

Social change was, in turn, built on economic developments ongoing in Europe, though very unevenly. These, too, are an important context of the wars. Britain, France, and the Netherlands, in particular, had by the late eighteenth century moved to the center of a global system of world trade that was lucrative and, in the form of the slave trade, often brutal. Caribbean sugar production was especially important—the annual value of Britain's trade in sugar exceeded the total value of its trade with the Far East—and the protection and exploitation of this source of wealth was intimately tied up with the development and extension of European sea power (see Chapter 25), which Britain came definitively to dominate in the course of these wars. The wealth of the Caribbean sugar trade specifically and the resources of the Americas more generally were already contributing to the early stages of industrialization in England. Industrial output was of limited importance in itself as a factor in Britain's wars with Napoleon, although the influx of cheap British cotton goods had contributed to the increasing poverty of French peasants, who had been used to extending their farming income with home weaving, and so contrib-

uted to the unrest that exploded in the revolution. But it indicates the unusual development of the British economy, whose broad social basis led Napoleon to dismiss the British as a "nation of shopkeepers." He underestimated the shopkeepers to his detriment.

The French economy was itself quite rich and sophisticated, and supported the largest population in Europe outside of Russia. Russian economic backwardness, in contrast, was disguised by the sheer size of the country and its population; in a world that was effectively still totally preindustrial, and in which technological change was incremental, such scale counted for a lot. It should also be noted that, despite the centrality of the Atlantic seaboard of Europe to the global trade network, the economic powerhouse of the system was China, which also remained the world's strongest land power. This is a reminder that economic output, and the related but not identical ability of states to tap the economic production of the countries they ruled for fiscal wealth, constituted the sinews of war.

Ideological Contexts

A standard approach to the wars of this period identifies ideological conflict as their cause. Although this exaggerates its role, as we saw above in examining geopolitical factors, the radicalism of the French Revolution—specifically, its opposition from 1792 to the cause of kings and its espousing of the Rights of Man (encapsulated in the trinity of liberty, equality, and fraternity)—played a role. It led the advancing forces of the revolution to create republics (or, where republics already existed, more radical republics) in Italy, Switzerland, and the Low Countries. Although Napoleon, the French general who seized power in 1799, making himself emperor in 1804, abandoned this republican commitment (his traditionalist outlook shows in his adoption of the imperial title as well as in his disdain for shopkeepers), he also rejected much of the ancien régime, and helped codify many of the principles of the revolution in French law. He displaced long-established rulers, such as the Bourbon dynasty in Spain in 1808, and redistributed their territories, frequently to the benefit of his relatives.

Alongside this radicalism, it is possible to point to counterrevolutionary goals on the part of the ancien régime forces. These certainly motivated Austria and Prussia in 1792. Further, when Napoleon was overthrown, first in 1814 and then, more conclusively, in 1815, it was in order to restore Louis XVIII, a brother of King Louis XVI, who was executed by the revolutionaries in 1793. Ideology also played a role at the level of the individual soldiers. Many French troops in the 1790s were fired up by a commitment to the radical cause. So, too, were some of their opponents—most obviously, the Spanish guerrillas who resisted Napoleonic forces during the Peninsular War of 1808–14.

The radicalism of the French Revolution dissipated fairly quickly, however. The more lasting ideological effect of the wars, an effect that became part of the context of the wars while they were still going on, was to spread the idea of nationalism. Although British nationalism had begun to emerge organically as part of the ideological fallout of the Revolution of 1688, European nationalism was born, effectively, with the French *levée en masse* of 1793: Soldiers from every region of France, who probably conceived of their identity more in regional than national terms, were brought together and deluged with revolutionary propaganda. The effect was to forge a French national identity, a national army that fought as much for the abstraction of *la patrie* as for revolutionary principles. When it marched through Europe conquering in the name of the revolution, the idea that spread most effectively with it was that armies could be inspired to fight for Prussia, for Mother Russia, even for Bourbon Spain, and so forth—an effect that increased resistance to rather than acceptance of French conquest on the part of occupied populations. This is an effect whose parallels are visible in the Middle East today.

Not that the implications or effects of nationalism were simple or unproblematic. In the long run, it was an ideology that could inspire unification of separate states, as later in the nineteenth century in Germany under Prussian leadership or in Italy. But it could also threaten the territorial integrity of states suddenly viewed as multinational—what was the role of Hungarians in the Austrian Empire, after all, and what had happened to the Poles when Poland disappeared? Some of this complexity affected the dynamics of the Revolutionary and Napoleonic Wars even as nationalist ideology was in its infancy.

STRUCTURES OF WAR

Manpower and Organization

Numbers: The **Levée en Masse** The *levée en masse,* the general conscription ordered in August 1793, was the key to the successful deployment of France's human resources not just ideologically but organizationally, while the social and fiscal reforms made possible by the revolution allowed for the support and sustaining of a mass army despite the strains of prolonged conflict. Under this system, the entire population could be obliged to serve the war effort, and all single men age 18–25 were required to join the army.

With France turning to conscription in order to mobilize its large population, the armies it raised were far larger than those deployed by any European power hitherto. Previously, the size of the French army had peaked briefly under Louis XIV at around 400,000, a level that proved unsustainable, but had usually been between 300,000–350,000 men. The first conscription raised that number to over 800,000. Such numbers enabled France to operate effectively on several fronts at once, to sustain casualties, and to match the opposing forces of much of Europe. The availability of larger numbers of French troops told, particularly as Allied cohesion was limited. Superiority in numbers was important in both battles and campaigns. In addition to the obvious advantage of larger armies for battles, larger individual armies and total forces directly affected operational and strategic options. Fortresses that might have stopped an eighteenth-century army could be blockaded or invested with a secondary force larger than earlier main forces, while the primary force proceeded rapidly onward. The limitations of positional warfare were, in other words, overcome as much by numbers as by altered mentalities.

Divisions and Corps The armies raised by the first *levée en masse* and then continually reinforced by its institutionalization were systematized by Lazare Carnot, head of the military section of the Committee of Public Safety, who brought a crucial measure of organization to what, at first, had been mass military confusion. His success in forming and training new units was instrumental in the transformation of a royal army into a nation in arms. The creation of a streamlined training program and massive numbers of new regiments was only part of the organizational challenge, however. Deploying such numbers effectively on campaigns, especially in ways that would maximize French advantages in morale and flexibility on the march and in battle, demanded a second level of innovation during the course of the wars.

What emerged first was the combined-arms division, which grouped together a number of smaller infantry units with their own integrated artillery and support services. The division of 5000–6000 men

Certificate of Merit

A certificate of merit awarded to an officer of the French Army of the Rhine in the 1805 campaign. Promotions based on merit forged a French officer class of high quality and initiative out of men from varied social backgrounds.

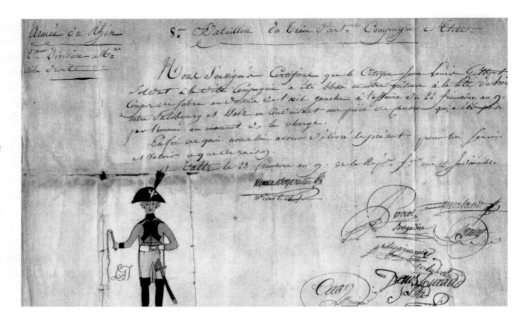

proved an ideal-size unit for battlefield command and control purposes, large enough to matter but small enough to retain flexibility. Under Napoleon, a second tier of organization developed that was aimed at solving the problems of command on campaign: the corps. The corps combined several infantry divisions with a corps artillery battery and cavalry, forming a small, self-contained army. Corps became the basic operational unit of command under Napoleon, often marching on separate routes and combining only when a battle developed, and were capable of fighting a battle independently. This was evident in 1806 when Davout's III Corps by itself defeated the main Prussian force at Auerstadt while Napoleon crushed a subsidiary force at Jena that he thought was the main Prussian army.

That very defeat inspired Prussian attempts to institute military reforms modeled on the French experience; similar imitation happened in the Austrian and Russian armies. By 1813, the Prussians were deploying an army reformed, in part, by a greater emphasis on merit in the appointment and promotion of both officers and enlisted men, so as to increase its operational flexibility and tactical fighting qualities. This also entailed a marked attempt to raise more troops by introducing a comprehensive obligation to serve either in the army or in the *Landwehr* (citizen militia), although initially it proved difficult to combine quality with quantity under the pressures of war and the limits of the Prussian political system. However, the Prussians still fought by brigades rather than using corps, and other forces moved haltingly toward the French model of higher level units.

Command and Control   The combination of infantry, artillery, and cavalry in a corps and, at a lower tactical level, of artillery, skirmishers, and assault columns on the battlefield (see below) ensured that command and coordination skills became more important to the officer corps of French Revolutionary (and eventually all Napoleonic-era) armies. The French benefited from young and determined commanders, and the average age of command was far lower than in the armies of France's opponents. Talent flourished under a strictly meritocratic system freed of aristocratic domination: Notable French commanders who rose through the ranks included Jean-Baptiste Jourdan, a former private; Lazare Hoche, a former corporal; and another corporal, named Napoleon Bonaparte. There was also, at least initially at the battalion level, a more democratic command system. The meritocracy of French command proved one of the hardest aspects of French innovation for France's foes to copy, as it was tied so deeply to the social and political implications of the revolution. Military professionalism and the social cohesion of an elite (whether Prussian Junkers or Englishmen from the playing fields of Eton) could certainly supply competent commanders, but not in the numbers or with the depth of quality that the French system did.

The "Art of War"

The Napoleonic Wars have been a major focus of the academic study in the West, both civilian and military, of the so-called Art of War. Here, too, both continuities and innovations are visible.

Technology There was no major technological transformation leading to new means of conflict during the wars of this era. This is particularly notable because there were signs of what would subsequently become major changes. The period saw experiments with steamships and submarines, the use of manned balloons for observation by the French in the 1790s, and the development of an artificial communication system in the form of the semaphore. The list of novelties included shrapnel, a new type of exploding shell, as well as the first use of rockets in the West, including land-to-land and sea-to-land missiles.

The semaphore was an important example of the increased application of the scientific method to aspects of military affairs during the period. Given official approval in 1793, Claude Chappe developed the semaphore telegraph, a set of arms pivoting on a post that provided opportunities for multiple positions and thus messages. The system had a capacity of 196 different combinations of signs and an average speed of three signs a minute. Furthermore, code could be employed. The network of semaphore stations, with an average distance of 7 miles between them, created from 1794 by the French Revolutionary government, was extended by Napoleon to reach Venice, Amsterdam, and Mainz, each of which the French controlled. In favorable weather, a message could be sent the 150 miles from Paris to Lille in five minutes, although fog, poor weather, and darkness gravely limited the system. Telescopes on towers constructed about 5–10 miles apart were used to read messages. No better system of communications was devised until the electric telegraph. The Paris-to-Lille route was important because Lille was a key base for French operations on the northeastern frontier. This frontier was under attack from allied forces in 1792–94, and, in turn, the French made decisive advances there in 1794.

The semaphore system was copied abroad, an aspect of the way in which what appeared to be best practice was rapidly diffused within the Western world. Chappe's work was translated into English by Lieutenant-Colonel John Macdonald, a military engineer who did much work himself on improving telegraphy, publishing *A New System of Telegraphy* in 1817. In the 1790s, the British Admiralty in London was linked to the major base of Portsmouth by semaphore, while Sweden also built some stations. Furthermore, nine stations were constructed along the Lines of Torres Vedras, fortified positions built in 1810 by the Duke of Wellington to protect Lisbon against French attack. In good weather, a message could be sent the 22 miles from the Atlantic to the River Tagus in seven minutes.

Nevertheless, semaphore networks were very limited, in part because of visibility problems but also because the stations were vulnerable to attack. Indeed, British naval forces in the Mediterranean put ashore parties in order to attack the stations. Napoleon investigated the possibility of a mobile semaphore system for his 1812 invasion of Russia but decided it was not viable. Most orders and reports were still handwritten and communicated by mounted messengers, both on the battlefield and at the operational level.

Indeed the overwhelming technological reality was of continuity in weaponry. In 1815, as in 1792, armies relied on muzzle-loaded smoothbore muskets and cannon. Armies marched or rode on campaign and in battle, and their supplies were transported in wagons drawn by draught animals. Alongside these were other profound continuities linked to the constraints created by exposure to disease and those arising from the difficulties of food preservation. These again had important consequences both for individual soldiers and for operational possibilities. Such continuities need emphasizing because there is a tendency to stress the main changes that characterized the warfare of revolutionary France. Further, it is in part because all the major powers were fighting with essentially the same well-understood technologies that generalship and Art of War factors can loom so large in analyses of these wars.

New Tactics The French Revolution stimulated French interest in new tactics. This continued the widespread discussion about new ideas that had been a feature of military circles in ancien régime France, notably from the 1720s and especially after the experience of defeat at the hands of Frederick the Great of Prussia at Rossbach in 1757. There had been considerable interest in how best to restore the offensive to the battlefield and, in particular, how to overcome the apparent impasse created by the massed firepower of linear formations of musketeers. This anticipated the comparable interesting new ideas after the experience of trench warfare during World War I.

Columns appeared to be the answer and became the characteristic battlefield maneuver of French Revolutionary forces. The most effective way to use the mass of inexperienced soldiers called up for the revolutionary armies was in independent attack columns. This was also best for an army that put an emphasis on the attack. Column advances were far more flexible than those in lines, as it was difficult to maintain line formations during an advance. Columns were used in victories such as Jemappes in 1792, a key battle in the conquest of the Austrian Netherlands (modern Belgium). A reliance on columns helped give the French an edge in battlefield mobility, which was to be important to Napoleon's effectiveness. Frontal attacks by columns were not without disadvantages, of course. They could suffer heavy casualties due to firepower wielded by defending line formations, while only those at the front of the columns could use their firepower. Columns were also more vulnerable than lines to concentrated defensive cannon shot, as one ball could take out an entire file of men.

On the other hand, the French combined columns with an increased use of offensive cannon fire, especially massed batteries that would blast holes in enemy formations in preparation for an infantry attack. This practice built on ancien régime reforms in French artillery, not least a standardization of gun types. Napoleon, originally an artillery officer, proved adept early in his career at improvising artillery concentrations at decisive moments and points in a battle, contributing in no small part to his success.

The French also used large numbers of skirmishers. This proved to be a successful meshing of tactical elements matched to the technology of the times and the character of the new republican soldiers, who, because of their ideological training and commitment, were seen by their commanders as less likely to desert if freed from the confines of a mass, disciplined formation. Sent in advance of the columns and deployed in open order so that they were less vulnerable to volley fire or to cannon, the skirmishers used individual fire to inflict casualties on the close-packed lines of their opponents. This affected the morale of the latter and also disrupted their formations. Skirmishers were deployed in whole units from line regiments and were thus more integrated into the French force structure than, say, their Prussian counterparts, who composed separate units specially trained for skirmishing. Any French infantryman could in theory deploy as a skirmisher, in line, in column, or even in square, a forma-

tion generally used by infantry units faced with large masses of cavalry. Napoleon deployed his army in several large squares against the Egyptian Mamluks at the battles of Shubra Khit and Embabeh, the latter known as the Battle of the Pyramids, in 1798, combining the firepower of densely packed infantry with the tactical flexibility of formations that could not be put at a disadvantage by being attacked in flank or rear by more mobile cavalry. Turning the tables, in 1815, the center of Wellington's line at Waterloo formed into regimental squares to face a great French cavalry charge led by Marshall Ney. Squares were relatively immobile, however, and vulnerable to artillery, and so saw much less frequent use than lines and columns.

Most of France's enemies gradually adopted at least some of the French emphasis on columns and artillery. However, they remained limited at times by organizational and ideological factors, and man for man, few infantry forces could match the French until late in the wars, when Allied improvements met the declining quality of the French army under the pressure of massive losses, especially in the Russian campaign. One exception was the British infantry. The disciplined firepower of the British infantry played a major part in Wellington's victories in the Iberian Peninsula. The infantry almost always deployed in lines a mere two deep, capable thanks to excellent training of maintaining almost continuous fire, making defensive stands by this "Thin Red Line" formidable. Wellington often made optimal use of these qualities by combining an operational or strategic offensive with the tactical defensive, using an incursion into enemy territory to provoke a battle on his own terms. British infantry firepower was not necessarily immobile, however, but rather was often used as a prelude to a bayonet charge. Ably executing fire and movement tactics, the British succeeded in balancing the well-drilled line that represented the legacy of Frederick the Great with extensive use of light infantry in battle, combining linear firepower formations with a greater role for troop maneuverability and tactical flexibility. The corresponding cost was that the professional British army could not hope to match the overall numbers of troops raised by major continental powers.

As in eighteenth-century warfare, the short range and relatively slow reload rate of smoothbore muskets and artillery left a substantial role for cavalry on Napoleonic battlefields. Well-timed charges in support of artillery bombardments and infantry attacks could deliver a decisive blow to the morale and cohesion of

The Battle of Waterloo
This engraving shows French cavalry attacking a British infantry unit formed up in square formation in the Battle of Waterloo. The square was excellent against cavalry but vulnerable to artillery fire. Success in battle relied on skillful use of combined-arms tactics.

enemy infantry formations and also often served as effective counterattack forces against spent enemy infantry or cavalry attackers. But cavalry units were fragile, tending to lose cohesion rapidly in a charge, and a blown and disordered formation was itself extremely vulnerable to counterattack. The quality of French horses and many of the same elements of morale and leadership that contributed to the effectiveness of French infantry also made its cavalry among the best. Further, Napoleon developed the technique of gathering much of his cavalry into a large central reserve cavalry corps, regularly under the daring leadership of Joachim Murat, which multiplied its battlefield impact. Cavalry remained indispensable for scouting and pursuit.

Grand Tactics It is at the larger level of maneuvering entire units on the battlefield (and, at the operational level, maneuvering that led up to a battle, treated below) that issues of generalship, as opposed to unit-level command and control, begin to emerge more clearly, and where much of the interest in the Napoleonic-era Art of War has focused. However, it is also where historians' construction of reality after the fact is most potentially distorting. Battles are inherently chaotic, confused, and difficult to control centrally—no Napoleonic commander had as much impact on the shape of a battle as the command choices of a board game or computer simulation of Napoleonic warfare seem to convey. But it was in the interests of successful generals, not least Napoleon, to play up their role in victories, a tendency that fitted with the general emphasis of European military history and analysis at the time and subsequently. The great historiographical counterstatement against this "Great Man" tendency in analyses of battlefield generalship is Leo Tolstoy's account of the Battle of Borodino in his epic novel *War and Peace*. Tolstoy's focus is on the lack of control exerted by the top generals, the fogginess of information flows, and the contingency and near-randomness of the many small events that added up to battlefield success—a focus that calls into question any analysis of generalship at the grand tactical level.

We may accept Tolstoy's critique as a strong caution without giving up such analysis altogether, however, for some patterns are discernible through the cloud of contingency and partisanship. Indeed, a sort of historiographical middle ground has emerged about Napoleon himself. Historian Owen Connelly has characterized Napoleon as an effective battlefield improviser, not necessarily controlling the flow of events but reacting to the opportunities chance laid at his feet more rapidly and effectively than most of his opponents: In the terms of Connelly's book title, he "blundered to glory." This is probably a fair assessment, especially if this is taken as a model of the upper limit of battlefield command effectiveness. One key to effective improvisation was Napoleon's ability to gain and use the initiative, the most impressive feature of his generalship. In modern terms, he got within the decision loop of his opponents and, as a consequence, was able to maximize the fighting capabilities of his men. His ability to maneuver on the battlefield brought victory over the Austrians at Arcole (November 15–17, 1796) and Rivoli (January 14–15, 1797), and associated Napoleon's name with military success.

For all his reputation as a tactician, though, Napoleon actually was more effective at the operational level, where many of his battles were won virtually before they began (see below, including the Highlights box). Although he pushed innovations in the massing of artillery and cavalry, was a master at siting cannon, and early in his career showed skill at maneuvering units onto his enemies' flanks and rear, later in his career his battles became steadily more blunt, less characterized by finesse than by brute force and frontal attacks. In addition to personal factors that may relate to his declining energy as he aged and to an ill-considered lack of respect for his opponents stemming from his early success, a large part of this probably relates to the increasing size of battlefield armies across the span of the wars. The difference between controlling 30,000–50,000 men, as at Marengo (1800), and 80,000–90,000, as at Borodino (1812) is significant, and undoubtedly makes the latter conform more closely to Tolstoy's model of contingent chaos. When armies of well over 100,000 met at Leipzig, the numbers exceeded any one man's ability to respond to events rapidly or creatively given the limited communications technology of the time, even with the best staff. Brute force was all that was left to either side, and in that event, the numbers told against Napoleon.

Further, a number of his opponents showed certain skills as battlefield commanders. Wellington was at least his match in assessing and using terrain effectively, a number of Russians showed tenacity in defending positions, while the Prussian Blücher was second to none at least in a dogged determination born of utter hatred of his opponent. Where Napoleon gained another advantage on the battlefield was in the excellent set of corps commanders he depended on, whose initiative and talent won a number of engagements, including Davout's remarkable victory at Auerstadt.

Operations   It was at the operational level, the maneuvering of troops within a particular campaign and theater, that Napoleon excelled, and it is where the interest of military professionals in Napoleonic warfare probably peaks as well. The main features of his operational motif were visible as early as the northern Italian campaign of 1796. He showed great self-confidence, displaying in particular determination to gain the initiative. Napoleon also displayed his commitment to swift decision making using rapidity of movement to enhance the impact of his forces. He got his troops to march faster than his opponents in part by arranging for careful staff work that minimized logistical obstacles. He also used the army's divisional and corps structure to advance along many routes toward one objective. This allowed him to concentrate strength at what he chose as the decisive point. In addition, he was concerned to secure the exploitation of interior lines. In northwestern Italy, Napoleon seized a central position between the Austrians and the king of Sardinia (ruler of Piedmont), defeating both in turn and knocking Sardinia out of the war. He made similar uses of rapid marches, concentration of forces from converging routes, and exploitation of interior lines on much larger scales in the 1805 Austerlitz campaign (see the Highlights box "The Campaign and Battle of Austerlitz, 1805") and the 1806 Jena-Auerstadt campaign. In the latter case, he actually analyzed the strategic position so much more effectively than the Prussians that he converged on where the latter should have been rather than where they really were, setting up Davout's victory over what Napoleon thought would be at best a supporting force.

It is important to note the conditions that made such operations possible, however, as well as their limitations. Western and central Europe were economically prosperous, which meant that troops could forage relatively easily across broad swathes of territory. The region also had a fairly extensive network of good roads. The combination of these factors meant that Napoleon's (and his opponents') divisions and corps were not dependent on depots, nor were they confined to a few main roads, allowing them to march along parallel or convergent routes and increasing their operational flexibility. In areas such as central Spain and, above all, Russia, where these basic conditions did not hold, operational options were far more

Camps at Boulogne
Napoleon's *Grande Armée* waits in camp at Boulogne for the invasion of England that never came. British control of the seas proved decisive at the global strategic level of the Napoleonic Wars.

restricted, and French armies proved far more vulnerable to guerrilla resistance, scorched-earth policies, and ambushes. It was precisely these two theaters that saw Napoleonic France's longest-running problem and its greatest disaster, respectively.

WAR ON THE CONTINENTAL SCALE

Grand Strategy

The grand strategies, such as they were, of many of the players in the Napoleonic Wars came down essentially to survival as independent political entities. From this perspective, Poland failed and Prussia came close to failure, enduring a period after 1806 of clientage to France. This same grand strategic aim can loosely be said to have animated the Spanish resistance to an enforced change of royal dynasty and Portugal's alliance with Britain. Only France, Britain, and Russia had grand strategies extending much beyond survival.

Power Projection   For each of these three powers, the key to their grand strategy was ensuring the projection of their own power and, conversely, limiting the ability of their chief enemy or enemies to project power into the sphere of influence each had defined for itself. None conceived of the elimination of the other, though the British and Napoleon saw the continued existence of their respective political regimes as incompatible with their grand strategic goals. Analysis of each power's conception of its sphere of influence reveals a certain asymmetry that had important implications.

The French, especially under Napoleon, and the Russians in some sense met head on, as each aimed at army-based domination within Europe so as to protect their political core. Russian grand strategy, however, included power projection not just westward, which met the eastward thrust of French power, but southward toward the Ottoman Empire and eastward into Siberia as far as its borders with China. Meanwhile, British grand strategy was oceanic and navy-based: As long as no power so dominated continental Europe as to pose a threat of invasion of the British Isles, Britain saw its sphere as its colonial possessions in particular and its global economic connections in general. Thus, while British and Russian conceptions were, if not complementary, at least not conflicting, French aims ran afoul of both Britain and Russia and in the event could negate neither.

British and Russian ability to pursue a grand strategy beyond mere survival suggests that the powers on the edge of Europe had a strategic depth that enabled them to resist Napoleon. Yet, the ability to resist was not the same as that of ensuring success. It would be convenient to say that Britain and Russia, as powers

The Campaign and Battle of Austerlitz, 1805

Austerlitz is often called Napoleon's greatest victory, and it is, in fact, a masterpiece of strategic, operational, and tactical planning and execution that illustrates why the Napoleonic Art of War held such a central place in military studies for so long (Figure 22.2).

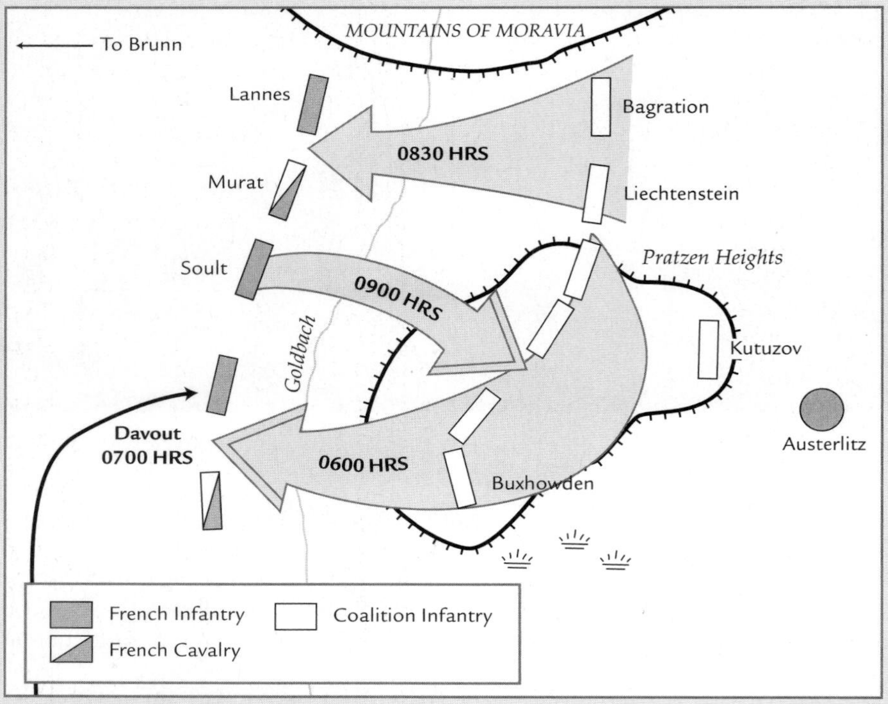

In the summer of 1805, Napoleon had assembled what he would come to call *La Grande Armée* (The Great Army) in camps around Boulogne in preparation for an invasion of England. England, however, had organized the Third Coalition with Sweden, Austria, and Russia, and it became increasingly clear that the cross-Channel invasion was not viable. As Russian forces marched to join up with their Austrian allies, and an Austrian army moved toward the Rhine, occupying the strong Bavarian fortress of Ulm, Napoleon force marched 200,000 men in seven corps away from the Channel. They crossed the Rhine on September 25 on a broad front, sweeping eastward to the north of Ulm, and then wheeling southward onto the rear of the 37,000-man Austrian army. It surrendered on October 20 without a fight: Strategic maneuver had done the fighting.

Leaving Ulm garrisoned, Napoleon then marched rapidly eastward. Austrian defenses were so disordered, even though Russian forces arrived

Figure 22.2 The Battle of Austerlitz

that had highly varied military tasks and experiences, were thereby more effective and better able to defeat Napoleon; but it is difficult to show that any such transferability of military quality took place. For much of the period, the French and Russians essentially remained in a standoff. French successes were more visible, as the French center of power was closer to the areas (especially Germany) where the two met, while the Russian ability to transcend the vast distances between the two centers was superior, as the campaigns of 1812 and 1813 demonstrate. France and Britain, too, appeared to face a standoff, as Napoleon could not readily invade Britain, nor could the British muster the force to challenge Napoleon directly within Europe.

But British defensive success was consistent, and the victory at Trafalgar in 1805 virtually ensured more slowly than expected, that Vienna fell in mid-November, giving Napoleon 100,000 muskets, 500 cannon, and, most important, undamaged bridges across the Danube. The Russians withdrew to the northeast of the city to link up with the rest of their forces and scattered Austrian units in the campaign.

The campaign had been a brilliant success so far, but it was far from over or secure. Napoleon's line of communications back to France was long and vulnerable, and occupied by so much of his army that he had only about 67,000 men left to face about 73,000 Allies in a potential battle. Yet the Prussians might join the war at any time, so a battle was what Napoleon needed, despite the misgivings of his subordinates. He followed the Allies to the northeast, and Tsar Alexander of Russia obliged him by convincing the Austrians and his generals to attack.

Napoleon's plan was to entice an Allied attack on his right wing, which he left lightly guarded (indeed, 7000 men of Davout's III Corps had to force march seventy miles in forty-eight hours to arrive on the right wing as the battle was already underway, a daring but risky bit of operational timing). Once enough Allied reserves had been committed to that attack to weaken their center, Soult's IV Corps would break through the Allied center, splitting and destroying the Allied force. Things did not go exactly as scripted—the Allies' handling of the successive attacks on the French right went awry in such a way as to leave more units than Napoleon expected in the path of his attack in the center, and any number of Russian units distinguished themselves by fighting hard and well, creating some nervous moments for the French command. But in larger terms, the plan worked perfectly. Davout arrived in time to help hold the right against the Allied attacks there, Soult's attack carried the day, and the Allied army broke in panic as many of its officers fled. Some Russian units, retreating southward toward Vienna across frozen ponds, died when Napoleon had his gunners open fire on the ice. The Allies lost 27,000 casualties to 9000 for the French.

Austria came to terms shortly after the battle, signing a humiliating but not disastrous peace treaty, while the Russians went home. Napoleon organized a set of German states into the Confederation of the Rhine to serve as a buffer zone for France, which provoked Prussia to declare war in 1806, when its armies were crushed at Jena-Auerstadt. Napoleon was at the height of his power and fame and had written a chapter in the annals of decisive land warfare. And yet . . .

Russia had withdrawn but was not decisively defeated. A solution to the British problem was further away than ever—indeed, Nelson had destroyed any remaining hope of a direct invasion by crushing the Franco-Spanish fleet at Trafalgar the day after Ulm surrendered (see the Highlights box on page 488). And Napoleon never again managed such battlefield brilliance. The lessons of Austerlitz are therefore, shall we say, ambiguous.

British immunity from invasion (see Chapter 25). Due to British success, France was unable to enjoy the benefits of the European hegemony it had gained. The colonial empires of its European allies were outside France's (and their) control, and the resources that Napoleon deployed could not be used to project French power. This was a failure that was not inherent in France's position, but one that reflected the rela-

tively low priority given to maritime as opposed to continental activities, as well as the successes of the British navy; in short, contingent factors were crucial. Like Louis XIV, Napoleon wanted colonies and a strong navy, but under pressure, the army very much came first. Like Hitler, Napoleon pursued his colonial plans within (rather than outside) Europe, and this was clearly the focus of his worldview. After the Egyptian expedition of 1798, Napoleon's interest in, let alone commitment to, the world outside Europe was episodic. Further, it essentially arose from interest in harming European rivals, rather than from any sense of France's role in an expanding Western world.

Economic Warfare   Moreover, Napoleon did not truly understand either the means to further trade or the dynamics of commercial activity and its relation with public finances. This failing was critical when military stalemate led Britain and France to pursue their grand strategic aims through economic warfare. Here it should be said that the fact of economic warfare was not new, but the scale on which it was pursued, and the theoretical sophistication that lay behind British economic and fiscal policy, was. The British blockaded Europe (in the process provoking war with the United States); Napoleon responded with the "Continental System," an attempt to bar British imports into the European mainland and thus cripple Britain's economy, whose misunderstanding of the global nature of the British economy is telling. Russia stood essentially outside this conflict, vaguely cooperating with Napoleon for a time, then subverting the Continental System enough that Napoleon launched the ill-fated 1812 invasion. Meanwhile, the British poached French colonies in the Caribbean and India, while one French colony, Haiti, entered into its own revolution that France proved unable to counter.

Specific Strategy

The grand strategies each power pursued had significant bearing on the strategies each followed in particular campaigns. In fact, a consistent strategic approach can be discerned in French, British, and Russian campaigning throughout the Napoleonic Wars, at least.

The Europe-dominating thrust of French grand strategy meant that Napoleon regularly faced coalitions of foes raising multiple armies. The consistent pattern of Napoleon's strategy was in essence an extension of the operational principle of interior lines: to seize a position from which he could strike with superior force at each enemy army in turn, before they could combine and achieve superiority of numbers. In this, he was aided by poor communications that made coalition warfare difficult to coordinate and by diplomacy that aimed at preventing or breaking

up coalitions politically. The problem was that experience taught his enemies both to be cautious of this approach and not expose individual forces rashly, and to better coordinate Allied armies across entire campaigns and regions. Thus, his task became harder even as his instrument, the French army, wore down from constant campaigning. (See the Issues box "The Significance of Napoleon" for a discussion of his actual historical import.)

The essentially extra-European focus of British grand strategy and the vast numerical superiority of the French army over the British forced Britain to pursue an indirect approach to strategy—indirect in two senses. First, Britain created armies to oppose Napoleon indirectly, by funding the war efforts of coalition partners. Second, when British forces did enter the field directly (at least before the Waterloo campaign of 1815), it was via a secondary front in the Iberian Peninsula. In 1807, the French successfully invaded Portugal, a major British trading partner. But in 1808, Napoleon's attempt to place his brother Joseph on the throne of Spain led to a popular uprising that the British exploited by sending an expedition to Portugal under General Sir Arthur Wellesley, later Duke of Wellington. He proved an adept general. His eye for the terrain and the superior firepower of his troops defeated attacking French forces at Vimeiro in 1808. Though the subsequent British advance, under Sir John Moore, into Spain, proved unsuccessful in the face of overwhelming French strength, continued British defensive triumphs in Portugal, combined with operational offensives into Spain, kept pressure on the French until 1813. Then Wellington invaded Spain successfully, winning a key victory at Vitoria; his armies entered southern France in 1814.

The key strategic problem faced by the Russians was the distance of their political and economic centers from the theaters of operations in central Europe. Thus, Russian strategy often focused first on establishing forward bases, usually in conjunction with allies, for the projection of their power. Space, on the other hand, became their ally in 1812, and they pursued a scorched-earth strategy against Napoleon's invading force in order to maximize the impact of space. Their success in that campaign, and their subsequent role in the victorious Allied campaigns in Germany in 1813 and the decisive invasion of France itself in 1814, demonstrate Russian skill at both using and overcoming the limitations of space and distance strategically.

The Significance of Napoleon

Why is Napoleon such a major figure in Western military history and military analysis? Despite stunning initial successes, he was ultimately a failure, not only in hindsight but also in his lifetime. If there was no perverted *Götterdämmerung* equivalent to the Berlin bunker in which Adolf Hitler was to commit suicide in 1945, Napoleon discovered hell in his own terms when imprisoned by the British on Saint Helena, an isolated island in the storm-tossed South Atlantic. Why, then, has Napoleon been for so long the focus of attention among military commentators, both intellectual and popular, from theorists, via teachers and war-gamers, to reenactors? Why study failure, in short—a question that recurs when we think about the Germans in World Wars I and II?

Several reasons offer themselves, some historical and some directly relevant today. As far as historical factors are concerned, Napoleon's initial success in the 1790s and 1800s forced others to study the basis of his success in order to try to imitate it or to learn how best to avoid suffering from its repetition. In short, there was a clear tasking in terms of an obligation to understand Napoleon. This remained apparently relevant because the European great-power system did not change substantially for several decades after 1815. Indeed, France was to find itself at war, separately, with Russia, Austria, and Prussia within a half-century of the fall of Napoleon, in 1854–56, 1859, and 1870–71, respectively. The battlefields in the wars with Austria and Prussia, in northern Italy and eastern France, were some of the same ones fought over under Napoleon. So Napoleon seemed relevant, particularly so because weaponry changed relatively little in the 1820s and 1830s, while operational and strategic goals remained similar even after the nature of weaponry altered in the 1850s and 1860s. Several major figures from the wars, furthermore, including Wellington, remained in influential positions long after the wars.

In academic terms, the works of the leading nineteenth-century Western writers on war, Clausewitz and Jomini, on the warfare of the Napoleonic years provided a ready fixing of lessons from the period. The expansion of military education in the nineteenth century was particularly important in this light, as Napoleonic warfare became a key topic. Once established, this pattern proved very durable. There was also a confidence that Napoleonic warfare was crucial to the grand narrative of Western conflict. For the twentieth century, this seemed self-evident, as warfare between major states, the basic theme of Napoleonic conflict, commanded attention.

The applicability of this model, however, is less apparent from the perspective of the early twenty-first century. Now, the focus is on a wider range of conflict, reflecting the trajectory of military history in recent decades (see Chapter 30). Two spheres are of particular importance: first, conflict between Western and non-Western powers, and, second, the dialectic of insurrectionary and counterinsurrectionary warfare. In each case, there is relevant material in the Napoleonic period. The Egyptian campaigns of 1798–1801 provide instructive instances of the former; those in Calabria, the Tyrol, and Spain, of the latter; and that in Haiti, of both. Possibly, had work on Napoleonic warfare included such a focus, it would continue to have the necessary broader reference and relevance, but all too often, this has not been the case. However, this represents a challenge for Napoleonic military historians. The challenge is particularly acute because any assessment of relative effectiveness requires looking at both combatants. Thus, those working on Egypt and Haiti need to match the fine work, particularly by Charles Esdaile, on the Spanish resistance to Napoleon. For the British in India, there is comparable work by Randolph Cooper on their major opponents, the Marathas, which throws considerable light on British operations. Such work needs to be replicated.

If Napoleonic-era warfare can tell us about conflict between the West and the non-West and about irregular warfare, however, Napoleon himself may not. In Egypt, he won the battle but lost the war, and popular resistance seemed to baffle him. It need not detract from our assessment of his operational brilliance to question how relevant his example remains today.

SOURCES

Western Fighting Techniques in India

Some British soldiers recorded their impressions of warfare in India, commenting on the fighting quality of their Indian opponents and on the conditions of the country that affected campaigning. The following passages give a sample of these European impressions.

■ ■ ■

In the following passage, Major Skelly of the British 52nd Regiment recorded the British advance on Seringapatam, the capital of Tipu Sultan of Mysore, on May 13, 1792.

The enemy for some time stood firm and their fire was heavy, but on our troops charging, they abandoned their guns, and fled, in confusion, towards the island of Seringapatam, which everywhere presented batteries of heavy cannon to cover their retreat . . . on the left . . . when we arrived within reach of their musquetry they gave us their fire, which, though heavy, was ill directed, and did little execution, few of our corps even returned the fire, but moved on in such perfect order, and with such fine resolution as might have commanded victory from better mettled troops than Tipu can bring into the field.

Skelly also commented on the hardship of war. He recorded an earlier attack on British troops in a redoubt outside Seringapatam.

. . . the enemy now brought three field pieces against us from which, as well as with their musketry and rockets . . . our loss soon became serious . . . the want of water was severely felt . . . these different attacks were still attended with loss on our side, and the redoubt was now become a horrid scene of carnage—many had fallen, and the rest, through heat, exertion, and thirst were almost exhausted most of them, however, stood gallantly to their duty, though in a few signs of despondency began to appear.

A letter from Major Lachlan Macquarie from the British camp at Seedaseer described a major battle between the British and a Mysorean army of 20,000 men under the command of Tipu Sultan on March 5, 1799.

On the 5th. of March a Camp was seen, from the Look-out on the Top of the Seedaseer-Hill, to be forming to the Right of Periapatam.—Before Evening it had become very extensive, and a large

GLOBAL PERSPECTIVES

Expanding Western Power

At the global scale, the period of the French Revolutionary and Napoleonic Wars, from 1792 to 1815, and, even more clearly, that of the Napoleonic Wars from 1799 to 1815, were of great significance for the expansion of Western power relative to that of non-Westerners. Britain achieved key successes in southern and western India, at the expense of Mysore and the Marathas, and this secured its hegemony in the subcontinent (see the Sources box "Western Fighting Techniques in India"). Russia was able to establish itself in Georgia in the Caucasus Mountains and subsequently, in 1806–12, to defeat the Turks at the same time as it faced the challenge of Napoleonic France. And the United States made important gains at the expense of Native Americans.

It was not the case, however, that Western powers were invariably successful or dominant, as the British discovered in the eastern Mediterranean in 1806–7. An invasion of Egypt failed when it became a question of moving into the interior as opposed to establishing a coastal presence. In 1807, moreover, French advisors helped Ottoman forces deploy cannon to prevent a British fleet seeking to force acceptance of British mediation of their war with Russia. In those presteamship days, the British warships were also held back by contrary winds. As far as dominance was concerned, British caution in responding to China—for example, when the Gurkhas of Nepal requested assistance in

Green Tent could be distinctly observed in the Center of the Line. —The Post of Seedaseer was therefore ordered to be reinforced by the two Battalions of the Muddy-Tank; and all the Troops in the Rear were directed to hold themselves in readiness to move at the shortest notice.—

On the morning of the 6th. of March a Column of Six Thousand Men (—as we since understand) attacked the front of the Post at Seedaseer: —while two others of equal Force, making a great circuit through the Jungle, came round by the Right and Left into the Rear of it, apparently for the double purpose of intercepting and succours which might be sent forward, and attacking the Post in every Quarter. —No part of the Plan, however, succeeded.—

The Column in front, after continuing its attacks from Nine in the morning till Two Oclock in the Afternoon, was finally repulsed by Lieut. Colonel Montresor's Brigade, which occupied the Pass; and the two Columns in the Rear were dispersed or driven back by a part of the European Brigade under Lieut. Colonel Dunlop, which had moved to the support of the Post when the first report was made of an attack being threatened. —We have lost two officers killed; —three others are wounded; and the total of our killed and wounded and missing amount to one Hundred and Forty three. —We cannot ascertain the loss of the Enemy; —but for two miles and a half in the Rear of the Post, their dead and wounded are to be seen scattered on the Road and in the Jungle in great numbers—besides those who fell in front of the Advanced Post. —From the nature of the Country very few Prisoners could be taken; —amongst these few is Murzeem Kaun, who commanded and was Bukhsy of a Cutcherry, or Brigade; Mirza Bokhar, a Bukhsy and Commandant of a Cutcherry; and Seid Ghofar—since dead of his wounds—an officer of high rank and favorite General of Tippoo's—who commanded one of the Columns of attack.—

All the Prisoners agree in saying Tippoo commanded in Person, and they estimate his Army at Twenty Thousand Infantry, and a few Hundreds of Horse: —the greatest part of his Cavalry having gone to the Eastward to oppose the Madras Army. —From the Prisoners we also learn the Strength of the different Columns which marched against us; the thickness of the Jungle having prevented our obtaining an accurate and connected view of them.—

SOURCE: www.lib.mq.edu.au/digital/seringapatam/intro.html.

1792—indicated a clear sense of relative power. Furthermore, there was reluctance to accept commitments arising from the establishment, in 1786, of Georgetown, the first British base in Malaya.

Yet, at the same time, there had been an important shift toward Western powers, and this is one of the most noteworthy developments of the period. Given modern concern about relations between the West and the Islamic world, it is instructive to consider the ability of Western states to project their power into this world. This can be seen in the treatment of what were regarded as rogue polities. For example, from their base in the Persian Gulf, the Wahhabi (Arab) pirates attacked British East India Company ships and British warships in the Arabian Sea. A British punitive expedition of 1809 freed British trade from attack, but a fresh pirate campaign was launched in 1816, leading to another British expedition in 1819–20. The latter indicated the difficulty of establishing a permanent presence. The British commander was badly defeated by the Bani Bu Ali, desert Arabs whom he had accused of piracy, and the British presence was wound down. More prominently, in 1816, the British took action against the Barbary states of North Africa, whose longstanding piracy was seen as an attack not only on British interests but also on the general freedom of navigation and trade with which the British associated themselves and from which other Western powers benefited when not at war with Britain.

This was seen, in both Britain and Europe, as a great triumph, and it established a pattern of what was seen as exemplary conduct. Unlike operations on land, some of which had to be presented as glorious failures, and few of which could be seen as of general value to humanity, it was possible to present the *Pax Britannica* at sea as invariably successful and praiseworthy. Further, at Algiers the British fleet had assumed a responsibility formerly undertaken by the Bourbon powers, and its success contrasted markedly with Spanish failure there in 1784. Combined with Russian successes in the early nineteenth century at the expense of Turkey and Persia, this represented a dramatic shift in the relative effectiveness of Islamic and non-Islamic powers.

Spreading European Influence

The relative advantage Western armies were gaining in this period, especially over their close neighbors, did not go unrecognized, and there were attempts to borrow Western practice. The Egyptian army was trained by French officers after 1815 and was supplied by France until 1840. However, few areas had metallurgical capacity comparable to that of the industrial sectors of the leading Western powers, and none had anything to compare with their fleets of heavily gunned specialist warships. The challenge of Western influence around the world in the nineteenth century is the topic of Chapter 24.

The limits of Western power and influence in 1815 deserve emphasis, however. It was only with significant technological change consequent on industrialization that Europe presented a serious challenge to the political independence of much of the nineteenth-century world, change that had barely begun in 1815. European influence remained confined largely to coastal areas outside of British India and Russian Asia, and China remained the world's leading land power during this period, as indicated by its relative advantage along its border with Russia.

CONCLUSION

The Napoleonic legacy was a weaker France in Europe, with Russia dominant in eastern Europe and influential further west, and a European overseas world dominated by Britain. France's colonies in 1815 were only those allowed them by Britain, such as a number of now inconsequential bases in India, most prominently Pondicherry, as well as other territories that the British were confident of capturing if necessary. Britain dominated the Western world, and France was in a weaker transoceanic position, both absolutely and relatively, than had been the case since the seventeenth century. Russia in 1815, on the other hand, was in many ways at the height of its global influence.

The impact of the wars within Europe was complex. On the surface, especially politically, the status quo ante bellum was restored by the peace of 1815. Yet this is a somewhat misleading picture. Napoleon's conquests had carried elements of revolutionary ideology across Europe, and the adjustments his opponents had had to make to resist him in many ways reinforced the impact of those ideas. Western Europe in 1815 was a more bourgeois world, though it would take the revolutions of the 1830s and 1848 to solidify the implications of this, and it included more of Germany. From this perspective, the French Revolution and the Napoleonic Wars that conquered in its name had reconfigured western Europe socioeconomically so as to be more compatible with British-style industrialization. This effect did not extend into Russia, of course, which created the potential for the erosion of its dominant position, which derived from vast human and natural resources applied during a period of incremental technological change.

But above all, Europe in 1815 was a world more consciously animated by—and divided by—nationalism. The importance of this is hard to underestimate. It is to the effects on European warfare of the combination of industrial development and nationalism, effects with global implications, that we will turn in Chapter 23.

SUGGESTED READINGS

Bertaud, J.-P. *The Army of the French Revolution*. Princeton: Princeton University Press, 1988. A study of how the Revolution changed the French army and made it more effective.

Connelly, Owen. *Blundering to Glory: Napoleon's Military Campaigns,* 2nd ed. Wilmington: Scholarly Resources, 1998. Presents Napoleon as an effective improviser. See also his *The Wars* of the French Revolution and Napoleon, 1792–1815 (London: Routledge, 2006), an up-to-date survey that is narrative in its approach and provides a clear account.

Esdaile, Charles. *The Peninsular War: A New History*. London: Penguin Books, 2002. An excellent case study that is particularly valuable because of its consideration of the Spanish perspective.

LeDonne, John P. *Grand Strategy of Russian Empire, 1650–1831*. (Oxford: Oxford University Press, 2004. A provocative reconceptualization of the Russian role in Europe before, during, and after the Napoleonic age.

Lynn, John. *The Bayonets of the Republic: Motivation and Tactics in the Army of Revolutionary France, 1791–4*, 2nd ed. Boulder: Westview Press, 1996. A key work on the effectiveness of the army of Revolutionary France.

Rothenberg, Gunther. *The Napoleonic Wars*. London: Cassell, 1999. A clear and well-illustrated introduction from a specialist on the Austrian army; gives an instructive perspective. See also his *The Art of Warfare in the Age of Napoleon* (Bloomington: Indiana University Press, 1978), the key work on the practice of war in this period.

Schneid, Frederick. *Napoleon's Conquest of Europe. The War of the Third Coalition*. Westport: Greenwich Press, 2005. A major work of wide-ranging importance for the whole of Napoleonic war making.

CHAPTER 23

Rifles and Railroads: War in the Age of Industry, 1815–1914

The Industrial Revolution ranks with the taming of fire and the invention of agriculture as a fundamental turning point in human history. Industrial capitalism drew on energy sources far more powerful than the wind, water, and muscle power that had driven all previous human endeavors. It then harnessed them in tandem with a scientific worldview that could produce increasing numbers of technological breakthroughs, and it hooked everything to a system of predatory, expansionist economics. The results in all areas of human existence were truly revolutionary, including—and often led by—military affairs. The century from 1815 to 1914 in Europe and North America saw a transformation of armies and warfare far more radical and complete than any before in history, a transformation that propelled the West to world dominance but left everyone uncomprehending of and unprepared for the results of this revolution.

This chapter will first present an overview of the military consequences of the rise of industrial capitalism for Western armies, warfare, and society. The interplay of these developments with the political and military changes already underway due to the French Revolution and the Napoleonic era is central to this story. We will then examine a number of wars that were crucial to the development of modern war. The American Civil War was the first modern war: one fought by mass popular armies aided by new technologies. Many of its tactics, especially in the trenches of Petersburg and its effects on the wider societies of the combatants, gave the first accurate indication of the shape twentieth-century war would assume. But for all its modernity in technique and result, it remained a typically American, and therefore somewhat ad hoc, war. It was in the various European wars of the second half of the century that the organization, if not the full implications, of modern warfare were forged by the Prussian General Staff system, while the Franco-Prussian War, the

campaigns of Garibaldi in Italy, and conflicts in the Balkans showed the growing importance of popular involvement in war.

INDUSTRY AND THE MASS ARMY REVOLUTION

War and Industrial Economics

Mass Production and Logistics The key concept with the coming of industrialization is *mass*. The vast productive powers of industrial capitalism allowed mass production that could meet the needs of mass consumption in a mass society increasingly organized around various forms of mass (but not necessarily democratic) politics. Industry also allowed the explosive population growth that took people of European descent from one-fifth of the world's population in 1800 to one-third by 1900. And here, therefore, was the demographic and productive capacity capable of supporting the mass armies that the French Revolution and Napoleonic era had begun to create but that the economies of that time could not sustain for long.

Mass production of uniforms, boots, and so forth could clothe larger armies while mass production of ammunition and weapons, facilitated by the eighteenth-century invention of interchangeable parts, could arm them. New modes of transport—steamships and railways—could bring these supplies and food to them, provided they remained within cartage range of their ports or railheads. The invention of canned rations in midcentury brought further industrialization to logistics. Ships and railways could also move the armies, creating a potential revolution in strategic mobility, again provided that ports and rails were where they were needed. And the importance of rail networks soon made them a new object of strategy.

Mass production therefore allowed the creation of mass armies. It did not, however, necessitate them. Raising mass armies was fraught with political dangers, and it was politics, not economics, that determined army size in Europe and the United States, as we will see. In any event, industrialization brought changes even to smaller professional armies, as mass production could not only equip a large army but rapidly reequip a smaller force with the latest weaponry, ending the period of slow technological evolution and introducing an age of nearly constant innovation.

Technological Innovation   Constant creation of new technology was built into the system of industrial capitalism, since economic imperatives encouraged new machinery both as more efficient means of production and as commodities for sale. In some important cases, such as railroads, nonmilitary inventions became militarily significant. But military and economic competition, combined with powerful national governments as buyers, guaranteed an increasing range of new and improved war machinery, as well as spurring the growth of companies such as the German Krupp armaments works into a network of military-industrial complexes. The biggest changes affected transport and firepower.

Rail networks developed first under the direction of private interests for commercial reasons. By mid-century, however, the strategic significance of rail networks was becoming apparent, leading to more pervasive forms of government–private sector cooperation in the building of railroads. In some areas, such as the United States, private and commercial interests remained dominant, with the government contribution consisting of gifts of land. (Not that this hindered growth: By 1860, the United States had the world's most extensive rail network.) In other areas, such as Prussia (and Japan—see Chapter 24), the government intervened more directly, dictating the growth and placement of rails for military more than commercial purposes. Railroads were the first step in an ongoing revolution in army mobility.

A concurrent revolution in firepower began with the invention of easy-to-load rifled muskets in 1830. Rifles had been produced for centuries, but the tight fit between ball and barrel necessary in rifling made the process of loading so slow that such guns were useful only for hunting. But a soft bullet with a hollow base that expanded to fit the barrel on percussion made rifled muskets as quick to load as smoothbores.

And the spin imparted by rifling turned the old smooth-bore knuckleball into a fastball, tripling effective range and vastly improving accuracy. The result was to render cavalry charges virtually obsolete, to temporarily drive artillery beyond the range where it could support an attack, and so to make any attack on a prepared infantry line much more difficult. Subsequent improvements included the replacement of flintlocks with percussion caps struck by a firing pin (giving the name to "needle guns"), the replacement of muzzle loading with breech loading, the invention of magazines and repeat-firing rifles, and the introduction of smokeless powder. Thus, during the century, the firepower of a company of infantry went up steadily while their ability to make use of natural cover by reloading in a prone position and to conceal the source of their fire further enhanced their defensive capabilities. By the 1870s, rifling and breech loading were coming to the artillery as well, followed by recoilless carriages in the 1890s. Meanwhile, at sea, transport and firepower came together in new forms of warships (see Chapter 25).

The Potential for Total War   The explosive new importance of industry in war created the potential for what would come to be known as *total war*—that is, war on an enemy's entire population, industrial base, and capacity to make war. Though in some senses merely an extension of the ancient practice of ravaging the countryside, industrial technology provided the means to significantly extend the idea of attacking resources and infrastructure, which came to include attacking the enemy population's will to make war. Physical attacks played the major role, an early example of which is General William T. Sherman's march through Georgia in the Civil War. Sherman carved a swath up to 50 miles wide and 425 miles long through the South, leaving no barns, farm animals, or valuable household goods in his rear. As Sherman himself explained, "We cannot change the hearts of these people of the South, but we can make war so terrible . . . [and] make them so sick of war that generations would pass away before they would again appeal to it." Increasingly, however, propaganda aimed at the enemy population would come to supplement actual physical attacks as a means of undermining an opponent's political will. This focus on political will resulted from the new mass nature of society and politics in industrial countries, a development with significant implications for the military and military-civil relations. But the concept of total war (as opposed to its growing practice) was slow to develop and is more useful for retrospective analysis of trends than for understanding how nineteenth-century people viewed the challenges of industrialized war. For they, necessarily, looked back to the Napoleonic era and the nationalist mobilization of society rather than forward to the great wars of the twentieth century for insights. This was true of strategy and tactics as well and accounts for some of the problems armies (and navies—see Chapter 25) had in adapting to constantly changing technology and economics.

Armies and Mass Society

Industry, War, and the Nation-State   Industrialization reconstructed society, creating new classes and class conflicts. In Europe, the old aristocracy remained powerful but increasingly shared influence over state policy with a vastly expanded bourgeoisie, or middle class, especially its upper levels of wealthy industrialists. And both classes mistrusted the growing urban proletariat drawn to the factory system. The rise of self-conscious ideology, indicated by the invention of "ism" words and including nationalism, liberalism, conservatism, socialism, and communism, reflected the political struggles of an age of revolutions and the gradual extension of democratic forms (if not full content) to many of Europe's governments.

Political class struggles were given impetus by the increasing power of the state. Industrialization and the scientific culture that accompanied it gave to states new resources in finance, administration, and manpower, while nationalism gave a new moral backing to those states whose boundaries coincided more or less with ethnic populations. The problems raised by industrialization drew the state into an increasing number of areas of people's lives. And the partnership between states and industries for the production of armaments (and, at times, for the development of transportation networks) created national military-industrial complexes across the continent. This meant that the interests of industrialists began to have a significant influence on military policy, contributing to the development of military-industrial complexes and to arms races on land and at sea.

The new capacities of armies expanded their potential role as the ultimate enforcers of state sovereignty and gave them a key role in political conflicts. That is, rifles could be used against internal as well as external enemies. The tensions between the sorts of forces needed to meet those two different foes shaped military policy for much of the century. Used for internal security, armies could easily be seen as oppressive tools of a narrow ruling class. But at the same time they could be both symbols and active forgers of national unity across divisions of both region and class. In the United States, the absence of a large standing army and the early triumph of democratic ideology made popular mass armies a relatively uncontroversial option during the Civil War. But in Europe, the century divides at 1870 with respect to the dominance of one or the other of these paths.

Professional Armies, 1815–1870   After the final defeat of Napoleon, the Great Powers attempted to put prerevolutionary Europe back together. Conservative regimes took power everywhere, as bourgeois aspirations for change unleashed by the French Revolution and Napoleon's conquests were everywhere suppressed. When conflict boiled over in 1848, the revolutions were put down, and order was reestablished based on an accommodation between the upper bourgeoisie and the aristocracy, who now took radicals among the working classes as their common enemy. Meanwhile, tensions between states were at a low ebb. In this climate, armies were almost universally constructed with social control as their primary mission.

This meant moderately sized armies of long-term professionals, enlisted for terms ranging from seven to twenty years. An extended term of service was considered necessary to separate the army from society and to impose enough training that soldiers would be reliable tools of the government—that is, could be counted on to fire on their fellow countrymen. In multicultural states such as the Austro-Hungarian Empire, under whose umbrella governments nationalist sentiments simmered, units served away from their districts of origin to make such obedience to state authority even more likely. Armies with extensive colonial roles, such as the British, also required long-term enlistees. Quality was seen as more important than quantity, which meant smaller forces with more training in the new weapons of the day. Cost-consciousness further reinforced this consideration, while an officer class dominated by the aristocracy helped maintain political reliability. The size of such forces did increase significantly over the course of this period: External threats were not nonexistent, larger populations demanded larger policing forces, and the capacity to support larger forces increased. But the increases after 1870 were far larger.

Only Prussia departed from this model. As elsewhere, the aristocracy dominated the officer class. In Prussia, however, the system of universal military obligation and conscription created to fight Napoleon remained in force after his demise. Each class of recruits served three years in the regular army followed by a term in the reserves. Not only was Prussia capable of raising a larger army than states using the long-term enlistment system, but, as it proved against France, its citizen-soldiers were the professionals' equals. Prussian victory in 1870–71 moved foreign competition ahead of internal security for every European state, and the era of mass conscript armies began in earnest.

Conscription, 1870–1914

All the major European states except Britain, and most of the minor ones, moved quickly after 1871 to copy the Prussian system, with details varying according to political and economic constraints. For their part, the British copied many aspects other than conscription. The basis of the system was the universal obligation to military service on the part of every male citizen of a certain age, a principle established in law during this period. Some percentage of each age cohort was called up when it first became eligible, served from 2 to 3 years in the regular army, then entered the reserves for periods ranging from 7 to 30 years, depending on the country. The regulars served as a cadre for the mobilization and organization of the reserves in case of war, a system made possible by the rail networks that could draw units together and move them to the front.

The rapidity of the system's spread does not, however, mean that the decision to implement it was taken lightly. Mass conscription raised acute fears of arming the working classes for a revolution, and every army took care to guard against that possibility. The officer corps remained largely monopolized by aristocrats. Training routines stressed not just proficiency with arms but education in national ideals and automatic obedience to authority. Thus, armies were designed to train not only soldiers but supportive, even docile, citizens. To a large extent, they succeeded, though the continued tendency for armies to become separated from civilian life made their popularity as institutions among the general populace uncertain. But rising international tensions in this period meant that considerations of military efficiency increasingly outweighed political fears. Units of the Austro-Hungarian army, for example, came to be stationed in their areas of recruitment so that they could be near their reserves for mobilization, despite fears of nationalist divisiveness.

Rising tensions also forced the numbers of every army upward, while conscription itself contributed to the spread of military values through society. Statesmen became obsessed with birthrates, as the size of each age cohort mattered to the overall size of the army, and diplomatically, the military tail threatened more and more to wag the dog of state, shaping policy to mobilization plans. There was certainly a growing acceptance of the inevitability of warfare to settle diplomatic logjams, an acceptance fostered by the belief that any war would be (indeed had to be) short.

Professionalism and the Staff System

That belief stemmed from the success of the Prussian army in the Wars of German Unification (1866 and 1870–71). The institution thought responsible for that success was the General Staff, which controlled a professional, technically trained and oriented officer corps. The General Staff was the brains needed to make the vast body of a cadre and reserve conscript army work. Only such a control center, manned by officers educated in the professional military academies that sprang up in this period, could create and implement the intricate mobilization and operational plans by which such armies fought. Increasingly, such plans came to determine diplomatic options rather than serving them. That narrow technicalism was a poor basis for diplomacy got lost in the rising fears of the age. The full strengths and weaknesses of the General Staff system would become apparent in 1914, as World War I reinforced and expanded the lessons about modern war first evident in the American Civil War and the European wars of the later nineteenth century.

THE AMERICAN CIVIL WAR, 1861–1865

Overview

The Civil War is a central event in American history and continues to generate a more massive bibliography than any war in history except perhaps World War II. No survey this brief can do justice to a topic subject to such intense scrutiny, but the highlights and central features of the war can be outlined.

The Civil War started somewhat slowly, as neither the Union nor the Confederacy was prepared for war.

The standing army of the United States was tiny and mostly stationed out West, and both sides had to develop strategic plans on the run. Early Confederate success in the East was matched by more important Union success in the West, but by the end of 1861, it was clear that hopes on both sides for a short war were in vain. Despite further Union advances in Tennessee in early 1862, the summer of that year saw the first Confederate high tide. But at Antietam, Perryville (Kentucky), and New Orleans, Yankee successes turned back rebel threats and pushed the Union cause forward. But the Northern advance then slowed, and by the summer of 1863, the Confederate States of America (CSA) seemed poised again to strike north and possibly win the war. This time, however, major Union victories at Gettysburg and Vicksburg ended hopes for a Confederate knockout punch. Forced into a purely defensive strategy, the CSA's hopes for a win through Northern war weariness seemed tantalizingly close in the fall of 1864, but once again, a set of Union breakthroughs came just in time, at Atlanta and Mobile, and in the Shenandoah Valley. The remainder of the war was a foregone conclusion, with the shape of the peace emerging as the major issue.

Such a brief sketch hides the complexity of a war fought at many levels. It was also a war that either side could have won, as a closer look at key aspects of the war reveals.

Nations at War

Politics and War Aims   The Civil War was a modern war first by virtue of being a war of popular politics that combined issues of economics and human rights. Slavery was not the spark that ignited the explosion, but it was the fuse, the gunpowder, and the barrel. Slavery created the differential economic development of North and South that itself became a problem; slavery was the moral issue that polarized debate in the decades before the war; and the extension of slavery fueled the constitutional crisis of federal power versus states' rights behind which both sides initially fought. As a mass political war, both sides fought against the backdrop of frequent elections and with the need for popular support. A striking result of this aspect of the war was the rise of the *political generals*—men whose qualifications for command rested in their popularity or political connections in a key state—who plagued both sides' war efforts.

In terms of war aims, the North had the simpler time of it. Yankee forces fought to preserve the Union: Quelling the rebellion was the only Northern goal as the war started. Emancipation emerged gradually but inevitably as a second goal, in large part because its proclamation aided the effort at preserving the Union. Going directly after slavery exposed the internal contradictions in Southern war aims, weakened the CSA abroad, and contributed to solidarity in the Republican Party, the party that conducted the war in the face of a Democratic Party that wavered between qualified support and qualified opposition. The clarity of the division in Northern politics made the elections of 1862 and, above all, 1864 crucial; Republican victories in each assured the continuation of the war. Most active soldiers could vote absentee in the latter contest, and they cast their votes overwhelmingly (over 80 percent) for Lincoln. The army as a school of nationalism was clearly at work.

The CSA fought for its independence and, though some Confederate leaders soft-pedaled the issue, for the preservation of "the Southern way of life," that is, slavery. But the lack of clear party lines in Confederate politics muddied rebel war aims, as the CSA faced opposition from various quarters on numerous issues. Two key problems dogged the rebel war effort. First, a government set up to preserve states' rights had a difficult time imposing unity on and obtaining cooperation from its constituent parts. Second, the institution of slavery itself came to conflict with an efficient war effort in modern terms. The slave population formed a workforce that became more uncertain and threatening the less it was supervised by the South's absent men, and it represented an untapped pool of manpower. There is no better illustration of the magnitude of the pressure total war exerts than the calls within the Confederacy during its last year for the arming of slaves in support of the war effort.

Demography and Industry   The Civil War was a modern war second by virtue of the key role that modern economics played in its prosecution. Each side drew on its population, industry, and infrastructure to the fullest. Major Union advantages in each area made possible (but did not guarantee) the North's ability to overcome the South's advantages in fighting on the defensive in a region larger than Russia.

The North had almost three times as many white males of military age as the South, though slavery did allow, at first, a greater proportion of Southerners to fight. The Union's effective manpower advantage, reflected throughout the war in actual army sizes, was slightly more than two to one, roughly the same as its overall population advantage. In addition, population had long grown faster in the free states than in the slave states. Greater economic opportunity both encouraged economic growth and drew immigrants. Indeed, immigration during the war more than made up for deaths in Union armies: The free-state population grew and westward expansion continued even during the war. Thus, a basic demographic difference between an industrial and an agrarian economy told in favor of the North.

The Union advantage was even greater in terms of actual industrial production. Over 90 percent of the country's manufacturing was in the North when the war broke out, including munitions, clothing, and shoes, a fact rebel armies would come to know only too well. Even food production gave no advantage to the South, since so much Southern land was tied up in cotton production when the war began. The Northern industrial economy brought another advantage, in that it produced wealth of a more liquid sort than did plantations. The South had over 40 percent of the nation's capital in 1860, but much of that was in the form of land and slaves. Such wealth was hard to tap for financing war. The result was that, with both more resources and a much more efficient treasury, unhampered by considerations of states' rights, the Union had access to substantial funding through taxes and loans. In contrast, the CSA basically printed money to finance the war, ruining the Southern economy while failing to fund the army adequately.

As the war progressed, Northern industry kept Union armies well supplied. The Confederacy had surprising success at setting up war industries, notably munitions, of which rebel armies were never really short. But uniforms and shoes were always a problem, and by 1864, even the successes were being rapidly undone by a combination of Union destruction and transport problems.

Transportation Over two-thirds of the country's railroads and almost all its canals were in the North in 1860, as was all the technical expertise for the repair and extension of the rail network. The CSA, short on railroads to begin with, did not have the industrial capacity to maintain its own network through the war, never mind repair the destruction wrought by Union cavalry raids. The breakdown is shown by the fact that in 1864 the South still produced plenty of food—Sherman's army ate magnificently from Atlanta to Savannah—but its own armies and many cities went hungry for lack of transport.

The economic squeeze was further exacerbated by the Union naval blockade (see Chapter 25 for details). Southern cotton did not go out, earnings from it therefore did not come in, and many imported products became scarce and expensive. The blockade's effectiveness has been questioned by some historians, but it clearly contributed not just to notable victories at New Orleans and Mobile but to the collapse of the Southern economy and war effort. The blockade was also the most visible sign that economic calculations, as well as the Union advantages in population, industry, and infrastructure outlined here, directly influenced the strategy on both sides, accounting not just for grand strategic patterns but for the importance within specific theaters of productive centers such as the Shenandoah Valley in Virginia. In other words, a modern combination of politics and economics shaped both sides' strategic approach to the war (Figure 23.1).

Strategy

Grand Strategy Union grand strategy developed under the inspired leadership of President Abraham Lincoln, and from the time of General Winfield Scott's first formulation of the Anaconda Plan, the North had a fairly coherent vision of how to subdue the South. The slow strangulation of Scott's blockade-and-contain strategy might have succeeded in purely military terms, but politically it was unworkable. So on top of the blockade emerged plans to attack down the Mississippi to slice the Confederacy in half, combined with campaigns to "liberate" Union-sympathetic east Tennessee and to take the Confederate capital at Richmond, Virginia. Further moves focused on key rail junctions in the South, so as to slice the CSA into economically nonviable units incapable of sustaining a war effort. Of course, execution proved more difficult than planning, and it was only with the emergence of Ulysses S. Grant that Lincoln found the general to finish the job everywhere that he had started in the West. Grant and Sherman then moved toward total war: As Grant pinned Robert E. Lee's Confederate army in Virginia and George Thomas contained the remaining rebel forces in the West, Sherman ripped the economic heart out of the Confederacy.

Figure 23.1 Civil War Strategy

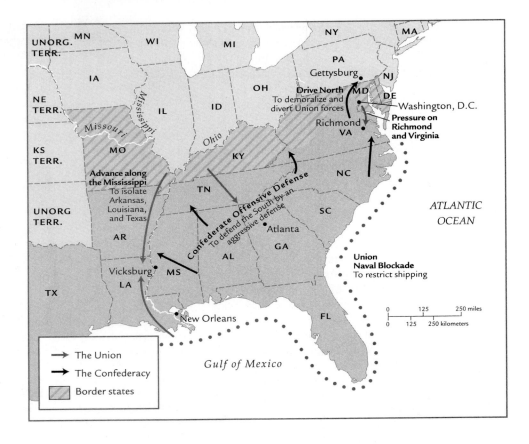

For its part, the CSA lacked as clear and unified a vision of grand strategy. President Jefferson Davis proved a poor war leader, alienating subordinates and meddling in operations. Davis's lack of effective leadership left overall strategy to develop in an ad hoc way out of the proposals and actions of departmental commanders. And here the early success of Lee in northern Virginia proved a mixed blessing. Success and Lee's own inclination, combined with the decision to put the Confederate capital in Richmond, probably led the CSA to devote too many resources in men and material to that theater and not enough to the West. Lee did not have Grant's clear vision of the war as a whole, and for all his undeniable success in defensive campaigns, his offensives were not only outright disasters for the rebel cause but probably a bad idea in principle, given the South's limited resources and the difficulties of offensive campaigns. They at least demonstrate that Lee, like most Southern leaders, had a deeply flawed understanding of Northern political dynamics: Neither in Maryland nor in Kentucky did Southern sympathizers emerge as expected in response to rebel invasions.

The South did have the advantage of fighting on the defensive, which allowed it in some places to trade space for time and to take advantage of interior lines. But the latter advantage was in practice more than offset at the grand strategic level by the Union's greater ability to transfer troops between theaters by rail and sea.

Campaigns   The defense had an advantage at the level of individual campaigns as well. Well-placed fortifications greatly aided the defense and became the focal points of a number of important campaigns, especially in the West. Organizing the logistics of an offensive was more difficult, as defending forces were closer to and could fall back on their lines of supply. Inadequate logistical planning was a major problem with Lee's offensives, for example, and also slowed many Union advances. Coordinating the units of an invading army was also more difficult than for the defense, as Lee also discovered when he moved north. And at this level, interior lines did count. The most spectacular Confederate successes in Virginia—

Stonewall Jackson's Shenandoah valley campaign and Lee's victory at Chancellorsville—involved smaller forces defeating larger forces through rapid marches, surprise concentrations of force, and judicious use of the tactical offensive. But the latter was risky, as the defense also had a big edge tactically (see below). Thus, even successful offensives tended to wear down as battles were fought.

In fact, many of the most successful offensive actions of the war were indirect. These included cavalry raids of the sort in which Confederates such as Nathan Bedford Forrest made their names, though after holding the advantage in such warfare in the first year of the war, the Confederacy saw the Union catch up and eventually make more effective use of this technique. Fast-moving cavalry units could cut loose from their supply lines more easily than larger, slower infantry forces, and they could strike deep into enemy territory, destroying railroads and supplies. Such raids could also sow confusion in the enemy camp and keep enemy forces dispersed, unsure of where the next strike would come and unable to mass. This highlights the key role of intelligence in campaigns, another area in which the defense, operating on its own ground among a supportive populace, had an edge. In this respect, cavalry continued to act in their traditional scouting role as the eyes of an army.

Indirect approaches also characterized the most daring and successful campaigns by infantry armies. Again, rapid movement, deception, and a growing willingness to abandon conventional supply lines and live off the land were keys to such campaigns. Jackson's masterful valley campaign is probably the most intensely studied episode of the war from a purely military point of view, as his "foot cavalry" exploited each of these factors in classic fashion. Grant's Vicksburg campaign (see the Highlights box "The Vicksburg Campaign") was equally daring and successful; even Sherman's "March to the Sea," obvious in retrospect, was a calculated gamble initially opposed by Grant. But careful logistical planning and clear objectives contributed to the success of even such apparently improvised maneuvers. In contrast, truly haphazard logistics undermined Lee's offensives, as noted above. In no campaign could be completely indirect or based solely on maneuver. A tension existed for both sides between territorial gain and destruction of opposing armies as the goal of any campaign, and the modernity of the Civil War shows up at this level in the greater ultimate importance of

the latter in winning the war. Even Sherman's march was complemented and made possible by Grant's pinning Lee down at Petersburg, Virginia, and by Thomas's destruction of John B. Hood's army in Tennessee.

Tactics

Civil War tactics were dominated by the defense. Rifled muskets that could be reloaded lying down let defending infantry take cover behind stone walls or logs or in shallow ditches and deliver effective aimed fire at an advancing opponent from over 300 yards away. The effect on massed formations of infantry or cavalry attempting to charge was devastating, but the pattern was repeated throughout the war because generals had no other way to launch and control a major attack. Probably the most famous such charge was by Pickett's division of Lee's army at Gettysburg: Of the 14,000 men who set out against the Union lines, fewer than half returned, despite support from a massive artillery barrage before the attack.

Part of the problem was that the range of rifles drove cannon back to the limits of their effective range. Batteries could no longer deploy aggressively in front of their infantry lines in preparation for an attack, as they had in Napoleonic armies, because the gunners rapidly fell to accurate rifle fire before they could inflict much damage. But cannon supporting the defense had no such problem. They could choose a site with some protection and infantry support and wait until massed attackers were well within range. Indeed, defensive artillery became devastating at close range, as grapeshot spewed shrapnel across a broad front.

Attacks were also likely to suffer from increasing lack of capable leadership. Again, the accuracy of rifles as opposed to smoothbores made the difference, as any officer who made himself conspicuous either by position in front of an attack or by uniform and insignia became a target in a deadly shooting gallery. Officer casualty rates were significantly higher in the Civil War than in the Napoleonic Wars, and many higher-ranking officers, including Grant, took to wearing a uniform that was distinguishable from a private's only by its inconspicuous shoulder bars in order to reduce their targetability.

Another problem for the offense was that while rifles made massed infantry attacks difficult, they rendered the traditional cavalry charge, long an offensive masterstroke, completely obsolete. The defensive

The Vicksburg Campaign

Grant's army had reached the shores of the Mississippi opposite Vicksburg in November 1862. The city, the Confederacy's last great fortified outpost on the river, stood high on bluffs, protected to the north by the 175 miles of swampy bottomland of the Yazoo River delta. Grant's problem, therefore, was how to get his army from the west bank of the river north of the city to the high ground east of the city. He had about 50,000 men in three corps opposed by 31,000 under John C. Pemberton in and around Vicksburg.

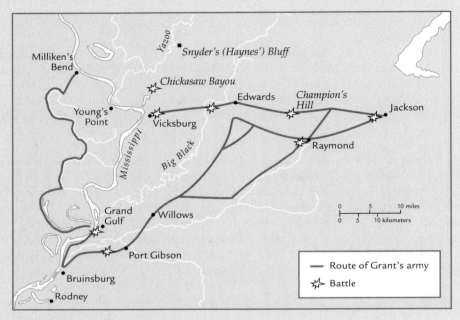

Figure 23.2 The Vicksburg Campaign

Through the cold and rainy winter, he kept his troops and a gunboat squadron under Admiral Porter busy in attempts to reach the city. Two attempts to navigate the Yazoo swamps failed, while other attempts to cut canals across the neck of land opposite Vicksburg, and thus to bypass the city's batteries or even to reach the Red River by canal, proved fruitless. It is not clear that Grant expected any of these efforts to work, but they kept his army busy, the rebel forces uncertain, and the president (who pushed the canal project) happy.

Then, in late March 1863, when the weather dried, he launched one of the most daring campaigns of the war (Figure 23.2). Leaving Sherman's corps to continue demonstrations opposite and north of the city, he marched his other two corps southward, well to the west of the river, to a point nearly sixty miles below Vicksburg. There they linked up with Porter's fleet of gunboats and transports, which had slipped past the Confederate batteries in two stages on the nights of April 16 and 22. While these movements were going on, a large force of Union cavalry

swept into Mississippi unopposed (the rebel cavalry all being in Tennessee), plundering supplies, wrecking railroads, and sowing further confusion as to Grant's intentions until they reached Union lines around Baton Rouge—perhaps the most successful cavalry raid of the war.

On April 30, Grant's army crossed the river, defeating a small rebel force at Port Gibson the next day. However, instead of turning north toward the city and into the teeth of Pemberton's defenses, Grant abandoned his supply lines and struck northeast toward Jackson. His men, carrying their supplies and living off the land, defeated Confederate detachments in detail before Jackson on May 12. Having taken Jackson and cut the rail lines into Vicksburg, Grant turned west, defeated more of Pemberton's army at Champion's Hill on May 16, and arrived before the city on May 18. Though a costly assault followed by a siege would be required before the city fell on July 4, that result and the splitting of the Confederacy were already assured by Grant's careful planning, logistical daring, and rapid marching.

firepower even of retreating infantry meant that cavalry were limited not only in attacking but also in pursuing, so that Civil War armies proved remarkably difficult to finish off in the field. Most armies defeated on the battlefield escaped bloodied but still intact, and indeed, many managed to inflict greater casualties on their victorious attackers. Again, the advantage of the defense meant that a heroic stand by one unit in an army, such as Thomas's at Chickamauga, could save the rest from being surrounded or overrun.

The recognized advantages of defensive tactics encouraged a new development: entrenching. If some natural cover were not available, such as the sunken lane at Fredericksburg, quick use of shovels could create cover. By 1864 in Virginia, Lee's army was routinely digging in wherever it stopped, and given any amount of time, such earthworks became formidable indeed. Little except the presence of interlocked, pointed wooden stakes instead of not-yet-invented barbed wire distinguishes the trenches at Petersburg from those on the western front in World War I.

Given all these advantages, it is no wonder that massed attacks succeeded so rarely and often appeared suicidal. The occasional success—most notably, the Union's astonishing storming of rebel positions on Missionary Ridge outside Chattanooga—appears all the more spectacular in contrast and must be explained in terms of total failure of morale on the part of the defenders rather than in tactical terms. More often, attacks succeeded because of the element of surprise (the first that many Union units at Shiloh knew of an impending battle was the sudden low roar of Confederate musketry) or because units got on the flank or rear of the defense and enfiladed an entire position. This put a further premium on prebattle marching and maneuver, which could either drive an enemy from its position without a fight, as Sherman was able to drive Johnston from Atlanta by cutting all the rail lines into the city, or set up surprise flank attacks, such as Jackson's at Chancellorsville. Even then, hard fighting was necessary and, as Shiloh shows, could not guarantee victory, especially if fresh troops showed up to oppose the weary attackers. When victory did come from such attacks, it was often, not because entire units were routed or captured, but because the defending general lost his nerve and conceded defeat. Some of Lee's victories, such as in the Seven Days Battle against McClellan, resulted from his successful psychological warfare against his hapless opponents and were achieved despite higher casualties in his army than in his opponents'. He met his match in Grant,

Confederate Dead at Marye's Heights After the Battle of Fredericksburg   The vastly improved range and accuracy of rifled muskets made attacks expensive, but even defenders behind earthworks suffered increased casualties.

who could not be cowed and who, despite his reputation in some quarters for unimaginative bludgeoning of his foes, had a lower casualty rate in all of his campaigns than Lee did in all of his. (See the Sources box "The Passing of the Armies" for a first-hand account of what it was like to serve under Grant.)

In short, such defensive tactics meant massive casualties. Antietam, where 3654 died, is the bloodiest single day in American history, and more Americans died in the Civil War—at least 618,000 and perhaps as many as 700,000—than in all its other wars combined. The sheer number of deaths and injuries of the war accounts for at least some of the continuing impact of the war on the American psyche.

Assessment

Why the North Won   The Civil War makes a good historiographical case study in the dangers of explaining victory or defeat in war. In particular, there is a tendency to think that because one side won, it was inevitably going to win, and so to explain the outcome in terms of deterministic factors. Thus, some historians have cited the North's vast manpower and

The Passing of the Armies

Joshua Chamberlain was a Union general who accepted the Confederate surrender at Appomattox, won a Congressional Medal of Honor for his actions at Gettysburg, and returned after the war to college teaching and a university presidency in Maine. Chamberlain here summarizes the late-1864 campaigns by the Army of the Potomac under Grant.

■   ■   ■

A similar fate befell the new hope kindled by Grant's sudden change to a new base of operations, —a movement bold if not hazardous, being practically a change of front under fire for the whole army on a grand scale. Skillfully withdrawing from the enemy's front by secret orders and forced marches, swiftly crossing the James River on transports and pontoons, hurrying forward to strike a surprise on weakly defended Petersburg, and thus cut Lee's main communications and turn his entire position— seemed good generalship. But the bold plan and generous following stultified by confusion of understandings and supine delays of subordinates, brought all to nought once more with terrible recoil and reckoning. Then the long slow fever of profitless minor action and wasteful inaction, with the strange anomaly of a mutual siege; crouching in trenches, skulking under bomb-proofs and covered ways, lining parapets where to show a head was to lure a bullet, picketing a crowded hostile front where the only tenure of life was the tacit understanding of common humanity, perpetual harassing by spasmodic raid or futile dash, slow creepings flankward yet never nearer the main objective, —such was the wearisome, wearing experience, month after month, the new year bringing no sign nor hope that anything better could be done on that line than had been so dearly and vainly tried before.

The resultant mood of such a front was not relieved by what reached us from the rear. The long-suffering, and helpless grief of homes; the sore-tried faith and patience of the whole North almost faltering; recruiting disenchanted, supplemented by enormous bounties and finally by draft and conscription; newspapers jeering at the impotence of the army; self-seeking politicians at the Capitol plotting against the President; . . .

The number of men of all arms present for duty equipped in the Army of the Potomac at the opening of Grant's campaign, as shown by the consolidated morning reports of May 4, 1864, was 97,162. . . . The number of men available for battle in the Fifth Corps at the start was 25,695. . . . And the casualties of the six weeks from the Rapidan to the James . . . total 16,245. This is 3398 more than half the present for duty at the start. . . .

And the restless, fruitless fighting before Petersburg during the remainder of that year brought the total loss in the Corps up to 18,000, —this being almost a thousand more than two thirds of the bright faces that crossed the Rapidan in the starlight of that May morning, now gone down to earth, or beneath it, —and yet no end!

SOURCE: Joshua Lawrence Chamberlain, *The Passing of the Armies: An Account of the Final Campaign of the Army of the Potomac* (New York: Bantam Books, 1992).

industrial advantages as making the outcome of the war a foregone conclusion. Others have said that the North was bound to win because in the end it had the better generals. Still others have asserted that the South lost the will to fight or that the population of the Confederacy was unwilling or unable, because of their political traditions of states' rights and other factors, to do what was necessary to win.

But as late as September 1864, the outcome of the war was still clearly in doubt. Lincoln himself was convinced he would lose the 1864 election, and rebel victories in key battles in the summer of 1862 or 1863 might have made the cause hopeless for the Union. The South could have won, and if it had, historians might be explaining victory in terms of the inadequate Union material edge, the advantages of the defense, better Southern generalship, or the loss of Northern will to prosecute the war.

Resources mattered. Generalship mattered. But the North triumphed because, at crucial turning points and in key battles of the war, it managed to win more of these uncertain encounters. Southern loss of will was then a result, not a cause, of Southern defeat. Luck, skill, and the unpredictable sequence of events led to one outcome out of a range of possible outcomes. Some wars do seem, in retrospect, to have been foregone conclusions, but the Civil War was not one of them.

Results of the War   The results of the war reflected the aims and methods of the war. The apparently obvious political result was the end of slavery. But the country's race problem was not to be solved on the battlefield, and a century would pass before the seeds of freedom finally began to bloom for the nation's African American population. The continued suppression of African American rights crippled the South's ability to recover from the war economically. The South became an economic backwater for most of the same hundred years prior to the Civil Rights Movement, unable to overcome the drag of a subject (though not legally enslaved) labor force.

This was because the most important result of the war reflected its modernity: The industrial capitalist social and economic system of the Northeast was the real winner of this war. Its growth had contributed to the sectional tensions that preceded the war; its workings supplied Union armies, built Union railroads, and attracted new immigrants to the Union; and its victory led to the reshaping of the country in its image. For it triumphed, not just over the traditional labor system of the South, typical in 1860 of far more of the world than industrial wage labor was, but also over the economics and political culture of free and independent small farmers and craftsmen that had given birth to the country. The Civil War transformed the United States from a Jeffersonian democracy into a modern, centralized, industrial nation-state.

Lessons of the War   The military lessons of the war were even simpler than its results. The lessons were these: that a major war between industrialized countries would be a total war, drawing on political and economic resources that had not existed prior to industrialization; and that the defensive effectiveness of firepower had increased dramatically. A half-century would pass before these lessons were hammered home

to the world, but they found strong echoes in the European wars of the nineteenth century.

WARFARE IN EUROPE, 1815–1914

Conflict in Europe in this century reflected both the growing power of nationalism as a source of identity and demand for change, and the increased competition between states that were in a stronger position, due to population growth and industrialization, to sustain major wars. The teleological pull of the First World War has made it commonplace among military historians to focus on the Wars of German Unification (1864–71) as the key wars of this period, but other episodes of conflict or confrontation after the First World War, such as the Cold War, suggest that it is pertinent to focus on different wars in the period 1815–1914 when considering the development of warfare.

The Crimean War, 1853–56

The first major conflict in the second half of the nineteenth century was the Crimean War, which reflected British and French concern about Russian expansionism and the fate of the Near East. Begun between Russia and Turkey in 1853, this war widened when Britain and France came to the support of the Turks in 1854 in order to prevent Russia from dominating the Black Sea and the Balkans and, thus, apparently threatening the overland route to India. This led Britain in particular, which exaggerated the threat from Russia, to come to Turkey's aid. Domestic factors also played a role, as Napoleon III of France sought prestige to strengthen his political position and to satisfy his desire for glory.

The war showed the difficulty of defeating a continental (major land) power and the contrast between being able to project force and being able to achieve outcomes. Despite French suggestions of a march on Moscow, the Allies lacked the land resources of Napoleon I. Conversely, they were far more powerful at sea. Indeed the Russian navy, while capable of conclusively beating the Turks off Sinope in the Black Sea in 1853, did not dare take on the British. As a result, the war focused on naval and amphibious action against the Russians. Naval operations by the Allies in the Baltic, which threatened Saint Petersburg, were matched by a full-scale expedition to Crimea to take the Russian Black Sea naval base of Sevastopol.

The difficulty of the task, however, had not been properly gauged and the Allies lacked the necessary manpower. In besieging Sevastopol, the Allies also surrendered mobility and exposed themselves to Russian relief attempts, which focused on the ports through which the Allies were landing all their supplies—the cause of the battles of Balaclava and Inkerman in 1855.

The Russian failure to breach the supply links was an Allied defensive success matched by that of the Russians at Sevastopol. Despite heavy artillery support, Anglo-French land assaults on the base initially failed. Furthermore, in a harbinger of warfare to come, the Allies had to face a type of trench warfare that was different from earlier sieges. Strongly entrenched outside the town and making able use of earthen defenses, the Russian forces were supported by over 1000 cannon, while the Allies fired 1,350,000 rounds of artillery ammunition during the siege. In the end, Sevastopol fell in 1855 after a successful French surprise attack on a part of the defenses, while the Treaty of Paris of 1856 severely limited Russian naval activity in the Black Sea.

The Crimean War also illuminated the deficiencies of contemporary military operations. Troops lacked adequate food, clean water, shelter, clothing, and medical assistance, and this helped lead to heavy losses from disease. The commanders, particularly the British, lacked professionalism, and, due to poor planning, strategy occurred almost by accident.

Yet, as later with World War I, in which generalship also has been criticized, it is possible to underrate the achievement of deploying, supplying, and controlling large forces, as well as the extent to which each war ended with victory for one side. In the Crimean War, the Allies successfully deployed forces into Russia and kept them there until they had achieved their task, a goal that had eluded Napoleon I in 1812. And while Britain and France combined lacked Napoleon's manpower, the ability to move forces had been altered by the Allies' embracing of new technology, in the form of steamships, that enabled them to sustain their presence. These steamships were not matched on the Russian side by railways capable of moving large numbers of troops and sufficient supplies. Once ashore, the Allies preserved this advantage by making a port their target; there was no deep deployment into the interior comparable to that in 1812 (or in 1941–42, when the Germans invaded Russia).

Another point of more general relevance is the improvement in the British war effort during the conflict. It is generally a mistake to judge effectiveness from initial campaigns, and the Crimean War was no exception. Better transport, medical, and supply provisions helped improve the health of the army. And in another harbinger of things to come, the Crimean War saw major advances in war reporting in the press, with news sent home by telegraph, and in war photography.

The Wars of Italian Unification, 1848–60

The nationalist-inspired quest by the leaders of some Italian states to drive Austria from Italy and to unify the states led to conflict earlier in the century, with the Austrians victorious in 1848–49 over Piedmont-Sardinia, the Italian state in the forefront of nationalist activity.

In 1859, war resumed as Napoleon III sought to use Italy as an opportunity to unravel the 1815 peace accord that had marked France's earlier failure and instead to assert French superiority. The resulting Franco-Austrian war in Italy anticipated many features of later conflicts between major states. Both sides employed railways in the mobilization and deployment of their forces. In the opening stage of the war, the French moved 50,000 men to Italy by rail, thus helping to gain the initiative. Moreover, the total forces deployed were substantial. At the battle of Solferino on June 24, there were 160,000 men on each side, which helped lead to heavy casualties—39,000.

Larger numbers also led to serious problems for command and control. Indeed, the high commands of both sides largely lost control of the course of battles; instead of being the masterpieces of Napoleonic encirclement that were held up as an ideal, they were more attritional in character. More generally, there was a lack of planning and of command coherence. This reflected the more general midcentury prevalence of personal rivalries within command structures that did not act as effective hierarchies. Thus, it was difficult to get subordinate commanders to carry out their orders. In 1859, the French also suffered from the poor military leadership of Napoleon III, who did not match his famous namesake in operational or tactical skill. There were problems as well with transporting and supplying the numbers of troops deployed. The French were fortunate that their battlefield determination in what turned out to be a short war enabled them to overcome the effects of these deficiencies. At Magenta (May 4) and Solferino,

French infantry advances with the bayonet were successful against poorly trained and led Austrian infantry, who were unable to draw much benefit from their technically advanced (although still muzzle-loading) rifles. The Austrian infantry had had inadequate training in range finding and sighting, and as a consequence, the French were able to close and employ their bayonets. Using tactics similar to those of the Napoleonic period, such as dense deployments and column formations, the French also benefited from superior artillery. Their new rifled cannon were better than the Austrian smoothbores and destroyed most of them with highly accurate counterbattery fire, before devastating the Austrian infantry.

Having won the battles, however, the French did not exploit the victory as Napoleon I had done in Italy in 1796–97. Instead of attacking the rest of Austrian Italy, Napoleon III, affected by the heavy casualties at Solferino, a lack of reserves, and concern about Prussian views, negotiated a peace that led to his ally, Sardinia, gaining Lombardy and Parma from Austria, and, in turn, ceding Savoy and Nice to France. France seemed the leading power in Europe, and it appeared inconceivable that within twelve years German troops would be shelling Paris.

Again, it would be all too easy to press on to consider the Wars of German Unification. But this would neglect not only continued conflict in Italy but also what it indicates about the diversity of types of warfare in nineteenth-century Europe and the variety of successful military organizations.

The end of the war in northern Italy led Giuseppe Garibaldi, a radical supporter of unification, to sail with 1000 red-shirted volunteers to Sicily in 1860 to help a revolt against the Kingdom of the Two Sicilies (Sicily and southern Italy) of the reactionary Neapolitan Bourbons. Neapolitan forces were defeated, and Garibaldi then captured Palermo, the capital of Sicily, after three days of street fighting. He went on to conquer southern Italy before handing it over to Piedmont-Sardinia, whose ruler created the Kingdom of Italy.

This was one of the most rapid and complete victories of the period 1816–1913. In place of a defeat of the main field army of an opponent, as by the French in 1859 or the Prussians in 1866, there was a conquest of a state. The domestic dimension of what was in part a civil war was also notable. The Bourbon regime was fairly weak, especially in Sicily, much of which was close to ungovernable as a result of widespread brigandage, and its overthrow was partly a revolution rather than a straight conquest.

Similarly, in Spain, during the civil wars known as the Carlist Wars (1833–40 and 1873–76), there was an interaction of battle with insurrectionary conflict. As in other civil wars, strategy, operations, morale, and generalship were shot through with political considerations.

Prussia and the Wars of German Unification, 1864–71

This dimension of civil war was not present in the Wars of German Unification—the conflicts between Prussia and Denmark (1864), Austria (1866), and France (1870–71)—and this helped ensure that they were less useful as a template for military success than was to be subsequently assumed, both by the German state created by Prussia and more generally (see Figure 23.3). Indeed, a characteristic of subsequent Prussian-German war making was that it sought military solutions in warfare rather than also directing sufficient attention to the wider political contexts.

The key to Prussian military success in 1864–71 at the strategic level was sequential warfare: The Prussians fought their opponents separately, avoiding the two-front wars that were to bedevil Germany in 1914–18 and 1941–45. At the operational level, the key factor was the development by Prussia of a General Staff system that provided the basis for effective and rapid decision making, not least with the implementation of strategic plans in terms of timed operational deployments, effective exploitation of railway networks for strategic and operational troop movements, and interrelated tactical actions. Coordination during combat proved a key characteristic of the Prussian system, and one that opponents lacked.

There was also a determined engagement with new technology, both military and nonmilitary. Helmuth von Moltke, the chief of the Prussian General Staff, sought to counter the benefits that rifled weapons and the scale of conflict had given the defense by avoiding frontal attack, instead seeking to envelop opposing forces and obliging them to mount such attacks themselves in an effort to regain freedom of maneuver. Moltke also adapted Napoleonic ideas of the continuous offensive to the practicalities of the industrial age, including railways. He sought battle as well, because, through decisive victory in battle, which destroyed the ability of the enemy forces to continue effective resistance, he hoped to obtain a rapid close to his wars. In 1864, for instance, the

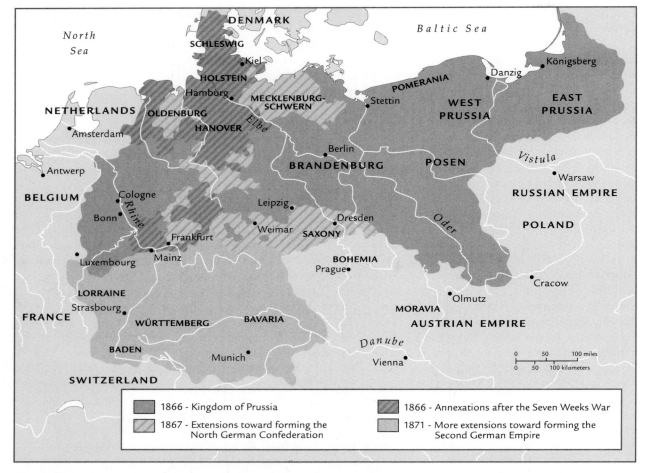

Figure 23.3 German Unification   The German Empire came to include Prussia and the many smaller southern and western German states but to exclude Austria, leaving Prussia as the dominant power in the federation.

outnumbered Danes suffered from the better rifles, cannon, and training of the Prussians and yielded Schleswig-Holstein as the price of peace.

The Austro-Prussian War, 1866   Two years later, in the Seven Weeks War, the Prussians achieved a speedy triumph over not only the Austrians but also their German allies, such as Hanover and Hesse-Cassel. The Prussians gained the initiative thanks in part to their more effective mobilization and deployment plans. Each side deployed a quarter of a million men on July 3 at Sadowa, the decisive battle. The Austrians were in a reasonable defensive position, had better artillery, and had the possibility of using interior lines to defeat the separate Prussian armies in detail, but they were outmaneuvered by the Prussians, who

demonstrated Moltke's strategy of exterior lines. Whereas Napoleon I had used separately operating corps within his army, Moltke employed independently operating armies, and whereas Napoleon had concentrated his forces prior to the battle, Moltke aimed for a concentration of his armies during the battle. The rapidity of Prussian operational movement obviated the theoretical advantage of Austrian interior lines and resulted in the Prussians consistently turning Austrian flanks and threatening Austrian lines of communication.

The Prussians also proved superior on the battlefield. Prussian units possessed a flexibility and command initiative their opponents lacked, ensuring that the Austrian positions were caught in the flank and hit by cross fire, whereas massed Austrian attacks led

The Franco-Prussian War This highly romanticized painting shows a Prussian cavalry charge against French infantry. Rifles and ever-improving artillery were already driving cavalry to the margins of most battles.

to heavy losses. The Prussian tactic of concentrating strength on the skirmishing line and adopting more extended formations that were less dense than columns or lines and thus less exposed to fire, was effective. Defeat led to the collapse of the coherence and morale of the Austrian army and to the end of governmental determination. The Austrians sued for peace, paid an indemnity, and formally recognized the Prussian annexation of their allies in North Germany. The two-power system in Germany, with Austria the senior power, was defunct.

The Franco-Prussian War, 1870–71

Outmaneuvered diplomatically by the German chancellor, Otto von Bismarck, Napoleon III declared war on July 16, 1870, but without having an appropriate plan or an adequately prepared army. In contrast, Moltke rapidly deployed a force capable of seizing the initiative and taking the war to France. Rail mobilization worked as never before, and the French were outnumbered. As the Germans gained the initiative, the French lost confidence, and the French commanders surrendered mobility and the opportunity to block the Prussians. The latter's superior breech-loading, steel-tubed artillery proved crucial on the battlefield, although, as ever, it was the use made of technology that was key. Departing from the Napoleonic tradition

of gun lines laying down frontal fire, the Germans organized their artillery at corps level and operated in artillery masses: mobile batteries formed by enterprising officers, which converged on key points, annihilated them with cross fire, and then moved on.

The effective use of artillery as an integral part of tactical and operational planning and execution overcame the impressive defensive capabilities of the French infantry, which, in part thanks to the *chassepot* rifle, inflicted heavy casualties on German attacking formations. The chassepots' rounds had a tendency to tumble through the body, smashing bones, tearing tissue, and blowing exit holes four times bigger than the entry wound: Wounded Germans mentioned the "razor pain" of the French bullet.

The French Army of the Rhine under Achille Bazaine was cut off in Metz as a result of Prussian pressure in the battles of Mars-la-Tour (August 16) and Gravelotte (August 18). The attacking German forces suffered heavy losses to French defensive fire at Gravelotte, but Bazaine thereafter failed to act, providing Moltke with the opportunity to outmaneuver the Army of Chalons and trap it at Sedan. With the surrounding hills occupied by German artillery, French attacks were beaten back on September 1. The next day, the French under Napoleon III surrendered, but the Third Republic, under a Government of National

Defense that replaced Napoleon on September 4, determined to fight on and not to surrender territory as the price of peace. It was able to appeal to the tradition of republican enthusiasm, reviving the idea of revolutionary war associated with the 1790s.

The Germans, therefore, pushed on, surrounding and bombarding Paris and fighting off French attempts to relieve the city. In these attempts, the French discovered, as the Americans had done in the Civil War, that rapidly raising large forces created serious problems of supply, training, and command. Numbers alone could not suffice: It was the way in which men were integrated into already existing military structures that was crucial, as the Germans showed.

The new French armies were outfought, and the insurgent tactics of the *francs-tireurs* (French deserters or civilians who fought back) also did not seriously inconvenience the Germans. Nevertheless, the Germans responded harshly, treating the francs-tireurs as criminals, not soldiers. Summary executions helped dampen opposition, but they were also part of a pattern of German brutality that included the taking of hostages, the execution of suspects (as well as of those actually captured in arms), the mutilation of prisoners, and the destruction of towns and villages, such as Châteaudun. In part, this reflected German frustration at the difficulty of protecting increasingly lengthy supply routes, as well as the problems posed by hostile citizen volunteers who did not wear uniforms and were impossible to identify once they had discarded their rifles. In response, the Germans adopted a social typology that prefigured those of the following century, treating every "blue smock," the customary clothes of the French worker, as a potential guerrilla.

In practice, guerrilla warfare played only a minor role in the conflict and led to fewer than 1000 German casualties. However, the idea of such violence threatened not only to introduce a level of friction and uncertainty that the Germans did not want operationally but also to usher in a chaos that they could not accept psychologically. The use by regulars of violence against civilians suspected of opposition, in order to ensure that the regulars had a monopoly of force, was not new, but it entered a deadlier cycle when it was seen by the Germans as necessary and became for them an automatic response.

French defeats led to an armistice signed on January 28, 1871, and to the French accepting German terms. But these terms, which included the cession of Alsace and part of Lorraine, as well as the payment of an indemnity, were far harsher than necessary to achieve Bismarck's initial war aims, which largely had to do with incorporating the remaining independent, mostly southern, German states into the Prussian confederation that would after the war become the German Empire. Germany's, and in particular Bismarck's, reaction to the strains of guerrilla and irregular warfare thus arguably had a far larger effect after the war than during it, for the peace terms of 1871 conditioned the war terms of 1914 (see Chapter 26).

Conflict in the Balkans, 1876–78

The diversity of European warfare is indicated by the next major conflict after the Franco-Prussian War—the strife among the Turks, Bulgarians, Serbs, and Russians in the Balkans in eastern Europe. In anticipation of the Balkan conflicts in the 1990s, reports of atrocities played a role in the unfolding of events. Such atrocities were far from new, but the press attention to the brutal nature of the Turkish crushing of the Bulgarian uprising in 1876 was novel and helped to discredit the Turks in the eyes of European public opinion. The extent to which the Bulgarian rebels massacred many Muslims was ignored, while the numbers of Bulgarians killed were considerably exaggerated. Nevertheless, Russian Pan-Slavism led to the dispatch of many volunteers to help the Serbs when they declared war on the Turks in 1876, only to be defeated at Aleksinac and Djunis. The Russians formally entered the war later in 1876 and proved a far more formidable foe. However, the war underlined the tactical problems with frontal attacks, especially when poorly coordinated. The war demonstrated as well the operational disadvantages arising from essentially untrained commanders appointed through patronage—in this case, the relatives of the Russian ruler Tsar Alexander II—a system that also undermined efforts at military reform.

At the same time, the potential of the offensive was fully demonstrated. The Russians crossed the Danube at Svistov in June 1877, rapidly bombarded the garrison at Nicopolis into capitulation the following month, and finally, after costly and unsuccessful attacks, starved the garrison at Plevna into surrender in December 1877. The Russians encircled another Turkish army at the Shipka Pass the following month and then pressed on to take Plovdiv and Adrianople and to threaten Constantinople. Peace was dictated at San Stefano outside Constantinople in February 1878,

ISSUES

The Balkan Wars, 1912–13

The Balkans were a major area of European conflict in the 1870s, 1910s, 1940s, and 1990s. As such, they registered both changes in the nature of war and the continued potency of ethnic animosities. The desire for territorial control was the key objective, seen as the way to ensure ethnic survival and success.

As with the conflicts in the 1990s that caused, and arose from, the collapse of Yugoslavia, so the key in 1912–13 was the fall of the Turkish Empire in Europe. The First Balkan War (1912–13) saw Turkey attacked by its neighbors—Bulgaria, Greece, Montenegro, and Serbia—and most of its European empire conquered. At the tactical, strategic, and operational level, this war demonstrated the risks associated with the absence of mass formations, as Turkish strategic dispersal—designed to prevent territorial loss in the face of attack from a number of directions—enabled their opponents to achieve key superiorities in particular areas of attack. This was similar to the problems that faced Poland in 1939 and Yugoslavia in 1941, as a result of the dispersal of forces to protect long perimeters, when they were successfully attacked by Germany and its allies. Operationally, in 1912–13, the Turks squandered the tactical advantage of the defensive through unsuccessful attempts to encircle their opponents. And the lack of rehearsal in yearly military maneuvers comparable to those of Germany and other powers at the time greatly lessened Turkish effectiveness.

At the tactical level, although the use of air power was small-scale and had little effect, effective artillery played a crucial role. Conversely, in the absence of artillery superiority, the Bulgarian attack on the entrenched positions of the Çatalca Line was defeated in November 1912, saving the remaining Turkish positions in Europe near Constantinople (Istanbul) and prefiguring tactical positions in the First World War. The Turkish artillery was outnumbered in this battle, but its superior centralized command and control enabled it to damage the Bulgarian artillery and to repel Bulgarian attacks. The Bulgarian emphasis on bravery in attack and on the use of the bayonet cost them dearly, although the absence of surprise was also important, as was the extent to which the Turks had defense in depth. The Bulgarians suffered 12,000 casualties.

The strength of the defensive was also indicated at Scutari, a Turkish fortress besieged by Montenegro in 1912–13. Several costly attacks, which led to the death of close to 10,000 Montenegrin troops, were required before the fortress surrendered.

The dynamics of power politics quickly led the victors to fall out, and in the Second Balkan War (1913), Bulgaria unsuccessfully fought its recent allies, as well as Romania and Turkey. The Bulgarians fought well in Macedonia, where they concentrated their forces, but this allowed the Turks to recapture Adrianople and the Romanians to advance on the capital, Sofia. Bulgaria capitulated and surrendered territory. Renewed conflict in the Balkans—what became the First World War—was to begin a year later.

---

with Bulgaria established as a major state including Macedonia and stretching to the Aegean Sea.

Nevertheless, as a reminder of the interaction of local conflict with great-power politics, an interaction that was to lead to the outbreak of World War I in 1914 (see the Issues box "The Balkan Wars, 1912–13"), Britain and Austria intervened, and, having threatened war, successfully insisted that Bulgaria receive less territory. Conversely, in 1897, in a much neglected war between Greece and Turkey, Russian intervention deterred the victorious Turks from advancing on Athens.

Copying Germany

Prussian success in the Wars of German Unification led other states to see united Germany as the model of military excellence as they sought to prepare for future wars in an intensely competitive atmosphere in which rationalizations for territorial aggrandizement focused on nationalism and state interest. Planning and preparation were the keys to modern warfare. As Western militaries became more institutionalized and professional, so planning came to play an ever-greater role. Military education was emphasized, and in the new staff colleges, Clausewitz's hitherto obscure *On War* (1832) became widely known, reflecting the prestige of German war making. In planning, stress was placed on the offensive, which, based on study of the Wars of German Unification, was seen as the sole way to secure success.

A wider cultural context affected both military planning and the willingness of the average male citizen to acquiesce in the burdens of military spending and, in continental Europe, of peacetime conscription. The Social Darwinism of the late nineteenth century, with its emphasis on the competitiveness inherent in human existence, encouraged interest in aggressive military planning. This was supported, both with resources and psychologically, by the tremendous population expansion of the period and by the major increase in industrial capacity in the West and also in Japan. Academics, scientists, artists, clerics, and intellectuals also played a major role in formulating rationales and objectives for expansion and conflict. War was seen as a glorious means to renew a people's energies and escape cultural and moral decadence. Most intellectuals were ardent nationalists, and internationalism had only limited appeal. A concept of triumphant will, as well as millenarian theology and providentialism, contributed to a sense of the rightness of conflict. Educated elites believed in the moral value of war; this was a "rationality" centered on themes of sacrifice and ideas of vitalism. Contributing to the same end, industrialists pressed the economic and social utility of weapons programs.

Such ideas proved more influential than those that lay behind the attempt to decree accepted laws of war, although the latter led to a series of international congresses, the decisions of which were to influence the post-1945 move to establish international codes of behavior. The absence of major wars in the last three decades of the nineteenth century helped boost the popularity of the idea of war and the acceptability of military service: it was a no-risk rite of passage, at a time when other male rites of passage had been discredited. Military parades, flags, uniforms, and medals symbolized the appeal of military service.

With the offensive in vogue, Clausewitz's chapter on defensive warfare (the longest in *On War*) was largely ignored, and some translations omitted it altogether. To sustain the offensive and achieve victory in the face of ever-more-lethal technology on the battlefield, strategists and tacticians called for ever-larger forces. As a result, planners and commentators emphasized the value of conscription and the maintenance of substantial reserves. Having fulfilled their allocated period of permanent military service, conscripts moved into the reserves, where their military effectiveness was maintained by annual maneuvers. Choice played no role in this system. The net effect of conscription was the availability of millions of men trained for war.

Industrial capability underwrote a major increase in military strength. Thanks to the nature of industrial culture and the availability of organizational expertise, investment capital, and trained labor, it was possible to translate novel concepts rapidly into new or improved weapons, and, with mass production, such weapons could be deployed rapidly in large quantities. The improvement in artillery was of particular significance as it became the most destructive battlefield weapon of the first half of the twentieth century. More generally, a sense of new opportunities stemmed from technological advances. In 1909, Colonel Frederick Trench, the British military attaché in Berlin, reported that the Germans were developing power traction vehicles "of a type suitable for military use."

These developments also affected nations that for political and cultural reasons did not have peacetime conscription—most obviously, Britain and the United States. Indeed, these developments contributed to anxiety about the effectiveness of their military arrangements. Mindful of the prestigious German system, the Esher Committee of 1904 recommended the foundation of a British General Staff, whose creation led to the strengthening of command and planning structures. The General Staff was designed to ensure a trained body of senior officers across the army, and this led to staff tours and conferences. The contrast between British activities in the Second Boer War in South Africa (1899–1902) and the deployment and operations of the British Expeditionary Force in Belgium and France in 1914 suggested a marked rise in British military efficiency.

CONCLUSION

Meanwhile, commentators studied the wars that did occur in order to have some idea of the likely nature of a future major war in Europe. The Russo-Japanese War of 1904–5 (see Chapter 24), for example, was seen as evidence that the attacker would win and that it was possible to wage a modern war successfully and relatively quickly, even in the face of defensive firepower. Clearly, the cultural context noted above colored such interpretations.

Industrialization in the context of nationalist competition, as well as the growing dominance of Europeans globally in the last quarter of the nineteenth century, had a deep effect on the culture of the major military powers of Europe. An optimistic belief in "Progress"—defined not just materially but morally—dominated the intellectual culture of European leadership. The road to 1914 was paved with confidence; the destination would thus prove all the more shocking when the road reached the trenches of World War I (see Chapter 26).

SUGGESTED READINGS

Black, Jeremy. *Western Warfare, 1775–1882*. Bloomington: University of Indiana Press, 2001. An analysis that avoids a simplistic account of change.

Boemke, Manfred, Roger Chickering, et al., eds. *Anticipating Total War: The German and American Experiences, 1871–1914*. Cambridge: Cambridge University Press, 2004. A collection of articles examining aspects of the historiography of the concept of total war and the cultural history of the growth and impact of the idea of total war.

Craig, Gordon. *The Politics of the Prussian Army, 1640–1945*. New York, Oxford University Press, 1964. A masterful overview of the development of the leadership of the Prussian army and its role in politics.

Foote, Shelby. *The Civil War: A Narrative*. 3 Vols. New York: Vintage Books, 1986. A comprehensive narrative of the war, with a wealth of illustrations.

Howard, Michael. *Franco-Prussian War: The German Invasion of France, 1870–1871*. London: Routledge, 1985. Still useful, though see now Wawro.

McPherson, James. *Battle Cry of Freedom: The Civil War Era*. New York: Ballantine Books, 1988. An authoritative overview of the Civil War by the dean of Civil War historians; sets the military action firmly in its political, social, and economic contexts.

Palmer, Michael A. *Lee Moves North: Robert E. Lee on the Offensive*. New York: Wiley, 1999. A critical reexamination of Lee's Northern campaigns, focusing on the weaknesses in strategic vision, planning, and logistics that characterized the Southern icon's offensive generalship.

Showalter, Dennis. *The Wars of German Unification*. New York: Oxford University Press, 2004. A dense but valuable overview of the German midcentury wars. See also his *Railroads and Rifles: Soldiers, Technology and the Unification of Germany* (New York: Oxford University Press, 1976), the seminal work on the topic.

Smallman-Raynor, M. R., and A. D. Cliff. *War Epidemics: An Historical Geography of Infectious Diseases in Military Conflict and Civil Strife, 1850–2000*. Oxford: Oxford University Press, 2004. An excellent analysis of the relationship of war and epidemic disease, including both the effects of disease within armies and the role of armies as vectors of disease spread.

Wawro, Geoffrey. *The Franco-Prussian War: The German Conquest of France in 1870–1871*. Cambridge: Cambridge University Press, 2003. A superb narrative and analysis of the war, with balanced assessment of the strengths and weaknesses of both sides and incisive criticism of Bismarck's peace terms. See also Wawro's *The Austro-Prussian War: Austria's War with Prussia and Italy in 1866* (Cambridge: Cambridge University Press, 1997), which focuses on the Austrians. Also of interest for putting the entire period into perspective is his *Warfare and Society in Europe, 1792–1914* (London: Routledge, 2000), a good overview with the heaviest coverage for the period from 1848–1914.

Weigley, Russell. *A Great Civil War: A Military and Political History, 1861–1865*. Bloomington: Indiana University Press, 2001. Another authoritative overview of the Civil War that sets the military action in its political, social, and economic contexts.

CHAPTER 24

Guns and Government: Global European Dominance, 1800–1914

Professional national armies, armed and equipped by the forces of industrial capitalism and motivated by nationalism, represented a quantum leap forward in the ability and desire of westerners (essentially, Europe and the United States) to project military force. Despite the fact that the vast bulk of this military capacity was deployed within Europe, those contingents sent overseas presented nonwesterners with a critical challenge in the nineteenth century. Their indigenous modes of military organization—all of them—were suddenly rendered uncompetitive, and therefore, their political independence was often threatened. What responses were possible?

On King Street in Honolulu stands a statue of King Kamehameha I. Kamehameha had united the Hawaiian islands into one kingdom at the end of the eighteenth century, winning the decisive battle in part by using European ships and cannon. The statue was erected in 1878 by King David Kalakaua. Kalakaua, whose library included Prussian and French volumes on military organization, was working to maintain the independence of his small kingdom against increasing economic (and implicit military) pressure from Western powers. Though the statue puts Kamehameha in traditional Hawaiian garb, the pose would have been instantly recognizable to any Western diplomat: It is triumphant Caesar Augustus. It thus represented Kalakaua's effort to legitimize his kingdom to those threatening it. But Kamehameha as Augustus also symbolizes the central problem facing nonwesterners at this time: To what extent did they have to become western to defend themselves? Did defense of their cultural traditions necessitate abandonment of those very traditions? Or was there a way to modernize without westernizing, to dress Caesar in Hawaiian garb?

The problem was a difficult one because Western military organization by the eighteenth century had already become inextricably tied to modes of social, economic, and political organization foreign to much of the traditional world. The addition of industrial economics and nationalist ideologies only made the importation of European-style armies and the leap to modernism more difficult. Many areas could not meet the challenge and fell under Western imperial control. Attempts to import modern military organization in Russia, under Peter the Great (r. 1689–1725), and subsequently in the Ottoman Empire and China, highlight the difficulties of the challenge even for great powers. Only Japan succeeded in meeting the West on its own terms and, in so doing, then joining the imperialist powers. This chapter surveys and analyzes these varying responses to the new power of the West and the challenge it posed to the cultural identities of the peoples of the world.

WARFARE IN LATIN AMERICA

The Latin American Wars of Independence arose from the disruption caused by Napoleon's conquest of Spain in 1808 and the subsequent Peninsular War of 1808–13, which created great confusion in the Spanish Empire. Once Napoleon had been defeated, there was a major attempt to reestablish royal authority in Spanish America, but this effort was handicapped by Spain's financial and economic weakness. After Argentina gained independence in 1816, forces under José de San Martin crossed the Andes and defeated the royalists (pro-Spaniards) in Chile in 1817–18. Further north, after repeated failures, Simon Bolívar overran Colombia (1819), Venezuela (1821), Ecuador (1822), and Peru (1823–24). Mexico declared independence in 1821, while in 1822–23 a successful rebellion ended Portuguese rule over Brazil.

These wars indicated the difficulty both of sustaining a revolutionary struggle and of mounting effective counterinsurgencies. The force-space ratios of conflict in Latin America were different from those in western and central Europe, and the problems of political control were greater. The need of both revolutionaries and royalists to create new armies put a premium on overcoming problems in recruitment and on limiting desertion. The creation and legitimization of government structures were important in providing the context for harnessing human resources. And remedies were often brutal. Recruitment was enforced with violence and the threat of violence; desertion was punished savagely, frequently with executions; and, faced with major logistical problems, armies raised supplies through force. These would become the norm in the independence struggles across the world in the late twentieth century—for example, in sub-Saharan Africa. In these cases there was much burning and destruction—of crops, haciendas, and towns—in order both to deny resources to opponents and to punish those judged disloyal. As it would in the late twentieth century, a shortage of arms put a premium on foreign supplies but also ensured that weapons other than firearms were used. To the extent that the wars were civil conflicts, the emphasis was on political factors in strategy, political factors that differed from those seen in the state-to-state conflict of the Napoleonic Wars in Europe. There was also a concern with the social order and with the postwar structure of society. This led the South American rebels to endorse a policy of moderation toward loyalists that was ultimately successful.

Subsequently, the military history of Latin America was dominated by a small number of international wars, principally the Paraguayan War of 1864–70 and the War of the Pacific of 1879–83, and by a much more extensive and incessant process in which the militaries of the newly independent states played a key role in the contesting of authority and the consolidation of power within those states. Force was the key element in attempts to gain political power in the metropole: Military coups were common, and contested elections led to uprisings, as in Argentina in 1874. In addition, there were serious problems due to rebellions in particular regions, as in Argentina in 1870. Military influence, indeed rule, was a major aspect of Latin American politics.

IMPERIALISM: THE IMPOSITION OF EUROPEAN RULE

The European capacity for imperialist expansion increased steadily throughout the nineteenth century. This was partly a result of the growing economic resources and organizational muscle of European states supplied by emerging industrial economies. Steamships, railroads, and telegraphs provided an infrastructure of communications and transport capable of linking and controlling far vaster and more widespread possessions than ever before. Weapons such as machine guns began to give European armies and navies serious advantages in battle; steamboats and gunboats equipped with rifled cannon could dominate previously inaccessible rivers. Medical advances, especially the use of quinine to combat malaria in tropical zones, opened new areas to permanent European occupation.

But capacity and motive are different things, and for much of the nineteenth century, European powers remained focused on each other while their overseas holdings, especially in Latin America, actually freed themselves from European political control. Only India saw major advances in European (British) rule before 1870, and that represented the continuance and consolidation of an older eighteenth-century colonialist impulse that was largely in private hands until 1857. Still, the threat of European military power loomed over the globe.

From 1870 on, however, the major (and some minor) European powers engaged in a scramble for imperial possessions in Africa and Asia, joined several decades later by the United States and Japan. What prompted this sudden increase in imperial ambitions? The answer involves a complex set of factors that interacted in sometimes unpredictable ways. Rising economic competition played a role: Prior to 1870, only Britain was a major industrial power; by 1870, other nations had joined the ranks, and a perceived need to secure the raw materials of the rest of the world drove some imperial competition. (Not all colonies proved profitable, but a vast flow of resources headed to Europe at less than market rates, thanks to rising political control.) Nationalism prompted some land grabbing simply because having a large empire became a point of national pride. A revived Christian missionary impulse added further motivation, as well as contributing to rationalizations for European rule that ran the gamut from "civilizing the savages" to "scientifically" supported racism. This mix of motives tremendously complicated the task of responding to European aggression for peoples around the world.

India

The British became the key power in South Asia, creating in the process a key hybrid form of military power. Victories in 1799–1818 were crucial. Tipu Sultan of

Drilling Sepoys Drill was a key to producing not just effective but loyal Indian soldiers serving in British-led forces.

Mysore, the leading ruler in southern India, was defeated and killed in 1799; next to succumb were the Maratha Confederation in 1803–6 and 1817–18, the Kingdom of Kandy in Sri Lanka in 1815, and the Gurkhas of Nepal in 1815–16. Key episodes in these hard-fought wars included the storming of the Mysore capital of Seringapatam in 1799 and the Duke of Wellington's victories at Assaye (1803) and Argaum (1803), in which British bayonet charges played a decisive role. Casualties claimed over a quarter of the British force at Assaye.

Aside from British units, the British relied on Indian manpower. The first Indian troops raised by the East India Company appear to have been two companies of Rajputs enlisted at Bombay in 1684. The mostly native army of the British East India Company rose from 18,200 in 1763 to 154,000 in 1805. Britain had come to dominate the market for Indian military manpower, but this was an active relationship in which the British molded the situation. In Bengal in the 1800s, for example, an effective force of cavalry supported by light artillery was created, greatly enhancing mobility, while a company of skirmishers was added to each regiment of native infantry. This reflected both responsiveness to developments in Europe and a degree of hybridization between British and Indian military practices. (For a look at the darker side of

British-Indian military collaboration, however, see the Issues box "Presenting the Indian Mutiny.")

Methodical, relatively orderly military and administrative structures were important to British success, as was the crucial ability to buy military service. The systematic application of power ensured that the British army in India was not one that, like most forces there, dispersed in order to forage and ravage or one that had to be held together by booty and that thus dedicated itself to a strategy of pillage. Furthermore, the British succeeded in combining firepower with a reasonable degree of mobility. They also benefited from the inability of potential opponents to cooperate: The Marathas were very divided, and in 1815–16, the Marathas and Sikhs failed to support the Gurkhas.

In the mid-1820s, British forces defeated Burma (1824–26), and in the 1830s, they consolidated their position in India. But in the 1840s, they badly mishandled an intervention in Afghanistan, with an army being destroyed in the mountain passes in January 1842 as it retreated from Kabul. However, victories over the Baluchis (1843) and Sikhs (1845–46 and 1848–49) left Britain dominant in what is now India and Pakistan. Control of Burma followed as a result of wars in 1852–53 and 1885–86, but intervention in Afghanistan in 1878–80 again proved problematic. The British were able to advance and hold positions,

ISSUES

Presenting the Indian Mutiny

Many factors contributed to the discontent among the Indian troops that led to rebellion against British control in 1857–59. The reluctance of many soldiers to serve abroad for caste reasons conflicted with the determination of the authorities that they do so. The trigger for the uprising was the British demand that their Indian soldiers use a new cartridge for their new Lee-Enfield rifles, allegedly greased (to keep the powder dry) in animal fat, a measure that was unacceptable to Muslims and Hindus for religious reasons. However, there had been a concerted plan for mutiny, with communication between the plotters, long before the issue of the cartridges arose.

Most of the Indian troops in the army's largest section, the Bengal army, mutinied in May 1857, while there was also a large-scale civilian rising in north-central India. Fortunately for the British, much of the Indian army remained loyal. No major prince joined the rebellion; indeed, the rulers of Hyderabad, Kashmir, and Nepal provided the British with assistance, while the rebellion had no foreign support. Furthermore, the movement of British troops into the region, and the inability of the badly led rebels to spread the rebellion, helped the British regain the initiative, storming Delhi and clearing the city in bitter street fighting in September 1857.

The brutal treatment of captured British women and children at Kanpur during what the British termed the Indian Mutiny was used by the British to justify their claim to be morally superior and thus to legitimate empire. The mutineers' massacre of British prisoners at Kanpur was commemorated with the Kanpur Memorial Well. The historiography and publicly projected historical memory of the events of 1857 were thus dominated by British perspectives for nearly a century.

After India gained independence in 1947, the emphasis moved to what were presented as British atrocities, especially the treatment of captured sepoys (Indian soldiers from the army), although, in practice, the execution of mutineers was normal around the world in this period. The mutiny itself was reinterpreted and renamed as a rebellion that was intended to begin a war of independence—indeed, the First War of Independence. In 2007, the 150th anniversary of the mutiny/rebellion was used by the Indian government to counter potent religious and caste divisions, and, in particular, Hindu sectarianism. The prime minister, Manmohan Singh, declared, "The fight for freedom united people from different religions and speaking different languages. Hindus and Muslims stood together shoulder to shoulder. We cannot forget the Hindu-Muslim unity that 1857 represented and held out as an example for subsequent generations."

This new "nationalist" interpretation tended to ignore the role of Indians in supporting Britain in this crisis of power, although the suppression of the rebellion depended on this support. More recent interpretations of the mutiny/rebellion coming from Western historians have moved toward cultural interpretations of the various participants' motives and actions, understood as far as possible in the context of their own times.

but they had difficulty ending resistance, let alone stabilizing the situation.

The Scramble for Africa

Most of Africa was partitioned by European powers between 1830 and 1910, particularly from 1885 (Figure 24.1). This reflected the flexibility of Western military imperialism. Along with the benefits derived from the use of modern armaments and communication technologies, it was important for imperialists to be able to adapt to different physical and political environments. Attitudes were crucial. Expansion was normative, motivated by an attitude that increasingly drew on triumphalism, racism, and cultural arrogance. Divine purpose, natural right, geographical predestination, the appropriate use of natural resources, and the extension of the

Figure 24.1 The Partition of Africa by the European Powers from 1878 to About 1914

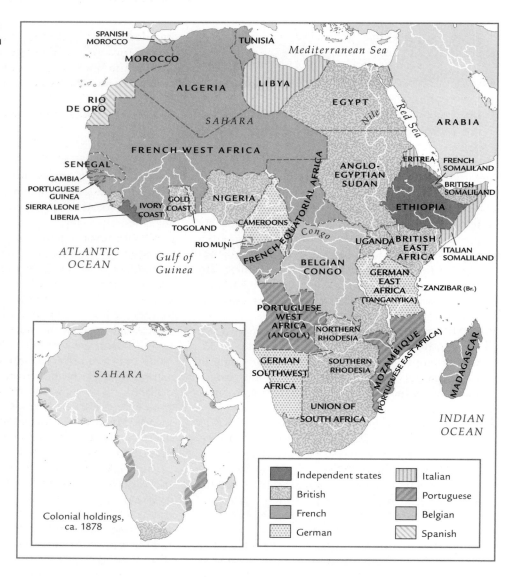

area of freedom and culture—all apparently combined to support the cause of territorial expropriation. The sense of mission that underlay late-nineteenth-century Western imperialism led to a determination to persist even in the event of setbacks, as with the British against the Zulus in southern Africa in 1879.

Western expansion also owed much to an ability to exploit native divisions and to win local support. For instance, the French used soldiers recruited in Senegal to conquer the interior of what became French West Africa—the modern states of Niger, Mali, Burkina Faso, and Chad. Thus, imperial gains in turn provided the basis for fresh conquests.

Local support was important as well when rebellions had to be confronted. From the city of Algiers, which they captured in 1830, the French, in the face of considerable opposition, expanded their power into the interior of modern Algeria. In the 1840s, they sought to build up a network of favorable tribes; and, when there was a major rebellion there beginning in March 1871, much of the population did not take part. Thus, the uprising was put down by January 1872.

In addition to superior weaponry, other aspects of Western technology were important in aiding and encouraging imperial expansion. Communications were greatly enhanced by steamship, railway, and telegraph. The building of a railway was crucial to the logistics of Britain's successful campaign in the Sudan from 1895 to 1899. (See the Highlights box "Omdurman, 1898," for an account of one British campaign in the Sudan.) Medical progress in understanding and counteracting tropical diseases was important as well.

There was also considerable brutality, especially the German suppression of the Nama and Herero uprisings in Namibia (1904–7) and the Maji Maji uprising in Tanzania (1905). Their scorched-earth policy against guerrilla resistance in Namibia led to hundreds of thousands of deaths, mostly of civilians denied water.

By then, most of Africa had been partitioned. Effective resistance to the British in northern Nigeria and to the French in the Sahara ended in 1903 and 1905, respectively; although, having invaded Libya in 1911, the Italians were unable to suppress resistance among the Senussi tribesmen in the interior. This was also the first war in which armored cars and airplanes were used.

Southeast Asia

Southeast Asian kingdoms struggled to meet the challenge of Western arms and modernization with varying degrees of success. As in other areas, Western superiority in battlefield technology was not always their major advantage and indeed, at times, was nonexistent. Rather, it was their social and political organization, and the accompanying effects in terms of army organization, discipline, and officer training, that often carried the day. The key Western technological advantage was steamships and the mobility and control of seas and rivers that they conveyed.

Burma In the eighteenth and early nineteenth centuries, both British India and Konbaung Burma were expansionist empires seemingly destined to come into conflict. The Burmese fought British military forces three times, in the 1820s, 1850s, and 1880s; the result was the gradual elimination of Burmese independence.

The Konbaung dynasty was on an almost constant military footing, with an elite force of highly trained hereditary warriors leading a mass of conscripts who were called up for particular campaigns. Overconfident, the Burmese court realized too late the military advantages possessed by the British.

Superior British weaponry and fire discipline won early battles and attracted support from traditional enemies the Burmese had subjected. Steam warships seized control of ports and rivers, depriving the Konbaung court of its richest regions. A late appeal for help to the French simply provoked the British into completing their conquest. Poor weather and disease were the only allies the Burmese had—close to half of a British force of 11,000 that took Rangoon in 1824 subsequently died in the occupation. Thus, Burma's traditional military structure failed, and it became a Western colony.

Vietnam The founder of the Nguyen dynasty, Gia-long, had attained the throne in 1802 partly with the aid of French Catholic missionaries and military men who sold him weapons and provided his army with advisors. In addition to instructing Vietnamese soldiers in the use of the latest European artillery and handguns, these advisors organized several units along European lines of drill, formation, and tactical use of their acquired Western weapons. Also, French military engineers constructed a European-style fortress (incorporating Chinese wall-building techniques as well) at the new capital city of Hue. Gia-long and his two successors expressed their gratitude for French assistance by allowing French Catholic missionaries nearly unlimited access to the country.

These moves provoked a Confucian-inspired anti-Western reaction, however, expressed in increasing persecution of Vietnamese Christians and Western missionaries. Unfortunately, this reaction coincided with rising French nationalism and empire building in competition with other European powers, and French forces moved in. They used naval superiority to destroy the Vietnamese navy, provide mobility to their ground forces, and enforce a blockade of the sea routes bringing rice to the center and north, a strategy similar to that utilized by the British in the Opium Wars in China (see below). There was no unified Vietnamese policy regarding modernization of their military forces. Loss of territory undermined the legitimacy of the Nguyen court, and severe economic problems led to recurring disturbances and uprisings that sapped much of the energy of the imperial government. Officials lashed out at Vietnamese Catholics, who called on the French for protection, which led to demands by the French for ever more territory and concessions.

But the final conquest of the rest of Vietnam in 1884–85 proved to be no walkover for the French.

Omdurman, 1898

The British had conquered Egypt by 1882, but an uprising of religiously inspired rebels, the dervishes, led by the Mahdi Mohammed Ahmed of Dongola, freed the Sudan from Egyptian control. In the process, the rebels wiped out one Anglo-Egyptian army and massacred another, led by General Charles "Chinese" Gordon, after a siege at Khartoum in 1885. This prompted the British to begin a methodical reconquest of the Sudan. Major General Sir Horatio Kitchener led a mixed force of about 8000 British and 17,000 Egyptian troops south along the Nile against the forces of the Mahdi's successor, the Khalifa Abdullah, which numbered perhaps 50,000.

Kitchener camped at Kerreri, about six miles north of Omdurman. His forces formed a shallow arc around the village, anchored by cavalry at either end on the Nile, where steam gunships provided artillery support to the army. Around 6:00 AM on September 2, the center units of the Mahdist forces, around 16,000 spearmen and riflemen, attacked, charging into the teeth of fire from howitzers and Maxim machine guns even before they got within range of the disciplined infantry fire of the Anglo-Egyptian forces. Leaving 4000 casualties on the field, they retired in disorder.

Thinking the battle won, Kitchener ordered his army to march south to occupy Omdurman before the rebels could recover. The march was spearheaded by light cavalry that ran into unexpected resistance in the hills to the southwest, losing almost a quarter of their force before driving the defenders away. The march was covered in the rear by a brigade of 3000 mainly Sudanese troops commanded by the Scotsman Hector MacDonald. The Khalifa, rapidly rallying his remaining troops, ordered his reserves to attack from the west while several units hidden behind the Kerreri hills fell on MacDonald's brigade from the north and west. MacDonald kept his outnumbered forces together while their steady fire barely held off the attacks. Belatedly learning of the trouble his rearguard was in, Kitchener directed relief forces back north while repulsing new but belated attacks on his main position. Finally, around 11:00 AM, the last desperate dervish charge was shot to pieces and the remaining Mahdists scattered, and the march to Omdurman continued.

The battle revealed the effectiveness of British artillery and machine gun fire against massed infantry charges. The Khalifa's army left over

The Vietnamese had turned to China for help, and together they outnumbered the French and were at times equipped with superior firearms such as Winchester repeaters. After a series of defeats and costly victories, the French finally achieved success by capitalizing on Western tactics, organization, and naval mobility rather than technology. Time and again, French commanders used disciplined flanking maneuvers to force Chinese retreats. China finally pulled out of the war when a French fleet sailed to the port city of Fuzhou, where most of the Chinese southern fleet was based. Within a few hours, every Chinese vessel was either destroyed or on fire, with the loss of at least 2000 Chinese and only 10 French killed and 48 wounded. According to the terms of the resulting treaty, China accepted French control of Vietnam.

Thus, in Vietnam, anti-Western reactions undermined early moves toward modernization, and Vietnam joined Cambodia and Laos as French Indochina.

Thailand Geopolitics and skillful diplomacy came to the aid of Thailand. Between 1851 and 1910, under kings Mongkut and Chulalongkorn, Thailand pursued a vigorous policy of modernization. The kings built railroads and telegraphs, opened trade routes, abolished slavery, and introduced Western education while preserving Thai literature and culture. They also remodeled the army along European lines but stressed its role as an internal police force and actively reversed the Thai tradition of aggressive expansionism so as to avoid conflict with the European powers. By modernizing, projecting a peaceful and stable image,

10,000 dead on the field, had 5000 captured by the Anglo-Egyptians, and suffered an unknown number of wounded—according to one British account any enemy wounded turned into dead because even those who appeared incapacitated would spring up as British troops passed and fire a rifle or throw a spear, and so had to be shot. Kitchener's army had only 48 men killed and 382 wounded, mostly from the light cavalry and from MacDonald's brigade.

MacDonald's Brigade in Action at Omdurman   The Sudanese troops of Hector MacDonald's brigade maintain steady fire against dervish attackers, not shown in the photograph.

Kitchener became a national hero. But the bravery and commitment to their cause of the Mahdists are also notable, as is the critical role played in the British victory by the black Sudanese troops of MacDonald's brigade. Discipline and training combined with the technology of firepower to yield heightened effectiveness. Against foes who combined their own aimed rifle fire with discipline and intelligent use of terrain, as in the Boer War of 1899–1902, the British found their technological advantage much less decisive.

and playing off European powers against each other—both Britain and France found an independent Thailand to be a useful buffer between British Burma and French Indochina—Thailand maintained its independence. This was an achievement comparable to, though very different in character from, Japan's modernization (see below).

The Philippines   "Europeanized" to some degree by centuries of Spanish rule, Filipinos had nearly succeeded in expelling Spain with U.S. help when the latter stepped in as a new colonial master. It is no coincidence that U.S. overseas imperialism followed the closing of the domestic western frontier, where a century of small-scale warfare had pitted a Western power against Native Americans who often obtained modern weaponry but who were at a severe disadvantage demographically, epidemiologically, and organizationally. This internal imperialism carried over into the U.S. war in the Philippines, where a partially modernized Filipino force resisted the United States in a bloody war from 1899 to 1902.

Superficially, the two sides appeared unevenly matched, with the Filipinos holding the advantage. The Filipinos fielded an army of over 120,000, including several regiments that had served in the Spanish constabulary forces. Most were only partially trained, but they had a fairly good supply of German rifles, in addition to weapons originally acquired from the Americans or seized from captured Spanish garrisons. They were also equipped with a few artillery pieces. What the Filipinos lacked was a large enough core of trained, experienced officers. The Americans began the war with only about 24,000 officers and men and poorer firearms than the Filipinos had. Eventually, however, over 75,000 troops (nearly two-thirds of the American army), equipped with better weapons, became involved.

The initial Filipino strategy of fighting large engagements proved disastrous: Slow-reacting Filipino armies and strongholds fell to a superior American navy, which swiftly transported troops from one area to another and supported ground forces with naval artillery. A shift to guerrilla war aimed to keep forces in the field and inflict enough damage so that the American populace would elect a more sympathetic administration in 1900. Filipino and American atrocities did affect American opinion, leading to congressional hearings and changes in American military organization, but such tactics failed militarily. American commanders, often utilizing tactics learned in the Native American wars at home, isolated and destroyed Filipino guerrilla forces while successfully waging a hearts-and-minds campaign to win the support of Filipino civilians. But the conquest of the Philippines was costly. Over 4000 American soldiers died in the fighting, as well as several hundred allied Filipinos; the Filipinos lost at least 20,000 guerrillas and over 200,000 civilians, mostly to disease. Against a force at least partially modernized, the U.S. victory resulted primarily from superior organization, logistics, and a naval force.

MEETING EUROPE: ATTEMPTS AT REFORM

The Ottomans

Militarily, the decline of the Ottoman Empire was not clearly evident until the early eighteenth century, which saw the Ottomans steadily pushed out of their European territories. Much of this rollback was caused by a new opponent, imperial Russia, but traditional enemies such as Austria also made inroads. At times in the seventeenth and even eighteenth centuries, Ottoman armies scored impressive victories, but these masked the fact that the Ottoman military was dependent on numbers rather than tactics and technology. As we saw in Chapter 17, the Ottoman defeat at the gates of Vienna in 1689 was due in part to European advances in weaponry and uses of those weapons and in part to Ottoman decline. In addition,

economic difficulties resulting from direct European access to the Far East and European inflation (see Chapter 17) undermined the Ottoman ability to pay for its army. Further, the Janissaries, once a pillar of Ottoman power, had by 1800 become corrupt political meddlers, ineffective even when they could be persuaded to fight. And weak sultans made things worse: Feeble central authority allowed both internal fragmentation and external aggression against Ottoman territory. The Ottomans came late to realize that reform of their military was essential.

Early reformers believed that revitalizing the Janissaries, especially along European lines, was the solution. But in all instances, these reforms were resisted by the Janissaries, sometimes violently, out of a combination of traditionalism and fear. The new European style of warfare was seen as an attack on Janissary traditions, threatening their concept of themselves and their role in society; further, if they acceded to this new style of fighting, they would be expected to actually fight instead of collecting graft in the capital.

Serious Reforms: Destruction of the Janissaries

In the 1790s, the sultan Selim III determined to create a New Order military force, called the Nizam i-Cedid. Recruited from prisoners of war, army deserters from Russia and Germany, Turkish street gangs, and homeless men in the capital, these units trained secretly, away from the capital. Early results were encouraging. But once again, the Janissaries and their allies forced Selim to abandon his efforts. The sultan attempted to quell an open rebellion peacefully by ordering the New Order soldiers to remain in their barracks. This was not sufficient for the rebels, and the Nizam i-Cedid was abolished and Selim forced to abdicate. Many of the new troops were slaughtered, but some units that had been posted in the northern parts of the empire survived to form the nucleus of later, somewhat more successful, reformed forces under Selim's son Mahmud II. Mahmud became convinced that military reform had to follow the European model when, during the Greek revolt of 1823, the Egyptian governor Muhammad Ali (see below) achieved significant results with a European-style military force.

It was obvious to the sultan that the main obstacle to reform was an alliance of the Janissaries and the religious establishment. Therefore, he followed a patient strategy of gaining the support of the religious authorities while forming a new military force of men plucked out of the Janissary corps. The new units were explicitly modeled on the Egyptian army of Muhammad Ali, effectively countering the argument that the Ottomans were copying the infidels. When the Janissaries finally realized what was up in 1826, Mahmud moved swiftly and literally destroyed the Janissaries with his new units.

The Tanzimat Reforms and the Young Turks

Like China in the late nineteenth century, the Ottomans discovered that forming a modern military system able to both defend the empire and maintain order within it would require reform of society itself, including an industrial revolution. First, it was necessary to rein in the autonomous elements of Ottoman society, including the strong governors. After losing several battles to Muhammad Ali, the Ottomans were forced to rely on European assistance to restore their authority. Then, during the Tanzimat (Turkish, "reorganization") era, beginning in 1839 under Sultan Abdulmecid, European financial assistance was acquired to effect more far-reaching reforms. These reforms affected everything from the financial and education systems to agriculture, as well as the military. As in the past, reform met with resistance, and civil unrest was a constant feature of Ottoman life in the later nineteenth century. Meanwhile, Ottoman territory continued to be taken by European enemies.

Ironically, during these chaotic times, much of the military was successfully reformed. In particular, a new officer corps came into being, based on the European model and imbued with a great deal of professionalism and nationalism. This modern military force was still not capable of preserving the Ottoman Empire, but it would form the successful core of a modern military force for the subsequent Republic of Turkey.

Muhammad Ali in Egypt

While the sultan and the central government of the Ottoman Empire had much difficulty in modernizing their military institutions to cope with the European threats of the early nineteenth century, one of the semi-independent Ottoman provinces came close to succeeding. Egypt had been only tenuously governed by the Ottoman court when the invasion of Napoleon in 1798 disrupted affairs such that the Ottoman authorities were able to reclaim a measure of control. An Ottoman army composed primarily of Albanians

became the dominant power in Egypt, and its commander, Muhammad Ali, was named governor of the province in 1805. An extraordinarily deft political operator, within a few years Muhammad Ali was in firm control of the province, and once again, Egypt was only formally under the rule of the Ottoman sultan. Once in power, Muhammad Ali launched a series of economic, financial, and especially military reforms that allowed him to strengthen his base in Egypt, engage in successful military campaigns outside of Egypt, and even challenge the sultan for ultimate control of the Ottoman Empire.

Muhammad Ali took advantage of the great resources and wealth of Egypt to finance his military modernization efforts. Land was confiscated from Muslim schools, mosques, and other formerly powerful institutions and put to use producing cash crops for the state. Profits from the export of these crops—cotton, tobacco, and sugar in particular—provided the funds he needed to invest in a vast road, canal, and irrigation works program, which in turn boosted agricultural production. He significantly improved the tax collection bureaucracy, which also contributed to the revenues needed for industrial and military development. And his mostly state-run factories produced much of the weaponry and other equipment needed for his European-style military force.

The Albanians who made up the majority of his military force resisted efforts to impose European uniforms and drill on them; they particularly resented the use of European officers as trainers. Muhammad Ali responded by conquering part of the Sudan and creating a military force of mostly black slaves. When this proved insufficient, Egyptian peasants were conscripted into the army, although officer ranks were reserved for Turks, Albanians, and Circassians (from southern Russia). Force was needed to overcome peasant resistance (much as in Japan later in the century), but by the late 1820s, Muhammad Ali's army numbered over 150,000—a large proportion of the available adult male population of Egypt.

Organized along French lines and emphasizing such things as constant training and drill, this new army paid dividends in just a few years. Egyptian power was successfully projected into Arabia and down the Red Sea. Moreover, it was the success of the Egyptian force against the Greek rebellion in 1824 and 1825 that convinced the Ottoman sultan Mahmud II to speed up his own reform efforts. In 1829, modernized Egyptian forces took Syria from the Ottoman sultan, and by 1833, Muhammad Ali had control of almost all of the Fertile Crescent. The very existence of the Ottoman throne was threatened as Egyptian forces moved into Anatolia, and a major Ottoman effort to retake lost territory in 1839 was soundly defeated. It appeared to be merely a matter of time before Muhammad Ali became master of the rest of the Ottoman Empire. However, at that point, the European powers stepped in and demanded that he return to Egypt and limit his army to 18,000 troops. Muhammad Ali was in no position at that time to resist the Europeans, and so he bitterly complied.

During the nineteenth century, only Japan underwent a more impressive—and successful—military reform effort. However, unlike Japan, the Egyptian case depended heavily on the abilities and force of will of one man. Muhammad Ali persisted in the face of tremendous resistance among many segments of Egyptian society, but his attempts to impose his reforms on Syria failed miserably. Peasant rebellions were an almost constant feature during his rule, and in the 1840s, he was forced to break up his agricultural monopolies, the main source of funding for his efforts. His successors carried on some of his military reforms, but within a few decades, Egypt was bankrupt and dependent on foreign loans—no longer a showcase for successful military modernization by a non-European power.

China

After suffering a series of defeats at the hands of Western militaries, in the 1860s, Qing China responded by initiating a policy of adopting aspects of the military systems of the West, especially its technology. But several factors militated against the success of China's modernization policy. First, the sheer size of the country in geographic and demographic terms complicated any modernization program. Second, unlike many areas of the world where a traditional warrior elite resisted military modernization, China had a long tradition of civilian control of the military. But the Confucian scholars who dominated the Chinese bureaucracy had little interest or expertise in military matters and tended to underestimate the threat posed by Western military force and the difficulty of meeting it. Finally, the Chinese military had been constructed to minimize the possibility of rebellion by powerful generals. The result, a decentralized military structure, proved hard to reform from the center. Although China's military made some

gains, the ultimate inadequacy of its policy became clear in the Sino-Japan War of 1894–95.

Decline of Chinese Military Systems The two main Qing military organizations, the Eight Banners and the Green Standard Army (see Chapter 19), were equipped with firearms (matchlock muskets and various types of artillery), but these troops were scattered in numerous garrisons throughout the empire, as the Qing court preferred to manage external and internal threats at the local level. When this proved insufficient, neighboring garrisons were tasked to contain disturbances while a major expedition was ponderously organized from forces throughout the realm.

The eighteenth-century increase in China's population led to a proliferation of internal disturbances by the early nineteenth century that undermined Qing military and civil institutions. Major expeditions took longer and longer to organize, and increasing corruption and inefficiency interfered with the logistical system. By the 1830s, Qing armies had come to rely heavily on militia forces organized by local gentry. It was in this setting that the Qing military came to face the challenges of the Opium Wars.

The Opium Wars Britain had begun exporting opium from India to China in the late eighteenth century. A drug whose addictiveness sustained Chinese demand in spite of official prohibitions, opium generated profits that finally balanced a European trade deficit with China that had persisted for centuries. Therefore, when the Qing dynasty attempted to shut down the trade in the 1830s, the British responded with force to the Chinese taking British merchants and diplomats hostage. The war exposed the new weakness of China in relation to modern British forces.

The Chinese were largely ignorant of the West. But many of China's best troops were garrisoned in the port cities that were the main battleground of the wars, while the British never fielded more than 10,000 men against a Qing army of several hundred thousand (though British weapons and training were vastly superior). The Qing court, then, even if it had had more information, could have felt confident in the efficacy of its typical strategy of engaging the enemy with local forces while organizing a large expeditionary force.

The British upset this strategy through the mobility of their fighting forces provided by their command of the sea. British commanders could move at will along the coast, bombarding coastal forts and troop

Firepower in the Opium Wars British naval artillery made short work of Chinese war junks, both in harbors and, mounted on steam gunboats, on Chinese rivers.

concentrations, landing their troops wherever they wished, and embarking them before significant Qing reinforcements could arrive. China had never faced a serious naval threat, and the war was nearly over before Qing commanders appreciated the difference between the British strategy and mere piracy. The Qing had virtually no navy, and British vessels could fire on Qing coastal targets while staying outside the range of Chinese artillery fire. And the steam gunboat *Nemesis* gave the British an incalculable advantage along Chinese inland rivers. In addition to its own firepower, the *Nemesis* could tow other British sailing warships into range.

High Qing officials, having witnessed the near invulnerability of the British warships at the Battle of Tianjin, decided to negotiate. When a *Nemesis*-led British fleet sailed at will along the Yangzi, threatening to cut off the transport of grain from the south to the capital, even the emperor realized that Qing forces did not have time to organize a major expeditionary force before disaster might strike. Besides, the British were primarily interested in trade and did not challenge the right of the dynasty to rule China once they had negotiated preferential trade terms.

Subsequent agreements with the United States and other European powers further opened up China to Western trade and influence, but this led to little change in Qing military structure or doctrine. Al-though some officials and intellectuals argued for a program of reform, the dominant view continued to be that Chinese moral superiority would eventually give China the ability to control the foreigners. It took the Arrow War (sometimes called the Second Opium War) to seriously shake the Qing court out of its complacency.

In 1856, Chinese unwillingness to carry out its treaty obligations led Britain and France toward military action. In August 1860, a joint British-French force of about 20,000 marched on Beijing. While the Chinese military managed to delay and even at times repulse the allied military force, within two months, the allies had control of Beijing, and the emperor fled. Despite some successes in battle, Qing military forces had proven inadequate to defend China from determined Western military efforts. Also, while the Arrow War was in progress, the Qing was embroiled in a domestic uprising, the Taiping Rebellion. Traditional Qing military forces suffered a series of defeats during the fighting, and success came only through the use of new military forces armed with more modern weapons. These events prompted reform.

The Taiping Rebellion The Taiping Rebellion (1853–64) was a massive peasant revolt with religious and ethnic overtones. Qing forces were not designed for rapid mobilization against a large enemy, and at first, the Taipings scored one victory after another. As the Qing court frantically searched for a means to stop the Taiping advance, the provincial governor of Hunan, Zeng Guofan, responded by creating a new type of military force. Learned in Chinese history, Zeng essentially copied the system devised by the Ming general Qi Jiguang in the sixteenth century (see Chapter 19).

His *yongying,* or "brave battalions," were an expansion of the traditional Qing militias. Officers and men were recruited largely through personal connections and were constantly trained and drilled; many were also equipped with modern weapons purchased from the West. Training included indoctrination in Confucianism and Chinese cultural traditions, in effect a form of nationalism. Pay was high by Chinese standards, and the men were expected not to molest the population. By 1864, Zeng's Hunan Army and other forces modeled on it had succeeded in completely exterminating the Taiping Rebellion.

The Qing defeat in the Arrow War had convinced the court that China could not compete with the West in military affairs. Yet the victory of the new-style forces in the Taiping Rebellion persuaded many that the problem was a narrow one. They believed that it was really only in the field of military technology and its application that China lagged behind the West. Similar to the prevailing sentiment of most contemporary Ottoman reformers, the Chinese considered that in most matters, particularly regarding culture and morality, China retained a significant edge over its Western adversaries. This attitude limited the willingness and ability of Qing officials to innovate.

Reform: The Self-Strengthening Movement

The reform program that did emerge, called the Self-Strengthening Movement, centered on training the *yongying* army forces along Western lines. It also involved the construction of arsenals to produce Western-style arms and reduce China's dependence on imports. Most of the program was carried out at the provincial level. Zeng Guofan led the effort, followed later by his protégé, Li Hongzhang. Li tried to go beyond merely borrowing Western military technology, arguing that China had to industrialize as well. In this, as with much of the reform program, he had only limited success.

The Self-Strengthening Movement reforms aimed at creating a Western-style army and navy. Much of the equipment needed for the new forces was purchased

from abroad, but the Qing reformers did not want China to be dependent on foreigners for its military needs. Therefore, arsenals, shipyards, and other factories were constructed for the production of ships, arms, and ammunition. The largest of these arsenals were built in Shanghai and Fuzhou; indeed, the "Jiangnan Arsenal" in Shanghai was one of the largest in the world. To provide the raw materials for the arsenals, modern iron and coal mines were begun under imperial sponsorship, and rail lines were constructed to bring the materials to the factories. The major arsenals also contained a translation bureau to translate Western military and technical books into Chinese. In the late 1880s, a European-style military academy was established, though there were too few graduates to have much effect on the Chinese military. *Yongying* units, the focus of reform, were equipped with the latest weaponry, and European instructors provided training. But almost no effort was made to adopt the military staff systems of the West, and central control of policy and strategy remained weak and fragmented along provincial lines. The deficiencies of this organizational system became painfully clear when war with Japan broke out in 1894.

The Sino-Japanese War

Fought for control of Korea, the Sino-Japanese War of 1894–95 reflects to China's disadvantage the relative success of two military modernization programs. Japanese forces swiftly forced the Chinese out of Korea and Manchuria and then, after securing a foothold on the Shandong Peninsula, prepared a two-pronged assault on the Qing capital of Beijing, whereupon the Qing court sued for peace. What went wrong?

Qing armies proved incapable of swift mobilization or, once in place, of quick reaction to Japanese moves on the field. Time and again, the Japanese forces were able to turn the flank of nearly immobile Chinese units. In contrast, when Japanese forces chose to fight in a frontal attack, Qing troops often acquitted themselves well. Qing troops also had some of the latest modern weaponry—some even more advanced than those used by the Japanese. But these weapons were not always evenly distributed, and many of the soldiers had been provided little training in their use. In other cases, corruption in the procurement process meant that many shell casings for artillery rounds were filled with sand rather than gunpowder. Yet for all these problems, the fact that soldiers in some of the early battles demonstrated discipline against Japanese

Admiral Perry's Black Ships in Tokyo Bay   In this Japanese illustration, the attention to the detail of the American ships and the contrast between them and the Japanese sailboats shows that already some Japanese were eager to learn from the foreign barbarians.

frontal charges provides evidence that the new training regime was not a complete failure.

Above all, the war against Japan was fought, not by the national military forces of China, but by local provincial armies. Only in the latter months of the war was an imperial edict issued ordering the mobilization of forces of provinces other than those directly affected by the fighting. Even then, the provincial governors and military commanders dallied in carrying out the directive or refused to do so altogether. This lack of national commitment to the defense of China was a result of the whole modernization effort having been conducted through provincial authorities rather than as a centrally directed program.

Defeat led within fifteen years to the collapse of the Qing dynasty. China's struggle to modernize would then continue in very different ways in the twentieth century.

JAPAN: THE SUCCESS STORY

The arrival of the American Commodore Matthew Perry off the coast of Japan in 1853, demanding open trade and normal diplomatic relations, came as a shock to a Japan that had been closed to almost all foreign contact for over 200 years (see Chapter 19).

But it was not an entirely unexpected shock: The Japanese had followed the Opium Wars with alarm, and elements among the political class had been warning that this day would come.

Nor was Japan completely unprepared to meet the challenge to her independence and self-image that Western contact brought. In immediate terms, Japan *was* completely unprepared, its armed forces obsolete and fragmented among the domains that made up a federation under the hegemony of the Tokugawa shoguns. But two centuries of internal peace provided resources that Japanese leaders could draw on. Economic development had created a thriving market economy whose merchants already chafed under the restrictions of isolation. The samurai class, while retaining a military ethos, had become skillful administrators. The population was unusually well educated for the time, and a revival of the native Shinto religion had reinforced a sense of cultural identity and unity in the population as a whole, despite political divisions.

Against this background, Western contact and forced opening of the country created a political crisis for the Shogunate. Factional struggle simmered between the Tokugawa house, with its supporters, and several major southwestern provinces whose partisans gained control over the imperial family. This intersected with ideological conflict characterized by a three-way split similar to that found in many areas of the world facing Western intrusion. At one extreme were those who, completely impractically, wanted to "expel the barbarians," as the emperor ordered, and maintain isolation. At the other extreme were those who wished to abandon all Japanese traditions and westernize totally. Finally, some took a middle position, advocating adoption of Western scientific, military, and technological advances in the context of Japanese ethics and culture (see the Sources box "Reflections on My Errors"). One oddity about Japan's response to the West is that the middle position in effect won out, especially once the anti-Western extremists were defeated by Western forces retaliating against attacks on Western shipping and merchants, convincing the extremists of the need to adopt modern weaponry. When the last shogun abdicated in 1868, the modernizers took control under the emperor Meiji, who was restored to full power using the German model of government.

Modernization: Industry and the Military

The Meiji leadership, many of whom spent time in the West for education and experience, remained in some ways divided between westernizers and modernizers but agreed on their fundamental practical goals. They wished to earn for Japan respect as an equal among the powers of the world. This required a strong military, which in turn required (and would support) a strong central government. For their part, government and the military needed a strong, industrialized economy as a base to build on. And, all of this depended on a unified Japanese people. These interlocked goals were achieved with remarkable rapidity.

Society, Economy, and Government   The restoration of the emperor helped create a powerful symbol of national unity, one reinforced by a universal system of education that inculcated loyalty to the emperor as a central value. Education extended to the armed forces, where new conscripts received political as well as military training. Conscription also assisted in breaking down the old class barriers that had been formally abolished by government decree. In the context of conscription and national defense, elimination of the samurai class in particular meant, not the extinction of samurai values, but their extension to the population as a whole.

To avoid borrowing capital from abroad for industrial development, and thus risking foreign control of industry, the government subsidized the rapid growth of silk textile mills. Largely staffed by cheap female and child labor and aimed at the export market, silk brought profits that supplemented crushing taxation of farmers in funding the development of strategic heavy industries. Coalitions of government and private interests built factories for steel, machinery, and shipbuilding; once these became going concerns economically, the government usually divested itself of its ownership, often on favorable terms to powerful ex-samurai families to compensate them for their loss of formal status. Railroad and telegraph networks spread through Japan, and the first telephone line came only a few years after Bell invented the device. Foreign advisors and managers were retained only until they could be replaced by Japanese. The first trans-Pacific voyage by a Japanese-crewed ship came as early as 1860, reflecting this rapid learning process. Foreign trade and markets stimulated economic growth, and by 1876, just thirteen years after being "opened," Japan was pressuring Korea for trade liberalization.

In addition to abolishing the Tokugawa class system, the Meiji government eliminated the old domains and divided the country into standard prefectures for civil and military administration. The financial and military responsibilities of the various domains were centralized in the hands of the imperial government. And reform created its own momentum and demands among the population. In 1890, the first session of the Diet, the Japanese parliament, opened as a new wave of westernization, this time focused on politics, took hold. But greater democratization, limited though it was, met resistance among some members of the Meiji leadership. This struggle had a significant bearing on the role of the military in the new Japanese government.

A New National Military   The central problem for military reformers involved breaking the resistance of the old samurai to the end of their military monopoly. The earliest moves toward military reform and the adoption of Western military organization had come about before the restoration of the emperor, in the southwestern domains of Satsuma and Choshu. Anti-Western leaders in Choshu, defeated by Western expeditionary forces, created a volunteer force drawn from all classes and armed with Western weaponry. When

SOURCES

"Reflections on My Errors"

Sakuma Shozan was the leading exponent of a middle way between the extreme but impractical rejection of all things Western and the equally extreme rejection of Japanese tradition in favor of complete westernization. His program is summed up in the slogan "Eastern ethics, Western science." His reflections on his "errors" is actually a defense of this middle way.

■ ■ ■

20. The gentleman has five pleasures. . . . That he employs the ethics of the East and the scientific technique of the West, neglecting neither the spiritual nor material aspects of life, combining subjective and objective, and thus bringing benefit to the people and serving the nation—this is the fifth pleasure.

28. The principle requisite of national defense is that it prevents the foreign barbarians from holding us in contempt. The existing coastal defense installations all lack method; the pieces of artillery that have been set up in array are improperly made; and the officials who negotiate with the foreigners are mediocrities who have no understanding of warfare. The situation being such, even though we wish to avoid incurring the scorn of the barbarians, how, in fact, can we do so?

30. Of the men who now hold posts as commanders of the army, those who are not dukes or princes or men of noble rank, are members of wealthy families. As such, they find their daily pleasure in drinking wine, singing, and dancing; and they are ignorant of military strategy and discipline. . . . For this reason, I have wished to follow in substance the Western principles of armament [conscription]. . . .

35. Mathematics is the basis for all learning. In the Western world after this science was discovered military tactics advanced greatly, far outstripping that of former times. . . . In the *Art of War* of Sun Tzu, the statement about "estimation, determination of quantity, calculation, judgment, and victory" has reference to mathematics. However, since Sun Tzu's time neither we nor the Chinese have ceased to read, study and memorize his teachings, and our art of war remains exactly as it was then. It consequently cannot be compared with that of the West. . . . At the present time, if we wish really to complete our military preparations, we must develop this branch of study.

46. [In 1843] the English barbarians were invading the Ch'ing empire, and news of the war was sensational. I, greatly lamenting events of the time, submitted a plan in a memorial. . . . [I] wish to promote to the full the teaching of techniques for using armored warships and to form a plan of attack whereby an enemy could be intercepted and destroyed, in order that the death sentence may be given to the plunderers before they have reached the country's shores.

47. In order to master the barbarians there is nothing so effective as to ascertain in the beginning conditions among them. To do this, there is no better first step than to be familiar with barbarian tongues. Thus, learning a barbarian language is not only a step toward knowing the barbarians, but also the groundwork for mastering them. . . .

48. The main requirement for maritime defense are guns and warships, but the more important item is guns. . . .

SOURCE: Sakuma Shozan, "Reflections on My Errors" in *Sources of Japanese Tradition, Vol. 2,* ed. Ryusaku Tsunoda, Wm. Theodore de Bary, and Donald Keene (New York: Colombia University Press, 1958).

this force defeated a shogunal invasion in 1866, it not only hastened the fall of the Shogunate but convinced many conservatives of the merits of a national conscript force, as peasant recruits had fought as bravely as, and more effectively than, traditional samurai.

With the already partially westernized armies of Choshu and Satsuma at its core, therefore, a national army began to emerge in the decades after the imperial restoration. It was based on a system of cadres and reserves filled by universal conscription that did much to help break down old class and political division, as we have seen, thereby contributing significantly to the material and ideological unity of Japan. Though the army's growth was slow at first due to financial constraints, it proved capable of suppressing a major rebellion of ex-samurai in 1877, and by the 1890s, it was large and effective enough to begin playing a significant role on the world stage (see below). At the same time, an imperial navy was created, with Japanese-constructed ships slowly supplementing and then replacing ships ordered or leased from Western shipyards (see Chapter 25 for naval developments).

The Meiji leadership initially took as their military models the French army and the British navy. But Yamagata Aritomo, the architect of the Japanese military establishment, successfully exerted his leadership on behalf of German models of army organization. He saw the creation of a Prussian-style General Staff in 1878, the appointment of an inspector general for military education in 1879, and the establishment of a military academy for officer training in 1882. He also instituted a modern divisional structure in 1886.

Furthermore, Yamagata was a conservative who mistrusted civilian bureaucrats, hated political parties, and wished to see the army independent of and above factional politics. With the reorganization of the General Staff in 1886, he achieved his goal. The chief of the General Staff reported not to any cabinet minister but directly to the emperor, and top defense ministers were required to be active generals or admirals. While Yamagata intended this structure to place the army above partisan politics, the actual effect was to separate the army from the emergent political parties and thus force it to play an active role in politics itself to defend its interests. A politicized army outside the control of civilian policy makers would prove a baleful legacy to Japan in later decades.

In the meantime, the new army proved a leading force in the westernization of sometimes unexpected areas of Japanese life beyond education, class, and political divisions. Military uniforms led a trend toward Western styles of dress, and short haircuts, hitherto unknown, spread from the army, where they were found necessary for safety in weapons handling. Even the eating of bread started with military rations. But such matters of style often proved to be short-lived fads, and modernization, rather than westernization, may in fact be the better term for Japan's overall transformation. For while Japan adopted industrial modes of economic organization, mass political forms and ideologies, and a mass national military structure, it usually did so in ways that consciously retained a Japanese flavor. Western styles called forth reactions stressing traditional Japanese values and spirit, a formula vague enough to accommodate much change but still foster a sense of Japanese cultural identity. This cultural strength with flexibility was probably a key factor in allowing Japan to enter rapidly and successfully into the modern world— not without major internal stresses and hardships, to be sure, but as a unified and increasingly powerful nation-state.

Wars with China and Russia

The Sino-Japanese War The first proof of the effectiveness of Japan's modernization program came for the outside world in 1894 when war broke out between Japan and China. At issue was effective control over Korea. Many observers had suspected some weakness in China's armed forces, but Chinese attempts at modernization (see above) also made many wary of arousing a sleeping giant. And few expected Japan to have much success. But Japanese forces rolled through Chinese armies and advanced on Peking, forcing the Qing government to sue for peace.

Japan's favorable terms and territorial gains agreed to in the peace treaty were, however, largely reversed under pressure from Western imperial powers, which moved both to prop up the now-collapsing Qing dynasty and, even more, with Qing weakness suddenly exposed, to carve up the Chinese empire for themselves. This outcome further convinced Japan's leaders of the need for an even stronger military if the full respect of the Western powers were to be earned.

The Russo-Japanese War That respect would come in 1904 in a war with Russia. The two powers had been on a collision course for several years over Manchuria,

Korea, and the Kurile Islands north of Japan, as Russian Pacific expansion brought it increasingly into conflict with a newly assertive Japan. And this time, Germany, England, and the United States all lent a supportive neutrality to Japan's cause, as each for different reasons wished to see Russia's Pacific ambitions checked. Still, none hoped for more than a hard-fought defeat for Japan against one of the great European powers—enough perhaps to check Russia for a time.

Supply lines, however, were a key factor in the war and gave Japan an initial advantage. Only 83,000 of Russia's 4.5-million-man army were stationed east of Lake Baikal, and both supplies and reinforcements at the rate of no more than 40,000 a month had to come via the 5500 miles of the single-track Trans-Siberian Railway. Japan, on the other hand, could move its entire standing army of 283,000 men plus 400,000 reserves and supplies quickly to the mainland provided it had control of the seas. This it seized immediately in February 1904 with surprise torpedo attacks on the Russian Pacific fleet at anchor in Port Arthur. Admiral Togo blockaded the surviving Russian ships until they were destroyed by Japanese artillery late in the siege of Port Arthur, then sealed Japanese victory at sea and in the war with a crushing victory at Tshushima in May 1905 over a Russian fleet sent from the Baltic (see Chapter 25 for details of the war at sea).

Japan thus looked to end the war quickly while it had the advantage of numbers. One army marched to besiege Port Arthur while three others moved to halt Russian forces advancing to the port from Manchuria. The siege lasted six months, from early June 1904 to January 1905, while the other armies steadily pushed the Russians farther into Manchuria. The fighting in both cases was fierce and should have provided Western observers with lessons about the changing nature of warfare. At Port Arthur, the 40,000 defenders were well entrenched and supported by fortified positions on hills around the city. Machine gun and artillery fire from these prepared positions mowed down assaults by massed Japanese infantry time and again. But mismanagement, starvation, heavy bombardment by siege artillery, and sheer weight of numbers finally wore down the defenders, who lost 30,000 men, compared to 59,000 killed, wounded, and missing among the besiegers. In the field battles, entrenchments played a large role on both sides, with machine gun and indirect artillery fire proving effective in defense and attack. The battles were mostly

tactical draws, with neither side able to gain a decisive victory. Japanese success came from superior leadership, as hesitant Russian generals failed to press advantages or withdrew, conceding defeat from stalemate. But many observers also came away impressed by the morale (verging on fanaticism) and discipline of Japanese infantry in the attack and thus, despite suicidal results at Port Arthur, a renewed faith in bayonet assaults.

The war also foreshadowed the vastly increased national commitment necessary to fight a war in the age of firepower and industry. When President Theodore Roosevelt mediated a peace agreement in September 1905, both sides were on the verge of collapse. The war, unpopular in Russia except among the Tsar's closest advisors, brought the state close to revolution. Japan's war effort had the full support of the nation, but by mid-1905, the government was nearly bankrupt, the economy was under severe strain, and, above all, the army was beginning to suffer critical manpower shortages. Japan had won the war, but barely. Furthermore, government censorship of the press had created the impression of a victory more decisive than was the case—a policy that backfired because the peace agreement was seen by the Japanese population as soft on Russia, leading to the cabinet's resignation.

The peace did, however, bring Japan greater security, a freer hand in Korea, and possessions on the Chinese mainland. New territory brought in new resources and opened new markets to Japanese industry. The economy, government finances, and the military all recovered rapidly from the strains of war. And Japan had achieved its goal: It was now recognized in the West as one of the great powers. But this achievement itself created complications. Japanese relations with the United States, long on friendly terms, became strained after the war because Japan's new power was now seen in the United States as a potential threat to American Pacific interests. Similarly, Britain awoke to the possibilities of a new rival for naval dominance, as Japan's navy was now the third largest in the world. Also, the war raised the prestige of the military within Japan to new heights. The army and navy were increasingly seen as the architects of Japan's new position in the world and as the most efficient and glorious of all Japan's institutions. Combined with the military's constitutional position outside the normal channels of political control, this prestige opened the door to the disastrous militarism of the 1930s (see Chapter 27).

In 1905, though, what stood out was that a non-European power had beaten a major European power in a significant war. The Japanese achievement in rapidly modernizing, meeting the West on its own terms, and still retaining a sense of its unique cultural identity was unprecedented and would remain unique for many more years. But it proved to the rest of the world that it could be done, and therefore created the first fatal crack in the structure of European global hegemony.

CONCLUSION

The scarcity of success stories in the rest of the world's attempts to meet the West on equal military terms during the nineteenth century attests to the difficulties of the process of modernization. Adopting European-style armies was no simple matter of acquiring the newest technology. Making effective use of the technology required systems of officer education and mass conscription that frequently clashed with existing political arrangements, especially the status and privileges of traditional military elites. Even in Japan, the lone success story, the biggest obstacle to modernization was probably the resistance of much of the samurai class to the ending of their military monopoly. Elsewhere, such resistance often proved fatal to the plans of modernizers. Furthermore, effective long-term use of European-style armed force depended on an industrialized economy for the production of weapons and wealth in general, and required levels of bureaucratic and fiscal competence in government that were also hard to meet in the context of opposition from traditional elites. Industry rested on social and legal arrangements for market economics and private property that again conflicted with many traditional aristocratic privileges, as well as with the autocratic and arbitrary powers of many of the world's governments. Finally, the tendency, encouraged by Europeans, to equate modernization with westernization almost always polarized the cultural responses of non-westerners to the challenge of Western force. Again, only in Japan did a middle way emphasizing Western technology and science in combination with non-Western cultural values emerge as a dominant view. Elsewhere, the close association of aristocratic ways of war with the cultural identities of various peoples tended to squeeze this option out between extremist antiwesterners and extremist westernizers.

Nevertheless, the very success of Western imperialism and ways of war in this period sowed the seeds of future reactions. Most important, nationalist ideology would prove a powerful force in favor of anti-imperialism, as the peoples under European rule invented for themselves, as the Europeans had done, unifying myths and traditions in opposition to those of their imperial rulers. In addition, the obvious power of the Western way of war encouraged resisters not to meet Western armies head on, but to use Western weapons in non-Western ways. Ideologically motivated guerrilla forces armed with modern weapons would present a difficult challenge for Western armies throughout the twentieth century.

But the full emergence of such forces had to wait for some breaks to appear in the structure of European dominance. While the success of Japan created a crack, it would take two world wars, both of which were at least in part European civil wars, to bring the structure down.

SUGGESTED READINGS

Asher, Michael. *Khartoum: The Ultimate Imperial Adventure.* London: Penguin Books, 2005. A popular but reliable account of the campaigns centered on Khartoum that included the Battle of Omdurman.

Black, Jeremy. *Introduction to Global Military History: 1775 to the Present Day.* London: Routledge, 2005. An important treatment of the nineteenth century that avoids the pitfalls of Eurocentrism.

Headrick, Daniel. *The Tools of Empire: Technology and European Imperialism in the Nineteenth Century.* Oxford: 1981. Still the standard work on the connection of technological advance and imperial systems of conquest and control.

Kolff, Dirk. *Naukar, Rajput, and Sepoy: The Ethnohistory of the Military Labour Market of Hindustan, 1450–1850.* Cambridge: Cambridge University Press, 2002. Roots the British sepoy system in the dynamics of India's medieval market for military manpower.

Linn, Brian. *The Philippine War, 1899–1902.* Lawrenceville: University of Kansas Press, 2002. A nuanced treatment of the problem of fighting an insurgency, based on a broad range of sources.

Ralston, David. *Importing the European Army: The Introduction of European Military Techniques and Institutions in the Extra-European World, 1600–1914.* Chicago: University of Chicago Press, 1996. A comparative study of Russia, China, the Ottomans, Egypt, and Japan that analyzes the difficulties non-European powers faced creating European-style armies.

Roy, Tapti. *The Politics of a Popular Uprising: Bundelkhand 1857.* Delhi: Oxford University Press, 1994. A regionally focused study of the conflicted politics of the Indian uprising.

Scheina, Robert. *Latin American Wars: Vol. I, The Age of Caudillos, 1791–1899.* Washington, DC: Brassey, 2003. A detailed narrative and analysis of the whole range of Latin American wars, from revolutions to internal conflict; especially good for the complex relationship of military power to the failures of state formation in the region.

Spiers, Edward. *The Victorian Soldier in Africa.* Manchester: Manchester University Press, 2005. A detailed reexamination of the experience of the common soldier in the British armies that spearheaded imperialism in Africa.

CHAPTER 25

From Sails to Steam: Naval Warfare, 1750–1914

The industrialization that revolutionized warfare and vaulted western Europe and the United States to world dominance in the nineteenth century contributed equally, if not more radically, to transformations of naval warfare. Indeed, naval power was often the key to the successful projection of Western military force around the globe, from steam-powered riverine gunboats in China in the Opium Wars, to American steamships forcing open Kamakura Japan, to the even more important but often unseen maritime supply lines that connected European capitals to their far-flung imperial possessions. Technological transformations were at the heart of changes in naval warfare, but as with land warfare, modern naval technology came inseparably tied up with political, social, and economic structures that generated and supported the technological breakthroughs.

Yet in some ways, the age showed a curious continuity. The last half of the eighteenth century saw Great Britain cement its naval dominance in the climax of the age of sailing ships and smoothbore cannon. Having already pioneered the systems of finance and manufacturing necessary for maintaining a globally powerful fleet of warships (see Chapter 20), Britain's navy sought ways to apply its strategic superiority more decisively at a tactical level. The search was apparently crowned by the brilliant career of Horatio Nelson, perhaps the most famous admiral in history, in his decisive victories over large fleets of enemy ships of the line, especially at Trafalgar, off the coast of Spain, in 1805. But tactical control of fleets continued to present problems throughout this century. Despite this, in 1905, Britain remained the world's top naval power, and battle fleets led by battleships that were the lineal descendants of Nelson's flagship HMS *Victory*, however transformed technologically, still constituted the key to naval power. Indeed, the Royal Navy in 1905 laid down a new battleship that would synthesize a half-century's tech-

nological change and further reinforce the prestige of capital ships as the symbol of command of the seas. The rise of Germany and the United States as naval powers challenged British supremacy even as it confirmed the vital link between industrial might and naval strength. Around the world, 1905 also saw the biggest and most decisive fleet action since Trafalgar, at Tsushima Bay in Japan. Theorists such as Alfred Thayer Mahan saw in the results of Tsushima Bay confirmation of principles they had derived from studying the warfare of Nelson's age.

On the other hand, the victor at Tshushima was Japan—a non-Western power allied to Britain, an admission on the latter's part that it could no longer patrol the whole world on its own. And by 1914, the effective extension of naval warfare under the sea and into the air appeared far more possible than it had even nine years earlier, casting doubts on the future role of the battleship as the arbiter of naval conflicts. In short, naval history between 1750 and 1914 demonstrates the contradictions of a complex age, full of change and continuity, and confusing to the makers of navies and naval policy who lived through it.

CLIMAX OF THE AGE OF SAIL, 1750–1830

Incremental and sometimes contradictory developments in naval tactics after 1750 coexisted with fundamental continuity in terms of strategy and with slow gains in the efficiency of naval administration based partly in accumulated experience and partly in the application of the rational and scientific method so characteristic of the late eighteenth century. The fundamental context for all these developments was the intensifying rivalry between Great Britain and

France that carried European naval warfare to practically every ocean on the globe during this period.

Anglo-French Rivalry

France was the largest kingdom in Europe outside Russia, as well as the richest, though the limitations of public finance imposed by the political contradictions inherent in absolutism, especially the tax-exempt status of the nobility, prevented the French government from exploiting that wealth as efficiently as it could have. Britain, though far smaller than France in population and total economic output, had perfected systems of public finance that allowed it to match its great rival in military spending with few adverse political consequences (see Chapter 20). Britain had the further advantage of a single focus for its grand strategy. After its success in containing Louis XIV's bid for European hegemony climaxing in the War of Spanish Succession, which had entailed sending large armies to the Continent, Britain thereafter limited its direct engagement in land warfare on the Continent. Instead, Britain pursued what was called a *blue water strategy* of ensuring the island's immunity from invasion, protecting commerce, and extending the reach of its commercial and colonial empire through the strength of the navy. While Britain did maintain a standing army, it was small by European standards and was stationed largely not in England, where it was seen as a potential threat to political liberty, but in Ireland (effectively a colonial possession), with contingents deployed to other colonies as necessary. The protection afforded by the fleet against French invasion was reinforced by subsidies paid to allies on the Continent who opposed the French army, though the Napoleonic Wars did bring significant British armies back to the Continent.

France, on the other hand, found itself in the difficult position of attempting to maintain both a powerful army and a navy capable of challenging the British at sea—in the process, stretching its resources thin. The threat of direct invasion made France's land frontiers of necessity its primary focus, pushing attempts to expand its colonial and global commercial enterprises, and therefore its naval effort, into secondary status. Nevertheless, the French navy was a serious threat to the British and often surpassed its island rival in purely technological developments. The strategic imperatives of geography are reflected in the continuity of French and British policies even across divides such as the French Revolution. But each did

have a range of choices in implementing their grand strategies: The technological, administrative, strategic, and tactical efforts of both powers were shaped by this ongoing rivalry. In the end, the British triumphed, launching a century of British dominance at sea after 1805.

The Infrastructure of Naval Power

Shipbuilding and Technology   As we saw in Chapter 20, the full-rigged warship was the most complex, expensive military technology of the age, and production and maintenance of such ships required extensive infrastructure: shipyards, dry docks for cleaning and repair, storage for vast quantities of naval stores, and munitions manufacturing (a small squadron of ships of the line carried far more heavy firepower than any army). There were no radical changes in naval technology during the latter half of the eighteenth century, but steady incremental improvements gradually extended the range and fighting power of battle fleets. Scientific and mathematical testing brought some improvement to naval architecture, with the French usually leading the way—French ships often sailed better than their British counterparts. Designers steadily added greater sail area per ton of displacement, aiding speed and maneuverability. Copper plating on the underwater portions of hulls reduced fouling from barnacles and seaweed, also improving speed, and extended the time ships could cruise between refits. Naval medicine made small improvements: The British started carrying supplies of limes on board to reduce scurvy and thereby earned a national nickname. Improvements in signaling, designed for control of fleets in battle (see below), actually helped most in keeping fleets together while cruising. Gunnery got better both through improvements in cannon design and, for the British, through constant practice. Perhaps the most significant scientific breakthrough came in navigation, where the British invention of an accurate shipboard chronometer allowed direct tracking of longitude for the first time. The cumulative result of such changes was that fleets could stay at sea longer, cruise farther, and deliver more firepower. But change was slow enough that many ships of the line remained in commission for decades.

Administration   The complexities of managing navies and their infrastructures spurred increasing professionalism in the government departments responsible for this task. The British Admiralty, though subject to political favoritism in the appointment of senior admirals to its ranks, developed oversight procedures and kept voluminous records. French administration often promoted rationalization of procedures and doctrine but suffered a severe blow to its continuity during the Revolution. But the tendency of both administrations was to try to extend central control over naval operations, a philosophy limited by slow communications at the strategic level and that had less than optimal consequences at the tactical level (see below).

Manpower Perhaps the most difficult task for any naval administration was obtaining sufficient manpower to crew all its ships, especially during rapid wartime buildups. Merchant captains often complained that the hiring of merchant crews for military duty did as much damage to trade as enemy action. Recruiters regularly offered signing bonuses, and ultimately, most navies resorted at times to impressing crews from among the general population (including vagabonds, criminals, and other marginal types) and from merchant shipping, sometimes causing diplomatic trouble with neutral powers. Impressment became a key issue leading to the Anglo-American War of 1812, for example. Once aboard, crews faced harsh discipline (though brutality varied greatly from ship to ship and between fleets) and unhealthy conditions that spread disease. Desertion of crews in port was a constant problem. Still, naval operations were rarely hampered by manpower problems except at times in the West Indies, when epidemics could disable entire fleets.

Strategy

Blockades, Convoys, and Control of the Seas The grand strategies of Britain and France, discussed above, shaped their naval strategies, but neither geography nor grand strategy were deterministic of strategy. Each side had choices, and the consistency of their choices over the century after 1715 reflected institutional cultures as much as necessity.

British naval strategy aimed aggressively at what is often called *control of the seas*, though absolute control was an impossibility given the technology of the day. What it really meant was ensuring British merchant and naval access to sea-lanes free of enemy interference, while limiting enemy use of those sea-lanes as much as possible. This entailed a three-pronged

mission for individual fleets, with the details of how to accomplish the mission left to the admiral on station. First, the main contingents of the French fleet were to be blockaded in port at the opening of hostilities. There were periodic disputes between advocates of close blockades, which entailed the British fleet cruising constantly offshore in all weather so as to meet immediately any French fleet trying to sail and defeat it in battle, and advocates of loose blockades, in which the British fleet would base in the closest friendly port and keep watch on the blockaded fleet with fast frigates, chasing it down if it sailed. Despite reasonable-sounding arguments in favor of loose blockade—that it kept the ships in better repair, avoided the risk of storms, and allowed greater flexibility for executing the other tasks of the fleet—close blockade almost invariably worked better. And it had the additional major advantage of providing constant practice in sailing and gunnery for the ships' crews. It was the skills honed in constant cruising that consistently gave British crews the advantage over other navies when it came to combat, even when their ships were not as good. Second, the fleet was to provide protection to British merchant convoys, especially in areas such as the English Channel where blockade stations coincided with major shipping lanes. Clearly, bottling the enemy combat fleet up in port accomplished this task preclusively. Third, the same fleet would also be tasked with intercepting enemy merchant convoys and their escorts. This conception of strategy assumed naval superiority from the start of any hostilities, an assumption almost always supported by peacetime building programs.

French strategy usually assumed inferiority, in contrast, even when building programs were instituted with the express purpose of challenging British dominance. French fleets rarely aimed at instigating large-scale battles with British fleets, preferring instead to attempt forays into the open sea to prey on British merchant shipping. This emphasis on economic warfare and a *guerre de course* owed something to mercantilist theory and something to expedience, as preclusive control of shipping lanes was out of the question due to British dominance. French fleets were also tasked with escorting convoys of French merchantmen into port. A similar dichotomy showed up in each country's strategy regarding overseas colonies. The French generally adopted a defensive posture, posting fleets to protect their key Caribbean sugar islands, for example. The British adopted an offensive approach that sought to cut off and seize French colonies in the

Caribbean, Quebec, and India, where French coastal outposts were especially vulnerable to being isolated and captured in detail. Most of the time, the British approach prevailed.

Amphibious Operations The other significant aspect of naval strategy in this period was amphibious operations, which included escorting of troop transports by battle fleets and coordinating land and sea forces in campaigns along a coast. The British specialized in the former type of operation, regularly landing British armies in Europe (and taking them off again when necessary) throughout the eighteenth century. After the landing, the fleet protected the naval supply line to the army. But the system failed to operate as smoothly across the distances involved in fighting the American Revolution and ultimately proved inadequate to crush the independence movement. The lessons the British absorbed from their failure in North America, however, were put to good use in the Iberian Peninsular campaign and in operations in the War of 1812 that included the burning of Washington, DC.

Coordinated operations between land and sea forces were harder to pull off than troop transport and protection, partly because most theaters of land campaigning were far from any coast. Ironically, the British were the victims of the greatest of such operations, the combined Franco-American siege at Yorktown (see also Chapter 21, including Figure 21.3). The opening move came when Admiral François de Grasse sailed from Brest on March 22, 1781, with 26 ships of the line and a convoy of troop transports. He arrived in the West Indies at the end of April, where his fleet engaged inconclusively with British forces. On May 21, George Washington and the French general Rochambeau agreed to urge de Grasse north to conduct joint operations against the main British forces in either Virginia or New York. A frigate conveyed the message. De Grasse sailed north on August 13, and Washington marched south from New York eight days later. De Grasse arrived off Yorktown on August 30 and repulsed a British fleet under Admiral Thomas Graves at the Battle of the Capes on September 5–9. On September 14, Washington and Rochambeau arrived at Yorktown, and the end of the war was in sight. The coordination of forces across such distances involved some luck but was above all a triumph of cooperation and of Washington's bold strategy and his appreciation of the potentially decisive influence of sea power in this campaign. Hesitant and indecisive British tactics

at the Capes also contributed (though de Grasse did have more ships of the line—24 to 19), which fueled a search by some within the British navy for more effective tactical methods to complement their (normally) successful strategy and operations.

Tactics: Command and Control

At one level, the tactics of British and French naval combat reflected fairly directly their strategic missions. The British, intent on engaging and destroying French battle fleets, tended to aim low, piercing the hulls of opposing ships so as to kill the crews and disable or sink the ships. They also tended to engage from upwind of the opposing line, so as to be able to close the gap, engage closely, and seek a decision. The French, in contrast, saw their main high-seas role as protection of their commerce, in which fleet actions would be defensive. They therefore tended to aim high, at opposing masts and sails, so as to prevent the enemy from pursuing, and to open engagements downwind of their opponents, so as to be able to draw away if things went badly or the merchantmen had already escaped. Circumstances could alter these stereotyped patterns (the French were at times on the offensive, especially in the West Indies), but training and habit influenced the effectiveness of gunnery, especially, even under abnormal conditions.

But the larger tactical issue that occupied admirals and theorists in all major navies had to do with the central problem of command and control in battle action, and how that affected the orthodox method of fighting battles in line-ahead formation (see Chapter 20). The line ahead, in which a fleet, usually divided into van, center, and rear squadrons, sailed one ship after the other in a line parallel to a similarly arrayed enemy fleet, had originally emerged as a solution to the loss of command and control inherent in mass melee battles. Compared to the melee, the line maximized firepower by making sure each ship had an open field of fire and theoretically allowed an admiral to maintain control over his fleet's movements throughout a battle. The introduction of the line ahead had also encouraged standardization, eliminating weaker ships from the line and so creating the concept of the ship of the line, and professionalization of the officer class, as captains were expected to follow the line, not sail off under their own agenda. But the line ahead solved the problem of command and control by severely limiting the tactical options a fleet could employ. A substantial line of ships, each around 100 feet long and with at least 300 feet between them, could stretch over the horizon. With simple signal flags, the only method of ship-to-ship communication, any action other than continuing to follow the same course in line risked degenerating into confusion. But while holding course in line made for a powerful defensive formation, it could not easily be employed for a decisive offensive stroke. One might have advantage in gunnery and drive off an enemy line but not destroy much of the enemy fleet.

Two strains of thought emerged in response to the restrictions imposed by the rigidity of the line ahead. They were not formalized enough to be called schools, nor were they exactly opposed, but they did represent different poles regarding the philosophy of command and control. At one end were the centralizers, who thought that the solution to tactical limitations would come from more effective control of battle fleets by admirals. Their position was a natural outgrowth of the forces that had created the line-ahead doctrine in the first place. Proponents called for strict adherence by captains to a set of written "Fighting Instructions" that attempted to cover the major possibilities that could arise during a battle, with signal flags keyed to the instructions raised by the admiral. The French, following the rationalist and scientific approaches of the time, actually pioneered this approach: The "Fighting Instructions" they introduced in 1689 would not be matched in level of detail by the British for a century. Improvements in the eighteenth century focused on better systems of signal flags, culminating in a numeric system that required only three flags to reference numbered rules in the instructions.

However rational and sophisticated the combination of flags and instructions might be, however, they could not cover the range of contingencies that arose in the everchanging conditions of combat at sea. Even more problematically, the length of a line made visibility iffy under the best of conditions; the smoke of battle and any kind of bad weather could rapidly make visual communications impossible. All admirals found improved signaling useful during cruising, though, and continued to use the line ahead as the foundation of tactics. However, some British admirals, led initially by Admirals Edward Vernon, George Anson, and Edward Hawke, concluded that no combination of doctrine, signals, and tactics could open the tactical door to decisive fleet actions. They did not formulate an opposing doctrine but

instead took a decentralizing approach to command and control of fleets. That is, they trusted and relied on the judgment of their captains rather than on vainly seeking improved central control. Anson at the First Battle of Finisterre on May 3, 1747, and Hawke at Second Finisterre on October 14 the same year put their ideas into practice by setting their fleets onto French squadrons under the signal for a General Chase, a signal usually reserved (if used at all) for the pursuit of an already broken and fleeing enemy line. The result in each case was a decisive destruction of the French squadron.

Their younger admirer Horatio Nelson would perfect this style of leadership. He consciously inculcated his approach to battles in the captains under his command, the Band of Brothers as he dubbed them. Before a Nelson fleet went into battle, the general plan was thoroughly discussed, but the execution was left to the initiative of the captains schooled in the "Nelson Touch." The results from 1797 to 1805 were an unprecedented series of decisive victories for British sea power, culminating in Nelson's masterpiece at Trafalgar (see the Highlights box "Trafalgar"). This tactical style reproduced the successful command and control style the Admiralty Board assigned to strategy: general, overarching instructions to squadron commanders, with detailed execution left to the commanders based on their assessment of conditions on the spot.

And yet Nelson's tactical approach died with him—it was far from universal even in the Royal Navy during his career. The Admiralty made some attempts to incorporate the surface features of Nelson's tactics into the "Fighting Instructions"—to convert spontaneity into doctrine—but the underlying reality was continued reliance on centralized implementation of doctrine through signals. No other navy even tried to copy Nelson's style. Why? There are two basic reasons, one general and one specific.

The general reason was that Nelson's decentralized style flew in the face of the rational, scientific, and centralizing tendencies of the age. The Admiralty's strategic approach was forced on them by the impossibility of communicating rapidly with a fleet on station; presented with at least some chance to micromanage by the invention of the telegraph later in the nineteenth century, the Admiralty happily seized it. Trusting individual captains on decisive throws of the dice seemed too fraught with risk, not least to the reputations of their superiors who would answer if the captains failed; centralizers sought certainty through

The Death of Nelson
Naval command in the age of sail was dangerous as well as difficult. Having lost an arm and an eye in earlier battles, Horatio Nelson died from a French sniper's bullet in the spine during his crowning victory at Trafalgar. This Romantic engraving illustrates the secular sainthood Nelson achieved in England.

unified decision making. (It was probably Nelson's intense religiosity, which also contrasted sharply with the rationalism of the age, that allowed him to trust his sacred Band of Brothers.)

The specific reason was that the institutional culture that fostered a cohort of captains who knew and trusted each other, their admiral, and the approach to battle he believed in was difficult to replicate even in the Royal Navy, never mind in other navies that had neither the number of ships constantly at sea nor the institutional continuity of the Royal Navy. Indeed, after 1805, the dense history of naval battle (fifty-six major engagements between 1715 and 1815) so thinned out (fifteen smaller battles between 1814 and 1914) that no navy could replicate the combination of training and experience on which the Nelson Touch depended. Forced to put to sea with more inexperienced captains and admirals without long records of success, it is no wonder most navies including the post-Nelson Royal Navy opted for attempts at micromanaging via doctrine and signals. Yet the limitations of centralized command and control inherent to fighting at sea remained, at least until the inventions of wireless telegraphy and later radio communications mitigated them somewhat. Navies in the nineteenth century would therefore continue to struggle with an almost impossible obstacle to implementing effective fleet tactics in combat.

NAVAL TRANSFORMATIONS, 1830–1914

Industrialization and Naval Power

The last significant naval battle between fleets reliant exclusively on wind took place in 1827, between British and Turkish fleets in the Greek waters near Navarino. Steam power had already been applied with commercial success to ships by Robert Fulton as early as 1807 and would soon become widespread at least as a backup system of propulsion for combat ships. Steam power heralded a widespread transformation of naval technology in the nineteenth century that would affect every aspect of ship design, as well as the relationship of naval power to economic and political systems. In other words, the vast transformations of economies, politics, social structures, and cultures brought about by the Industrial Revolution—a set of changes discussed in Chapter 23—affected naval warfare as much as land warfare. Indeed, given the vast capital and material investments needed to build and maintain

Trafalgar

In December 1804, Spain entered the war between Britain and France on the French side, bringing the third-largest fleet in Europe into the naval equation. Napoleon immediately began planning an invasion of England. The plan was to bring all the major Spanish and French fleets first to a rendezvous in the West Indies that would draw off British strength in the Channel, then dash back to the Channel to seize temporary control of the narrow seas and cover transport of the Grand Armée to England. But the scheme failed in the face of a central tenet of British strategy: When in doubt, concentrate in the Channel.

The Toulon fleet under Admiral Villeneuve united with a Spanish squadron and sailed to the West Indies and then back to Cadiz in southwest Spain between April and July. Nelson, who had been blockading Toulon while the main British fleet guarded the Channel, scoured the Mediterranean when the enemy escaped, then followed to the West Indies and back across the Atlantic, having driven Villeneuve's fleet away from Britain's lucrative sugar islands.

On September 27, Villeneuve left Cadiz on Napoleon's orders to rendezvous with another Spanish fleet at Cartagena in the Mediterranean and then sail to Italy to support a French campaign there. Nelson now had the Combined Fleet, 33 ships of the line of both France and Spain, where he wanted it. Nelson quickly closed in with his 27 ships from the west to confront the enemy entering the Straits of Gibraltar, his frigates shadowing the Combined Fleet and signaling with flares and rockets.

Nelson had already laid his tactical plan before his captains: to sail at the foe in two lines perpendicular to the allied line and cut it in two places (Figure 25.1). The lee division would overwhelm the enemy rear division while the weather division engaged the enemy center and held off the enemy van. With the enemy rear rapidly overwhelmed, the van would then be dealt with. Nelson's memorandum of October 9 summarizing the plan also noted the key tactical element: "But, in case signals can neither be seen or perfectly understood, no Captain can do very wrong if he places his ship alongside that of an Enemy." In the event, the only signal Nelson's flagship flew was the general one "England expects every man will do his duty."

The Combined Fleet turned back northward on the morning of October 21 to give battle. The wind, from west-northwest, was light, increasing the risk of Nelson's plan as the lead ships in each of his divisions had to endure unanswered broadsides for up to half an hour while they closed on the enemy line. Firing began about noon; ten minutes later, the lee division broke the enemy line at the

---

navies in the industrial age, naval power and industrial power became ever more closely linked—far more directly than land-based military power and industrial strength.

The impact of industrialization's multifaceted transformations on naval combat was often difficult to judge, however, for practitioners then, as it is for historians now, because the frequency of naval combat declined steeply after 1815, as already noted. Technological innovations therefore emerged within a context of strategic and doctrinal continuity. Feverish reevaluation followed the few actions that did take place, especially in the Crimea, the American Civil War, and the Russo-Japanese War. But theorists tended to find confirmation in recent action of theories built on eighteenth-century history. It was only in 1914, at the end of a century of change, that any of the new technologies began to pose problems for that basic continuity.

New Technologies

Surface Ship Technologies   Changing the design and technological profile of ships was not a simple matter of adding new inventions as they came along. Especially with ships designed for combat, a range of factors had to be balanced in any new design, the three chief of which were mobility (both top speed

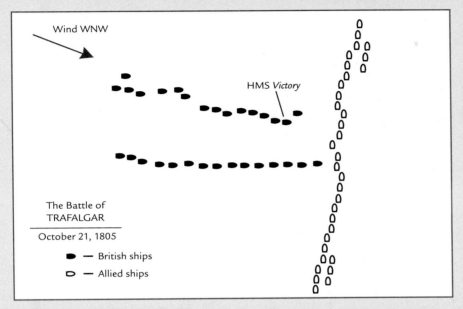

Figure 25.1 The Battle of Trafalgar

the time he died, he knew that a decisive victory was his: Eighteen allied ships were taken or destroyed; no British ship was lost; and the remainder of the allied fleet was bottled up or hunted down over the next two weeks. British control of the seas was assured, but decisive as Trafalgar was, it could not end the war against Napoleon, who achieved his greatest victory at Austerlitz two months later. Nelson and sea power could protect Britain from losing the war. Winning it was another matter.

Still, Nelson died a national hero, and his reputation as the greatest admiral in history survives to this day. It was a reputation built on tactical daring and decentralized command and control that made full use of the understanding and initiative of his captains.

sixteenth ship, and twenty minutes after that, Nelson's flagship *Victory* broke the line again. A fierce and bloody melee ensued. Nelson fell mortally wounded about 1:30, shot through the spine by a sniper, and was carried belowdecks where he lay in intense pain for nearly three hours. But by

and cruising range), firepower, and defensive protection. Increases in one usually had to be achieved at the price of decreases in one of the others, as when the introduction of side paddle wheels for steam propulsion cut down dramatically on the number of guns that could be mounted on a ship's broadside. Both for this reason and because large side paddles were very vulnerable to enemy fire, paddle wheel steamers were minority components of any nation's navy except in specific circumstances, such as the armored sternwheelers used for riverine operations during the American Civil War. Over the century, the size, speed, firepower, and armoring of battle fleets all steadily increased, but the balancing of factors still applied

at each stage of the evolution of ship design and accounted for many of the peculiarities in different approaches.

The invention of efficient screw propellers in the late 1830s allowed steamships to carry full broadsides, and screw-driven ships became standard in navies beginning in the mid-1840s. Further improvements in propulsion followed at regular intervals. Simple one-cylinder engines were replaced by much more efficient two-cylinder compound engines in the mid-1850s, increasing speed and dramatically raising fuel efficiency. Triple-expansion engines further boosted engine power and reduced coal consumption in the 1870s, by which time most navies had

La Gloire The first ironclad warship (center), it sat lower and carried fewer guns than a conventional ship of the line (right), but its armor-plated hull signaled the end of the days of wooden battle fleets.

abandoned sails even for auxiliary power. In 1894, a modern method of ship propulsion arrived with the invention of the turbine engine. Conversion to oil in the 1920s (and nuclear power in the 1950s) changed the fuel, and turbine designs improved incrementally, but the basic power plant for warships (and merchant ships) was in place by 1900. Steam turbines, while offering the prospect of radical increases in speed, were only slowly incorporated in new designs. The turbine, which ran most efficiently at high speed, proved incompatible with current propellers, which operated best at low speeds. The Royal Navy made turbines standard after 1906 because they were more reliable and saved weight and space. The development of special gearing, which reduced the rotational speed of the propeller, resolved the turbine-propeller incompatability problem, resulting in greater fuel efficiency and increased propeller life. By 1912, the Royal Navy had begun installing geared turbines in its destroyers, with the United States and Germany following suit. However, the Royal Navy was the only navy that used geared turbines to any great extent during World War I. Still, over the course of the century, speeds of the biggest battleships rose steadily from the 10–12 knots of early paddle wheelers, to 18–22 knots with compound engines, to close to 30 knots with turbines after 1914.

Steam power could be retrofitted to wooden ships, and many of the steam frigates of midcentury navies were former sailing vessels, though many were also purpose-built steamships. But changes in hull construction accompanied changes in propulsion. The maximum length a wooden ship can attain is about 400 feet, but in practice, a much shorter length is needed to maintain good sailing qualities. The problem was hogging: the tendency for long wooden ships to sag at the ends due to the structural weakness of wooden frames. Iron frames appeared as early as the 1820s, and ships with all-iron hulls shortly afterward. But most navies, even more conservative than commercial shippers, stuck with wooden planking even on iron frames, in part because thick wooden sides provided more protection than thin iron hulls. Thus, wooden ships of the line firing broadsides continued to rule the waves through the mid-1850s, though by then almost all were steam driven at least some of the time while retaining full rigging. Continuity to this point appeared more dominant than change.

But in 1857, prompted by improvements in naval ordinance (see below) and a desire to erase Britain's lead in conventional steam frigates, France began construction of the *Gloire*, which was launched in 1859 and completed a year later. It had a wooden hull plated with 4.5 inches of iron armor. Britain, which had held back constructing ironclads so as not to render its lead in conventional battleships obsolete, responded with its own ironclad designs. In each country, iron plating was applied both to wooden- and to iron-hulled ships. But these designs, still based on broadside arrangements of the guns, came into question in 1862, when the first battle between ironclad ships was fought at Hampton Roads in Virginia, in the American Civil War. The Confederacy had created its ironclad, the CSS *Virginia*, on the hull of the

The *Monitor* vs. the *Virginia* The first battle of ironclads; the CSS *Virginia* (rebuilt from the USS *Merrimack*) carried more guns in its casemate, but the future belonged to the turret-mounted guns of John Ericsson's revolutionary USS *Monitor*.

USS *Merrimack*, a steam frigate burned to the water-line when the Union abandoned the naval base at Hampton Roads. The Confederates raised the hull and built on it a casemate plated with 4 inches of armor housing ten heavy guns. On March 8, it steamed out into harbor and attacked the Union blockade ships. It rammed and sank the sloop *Cumberland*, then destroyed the frigate *Congress* with gunfire, while suffering no damage from Union gunnery. But soon after it retired for the day, the USS *Monitor* was towed into the roads (a partly sheltered area of water near a shore). The design of a Swede, John Ericsson, who had decades earlier invented a workable screw propeller, the *Monitor* was an odd craft. Essentially an armored raft atop an iron hull, it had only two structures projecting above its flat, near-water-level deck: a small pilothouse (really only a box over the pilot's head), and an iron-clad turret, holding two eleven-inch guns, turned by steam power at a rate of one revolution every thirty seconds. The *Monitor* and the *Virginia* fought to a standstill over several hours the next day, with neither able to do much damage to the other. But the tactical standoff was a strategic victory for the Union, as it maintained the blockade, and Ericsson's turret pointed the way to future battleship design in terms of the layout of guns (see further below).

The *Monitor* sank in a gale while being towed off Cape Hatteras, North Carolina, demonstrating the weakness of the "cheese box" design for open-seas cruising. Therefore, despite the great success of *Monitor*-class vessels in the rest of the Civil War, European navies began placing gun turrets on larger, more seaworthy, hulls. Engineers turned their attention to producing better armor, and designers attempted various ways of armoring ships that would not slow them down too much, including belts of armoring only at the water-line. The real breakthrough in both hull construction and protection, however, came with the application of modern chemical science to metallurgy in the 1870s. In 1880, steel began replacing iron as the material of combat ships. Steel hulls were stronger and lighter than iron hulls, and steel plate provided significantly more protection than iron plate of the same thickness. New techniques for producing steel plate and new alloys that strengthened the material appeared steadily through the 1890s and first decade of the 1900s. Steel also allowed ships to continue to grow in size; the biggest battleships of 1910 displaced nearly 30,000 tons, whereas the *Monitor* displaced under 1000.

HMS *Dreadnought* The first all-big-gun battleship, the *Dreadnought* triggered a new wave of the naval arms race between Britain and Germany when it was launched in 1906.

The search for better armor occurred in a reactive cycle with improvements in naval ordinance that began in the 1830s. Exploding shells proved far more effective against wooden hulls than the solid shot standard in Nelson's day. Their effectiveness was further enhanced by the design of aerodynamic shells, pointed at one end rather than round as solid shot had been. Combined with rifled cannon, such shells greatly increased the range and accuracy of naval guns. Breech loading improved rates of fire, and steel construction allowed both larger, more powerful, guns and the creation of armor-piercing shells. Between 1895 and 1915, the range of naval rifled heavy artillery increased sixfold, from about 6000 to about 35,000 yards. The accuracy of these weapons, abysmal in the late nineteenth century, improved with the advent of optical range finders, mechanical fire-control systems, and smokeless gunpowder. The armor-piercing shells packed with high explosives such guns fired consistently kept ahead of improvements in defensive armor. Meanwhile, new forms of naval weaponry were appearing, especially the self-propelled torpedo, introduced in the early 1880s and leading to a brief vogue for torpedo boats as against large capital ships.

But the most experimentation came in the arrangement of guns, both where to put them and what mix of large and small guns to include on a ship. The turret (or its unarmored cousin the *barbette,* used at times to save weight) allowed a new flexibility in the direction of a ship's firepower, but the optimal placement of turrets was far from clear to designers. Battleships of the 1870s and 1880s often combined one or two centerline turrets fore and aft with several placed amidships on either side, making it impossible for a ship to bring all its large guns to bear at once. And not every turret was armed with the biggest guns available; smaller guns were thought necessary for close-in action, especially against torpedo boats. The number of guns in a turret also varied.

The grand synthesis of nearly a century's technological development came in 1906, when Britain launched the HMS *Dreadnought.* Designed by First Sea Lord Sir John (Jackie) Fisher, the *Dreadnought* made all extant battleships obsolete. It combined unprecedented size (18,110 tons, 527 feet long) with 11-inch armor; a turbine-driven 21-knot top speed, greater than that of all existing battleships; and a main battery of eight 12-inch guns in four centerline turrets, which was twice the number of the largest guns used even on relatively recent battleship designs. Fisher was actually aiming at a new kind of capital ship, what would be the battle cruiser, but built the *Dreadnought* to satisfy battleship advocates. His cruisers were nearly as large and as heavily armed as battleships, but their lighter 6-inch armor helped them achieve a 25-knot top speed. But trading protection for speed proved a risky tradeoff, as increases in firepower dominated naval technological improvements.

It was thus the *Dreadnought,* built in an astonishing eleven months, that touched off a new round of the pre–World War I arms race. Warships of all types grew bigger and faster and carried larger crews servicing more specialized weapons. All earlier designs became known as *pre-Dreadnoughts,* a euphemism for general obsolescence. With this generation of capital ships, the linear transformation of battleships, from Nelson's *Victory* through the *Dreadnought,* reached a logical conclusion. Further transformations in the technology of naval power would involve taking naval combat under the sea and into the air.

Submarines and Airplanes

People had experimented with submersible boats since the 1600s, and David Bushnell's *Turtle* became the first submersible to engage in combat when, during the American Revolution, it was used unsuccessfully to attach a mine to a British warship anchored in New York Harbor. The CSS *Hunley,* named after its inventor, became the first submarine to sink an enemy craft, using a spar torpedo to blow up the USS *Housatonic* in Charleston Harbor during the Civil War. The *Housatonic* dragged the *Hunley* down with it, with the loss of all hands; in fact, it had gone down twice before, killing all aboard (including its inventor), during trials. A thirty-foot-long modified boiler with a ballast tank, diving planes, and a depth gauge, the *Hunley* was a recognizable ancestor of modern subs. But it was powered by a stern propeller hand-cranked by eight men, and it had to steer blind when submerged. Power and visibility continued to be the chief problems submarine designers worked to overcome. Battery-powered submarines appeared in the 1880s, but these had limited cruising range. Internal combustion engines, used from the 1890s, could power a surfaced ship while recharging batteries for underwater cruising, but the accumulation of gasoline fumes proved a constant hazard. A switch to diesel after 1908 solved the fume problem, though only the German invention in World War II of the *snorkel,* a tube for drawing in air and venting out exhaust when the ship was shallowly submerged, enabled long-distance concealed cruising. Meanwhile, in 1902 an American inventor came up with a workable periscope, solving the problem of submerged navigation

and sighting of enemy vessels. Such battery-and-diesel submarines, armed with self-propelled torpedoes, were ready to assume a central place in the naval side of World War I (see Chapter 26).

The year 1903 saw the beginning of the age of aviation, and visionaries quickly began to design ways to harness airpower to the needs of naval combat. But such efforts would bear even slower fruit than submarine technology, and sea-based aviation played little role in World War I, and none prior to it.

Infrastructures of Naval Power

The technologies of ships themselves were only a part of the transformation of sea power in the nineteenth century. Land-based technologies and organizations of production, communication, supply, and political symbolism also affected the building, deployment, and use of naval power.

At the most basic level, naval power, both actual and potential, through the century increasingly reflected the industrial capacity of maritime nations. Britain's early lead in industrialization meant that it spent the decades at least up to 1880 with few concerns about serious naval competition. France, for example, may have built the first ironclad, but its iron industry could supply only enough plate for one *Gloire*-class ship a year in 1860. Britain laid down its first ironclad after the *Gloire* but finished it almost at the same time and was building several others simultaneously. Each transformation of ship technology saw this same pattern repeated, with Britain rapidly outproducing most of its rivals even if when it did not innovate first. The increasing use of private contractors in an industrial capitalist model of naval construction—this was the age of Krupp, the great German steelworks and their like in industrial chemistry, munitions, and so forth—had several significant consequences for patterns of naval competition as well. British shipyards built not only the Royal Navy's ships but ships for navies in Latin America, East Asia, and North America (including contracts, mostly never fulfilled, with the Confederacy), and even for European rivals. British ironworks even supplied the plate and much of the engine machinery for many French warships after 1860, despite ongoing rivalry between the nations. In fact, this was not an age of industrial defense secrets. New designs, inventions, and processes, such as for steelmaking, spread rapidly to all competitors not just because of direct sales of components and whole ships but because of licensing agreements whereby, say, American steelmakers would buy the right to use a patented German alloying technique. Governments, perhaps strangely from the vantage point of the early twenty-first century, did nothing to inhibit this flow of information (though the flow of militarily sensitive information despite government regulations even today demonstrates the commercial value of military innovations to capitalist companies for whom political boundaries are mostly an inconvenience). The result was probably a greater level and pace of innovation, but with few asymmetrical results between major navies in terms of technology—the asymmetry developed between the industrial nations (including, after 1870, Japan) and the nonindustrial ones, who were left to buy the leaders' obsolete ships and designs on the market. Competition between the great navies therefore focused on numbers, as no technological lead was safe for long. And ability to build large numbers again reflected basic industrial capacity.

The global reach of navies and the aims of naval strategy were affected by two other aspects of naval infrastructure. First, the invention of the telegraph in midcentury and the subsequent laying of transcontinental and transoceanic cables created the possibility for greater central direction and management of distant fleets, though in practice this often turned out to be more mirage than reality. The application of technology to the problem of ship-to-ship communication and tactical fleet coordination was slower. Despite the use of Morse Code, derived from telegraph usage, visual signaling at the end of the century remained subject to vagaries of weather and the confusion of combat, as well as heavily reliant on doctrine (that is, coded, prearranged messages) for conveying content.

Second, the conversion of sailing fleets to steam power made access to fuel a critical problem for fleets tasked to sail beyond home waters. Early steam engines consumed coal at a prodigious rate, one reason auxiliary sail power was retained for so long. More efficient engines extended the powered cruising range of fleets, but global reach for navies such as Britain's required that a global network of secure coaling stations be established. Britain's already established colonial territories helped in this respect, with some outposts, such as the Cape Colony in South Africa, gaining in importance as a result. For other powers, the need to establish coaling stations added yet another dimension to the push toward imperialism in the last quarter of the nineteenth century.

A final and critical aspect of the infrastructure of naval power, given the steadily rising cost of technologically advanced capital ships and the rising level of

naval competition by the end of the century, was funding. In the competition for scarce government money, the navies of major land powers often found themselves at a disadvantage vis-à-vis armies with established levels of manpower and long historical traditions, reflecting the more central place of armies in national grand strategy. Faced with hard choices, France eventually opted out of attempting to maintain a truly first-rate navy, a decision aided by the gradual détente with Britain at the turn of the century. (As late as the 1880s, the strategy and building program of the French navy, which for a time focused on torpedo boats and commerce raiding, was aimed at Britain as the potential enemy.) Germany, on the other hand, with its navy under the leadership of Admiral Alfred von Tirpitz, ramped up its naval construction program in direct challenge to British naval supremacy despite the concurrent demands of the army.

Von Tirpitz and proponents of naval buildups in the United States, Japan, Italy, Austria, Russia, and elsewhere, as well as defenders of Britain's traditional emphasis on naval power, relied on three basic arguments for investment in capital ships. First, the possession of at least some battleships could act as a deterrent on the ambitions of rivals even if they were never used, and so they could be presented as a cost-efficient way of avoiding major conflicts, despite the apparent high cost of ships. Such reasoning gained force near the end of the century with the rise of the first popular theories of naval strategy, especially those proposed by Alfred Thayer Mahan and Julian Corbett (see below). These theories emphasized the role of naval power in preclusive national security and the competition for imperial possessions, which the theorists tied via historical examples to long-term national growth and greatness. Such theories were especially attractive in democracies such as Britain and the United States. In those nations, traditional mistrust of military spending based on fear of tyranny remained a potent political fact, but fleets did not pose the threat to democratic institutions that standing armies did. But perhaps the most powerful argument in favor of naval construction drew on the emotional power of capital ships and naval victories as symbols of national greatness. In some ways, it was a search, not for a new Nelson, but for a new Nelson's Column in a new Trafalgar Square that motivated politicians and the general public to open their wallets for programs of naval construction. All these factors combined fueled a race for naval dominance that has become an historical prototype of

Arms Races

Rapid technological change created problems for all navies. On the one hand, keeping up with innovations was critical if a navy were not to find its fleet threatened with obsolescence. On the other hand, new technology periodically seemed to offer the chance to leapfrog the leading naval power, though such opportunities usually proved illusory. After all, naval power rested not on specific technologies or even particular combinations of technologies, but on a broader basis of industrial might and political will that made the outcome of competitive building programs fairly predictable. Britain's Admiralty Board understood this clearly and so reacted calmly to each French challenge to British supremacy at sea through the 1880s. But they also understood the much greater threat posed by the German challenge that began in the 1890s, as well as the inevitability if not the threat of rising U.S. naval power at the same time, because the industrial strength of each country was clearly now on a par with (if not surpassing) Britain's own. Britain maintained its naval lead, but with more difficulty and by virtue of its ability to focus its resources almost exclusively on its navy, while Germany armed on land as well as at sea. And the introduction of the *Dreadnought*, which effectively wiped out Britain's significant lead in "modern" battleships (reducing it to 1–0 from a lead of over 20) illustrates the difficult decisions nations and navies faced in balancing overall numbers against new technology.

But for the most part, this was in fact an arms race driven by politics—based in a range of motivations including nationalism and imperialism—rather than by technology. The key technology and symbol of power, the battleship, was not new,

nor were most of its variations new (even the *Dreadnought* was simply a bigger, more specialized version of what already existed). Further, the doctrine for using this technology remained stable even as the technology changed. In this way, it resembled the buildups in European army strengths that characterized military competition on land between 1660 and 1720 (see Chapter 16) more than a technologically driven arms race.

But have there been arms races that were technologically driven? Historians here face the problem of technological determinism in a different form than in the Military Revolution debate (see the Issues box on page 306). New technologies have sometimes made a difference in military history, to be sure: the introduction first of chariots, then of horse riding, iron weaponry, gunpowder, the whole range of industrial technology, and finally nuclear weapons. But it is hard to see any of these as directly responsible for an "arms race." Rather, such technologies tended to create temporary asymmetries in military power that were then erased, more or less gradually, by diffusion of the new technology. Even the nuclear arms race was basically political: Both sides had fusion bombs after 1954, and the "race" was a matter of the buildup of numbers of such weapons, driven by ideological and geopolitical competition in a bipolar world.

The naval arms race of the late nineteenth century therefore appears to be an archetypal arms race, consisting of a politically motivated buildup in numbers of a technology shared by the competitors. The appearance of a technological race, whether in battleships or nuclear weapons, is mostly illusory.

---

arms races (see the Issues box "Arms Races") and contributed to the coming of World War I.

Naval Power in Practice

As already noted, the rapid technological changes that characterized navies in the nineteenth century took place in an environment short on actual naval

combat. As a result, hard lessons about the impact of technology were sparse. The few major engagements that took place ended up overanalyzed, but often without a clear lesson or even with wrong ones. Strategically, doctrine remained stable; tactical doctrine was by necessity more malleable, as the new technology altered the potential conditions for naval combat directly, but command and control of fleets of ships from an admiral's flagship remained the central tactical problem of the period. There is not room to narrate all the naval engagements of the period after 1830. This section will instead focus on a few key and representative naval conflicts and their impact on conceptions of sea power at the time.

The Crimean War   Two naval actions during the Crimean War affected naval thinking. At the Battle of Sinope on November 30, 1853, a Russian fleet destroyed an Ottoman fleet. This was taken, especially by Napoleon III, as proof that shell guns were rendering wooden ships obsolete, despite the fact that Russian shells were probably no more efficient than solid shot would have been. This belief was reinforced by the bombardment of Kinburn, a Russian fort at the mouth of the Dnieper, by a combined British-French squadron in October 1855. The key vessels were shallow-draft armored floating batteries that pounded the fort to rubble while Russian shot bounced harmlessly off their armor plate. The Russian guns were second-rate, and it is not clear that the batteries were in fact decisive, but Napoleon again thought they were, contributing to his decision to build an ironclad warship three years later.

The American Civil War   The tactical lessons of the naval side of the American Civil War had to do mostly with the effectiveness of turreted ironclads on the *Monitor* model, as discussed above. The advantage ships had in gun duels against stationary fortifications ashore (including the inability of forts to block the passage of ships on rivers) was also demonstrated repeatedly.

The more important lessons of the naval war were operational and strategic. The Union exploited the advantage that ironclad gunboats in particular had over shore defenses to facilitate army transport, bypass and then take Confederate forts, and open river communications for its own forces while denying rivers to the Confederacy. General Grant proved particularly adept at such combined river operations, from his first campaign around Paducah in Kentucky to his masterpiece in the Vicksburg campaign (see the Highlights box on page 450). The latter, by closing the last crossing of the Mississippi, split the Confederacy in two. Such operations expanded on the ability of steam gunships to exploit rivers in ways no oared or sailing ship could, a capacity first used to decisive effect by the British in the Opium Wars against China.

Combined river operations formed part of a larger Union strategy that aimed to isolate and strangle the Confederacy through naval blockade—the "Anaconda Plan" proposed by General Winfield Scott at the start of the war. The Union navy had enough forces only for the barest minimum of coverage when the war began, given the vast length of the Confederate coastline and its many sheltered harbors. But the Confederacy failed to challenge the blockade at its weakest because it thought (mistakenly) that placing an embargo on its cotton exports would pressure Britain into support for its cause. And by the time the Confederacy reversed the policy, a steady stream of reinforcements had augmented the blockading squadrons. The Union tightened the cordon by picking off major Southern ports with combined army-navy assaults. Admiral David Farragut led the two most famous of these efforts. In April 1862, he took a squadron of steam sloops, mortar flotillas, and gunboats, escorting 10,000 soldiers under General Benjamin Butler, up the Mississippi. Running through a barrier of abandoned ships and logs and the fire from Forts St. Philip and Jackson ninety miles below New Orleans, he then sank nine of eleven Confederate gunboats and sailed unopposed into New Orleans while his mortar boats and Butler's troops took the forts. And in August 1864, he ran a fleet of ironclads and other ships into Mobile Bay past heavily gunned harbor defenses and a minefield that sank one of his monitors (prompting his famous command "Damn the torpedoes, full steam ahead!"); the capture of Mobile provided President Lincoln's reelection campaign with a much needed boost. Although the Confederacy had minor successes using fast, shallow-draft blockade runners and commerce raiders to evade Union patrols, overall the Union blockade was a successful application of naval power to economic warfare that contributed materially (though probably not decisively) to Southern defeat.

The Battle of Lissa   Ironclad actions in the Civil War all took place either on rivers or in harbors. The first open sea battle between ironclad warships, and indeed the largest naval battle between Trafalgar (1805, see above) and Tsushima (1905, see below), occurred off the island of Lissa in the Adriatic on July 20, 1866, between an Italian fleet that included 11 foreign-built ironclads and an Austrian fleet of 7 armored frigates, 7 screw-propeller warships including a ship of the line, and some smaller gunboats. The Austrian admiral Tegethoff attacked in line abreast. The battle rapidly devolved into a confused melee pitting weak Austrian guns against bad Italian gunnery. The decisive blow thus came when Tegethoff's flagship rammed and sank an Italian ironclad. The battle should not have taught any lessons, as it reflected ad hoc tactics and incompetence on both sides, but Tegethoff's success meant that line abreast became the favored formation for two decades afterward, and battleships were built with useless bow rams into the early twentieth century.

The Russo-Japanese War: Tsushima With the war against Japan going badly on land, the Russians sent their Baltic fleet to reinforce their Pacific forces. It left home under Admiral Rozhestvensky in October 1904 and nearly brought on a war with Britain by mistakenly shelling a British fishing fleet in the North Sea. The larger battleships sailed round the Cape of Good Hope, rendezvousing off Madagascar with the cruisers and destroyers that used the Suez Canal. Further reinforcements of older ships followed in January 1905, when Rozhestvensky learned that Port Arthur and its ships had fallen; the entire fleet finally linked up off Vietnam in April 1905. In May, Rozhestvensky steamed north with 11 battleships, 8 cruisers, 9 destroyers, and a number of smaller craft. Many of the ships were old (only 5 of the battleships were near the quality of newer Japanese ships) and overloaded with coal for the long cruise, and their crews were undertrained.

The Japanese admiral Togo, with 4 battleships, 8 cruisers, 21 destroyers, and a flotilla of torpedo boats, cruised to meet the Russians in the Tsushima Straits, which they entered on May 27. Togo steamed west, "crossing the T" of the northbound Russian fleet, then reversing course to repeat the cross. The action opened around 1:30 PM with the Russians opening fire at 7000 meters and the Japanese at 6400 meters. Rozhestvensky altered course first to the east, then back northwest, trying to outrun Togo and make it to Vladivostok, but the greater speed of the Japanese ships prevented the Russians from escaping, and superior Japanese gunnery took a steady toll. By the end of the day, all the Russian battleships had been sunk or captured, and the Japanese destroyers hunted down the remnants of the fleeing Russian fleet overnight. Three cruisers escaped to Manila where the Americans interned them, and a small gunboat made it to Vladivostok. The rest were sunk, scuttled, or captured; over 10,000 Russian seamen were killed or captured, while the Japanese lost 110 men and three torpedo boats.

Tsushima was the largest naval battle since Trafalgar, and it was equally decisive both tactically and strategically, as the battle led to negotiations and peace that year. And unlike Lissa, it taught real lessons. The battle was dominated by big guns at long range; the *Dreadnought*'s all-big-gun design followed later in 1905. Though Japanese gunnery proved effective, fire control on both sides was inadequate, giving further impetus to the search for better ways to achieve accuracy. The improvements in guns and gunnery that followed Tsushima, however, complicated the lesson of the importance of speed. That is, the future would not lie with fast but underarmored battle cruisers on Jackie Fisher's model, but (however briefly) with bigger, faster, and still more heavily armored battleships.

The Development of Naval Theory

Naval strategy before the 1890s was not a science. Certainly, bodies such as the British Admiralty Board and individuals such as Nelson applied principles to their use of navies, and it is possible to see coherent strategy (especially in the British use of blockades) at work in eighteenth-century naval campaigns. But there was no systematic, written statement of the principles that should guide naval strategy, just the practical application of experience to particular situations. Given the professionalization of academia in the nineteenth century and the profusion of writing about the principles of land warfare, led by the massive popularity and influence of Clausewitz's *On War*, what is perhaps surprising is the time it took for such a statement to appear. In 1890, Alfred Thayer Mahan published his *The Influence of Sea Power upon History, 1660–1783*, and professional naval strategy was born. Partly as a result of the massive popular success of Mahan's work, in 1911, Julian Corbett published *Some Principles of Maritime Strategy*, challenging many of Mahan's conclusions but sharing certain fundamental insights and methods for analyzing sea power. Naval strategy had entered the public stage.

Mahan founded his theory in the study of history—specifically, the study of the great naval wars of the age of sail. From the lessons of these wars as he read them, he derived a set of "Elements of Sea Power," *sea power* being broadly defined to include a nation's maritime commerce and combat navy, and the entire infrastructure—economic, political, and cultural—that supported both (see the Sources box "Naval Strategy").

The core of Mahan's argument was that sea power, produced by the combination of maritime commerce, naval building, and economic strength, must in time

Naval Strategy

In this selection from Chapter 1 of his The Influence of Sea Power upon History, 1660–1783, *Alfred Thayer Mahan outlines the origins and principle factors affecting sea power. It should be read not as history, but rather as a foundation myth akin to John Locke's "state of nature": a simplified derivation of the principles of sea power from a portrait of "nature" whose underlying assumptions need careful examination by the modern reader. It is also a statement of Mahan's historical philosophy and method.*

■ ■ ■

The first and most obvious light in which the sea presents itself from the political and social point of view is that of a great highway, . . . both travel and traffic by water have always been easier and cheaper than by land. . . .

[For a modern country bordering on the sea,] foreign necessaries or luxuries must be brought to its ports, either in its own or in foreign ships, which will return, bearing in exchange the products of the country, . . . and it is the wish of every nation that this shipping business should be done by its own vessels. The ships that thus sail to and fro must have secure ports to which to return, and must, as far as possible, be followed by the protection of their country throughout the voyage.

This protection in time of war must be extended by armed shipping. The necessity of a navy, in the restricted sense of the word, springs, therefore, from the existence of peaceful shipping. . . .

As a nation, with its unarmed and armed shipping, launches forth from its own shores, the need is soon felt of points upon which the ships can rely for peaceful trading, for refuge and supplies. . . . In earlier days, the merchant seaman, seeking gain in trade and new unexplored regions, . . . intuitively sought at the far end of his trade route one or more stations, to be given him by force or favor, where he could fix himself or his agents in reasonable security, where his ships could lie in safety, and where the merchantable products of the land could be continually collecting, awaiting the arrival of the home fleet, which should carry them to the mother-country. As there was immense gain, as well as much risk, in these early voyages, such establishments naturally multiplied and grew until they became colonies. . . .

In these three things—production, with the necessity of exchanging products, shipping, whereby the exchange is carried on, and colonies, which facilitate and enlarge the operations of shipping and tend to protect it by multiplying points of safety—is to be found the key to much of the history, as well as the policy, of nations bordering the sea. The policy has varied both with the spirit of the age and with the character and clear-sightedness of the rulers; but the history of the seaboard nations has been less determined by the shrewdness and foresight of governments than by conditions of position, extent, configuration, number and character of their people,—by what are called, in a word, natural conditions. It must however be admitted, and will be seen, that the wise or unwise action of individual men has at certain periods had a great modifying influence upon the growth of sea power in the broad sense, which includes not only the military strength afloat, that rules the sea or any part of it by force of arms, but also the peaceful commerce and shipping from which alone a military fleet naturally and healthfully springs, and on which it securely rests.

The principal conditions affecting sea power of nations may be enumerated as follows: I. Geographical Position. II. Physical Conformation, including, as connected therewith, natural productions and climate. III. Extent of Territory. IV. Number of Population. V. Character of People. VI. Character of the Government, including therein the national institutions.

SOURCE: Alfred Thayer Mahan, *The Influence of Sea Power upon History, 1660–1783* (Boston: Little, Brown, 1898).

of war be exerted to achieve control of the sea, as only this control could guarantee a nation's commerce and coastal security. Control was to be gained by having a combat fleet capable of seeking out and destroying the enemy fleet in decisive battle, thereby securing the sea-lanes for commerce. This view, with its emphasis on decisive battle and offensive action, borrowed heavily from contemporary theories of land warfare and was in this sense unexceptional. What made Mahan so influential and popular was a combination of aggressive self-promotion—he wrote 20 books and over 150 articles, many for popular magazines, expounding his views—and the larger political context in which he set his work, which nearly guaranteed it a favorable reception. By stressing the importance of global reach and colonial possessions to national strength, and showing that imperial power need not entail a large standing army, he gave expression to the imperialist aspirations of many U.S. politicians and rationalized a shift in U.S. policy from isolationist to expansionist. Indeed, Congress authorized the country's first modern seagoing battleships shortly after the book's publication, and eight years later, a U.S. fleet helped the United States grab the Philippines from Spain.

Julian Corbett, writing in Britain two decades after Mahan, agreed that control of the sea was the crux of sea power. He derived his theories, as Mahan had done, from the study of British naval history, though his writings were not historical but theoretical. But he read the lessons of that history differently from Mahan, thereby working out more carefully and systematically, though less flashily and with less popularizing, an alternate theory of sea power. His concept of control of the sea was more nuanced and contingent than Mahan's: It focused on access to sea passage, which could be general or local, temporary or more permanent, depending on the situation. He also distinguished carefully between positive and negative objects of sea power (gaining access versus protecting extant access, for example) that called for offensive or defensive strategies, respectively. He denied that battle seeking was necessary or even wise in all circumstances. Rather, simply maintaining a "fleet in being" could accomplish many of the ends of sea power. Above all, he saw naval power as working in concert with land power, and he emphasized amphibious operations—in Jackie Fisher's words, "The army is the projectile to be fired by the navy"—since the ultimate decision, no matter how effective a naval blockade might be, would rest on land.

Both Mahan and Corbett saw protection of friendly commerce and interdiction of enemy commerce as central tasks of sea power, therefore, but Corbett fit blockades and convoys into a more multidimensional strategic picture that included land warfare more comprehensively than did Mahan. The irony is that tactical multidimensionality began to undermine both Mahan and Corbett's theories even before their authors died. Early-twentieth-century battleships, technologically in another world from Nelson's, still operated in a two-dimensional Nelsonian sea guided by principles and fulfilling tasks recognizably Nelsonian. Submarines and aircraft would open the undersea and the skies to naval combat and force a radical rethinking of the principles of naval power. Eventually, nuclear weapons, aircraft, and missiles would give sea power a combat range extending to every corner of the globe. The lessons of Britain's eighteenth-century naval wars to this world were far less obvious than they were to Mahan, Corbett, and their world.

Conclusion

As the world approached onset of World War I, naval power seemed to rest securely on the battleship, as it had a century and a half earlier. Backed by industrial and commercial might, and deployed according to strategic and tactical doctrines that also showed more continuity than change since 1750, the battleship's superiority as the weapon of sea power seemed to show that the vast technological revolutions of this period had in fact produced little real change.

In some ways, this view is correct: The largest single naval battle of the war at Jutland in the North Sea would be dominated by battleships, and blockades based on strategic control of sea-lanes would play a significant economic role in the war. But while the British version of this strategy relied on conventional ships, the German effort based on submarine warfare showed that changing naval technology was by 1914 close to creating the conditions for significant change in the tools of sea power. That story is taken up in Chapter 26.

SUGGESTED READINGS

Barnett, Gary. *Seapower and Strategy.* Annapolis: Naval Institute Press, 1989. A good analysis of the major elements of naval strategy.

Dunnavent, R. Blake. *Brown Water Warfare: The U.S. Navy in Riverine Warfare and the Emergence of a Tactical Doctrine, 1775–1970.* Gainesville: University of Florida Press, 2003. A scholarly examination of the U.S. Navy's development of a coherent approach to naval warfare on rivers, an area decisively influenced by steam power.

Harding, Richard. *The Evolution of the Sailing Navy, 1509–1815.* See Chapter 20.

Keegan, John. *The Price of Admiralty.* London: Hutchinson, 1988. A readable survey of the development of naval warfare from 1750 to 1945; especially good analysis of Trafalgar.

Landstrom, Bjorn. *The Ship.* See Chapter 10.

Massie, Robert. *Dreadnought. Britain, Germany, and the Coming of the Great War.* New York: Random House, 1991. An incisive analysis of the role of the naval arms race between Britain and Germany in bringing on World War I, emphasizing the role of Kaiser Wilhelm II's strategic and diplomatic blundering.

Miller, Nathan. *Broadsides: The Age of Fighting Sail, 1775–1815.* New York: Wiley, 2001. A readable history of the pinnacle of the wooden-ship age of naval war.

Palmer, Michael. "'The Soul's Right Hand': Command and Control in the Age of Fighting Sail, 1652–1827." *Journal of Military History* 61 (1997), 679–705. A clear analysis of the characteristics that made Nelson's command style so successful and so difficult to duplicate.

Reeve, John, and David Stevens, eds. *The Face of Naval Battle.* New York: Allen & Unwin, 2004. A set of examinations of the human side of naval battle in this period.

Sondhaus, Lawrence. *Naval Warfare, 1815–1914.* New York: Routledge, 2001. A fine survey of naval warfare, with attention to changing economic and political contexts.

Sweetman, Jack, ed. *The Great Admirals. Command at Sea, 1587–1945.* See Chapter 20.

COMMENTARY: PART 5, 1700–1914

The period 1700–1914 witnessed a historical revolution unparalleled since the invention of agriculture and a resulting military revolution unparalleled since the taming of the horse and the rise of the Eurasian steppe nomads. In broad terms, the Industrial Revolution changed the global landscape. In military terms, the twin engines of revolution were industrial capitalism paired with the ideologies and political structures of nationalism. These forces altered the contexts of warfare and the conduct of warfare from the grand strategic down to the tactical level. The implications are still being felt, both in current military affairs and in the study of military history.

INDUSTRY AND NATIONALISM

The creation and spread of industrial methods of production was slow at first and limited to Great Britain. But the spread increased rapidly in pace and international competitiveness after 1850 as other European Great Powers plus the United States and Japan joined the industrial world, effecting a fundamental transformation of life both inside and outside the industrial powers. This transformation extended from economic patterns and social structures to political institutions and cultural expression. And as the chapters in this part have shown, military activity was equally transformed, both directly by industrial methods and indirectly as a result of other changes. Mass production, mass consumption, mass communication, mass politics, and mass culture characterized this transformation. These effects were made possible by the harnessing of new forms of power that far exceeded the potential of wind, water, and muscle, in the context of capitalist systems of economic organization that generated rapid and ongoing technological change. Though eighteenth-century Europe was by the standards of the time technologically innovative and witnessed many incremental improvements in its weaponry, eighteenth-century change looks limited in scope and glacial in pace compared to the nineteenth century. Armies of 1900, with their rifles, machine guns, and breech-loaded artillery, operated on a different planet from Napoleonic armies. And the change at sea was if anything even more pronounced: The *Dreadnought* was a universe apart from Nelson's *Victory*.

Technological change was driven in part by the general dynamics of capitalism, but the rise of nationalism as a central ideology of the nineteenth-century world (especially in Europe), and the corresponding competition between newly emergent nation-states that nationalism both reflected and fostered, focused the energies of many scientists and engineers directly on weaponry, accelerating further the pace of change. One result was that arms races began to be a constant of military history, rather than sporadic and generally short-lived phenomena. Arms races were in part rational policy responses to changing technology and the potential threat new weapons posed. But national pride often pushed arms competitions beyond the bounds of rational analysis: Having the latest, most advanced weapons as a symbol of national power and prestige, whether the weaponry was strategically useful or not, could become an end in itself. Nationalism, in short, began to fundamentally alter the ideological context of warfare. The corresponding rise of the nation-state as the most important unit of international diplomacy likewise fundamentally altered the geopolitical context of warfare and strategy. While the connection of the rise of nationalism to the French Revolution and the Napoleonic Wars is clear, the change wrought in politics and diplomacy by a century of ideological and political development after 1815 is nearly as vast as in the realm of technology.

CONSEQUENCES: WARFARE

The twin engines of industrial capitalism and national competition affected every aspect of the conduct of warfare from grand strategy down to tactics. The consequences of warfare in the age of industry and nationalism also included the rise of European empires and a period of European dominance over the globe unmatched before or since. Also, the same contexts that altered warfare and international relations shaped the emergence of history as a modern academic discipline, with a significant impact on the shape of military history down to the present.

The expansion of European military capabilities in terms of transport and communications brought about by advances such as railroads, steamships, and telegraphs encouraged, in the context of national competition, a shift in grand strategies. European dynastic states had been fairly limited in their ambitions, operating within conceptions of a balance of power focused on and largely limited to Europe. The economic reach of eighteenth-century colonial states, especially Britain, had of course been impressively global. However, the influence of these largely maritime empires on hinterlands throughout the world was still limited, and the empire building that did take place was traditional in aim. That is, areas such as India as it fell under British rule were exploited in traditional ways for wealth generated by traditional means. But the industrial nation-states of late-nineteenth-century Europe aimed at global dominance in worldwide competition. Nothing in the eighteenth century or before compares with the "Scramble for Africa," for example. And the new imperialists aimed not at traditional exploitation but at reorganization of their colonial societies for efficient production of industrial raw materials, bringing far-reaching changes to peoples around the world. The heightened ambitions and stakes involved in this competition showed up in the dawning conceptions of "total war" visible in the American Civil War; such conceptions would become even clearer after 1914.

Like grand strategy, strategy adjusted to new transport and communications capacities. The cautious positional strategies of eighteenth-century European warfare disappeared as armies could be mobilized faster and moved farther on rail networks than ever before—for the first time, steppe armies no longer held the record for rapid movement of masses of men overland. Navies also could move faster, if not farther, though they became tied more closely to coaling stations than sail navies had been to their bases. Napoleon showed that mass armies could afford to bypass and screen fortifications instead of having to reduce them, which also expanded the pace and scope of campaigns. The new strategic challenges called forth new strategic theoreticians whose influence remained central to military thought well into the twentieth century. Clausewitz studied Napoleon's campaigns and extracted principles that rapidly became dogma: the power of the offensive and the search for the "decisive battle" that would annihilate the opponent, in a context expressed in the Clausewitzian cliché "War is the extension of politics by other means." Likewise, Corbett and Mahan produced influential works on naval strategy, though Mahan's use of the wars of the age of sail as the basis of his study shows that the tasks of eighteenth-century navies changed less than their technology did. Given the logistical, organizational, and strategic complexities imposed by the new technological environment, it is not surprising that the nineteenth century saw the emergence of general staffs to plan and manage strategy. In most cases, however, even this new institution struggled with these challenges, and execution usually failed to match conception, especially in larger campaigns. Telegraphs, for example, promised greater central control over campaigns, but the promise usually turned out to be an illusion that simply stymied the initiative of subordinate commanders while leaving the overall command in the dark.

The problems created by new technology were even more apparent at the operational level. Larger armies and the increased range and accuracy of infantry weapons exacerbated command problems in the field. Generals found themselves more cut off from the action, unable safely to get close enough to see what was happening on battlefields, which, in any event, were becoming too large to survey directly. Junior officers, meanwhile, became targets for whole armies of sharpshooters armed with breech-loading rifles. Cavalry, especially vulnerable to the new weaponry, first lost any significant combat role and then found even its ability effectively to carry out scouting functions impaired. Navies suffered the same problems. Steamships were capable of faster, more precise maneuvers than sailing ships, which simply put them even farther beyond the reach of the still rudimentary signaling technologies that connected an admiral to his fleet. Finally, the limits of the new technology also showed up at the operational level. Railroads (or steamships) could move armies and their supplies to the front, but once there, they faced a major logistical and transport bottleneck, as speed ended at the railhead or port, and the limits of foot and animal transport reasserted themselves.

Where the transport bottleneck set in, the tactical revolution also took hold. Vastly increased firepower, the result of rifling, breech loading (that also allowed infantry to load and fire while prone), machine guns, and better artillery, all multiplied the weight of metal a formation could throw against an enemy. Against non-European armies carrying spears, swords, or muskets, this firepower was deadly and allowed tiny forces to defeat forces of tens of thousands. But when arrayed against similarly armed foes, such deadly firepower emphasized the power of the defense. One ironic result was that strategy and tactics grew increasingly discordant, as strategy under the influence of Clausewitz increasingly emphasized offensive action and decisive battles while tactical defense made decisive results more difficult and expensive to achieve.

Unlike early gunpowder weapons, whose technology proved simple enough to transfer with relative ease and so gave no area a lasting advantage, the military technologies of the industrial age were based in a far more complex and extensive set of social and economic systems and relations. These proved difficult for many societies to adopt, and the Industrial Revolution and its military advantages remained confined almost exclusively to Europe throughout the nineteenth century. The United States, a European outpost, also industrialized, but as most of Latin America shows, a European population alone was not sufficient to create an industry-compatible environment. Japan was the only non-European power to join the industrial world, and it proved its military competence in 1905 against Russia.

A vast technological and organizational disparity between the industrial and non-industrial worlds thus opened up. This disparity laid the basis for an unprecedented age of competitive imperialism that saw a handful of European states dominate world politics and build global empires, with most of that activity concentrated in the period 1870–1914 when nationalist-inspired competition became most intense. Though brief, the period saw effects of European empire building that were significant and whose legacy continues to shape international relations (and the writing of history) to this day.

Consequences: Military History

Not only were industrial society, nationalism and nation-states, and imperialism the contexts of the momentous changes taking place in nineteenth-century warfare, but they formed the world into which the study of history in its modern academic form was born. This is too large a topic to go into in detail, but the main outlines and consequences, especially for military studies, of academic history's birth deserve some mention here.

"Modern academic history" emerged from the seminar system of instruction perfected by Leopold von Ranke in Germany in the 1840s. It stressed the careful, critical assessment of primary sources using methods as objective and scientific as possible (which turned out to be much less objective than von Ranke and his many followers thought) and adhering to standards of scholarly publication that emphasized careful citation of sources in footnotes. These standards were propagated and enshrined in the flagship publications of national historical societies, led by the *Historische Zeitschrift* in Germany and the *English Historical Review* in Britain. But these publications, founded in the mid-nineteenth century and each focused on its home country, also enshrined another principle first stated by von Ranke: that the political history of "nations" was the central object of historical enquiry. As von Ranke put it, "national history" was "universal history." In other words, nationalism deeply influenced the shape of modern historical study from the start.

As a branch of modern political history, military history took on this national character. It also drew inspiration from contemporary military theory, especially that of Clausewitz, and proved especially susceptible to the popular historigraphical theory, propounded forcefully by the English historian Thomas Carlyle, that "great men" are the makers of all that is important in history. These influences combined to create a military history exemplified by the book *Fifteen Decisive Battles of the World* by Edward Creasy, published in 1851. The principles: that the progress of history (and progress is a key word here, justifying military history by tying it to a triumphalist and nationalist conception of historical advance) was shaped at crucial junctures by "decisive battles" fought between armies led by great generals.

It is only in the past twenty-five years that military history has begun to escape this conceptual straightjacket imposed by the nineteenth century. And escape it needed to, for nationally focused, battle-oriented, great generals military history in a political context is a seriously distorting lens through which to view the military history of pre-nineteenth-century Europe and the rest of the world, as most of this book has, we hope, shown. (In fact, it isn't even very accurate for nineteenth-century Europe.) Such an approach is even less satisfactory for the vast global wars and complicated regional conflicts that would engulf the twentieth century. These wars are the subject of the next part of this book.

PART 6

THE AGE OF GLOBAL CONFLICT, 1914–PRESENT

CHAPTER 26

The Great War: World War I, 1914–18

The Great War to those who took part in it, World War I was larger than any prior conflict in world history. Like the wars between France (and its allies) and Britain (and its allies) waged between 1689 and 1815, this was a conflict fought in Europe, on the oceans, and overseas; but the First World War was different in scale and intensity for several reasons. First, it included, as other conflicts had not, both air and submarine warfare, and this directly contributed to a sense of a new form of conflict, one that reflected the great and murderous potential of new technology. So also did the first use of gas, tanks, and modern flame-throwers. Individually and collectively, these weapons engaged the imagination and transformed the perception of conflict, although most of the casualties were in fact inflicted by already established weapons, particularly by artillery and rifles. Moreover, innovations in established weapons—for example, in machine guns and mortars, which became more mobile—were, at least in the short term, more significant than the development of new weapons systems.

Second, this was the first European war in which a major East Asian power played a role. Japan entered the war on the side of the Allies (Britain, France, and Russia) in 1914. It played a relatively minor role in the conflict, capturing German bases in China and the Pacific, and sending warships as far as the Mediterranean, but this display of assertiveness anticipated the aggressive expansionism shown by Japan in 1931–45. Furthermore, Japan used the war as an excuse to increase its intervention in China.

Third, this was the first European conflict in which the United States played a role, again on the side of the Allies. American entry, in 1917, was late; America was not a leading military power at that juncture, and certainly not one with experience of the type of conflict being waged; and, unlike in the Second World War, the war was over before the full potential of American force could be brought to bear. Nevertheless, prior

French Infantry in Their Trenches   Life in the trenches consisted of periods of squalid boredom punctuated by intense horror.

to formal entry into the war, the American economy had provided crucial assistance to the Allied war effort, while the dispatch of a large American expeditionary force to France was an important geopolitical shift.

Fourth, the intensity of the struggle in Europe surpassed anything seen hitherto. Casualty rates were extremely high, with nearly 9 million troops dying in the war. The French lost 1.4 million men, with another 4 million wounded, 800,000 of them severely. Moreover, casualty rates were very high. For example, 1.1 million of the 8 million soldiers mobilized by Austria died. Even nations that did not fight for the entire war, such as the United States, suffered high casualty rates, which left a record in war memorials in towns and on college campuses across the country. Indeed, the war proved a traumatic experience for many of those who survived, leading to the definition and treatment of shell shock and other psychological conditions.

Fifth, the intensity of the struggle, especially of the trench warfare on the Western Front—the front line in France and Belgium—came, for many, to symbolize the barbarity and futility of war. This contributed greatly to a major cultural rejection of war and was influential not only in the years running up to the Second World War but thereafter. Indeed, the war eventually gripped the collective Western imagination as a murderous exercise in futility. Thanks to the combination of factual and fictional accounts—for example, the film *Oh! What a Lovely War*—there is a perception that the First World War is better known than other conflicts, a perception that is only partly true.

In particular, the extent to which the war led to a decision rather than a stalemate is underplayed. Given conflict between leading industrial powers that were willing to sustain the struggle, a high rate of casualties was to be expected. In 1914–17, this led, not to victory on the Western Front, but rather to the ability of each side to survive the heavy blows aimed by their opponent. Nevertheless, elsewhere decisive outcomes were obtained with states effectively knocked out of the war—for example, Serbia (1915), Romania (1916), and Russia (1917). In 1918, the Central Powers—Bulgaria, Austria, Turkey, and Germany—were also knocked out.

This represented a major military achievement. In terms of rapidity, it did not compare with the Napoleonic Wars or the Wars of German Unification. Instead, the more appropriate comparison is with the American Civil War, which also lasted several years and involved the mobilization of resources without the ability to deliver a speedy military verdict. All comparisons risk underplaying the specific character of individual conflicts, but they also bring out the value of searching for similarities and contrasts.

BACKGROUND

War broke out in 1914 as a consequence of the interaction of instability in the Balkans with European great-power rivalries (see the Issues box "Why Did the War Happen?"). This situation was exacerbated by the cultural dimensions of power—specifically, the dominance of militarist attitudes in Germany, Austria, and Russia. These three powers were responsible for ensuring that what could have been a limited clash in the Balkans became, instead, a trial by firepower in Europe. Moreover, because they did not wish to see their alliance system collapse, France and Britain also joined in.

On June 28, 1914, Archduke Franz Ferdinand, the heir to the Austro-Hungarian Empire (Austria for short), was assassinated in Sarajevo, the capital of Austrian-ruled Bosnia. The fact that the assassins were Slav nationalists supported by the Serbian secret police was used by Austria as an opportunity to end what it saw as the Serbian threat to its control over neighboring Slav territories. Franz Conrad von Hötzendorf, the chief of the Austrian General Staff, feared that war with Serbia would lead to a widespread conflict for which Austria was not ready. Nevertheless, he pressed for intimidation, and on July 23, an ultimatum was delivered to Serbia, one that it was correctly believed her government could not accept. As a result, Austria declared war five days later.

For its part, Russia feared that the defeat of its protégé, Serbia, would leave Austria too powerful in the Balkans, thereby endangering Russia's overall ability to compete with Austria and Germany. Thus, the focus of international relations on two competing alliance systems, centered on the rival alliances of France-Russia and Germany-Austria, ensured that a breakdown in a particular area—in this case, between Austria and Serbia—would rapidly expand. Other states acted because they thought that not to do so would lead to a weakening of their relative position. Thus, concerned that Russia would be weakened, France made its support clear, which encouraged Germany to attack France. To do so by outflanking the French defenses on their common frontier, the Germans attacked via neutral Belgium on August 4. This brought Britain, which had guaranteed Belgian neutrality, into the war.

The alliance of Serbia, Russia, France, Belgium, Britain, and Japan was to be joined by Italy (1915), Romania (1916), and the United States (1917). The Central Powers, Germany and Austria, were to be joined by Turkey (1914) and Bulgaria (1915).

WORLD WAR I ON LAND

The Opening Campaigns

In 1914, the Germans sought to repeat the successes of Napoleon in 1796–1809 and Moltke the Elder in 1864–71 by mounting and winning a war of maneuver. Owing to the alliance between France and Russia,

Why Did the War Happen?

Why did the European powers go to war? Was it an inevitable part of the international system or a product of particular decisions? A tendency to focus on the former was for long an aspect of the attempt to spread the blame, but in practice, key players made decisions that led to war, and those players must be held responsible for the war.

The elites who directed German, Austrian, and Russian policy played the central role. They were worried about domestic changes, including left-wing activism, as well as international challenges. Much nineteenth-century militarism and imperialism was rooted in the concerns of their traditional military and social elites, who felt threatened by modernization and who used militarism and imperialism to defend their privileges. Such regimes, like others of the period, operated in an increasingly volatile situation in which urbanization, mass literacy, industrialization, secularization, and nationalism created an uncertain and unfamiliar world. The temptation to respond by the use of force, to impose order on the flux, or to gain order through coercion, was strong. A growing sense of instability both encouraged the use of might to resist or channel it and provided opportunities for "unsatisfied" rulers and regimes that wished to challenge the diplomatic order.

Germany was the key player in 1914, because its support was necessary for its major ally Austria when the latter turned on Serbia. In large part, militarism fed itself in Germany, particularly after the failure of liberal revolutions there in 1848. Social and political groups that retained and sought power and that responded to the challenges of modernity by endorsing a militarism backed by rapidly changing weaponry and imbued with a nationalist-racialist notion of the collective will of "the folk" were prone to address problems by seeing both them and their solutions in military

terms. This was also to become a pronounced tendency in Japan.

Moreover, the German capacity to respond to challenges was greater than that of the absolutist European regimes two centuries earlier. In part, this was due to resource criteria, particularly the expansion of population and industry; in part to organizational developments, especially communications and bureaucracy; and in part to a population made more reachable and responsive by urbanization and by education under national control. Greater resources were necessary for the war plans of the major powers, not least because they required armies substantial enough to ensure effectiveness on several fronts. This was a particular problem for Germany as a result of the alliance between France and Russia, an alliance that threatened Germany with attacks from west and east.

The perception on the part of Austrian and German leaders that they were losing out in diplomatic and imperial competitions focused their anxieties on particular fronts in particular ways. This anxiety can be seen in alliances, such as the Triple Alliance of Austria, Germany, and Italy in 1882, but these alliances appeared inadequate in the 1900s and early 1910s as anxieties grew about shifts in international geopolitics and national politics. This was particularly so for an Austrian elite worried that the breakdown of Turkish power was leading to a degree of assertiveness in the Balkans, especially by Serbia, that threatened the cohesion of the Austrian Empire. Whether that empire was itself overstretched in the face of rising nationalism is a matter of controversy. In any event, internal political disputes related to nationalism made it difficult to pursue policy initiatives and also helped create a destabilizing sense of the enemy within. Ironically, the real danger to the Austrian Empire came not from Slav nationalism

however, there was now the need for Germany to plan for a two-front conflict (Figure 26.1). The war therefore could not be like Germany's last European war, the Franco-Prussian War of 1870–71.

The strategy of first strike underlay German planning, and it was influenced by Moltke the Elder's preference in 1864–71 for enveloping opposing forces, rather than relying on frontal attack. Concerned but from a bellicose German nationalism on the part of much of its ruling elite, and this accentuated both domestic and international weaknesses.

In the case of Germany, there was concern about both the problems of its Austrian ally and the problem of having Austria as an ally. Neither power was able to restrain the other sufficiently in 1914; instead, in the First World War, the geopolitical logic of alliances drew powers into actions that were highly damaging and that ultimately destroyed the logic of the alliances. There was also German concern about the developing Russian offensive capability, a capability financed by France, in part in the form of railway construction in Russian Poland. Ironically, the Russian attack on Germany was to be easily defeated in 1914, and much of Russian Poland was conquered by the Germans in 1915. The Germans, both the military leaders and the politicians they advised, had consistently overestimated Russia's military potential. There is nothing to suggest that this was deliberate, but the misperception proved very powerful. This underlines the general importance of perceptions and self-perceptions of political elites, especially in Austria and Germany, in shaping the decisions that led to war.

There was also, however, a specific German ambition that was a clear case of wishful thinking and strategic overreach: the ambition to build a navy capable of contesting the seas with Britain. In practice, this naval program was unnecessary to the attainment of Germany's goals within Europe. Moreover, German naval ambition was likely to alienate Britain and therefore to ensure that these goals became unattainable, as indeed was to be the case in the First World War. And the German assumption that Britain's differences with France and Russia would remain insuperable was a crucial mistake. The Japanese elimination of Russia as a

naval power in 1905 also undermined Germany's calculations as it helped to magnify the German challenge in British eyes, replacing Russia, which earlier had been seen as a challenge to British imperial and strategic concerns in India and the Turkish Empire.

In the Franco-Prussian War (1870–71), Germany had won despite French naval strength. In any future struggle, if Britain remained neutral, Germany could hope to trade both with her and with the United States, thus deriving economic benefits that would make it easier to pursue its goals within Europe. Such goals became an overreach only when combined with a navalist policy.

Germany's naval ambitions rested not so much on a rational assessment of the strategic situation as on Kaiser Wilhelm II's odd combination of admiration, envy, and hatred of Britain, attitudes probably traceable to his conflicted relationship with his English mother (Wilhelm was Queen Victoria's first grandson). Wilhelm dominated German politics from the 1890s, in part by concentrating political power, particularly by destabilizing ministries with his appointments policies and his use of ministerial reshuffles. Ultimately, it was his decisions, perceptions, and miscalculations that must bear the greatest share of the responsibility for the outbreak of the war.

The role of individuals is not readily compatible with determinist and structural explanations of international relations, but it emerges if particular crises are examined closely. Structural constraints and cultural patterns certainly matter and on a broad scale explain much about the conditions that led to World War I. But it does not necessarily entail a reversion to "Great Man" views of history to see the choices and agency of individuals—great and small—operating within the structural and cultural contexts that shaped those individuals.

about the ruinous consequences if the war became a lengthy positional conflict, Count Alfred von Schlieffen, chief of the German General Staff from 1891 to 1906, left his successor, Helmuth von Moltke (Moltke the Younger), a plan for an attack on France through Belgium. Moltke, however, failed to adapt this plan to changing circumstances, including the Russian recovery from defeat at the hands of Japan in 1904–5

Figure 26.1 An Overview of World War I

and buildup of an army that was more powerful than that of Austria. Furthermore, Russia was to mobilize more rapidly in 1914 than had been anticipated.

Moltke and his colleagues in the General Staff wanted war. By emphasizing future threats, especially faster Russian mobilization once Russian railways im-

proved, and stating that victory was still within their grasp in 1914, they helped to push civilian policy makers toward conflict. Unhelpfully, no alternative scenario to that of all-out war was offered to the politicians. Schlieffen, foolishly, had excluded nonmilitary elements from General Staff thinking, ensuring that planning failed to devote due weight to the political consequences of German military measures, most obviously British entry into the war.

Moltke planned for a short and manageable war, which would have made British entry of limited military value to France; but, paradoxically, he feared that it could be a long struggle for which Germany was not prepared. In the event, the 1914 campaign showed that Germany was unable to repeat the war-making success of 1870. Despite their emphasis on surprise, speed, and overwhelming and dynamic force at the chosen point of contact, the Germans were unable to overcome a French defense that retained the capacity to redeploy troops by rail during the course of operations. Aside from serious flaws in German planning and execution, there were also problems with equipment and discipline that tarnish the usual image of German competence. More generally, the "fog of war" discerned by Clausewitz—the distorting impact of circumstances and events on plans—was much in evidence.

French success in saving Paris and halting the over-extended, exhausted, and poorly deployed Germans in the Battle of the Marne in September 1914 ensured that there would be no speedy end to the war. Having won in the west, the Germans had planned to shift forces to the east in order to overcome Russia. However, with British and Belgian forces fighting alongside the French, even as the Germans had to respond to a Russian invasion, the French benefited from being part of a powerful coalition, a marked contrast with the situation in 1870–71. This coalition, nevertheless, was not able to mount a successful offensive of its own. French and Russian opening attacks in 1914, designed to gain the initiative and to seize territory, were both heavily defeated by Germany.

The Russian invasion of East Prussia was brought to an end by a crushing defeat at Tannenberg on August 27–28 and another at the Battle of the Masurian Lakes, September 7–14. German generalship proved superior, benefiting from the flow of the campaign and from the deficiencies of Russian commanders, although the latter were less acute than is sometimes suggested. As a consequence of Russia's defeat and of the punishing failure of the French offensive in Lorraine, the Germans were able to overcome the challenge of the two-front war at the operational level. But prior to Tannenberg, German concerns about Russian capabilities had caused them to shift troops needed for the offensive in France east-

ward; in the event, they arrived too late to help there while being acutely missed in the west.

In France and Belgium, the Battle of the Marne was followed by the "Race to the Sea" as both sides unsuccessfully sought to turn their opponent's line. The failure of the combatants in the First Battle of Ypres to win on the remaining open flank in Flanders, in October–November 1914, was followed by stalemate.

The Western Front

Strategy and Tactics   The campaigning in the First World War was for long intractable, particularly on the Western Front. The concentration of large forces in a relatively small area and the defensive strength of entrenched positions, especially thanks to machine guns with their range and rapidity of fire and to quick-firing artillery, but also helped by barbed wire and concrete fortifications, ensured that, until the collapse of the German position in the last weeks of the war, the situation there was essentially deadlocked. In attacking German positions, the Allies had difficulty translating local superiority in numbers into decisive success, while casualties were heavy. Fifty-eight percent of British battlefield deaths were from artillery and mortar shells, and just below 39 percent were from machine-gun and rifle bullets.

It was possible to break through trench lines but difficult to exploit such successes. As yet, airplanes and motor vehicles had not been effectively harnessed to help the offensive. Furthermore, once troops had advanced, it was difficult to recognize, reinforce, and exploit success: Until wireless communications improved in late 1917, communications and central control were limited. As a result, attacks, such as by the Allies at Loos (1915), the Somme (1916), and Arras and Passchendaele (1917), and by the Germans at Verdun (1916), led to heavy casualties without securing any breakthrough.

Most attacks were mounted by the Allies. Why then did they attack? First, the Germans had dug in after having seized much of Belgium and part of France. To prevent the Germans from realizing territorial gains in the eventual peace, the Allies had to drive them out. Second, the Allies felt it necessary to reduce German pressure on Russia and to prevent it from being knocked out of the war, as it was to be in 1917. Third, the Allies believed that only through mounting an offensive would it be possible to gain the initiative and, conversely, deny it to the Germans, and that both gaining the initiative and mounting an offensive were prerequisites for victory. This, indeed, was to be the case in 1918. Fourth, in early 1915, it was widely believed that the stalemate of the winter reflected the exhaustion of men and supplies in the previous autumn's campaigning and that it would be possible, with fresh men and munitions, to restart a war of maneuver.

It was not generally realized that stalemate and trench warfare were the natural outcome once both sides had committed large numbers but lacked the ability to accomplish a breakthrough. Furthermore, the strength of the German defensive positions was not appreciated. German lines were carefully sited on favorable terrain while Allied lines simply followed Germans lines, which gravely hampered Allied offensives by conceding the advantage of the terrain the Germans had chosen.

Similarities between attacks at the tactical level resulted from the emphasis on trench warfare. But this does not mean that there was a similarity in operational and strategic circumstances, planning, or political contexts. For example, the poorly coordinated Allied attempts in 1915 to ensure a strategic breakthrough on the Western Front by frontal attacks were designed, by compressing the front of attack, to overcome the problems posed by trench warfare. In contrast, in 1916, there was a more coherent and ambitious grand plan for a series of concerted assaults by the Allies on all major German fronts. Designed to inflict sufficient all-round damage on the German army, especially by forcing them to use up their reserves, so as to permit follow-up Allied attacks that would achieve the long-awaited breakthrough, this strategy was derailed by the preemptive German assault on French-held Verdun in February 1916. The resulting strain on the French obliged the British to assume a greater role in the eventual Anglo-French attack on the Somme in July 1916. However, this attack was poorly prepared, both in the sense of inadequate supporting firepower and in the definition of attainable objectives.

The relative stability of the trench systems made it worthwhile to deploy heavy artillery to bombard them. The guns could be brought up and supplied before the situation changed, as it did in maneuver warfare. It was also necessary to provide artillery support in order to batter an enemy's defensive systems. Artillery was designed to inflict casualties among attacking infantry, although it may, instead, simply have fulfilled its role of increasing casualties among the defenders. Whereas on the Somme in 1916 the British guns had been spread too widely to be effective, in April 1917, the British used 2879 guns—one for every nine yards of front—for their attack near Arras. Heavy casualties sapped morale—seriously so for the French and Russians in 1917. In fact, the army of the French mutinied, in effect refusing to conduct any offensive operations, though still defending their own positions, in 1917, prompting a change in the high command. The war effort of the Russians broke down entirely. What is notable, however, is that, on the whole, morale remained high until then, and prior to late 1918, it was only in Russia that there was a military breakdown. Indeed, in both the French and Russian cases, it was not casualties per se that led to mutiny or military breakdown, but the sense among the common soldiers that their sacrifices were being made on behalf of incompetent and uncaring leadership (see the Sources box "The View from the Front"). The French successfully addressed the problem; the less flexible and resilient Russian polity could not, and broke under the strain.

Technology: Gas and Tanks   The stalemate along the trench lines led to experiments with new technologies designed to create openings that conventional technology could not. Poison gas, first released from canisters along friendly lines (which required favorable winds that proved not always forthcoming or reliable) and later fired in artillery shells, was the first major innovation. Both the French and Germans had used tear gas canisters in the opening campaign, but the Germans deployed the first poison gas, chlorine. After failed experiments on the Eastern Front, a major chlorine gas attack opened a four-mile gap in the Allied lines at the Second Battle of Ypres on April 22, 1915. But the Germans were as surprised as the Allies by the success of the gas and could not exploit the gap before it closed. The initial success, however, led to increased use of poison gas throughout the war and a search for ever-more-deadly gasses, including phosgene and mustard gas. Without the element of surprise, however, and with defensive countermeasures built around gas masks rapidly adopted on all sides, gas simply added to the misery of the front without materially affecting the outcome of the war.

The development of self-propelled, armored firepower in the form of tanks would prove a more successful path of innovation. First used in September 1916, and largely developed by the British, tanks

The View from the Front

The following passages—from a classic novel whose auther served in the trenches and from the memoirs of a German officer—paint a vivid, harrowing picture of life on the front lines.

◼ ◼ ◼

[Erich Maria Remarque, *All Quiet on the Western Front*] The front is a cage in which we must await fearfully whatever may happen. We lie under the network of arching shells and live in a suspense of uncertainty. Over us, Chance hovers. If a shot comes, we can duck, that is all; we neither know nor can determine where it will fall.

It is this Chance that makes us indifferent. A few months ago I was sitting in a dug-out playing skat; after a while I stood up and went to visit some friends in another dugout. On my return nothing more was to be seen of the first one, it had been blown to pieces by a direct hit. I went back to the second and arrived just in time to lend a hand digging it out. In the interval it had been buried.

It is just as much a matter of chance that I am still alive as that I might have been hit. In a bomb-proof dug-out I may be smashed to atoms and in the open I may survive ten hours' bombardment unscathed. No soldier outlives a thousand chances. But every soldier believes in Chance and trusts his luck.

[Ernst Junger, *Storm of Steel*] Once seen, the landscape is an unforgettable one. In this neighborhood of villages, meadows, woods, and fields there was literally not a bush or a tiniest blade of grass to be seen. Every hand's breadth of ground had been churned up again and again; trees had been uprooted, smashed, and ground to touchwood, the houses blown to bits and turned to dust; hills had been leveled and the arable land made a desert. And yet the strangest thing of all was not the horror of the landscape in itself, but the fact that these scenes, such as the world had never known before, were fashioned by men who intended them to be a decisive end to the war. Thus all the frightfulness that the mind of man could devise was brought into the field; and there, where lately had been the idyllic picture of rural peace, there was as faithful a picture of the soul of scientific war. In earlier wars, certainly, towns and villages had been burned, but what was that compared with this sea of craters dug out by machines? For even in this fantastic desert there was the sameness of the machine-made article. A shell hole strewn with bully tins, broken weapons, fragments of uniform, and dud shells, with one or two dead bodies on its edge—this was the never-changing scene that surrounded each one of all these hundreds of thousands of men. And it seemed that man, on this landscape he had himself created, became different, more mysterious and hardy and callous than in any previous battle. The spirit and the tempo of the fighting altered, and after the battle of the Somme the war had its own peculiar impress that distinguished it from all other wars. After this battle the German soldier wore the steel helmet, and in his features there were chiseled the lines of an energy stretched to the utmost pitch, lines that future generations will perhaps find as fascinating and imposing as those of many heads of classical or Renaissance times.

For I cannot too often repeat, a battle was no longer an episode that spent itself in blood and fire; it was a condition of things that dug itself in remorselessly week after week and even month after month. What was a man's life in this wilderness whose vapor was laden with the stench of thousands upon thousands of decaying bodies? Death lay in ambush for each one in every shell hole, merciless, and making one merciless in turn. Chivalry here took a final farewell. It had to yield to the heightened intensity of war, just as all fine and personal feeling has to yield when machinery gets the upper hand. The Europe of to-day appeared here for the first time on the field of battle. . . .

SOURCES: Erich Maria Remarque, *All Quiet on the Western Front* (New York: Little, Brown and Company, 1929), p. 101; Ernst Junger, *The Storm of Steel: From the Diary of a German Storm Troop Officer on the Western Front*, trans. Basil Creighton (London: Chatto & Windus, 1929).

Tank Warfare A British tank plows its way through a trench and starts toward the German lines near Saint Michel. Though capable of breaking through trench lines, these early tanks had limited range and broke down frequently.

overcame one of the major problems with offensives against trenches: the separation of firepower from advancing troops and the consequent lack of flexibility in creating and exploiting breakthroughs. By carrying guns or machine guns, tanks made it possible for advancing units to confront unsuppressed positions and counterattacks. They offered precise tactical fire to exploit the consequences of the massed operational bombardments that preceded attacks.

Tanks, however, like gas, also had serious limitations, and these are instructive because of the tendency to emphasize new weapons when explaining military developments. There were problems with tank durability, firepower, and speed, as every World War I tank model was underarmored, undergunned, and underpowered, as well as unreliable. Moreover, it was difficult for the crew to communicate with each other, let alone anyone outside the tank, and this made it that much harder to get a tank to engage a target of opportunity. The value of tanks was affected as well by the difficulty of providing sufficient numbers of them, which reflected their late arrival in wartime resource allocation and production systems. German success in antitank measures was also important. To operate most effectively, tanks need

to support, and be supported by, advancing infantry and artillery, a lesson that had to be learned repeatedly during the century in the face of pressure from enthusiasts for tanks alone.

Nor was it tanks that broke the tactical impasse on the Western Front for the Allies in 1918. Instead, well-aimed heavy, indirect fire, ably coordinated with rushes by infantry, was crucial. The British army had 440 heavy artillery batteries in November, 1918, compared to only 6 in 1914.

Other European Fronts

Where the force-space ratio was lower than on the Western Front, it was harder to ensure concentration and mass in order to mount offensives on the same scale. On the other hand, weaker defenses, especially defenses in depth, ensured that armies could achieve breakthroughs, make major gains, and achieve decisive results. This was particularly the case on the Eastern and Balkan fronts, on which, from 1915 to 1918, the Germans and Austrians captured large swathes of territory and defeated opposing forces in campaigns of maneuver.

The Eastern Front Having smashed the Russian offensive in 1914, the Germans moved on to the attack on the Eastern Front the following year. They drove the Russians from much of Poland, outfighting the indifferently led and poorly supplied Russians, achieving far greater gains than the British and French did in their attacks the same year on the Western Front. The Russian army proved inadequate to the challenge in part because its command culture remained anachronistic. Although the Russian General Staff Academy graduates were a meritocratic group, open to a scientific approach to war, they were also a small group. In general, an emphasis on lineage, connections, and character did not guarantee an informed response to the problems posed by machine guns, entrenched defenders, and the like.

In 1916, in contrast, the Germans assumed a defensive posture in the east in order to switch to the offensive on the Western Front—the Verdun attack. Combined with greater success in tackling their serious supply problems, this enabled the Russians to fight more successfully that year. Their Brusilov offensive in June 1916 against Austrian forces gained much territory before German reinforcements stiffened the Austrian resistance. General Brusilov's forces managed to combine exploratory attacks, close artillery support, and reserves positioned for exploitation of weak spots in ways that prefigured both German infiltration tactics later in the war and Soviet "Deep Battle" operations in World War II.

In 1917, German strategy entailed going on the defensive on the Western Front, indeed retreating to a straighter line, the Hindenburg Line, to free up some forces. Instead, the Germans proposed to knock out Britain (using unrestricted submarine warfare), Italy (the Caporetto offensive), and Russia. They were successful only in the last. In Russia, defeat by the Germans interacted with internal problems in sustaining the war to create a crisis in support for Tsar Nicholas II (who had assumed personal command of the army) and led to his replacement by a republican government. Instead of suppressing rioters in the capital, Saint Petersburg, troops had fraternized with the rioters. The Soviet of Workers' Deputies pressed soldiers to seize control of their units from the officers and to send representatives to the Soviet. In the face of widespread opposition, the tsar abdicated on March 15, 1917.

The new Russian government sought to continue the war in order to maintain its treaty obligations to Britain and France, and so launched another offensive in Galicia (southern Poland) on June 30, 1917.

However, the Germans maintained their pressure on Russia, capturing Riga in August, and the continuation of the unpopular war led to a growth in support for the Communists. Large-scale Communist demonstrations in July were suppressed by force, but unable to rely on military support, the government was overthrown by a Communist coup in Saint Petersburg in November 1917. The new leadership, under Vladimir Lenin, negotiated the Peace of Brest-Litovsk with Germany the following year, accepting major territorial losses. This outcome contrasts with the indecisive warfare discerned by some commentators.

The Balkan Front Although not as significant, there were also important advances on other fronts. In 1914, the Austrians had failed to conquer Serbia, but it was overrun the following year by attacking Bulgarian, German, and Austrian forces. So too was Romania in the autumn of 1916.

The wide-ranging nature of the war ensured that it involved many different narratives. States entered the war for different reasons, and it is all too easy to neglect the perspective of the minor states. The focus on the Western Front, for instance, leads to a neglect of the Balkans, which in fact saw much fighting. By initially remaining neutral, Bulgaria with its large army ensured that it would be wooed by both sides. In the end, the Bulgarians joined the Central Powers because they were willing to promise Serbian territory. Furthermore, in 1915, the Allies made little progress in the war, which encouraged Bulgaria to join the other side. As a result, Bulgaria attacked Serbia on September 28, 1915, after which the Allies declared war on Bulgaria. Bulgarian success against Serbia in 1915 was followed by the invasion of Greece in 1916, in order to prevent Anglo-French forces from advancing from the port of Salonika, and also by participation in the successful Central Powers' invasion of Romania. The war, however, resulted in savage inflation, serious shortages, and growing public discontent, which also affected military morale, and the 1918 harvest was disastrous. Calls for peace grew.

Military defeat proved the precipitant for peace. In September 1918, British and French forces advancing from Salonika drove back the Bulgarians, who accepted an armistice on September 29. Bulgaria was the first of the Central Powers to abandon the war.

The Italian Front In contrast, a stasis more comparable to that on the Western Front prevailed for much of the war on the Italian Front. In the key Isonzo sector, the Italians launched eleven offensives from 1915 to 1917, suffering heavy losses to push the Austrians back a mere six miles, although they did inflict serious casualties on their opponents. The Austrians benefited from the defensive potential of the terrain and from the failure of Italian artillery fire to suppress Austrian defenses.

Mobility was added in October 1917 by the surprise Austro-German Caporetto offensive. Italy was nearly knocked out of the war, but the arrival of British and French reinforcements helped stop their opponents in the Piave Valley. In June 1918, the Italians checked a new Austrian offensive. Later that year, the Italians advanced anew, driving back the Austrians, who surrendered on November 3.

The War Outside Europe

The Allies dominated in this highly varied sphere, although success took longer to achieve than had been hoped and than had initially seemed possible in 1914–15. Thanks to British naval dominance, British amphibious capability, and imperial support from within the British and French empires, the German colonies in Africa were overrun (although resistance in German East Africa continued until the close of the war). In addition, the Suez Canal and the Persian Gulf oil supplies were both protected from Germany's ally, Turkey, and in 1917–18, the Turks were driven from Palestine (now Israel and Palestine) and Mesopotamia (now Iraq).

The war in Africa differed greatly from that in Europe. The ability to cope with disease was critical in protecting both men and pack animals. Further, given the distances and the nature of transport links, the movement of supplies played a major role. Operationally and tactically, maneuver and surprise were crucial in Africa, while firepower was less important than in Europe.

The war with the Turks was more similar to the conflict on the Eastern Front. Mobility was a key characteristic, but firepower and the attack on prepared positions were also important. This was particularly seen in the Gallipoli campaign (see the Highlights box "The Gallipoli Campaign, 1915"), where British forces failed to break out from their landing zones in order to clear the Dardanelles and make possible an attack on Constantinople (now Istanbul). There were times when a breakthrough was possible at Gallipoli, but the failure of Allied tactics helped doom the strategy.

With far more room to maneuver, the British were successful against the Turkish forces defending Palestine in 1917–18. Effective infantry-artillery coordination was important, as was skillful planning. The nature of the terrain meant that tanks and airplanes could be used to good effect, while, unlike on the Western Front, cavalry—the precursor to tanks and planes in the tactical dynamics of warfare—played a major role in the breakthrough.

The war also represented an opportunity, but even more reflected a need, to expand imperial control in order to contain possible discontent, preempt exploitation by rivals, and tap resources. Thus, in 1915–16, the French suppressed a revolt in Tunisia as well as opposition in modern Burkina Faso in West Africa, while the British made Egypt a protectorate in 1914, and in the Persian Gulf, Qatar gained independence, under British protection, from Turkish rule. In the Sudan, British control increased with the conquest in 1916 of the territory of Darfur, whose sultan, Ali Dinar, had heeded Turkish calls for Islamic action. The British used aircraft and light lorries to provide speedy firepower and mobility. In Somaliland, the Turkish call for pan-Islamic action was thwarted because their failure to break through into Egypt and their defeat in Arabia by an Arab rising meant that the anti-British dervishes under Mullah Sayyid Muhammed did not receive the foreign assistance they wanted. Moreover, the British naval blockade became more effective, hindering the supply of arms and ammunition to the dervishes.

WORLD WAR I AT SEA

Surface Warfare

Hoping for another Trafalgar (1805), and mindful of the Japanese success at Tsushima (1905), British naval commentators assumed that the naval war would be settled with a major victory over the German navy. Instead, there was no such decisive clash between them, nor indeed elsewhere, particularly in the Adriatic Sea where the French and Italian navies confined the Austrian navy without actually defeating it. Nor was there any key encounter between the Russian navy and either the German or the Turkish navy.

Blockade and Battle   This lack of decisive naval activity resulted because the key role for superior Allied (especially British) naval power was blockading

HIGHLIGHTS

The Gallipoli Campaign, 1915

The Anglo-French attempt to force the Dardanelles and besiege Constantinople, the capital of the Turkish Empire, was the major amphibious operation of the war. It was also a total failure. Initially, the emphasis was on a naval attempt to force the Dardanelles, the key straits en route from the Aegean Sea toward Constantinople. However, on March 18, 1915, this fleet fell victim to mines, with three British and French pre-Dreadnought battleships sunk. The naval experts had been aware of the hazards posed by the mines and the supporting shore batteries, not least because, before the war, the British naval mission had provided advice to the Turks on mine laying. However, their cautions were thrust aside by Winston Churchill, the first lord of the Admiralty, who was a keen advocate of a bold naval advance on Constantinople. The Turkish ability and willingness to risk attack had been seriously underestimated.

With the element of surprise lost, the Allies followed on April 25 with a landing of troops on the Gallipoli peninsula to the west of the Dardanelles. This was designed to ensure that the shore batteries could be overrun and the mines then cleared. However, the Turks had strengthened their local defenses under German direction. Allied advances were held up as a result of a combination of poor planning and generalship, Turkish fighting skills, and the general strength of defensive firepower in this period, especially when unsuppressed by artillery fire. The fighting rapidly became static, with Lieutenant-General Sir William Birdwood reporting in May that deficiencies in the attacking force had ensured that it was pushed back onto the defensive and "practically reduced to a state of siege." Gallipoli was an example of how, repeatedly during the war, strategic conception was not matched by tactical and operational success.

John Monash, an Australian commander, reported, "We have got our battle procedure now thoroughly well organized. To a stranger it would probably look like a disturbed ant-heap with everybody running a different way, but the thing is really a triumph of organization. There are orderlies carrying messages, staff officers with orders, lines of ammunition carriers, water carriers, bomb carriers, stretcher bearers, burial parties, first-aid men, reserves, supports, signalers, telephonists, engineers, digging parties, sandbag parties, periscope hands, pioneers, quartermaster's parties, and reinforcing troops, running about all over the place, apparently in confusion, but yet everything works as smoothly as on a peace parade, although the air is thick with clamour and bullets and bursting shells, and bombs and flares."

The Allied withdrawal the following winter was one of the few successful aspects of the operation.

---

the Central Powers, cutting off their access to neutral trade, as with the United States, and to their colonial resources.

The most significant naval battle, and indeed the largest battleship clash in history, Jutland in the North Sea (May 31, 1916), arose from the only German attempt (and a half-hearted one at that) to break the blockade. The battle was mishandled by the British, as a result of the caution of their commander, Admiral Sir John Jellicoe, and their problems with fire control and the unsafe handling of gunpowder. The British lost more warships in the battle, but a number of German ships were badly damaged in the big-gun exchange, and their confidence was shaken by the resilience and size of the British fleet. Thus, despite getting the better of the fighting tactically, the German fleet retreated to port and remained there for the rest of the war, a monument to the folly of Wilhelm II's destabilizing naval policy. Jutland must therefore count as a major strategic victory for the British fleet, as it allowed the British blockade of Germany to continue.

In any event, the Germans were unable to break the British naval blockade, which cut them off from world trade. This inflicted serious economic damage and undermined civilian morale, contributing to the popular unrest that brought down the German political system in November 1918. As early as January 1915, bread rationing had begun as the blockade took effect. The blockade was not a matter simply of British ships blocking the waters to Germany, a process eased by the need for shipping to pass close to the British Isles; it was also part of the broader economic warfare waged against Germany. This entailed the buying up of supplies and shipping that might otherwise have tried to circumvent the blockade, as well as a range of economic, financial, and political practices designed to affect the situation in neutral countries. Some estimates place the number of German civilian casualties of the blockade, mostly from malnutrition and starvation, as high as 800,000, making it more deadly than the Allied strategic bombing campaign against Germany in World War II.

In the Mediterranean, the decision of Italy to abandon Germany and Austria, with whom it had agreed to a naval convention in 1913, and instead to join Britain and France in 1915, ensured that the Mediterranean was dominated by the Allies, with Austria and Turkey unable to contest the position, while the small German squadron in the Mediterranean in 1914 had taken shelter with the Turks. A French squadron at Corfu and most of the Italian fleet at Taranto confined the Austrians to the Adriatic and prevented them from breaking out into the Mediterranean. Threatened by submarines, the French and Italians withdrew their major ships from the sea, while mines were laid in the Straits of Otranto to keep the hostile submarines in their Adriatic bases.

Submarine Warfare

With his only attempt at breaking the British blockade by conventional surface combat having been defeated at Jutland months earlier, and with the effectiveness of the British blockade serving as a grim model, on July 4, 1916, the German commander at Jutland, Vice-Admiral Reinhard Scheer, suggested to Wilhelm II that Germany could win at sea only by using submarines.

Submarines were a new type of an old challenge, the commerce raider. The geopolitics were different because, in the wars of 1689–1815, commerce raiders had benefited from France's many anchorages. In contrast, the Germans had only limited access to the high seas, not only because they had a shorter coastline and fewer anchorages but also because Britain could block the English Channel and the North Sea through antisubmarine measures, especially minefields. There was no comparison to the geopolitical challenge that was to be posed in the Second World War

when, in 1940, the Germans conquered Norway and France.

Submarines, nevertheless, were a formidable weapon, in part due to the limited effectiveness of antisubmarine weaponry. Submarines were difficult to detect once they submerged, and depth charges were effective only if they exploded close to the hulls. The tactical challenge from submarines was made more serious by doctrinal problems, namely inexperience in confronting submarine attacks.

This increased the vulnerability of British trade and the danger that Britain might succumb to a form of blockade. As a result, submarines were most effective, not in destroying warships, but in sinking merchant ships. During the war, the Germans sank 11.9 million tons of Allied shipping, mostly commercial, at a cost of 199 submarines.

Submarines and American Entry into the War

In 1915, the Germans launched unrestricted submarine warfare as part of a deliberate campaign to starve Britain into submission, only to abandon it when American protests about the loss of their citizens—for example, on the sunken British liner *Lusitania*—led to fear that America would enter the war.

A continuing desire to deliver a knock-out blow, however, led on February 2, 1917, to the resumption of such warfare. This indeed helped bring the United States into the war on April 6. German military leaders thus took a calculated risk that failed, but they feared the collapse of their coalition or of the German homefront, so desperate measures were warranted. The Germans hoped that Britain would be weakened and that defeating Russia would enable them to transfer forces to the Western Front, defeating France in 1918 before the United States could make its military might felt.

Despite inexperience in antisubmarine warfare, American entry into the war made a key difference, as it was again to do in 1941. In 1917, the United States had the world's largest economy, itself a crucial support to the Allied war economies, and also the third largest navy (after Britain and Germany). From May 1917, American warships contributed to antisubmarine patrols in European waters, just as the dispatch of five American battleships to Britain in late 1917 contributed decisively to the outnumbering of German surface warships.

Defeating the Submarines
Once unrestricted submarine warfare was declared in 1917, the initial rate of Allied shipping losses was high enough to make defeat

The German Submarine U20, on the Danish Coast   This sub is claimed to have sunk the *Lusitania*, reflecting the fact that unrestricted submarine warfare offered Germany a chance at victory over Britain, but at the risk of bringing the United States into the war.

appear imminent. From February to April 1917, over 1.9 million tons of shipping were sunk with only nine German submarines destroyed. As a result, there was pessimism among British military leaders about the chances of success. However, the introduction in May 1917 of a system of escorted convoys was a key measure. Convoys cut shipping losses dramatically, reducing the targets for submarines, and led to an increase in the sinking of German submarines. The monthly tonnage of shipping lost by Britain fell from 630,000 tons in the first four months of the unrestricted submarine attacks in 1917 to less than 500,000 tons in August 1917. Only 393 of the 95,000 ships that were convoyed across the Atlantic were lost, including only 3 troop transports. The German naval defeat was clearly demonstrated by the large number of American troops safely shipped across the Atlantic.

World War I in the Air

Aerial warfare in World War I involved not only airplanes but also blimps (gas-filled airships). From January 1915, zeppelins (German airships) bombed Britain. The material damage inflicted was relatively modest, but attacks on civilians were a preparation for a new type of total war. A total of fifty zeppelin attacks on Britain (208 sorties) during the war dropped 196 tons

of bombs that killed 557 people, wounded 1358 and caused £1.5-million worth of property damage. Zeppelins, however, lacked the maneuverability of airplanes, and their flammable gas was vulnerable to incendiary bullets.

Instead, airplanes were the key military technology for bringing warfare to the skies. Reconnaissance was their most important function; in fact, planes came to replace the reconnaissance functions of cavalry. For instance, the Turkish columns advancing on the Suez Canal in 1915 were spotted by British planes. Even at the close of the war, many aircraft in service were reconnaissance and observation planes. Aerial photo-reconnaissance also developed, leading to the production of accurate maps.

Aerial combat helped deny these opportunities to opponents, and air superiority operations were therefore seen as having value for conflict on the ground, making it difficult for opponents to plan attacks. Albeit with heavy casualties, the British were particularly keen to wage the air war over German lines and thus to maintain continued pressure.

Pressures of aerial combat led to steady enhancements in the capabilities of airplanes. Increases in aircraft speed, maneuverability, and ceiling made it easier to attack other planes, and synchronizing gear enabled airplanes to fire forward without damaging their

A Pilot and His Biplane Highly visible dogfights created for fighter pilots an image of individual heroism unattainable in the trenches.

propellers. Airplane production rose swiftly with mass production techniques pushed to the fore. By 1918, Britain had 22,000 airplanes, significantly more than the Germans had been able to produce. Airpower also exemplified the growing role of scientific research in military capability: Wind tunnels were constructed for research, and strutless wings and airplanes made entirely from metal were developed. Engine power increased and size decreased, and the speed and rate of climb of airplanes rose.

Technological enhancements in aircraft capabilities showed up most dramatically in their effect on the individual air-to-air combat of air superiority operations. In addition to developments in individual dog-fighting tactics, airplanes began to fly in groups and to develop formation tactics. But ground attack also developed as part of the enhancement of airplane effectiveness. This technique was used at the Somme in 1916 and, in a more sophisticated fashion, in 1917, both at Passchendaele and in support of tanks at Cambrai. In 1918, German supply links came under regular

attack, inhibiting German operations. The British used air strikes in their advance in Palestine, and their aerial antisubmarine patrols increased German losses.

Bigger, better airplanes could also be used for more ambitious, longer-range bombing runs. In September and October 1914, the British Royal Naval Air Service conducted the first effective strategic bombing raids of the war, when planes carrying twenty-pound bombs flew from Antwerp to strike zeppelin sheds at Düsseldorf, destroying one airship. Bombing was directed against civilian as well as military targets. In 1917, as a complement to their unrestricted submarine warfare, German twin-engine Gotha bombers flew over the North Sea, attacking London. This encouraged the British to establish the Royal Air Force on April 1, 1918, in response. Its strategic bombing mission was conceived of as another technological way to surmount the deadlock of the trenches: Airpower proponents envisioned the possibility of destroying the enemy where he was vulnerable, in his soft, unprotected rear areas, including the industrial and population centers on which a total war effort depended. But, as with zeppelins, tanks, and even submarines, with planes, hopes outran realities. The actual damage inflicted by British bombing raids in 1918 was minimal, and many planes were lost. This was in large part because antiaircraft capability increased considerably, in tandem with increases in aircraft capability. This provided another instance both of the action-reaction cycle of military advances and responses and of the increasing specialization of military power.

Still, the sense of what airpower could potentially achieve expanded. In 1915, the Committee of Imperial Defence considered using long-range planes, based in Russia and armed with incendiary bombs, to destroy German wheat and rye crops. This proved not to be feasible, while the war ended before it was possible to employ the large Handley Page V/500 bombers to attack Berlin. On October 7, 1918, Douglas Haig, the commander of the British forces on the Western Front, recorded that Major-General John Salmond of the "Flying Corps, in reply to my question as to whether he was ready to support the Cavalry Corps with large numbers of low flying machines, in the event of the enemy breaking; for instance, how many machines could he concentrate about Busigny?—he replied that all were quite ready to act, and he could concentrate 300 machines practically at once!"

However, at this stage, many of the hopes of airpower were based on a misleading sense of its operational and technological possibilities, especially of

Propaganda Poster

This poster shows a caricature of two devils, one of them Kaiser Wilhelm II, looking at a monthly report of murders. The pressures of total war led all sides to demonize their enemies, complicating the making of peace after the war.

bombing. In aerial combat, the Germans did not lose as they were to do in World War II, and this, in large part, indicated the significantly more limited capability of World War I aircraft.

HOMEFRONTS: TOTAL WAR

World War I saw societies mobilize for war, with large sections of their economies placed under governmental control and regulated in a fashion characteristic of military organization. Other sections of society, not brought under formal control, can still be seen as part of the informal organization of a militarized state.

The demands of war drove this process, as did the length of the conflict. To meet the unprecedented demand for munitions, governments extended their powers, a marked shift from the liberalism of much pre-war economic regulation. Government powers became more insistent, including the control of prices and wages and the imposition of rationing. In Germany, the military was given powers of arrest, search, and censorship, as well as opening mail, forbidding the sale of particular goods, and closing businesses. Indeed, the increase in government power during the war proved permanent in most places, though not at full wartime levels.

The demands of war also changed the position of women, although not equally so. Thus, in France, women's rights did not extend as they were to do in Britain. In the latter nation, new roles, many in industry, were filled by women; for instance, the female percentage of British trade unionists rose from 7.8 in 1900 to 17 in 1918. Women received higher wages than hitherto, although their wages remained lower than men's, and in the factories, women were supervised by male foremen. Whereas only 72 army sisters had been employed in British military hospitals in 1898, 32,000 women served as military nurses in 1914–19; women even had a place in the command structure and were able to give orders to male ward orderlies. In 1918, the vote was extended to women age 30 or older, as long as they were householders, wives of householders, occupants of property worth £5 annually, or graduates of British universities.

The social impact of the war years on women was even more extensive. New opportunities were related to increased mobility and independence, including a decline in control and influence over young women by their elders, male and female. As a consequence, there was a new sexual climate: Chaperonage became less comprehensive and effective, styles of courtship became freer, and the number of illegitimate births rose.

However, the notion of a home front was also an affirmation of established gender concepts and roles, with women seen as nurturers. Established gender roles were also seen in the forces. Women who served near the front lines—for example, nurses and telephonists with the American army—found that the military hierarchy expected them to fulfill traditional gender roles and made scant allowance for their war contributions.

ENDING THE WAR

The impasse on the Western Front was broken in 1918. The American entry into the war against Germany in 1917 had greatly altered the strategic situation,

British Women Working in a Munitions Factory Though total war put a premium on mobilizing all the productive and human resources of the nations involved, the degree to which women entered the workforce varied considerably according to the strength of preexisting cultural norms.

especially logistically, with not inconsiderable effect on Allied morale in the trenches. But by 1918, the Americans had taken over only a part of the front line. Their role would have been far greater had the war continued into 1919. As a result, it was the British contribution that was crucial in 1918, not least because Russia was knocked out of the war that year by the Germans, while the French, although still very important, had been gravely weakened by earlier casualties. By "British," we mean the British Empire, and indeed Australians, Canadians, and even some Indian troops made key contributions on the Western Front.

The British blocked the last German offensive in the spring of 1918. In this offensive, the Germans used the infiltration tactics they had employed from late 1917, both in Italy and on the Western Front. These tactics were part of a shift in the offensive from attrition to surprise and speed. German storm troopers advanced in dispersed units under cover of artillery barrages and broke into Allied trenches, bypassing strong points. Their firepower was increased by their lightweight arms, including submachine guns, flamethrowers, trench mortars, hand grenades, and machine pistols.

In blocking the Germans, the effective Allied conduct of the defensive, the general limitations of the offensive in this period even with improved German

infiltration tactics, and superior Allied resources were all important. In July–November, the British, with French and American support, then launched a series of attacks in which they outfought the Germans, overrunning their major defensive system in September. The development of effective artillery-infantry coordination, as well as far more sophisticated fighting practices and more varied unit structures than in 1916, played a large part in this success, although later attention tended to focus on the novelty of massed attacks by tanks. More generally, the Germans had lost their superiority in weapons systems, while their ability to supply basic foodstuffs, clothing, and weaponry to the soldiers at the front line was breaking down, with consequences for morale that were heightened by knowledge among German troops of the abundance of American-supplied Allied rations.

In 1918, Germany and its allies were defeated in the fighting, and not stabbed in the back by domestic opposition, as German right-wingers such as Adolf Hitler later claimed. The focus is properly on the German defeat on the Western Front, but the military failure of Germany's allies in Palestine, Mesopotamia, Macedonia, and northern Italy is also instructive. It contributed to a cumulative sense of defeat on the part of the Central Powers and also indicated the general superiority of Allied war making.

On the Western Front, the Germans were out-fought, but the balance of resources was also important: The Germans ran out of reserves of troops while the Allies could call on American support. The role of resources motivated such policies as the Allied blockade of Germany and the German determination to seize resources in eastern Europe.

It is also appropriate, when considering German failure, to give due weight to a range of operational factors. These included Erich Ludendorff's poor generalship on the Western Front in 1918—specifically, his emphasis, in the German offensive early in the year, on sequential attacks on different parts of the Western Front, rather than a sustained drive in one sector. Yet, as a reminder of the difficulties of discussing policy and explaining events, the switching of the point of attack was also one of the crucial factors in Allied success after August on the Western Front. Other key factors included the success of Allied artillery tactics, which ensured that their outshooting of the Germans had a considerable impact, and the extent to which the German army suffered more seriously from the savage influenza epidemic than did its British and French opponents.

CONCLUSION

The kaiser abdicated on November 9, and on November 11 an armistice ended conflict on the Western Front. The war led to the collapse of the German, Austrian, Russian, and Turkish empires, which ensured that territory in Europe and the Middle East was redistributed to an extent and at a rate that was unprecedented. Outside the Balkans and Scandinavia, European borders had been fixed since 1871, but the situation now abruptly changed. Furthermore, the successor states established in eastern Europe—Poland, Austria, Hungary, Czechoslovakia, Yugoslavia, Finland, Latvia, Lithuania, and Estonia—were relatively weak, and this created a volatile situation that was open to exploitation by aggressive states, and fatally so by Hitler's Germany in 1938–39. It was also necessary to confront the challenge posed by the triumph of Communism in Russia.

The war gravely weakened the European economies. The United States now became the largest creditor nation, but American military weakness interacted with a lack of sureness in foreign relations. Across the world, challenges to stability were very different from those of the early 1910s, but they remained all too present. The attempt by military planners to anticipate the evolving shape of war after 1918 is the subject of the next chapter.

SUGGESTED READINGS

Beckett, Ian. *The Great War, 1914–1918*. London: Longman, 2001. Particularly valuable for coverage of social and economic dimensions.

Black, Jeremy. *The Age of Total War, 1860–1945*. Westport: Praeger, 2006. A valuable overview.

Chickering, Roger. *Imperial Germany and the Great War, 1914–1918*. Cambridge: Cambridge University Press, 2004. An up-to-date account of the German war effort.

Doughty, Robert. *Pyrrhic Victory: French Strategy and Operations in the Great War*. Cambridge: Harvard University Press, 2005. Excellent on the French war effort, not least the multifront strategy and the difficulties of achieving success.

Gordon, Andrew. *The Rules of the Game: Jutland and British Naval Command*. London: John Murray, 1996. Locates battle command style in naval culture.

Halpern, Paul G. *A Naval History of World War I*. Annapolis: Naval Institute Press, 1995. An excellent all-round account, especially valuable as it does not neglect the Mediterranean.

Herwig, Holger. *The First World War: Germany and Austria*. London: Edward Arnold, 1997. Gives Austria appropriate coverage.

Neiberg, Michael S. *Fighting the Great War: A Global History*. Cambridge: Harvard University Press, 2005. A successful general history with appropriate emphasis on France.

Neiberg, Michael S., ed. *The World War I Reader*. New York: New York University Press, 2007. An effective collection of key texts.

Sheffield, Gary. *Forgotten Victory: The First World War, Myths and Realities*. London: Headline, 2001. Incorporates revisionist perspectives.

Strachan, Hew. *The First World War: To Arms*. Oxford: Oxford University Press, 2001. A detailed account of its early stages.

CHAPTER 27

Tanks and Tasking:
Interwar Developments, 1918–37

Military planners and thinkers after World War I had to decide how to respond to the experience of World War I, the apparent capability of new weapons, and the likely challenges of the future. Each, however, was uncertain and controversial. This was particularly the case of the challenges of the future; the significance of this was that different challenges apparently led to an emphasis on contrasting conclusions from the experience of the recent war and the value of and need for new weapons.

A focus on challenges is valuable because it underlines the modern approach of considering military history by concentrating on the tasks the military faced as opposed to the capabilities they possessed. The latter approach, in contrast, leads to a focus on weaponry. Conventionally, much of the discussion of the period is in terms of the impact of the new weaponry of World War I, especially tanks and aircraft, but it is necessary to note the extent to which their use was considered by contemporaries in terms of the challenges that had to be faced. We will begin with the challenges, not least because it provides an opportunity for surveying developments around the world.

CHALLENGES

Maintaining Imperial Control

The peace settlements that followed World War I saw the European empires reach their territorial high point. A leading non-Western power, Japan, also made territorial gains, but only because it had been a part of the winning coalition. As a result, Japan gained, as mandated territories, some of the German possessions in the Pacific: the Caroline, Mariana, and Marshall Islands (which the United States therefore had to conquer in World War II), as well as the Chinese port of Tsingtao. In contrast, Britain and France made more extensive gains from both the German and the Turkish empires, while Australia, Belgium, New Zealand, and South Africa made gains from the former. These were all officially mandated territories, which meant that Japanese or European rule in these lands was answerable to the League of Nations. This was a body for international arbitration set up in order to prevent wars, a precursor to the United Nations.

The distribution of territory reflected the determination of the victorious imperial powers to retain control of the colonial world. Indeed, it was intended as a closing stage to the process of territorial allocation by the imperial powers that had been so relentless in the decades on either side of 1900.

In practice, however, it proved far harder than imagined to control the global situation, and the devastating impact of World War I accentuated the already serious problems faced by Western imperialism. A combination of already established anti-Western feeling and the spread of a new impulse of reaction against imperial authority affected large portions of the colonial world in the 1920s (Figure 27.1). This sentiment was particularly intense in the Muslim world, where opposition was widespread. It had varied causes and consequences, but included hostility to British hegemony in Iraq, Egypt, Persia (Iran), and South Yemen and to control in British Somaliland; an uprising against French rule in Syria; resistance to Italian occupation in Libya; an upsurge in action against Spanish attempts to dominate the part of Morocco allocated to it; and the Turkish refusal to accept a peace settlement that included Greek rule over the Aegean coast and European troops in Constantinople. Much of this opposition came to be framed, ironically, in terms of Western-inspired nationalist ideology.

The imperial powers made major efforts to maintain their position and were willing to use considerable force to do so. The French shelled and bombed

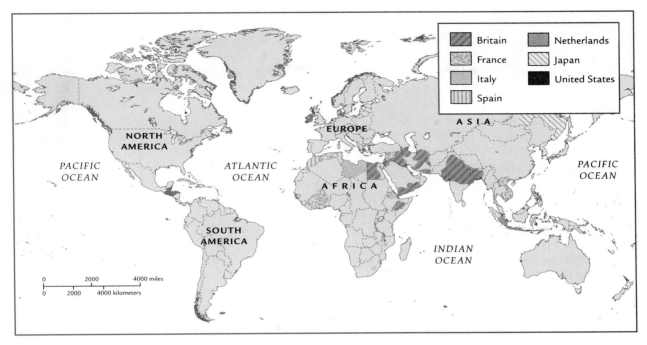

Figure 27.1 Imperial Trouble Spots in the 1920s

Damascus in 1926, while the British used the air power they had developed in World War I to strike at opponents in Afghanistan, Iraq, South Yemen, and British Somaliland. Air attack was seen as both modern and effective, and, crucially, as a force multiplier. That is, air power offered firepower and mobility without requiring the deployment of large forces.

Success, however, was mixed. In northern Morocco, the Spaniards responded to ferocious resistance in 1921–27 by using large quantities of mustard gas, dropped by air on civilians and fighters alike. Opposition to the Spaniards was brutally suppressed in 1925–27, albeit after considerable difficulties and largely due to French intervention. So also was the anti-French uprising in Syria and that against the Dutch in Java.

Nevertheless, the Turks under Kemal Ataturk were able to impose their will after defeating the Greeks in 1922 and facing down the British the same year. Indeed, Britain, the world's leading imperial power more generally, decided that its reach had exceeded its grasp. Therefore, British commitments in Iraq, Persia, Egypt, Turkey, Ireland (see the Highlights box "Nationalist Terrorism Succeeds: The British Fail in Ireland"), and Russia were abandoned or reduced.

After the mid-1920s, the extent and severity of resistance to imperial power declined. In part, this was a consequence of the use of brutal methods of reprisal. This was particularly true of the Italians, as with the harsh treatment of resistance in Libya in 1930–31. The Italians resorted to antisocietal warfare and more than 50,000 civilians were killed as the result of a ruthless suppression of the population in which wells were blocked and flocks slaughtered, both effective forms of economic warfare. Italian tactics included the dropping of gas bombs and large-scale executions. The surviving native population was disarmed and resettled in camps in which large numbers died.

Furthermore, in conquering Ethiopia, in 1935–36, the Italians employed poison gas and bacteriological weapons, as well as motorized columns. However, rather than seeing this as a triumph for modern weaponry, it is necessary to note other factors in Italian success, including the deployment of large numbers of troops—nearly 600,000 men. Furthermore, fortunately for the Italians, the Ethiopians chose to engage in battle rather than to avoid engagements and rely on guerrilla tactics. This misguided native strategy permitted the Italians to focus on their strengths rather than to face the problems arising from the

Nationalist Terrorism Succeeds: The British Fail in Ireland

The British failure in Ireland showed both the effectiveness of terrorism and the difficulties of responding to guerrillas. A nationalist uprising of about 1200 men had been firmly suppressed in 1916, but World War I had gravely undermined support for the option of autonomy within the British Empire. In 1919, the Irish Volunteers, soon to rename themselves the Irish Republican Army (IRA), began terrorist activity. They were opposed to conventional politics, which they saw as likely to lead to compromise. The British refusal to accept independence precipitated a brutal civil war in 1919–21 in which terrorism and guerrilla warfare destroyed the British ability to maintain control. In tones that were to become familiar from counterinsurgency operations elsewhere, Lieutenant-General Sir Philip Chetwode, deputy chief of the Imperial General Staff, claimed that victory was possible, but only if the army was given more power, including control of the police, and the full support of British public opinion: "The full incidence of Martial Law will demand very severe measures and to begin with many executions. In the present state of ignorance of the population in England, I doubt very much that it would not result in a protest which would not only ruin our efforts, but would be most dangerous to the army. The latter have behaved magnificently throughout, but they feel from top to bottom that they are not supported by their countrymen, and should there be a strong protest against severe action it would be extremely difficult to hold them."

Possibly Chetwode was correct, and, with a tough policy, the rebellion could have been put down, but public opinion would not have stood for it. Instead, there was a British withdrawal from much of Ireland, and a partition between a self-governing Irish Free State and a mainly Protestant Northern Ireland, which remained part of the United Kingdom. This partition was opposed by much of the IRA, the anti-treaty forces known as the Irregulars. They were unable to accept a settlement that entailed anything short of a united Ireland. The Irregulars mounted a terrorist campaign in Northern Ireland in 1921 and also fought the newly independent government in the south in 1922–23, but they were beaten in both conflicts.

logistical handicaps of campaigning in the difficult mountainous terrain.

Resistance to imperialism remained a factor within existing empires. The British faced a number of challenges including opposition in Waziristan on the northwest frontier of the British Empire of India from 1936 and the Arab uprising in Palestine in 1937–38. Yet the British were able to deploy substantial forces, thanks in part to the size of the Indian army, and to contain opposition. More generally, the severe economic depression of the decade did not lead to the breakdown of imperial rule, although it did exacerbate strains.

The informal American empire in Latin America also faced challenges. The marines sent to support American interests in Nicaragua in 1927–33 against the nationalist Augusto Sandino benefited from close air support in a struggle with rebels using guerrilla tactics, but it proved impossible to defeat them.

Fighting Civil Wars

In terms of scale, the key conflicts of the period were not those of imperial control, still less disputes between Western states, but rather civil wars.

Russia   The biggest war in the West was the Russian Civil War (1917–21). This began with efforts to overthrow the provisional government that had assumed power after the overthrow of Tsar Nicholas II in February 1917. Conservatives and Bolsheviks (Communists) both attempted coups that failed, but the Bolsheviks were successful in seizing power in November (October in the Russian calendar). Their determination to monopolize control led to a civil war in which the Whites (conservatives) were backed by Britain, France, Japan, the United States, and other powers.

Bolshevik victory owed much to divisions among their opponents and to the unpopularity of the White cause with the peasantry, which saw scant reason to welcome counterrevolution. The Bolsheviks held Moscow and Saint Petersburg and, with them, the central position and the industrial centers and communication nodes, and the White generals failed to coordinate their attacks on them.

China   Civil war was more sustained in China. Its importance was underplayed by Western commentators, but it was significant both politically, in that it undermined the attempt to create a non-Communist nationalist government, and militarily, in that civil war there indicated the limited success of regular forces in ensuring control, and, indeed, defining the nature of war. The conflict was three-part, with the Guomindang (Nationalist) forces under Jiang Jieshi (Chiang Kaishek) opposed by both warlords and the Communists (the warlords also competed with each other). Of course, in one light, Jiang Jieshi himself was a grand warlord, a view that captures the extent to which governance rested on force and served its ends. In the Northern Expedition of 1926–28, Jiang drove north from Canton, defeating warlords and capturing Nanjing, Shanghai, and Beijing; but this success depended on the cooperation of other warlords. Thus, combat was supplemented by negotiations, and indeed, defections by generals played a major role in ensuring success. The warfare in China underlined the extent to which increases in firepower did not necessarily lead to a loss of mobility. The Chinese forces employed advanced weaponry as well as large numbers of troops. This demonstrated the extent of China's military modernization, with the use of World War I–type equipment; the large-scale production of munitions, especially in Mukden in Manchuria; and the ability to move troops rapidly by rail.

China in the 1920s is a useful corrective against any assumption that the bases of politics and warfare were necessarily defined in terms of modern states. The same was true of Arabia, where, after the collapse of Turkish control and influence, tribal leaders operated rather like Chinese warlords. The most successful, Ibn Saud of Nejd, gradually extended his position, defeating the Hashemites, and gaining control of Mecca in 1924 and of Medina and Jeddah in 1925. This was a conflict of raids and loose sieges.

China also witnessed the ideological conflict that was so important to the nature of war during the twentieth century. In 1927, the Communists formed the Red Army. Initially, it suffered from a policy of trying to capture and hold towns, which only provided the Nationalists with easy targets. The Red Army was more successful in resisting attack in rural areas, where it could trade space for time and harry its slower-moving opponents, especially as the Nationalists lacked peasant support. The Nationalists, however, sought to control the peasantry, relocating them in order to deprive the Communists of local support, particularly in the form of food and information. They also sought to control the countryside through the establishment of large numbers of blockhouses.

In response, in what was the key doctrinal innovation of the period, the Communist leader Mao Zedong in 1937 published *Guerrilla Warfare*, a pamphlet in which he argued that, in response, unlimited guerrilla warfare offered a new prospect that was more effective than what was presented as more primitive guerrilla warfare. Indeed, Mao offered a prospectus for a major, not ancillary, effort for guerrilla warfare:

> In a war of revolutionary character, guerrilla operations are a necessary part. This is particularly true in a war waged for the emancipation of a people who inhabit a vast nation . . . the development of the type of guerrilla warfare characterized by the quality of mass is both necessary and natural. . . . We consider guerrilla operations as but one aspect of our total or mass war. . . . All the people of both sexes from the ages of sixteen to forty-five must be organized.

Operationally, the emphasis included words used to describe conventional warfare in the period, such as "mobility and attack . . . deliver a lightning blow, seek a lightning decision." Yet, in what truly was a prospectus for total war, general revolutionary wars were defined in terms of "the whole people of a nation, without regard to class or party, [carrying] on a guerrilla struggle that is an instrument of the national policy." Furthermore, this was seen in accordance with the historical process: "All these struggles have been carried on in the interests of the whole people or the greater part of them; all had a broad basis in the national manpower, and all have been in accord with the laws of historical development," the last a key ideological justification for Marxists. This type of "true" guerrilla war was contrasted by Mao with its use by counterrevolutionaries, which was seen as directly

The Spanish Civil War, 1936–39

The extent to which the Spanish Civil War provided an opportunity to test advanced Western weaponry and new ideas of war is a matter of some controversy. The foreign supporters of the left-wing Republican government and the right-wing Nationalist rebels certainly saw the conflict in part in this light. The Italian Fascist dictator Benito Mussolini was the principal supporter of the Nationalists, providing about 50,000 troops, as well as aircraft, while Adolf Hitler provided aircraft and other supplies. In turn, the Soviet Union helped the Republicans—support that could be very important. Thus, in November 1936, the Republicans blocked the Nationalist advance near Madrid, benefiting from the extent to which Soviet air support gave them control of the skies.

However, this attempt to internationalize the conflict underplays the extent to which foreign support was not only ancillary for both sides but also sometimes inappropriate. For example, in March 1937, an Italian advance east of Madrid became overly dependent on the few roads in the region, lost momentum and logistical support in poor weather, and finally was driven back in a successful counterattack. The terror bombing of civilian targets,

such as Madrid (1936), Guernica (1937) and Barcelona (1938), by German and Italian planes, though spectacular, did not play a significant role in the outcome of the conflict. However, it captured the imagination of many, sowing fears that the bombing of civilian targets would be decisive in a future war. The Germans found that their use of aircraft required effective ground-air liaison and developed it—tactics that were to be important in the early stages of World War II.

Rather than implementing the bold ideas of the Italians and Germans for rapid advances, the Nationalist leader Francisco Franco was more concerned to fit strategy to force structure and, in particular, to adopt a cautious approach. The Nationalist success was incremental, but in March 1939, the remaining Republican areas were overrun. The Republicans suffered from a poor military leadership that focused on outdated, static concepts of set-piece offensives, none of which were able to gain control of the tempo of operations.

Both sides found that the low density of defensive positions made it possible to break through opposing fronts relatively readily but that it was difficult to develop and sustain offensive momentum.

---

contradicting "the law of historical development." At the same time, Mao retained a major role for regular operations. As the history of the Chinese Civil War in 1948–49 (see Chapter 29) and also of the last stage of the Vietnam War, the conquest of South Vietnam in 1975, show, this was appropriate.

In the 1930s, however, civil war in China was increasingly overshadowed by foreign intervention. The Soviet Union had achieved success in 1929 when it intervened in Manchuria, but the Japanese had a more sustained impact, overrunning Manchuria in 1931–32 and launching an all-out war of conquest in China in 1937, capturing Beijing, Shanghai, and Nanjing (see Chapter 28). Their major gains, however, did not knock China out of what became World War II and in fact tended to push Chinese factions

toward a somewhat more unified front. (See the Issues box "The Spanish Civil War, 1936–39" for a discussion of another civil conflict of the era that had important implications for Europe as a whole.)

Preparing for Major Wars: Doctrine and Technology

The Japanese prided themselves not simply on what they saw as superior spirit but also on a better military, and this directs attention to the contemporary nature of doctrinal developments in this period. As already indicated, there was a degree of anachronism here, as such conflict seemed unlikely in the 1920s, especially once Russia had failed to overrun Poland in 1920, and only became probable after Adolf Hitler in

As a result, exploitation was inadequate. This was a product not only of the nature of the armies, which were poorly trained and inadequately supplied, but also of a lack of operational art, seen in particular in inadequate planning. All of this made the war attritional in character, lacking the more fast-moving maneuverist dimension of the Russian and Chinese civil wars of the 1920s. This attritional character ensured that resources, including foreign support, were crucial, but it also meant that much value accrued to the side that was better able to manage its economy, maintain morale, and retain political cohesion. On all three counts, the Nationalists under Franco were more effective.

The war was a brutal one, with the killing of those deemed an ideological threat common on both sides. The Nationalists alone executed at least 80,000 Republicans during and after the conflict.

Spanish Nationalists During the Spanish Civil War
Both sides' forces operated with limited training and logistical support; the Nationalists fit their strategy better to such constraints.

1935 launched Germany on a public and aggressive rearmament.

Nevertheless, there was considerable intellectual enquiry into the nature of war winning and much interest in the potential of tanks, in particular, and the potential of new weaponry in general, in a context of rapid changes in effectiveness. The search for a doctrine of rapid victory utilizing the operational capabilities of the new weaponry represented a desire at once to respond to the apparent possibilities of this weaponry and to avoid the devastation and prolonged struggle of World War I. Thus, interwar doctrinal thinking was characterized by a search for a limited war that could be effective, as opposed to what was presented as the ineffective total conflict of World War I. Interwar mechanization of armies led to a focus on the combination of firepower and mobility. General Sir Archibald Montgomery-Massingberd commented in 1929 on the need to develop vehicles able to withstand the rocky terrain of India: "Things advance so quickly now that things which seemed impossible a year or two ago are already practically accomplished."

Air Power   Proponents of air power argued for strategic bombing as the best way to overcome the impasse of trench warfare and to deliver an effective total war if that were required. Advocates such as Guilio Douhet and William Mitchell claimed that wars could be won through air power. In his *Il Dominio dell' Aria (The Command of the Air)* of 1921, Douhet claimed that "aeroplanes" would become the most successful offensive weapon and that there was no viable defense against them. Emphasizing the value of wrecking enemy morale and creating a demand for peace, Douhet advocated the use of gas and incendiary bombs against leading population centers. Mitchell, assistant chief of the American Air Service in 1919–25, also emphasized strategic bombing. The American Air Corps Tactical School even developed a policy of high-flying, daylight precision bombing designed to damage an opponent's industrial system. This later greatly influenced American policy in World War II.

Bombers were seen as able not merely to influence the flow of battle and campaign but also, as a strategic arm, to attack enemy industry and to sway the opponent's domestic opinion by bombing its cities. These arguments were pushed hard by those, particularly in Britain, who supported a separate service organization for air power. This emphasis led to a downplaying of close air support as a goal, a downplaying that would have detrimental effects for the British in World War II. The British played the key role in developing the concept of strategic bombing. This was based on optimism, institutional need (in the shape of the requirements of the Royal Air Force, an independent service), and the wish to have a great-power capability in European warfare without having to introduce conscription or incur the casualties of World War I. This British assessment of strategic bombing was not based on any informed analysis of what actually had been the impact of bombing in World War I, nor of subsequent developments in capability.

Ground Warfare and Doctrine   Around the world, preparedness for World War II was limited, understandably so as the shape of likely conflict was unclear, and its duration and intensity difficult to anticipate. Indeed, there was a widespread expectation that air power would bring any major war to a more rapid close than had been the case in World War I and that, in any case, the costs of the latter would deter nations and societies from risking a repetition. The move toward a major war between leading powers was hesitant on the part of many states. Under the Ten-Year Rule adopted by the British in 1919, it had been argued that there would be no "great war" involving the empire for another ten years, that therefore there was no need to prepare for one, a major restraint on expenditure demands, and that the army and air force should focus on imperial control. This rule was renewed until suspended in March 1932.

French Soldiers Inside the Maginot Line   Though formidable, the fortifications encouraged in the French a passive, reactive approach to war and made France vulnerable to German mobile warfare.

The American military similarly was not prepared for a major conflict. In 1938, the army could put only six divisions in the field while, with the exception of cruisers and aircraft carriers, the navy was smaller than it had been in 1925. In such conditions, doctrinal thinking remained sketchy and theoretical.

Interestingly, France, with its major investment in the fortifications of the Maginot Line along their common frontier, was better prepared for war with Germany. This was part of a pattern of expenditure that was exceptionally high for a major power in terms of the percentage of gross national product. Also, French tanks were technologically among the best in the world. In the event, however, the French doctrinal emphasis on defensive positions and the use of tanks in support roles led to its army being rapidly outmaneuvered in 1940.

German Tanks on Parade German tank technology did not lead the way in the 1930s, but their thinking about how to use armored forces fit well into preexisting notions of Prussian mobile warfare at the operational level.

From the low base of 100,000 troops permitted under the 1919 Versailles Peace Treaty, Hitler built up the German military, although rearmament took time, not least in creating the necessary industrial capability. In October 1934, Hitler ordered a trebling of army size to 300,000 troops, as well as the creation of an air force, which was illegal under the Versailles settlement. The German Four-Year Plan, initiated in 1936, was designed to ensure self-sufficiency and readiness to go to war in four years. Hitler also set out to strengthen the German position by negotiating agreements with Italy and Japan in 1936. His goal was to provide strategic flexibility for German aggression.

The Germans made much of their commitment to mechanization and created the first three panzer (armored) divisions in 1935. These were designed to give form to the doctrine of armored warfare that was developed in Germany beginning in the 1920s, in particular by Heinz Guderian. Initially drawing heavily on Britain's use of tanks in World War I and on subsequent British thought, the Germans developed their own distinctive ideas from the late 1920s through the late 1930s. The Germans planned to use tanks in mass in order to achieve a deep breakthrough, rather than employing them, as the French did, as a form of mobile artillery in support of infantry. The panzer divisions were designed to seize the initiative and to move swiftly as combined-arms units incorporating artillery and infantry. And the Luftwaffe, the German air force, focused on developing its close air support capabilities as part of this doctrine. Indeed, tanks and planes were to be the cutting edge of the successful German blitzkrieg, "lightning strike," operations in 1939–40.

German armor doctrine worked in part because it attached readily to an older Prussian doctrinal commitment to rapid, mobile, and aggressive operations. In practice, however, although the Germans aspired to create what they saw as a modern force, their army did not match the claims made for it by propagandists and was less of a war machine than they suggested. On the one hand, Germany's industrial and logistical bases were thin and ill organized—a result in part of the army's operational emphasis on short, decisive campaigns that would obviate the necessity for long-term logistical and economic planning. The mechanization of the infantry was limited, German logistics were overly dependent on horse transport, and the *Luftwaffe's* strategic bombing capabilities were minimal. On the other hand, the operational brilliance of German concepts was not fit into a coherent grand strategic outlook—again, partly a result of the emphasis on short, decisive and contained campaigns. Both problems would haunt Germany in World War II.

The Soviet army had also developed an innovative approach to mechanized doctrine. Soviet notions of "deep battle" shared with German doctrine an emphasis on massed tank assaults, close air support, and breakthroughs leading to encirclements. But "deep battle" envisioned a higher rate of attrition on both sides (or, put another way, was much less concerned with casualties among its own troops) and therefore, perhaps perversely to a modern democratic view, fit much more coherently into Soviet grand strategic and political perspectives. But these doctrinal developments were cruelly interrupted when Joseph Stalin, the paranoid Soviet leader, doubting their loyalty, turned on his officer corps in 1937. Marshal Mikhail Tukhachevsky, the able commander of the Red Army, who had been interested in mechanized warfare and seizing the offensive, and who had been responsible for the creation of mechanized corps in 1932, was shot, as were over half the generals. Stalin's brutal purges represented a colossal waste of talent that also stymied innovative thought, including the mechanized corps and the use of operational conflict to combine mass and maneuver. Stalin thus removed the cadre committed to operational warfare. The consequences were seen in the poor showing of the Red Army when it attacked the tiny state of Finland in 1939–40, although Soviet forces were more successful against the Japanese in border clashes at Zhanggufeng (1938) and Nomohan (1939). At the same time, the purges served as a reminder that one of the key roles of the military was as a reliable arm of the state, and this entailed issues of effectiveness different from those of combat readiness.

THE LESSONS OF INTERWAR DOCTRINAL DEVELOPMENTS

It is useful to reconsider the period from the perspective of the recent discussion of a "Revolution in Military Affairs" (see Chapter 30). In both cases, belief in the possibility of major change was a product of need. In the interwar years, the problem was tactical, operational, and strategic in military terms—the varied difficulties of winning World War I—but also, in a broader sense, social, political, and cultural, in terms of a widespread reaction, especially in Britain and France, to the unprecedented losses of that conflict, with all this entailed for military tasking. The war had ended in Allied victory, and in large part, doctrinal thinking

reflected extrapolation from the supposed lessons of this victory. This was driven further by a determination to ensure that, in any future conflict, there was no repetition of the war making of World War I and, in particular, of its longevity and casualties.

These goals led to a determination to argue that the new weaponry of World War I, if properly understood and applied, could be employed to further ensure, indeed constitute, a doctrine that was effective and decisive. However, as today, this entailed the misapplication of tactical capabilities and lessons to operational goals, and of operational lessons to strategic goals, a misapplication that readily stems from the tendency to take an overly optimistic view of technological capabilities (see the Sources box "The Spanish Civil War"). Thus, in the 1920s and 1930s, as in the 1990s and 2000s, there was much interest in the apparent potential of air power and mechanized warfare. As today, this involved evaluating what had occurred causally, always the most difficult and contentious aspect of historical analysis, and addressing the problem of reconciling theory and practice— that is, of deciding how best to integrate the supposed lessons of real and contemporary campaigning with doctrine.

Again, as today, there was also the question of which war or type of war was likely to occur. The range of present possibilities may seem extensive—the United States having to prepare to fight China, to persist in the "War on Terror," or to address issues in Latin America—but the situation was little different for the major imperial powers in the 1920s. It was unclear at the start of that decade whether it would be possible to stop Soviet expansion short of full-scale war, in part because, prior to the Battle of Warsaw, Soviet strength seemed particularly potent; and, thereafter, it was unclear whether there would be subversion as a result of pro-Soviet activity. States, in the end, did not succumb to labor activism in this fashion, but such problems had been anticipated, as in the United States, where War Plan White was designed to tackle this threat.

It was unclear how far it would be necessary to fight in order to defend imperial possessions, and the problems this tasking entailed were greatly extended by the expansion of these possessions into the Middle East as Britain and France realized gains from the Ottoman Empire. New technology seemingly could solve these problems and the specific problem of strategic overreach. Aircraft seemed a key capability advantage, providing both firepower and mobility,

SOURCES

The Spanish Civil War

The extent to which the warfare of the period did not conform to advanced ideas of modern warfare is indicated by a report about the Spanish Civil War sent in March 1937 to British Military Intelligence by J. F. C. Fuller, a retired general and a newspaper correspondent.

■ ■ ■

It is in no sense a great war, a trench war . . . had Franco a highly organised army and plenty of transport he could take Madrid. But he has not. For instance, General Queipo de Llano told me himself that when he launched his advance against Malaga he had only 28 lorries. . . . Nothing like the full manpower has been called up, in fact it cannot be, as the military organisation is not able to absorb more men . . . though the nominal front is immense . . . its garrisons are minute. . . . The front is totally unlike the fronts in the World War. Not only is it in no way continuous, but, generally speaking, hard to discover. . . . Of tanks I saw few. . . . Tank tactics are conspicuous only through their absence. Machines are generally used singly, or, if in numbers, they split up over a wide front. The result is that they are met by concentrated fire. . . . In fact, there are no tactics, no proper training or maintenance. One of Franco's officers told me that the largest number so far used in an attack was 15! I do not think we have to learn from either tanks or anti-tank weapons in this war, because the basis of tactics is training, and this is mainly a war of untrained men with a sprinkling of foreign mercenaries.

SOURCE: National Archives, War Office Papers, Vol. 106/1578, pp. 1–7.

and, albeit less dramatically, the same case could be made for mechanized vehicles. Indeed, aircraft were used extensively, not least by the British in Iraq.

The variety of tasks that the military might have had to face in the 1920s is a reminder that "transformation," in the shape of new capability, the dominant theme in accounts of revolutions in military affairs, is of limited value as an analytical concept unless it is understood in interaction with tasking. What, for example, was the use of air power expected to achieve: overawing opposition or gaining control on the ground? It is pertinent to remember that this is a two-way process: Capability can help shape tasking and, indeed, affect the assumptions referred to as *strategic culture,* as with the recent return of Western forces to Afghanistan. Nevertheless, on the whole, it is tasking that sets the terms within which capability becomes operative, not only because of procurement issues but also due to priorities for training and to the very decision to embark on conflict.

The crucial, and related, issues of procurement and prioritization indicate that, far from capability flowing automatically or semiautomatically from new developments, it is necessary to understand that, at any one time, there is a range of military options available for fresh and continuing investment. Indeed, the possibility for enhanced capabilities that stem from technological developments has made this situation more difficult, because the range of possibilities has grown at the same time that their real cost has risen. As a cause of further difficulty, at the same time, the possibility of interchangeability among weapons and indeed personnel has diminished as a product of the need for specialization in both weapons specification and training in order to obtain a cutting-edge advantage.

These problems both ensure the need for greater claims for proficiency on behalf of particular options, in order for them to justify support, and lead to a related need to rank options, whether weapons systems, organizational models, doctrines, or tactical and operational methods. This competition is one of the contexts of discussions about military change. Claims about change become a prospectus that encourages support or, looked at more harshly, a key aspect in a bidding war—and one in which the so-called military-industrial complex is to be understood not as a monolith but as a sphere of competing interests each advancing their case through bold claims. This is very much the case with the politics of procurement, and it receives insufficient attention.

Linked to this is the issue of prioritization. This involves the need to consider the range of tasks and the best way to respond to this variety. Thus, for example, in 1936–37, it might have seemed necessary in Britain to invest in tanks in order to confront the possibility of a continental war with Germany, but as far as the threat environment was concerned for Britain, there was also the prospect of naval action against Italy in the Mediterranean and against Japan in the Far East. Furthermore, there were large-scale obligations in the shape of the Arab uprising in Palestine and the Waziristan campaigns on the northwest frontier of India. Even if the colonial dimension were neglected (and for Britain, France, and Italy, this was not feasible), there were serious choices. Should France have focused on defense against Germany, or should it also have assumed Italian antipathy, which challenged the maritime routes from France to North Africa and Lebanon/Syria and required more investment in the navy? More generally, how far should any interwar revolution in military affairs have focused on offensive or defensive capabilities, and how far were weapons systems suited to one appropriate for the other?

CONCLUSION

Evaluating World War II from this perspective casts further doubt on the idea that military change is straightforward, either in terms of analysis of what is occurring or with reference to its consequences. Few countries were truly prepared for what was to happen. For example, the Germans were not really preparing for blitzkrieg and instead learned from their successful war of maneuver in Poland in 1939 what could be achieved. Furthermore, the tasks the German military were set did not arise in a predictable fashion.

Thus, an air force designed essentially for tactical purposes was called on to play a strategic role against Britain in 1940–41. Similarly, prewar navies sought carriers and submarines only as a subordinate part of fleets that emphasized battleships, with the Japanese navy providing a particularly good example. In short, force capabilities were developed for particular goals, and it was then discovered that they could be used in other contexts. We will explore these decisions in detail in the next chapter.

SUGGESTED READINGS

Beevor, Antony. *Battle for Spain: The Spanish Civil War 1936–1939.* London: Penguin Books, 2006. Unusually for work on this conflict, focuses on the military, not the political, aspects of the war.

Bond, Brian. *British Military Policy Between the Two World Wars.* Oxford: Oxford University Press, 1980. A scholarly treatment of the complexities of British military planning.

Budiansky, Stephen. *Air Power.* New York: Viking Press, 2004. A readable general survey that contains useful discussions of doctrinal developments in the interwar period.

Corum, James. *The Roots of Blitzkrieg: Hans von Seeckt and German Military Reform.* Lawrence: University of Kansas Press, 1992. Important for the origins of German effectiveness.

Danchev, Alex. *Alchemist of War: The Life of Basil Liddell Hart.* London: Weidenfeld & Nicolson, 1998. A lively biography of a key military figure.

Habeck, Mary R. *Storm of Steel: The Development of Armor Doctrine in Germany and the Soviet Union, 1919–1939.* Ithaca: Cornell University Press, 2003. Highlights the connections between German and Soviet thinkers in the early interwar period.

Mawdsley, Evan. *The Russian Civil War.* London: Allen & Unwin, 1987. An effective introduction to a complex conflict.

Simpkin, Richard. *Deep Battle: The Brain Child of Marshal Tukhachevskii.* London: Brassey's Defence, 1987. Explicates the origins of innovative Soviet thinking at the operational level.

CHAPTER 28

The Good War: World War II, 1937–45

The German, Italian, and Japanese determination to overthrow the existing order in order to push through major territorial changes that would advance, represent, and secure their self-images as imperial powers was responsible for World War II. And their failure set the scene for much of post-1945 political history.

But that failure came only after the largest war in world history, one fought at a truly global scale involving vast coalitions of forces. And it is rightly often cast as a "good war"—a war not just against imperial aggression but against fascism and the racism and genocide that accompanied it in the ideologies of the Axis powers. However, World War II was fought by a "good" Allied coalition that cut across ideological lines, sometimes uncomfortably, including as it did not just the Western democracies but Stalin's Soviet Union and both Mao's Communists and Chiang Kai-shek's authoritarian Nationalists in China. That such a diverse coalition coordinated their efforts effectively was one of the great achievements of the war; that the coalition barely survived the war and split into the competing antagonists of the post-1945 period was hardly surprising.

World War II was also arguably the first truly and fully modern war technologically. The promise of tanks, submarines, and airpower, glimpsed during World War I and developed in the interwar years, was much more fully realized—indeed, in the naval realm, airpower revolutionized combat and brought the eclipse of the battleship as the capital ship of modern navies. This is simply the most prominent example of the increasing interrelationship of land, air, and sea power, also exemplified by extensive amphibious operations; thus, an integrated analysis of these different realms of combat is warranted. Less visible but just as important was the widespread application of the internal combustion engine in the shape not of tanks but of trucks, which vastly increased the potential speed and range of troop movements and logistics. At the same time, a far higher proportion of World War II men and supplies continued to move on foot and by animal power than popular images of the war sometimes suggest.

Indeed, the war's obvious importance, its good-versus-evil story line (however oversimplified that notion may be), and its technological modernity, along with widespread documentation of the fighting in newsreels and official movie footage, continue to make World War II one of the most prevalent subjects for both academic and popular military history. World War II dominates the military history shelves of large bookstores (rivaled in the United States only by the American Civil War publishing industry) and is a staple of the History Channel. The Nazis as a paradigm of evil are so deeply embedded in the popular imagination that the shape of their helmets instantly characterized the nature of the imperial storm troopers in the Star Wars movies.

All of this makes summarizing the war in a single chapter a difficult task. We will not attempt a detailed narrative, but rather will focus on the main themes and developments of the war. As with every chapter of this book, but more obviously here, we can provide only an overview, an interpretation, and a brief roadmap to further exploration of the topic in the Suggested Readings.

MAJOR THEATERS OF OPERATION

The German War

Opening Moves The war in Europe began in September 1939. The German invasion of Poland led France and Britain to declare war on Germany, but the well-prepared Germans, aided by the Soviet Union, swiftly overran the outnumbered Poles. The unprepared

Anglo-French forces were unable to provide any assistance to Poland directly or even indirectly by attacking German forces on the French frontier.

Despite the rapid fall of Poland and Adolf Hitler's subsequent call for negotiations, Britain and France were determined to fight on in order to prevent German hegemony. Distrustful of Hitler, skeptical about Germany's ability to sustain a long war, and confident that, as in the First World War, the Allied forces in France would be able to resist attack, Neville Chamberlain, Britain's prime minister, sought to intimidate Hitler by a limited war waged through blockade. The strategy was intended to put such pressure on Germany that either Hitler would be forced to negotiate or he would be overthrown.

Instead, however, the Germans invaded Denmark and Norway in April 1940, undeterred by Anglo-French intervention in Norway. There, despite terrain that was unsuitable for their attacks and, in particular, for tanks, the Germans, thanks in part to effective air support, proved better able to seize and maintain the initiative and to overcome successive defensive positions. British failure in Norway led to Chamberlain's replacement by Winston Churchill.

In May 1940, the Germans conquered the Netherlands, Belgium, and France. The rapid German victory reflected German military strengths at the tactical and operational levels, as well as the lessons the Germans learned from the Polish campaign. But it also owed much to the serious deficiencies of French planning, particularly the use of reserves.

Blitzkrieg in France

German victories in Poland and Scandinavia had been impressive, but they had come against smaller enemy forces and been aided in Poland by the Soviets. It was the lightning victory in France that cemented the reputation of the *Wehrmacht,* the German Army, for operational brilliance and for bringing to perfection a new style of mobile warfare, dubbed *blitzkrieg,* or "lightning war," by its victims. Whether the reputation is fully deserved, just what constituted the principles of blitzkrieg, and how new blitzkrieg truly was remain heavily debated questions, but there is no denying the actual success of the German invasion of France and the Low Countries that began on May 10, 1940.

German forces were organized in three Army Groups and totaled 2.5 million men in 123 divisions, of which 10 were armored and 9 mechanized. Over 2 million Allied troops, the bulk of them French, in 103 divisions faced them. But though the Allies had

more tanks (3600 to 2500) that were better individually than the Germans', they deployed only three armored divisions, the rest of the tanks being scattered in divisional attachments. The *Luftwaffe* outnumbered the Allied air forces 3500 to 1500 in combat aircraft.

French planning lacked coherence but generally prepared to refight World War I: More than half the army sheltered behind the Maginot Line, the complex fortifications that guarded the German frontier; while most of the rest planned to move into Belgium to join the British and Belgians in meeting the expected German right-wing sweep. The hinge between these groups was the lightly defended sector of the Ardennes, a hilly and densely wooded area considered impassable to modern armies. The German plan would literally unhinge the Allies.

Army Group B in the north rapidly overran the Netherlands and northern Belgium, making effective use of paratroopers and glider troops to seize rearward communications centers and vital bridges and to help neutralize key fortifications, while Army Group C in the south watched the Maginot Line. While the Allies moved into Belgium to meet the expected attack advertised by Army Group B, Army Group A in the center, with the bulk of the armored and mechanized divisions, rolled virtually unimpeded along the east-west roads of the Ardennes, emerging around Sedan on May 12 and smashing the unprepared French center. All the initial German attacks featured aggressive use of massed armor supported by mechanized infantry and close air attacks by Stuka dive-bombers, some of which also hit Allied communications centers and terrorized the civilian populations in the Allied rear. Allied commanders reacted slowly and with stunned confusion as all their preconceptions about the campaign collapsed.

The leading German armored units reached the English Channel on May 21, cutting off the French 1st Army with the British Expeditionary Force (BEF) and the remains of the Belgian army. Only a heroic perimeter defense around Dunkirk, made possible by Hitler ordering the army to stop its assault on the defenders from May 26–28 in order to let the *Luftwaffe* finish them off—a task at which it failed miserably, as the weaknesses of the Stuka in the face of substantial fighter cover based in Britain were spectacularly exposed—allowed the evacuation of the BEF and a 100,000 French and Belgian troops between May 28 and June 4. On June 5, the Germans redeployed southward, and by June 21, they had overrun the rest of France. Hitler spent hours contemplating Napoleon's tomb in Paris, a destination the kaiser's armies never reached in four years of World War I.

It was certainly a brilliant victory, but it was not as complete as it might have been, thanks to Hitler's politically motivated "stop order" to the army, nor was it operationally or tactically unproblematic. The armored divisions tended consistently to outrun both the regular infantry divisions and their own logistical support, a problem that would recur in Russia. Though they had been effective, both the lightly armored German tanks and the Stuka bombers were already looking technologically obsolete. In terms of novelty, while tanks and air support played crucial tactical roles, the superiority of Allied tanks in numbers and quality emphasized the importance of German doctrine, which followed essentially traditional Prussian notions of mobile warfare into which the new technology was effectively integrated.

Grand Strategy and Resources   A more successful Anglo-French defense in 1940 might have led to a repeat of the situation in 1914, enabling the Western allies to make more effective use of their superior economic and financial resources and their geopolitical position—specifically, their location on the oceans and their ability to thwart access to them by the continental powers. This would have contributed to the attritional strategy the British intended to pursue and would have posed serious problems for Nazi Germany. As the First World War had shown, French defensive strength was thus a crucial adjunct to British power, and therefore an important aspect of a world in which American economic power was not yet matched by political and military primacy.

On the German side, the real failure of their conquest of France was that neither Hitler nor any of the High Command had asked beforehand what the next move of the war should be. The failure to match operational brilliance to strategic vision and planning remained the fundamental flaw in German war making throughout the war. In the event, after an awkward pause, Hitler faced essentially three potential foci for his next move: Britain, the Mediterranean theater (in support of his hapless Italian allies), or a turn eastward toward Russia. In the end, he chose, without much apparent rhyme or reason, all three at one point or another (Figure 28.1).

Britain, understood to mean the United Kingdom of Great Britain and Northern Ireland, its imperial possessions, and its Dominion allies, was not alone in the face of the now-nearby German juggernaut, as is often claimed. Rather, it was supported by the largest empire in the world and able to trade with the most powerful economy, the United States. Indeed, greater engagement with both Britain and China was also affecting American foreign policy by 1940–41. Albeit with the powerful additional challenges of air and submarine power, the Germans posed another instance of the naval threat to Britain earlier offered by Philip II of Spain and by successive French rulers (see Chapters 20, 22, 25). Britain, however, was in a stronger position than it had been in the sixteenth, seventeenth, and eighteenth centuries because of the size and resources of the British overseas system and the economic strength of the United States. For example, the British were able to obtain strategic metals, such as tungsten (from Canada and the United States) and manganese (from Africa) to strengthen steel. This was of great value for munitions, especially, in the case of tungsten, for armor, armor-piercing shells and high-speed cutting tools. The Germans did not have this access to transoceanic sources of supplies.

Furthermore, in 1940 and early 1941, when they were allies, Soviet cooperation in providing resources was important in enabling the Nazi economy to draw on raw materials. Conversely, in late 1941, after the German invasion of Russia, Soviet resources were indicated by their continued ability to sustain further fighting and produce fresh forces, despite major losses of territory, manpower, and productive capacity. This ability became even more apparent in 1942–43.

German military and political ambitions expanded rapidly in the early stages of the war. There was interest in acquiring naval bases in the Atlantic, from which it would be possible to threaten British convoy routes, increase German influence in South America, and challenge American power. This was an aspect of the goal of the German Naval Staff that Germany become a power with a global reach provided by a strong surface navy.

The Second World War was ultimately to see successful deployment of American and Soviet resources in order to secure the crushing of Germany and Japan in 1944–45. The extent of these resources was already apparent earlier in the war, and indeed prior to the entry of either power into the conflict. Thus, in 1940–41, the ability of Britain to continue trading with the United States was important to its survival, although, per capita, Britain derived much more support during the war from the Canadians.

Figure 28.1 The High Tide of Axis Expansion in Europe and North Africa, in late summer 1942

Ideology   Resources were important, but the tangled web of diplomacy in the early years of the war indicates the degree to which ideological factors played an important role in developing the narrative of conflict. In place of a common tendency to emphasize the struggle between fascism and communism, and thus between Hitler's Germany and Stalin's Soviet Union, as crucial in the war, it is pertinent to note that opposition to Britain and to liberal values was a key to the policies of both Hitler and the Soviet dictator, Josef Stalin. Indeed, the latter's positive response to Hitler in 1939–41 powerfully reflected his animosity toward Britain. In each case, there was hostility to Britain's political position but also a rejection of its liberalism. This was a product not only of a

rejection of liberal capitalism as a domestic agenda for liberty and freedom but also of hostility to liberalism as an international agenda focused on opposition to dictatorial expansionism and on support for the independence of small states. This was seen when Britain entered both world wars in support of such states—for example, Belgium in 1914 and Poland in 1939. Both Hitler and Stalin were reacting against Enlightenment, liberal, and capitalist values.

The Eastern Front   Operation Barbarossa, the German invasion of the Soviet Union, launched in June 1941, was in part designed to put pressure on Britain by making Germany appear more powerful: Worried about the United States, Hitler was anxious

Slave Laborers in Buchenwald Concentration Camp near Jena, April 16, 1945 This photo gives graphic evidence of the extent of Hitler's racial war; after all, these were some "lucky" survivors.

about his narrowing options. Thus, Hitler repeated Napoleon's attempt to get at Britain in 1812 by invading Russia in order to strengthen the Continental System, which was designed to block trade between Britain and continental Europe. However, this comparison does not capture Hitler's concerns that he had not much time left to fulfill his goals nor the extent to which, during their alliance, the resources of the Soviet Union contributed to the German war economy.

Napoleon, moreover, lacked the German concept and practice of race war, which was to play a central role in Hitler's quest for power in eastern Europe, including categorizing elements of the conquered population in preparation for the brutal treatment or slaughter of whole groups. To Hitler, war with the Slavs was a racial war in which the Germans would earn their right to survive and triumph, creating a Europe that they would dominate. What might be termed a racialized aspect of the quest for power was not new. Indeed, the concept of martial races, employed by Western powers when developing client military forces in the Third World, was based in part on constructed ethnographical identities. But Hitler carried it to an extreme that shaped German grand strategy in significant ways.

Many German commentators do not appreciate the extent to which, from the outset, and not only on the Eastern Front, the *Wehrmacht* was involved in atrocities (see the Issues box "The German Military and Race War"). Indeed, the army's military violence against unarmed civilians was not a matter of rogue commanders acting on their own initiative but instead was integral to its conduct during the war. The widespread German failure to appreciate this is a reflection of the sanitizing of the *Wehrmacht*'s reputation during the Cold War.

As a reminder of the contingencies stemming from the unpredictable nature of developments, Stalin had a nervous collapse of will on June 28–30, 1941, when the German advance, initially wildly successful especially at the tactical and operational levels, reached Minsk, the capital of Belarus. There was possibly consideration of a settlement with Germany, similar to that reached by Lenin in 1918, which might have been used to justify such an agreement. Again under the pressure of German advances, there was also a panic in Moscow in mid-October that owed much to official actions, including the evacuation of industrial infrastructure. Managers and other fleeing officials were attacked by the workers they were abandoning in

The German Military and Race War

The German advance into the Soviet Union in 1941, launched on June 22, brought far more people judged unsuitable by Hitler, both Jews and Slavs, under his control, providing a problem and opportunities for the implementation of Nazi plans. The war against the Soviet Union was conceived as genocidal, and the *Wehrmacht,* in conjunction with the Ministry of the Eastern Territories, planned for 30 million Soviet deaths. At the same time that plans were entertained for detaining and deporting Jews to Siberia, which the Germans did not intend to occupy, four *Einsatzgruppen* (SS Action Groups), advancing close behind the troops from the opening day of the invasion, killed Jews, political commissars, and others deemed "undesirable." Police battalions also played a prominent role in the killing, as they did in mass shootings in Polish Galica.

In general, the killing was with the cooperation of the army, which in Ukraine was willing to complain about harsh German treatment of Ukrainians but also to support the slaughter of the Jews and to see them (erroneously) as the key source of resistance. The harsh content and tone of orders for the day by many army commanders to their units scarcely encouraged a reasonable treatment of Jews, Communists, and prisoners. Instead, many called on their troops to annihilate Hitler's targets. SS military units were particularly murderous, but the *Wehrmacht* were also killers, as seen in both the Soviet Union and Serbia, where the Jews were killed in mass shootings in late 1941 and early 1942. They were the prime group shot in response to Serbian partisan activity, with the army officers accepting the identification of Communists and Jews and willingly having the latter shot because they could not catch the former or other partisans.

Violence by the German military against civilians looked back to a recent tradition of such action by German forces both in Europe and overseas. Shootings of civilians in the Franco-Prussian War (1870–71) (see Chapter 23) were followed by German atrocities in Belgium and France in 1914, which in part appear to have reflected fury that

Belgium unexpectedly resisted the German advance. German losses at the hands of Belgian regular units led to reprisals against civilians, as well as the killing of military prisoners. A high degree of drunkenness, confusion, and friendly fire among German units contributed directly to their belief that they were under civilian attack, which encouraged their attitude that it was acceptable, and indeed sensible, to inflict reprisals on the innocent.

While indicative, these actions were very different from the overlap between operational and genocidal warfare seen in the Second World War. Earlier violence against civilians in 1870–71 and 1914 was not the German goal, but rather was a response to an uncertainty and fear that they could not accept psychologically. The use by regulars of violence against civilians suspected of opposition was deadly when it was seen as necessary and became an automatic response, but prior to 1941, this was very much a secondary aspect of German conduct.

A far more pertinent background was that of German campaigning in Africa, particularly in the early 1900s when antisocietal practices with genocidal consequences, such as driving people into a waterless desert, were followed. The Herero prisoners sent to prison and labor camps were treated with great cruelty, such that large numbers died. In responding to the Herero rebellion in German Southwest Africa (now Namibia) in 1904–5, the Nama rebellions there in 1890 and 1905–9, and the Maji-Maji rebellion in German East Africa (now Tanzania) in 1905, the German army had become used to seeing entire ethnic groups as race-enemies and had developed the practice of racial conflict.

In part, these assumptions and practices were transferred to Europe in the twentieth century, first with massacres in Belgium during World War I, and far more clearly, consistently, and violently in eastern Europe during World War II. A key prelude to German policy there was possibly set during German campaigning on the Eastern Front in the First World War. A disparaging sense of the Russian people they overran as weak, dirty, and diseased became commonplace, in part in response not only to those who were conquered but also to the vast areas that now had to be psychologically understood and overcome. This history has been seen as important to the development of a hostile and violent response to conquered peoples as a central aspect of German war policies, although it is possible that, in part, this represents a retrospective perspective owing something to knowledge of what was to happen in the Second World War. Indeed, a less critical view of the German army in the First World War has been advanced.

In World War II, racial violence was displayed by the Germans in Poland in 1939, while the massacres of about 3000 French-African soldiers in 1940 showed that the German military was also willing to embrace the Nazi notion of racialized warfare and its murderous applications in western Europe. Both the regular army and the SS were responsible for massacres of African soldiers in France. These massacres were not a response to official policy but, instead, were a sporadic product of racial violence from below, albeit a violence that reflected Nazi ideology and also propaganda from the 1910s on against the French use of African soldiers.

On the Eastern Front from 1941, the institutionalized ruthlessness of the army was accentuated by Nazi ideology. Many members of the army appear to have accepted the identification and conflation of Jews with communism, a conflation interpreted to mean that the slaughter of the first would ensure the weakening of the second, thus stabilizing German conquests. German generals also personally benefited, as Hitler felt it necessary to bribe them and used seized Jewish property as a means to do so. This was an aspect of the close relationship between Hitler and the military elite, one the latter played down after the war. The navy also provided eager support for the regime, while the major role of the SS in creating military units—the Waffen-SS—indicated the eventually close relationship between ideology and the German war effort. Over 800,000 men served in the Waffen-SS, and it became an important part of Germany's fighting forces, serving under the operational command of the army, although it was a separate structure.

Field Marshal Walter von Reichenau issued an order urging soldiers to support the systematic killing of Jews as "a hard but just punishment for the Jewish sub-humans," an instruction at total variance with international law. His superior officer, Field Marshal Karl von Rundstedt, the commander of Army Group South, signed a directive to his other subordinate commanders suggesting they issue comparable instructions. In the postwar war crimes trials at Nuremberg, Rundstedt denied any knowledge of the episode, and it is typical of conventional military history that his role is not mentioned in standard guides. For example, the entry in Trevor Dupuy's *Encyclopedia of Military Biography* refers to Rundstedt as "an example of the best of the old Prussian officer corps." In 1941, the complicity of German commanders in atrocities was true both of Nazi sympathizers, such as Reichenau, and of others, such as Field Marshal Wilhelm von Leeb, the commander of Army Group North until January 1942. Erich Hoepner, the commander of Fourth Panzer Group, referred in May 1941 to the forthcoming war as the "warding off of Jewish Bolshevism." There was not only a lack of interest in the fate of civilians and prisoners of war but a wish to see them removed so as to make military operations easier.

In some circumstances, German generals were willing to defy orders. When, in December 1941, Hitler ordered Rundstedt, at the furthest point of his advance, to stand fast at Rostov rather than to retreat to a better defensive position, he resigned. More generally, in the face of the Soviet winter counteroffensive, commanders who responded to Hitler's "stand or die" order by advocating withdrawal were ignored and even dismissed. In total, thirty-five generals were removed, including Guderian and Hoepner, However, Hitler did not face comparable opposition over his treatment of the Jews. This indeed casts a harsh light on postwar justification of the actions of German generals. The brutal use of forced labor was one aspect of the way in which German companies were also complicit in this race war.

scenes described by the head of the Moscow NKVD (secret police) as "anarchy." Stalin, however, decided not to flee, and the NKVD was used to restore order, just as it accompanied the winter Soviet counteroffensive, meting out punishment and terror.

Nevertheless, despite serious Soviet deficiencies in command, training, weaponry, and operational strategy—the latter including a dangerous reliance on forward defense that facilitated the massive encirclements spearheaded by panzer units that characterized German operational practice—the German attack suffered from a major failure of planning and preparation. Overconfident of the prospects for a swift offensive, and completely failing to appreciate Soviet strength (they underestimated the number of Soviet divisions by more than half), the Germans also suffered from a lack of consistency. Goals shifted over the emphasis on seizing territory versus defeating Soviet forces and also over the question of which axes of advance to concentrate on. This led to a delay in the central thrust toward Moscow in September 1941, with forces instead sent south to overrun Ukraine and its resources and to destroy the Soviet forces there. The delay hindered the Germans when they resumed the attack as the autumn rains turned roads into impassable quagmires. Winter then froze the roads, restoring mobility, but the Soviets proved better than the Germans at operating in the bitter cold, for which German troops and equipment were utterly unprepared, as were German production and logistics when they attempted to respond to the crisis.

Although the Soviet government was evacuated to Kuibyshev on the River Volga, there was no military or political collapse comparable to that in France in 1940, and the Red Army was able to hold the assault on Moscow, their communication and command center, and to mount a counterattack from December 5–6, 1941. The Germans lacked operational reserves to cope with counterattacks and so found it difficult to stabilize the front.

Having failed to translate conquest and killing into victory in 1941, the Germans returned to the task in 1942, although they now lacked the resources and organization to attack along the entire Russian front, as they had done in 1941, or to open the attack as early as they had a year before. Indeed, the 1941 attack had come later than initially planned, and German offensives started later and were more limited in each year of the war. Moreover, the 1942 campaign revealed not only Soviet resilience but also serious German deficiencies in strategy and operational art. From the outset, Operation "Blue," the German 1942 campaign, was jeopardized by a poorly conceived and executed plan. The Germans sought the seizure of the Caucasian oil fields in order to better prepare for the lengthy struggle that American entry into the war appeared to make inevitable: Most of the world's oil supplies were under Allied control (the United States, Iran, Iraq) or closed to the Axis by Allied maritime strength (Saudi Arabia, Venezuela). Hitler, however, underestimated Soviet strength and also failed to make sufficient logistical preparations. Furthermore, there were major flaws in the development of the operation—specifically, in the decision to attack simultaneously toward the Volga and the Caucasus—while Hitler's conviction that the city of Stalingrad on the Volga had to be captured foolishly substituted a political goal for necessary operational flexibility. German strategy was therefore both misguided and poorly implemented. Despite a massive commitment of resources, the Germans were fought to a standstill at Stalingrad, which had been turned by their air and artillery attacks and by a determined Soviet defense into an intractable urban wasteland.

Furthermore, the lack of German preparedness that had made improvisations necessary in 1941 had not been overcome. The German army was divided between elite mechanized units, capable of acting as mobile striking forces, and the bulk of the army—infantry that relied heavily on horses for moving supplies. The problems of distance and weather posed by operating in the Soviet Union accentuated and exposed the difficulties arising from this contrast.

In addition, German war making was affected by an improvement in Soviet fighting quality that was clearly demonstrated by the differences in Soviet offensives. The large-scale Soviet counteroffensive in the winter of 1941–42 had eventually run out of steam. But the one in the winter of 1942–43, mounted by divisions formed the previous winter, was more focused as well as better prepared and managed. The development of Soviet offensive doctrine, which had been interrupted by Stalin's prewar purges of army leadership, had resumed with Soviet difficulties in their Winter War with Finland in 1940 and now picked up in pace. In contrast to German blitzkrieg operations with their emphasis on armor-led breakthroughs and vast encirclements, the Soviet aimed at greater coordination between armor, artillery, infantry, and close air support, with attacks by successive echelons along broad fronts. Designed to chew vast holes in the German lines and exploit breakthroughs where they happened, rather than planning precise breakthrough points, Soviet doctrine was implemented with increasing skill and success as the war progressed and proved much better able to cope with defenses in depth than German doctrine had. It was a style that could be costly, especially in terms of infantry lives, but that was a cost that the Russian regime could afford to bear. It also serves as a reminder that no doctrine can be evaluated in the abstract, but it must meet the needs and resources of the society it serves.

The interplay of production, doctrine, and leadership attuned to immediate lessons can be seen in Operation Uranus—the encirclement of the German Sixth Army in and near Stalingrad—in November 1942. The Soviets benefited greatly in this operation from their buildup of forces, especially tanks, made possible by the recovery and development of their munitions industry. But their advantages were magnified by the success of their planning and preparations, which contrasted with the poor quality of German command decisions. These latter included allocating weak, less motivated, and less well-armed Romanian forces to peripheral sectors that became, as a result of Soviet attacks, key flank positions for the German forces in Stalingrad that provided an inflexible response to the Soviet breakthrough. Hitler forbade a retreat from the city by the Sixth Army, leaving it to be encircled; it was then forced to surrender in early 1943. By midyear, with the complete defeat of the German summer offensive at Kursk, the Soviet army began rolling inexorably toward Berlin.

The German leadership thus made fundamental errors in understanding the nature of the war and their enemies. In addition, by 1944, the Soviet army certainly had acquired a superiority of technique over the Germans that produced a series of massive, overwhelming victories that destroyed nearly 100 German divisions. Had the Germans won over the population of the Soviet areas they occupied and had an effective anti-Communist cement for their system, this might have affected American policy as well as developments on the ground. However, the nature of German policy and rule made this outcome impossible. And given the thoroughness, skill, and brutality of the Soviet advance in eastern Europe in 1944–45, the period of the greatest German numerical losses, and the resources enjoyed by the Allies in the Second World War, it would probably not have mattered had the Germans enjoyed more support in the areas they occupied.

The Mediterranean The Mediterranean theater showcased on a small scale many of the themes of the larger war in Europe. Blunders and incompetence on the part of Mussolini and the Italians in invasions of Egypt from Libya and Greece from Albania virtually forced Hitler to send German reinforcements to both areas in late 1940. Masterful German tactics and operations led to victories: Greece was overrun and Crete taken in a dramatic (and costly) paratrooper operation. These at least denied Greek airfields to the RAF. But for all the brilliance of Erwin Rommel's campaigns in North Africa, which showcased German abilities in mobile warfare, they served little strategic purpose, diverted two valuable panzer corps from Russia, and were ultimately doomed in the face of superior Allied resources and control of the seas and skies. It was also in North Africa that the Allied ability to decode German communications first paid major dividends, both in anticipating Rommel's moves and in targeting vital supply ships. Allied code breaking remained a consistent and important advantage throughout the war. North Africa arguably provided American forces with a relatively restricted target against which to tune up for harder fighting in Europe itself.

America in Europe By the end of 1942, American entry into the war was making an impact directly as American forces advanced east in French North Africa after landing on November 8 at Casablanca, Oran, and Algiers, in Operation Torch. Already American industrial might had made a major difference in the Battle of the Atlantic against German submarines (see below). Responsible for 31.4 percent of world manufacturing in 1938 (compared to 12.7 for Germany, 10.7 for Britain, and 9.0 for the Soviet Union), the United States, helped by its sophisticated economic infrastructure, successfully adapted its economy for war production. Now, American forces first helped the British drive Rommel's Italian-German army from Africa, then launched amphibious invasions of Sicily and Italy, learning strategies that would be applied in Normandy in 1944.

The speed of Allied success in 1944 is striking. Having landed in Normandy on June 6, the Allies forced the surrender of the German commander in Paris on August 25, and on September 3, Brussels was captured. It had proved difficult to make progress against German prepared positions in Normandy, and the Allied effort was not perfectly run, but the Germans eventually were defeated and forced to flee. Similarly, having landed in southern France on August 15,

The Liberation of France   Crowds of French patriots line the Champs Elysees to view Allied tanks and half-tracks passing through the Arc du Triomphe, after Paris was liberated on August 25, 1944.

the Allies liberated Marseille on August 28. Allied success in different types of conflict was also significant. For example, the massed use of tanks in mobile warfare by the Germans in France in 1940 and by the Germans and British in North Africa in 1941–43 provided scant guidance to their subsequent less successful use in the mountainous terrain of Italy, which Anglo-American forces conquered in 1943–45, and in the *bocage* country of Normandy, with its deep hedgerows, perfect for antitank guns.

Still, total defeat of the Nazi regime proved necessary. After the unsuccessful assassination plot of July 1944, the bulk of the German military command rallied to Hitler, while Nazification was pushed by Guderian, the new chief of the General Staff. The repression of disaffection and any sign of defeatism by the Nazi surveillance system presided over by Heinrich Himmler helped ensure that there was no repetition of the German collapse of 1918: Allied forces were not on German soil at the Armistice then. Instead, it was a very different German regime and society that waged the Second World War until Hitler committed suicide on April 30, 1945, to avoid capture by the Soviet forces overrunning Berlin. The remaining German forces in the city surrendered on May 2.

The Land War in Asia

Japan and China   World War II opened on land with the Japanese army's occupation of Manchuria in 1931, initiating a new round of Sino-Japanese hostilities that dated back to the Sino-Chinese War of 1894–95. Though neither side officially declared war, sporadic fighting continued but failed to escalate into all-out warfare prior to 1937 only because the Chinese Nationalist leader Chiang Kai-shek preferred to focus his efforts on attempting to eliminate the Communists as rivals for power in China, while Japan did not yet judge it expedient to mount a full-scale attack. This changed in 1937 when the Japanese captured Beijing, Shanghai, and Nanjing.

Forces and Grand Strategies   Divisions not just between the Nationalists and Communists but within nominally Nationalist forces split along provincial and regional lines would hamstring Chinese grand strategy for most of the war, exacerbating Chinese tactical and operational inferiority grounded in a massive disparity in firepower and mechanization compared to Japanese forces. Contemporary American estimates put the effective firepower of Chinese units at about a twelfth of Japanese units. Serious command problems were intensified by Chiang's distrust of any successful general as a potential rival. China had no navy to speak of and an insignificant and outmoded air force. The advantages China enjoyed came down to manpower and motivation. China could mobilize about 2 million men at the start of the war, badly equipped and trained though they might have been. And this manpower was fighting on home turf for its homeland, inspired by increasingly sophisticated nationalist sentiment as the war progressed.

In contrast, Japan deployed a modern combined-arms force of about 300,000, along with 150,000 Manchurian and Mongol troops under Japanese officers, with another 2 million reservists in Japan. Japan also had thousands of tanks and modern aircraft, and the third-largest navy in the world. Japan aimed to knock China out quickly with mobile combined-arms strikes at the political centers of Nationalist government, counting on regionalism and the decrepit state of Chinese government to do much of its work for it. However, Japan seriously underestimated the popular will of the Chinese people even under bad leadership. Japan also aimed to occupy the richest industrial and resource-producing parts of China in the north and along the coast as part of its overall drive, from 1941, to bring East Asia as a whole under its rule. As the war broadened and Chinese forces held on, Japan also sought to isolate China from its allies by seizing French Indochina and Burma. For a time in 1942–44, only a tenuous air supply route from British-ruled India over the Himalayas—dubbed "The Hump" by American pilots—connected China to American and British supplies and aid.

Faced with the material disadvantages outlined above, never really overcome during the course of the war, and suffering massive defeats in large-scale fighting in the opening year of the war, the Chinese grand strategy by 1938 had become survival in a war of attrition, conducted with a minimum of conventional battles where superior Japanese firepower could be brought to bear. The Communist forces in the north took this one step further by conducting active guerrilla campaigns behind Japanese lines. This "protracted war" strategy looked more viable with the expansion of the war in the Pacific, as the focus of Japanese effort shifted elsewhere after 1941. Japanese control of most of the Chinese rail net, in addition to their edge in firepower, meant that their forces retained the operational and tactical initiative until the end of the war. But Japan went on a major offensive only in 1944, successfully assaulting American air bases in Chinese territory, from which bombing raids were reaching Japan.

Jungle Warfare   After 1939, Japanese efforts focused on securing the resource-rich areas of Southeast Asia and the Pacific Islands and on cutting China off from its allies. With troops specially trained and equipped for jungle warfare, Japanese campaigns rolled up British opposition in Malaya in 1941 and British, Chinese, and a few American forces in Burma in 1942. The Japanese made skillful use in these campaigns of preliminary air strikes, amphibious landings, infiltration tactics, and tanks equipped for river crossings. They timed operations so that the gains from successful dry-season offensives could be consolidated during the monsoon season. In some ways, the Japanese army showed at its best in Southeast Asia, though again the quality of opposition early in the war was not of the highest caliber. In 1944, British forces checked renewed Japanese offensives at the Indian border, and in 1945, they reconquered Burma, a more complete defeat of a large Japanese force than anything seen in the Pacific.

The War in the Pacific

Grand Strategy   The expansion of the war into Southeast Asia and the Pacific by Japan in part represented an attempt to take advantage of the opportunities provided by French and Dutch defeat at the hands of Germany in 1940, as well as the extreme pressure Britain was under. But there was also a concern about the apparently intractable nature of the Japanese commitment to defeating China and the need for resources that conflict raised. Alongside this tension, however, there were differing views in Japan on the desirability or need for conflict with individual powers, including the Soviet Union and the United States, as well as disputes over the institutional priorities and interests of particular army and navy lobbies, including the powerful army in Manchuria. This all amounted to a range of possible tasks, and thus a lack of clarity in the goals set for Japan's military-industrial complex. For Japan, there was also the more profound uncertainty, seen repeatedly with major powers, as to whether to act in order to retain and secure great-power status or whether such action might actually jeopardize it. This uncertainty looked back to a self-perception developed from the 1880s that emphasized Japan's weaknesses relative to the United States, and also to China and the Soviet Union, in terms of land and resources. The jeopardizing of Japanese power was the likely result predicted in the summer of 1941 by the *Soryokusen kenkujo* (Institute of Total War Studies) that had been instructed to investigate the matter. In the event, war with the United States ensured this outcome.

Opening Moves   By the end of May 1942, the Japanese had overrun Hong Kong, Guam, the Philippines, the Dutch East Indies, Malaya, Singapore, British Borneo, and Burma, lands whose combined population was far greater than that conquered by Nazi Germany. The Japanese also captured Attu and Kiska in the western Aleutian Islands. Despite having much of their military tied up in China, Japanese forces benefited from the weakness and poor preparation of their enemies, from air superiority, from the operational flexibility of their plans, and from the combat quality and determination of their units. This was particularly evident in Malaya, where the Japanese were outnumbered by the British. There were also serious Allied command and operational lapses, as with the loss of most of the American planes in the Philippines on the ground to Japanese attack on December 8, 1941 (one day after Pearl Harbor), and the British failure to provide adequate land-based air cover to their leading warships in the region, the *Prince of Wales* and the *Repulse,* off Malaya two days later: Both were sunk by Japanese planes. Land-based air support was necessary: Had the warships been escorted by a carrier, there is a good chance that the carrier would have been sunk as well. Furthermore, the British conduct of operations on the ground in Malaya and Singapore was badly flawed.

Initial Japanese successes left the Allies with an unprecedented amount of territory to regain. The situation was very different from that in Europe. Drawing equivalence is compromised by different force-space ratios, let alone the role of sea as opposed to land, but the distance between Stalingrad and Berlin did not match that between, say, Guadalcanal and Tokyo. The problems facing the Americans in the Pacific were compounded by a number of factors that included inexperience: Rehearsal in 1942 for the landing on the island of Guadalcanal revealed serious difficulties with traversing the coral and coordinating naval gunfire support. Nevertheless, the Japanese failure earlier to knock China out of the war indicated that their ability to plan and execute major advances and to inflict major defeats (equivalent to German blitzkrieg offensives)

did not necessarily lead to victory, especially when operational excellence failed to match strategic goals or geopolitical realities. If China could only deny Japan triumph (a defensive victory of sorts), the United States, in contrast, waged offensive warfare against Japan successfully.

The American-Led Offensive   It was not necessary for the Allies to reconquer the bulk of the territories Japan had seized in order to ensure its defeat. Indeed, at the close of the war in 1945, the Japanese still occupied Malaya, Singapore, Vietnam, Hong Kong, most of the Dutch East Indies, and much of China. Instead, the foci of Japanese power—in the shape of the fleet, the Manchurian army, and the homeland's security—were all overwhelmed in 1944–45, by the American navy, the Soviet army, and the American strategic bombing offensive, respectively.

In the Pacific, the Americans had to develop a host of skills. Improvement in amphibious operations entailed, for example, redesigning reconnaissance and firepower systems. It was also important to improve carrier warfare techniques, a formidable task because of limited prewar experience in this field. These techniques and doctrines had also to include the unfamiliar sphere of cooperation with other surface warships. A variety of factors, aside from carrier numbers, were involved in American victory. In the crucial Midway campaign in 1942 (see the Highlights box on page 556), Japanese failure reflected factors particular to the battle as well as more general issues, including the use of their submarines. In the campaign, the Japanese were seriously hindered by flawed planning and preparation. They underestimated American strength, and their deployment in pursuit of an overly complex plan and their tactical judgment were both poor. Admiral Yamamoto also exaggerated the role of battleships in any battle with the Americans.

In contrast, although there were major problems, particularly with torpedoes that did not work, American preparation was superior. This included the ability to intercept and decipher coded Japanese radio messages, enabling the Americans to out-think their opponents: The American intelligence failure of Pearl Harbor was more than rectified. In addition, the Americans were able to mount an effective repair effort, returning to service the carrier *Yorktown,* damaged at the Battle of the Coral Sea earlier in 1942. Furthermore, Japan had violated its initial strategy of seizing the key resource areas and sufficient land to provide defense in depth and waiting for the inevitable American counterattack

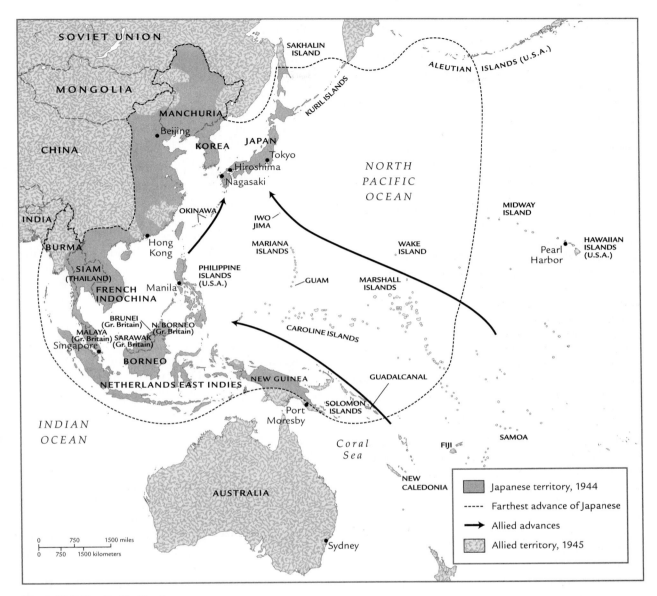

Figure 28.2 The Pacific Theater

by building up the defense from Japan's rather limited industrial base and hoping that the United States would shy away from the cost of battle. Instead, the Japanese gave in to "victory disease," to use their own phrase, and stayed on the offensive, weakening, if not wasting, forces. In part, this was a response to the American carrier-based Doolittle air raid on Tokyo and other cities on April 18, 1942, which helped lead the Japanese to the failed, flawed attack on Midway.

Despite these systemic American advantages, the Battle of Midway still had to be won on June 4, 1942. Far from being an inevitable result, it was a near thing that reflected American tactical flexibility. Having gained the advantage at Midway, the Americans were now safe from Japanese carrier offensives and were also in a position to provide carrier support for amphibious operations in the Pacific, although the Americans still had to develop an effective doctrine for carrier use in offensive operations. The Japanese were to stage renewed offensives on the Burma/India frontier and in southern China, both in 1944, and the latter with particular success; but they were no longer in a position to mount one in the Pacific (Figure 28.2).

The Americans focused on island hopping (see below). They could decide where to attack and could neutralize bases, such as Rabaul, that they chose to leap-frog. This lessened the extent of hard, slogging conflict and thus compromised the strategic depth represented by the Japanese defensive perimeter. It also helped the Americans maintain the pace of their advance.

The contrast in resources in the closing stages of the war in the Pacific was readily apparent. For example, although the Japanese XIV Area Army in Luzon in early 1945 had more than 250,000 troops, its condition reflected the degradation of the Japanese war machine. There were only about 150 operational combat aircraft to support it, and their planes and pilots could not match the Americans in quality; most were destroyed by American carrier planes before the invasion. The Japanese troops lacked fuel and ammunition, and the relatively few vehicles available had insufficient fuel, one result of the highly effective American submarine offensive against Japanese shipping (see below). Nevertheless, although the Americans, with Filipino support, overran the key parts of Luzon in 1944–45, they suffered over 140,000 casualties. The fanaticism of Japanese resistance even in the face of overwhelming material imbalances convinced American planners that, as in Germany, complete conquest of Japan would be necessary. The potential casualties—Japanese as well as American—an invasion of the Japanese homeland would entail was a major factor in the U.S. decision to use its newly developed atomic bombs to bring an end to the war in the Pacific.

AIR WARFARE

Air warfare matured in World War II as a third element of military power, a development reflected institutionally in the establishment of separate air forces with their own command structures in the military organizations of all the major combatants. But the political struggle entailed in creating a new service had already caused air power advocates to make grandiose claims for the ability of strategic bombing alone to win wars. This political-institutional history shaped, and in fact often hindered, the effective deployment of airpower, for it put emphasis on long-range strategic bombing at the expense of the development of tactical airpower. As with the war on land and at sea, the history of the air war demonstrates the interaction between doctrine, technology, and production.

Tactical Airpower

Tactical airpower had three main missions: gaining or maintaining air superiority against enemy fighters, providing close air support for ground combat units, and providing tactical interdiction, that is, attacking the immediate supply and communications network of enemy ground forces. The *Luftwaffe,* the German air force, designed like so much of the German war machine with tactical and operational imperatives in mind, rapidly gained air superiority over unprepared opponents in its early campaigns in Poland and France and was thus able to demonstrate its effectiveness in close air support and, especially, tactical interdiction. The *Luftwaffe's* problem was that it was then asked to become a strategic bombing force. Not only did it fail to win the air superiority contest in the Battle of Britain, but its medium and dive-bombers proved highly vulnerable to fighter interdiction and incapable of an effective strategic bombing campaign. When the invasion of Russia opened, mission schizophrenia led to scrambled production priorities, and the *Luftwaffe* found itself overstretched and then fighting a war of attrition for air superiority that it could not win against the Soviets.

Nor was its close air support ever more than psychologically effective (though the screaming Stukas were that, especially at first). It was in tactical interdiction that the *Luftwaffe* was most effective, and this continued to be true of all tactical airpower throughout the war as problems of inaccurate targeting and the vulnerability of tactical bombers to ground fire and enemy fighters limited the ability of planes to kill tanks and hit combat formations. Only the Russians continued to deploy a specialized ground attack plane, and its (significant) effectiveness depended on massive numbers and a willingness to take heavy losses.

The Allies, with air forces led ideologically by strategic bomber commanders, entered the war with nonexistent or misguided tactical air doctrines that scattered planes in small units subject to ground commanders' orders. This resulted in wasteful attacks on minor targets and useless continuous air cover for advancing units. Interservice mistrust also hindered efficiency. The British in North Africa finally worked out arrangements that unified tactical air command and focused on unrelenting offensive action against Rommel's supply and communications lines, which in turn drew German fighters into attritional battles for air superiority that they could not win. Lacking specialized ground attack bombers, the Allies also hit on using fighters as fighter-bombers, which proved to be

St. Paul's Cathedral, London, During the Great Fire Raid, December 29, 1940 Strategic bombing of civilian targets failed to produce the widespread demoralization predicted by some airpower theorists.

the right solution: They could defend themselves in dogfights, and they also were fast and maneuverable enough to heighten their survival rate in ground support and deliver much more accurate bombing missions against tactical targets such as bridges than medium and heavy bombers flying at high altitude ever could. When finally given the chance by a reluctant high command dominated by bombers, tactical interdiction proved spectacularly successful in Normandy, severely limiting the reinforcements and supplies the Germans could move into the campaign theater.

Indeed, the destruction of the *Luftwaffe* resulted not from strategic bombing of its manufacturing base, which strategic bombing proponents claimed would be decisive—German aircraft production actually increased in the last year of the war—but from a shift in the priorities of the strategic bombing campaign that emphasized the bombing runs, whatever their targets, as ways to lure German fighters into fights with the bombers' escorts. And this battle of attrition worked not because the Germans ran out of aircraft, but because they ran out of trained pilots. Similarly, in the Pacific, there was a growing disparity in quality between American and Japanese pilots, a matter of numbers, training, and flying experience. As a result, the Japanese could not compensate for their growing numerical inferiority in the air (see more on air combat at sea below). Nor could they keep pace with American technical

innovation: American forces got not only more but better aircraft throughout the war. The Germans did continue to innovate, introducing near the end of the war the first jet-powered fighter, but in insufficient numbers to make any difference.

Strategic Bombing

Europe The Germans initiated the use of strategic bombing in the war, but with an ill-designed force for the task, as noted above, and with a somewhat ill-defined strategy that devolved from destroying the RAF on the ground, in order to pave the way for a possible invasion, to destroying the RAF in the Battle of Britain, to night bombing runs of civilian and military targets that would, in theory, demoralize the island nation into surrender. By 1944, the Germans had introduced unmanned rockets, the V-1 and V-2, as weapons in this battle of will. They therefore arrived via expediency at the airpower doctrine that dominated the RAF and the U.S. Air Force, though in contentiously different ways. The RAF under "Bomber" Harris, forced early on in their bombing campaign to abandon daytime runs as too costly, also justified nighttime area bombing of German cities as a way to break the morale and productivity of the population and thus cause the collapse of the German war effort. The Americans stressed daytime precision bombing of military targets on the theory that hitting carefully selected choke points in the German economy would cause the rapid collapse of the German war machine.

To be blunt, neither approach worked, at least not until late in the war and then only in specific ways, and at an exceptional cost in Allied manpower. RAF area bombing of cities did lower morale among German workers, but this had no measurable effect on their productivity, nor did it lead to political revolt (just the opposite, as the government provided relief to those displaced), and it had minimal effects on the German manufacturing infrastructure, much of which was decentralized and not urban-based. American precision bombing was not precise, though accuracy improved during the war, and the choke-point theory, when applied to ball-bearing manufacture or other industrial targets, failed to put much of a dent in the German war economy, which proved both more resilient and less stretched than planners anticipated.

One precision bombing campaign did eventually yield results, however. In the summer of 1944, American bombers began to target the German oil industry, especially its refining facilities. Germany was heavily dependent on synthetic coal-based oils, and the attacks had an immediate and dramatic effect on fuel production. Aviation fuel production ceased by the end of the year, leaving the Germans with only a month's reserves. In fact, gasoline and diesel supplies were so low that entire panzer units ran out of gas on the Eastern Front. What would have happened had the Allies devoted a larger proportion of their bombing effort against the German oil industry, and started much earlier, remains one of the great "what ifs" of the war.

Air attacks on Germany did lead to the Germans diverting much of their air force and anti-aircraft capacity to home defense, rather than supporting frontline units. And the strategic bombing campaign in some form was necessary: The Anglo-American coalition faced expectations, from both the domestic front and the Soviet Union, that they would strike major blows against Germany prior to the opening of the "Second Front" by means of an invasion of France. The delay of this invasion, first in 1942 and then in 1943, led to pressure for action. But by the end of the war, moral questions were being raised about the targeting of civilians, one reason the Americans insisted, even when the practical difference was minor, that they hit only military targets. But the firebombing of Hamburg in 1943 by the British and of Dresden in 1945 by a combined Anglo-American

Nagasaki   As this shot of the fireball and mushroom cloud over Nagasaki, taken from a plane nearby, shows, the dawn of the atomic/nuclear age had arrived.

force raised persistent questions about this policy, as even collateral damage, and the general brutality of the war, tended to blur the distinction between military and civilian targets. This problem played out even more fatefully in Japan.

Japan   American carrier-based bombing raids against Japan began as early as 1942, again targeting industrial plants without much effect for the first two years. By early 1945, with new, giant B-29 bombers staging runs from China and the Marianas, the devastation of Japanese cities became extensive, culminating in the firebombing of Tokyo in April that left over 100,000 civilians dead. But far more effective in shutting down Japanese war-making capability was the secret aerial mining of Japanese ports in 1945; in conjunction with a tightening submarine blockade (see below), this virtually shut down vital Japanese oil imports, and the Japanese war machine, like the German, ground to a halt.

Task Group 38.3 in the Philippines, December 1944 Carriers and naval airpower dominated the war in the Pacific, as carriers replaced battleships as the ultimate capital ships of all major fleets.

The debate over the use of the atom bomb as the culmination of the American strategic bombing campaign in Japan remains a vexed one, with claims from some that they were used to make the Soviet Union more manageable in Europe and to restrict its gains in the Far East. Given the fighting determination and ferocity the Japanese had already displayed in defense, it is understandable that these bombs were used to try to ensure Japanese surrender. That they did so probably owed more to their status as new and unexpected weapons than to their destructiveness, which was less than, say, the conventional firebombing of Tokyo months before, as their novelty allowed a face-saving surrender by the emperor, obsessed to the end with honor. (See the Sources box "An Eyewitness Account of Hiroshima" to get a small sense of the large-scale horror.)

WORLD WAR II AT SEA

The Second World War, in both scope and cost, was the largest sea war in history. By midcentury, following a period marked by prolonged global conflicts, bloody political upheavals, and rapid advances in technology, none but the wealthiest of the great naval powers that had begun the century maintained a substantial presence on the world oceans.

At the same time, navies became arguably more important than ever. The ability of submarines to conduct devastating attacks on commerce and, even more, the ability of carrier-based aircraft to project state power over vast stretches of ocean and far inland, brought fleets into closer contact and cooperation with land-based forces than ever before. This development was epitomized in the amphibious warfare that characterized many of the major campaigns of World War II. This new importance made decisions about production of naval armaments and their use even more crucial. Given the swift pace of technological change, however, it was difficult for the makers of doctrine to adjust, and effective tactical, operational, and strategic systems were often developed on the fly. Therefore, naval warfare between 1937 and 1945 was, like air and land war, a story about the interaction of doctrine, technology, and industrial development.

Surface Warfare

German surface forces could exert little influence over the conduct of the war. The battleships and cruisers the Germans deployed as surface raiders turned out to be dismal failures. Operating essentially alone, they found it difficult to conceal their

SOURCES

An Eyewitness Account of Hiroshima

Hiroshi Sawachika was 28 years old when the atom bomb was dropped. He was an army doctor stationed at the army headquarters in Ujina. When he was exposed, he was inside the headquarters building, 4.1 kilometers from the hypocenter. Being rather far from the hypocenter, he was not seriously injured. Afterward, he was very busy getting medical treatment to the survivors.

■ ■ ■

I was in my office. I had just entered the room and said "Good morning" to colleagues and I was about to approach my desk when outside it suddenly turned bright red. I felt very hot on my cheeks. Being the chief of the room, I shouted to the young men and women in the room that they should evacuate. As soon as I cried, I felt weightless as if I were an astronaut. I was then unconscious for 20 or 30 seconds. When I came to, I realized that everybody including myself was lying at one side of the room. Nobody was standing. . . . At the windows, there was no window glass and the window frames had been blown out as well. I went to the windows to find out where the bombing had taken place. And I saw the mushroom cloud over the gas company. . . . After a while, with the guide of the hospital personnel, the injured persons reached our headquarters. With lots of injured people arriving, we realized just how serious the matter was. We decided that we should treat them also. Soon afterwards, we learned that many of them had been badly burned. As they came to us, they held their hands aloft. They looked like they were ghosts. We made the tincture for that treatment by mixing edible peanut oil and something. We had to work in a mechanical manner in order to treat so many patients. . . . Later on, when I felt that I could leave the work to other staff for a moment, I walked out of the treatment room and went into the another room to see what had happened. When I stepped inside, I found the room filled with the smell that was quite similar to the smell of dried squid when it has been grilled.

The smell was quite strong. It's a sad reality that the smell human beings produce when they are burned is the same as that of the dried squid when it is grilled. . . . When I felt someone touch my leg, it was a pregnant woman. She said that she was about to die in a few hours. She said, "I know that I am going to die. But I can feel that my baby is moving inside. It wants to get out of the room. I don't mind if I had died. But if the baby is delivered now, it does not have to die with me. Please help my baby live." There were no obstetricians there. There was no delivery room. There was no time to take care of her baby. All I could do was to tell her that I would come back later when everything was ready for her and her baby. Thus I cheered her up and she looks so happy. But I have to return to the treatment work. So I resumed to work taking care of the injured one by one. There were so many patients. I felt as if I was fighting against the limited time. It was late in the afternoon towards the evening. And image of that pregnant woman never left my mind. Later, I went to the place where I had found her before, she was still there lying in the same place. I patted her on the shoulder, but she said nothing. The person lying next to her said that a short while ago, she had become silent. I still recalled this incident partly because I was not able to fulfill the last wish of this dying young woman. I also remember her because I had a chance to talk with her however short it was.

SOURCE: Retrieved from http://www.inicom.com/hibakusha/hiroshi.html.

movements, particularly from aircraft, at which point superior Allied forces of ships and planes could be brought to bear. Few German ships survived the first year of the war.

Almost all the major traditional battles elsewhere involved cruiser and destroyer task forces. The new, fast battleships were almost always grouped with carriers, if only loosely, for mutual protection, with the carriers providing vital air cover for the battleships and the latter both protecting the carriers against surface attacks and contributing their heavy volume of anti-aircraft fire to cover the carriers against air assault. In other words, both battleships and carriers were too valuable to risk unsupported, leaving cruisers and destroyers to do independent jobs. The old prewar battleships, meanwhile, found highly useful employment as gunfire support ships in the war's major European and Pacific amphibious operations.

The successful execution of such fundamental tasks as gathering, disseminating, and using intelligence; providing effective command, control, and communication; and coordinating logistics and supply systems of unprecedented size proved key. Though there are remarkable examples of the survival of damaged ships, particularly in the U.S. Navy, which considered damage control the last line of defense, these engagements also demonstrated the continuing advantage of firepower over defensive armor. The powerful and long-range Japanese "Long Lance" torpedo, to cite a well-known example, wreaked havoc with the lightly protected cruisers and destroyers. As the war advanced, American warships benefited from technological advances, such as fire control radar, which greatly enhanced their night fighting ability. In combination with their greater numbers, their technological advances meant that later gunnery battles with the Japanese became fairly one-sided.

Submarine Warfare

The Battle of the Atlantic   During the interwar years, submarines profited from a number of technological advances. Able to cruise faster for greater distances and for longer periods submerged, linked to the shore by long-range radios, and carrying better torpedoes, submarines clearly should have been higher on the list of British concerns before 1939. But the British believed that their sonar system, known as ASDIC, would effectively counter the German U-boat threat. Unfortunately for the British, new German doctrine, centered on night surface attacks, would confound Allied defenders. In the first seven months of the war, U-boats sank 222 merchant ships while losing 18 of their number. The German conquest of Norway, the Low Countries, and France in April–June 1940 exacerbated the situation, as newly conquered areas provided forward bases for the U-*waffe*. In August 1940, Hitler declared a total blockade of the British Isles and warned that all

shipping of any nationality would be sunk on sight. The period from July through October 1940 became known as the "Happy Time" among German submariners, which sank 217 ships, most of which sailed alone and unescorted.

The German U-boat fleet went to sea under the guidance of Admiral Karl Dönitz. The submarine force commander coordinated his boats, supported by a handful of Italian boats, in a manner designed to sink the maximum amount of tonnage, regardless of its military value, while minimizing the risk to his forces. The Germans planned to use *wolf pack attacks*— operations involving several U-boats converging under central control from U-boat headquarters, to launch concerted nighttime assaults on convoys. Despite the fact that the Germans rarely possessed a sufficient number of submarines at sea to mount these wolf pack attacks, Allied losses reached an average of 450,000 tons of shipping per month by early 1941. Although the British reinstituted convoys quickly after the outbreak of hostilities, resources for antisubmarine warfare were scarce, and it took time to work out effective tactics and incorporate new technologies into the antisubmarine arsenal. The Royal Navy's global commitments stretched its antisubmarine warfare (ASW) assets dangerously thin.

As convoy escort became routine, wolf pack attacks increased in both frequency and intensity. Moreover, the entry of the United States into the Atlantic war in December 1941 opened up a new and vulnerable arena for the U-boats. The German's "Drumbeat" offensive off the East Coast of the United States marked what became known as a second "Happy Time." Losses of Allied shipping increased throughout 1942.

But so, too, did German losses. The advent of new ASW technologies, the development of new escort tactics, the increasing experience level of the escort crews, ever-expanding areas of air coverage for convoys, and increasingly effective breaking of the Germans' naval Enigma ciphers—all made the North Atlantic an increasingly dangerous place for U-boats. The provision of continuous air cover across the North Atlantic from a line of bases stretching from Northern Ireland to Iceland, Greenland, and Canada made the execution of wolf pack attacks more difficult. Not only could aircraft attack surfaced U-boats, but the mere threat of their presence drove submarines underwater, reducing their range, cruising time, and ability to spot targets. Allied losses declined, while at the same time a massive building program in the United States produced "Liberty Ships" faster than the Germans could sink Allied vessels. By the late spring of 1943, the tide turned dramatically, with the Germans beginning to lose almost as many U-boats as they were sinking Allied merchant ships. Dönitz withdrew his U-boats from the main North Atlantic routes.

The Germans U-boats renewed their offensive later in the year, increasingly armed with new technologies, primarily snorkels, which allowed submarines to run their diesel engines while submerged, and homing torpedoes. But the Allied escorts mounted new weapons and devices of their own—most notably, ahead-thrown weapons and improved radar and sonar. In combination with continued Allied code breaking, the German submarines stood little chance.

Submarines in the Pacific

On the other side of the world, the U.S. Navy prosecuted an aggressive and systematic war on Japanese merchant shipping throughout the war. Because Japan lacked such natural resources as iron ore, oil, coal, bauxite, and rubber needed to support a modern economy and armed forces, the war was critically about production, supply, and communications as much as it was about the outcomes of particular battles. In addition to her vital imports, Japan needed to transport arms and men to captured possessions.

The Japanese did not ignore the threat American submarines posed to their merchant shipping. Rather, they chose to invest their limited industrial resources in weapons systems designed to fight and win the quick victory they sought. Thus, they designed their submarines to support the fleet and to hunt not merchantmen but American warships. In so doing, they were running a calculated risk. In the absence of a quick victory, the destruction of the ill-defended but critically important Japanese merchant fleet would be a distinct possibility.

In mid-1943, with the U.S. submarine order of battle expanding, Admiral Charles A. Lockwood, who commanded all American submarines in the Pacific, planned a major offensive against Japan. U.S. submarines, which had operated in Japanese home waters since the beginning of hostilities, now boldly penetrated the Sea of Japan. A few formed three-boat wolf packs, but without the level of success achieved by the Germans in the Atlantic. Japan, sorely strapped for aircraft and shipping, lacked the resources and doctrinal flexibility to rapidly remedy its unpreparedness for antisubmarine warfare. Shipping losses soared in September 1943, but an independent command for shipping protection was not created at Japanese navy headquarters until November, a full two years after

Japan's decision to go to war. However, giving anti-submarine warfare an institutional voice failed to compensate for the lack of adequate numbers and types of vessels, aircraft, radar, effective systems of communications, and even political support within the government for implementing a system of convoys. And when Japan did turn to convoying, its escort vessels lacked tactical doctrine and training. By the end of 1943, Japan had lost 1.8 million tons of merchant shipping, two-thirds of it to submarines. In 1944, the onslaught continued, and American submarines achieved dramatic results, as oil imports from the East Indies dropped to half by midsummer. U.S. subs steadily strangled Japan's war machine.

The differing results of the submarine campaigns against shipping in the Atlantic and the Pacific highlight the key features of underseas warfare in World War II. Cruising virtually without opposition, submarines could interdict seaborne lines of supply. Effective counters required first the existence of an institutional and doctrinal will to combat the problem. Japan never attained this stage of antisubmarine warfare. Britain, which had faced a submarine threat during World War I, did, although its interwar preparations proved to be inadequate. Too often, submarines were conceived as adjuncts of the battle fleet, useful for scouting and perhaps sinking the odd enemy warship, and not as deadly instruments of a *guerre de course*.

Air and Sea

Carriers and Combat at Sea

In the summer of 1940, the British Mediterranean Fleet launched a daring night carrier attack on six Italian battleships based at Taranto. Twenty-one obsolescent Fairey "Swordfish" torpedo biplanes flying from the carrier *Illustrious* penetrated heavy anti-aircraft fire to hit and sink the brand-new *Littorio* and the old *Conte di Cavour*, while a third battleship was disabled. The three survivors abandoned Taranto.

The lesson was not lost on the Japanese. The U.S. Pacific Fleet had moved to Hawaii from its usual home in California in the spring of 1940 to deter, not precipitate, Japanese aggression. But Japanese leaders, inspired partly by the British success at Taranto, chose to attack Pearl Harbor in an attempt to knock out the Pacific Fleet in one dramatic opening blow. The magnitude of Japan's goal dictated that its six most capable aircraft carriers deploy for the operation. Fighting their carriers as a tactical unit was novel but necessary, given the Japanese navy's lack of an effective early warning system and the need to pool its small number of fighter aircraft for fleet defense. Imaginative in concept and skilled in its execution, the attack exceeded all expectations and achieved complete surprise on December 7, 1941, exacting a substantial toll in American lives and land-based aircraft.

Sober estimates of the material results achieved at Pearl Harbor revealed that two Japanese attack waves totaling some 350 planes inflicted severe damage on the battle line (sinking four old battleships, two of which became permanent losses) and several smaller vessels. However, the fliers ignored the navy base's supply and repair facilities, fields of exposed oil tanks, and submarine force. This failure, given Japan's desire to cripple the ability of the U.S. Navy to deter its expansion into Southeast Asia and so force the United States to acquiesce to its ambition, proved fatal. Also, the American aircraft carriers, which were at sea during the attack, escaped unscathed. Even though the Japanese had missed the carriers, the U.S. Navy might have found it necessary to retreat to the West Coast if the enemy had assaulted its base infrastructure as vigorously as it had the obsolescent battleships. Instead, with its carriers intact and operating from a fully capable advance base, the timetable for a U.S. counteroffensive in the Pacific was measured in months, not years. The carriers would prove to be the spearhead of this counteroffensive (see the Highlights box "The Battle of Midway, June 4–7, 1942").

In early 1942, American carrier task forces demonstrated their great mobility by raiding Japanese air and naval bases in the Marshall and Gilbert Islands and on New Guinea, temporarily deflecting Japanese attention from Australia. But it was in the Battle of the Coral Sea (May 7–8, 1942) that U.S. and Japanese carrier forces traded aerial blows in the first battle in history in which the opposing fleets remained beyond visual range. American aircraft sank a light carrier, severely damaged a heavy carrier, and eviscerated the air group of another, while Japanese aircraft badly damaged the *Yorktown* and sank the *Lexington*. The battle was a draw tactically, yet because Japan was forced to withdraw an invasion convoy headed to occupy Port Moresby in New Guinea, the U.S. Navy could claim a strategic victory in blunting the enemy's march toward Australia.

Still, heavy losses in carriers during 1942—by the end of the year, only two of the six prewar carriers committed to the Pacific remained afloat—revealed to American leaders shortcomings in ship design, damage control procedures, types and numbers of anti-aircraft weapons, and the handling of fighter protection. The improvements made by the U.S. Navy in all these areas paid great dividends, as the navy lost no fleet carrier after October 1942.

The addition of the new fast battleships to a carrier's escort screen dramatically increased the volume of anti-aircraft fire that incoming attackers faced. With improvements in radar, carrier task forces received a much earlier warning of approaching aircraft and thus had more time to prepare their defenses. The ranges at which an enemy air strike was spotted by radar, however, were still not large enough to give carrier fighter aircraft the time needed to engage the enemy striking force (which was also screened by fighters) and inflict sufficient casualties to diffuse or thwart the attack. As a result, on the approach of the enemy aircraft, the carrier task force would go to full speed and depend on radical maneuvering and its batteries of heavy (5-inch) and light automatic (1.1-inch, 40-mm, and 20-mm) anti-aircraft guns to foil the attack.

As U.S. improvements in fleet air defense took a heavier toll on Japanese squadrons, the Imperial Navy found it increasingly difficult to replace its losses. Not only was the production of new planes inadequate to keep up with demand—on top of which, new designs could not be produced to match American innovations—but also the supply of trained pilots dramatically decreased, further debilitating the combat capabilities of the Japanese air arm. The results were visible in air battles that became more and more one-sided. The trend culminated in the Battle of the Philippine Sea on June 19–21, 1944. A Japanese fleet sent to contest the American attack on Saipan met an American fleet that included carrier Task Force 58, organized to give more flexibility to carrier operations than strict support for amphibious assaults allowed. Inferior Japanese pilots were no match for TF 58's flyers. American aircraft and anti-aircraft defenses shot down some 400 Japanese aircraft, so that the battle was dubbed "The Marianas Turkey Shoot." Meanwhile, U.S. submarines attacked the Japanese fleet of 5 heavy carriers, 4 light carriers, 5 battleships, 13 cruisers, and 28 destroyers, sinking the 2 new heavy carriers. The Japanese took flight pursued by TF 58, which sank another heavy carrier and 2 tankers and destroyed the Japanese fleet's remaining 35 aircraft. No American ships were lost, though 76 pilots and air crewmen failed to return. The Japanese losses in aircraft and pilots were insurmountable; the Japanese never again seriously contested American air superiority.

The Battle of Midway, June 4–7, 1942

The American Doolittle air raid on Japan of April 1942, staged by aircraft carriers operating from Pearl Harbor, reinforced Admiral Yamamoto's belief in the need to extend Japan's defensive perimeter and, most important, draw the U.S. Navy into a decisive, Tsushima-style battle. In early May, however, American naval forces had thwarted a Japanese advance on Australia in the Battle of the Coral Sea. Moreover, clever cryptographic analysis of the Japanese naval code had alerted Admiral Chester W. Nimitz, commander-in-chief of the U.S. Pacific Fleet, to Yamamoto's next move, which was to capture Midway Island. Nothing short of disastrous describes what unfolded for the Japanese fleet.

The Doolittle Raid   Taking off from the USS *Hornet*, an army B-25 spearheads the first air raid on Japan in April 1942. The raid provoked the disastrous Japanese campaign against Midway.

Yamamoto devised an overly intricate operation that sought to dissipate American naval forces in the central Pacific while drawing the U.S. Navy's carriers into a decisive clash near a Japanese-controlled Midway. A small Japanese force built around several light carriers would strike into the Aleutian chain, while the main force of four heavy carriers pounded Midway, preparatory to an invasion. Japanese submarines would report the departure of, and then strike at, the American fleet as it sortied from Pearl Harbor and steamed into an ambush.

This was the context for the last desperate Japanese use of airpower, the kamikaze attacks of the last year of the war. As suicide missions, they needed pilots with less training who could be more reckless in penetrating anti-aircraft fire. Named "Divine Wind" after the typhoon that had destroyed the last fleet to threaten Japan with invasion, a thirteenth-century Mongol force (see Chapter 15), the kamikaze inflicted some damage but were never a threat to repel the by-then-overwhelmingly superior American naval forces. They did, however, contribute to the Japanese reputation for fanatical defense, a factor in debates about the invasion of Japan and the use of the atomic bomb (see above).

Amphibious Warfare

"Island Hopping" in the Pacific   Having created an island empire, Japanese leaders set out to turn it into a fortress, especially when the battles of the Coral Sea and Midway forced them onto the defensive

But it was the Japanese who would be ambushed. Nimitz, made aware of the Japanese plans by his code breakers, moved all his available carriers to a position northeast of Midway before the Japanese submarines arrived on station.

The carrier *Yorktown,* which had been hastily patched up following considerable damage received at the Battle of the Coral Sea, joined the *Enterprise* and *Hornet,* as well as aircraft based on Midway itself, in the ambush. On June 4, still unaware of the presence of enemy carriers, Vice-Admiral Nagumo Chuichi, who commanded the Japanese navy's carrier arm, proceeded with the attack on Midway. Land-based aircraft stood up in defense of the island and executed an attack on the Japanese fleet but suffered enormous losses. On board the Japanese carriers, deck handlers prepared their airplanes for another attack on the island. When a floatplane discovered the presence of an American carrier, Nagumo at once ordered his aircraft rearmed with antiship weapons, entailing a significant delay. In the meantime, his adversaries had gained the upper hand, as some 116 carrier attack planes were winging through heavy clouds toward him.

The U.S. Navy's obsolescent torpedo-bombers found the Japanese fleet first and bored in without fighter cover, sacrificing themselves in courageous but futile attacks on the enemy carriers. Some 35 of 41 were lost, including the *Hornet*'s entire squadron, without scoring a hit. Yet, unwittingly, they had drawn the Japanese fighter screen down to low altitude at the moment the American dive-bombers arrived over the enemy carriers. Marveling at their yellow flight decks and aiming for the large, red rising sun that adorned them, dive-bombers from the *Enterprise* and *Yorktown* caught the Japanese in the middle of feverish efforts to refuel and rearm aircraft. They attacked virtually unimpeded and reduced the *Kaga, Akagi,* and *Soryu* to flaming wrecks in a matter of minutes. The last carrier, the *Hiryu,* escaped the encounter but was sunk later in the day after trading punishing air strikes with the *Yorktown,* which for the second time in thirty days suffered heavy damage. Without air cover, Yamamoto was forced to cancel the Midway landings. On June 6, U.S. carrier aircraft sent a heavy cruiser, straggling after being damaged in a collision, to the bottom. On the same day, a Japanese submarine fatally torpedoed the *Yorktown,* which was under tow, and an attending destroyer. The veteran carrier rolled over and sank the next day.

At the cost of 1 carrier, 1 destroyer, 132 carrier- and land-based aircraft, and 307 men, the American navy had sunk 4 Japanese carriers and a heavy cruiser, destroyed 275 planes, and killed some 3500 of the enemy. The catastrophe stripped the aura of invincibility from the Imperial Navy. Strategically, just six months after its Pearl Harbor debacle, the U.S. Navy had crippled its rival's offensive capability, forcing Japan permanently onto the defensive. The Battle of Midway was perhaps the most decisive battle in American military history.

strategically. Facing the vastly greater industrial and population base of the United States, Japan's only hope was to make U.S. offensives so costly and slow that the Americans would tire of the war and leave Japan in control of at least the western half of its Pacific holdings. Thus, the Japanese garrisons on the many island groups throughout the Pacific dug in, fortified, and prepared for a desperate defense.

The bloody process of rolling back Japan's defense perimeter began in August 1942, when elements of the First Marine Division completed a surprise landing with overwhelming force on Guadalcanal and Tulagi. But success was not without costs or disputes over assault doctrine between the marines and the army. Nevertheless, some key elements of successful amphibious operations, involving the coordination of ground, air, and sea forces, emerged. The navy-marine team learned from their mistakes, scheduling better reconnaissance and longer gunfire support missions, gaining better knowledge of tide and surf conditions,

Bodies on the Beach of Tarawa, November 1943 Amphibious assaults were complicated and often costly, involving careful calculation of tides and currents and careful reconnaissance of coral reefs, as well as coordination of land, air, and sea power.

improving landing craft, and dedicating and equipping greater numbers of ships specifically to amphibious duty—all of which contributed to the success and lower casualty rates experienced by the landing forces in subsequent operations. As for the idea of bypassing certain Japanese-held islands and reducing their threat by choking off their lines of supply, that began as a strategy in response to the high casualties suffered earlier in 1943, in the Solomon chain, and was mastered not only by the navy but also by the army under General MacArthur in the southwest Pacific. While the Japanese attempted to resupply and reinforce bypassed garrisons, they did so at great cost. As they lost greater numbers of transports, they used first surface ships and then submarines, but eventually they gave up trying.

Nevertheless, despite the advances in American tactics and technology, the island-hopping strategy remained costly. The Japanese, too, refined their doctrine and tactics. At times, they defended forward, along the beaches; other times, they fortified positions inland. In late 1944, the Japanese adopted a new strategy. They no longer pursued victory in the conventional sense—the defeat of an invading American force. Instead, they accepted the fact that they would lose their isolated island fortresses, but in the process of so doing, they sought to maximize American casualties.

Amphibious Warfare in Europe   Allied military operations in the European theater included army-navy seaborne assault operations of all sizes. In contrast, the amphibious operation most associated with the Axis was one Hitler did not attempt—the invasion of Great Britain, code-named Operation Sea Lion. When the war turned in favor of the Soviet Union, the Red Army used coastal amphibious operations in both the Baltic Sea and Black Sea regions to capture enemy strongholds, bypass others, or cut off a route of German retreat. Though these were relatively minor affairs, Soviet forces (including marines, known as "naval infantry") improvised a motley array of native and imported vessels, such as American-built subchasers, into an effective amphibious force.

By exploiting their maritime superiority and control of the sea, as well as building a vast inventory of specialized amphibious ships, boats, and craft, Anglo-American forces carried out the most ambitious landing operations of the war. Even before the start of hostilities, navy planners in the United States had recognized that the procedure of disembarking assault troops from transports lying offshore and landing them on a hostile invasion beach in small, davit-carried craft would often prove impractical. As a result, the American government gave high priority to the production of vessels, vehicles, and other equipment dedicated to the conduct of amphibious warfare. Not only did

Landing on D-Day
Shown just as they left the ramp of a Coast Guard landing boat, these American soldiers were under heavy German machine-gun fire.

American industry equip U.S. forces with such equipment, it supplied large numbers of ships and craft to Allied navies around the world.

Active American entry into the European war began with an amphibious landing in Vichy French Morocco and Algeria. The American component had sailed undetected directly to Africa from Norfolk, Virginia. A bombardment force of battleships, cruisers, escort carriers, and destroyers helped the Allied forces overwhelm the French, who soon surrendered and switched their allegiance to the Allies. Success in North Africa led to the Sicilian and Italian campaigns of 1943–44, both of which began with major amphibious landings. In Italy, just as they had in North Africa and Sicily, the Allies exploited the element of surprise and got ashore relatively smoothly.

Allied amphibious operations climaxed with the greatest amphibious invasion in history, the Normandy invasion. American forces carried the bulk of the assault responsibilities, while the British navy supplied the majority of bombardment ships and most of the 2500 or so landing craft. The proximity of the target to the staging area, where nearly 13,000 Allied aircraft were based, made carriers unnecessary. The ability of the Allies to project enormous power—175,000 men—ashore established a viable second front, which, in combination with the movement west of Soviet forces, brought an end to the war just eleven months later.

ASSESSMENT

Impact: The Home Fronts

War and Society   Larger and longer than World War I, World War II was also even more of a total war. Strategic bombing and the fluidity of the front brought warfare directly to massive numbers of civilians in Europe and Asia. Even those areas untouched directly saw shortages and rationing, and felt the impact of more than 50 million dead. Though the war brought an end, finally, to the Great Depression in the United States, as preparations for war had done in Hitler's Germany and in 1930s Japan, human and material destruction during the war overshadowed this effect in most places. Economic historians have tried to calculate the vast negative impact of the war's casualties not just on the productive economies of the industrial nations but also on the rest of the world, which lost millions of potential consumers for its raw materials, hindering their economic development for decades. The United States would dominate the world economy for at least three decades after 1945, the war having magnified its position as the globe's leading industrial power.

The mobilization of the resources and manpower necessary to fight such a war was bound to affect the societies that made the effort, but there is no simple cause-and-effect relationship between mobilization

B-29 Nose Cones at Douglas Aircraft's Long Beach, California Plant, October 1942 Mass production of weaponry made industrial capacity a crucial element of military strength.

for war and social transformation. Americans are accustomed to thinking of the Second World War as a force for positive transformation at home as well as abroad. The war effort brought women into the workforce in record numbers, and the ideals for which the war was fought and the overtly racist nature of the main foes emphasized the social inequalities that remained at home. The war did not change things overnight, however: It took President Truman another three years after the war to desegregate the military, and it was another fifteen years before the civil rights movement bore substantial fruit in society at large. Similarly, the return of demobilized soldiers pushed women back into the domestic roles that gave the 1950s their *Leave It to Beaver* image, and it took another decade for women's rights to reemerge as a major issue.

And despite even more intense pressures and manpower shortages, Germany saw little movement of women into the workforce during the war: Nazi ideology, which stressed women's roles as childbearers for the regime, kept women largely shut out of roles in the formal economy. Much the same is true of Imperial Japan. France gave women the vote after the war, but the complexities of France's wartime record make it hard to draw simple conclusions.

The direct impact of the war in terms of casualties varied greatly. The United States ended the war with 292,000 military fatalities, compared to 397,800 for Britain, 1.75 million for Japan, 3.5 million for Germany, and about 7.5 million for the Soviet Union. In addition, almost 20 million Russian civilians died, along with 2.5 million Poles; part of those totals contributed to the 6 million Jews killed by the Nazi regime. Germany lost 2 million civilians, and Japan close to 1 million. And in China, 20 million civilians lost their lives, and another 100 million were refugees at some point during the war. The economic destruction was equally vast. The trauma of the Sino-Japanese conflict shaped a generation and more of the Chinese people in ways comparable to (and probably more far-reaching than) what World War I had done to Europe; the same was true around the world. Furthermore, Russia and China, the two nations that suffered by far the greatest casualties and destruction, rebuilt without the U.S. aid that reconstructed Germany and Japan, a significant factor in postwar political tensions.

War and Ideology The vast scope of Axis conquests brought the impact of the war to home fronts in many occupied territories. The failure of the Nazi and Japanese empires as integrating systems capable of winning mass support was important in their defeat. In each case, they elicited a considerable amount of backing in some conquered areas, such as Croatia in 1941–44 and Albania in 1943–44, and from Germany's Bulgarian ally in Macedonia; but there was no equivalent to the range or extent of support that the Western powers were able to secure in parts of their colonial empires. There was certainly considerable opposition to the Allies, including from nationalists in India, some of whom helped the Japanese, although to negligible military effect. The key point, however, was that the Indians held the line with the British and did not break even in the darkest hours of the Blitz and the German and Japanese advances in 1941–42. As 2.3 million Indians served outside India, the British ability to limit opposition on the Indian home front was key to their success in the Middle East and, far more, in neighboring Burma.

In contrast, the Germans and Japanese embraced beliefs in racial superiority that, to a considerable extent, precluded cooperation with other peoples: The Japanese never understood the force of any nationalism other than their own, and the Germans never wanted allies, only associates who would do what they were told. The Japanese were generally seen as new conquerors, not liberators from Western rule. The brutality and exploitation of the Germans and Japanese as occupiers or allies seriously compromised possibilities for support—for example, in Ukraine, for the Germans—and also accentuated serious economic mismanagement. In New Guinea, where some of the population had treated Japanese forces as liberators in 1942, there was a reaction against Japanese conduct that led to cooperation with Allied reconquest, not least in providing crucial carriers for supplies. The forced employment of millions of foreign workers, especially Russian, Polish, and French, who were brought to Germany and generally treated harshly, if not murderously, was not a way to ensure labor commitment or efficiency; it also compromised the appeal of cooperation with Germany. However, large quantities of matériel were also produced by the inmates of Soviet *gulags* (forced labor camps).

Success and Morale   The results of campaigns and battles were important not only to the course of the struggle but also to home fronts in terms of civilian morale. In June 1940, General Archibald Wavell, commander of the British forces in the Middle East, wrote, "The internal security problems in Egypt, in Palestine, and in Iraq, and elsewhere occupy a very great deal of the attention and time of the Middle East Staff. An improvement in propaganda may help the situation, but only military successes or evidence of strength and determination will really do it." Propaganda reflected the sense, even among the totalitarian powers, especially Germany and the Soviet Union, that popular support had to be wooed and was an aspect of a reeducation of the public that ranged from eating habits to political goals. Posters, films, radio, newspapers, photographs, and even animated cartoons were used to recruit, to boost production, to motivate, and to assist rationing and conservation of resources—and they linked the home front to the front line.

Confidence in popular responses, however, was less pronounced, particularly in Germany and Russia, than might be suggested by a focus on the wartime propaganda of togetherness. The Nazis, for example, had to confront the lack of popular celebrations when war broke out in 1939. In the Soviet Union, the stereotype of the heroic Red Army soldier bore scant reference to the reality; for example, in terms of the marked contrast between nationalities, Central Asian recruits had little understanding about the purposes of the war. The Western democracies enjoyed more popular support, in part because of better news from the front and because of the reduced direct impact of the war on the civilian population. But even there, government mistrust of segments of the population emerged and reflected popular perceptions—most clearly demonstrated by the U.S. internment of huge numbers of its Japanese-American citizens. On the other hand, Western propaganda efforts were bolstered by fairly open and trustworthy war reporting in the media, which enjoyed access to events and freedom to report that put recent restrictive U.S. policies in Iraq to shame.

The importance of civilian morale was recognized and targeted by the combatants. The air and submarine attacks launched by the Germans from 1940 were designed to damage the British war economy and, to that extent, reflected a materialist conception of conflict. However, they were also seen as a way to sap British morale. This reflected Hitler's presentation of war as a struggle of will, a widely held view. The idea that strategic bombing could dislocate and demoralize an opposing society shaped air policy. Thus, the 1940 War Manual of the Royal Air Force claimed that a nation was defeated when its people or government no longer retained the will to prosecute their war aims, and that strategic bombing was a means to this end. If bombing was designed to destroy will as well as resources, it was but one of the means employed to transform societies as an aspect of total war.

Overall Impact   In short, there is no denying the impact of the war on the societies that experienced it. It left deep cultural imprints—oddly, generally less negative imprints than those of World War I, perhaps because the outcome seemed less pointless—and the generation that came of age during the war dominated the postwar political world for decades. But the effect of the war varied with the values and structures of each society that participated, making further generalization difficult.

Military Lessons

The war indicated that resources alone were not the key factor; fighting quality (including doctrine) was also important on land and sea and in the air. The interaction of doctrine, technology, and production created a synergy that the Allies proved best able to harness. The Axis enjoyed an advantage in fighting quality in 1939–41 but had lost it by 1944. This reflected the ability of the Allies to close the gap in tactical terms and to gain important operational advantages. Strategically, the Allies had a clearer view of the war from early on.

Historiography   Interpretations of success in the war focusing on resources, economic mobilization, and home fronts tend to underrate the extent to which the Axis was eventually outfought on land, in the air, and at sea, in Europe, in the Pacific, and in Asia. Such interpretations appear to support self-serving German and Japanese interpretations that emphasize their wartime fighting quality and suggest that they lost only because they were outnumbered. These arguments, in turn, take up themes from the war itself—for example, the Nazi argument that they were defending civilization against Asiatic "hordes" in the shape of the large Soviet army. To this day, on the German side, there remains a tendency to regard their defeat as due to being beaten in resource production by the Allies and to minimize or ignore the extent to which they were outfought. This is a parallel to the earlier tendency, after 1918, to blame defeat in the First World War on everything other than the Allied ability to best German forces on the Western Front, an interpretation that served Hitler's purposes as he searched for domestic culprits.

For the Second World War, all too much of the literature on German war making is based on postwar analyses of their own campaigns by German commanders and staff officers. These place the responsibility for defeat on resource issues, as well as the size and climate of the Soviet Union, and, above all, Hitler's interventions. Hitler indeed was a seriously flawed commander, especially in defense, due to his unwillingness to yield territory and his consequent preference for static over mobile defense. By concentrating decision making and failing to match Stalin's ability to delegate, Hitler ensured that there would be no alternative way to provide sound command decisions, and by 1944, his diminished grasp on reality had seriously exacerbated the difficulties of German command. Alongside this approach, it is argued that, probably by early September 1942, Hitler had realized that final victory was out of reach but was determined to fight on in order to destroy Europe's Jews, as well as to achieve what he saw as a moral victory for his conception of the German people. This notion of self-destruction became a decisive part of the regime's ideology.

It is important, however, to stress that Hitler's deficiencies were part of a more general failure of German war making, not least its emphasis on will. In the event, the Germans proved unable to make opposing states accept their assumptions about how wars are won. As in 1914, when the Germans invaded France and Belgium, launching what became the Western Front of the First World War, the will to win could not be a substitute for a failure to set sensible military and political goals, and to establish attainable fall-back positions. Postwar German analyses also tend to ignore archival evidence that highlights battlefield mistakes by German commanders and do not consider the issue of Soviet fighting quality—a subject emphasized by excellent American work that has benefited from the opening of some of the Soviet archives after the fall of the Communist regime.

Resources, Industrial Capacity, and Military Skill   In the early stages of the war, the Germans and Japanese had a marked tactical and operational military advantage, the result of both better doctrine and accumulated experience, and it took until late 1942 for the Allies to fight their enemies to a standstill. Winston Churchill, the British prime minister, told a Joint Session of the U.S. Congress on May 19, 1943, "The enemy is still proud and powerful . . . still possesses enormous armies, vast resources, and invaluable strategic territories . . . it is in the dragging-out of the war at enormous expense, until the democracies are tired or bored or split, that the main hopes of Germany and Japan must now reside." Thereafter, it was a combination of superior Allied resources and technique that was important. Resources and military skill were complementary and also separate.

A narrow focus on industrial strength—specifically, the manufacture of weapons—underrates the agency of military skill. This skill was not a single factor but, instead, an interacting range, stretching from strategic insight and planning to unit cohesion and tactical competence. These factors changed. Crudely, there was a marked increase in Allied fighting quality, one seen, for example by comparing the British army fighting the Germans in 1940–41 and Japanese in 1941–42 with the same army fighting both in 1944–45, or the Soviets fighting the Germans in 1941 with their success in 1944–45, or the Americans fighting the Germans in Tunisia in 1943 with their success in 1944–45.

The latter stages of the Second World War more clearly demonstrate the role of resources than do the earlier years, because the sides were by then fully defined (although the Soviet Union did not attack Japan until the closing month), and the conflict was far more attritional than in its early stages. This did not mean that strategy played no role, but it pushes attention back to the respective strength of the war economies. For example, in 1944, the availability of oil helped determine Japanese naval dispositions, affecting their response to the American movement against the Philippines. Numbers and power were crucial to the disparity of force, but there was also a strategic dimension, and in 1944, the Americans out-thought and out-fought the Japanese. The Americans were able to fight the battle with Japanese air and naval power in the certain knowledge that such a battle could be won, and the ability to bring major superiority to bear was an expression of skill as well as strategic capability.

Leadership, Production, and Changing Capabilities

It is also necessary to give due weight to serious policy and planning flaws in both the German and the Japanese war efforts. In part, these relate to production issues linked to industrial mobilization, but the use of military resources is also at issue. German and Japanese planning became increasingly grandiose and divorced from reality as the war progressed, with wishful thinking replacing sober calculation. Losing the intelligence war, the Germans were unable to out-think their opponents, while the Allies also proved superior in applied research. The consequences were shown in weapon procurement. One example was the German failure to accept innovations in submarine design and the misplaced conviction that the existing Type VII submarine did not require improvement. Moreover, in early 1942, Admiral Erich Raeder, the head of the navy, decided to meet the shortage of shipyard workers for submarine maintenance by drawing on labor engaged in the production of new submarines. As a result, a useful short-term increase in the number of operational submarines was achieved at the cost of cutting new production.

More generally, the tasks the German military were set did not arise in a predictable fashion. Thus, an air force designed essentially for tactical ground support purposes was called on to play a strategic role against Britain in 1940–41. This proved to be a general problem for all combatants. For example, all pre-war navies sought carriers and submarines only as a subordinate part of fleets that emphasized battleships, the Japanese navy providing a particularly good case. In short, force capabilities were developed for particular goals, and then it was discovered that they could be, and had to be, used in other contexts. One consequence was that those economies with greater and more flexible productive capacities could respond more rapidly and effectively to the weapons demands created by new tasks. But the economies' responses were necessarily mediated and often directed by the policy and strategy decisions of the political leadership in all combatant countries, and here, too, flexibility proved both crucial and seriously lacking on the Axis side. One sign of this is that the German army never really solved the problems that plagued it on the Eastern Front, whereas the Soviets, as well as the British and Americans, improved their capabilities steadily at all levels—tactical, operational, strategic, and logistical—throughout the war.

CONCLUSION

Ironically, the lessons of World War II regarding mechanized operations, battlefield tactics, and the need for a coherent, long-term, grand strategy would be studied intensively on both sides, even as changes in global politics, especially decolonization, shifted warfare to new sorts of conflicts under the growing nuclear shadow. The eventual demise of the Soviet Union completed the global transformations set in train by World War II, moving much warfare even further from the "clash of great powers" paradigm of which World War II was the climax. These developments are taken up in Chapters 29 and 30.

Suggested Readings

Ambrose, Stephen. *The Supreme Commander: The War Years of General Dwight D. Eisenhower.* Garden City: Doubleday, 1970. An analysis of the role of the Allied commander by the historian who edited Eisenhower's wartime papers.

Black, Jeremy. *World War Two. A Military Hisory.* New York: Routledge, 2004. An effective short introduction, particularly on some aspects of the war frequently overlooked in works of this type.

Budiansky, Stephen. *Air Power.* New York: Viking Press, 2004. A comprehensive history of airpower in the twentieth century that does a good job of separating reality from the claims of airpower proponents.

Citino, Robert. *From Blitzkrieg to Desert Storm: The Evolution of Operational Warfare.* Lawrence: University of Kansas Press, 2004. An excellent analysis of World War II (and later) campaigns at the operational level, relating the shape of operations to the different needs and capabilities of the societies at war.

Evans, David C., and Mark R. Peattie. *Kaigun: Strategy, Tactics, and Technology in the Imperial Japanese Navy, 1887–1941.* Annapolis: Naval Institute Press, 1997. A seminal work, based on Japanese sources, that provides insight into the development of Japanese naval power from the Mejii Restoration to the eve of the Second World War; concludes that, despite earlier successes and preparation for a war against the United States, Japan's navy failed to prepare for the modern naval conflict that the Pacific war became.

Glantz, David M., and Jonathan M. House. *When Titans Clashed: How the Red Army Stopped Hitler.* Lawrence: University of Kansas Press, 1998. Based on recently accessible Soviet archives, a study that demonstrates the extent to which Soviet improvements shaped the fighting on the Eastern Front, correcting accounts long based on German sources.

Megargee, Geoffrey P., and Williamson Murray. *Inside Hitler's High Command.* Lawrence: University of Kansas Press, 2000. A crucial account of German decision making that undermines any attempt to place the blame for German failings solely on Hitler.

Murray, Williamson, and Allan R. Millet. *A War to Be Won: Fighting the Second World War, 1937–1945.* New York: Harvard University Press, 2000. A well-written one-volume history of the war that emphasizes the role of military skill as a necessary element in Allied victory.

Overy, Richard. *Why the Allies Won.* New York: Norton, 1995. Another history that undermines economic determinist accounts of the war, stressing that crucial Allied decisions were necessary for their material advantage to be effectively brought to bear.

Reynolds, Clark G. *The Fast Carriers: The Forging of an Air Navy.* New York: McGraw-Hill, 1968. A classic study of the evolution of wartime American carrier doctrine; blends a balance of official documentation and oral histories to explore the war-winning development of American fast-carrier battle groups.

Weinberg, Gerhard. L. *A World at Arms: A Global History of World War II.* New York: Cambridge University Press, 1995. A detailed study that significantly moves the historiography of the war away from German-centered accounts of Axis tactical superiority; stronger on Europe than Asia.

CHAPTER 29

The Nuclear Age: Decolonization and the Cold War, 1945–89

With recent history, we enter the age in which memory has a grip. Many people alive today fought in one or more of the conflicts that were waged from 1945. That is both an opportunity and a problem for the historian, for memory can both illuminate and mislead. This is even more the case when considering the far larger numbers who experienced conflict indirectly via a perception that was molded by the ways in which information and opinion were communicated: conversation, correspondence, radio and, increasingly insistently, the visual media, particularly television and the created memory of the movies. These offer an account not only of how war was waged but also, by choice and omission, of which wars were important. This, unfortunately, is often a misleading account, for the wars that tend to engage attention are those that involved "us": for the Americans, who dominate the production of films, most obviously the Korean and Vietnam conflicts. That, however, may lead to a misleading assessment of the nature of conflict in the period and, indeed, of the importance of particular wars.

This chapter examines the variety of conflicts that took place in the forty-four years after the end of World War II. Two major political contexts—the Cold War between the United States and the Soviet Union (USSR), and the unraveling of Western colonial empires—intersected with the development of nuclear weaponry to shape many of the conflicts of this age. But other factors, often local and often at odds with global trends, make for a complex and sometimes overlapping typology of wars whose relative importance depends on current perspectives. As those change, different features of recent warfare will appear more or less important to different analysts.

AFTER WORLD WAR II: THE GLOBAL CONTEXT

Warfare took place in a post–world war environment characterized by three major features or trends: U.S. economic dominance, political bipolarity focused around the United States and the USSR, and increasing globalism. The contradictions between these three features are real but may be understood by noting that the three trends, while overlapping, succeeded each other in importance over the period 1945–89.

The U.S. Position in the World

World War II was a wider-ranging struggle than World War I, in large part due to the greater degree of American and Japanese participation. Because the two powers were opponents instead of being, as in World War I, allies, there was also large-scale conflict in the Pacific, as well as a conclusive verdict to the struggle for influence between the two states. The war ended in 1945 with Soviet troops in Berlin, Vienna, and Manchuria (the most industrially advanced part of China), but America was the strongest power, in large part due to the strength of its economy. Germany and Japan had been greatly affected by bombing and were occupied by the victorious powers, Britain had large debts, and the Soviet economy had been devastated. The new economic order was thus established by the Americans. The international free trade and international capital markets that had characterized the global economy of the 1900s were slowly reestablished. The availability of American credit and investment was crucial. Among the major powers, only the United States enjoyed real liquidity in 1945 (Figure 29.1).

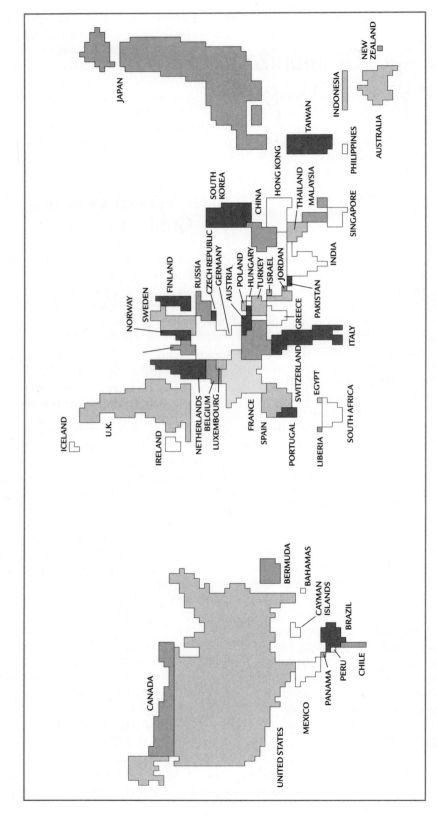

Figure 29.1 The Economic World of 1970   In this map, each country's size is proportional to its gross domestic product (GDP). This illustrates the economic dominance of the United States and its allies, Japan and Western Europe, in the post–World War II world.

Under the Bretton Woods Agreement of 1944, American-supported monetary agencies—the World Bank and the International Monetary Fund (each of which had American headquarters)—were established in order to play an active role in strengthening the global financial system. Free trade was also actively supported as part of a liberal economic order that the United States aimed to create. This was furthered by U.S. support of decolonization and the creation of independent capitalist states. This new economic order was intended as a counterpart to the United Nations, established in 1945 in order to try to ensure a peaceful solution to differences.

Bipolarity

This agenda was challenged by the USSR, a Communist dictatorship under Joseph Stalin based in Russia. There was a hotly contested though not always clear ideological division between communism on the one hand and either capitalism or liberal democracy (perhaps both, though they often proved contradictory) on the other. There was also an important political divide reflecting competing territorial interests, particularly initially in Eastern Europe and East Asia. As the United States and the USSR came to compete in the "Third World," which was created in large part by the end of the territorial control and extensive influence of the European empires, so this competition spread to include Southeast Asia, the Middle East, Africa, and Latin America. U.S. economic dominance was counterbalanced in this political competition by Soviet military power, embodied in its arsenal of nuclear weapons, its massive conventional army on the gates of Western Europe, and its military aid to allies and proxies. Bipolar competition complicated the reaction of the United States to decolonization at times by aligning some independence movements with communism.

Globalization

The bipolarity of the Cold War era was always at least partially illusory, as any number of nations, headed by postindependence India, aimed at nonaligned status. The split between the USSR and Communist China further complicated bipolarity while solidifying popular recognition of a Third World, those nations that did not fall into the camps of either the United States or the USSR. Economic and political developments over the course of the period further undermined both U.S. economic hegemony and political bipolarity. These included the gradual spread of industrialization

and economic development, especially the economic recoveries of Western Europe and Japan, the growing wealth of the Pacific Rim, and the diffusion of economic institutions and negotiations this entailed. The rise of what might be called *regional transnationalism,* in the form of treaty groups both political (NATO, SEATO, the Warsaw Pact, and so forth) and economic (above all, the European Economic Community and its expansion into the European Union), while often initially spurred by Cold War bipolarity, often ended up complicating that very bipolarity and the superpowers' job of managing it (Figure 29.2).

The complex intersection of these contexts represented a serious challenge to strategic planning and task forecasting.

THE COLD WAR AND NUCLEAR WEAPONS

Origins of the Cold War

Initially, World War II was followed by optimism in many circles in the United States. Germany and Japan had been defeated, and it was not yet clear to many Americans that the USSR would prove a serious threat. There was a widespread desire for demobilization and the return to civilian life, as well as optimism that America's monopoly of the nuclear bomb provided the nation with security. Thanks to the bomb, great-power status without the cost of continued large-scale military service or the problems posed by the war mobilization of much of the economy in support appeared a clear option.

However, this optimism ebbed rapidly (see the Issues box "Who Was to Blame for the Cold War?"). Ideologically and culturally, in 1945, each side felt threatened by the other. The American offer of Marshall Aid to help postwar recovery was rejected by the USSR as a form of economic imperialism, and this created a new boundary line between the regions that received such aid and those that did not. Soviet abandonment of cooperation over Germany, which was occupied by the victorious powers after World War II, and the imposition of one-party Communist governments in Eastern Europe, which culminated with the Communist coup in the Czech capital of Prague in 1948, led to pressure for a Western response. Soviet actions appeared to vindicate Winston Churchill's claim in March 1946 that an "Iron Curtain" was descending from the Baltic to the Adriatic.

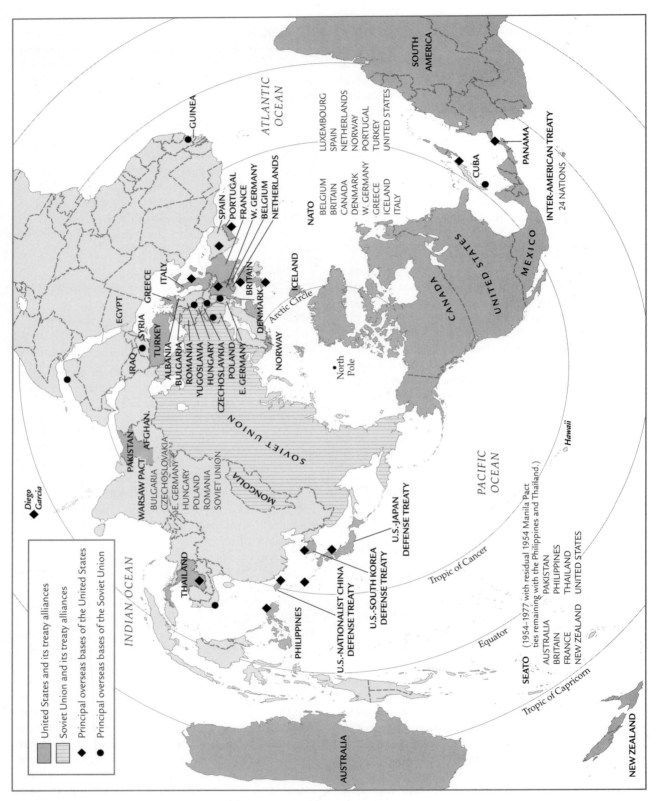

Figure 29.2 U.S. and USSR Overseas Commitments at the Height of the Cold War

ISSUES

Who Was to Blame for the Cold War?

In broad terms, the origins of the struggle for dominance between the American-led capitalist bloc and the Soviet-led Communist bloc lay in the revival of ideological and geopolitical tensions in the closing stages of World War II, as outlined in this section. But cast as a problem of assessing responsibility—or blame—for the failure of a peaceful postwar order to emerge, the origins of the Cold War have long been a contentious historiographical issue.

Earlier histories of the Cold War tended to follow (and reinforce) the ideological division between the sides. Thus, for many American historians, the Cold War had been necessitated by Soviet aggression—indeed, by the advance of "worldwide communism"—that aimed at global domination and was masterminded by the Soviets. The United States stood for them as a bulwark of political and economic freedom. Soviet historians, working in a Marxist-Leninist tradition, cast the Soviet Union in the defensive role and the United States as the capitalist, imperialist aggressor. This was also true of some Western historians, both American and European (especially French), and some who were inspired theoretically by Marxism. They were inclined to distinguish between capitalism (and its ties to imperialism) and democracy and to see the United States as a greater supporter of the former than the latter. The U.S. dropping of an atomic bomb on Nagasaki, in this view, had as much to do with demonstrating America's new atomic capability to the Soviets, who had joined the war against Japan after Hitler's defeat, as it did with reinforcing the message of Hiroshima to the Japanese.

Indeed, U.S. use of atomic weapons called into question, for some, the moral superiority of the U.S. side and led to a school of interpretation that downplayed ideology and instead saw both sides as major geopolitical, empirelike powers acting out of concerns readily analyzed in terms of *realpolitik*, or rational, state-centered motivations. While the downplaying of ideology had its limits, the influence of *realpolitik* political analysis was significant and has complicated the accurate interpretation of post–Cold War substate conflicts (see Chapter 30).

Yet-another strain of analysis that emerged later focused attention on the internal dynamics of each of the major players, recognizing that outward political stances often connected to internal political or economic struggles and challenges. In this view, for example, U.S. rearmament in 1947, in connection with the National Security Act and the founding of the National Security Council and the CIA, was motivated primarily by concerns about the U.S. economy slipping back into recession and even depression with the end of wartime production; the Soviet threat was merely a pretext. President Eisenhower's farewell address in 1961, in which he warned of the rise of an overly influential military-industrial complex, provided support for such interpretations.

Since the end of the Cold War in 1989, much of the heat has gone out of the historiographical debate about the origins of the Cold War, and more-nuanced interpretations combining many of the above strands of analysis in more dispassionate ways have begun to emerge.

Growing tension represented a failure of the hopes that it would be possible to use the United Nations to ensure a new peaceful world order. Instead, it provided the setting, not the solution, for growing East-West tensions.

The United States came to play the key role in the West. After World War II, there was interest in the idea of a Western European "Third Force" independent of the United States and the USSR, and Britain and France signed the Treaty of Dunkirk to that effect in 1947. However, in response to growing fears about Soviet intentions, an American alliance appeared essential. In February 1947, the British acknowledged that they could no longer provide the military and economic aid necessary to keep Greece and Turkey out of Communist hands. Instead, the British successfully sought American intervention. Similarly, in 1949, the British encouraged the Americans to become involved in resisting Communist expansion in Southeast Asia: The French were under pressure in Indo-China, and the British in Malaya.

Concerned about communism, the Americans did not intend to repeat their isolationism of the 1930s, when they had not responded to the expansion of Germany and Japan. Since then, the American economy had expanded greatly, both in absolute and in relative terms, and it had the manufacturing capacity, organizational capability, and financial resources to meet the costs of new military commitments. A more assertive American line was apparent by 1948. The Berlin Crisis of 1948, in which the Soviets blockaded West Berlin, led to the stationing of American B-29 strategic bombers in Britain. In the event of war, they were intended to bomb the Soviet Union. The threat of the use of the atom bomb helped bring a solution to the crisis.

In 1949, the foundation of the North Atlantic Treaty Organization (NATO) created a security framework for Western Europe. The United States abandoned its tradition of isolationism, playing a crucial role in the formation of the new alliance and thereby anchoring the defense of Western Europe. An analysis of World War II that attributed the war and Hitler's initial successes to appeasement led to a determination to contain the USSR. The establishment of NATO was followed by the creation of a military structure, including a central command, and, eventually, by German rearmament. The Warsaw Pact represented the USSR's response in kind.

The Cold War that emerged was not a formal or frontal conflict, but a period of sustained hostility involving a protracted arms race, as well as numerous proxy conflicts in which the major powers intervened in other struggles. The latter sustained attitudes of animosity, exacerbated fears, and contributed to a high level of military preparedness. Cold War theorists of international relations concentrated on confrontation rather than conciliation, affecting both political and military leaders and the public.

MAD: The Nuclear Arms Race

Origins   A feeling of uncertainty on both sides, of military vulnerability, and of the fragility of international links, political systems, and ideological convic-

tions, encouraged a sense of threat and fueled an arms race that was to be central to the Cold War. Indeed, in many respects, the arms race *was* the Cold War. Both sides claimed to be strong but declared that they required an edge to be secure: This was the inherent instability of an arms race, where only the threat of mutually assured destruction (MAD) from massive nuclear stockpiles eventually brought a measure of stability.

The United States and the Soviet Union competed to produce and deploy more and better weapons. The Soviet Union initially lacked the atom bomb, but its army was well placed to overrun Western Europe and could only have been stopped by the American use of atom bombs. Thus, nuclear strength was central to containment.

However, the American nuclear monopoly lasted only until 1949, when the USSR completed its development of an effective bomb. This had required a formidable effort, as the USSR was economically devastated by World War II, but it was pursued because Stalin believed that only a position of nuclear equivalence would permit it to protect and advance its interests. However, such a policy was ruinous financially; harmful to the economy, as it led to the distortion of research and investment choices; and militarily dangerous, as resources were tapped that might otherwise have been used to develop conventional military capability. Britain, France, and China followed with their own atomic bombs in 1952, 1960, and 1964, respectively.

Stages of Competition   Nuclear competition went through a number of stages, driven by developing technologies and changing politics. As far as the first was concerned, the key was not the shift from atomic to hydrogen bombs, but rather the development of delivery systems—in particular, the shift from long-range bombers to missiles, both land- and submarine-based. In 1957, the USSR launched *Sputnik I,* the first satellite, into orbit. This revealed a capability for intercontinental rockets that brought the entire world within striking range, and thus made the United States vulnerable to Soviet attack, both first strike and counterstrike. In strategic terms, rockets threatened to give effect to the doctrine of airpower as a war-winning tool advanced in the 1920s and 1930s, even as they rendered obsolescent the nuclear capability of the bombers of the American Strategic Air Command, particularly the B-52s deployed in 1955.

The development of intercontinental missiles also altered the parameters of vulnerability and ensured

Nuclear Powered Submarine Such subs, armed with ICBMs and capable of operating submerged for months, formed one leg of the nuclear triad, along with land-based missiles and strategic bombers.

that space was more than ever seen in terms of straight lines between launch site and target. As Nikita Khrushchev, the Soviet leader, declared in August 1961, "We placed Gagarin and Titov in space, and we can replace them with bombs which can be diverted to any place on Earth." The threat to the United States from Soviet attack was highlighted by a 1957 secret report from the American Gaither Committee. The strategic possibilities offered by nuclear-tipped, long-range ballistic missiles made investment in expensive rocket technology seem an essential course of action, since these missiles could go so much faster than airplanes and, unlike them, could not be shot down.

The United States had also been developing long-range ballistic missiles, using captured German V-2 scientists, particularly Wernher von Braun and many of his team from Peenemünde, the Nazi rocketry research center. The attempt to give force to the notion of massive nuclear retaliation entailed replacing vulnerable manned bombers with less vulnerable submarines equipped with ballistic missiles and also with land rockets based in reinforced silos. The Americans fired their first intercontinental ballistic missile (ICBM) in 1958, and in July 1960, off Cape Canaveral (subsequently Cape Kennedy), the USS *George Washington* was responsible for the first successful underwater firing of a Polaris missile. In 1961, the Americans commissioned the USS *Ethan Allen,* the first true fleet missile submarine. Submarines could be based near the coast of target states and were highly mobile and hard to detect. They represented a major shift in force structure, away from the air force and toward the navy, which argued that its invulnerable submarines could launch carefully controlled strikes, permitting a more sophisticated management of deterrence and retaliation, an argument that was also to be made by the Royal Navy.

Other nations followed suit. In 1962, in what became known as the Nassau Agreement, John F. Kennedy, the American president, and Harold Macmillan, the British prime minister, decided that the Americans would provide Polaris missiles for a class of four large nuclear-powered British submarines that were to be built, although American agreement was dependent on the British force being primarily allocated for NATO duties. In 1968, the first British Polaris test missile was fired from HMS *Resolution,* the British navy's first nuclear-powered ballistic missile submarine, which had been laid down in 1964. The Polaris remained in service until 1995, when it was succeeded by the Trident. The French commissioned their first ballistic missile submarine in 1969.

Nuclear Strategy The inhibiting effect of the destructive potential of intercontinental nuclear weaponry served as much to enhance the possibility of a nuclear war, by increasing interest in defining a sphere for tactical nuclear weapons and in planning an effective strategic nuclear first strike, as it did to lessen the chance of a great-power war or to increase the probability that such a conflict would be essentially conventional. The risk of nuclear destruction, nevertheless, made it important to prevent escalation to full-scale war and thus encouraged interest in defining forms of warfare that could exist short of such escalation.

In the early 1960s, U.S. concern about the nuclear balance increased. John F. Kennedy had run his 1960 presidential campaign in part on the platform that the Republican administration under Eisenhower had failed to maintain America's defenses. Kennedy aimed for a strategic superiority over the Soviet Union and increased defense spending accordingly.

Concern about missiles rose to a peak during the Cuban Missile Crisis of 1962, when the Soviet Union deployed them in Cuba. These missiles had a range of 1040 nautical miles, which made Washington a potential target. The Soviet intention was to protect Cuba from American attack, although it also shifted the balance of terror in the Soviets' favor. The United States imposed an air and naval quarantine to prevent the shipping of further Soviet supplies, prepared for an attack on Cuba, and threatened a full retaliatory nuclear strike. The Cuban leaders, Fidel Castro and Che Guevara, wanted a nuclear war, which they saw as a way to forward world socialism. However, the Soviet Union backed down, withdrawing its missiles, while the United States withdrew its Jupiter missiles (which carried nuclear warheads) from Turkey and agreed not to invade Cuba. Possibly the threat of nuclear war encouraged the Americans and the Soviets to caution, although both sides had come close to hostilities.

In the 1960s, both the United States and the Soviet Union built up their missile forces. In 1965, Robert McNamara, the U.S. secretary of defense, asserted that the nation could rely on the threat of "assured destruction" to deter a Soviet assault. Thanks in part to submarines, there would be enough missiles to provide an American counterstrike in the event of the Soviets launching a surprise first strike and inflicting considerable damage.

The logic of deterrence, however, required matching any advance in the techniques of nuclear weaponry, and this was one of the most intense aspects of the Cold War. In 1970, the United States deployed Minuteman III missiles equipped with multiple independently targeted reentry vehicles (MIRVs), thus ensuring that the strike capacity of an individual rocket was greatly enhanced. This meant that any American counterstrike would be more effective. The United States also cut the response time of its land-based intercontinental missiles by developing the Titan II, which had storable liquid propellants enabling in-silo launches, which reduced launch time.

Meanwhile, the destructive power of nuclear weapons increased when the atomic bomb was followed by the hydrogen bomb. The United States first tested the H-bomb in 1952, destroying the Pacific island of Elugelab, and was followed by the Soviet Union in 1953, Britain in 1957, China in 1967, and France in 1968. The hydrogen bomb employed a fission explosion to heat hydrogen isotopes sufficiently to fuse them into helium atoms, a transformation that released an enormous amount of destructive energy, far greater than that produced by a fission explosion. The precision of guidance systems was also increased.

Nuclear confrontation did not lead to conflict, but both sides also prepared for conventional warfare, either as part of a nuclear war or separate from it. This preparation encouraged a major development in conventional capability, not least as a result of pressure to make infantry and artillery more mobile. This owed much to the Soviet concept of Deep Battle, which was pushed from the 1970s, and to the American response, AirLand Battle. Both emphasized an abandonment of static conceptions of warfare in favour of a maneuverist emphasis. The Soviets focused on planning for an invasion of Western Europe, while the Americans moved from static defenses to the idea of a mobile defense that was also capable of counterattack.

Détente Diplomacy   The American position in the 1970s was challenged by the Soviet response, part of the action-reaction cycle that was so integral to the missile race. The Soviets made major advances in the development of land-based intercontinental missiles, producing a situation in which war was seen as likely to lead to mutually assured destruction, as both sides appeared to have a secure second-strike capability. Since the end of the Cold War, declassified Warsaw Pact documents have revealed that the Soviets then planned a large-scale use of nuclear and chemical weapons at the outset of any attack on Western Europe.

With the weapons race having reached a dangerous stalemate, diplomacy again came to the fore. President Richard Nixon confronted the nuclear standoff in two ways. His trip to China in 1972 led to the opening of diplomatic relations, explicitly recognizing an altered balance of power with China as a potential third player and complicating Soviet security calculations. This gave him leverage to pursue détente, or a lessening of tensions and increased cooperation, with the USSR that resulted in the opening of negotiations and eventually a Strategic Arms Limitation Treaty (SALT) agreement that set the first caps on the number and type of warheads each country would deploy.

The rise to power in the Soviet Union in 1985 of Mikhail Gorbachev, a leader committed to reform at home and improved relations abroad, further defused tension. Gorbachev was willing to challenge the confrontational worldview outlined in KGB reports. For example, he was convinced that U.S. policy on arms control was not motivated by a hidden agenda of weakening the Soviet Union, and this encouraged him to negotiate. In 1987, the Soviet government accepted the Intermediate Nuclear Forces Treaty, which, in ending land-based missiles with ranges between 500 and 5000 kilometers, forced heavier cuts on the part of the Soviets while also setting up a system of verification through on-site inspection. In 1991, START I led to a major fall in the number of American and Soviet strategic nuclear warheads.

The Cold War: Conclusion and Costs   Ultimately, the costs of military confrontation, particularly in the early 1980s, won the Cold War by bankrupting the Soviet Union. When President Carter initiated a major military buildup in the late 1970s, a buildup continued by his successor, Ronald Reagan, the overstretched and inefficient Soviet economy could not respond. In contrast, the resilient American economy was able to underwrite deficit spending and permit the mobilization of American resources. New technology often grabbed the headlines in this process. Concern about the threat from ballistic missiles led to American interest in a "Star Wars" program, for example. Supposedly, this program would enable the Americans to dominate space, using space-mounted lasers to destroy Soviet satellites and missiles, though the system has never worked and, according to most scientists, could not work even in theory. Alongside developments in conventional nuclear warheads, there was also investigation of the prospect for different warheads. One pursued by the Americans was the hafnium bomb, which was seen as a way to produce a flood of high-energy gamma radiation. As the release of energy from the nuclei does not involve nuclear fission or fusion, such a bomb would not be defined as a nuclear weapon.

It was the sheer scale of the buildup, however, in both nuclear and conventional arms, that proved decisive, because so far there have been major problems implementing most of the technological dreams of the 1980s. Meanwhile, Gorbachev sought to modernize communism, but economic reform led to demands for political change. This led to the successive collapse of Communist regimes in Eastern Europe in 1989, a collapse achieved with little violence and without Western military intervention. The same was true two years later when the Soviet Union was dissolved as the former republics, such as Ukraine, gained independence. (The Chinese government, in contrast, has so far proved more adept at managing the strains of change.) The Cold War with the Soviet Union was over.

The Cold War imposed tremendous costs on both sides and on the global community, however, and a full assessment of the conflict must take account of these. The pressure of a globally conceived bipolar struggle complicated and distorted the diplomacy of both sides in Third World decolonization struggles and other regional conflicts, topics taken up further below. The compromises such complexity forced on national policy could be destructive, especially on the American side, of the country's political ideals: The United States supported many brutal, right-wing, authoritarian regimes simply because they proclaimed themselves "anti-Communist." More starkly, the humanist and social-democratic ideals of Marxism had little chance of expression in the Cold War environment, and communism in practice simply legitimized totalitarianism.

The struggle shaped culture, spawning paramilitary competition (the Space Race) and symbolic competition (Olympic sports medal counting). More destructively, the Cold War context proved conducive to the rise of a National Security State mentality that led in the United States to Red Scares, McCarthyism, and an atmosphere in which civil liberties were at constant risk of erosion in favor of vaguely defined security measures, a trend that has intensified in the struggle against an even more vaguely defined and potentially more pervasive threat of terror. The institutional instantiation of this culture was the growth of *military-industrial complexes:* the close partnership between defense contractors and government that raises the specter of artificially created permanent threats that justify continued defense appropriations at levels beyond what might be optimal. For another cost of the Cold War was the diversion of incalculable productive resources into ultimately sterile military hardware, though military research and development did occasionally produce benefits for civilian economies.

Finally, the Cold War arms race created a vast stockpile of nuclear, biological, and chemical weapons of mass destruction whose safekeeping and safe disposal remain an ongoing problem. Concerned about the acquisition of such weapons by "rogue states" such as North Korea, the United States seeks, in reviving "Star Wars" schemes, a technological means to ensure security, a difficult goal at the best of times. Here, too, a hangover effect of the Cold War, with its emphasis on technology and confrontational state-level politics, may complicate the search for peace in the post–Cold War world (see Chapter 30).

DECOLONIZATION

The leading colonial powers, Britain and France, were among the victors in World War II, but their empires largely disappeared within two decades, one of the most important shifts of power in global history. This owed much to their military, economic, and moral exhaustion, although American and Soviet hostility to colonialism were also important, as was nationalist ideology in the colonies. Many possessions were given up by the colonial powers after singularly little violence aimed at them—most obviously, as in the British withdrawal from India and Pakistan in 1947—but elsewhere there was conflict. For example, returning to Indonesia after the Japanese withdrawal, the Dutch were unable to suppress nationalist resistance in 1947, although, with the support of local allies, they did limit the extent of Java and Sumatra controlled by nationalists who had declared independence in 1945. However, post–World War II weakness, American anticolonial pressure, guerrilla warfare, and nationalist determination forced the Dutch to accept Indonesian independence in 1949.

The Cold War Meets Decolonization

For much of the world, decolonization was the key political and military issue of the third quarter of the twentieth century. As such, it was an issue that was closely intertwined with the Cold War. This was true both of the goals of conflict, on each side, and of the means, not least intervention by other powers. For

the imperial powers, these wars also posed the problem for imperial rulers of maintaining support, both at home (the metropoles) and in the colonies, as a key aspect of defeating insurrectionary forces. This did not prove an easy equation, but instead interacted with divisions in the metropoles over the goals that should be followed. There was opposition to the maintenance of control but also to concessions. This complexity of goals created serious strategic, operational, and tactical problems for the colonial powers. In particular, they faced the problem of crushing rebels while winning the hearts and minds of the colonial population, the latter an objective thrown into prominence by the extent to which insurgencies sapped the consent on which imperial rule rested. In turn, the insurgents had, at least in theory, a simple strategy. They sought to wear out the imperial powers and their supporters in the metropoles and the colonies, and to make the price of continued imperial rule too high to pay. In operational terms, there was also a rivalry between the conventional forces and tactics of the imperial powers and the irregular forces and guerrilla tactics of their opponents. Indeed, warfare was characterized by a high level of asymmetry, not least in the use of massive firepower, including airpower, against scattered targets.

After the burst of decolonization in the late 1940s, the early and mid-1950s saw a determined attempt to maintain imperial power. Although Britain and France had reduced their global commitments, they were ready to fight for what remained.

The biggest effort was made by France. This involved bitter conflicts against nationalist independence movements in Indo-China in 1946–54 and in Algeria in 1954–62. In Indo-China, the Chinese-supplied Viet Minh succeeded in 1954 in defeating the French in position warfare at Dien Bien Phu, a forward base developed across Viet Minh supply lines by French parachutists in order to lure the Viet Minh into a major battle. Thanks to their mass infantry attacks, the Viet Minh suffered more casualties, but the isolated French stronghold, denied air support due to artillery bombardment of the airstrip, fell after a fifty-five-day siege. Despite their superior weaponry, the poorly led French had finally proved unable to defeat their opponents in either guerrilla or conventional warfare. They abandoned Indo-China in 1954, and American concern about the consequences sowed the seeds for the subsequent Vietnam War.

WARS: EMPIRES, HOT SPOTS, AND PROXIES

Cold War Opener: The Chinese Civil War, 1946–49

The Chinese Civil War was probably the most significant "hot" conflict between 1945 and 1989, but it generally receives insufficient attention, in part because of a lack of research and in part due to a tendency to mythologize. The victory of the Communists over the Nationalists in this conflict has traditionally been approached in the light of the views of the former. It was presented, accordingly, as a victory of hearts and minds that indicated the apparently superior virtues of the Communists over the corrupt and incompetent Nationalists, as well as the strength of the Communist People's Liberation Army and its brave peasant fighters. There was a focus on the three-stage revolutionary war model of the Communist leader Mao Zedong: clandestine political-social organization (stage 1), guerrilla warfare (stage 2), and conventional operations (stage 3), and, in particular, of the idea of taking the countryside, with the cities then falling.

More recently, in contrast, a greater emphasis has been placed on what actually happened in the fighting. Until 1948, the Nationalists, indeed, largely held their own, but that year, the Communist switch to conventional yet mobile operations led to the isolation and then destruction of the Nationalist forces in Manchuria. Communist victory there led to a crucial shift in advantage: The Communists made major gains of matériel, and Manchuria also served as a base for raising supplies for operations elsewhere. In the Huai Hai campaign in the winter of 1948–49, the Nationalists suffered from maladroit generalship, including inadequate coordination of units and poor use of air support, and they were also hit by defections, an important factor in many civil wars. Much of the Nationalist force was encircled thanks to effective Communist envelopment methods, and it collapsed due to defections and combat losses.

Communist victories that winter opened the way to advances farther south, not least by enabling them to build up resources. The rapid overrunning of much of southern China testified not only to the potential speed of operations but also to the impact of military success in winning over support.

Cold War Hot Spots: The Korean War, 1950–53

The competing Great Powers went toe to toe in sensitive areas of the world, particularly East Asia and Central Europe. Confrontation led to preparations for conflict, and several disputes were characterized by brinkmanship. This was particularly true of the Soviet blockade of West Berlin in 1948 and 1949 and of the Cuban Missile Crisis of 1962. Tension was accentuated by the Soviet willingness to use force to maintain its interests within its own bloc—most prominently, by invading Hungary in 1956 and Czechoslovakia in 1968, in each case with large forces, and suppressing liberal dissent.

In these cases, brinkmanship did not lead to conflict, but in East Asia, warfare did break out in 1950, leading to the sole occasion during the Cold War in which the regular forces of major powers became engaged in hostilities with each other. At the close of World War II, in a partition of Korea, a hitherto united territory that had been conquered by Japan, northern Korea was occupied by Soviet forces, and southern Korea by the Americans. In 1948, each established authoritarian regimes. There was no historical foundation for this division, each regime had supporters across Korea, and both wished to govern the entire peninsula.

The regime in North Korea, whose military buildup was aided by the USSR, was convinced that its counterpart in the South was weak and could be overthrown, and was likely to be denied American support. The bitter rivalry between the two states included, from 1948, guerrilla operations in South Korea supported by the Communist North. In June 1950, the North launched a surprise invasion of the South, using Soviet-supplied tanks and airplanes. The South Koreans were pushed back, but enough units fought sufficiently well in their delaying actions during their retreat south to give time for the arrival of American troops. As with the South Vietnamese during the Vietnam War, the role of the South Koreans has been underrated in most accounts due to a focus on American operations.

Concerned about the consequences of the Chinese Civil War, the Americans were determined that the Communists should not be allowed further gains in East Asia. The North Korean invasion led to intervention by an American-led UN coalition that was determined to maintain policies of collective security and containment.

A Korean Girl With her brother on her back, a war-weary Korean girl trudges by a stalled M-26 tank at Haengju, Korea, June 9, 1951.

After almost being driven into the sea at the southern end of the peninsula in the first North Korean onslaught, the Americans and South Koreans, who successfully retained the Pusan perimeter there against attack, managed to rescue the situation in Operation Chromite. This daring landing on the Korean west coast at Inchon applied American force at a decisive point far north of the front. About 83,000 troops landed in difficult, heavily tidal waters and pressed on to capture nearby Seoul, choking off the supply line to North Korean units farther south. UN forces then drove the North Koreans toward the Chinese frontier.

The UN advance, however, was not welcome to the Chinese, who suddenly intervened, exploiting American overconfidence. The Chinese dictator Mao Zedong felt that UN support for Korean unification was a threat, while success in the Chinese Civil War had encouraged him to believe that American technological advantages, especially in airpower, could be countered, not least by determination. As the Japanese did before Pearl Harbor in World War II, however, he underestimated American resilience, resources, and fighting quality. Nevertheless, the Chinese, who proved better able to take advantage of the terrain, outmaneuvered the UN forces and drove them out of North Korea.

In response, Douglas MacArthur, the American commander of the UN forces, requested an expansion of the war to include a blockade of China, as well as permission to pursue opposing aircraft into Manchuria and attack their bases, and to employ Nationalist Chinese troops against the Chinese coast or in Korea. These proposals were rejected by the American Joint Chiefs of Staff as likely to lead to an escalation of the war, with the possibility of direct Soviet entry. MacArthur was dismissed. American restraint therefore helped ensure that the conflict did not become World War III or a nuclear war, and the war also served as an important introduction for American politicians to the complexities of limited warfare. For his part, Joseph Stalin did not wish to take the risk of formal Soviet entry.

During the war, the Chinese made the full transition to a conventional, modern army, with tanks, heavy artillery, and aircraft. The UN forces, however, were now a more formidable opponent than when the war started. The Chinese were fought to a standstill in 1951 as Chinese human-wave frontal attacks fell victim to American firepower. Thereafter, the war became far more static. As trench replaced maneuver warfare, the role of artillery became more important, while, as the defenses on both sides became stronger, the tendency toward a more fixed front line increased.

Atomic weaponry was not employed, despite pressure from MacArthur. However, in 1953, the use of the atom bomb was threatened by the United States in order to secure an end to the conflict. This encouraged the view that such weaponry was important in helping resist Communist incursions.

The Korean War played a major role in raising the tensions and rivalries of the Cold War. It underlined concern about Communist expansionism and ensured that the major issue became that of the means rather than the goal of containment. In the West, military expenditures rose markedly as a result. The extent to which so much of this spending was applied to advanced weaponry led to frequent references in the United States to a military-industrial complex. More than equipment, however, was involved. There was also a need for large numbers of troops in order to man the front lines of containment, and this meant that conscription was maintained or revived. Indeed, the effort required both to support containment and to maintain imperial control in colonies put a formidable strain on Britain and France.

Decolonization in the Islamic World: Algeria, 1954–62

As in Indo-China, the French were unsuccessful in Algeria, despite committing considerable resources. Their forces there rose from about 65,000 men in late 1954 to 390,000 in 1956, after first reservists and then conscripts were sent. The dispatch of both these groups was unpopular and greatly increased opposition to the conflict within France. Algeria, which was treated politically as if it were part of France rather than a colony, was dominated by *colons* (a settler population) of more than 1 million, and the 8.5 million native Muslims had no real power and suffered discrimination. An insurrection by the *Front de Libération Nationale* (FLN) began in October 1954, but at first, it was restricted to small-scale terror operations. These destabilized the French relationship with the indigenous Muslims. Loyalists were killed, while the French found it difficult to identify their opponents and alienated Muslims by ruthless search-and-destroy operations; relations between *colons* and Muslims also deteriorated. In 1955, the scale of FLN operations increased, and the war heated up with massacres, reprisals, and a commitment by the French to a more rigorous approach. This also led to more effective

French tactics. Static garrisons were complemented by pursuit groups, often transported by helicopter. In some respects, the Algerian War prefigured that in Vietnam involving the Americans. The FLN was badly damaged in 1959, just as the Viet Cong were to be in 1968, but the continued existence of both created pressure for a political solution. This helped to turn General Charles de Gaulle, who had formed a government in 1958 and become president of France that same year, against the *colons* and much of the military leadership in Algeria, both of whom were against negotiations with the FLN.

The struggle thus became closely involved with political tensions within the French side, while these tensions in turn became militarized. In 1960, the *colons* tried to seize power in Algiers but were faced down by de Gaulle. In early 1961, de Gaulle ordered a truce with the FLN, and an attempt by some of the army to seize power in Algeria was thwarted. The *Organisation Armée Secrète* (OAS) then began a terror campaign against both the Gaullists and the Muslims, including an unsuccessful attempt to assassinate de Gaulle. The resulting three-pronged struggle among the government, the OAS, and the FLN led to extensive slaughter in 1962 as independence neared.

The Algerian War illustrated the general difficulty of counterinsurgency at the tactical, operational, and strategic levels. Tough measures, including torture, which was seen as a response to FLN atrocities, gave the French control of the city of Algiers in 1957. However, although undefeated in battle, the French were unable to end guerrilla action in what was a very costly struggle. And French moves were often counterproductive in winning the loyalty of the bulk of the population. Aside from the difficulty of implementing active counterinsurgency policies, there was also a need to tie up large numbers of troops to protect settlers and try to close the frontiers to guerrilla reinforcements.

It is easy to see France's failure as one of imperial counterinsurgency, but it is important also to understand the degree to which this was a more widespread problem facing states—and moreover, one that continues. For example, after independence, FLN-ruled Algeria also failed to preserve the peace as it was unable to meet popular expectations and was perceived as corrupt. From 1992, Algeria returned to civil war, as the Islamic fundamentalists of the *Front Islamique du Salut* destabilized the state by widespread and brutal terror tactics. In turn, the government adopted the earlier techniques of the French, including helicopter-borne pursuit groups, large-scale

"The Things They Carried"

This exerpt from Vietnam veteran and author Tim O'Brien's award-winning short story "The Things They Carried" conveys some of the experience of the Vietnam War on the ground.

■ ■ ■

Other missions were more complicated and required special equipment. In mid-April, it was their mission to search out and destroy the elaborate tunnel complexes in the Than Khe area south of Chu Lai. To blow the tunnels, they carried one-pound blocks of pentrite high explosives, four blocks to a man, 68 pounds in all. They carried wiring, detonators, and battery-powered crackers. Dave Jensen carried earplugs. Most often, before blowing the tunnels, they were ordered by higher command to search them, which was considered bad news, but by and large they just shrugged and carried out orders. Because he was a big man, Henry Dobbins was excused from tunnel duty. The others would draw numbers. Before Lavender died there were 17 men in the platoon, and whoever drew the number 17 would strip off his gear and crawl in headfirst with a flashlight and Lieutenant Cross's .45-caliber pistol. The rest of them would fan out as security. They would sit down or kneel, not facing the hole, listening to the ground beneath them, imagining cobwebs and ghosts, whatever was down there—the tunnel walls squeezing in—how the flashlight seemed impossibly heavy in the hand and how it was tunnel vision in the very strictest sense, compression in all ways, even time, and how you had to wiggle in—ass and elbows—a swallowed-up feeling—and how you found yourself worrying about odd things: Will your flashlight go dead? Do rats carry rabies? If you screamed, how far would the sound carry? Would your buddies hear it? Would they have the courage to drag you out? In some respects, though not many, the waiting was worse than the tunnel itself. Imagination was a killer.

On April 16, when Lee Strunk drew the number 17, he laughed and muttered something and went down quickly. The morning was hot and very still. Not good, Kiowa said. He looked at the tunnel opening, then out across a dry paddy toward the village of Than Khe. Nothing moved. No clouds or birds or people. As they waited, the men smoked and drank Kool-Aid, not talking much, feeling sympathy for Lee Strunk but also feeling the luck of the draw. You win some, you lose some, said Mitchell Sanders, and sometimes you settle for a rain check. It was a tired line and no one laughed.

Henry Dobbins ate a tropical chocolate bar. Ted Lavender popped a tranquilizer and went off to pee.

---

sweep-and-search operations, and the use of terror as a reprisal.

It is therefore inherently misleading to see Western military and political structures and methods as at fault in the failures of counterinsurgency operations in the 1950s and 1960s. This is not least the case because there were successes, as with the British suppression of Communist opposition in Malaya and of the Mau-Mau uprising in Kenya. In each case, after initial problems, the British benefited from a mixture of gaining the initiative militarily and adopting social policies that restricted opposition support. The British, however, were far less successful in Aden (South Yemen). Tactics seen in Malaya in the 1950s were used, but the guerrillas of the National Liberation Front forced an abandonment of the interior in 1967. Reduced to holding on to the city of Aden, a base area that had also to be defended from internal disaffection, and where the garrison itself had to be protected, the sole initiative left was to abandon the position, which the British did in 1967.

Decolonization Meets Cold War: Vietnam, 1954–74

Vietnam had been partitioned after the withdrawal of the French in 1954. Vietnam's struggle had started as a nationalist, anticolonialist uprising: The Vietnamese Declaration of Independence was modeled on the United States' 1776 document. But American support

After five minutes, Lieutenant Jimmy Cross moved to the tunnel, leaned down, and examined the darkness. Trouble, he thought—a cave-in maybe. And then suddenly, without willing it, he was thinking about Martha. The stresses and fractures, the quick collapse, the two of them buried alive under all that weight. Dense, crushing love. Kneeling, watching the hole, he tried to concentrate on Lee Strunk and the war, all the dangers, but his love was too much for him, he felt paralyzed, he wanted to sleep inside her lungs and breathe her blood and be smothered. He wanted her to be a virgin and not a virgin, all at once. He wanted to know her. Intimate secrets: Why poetry? Why so sad? Why that grayness in her eyes? Why so alone? Not lonely, just alone riding her bike across campus or sitting off by herself in the cafeteria—even dancing, she danced alone—and it was the aloneness that filled him with love. He remembered telling her that one evening. How she nodded and looked away. And how, later, when he kissed her, she received the kiss without returning it, her eyes wide open, not afraid, not a virgin's eyes, just flat and uninvolved.

Lieutenant Cross gazed at the tunnel. But he was not there. He was buried with Martha under the white sand at the Jersey shore. They were pressed together, and the pebble in his mouth was her tongue. He was smiling. Vaguely, he was aware of how quiet the day was, the sullen paddies, yet he could not bring himself to worry about matters of security. He was beyond that. He was just a kid at war, in love. He was twenty-four years old. He couldn't help it.

A few moments later Lee Strunk crawled out of the tunnel. He came up grinning, filthy but alive. Lieutenant Cross nodded and closed his eyes while the others clapped Strunk on the back and made jokes about rising from the dead.

Worms, Rat Kiley said. Right out of the grave. Fuckin' zombie.

The men laughed. They all felt great relief.

Spook city, said Mitchell Sanders.

Lee Strunk made a funny ghost sound, a kind of moaning, yet very happy, and right then, when Strunk made that high happy moaning sound, when he went *Ahhooooo*, right then Ted Lavender was shot in the head on his way back from peeing. He lay with his mouth open. The teeth were broken. There was a swollen black bruise under his left eye. The cheekbone was gone. Oh shit, Rat Kiley said, the guy's dead. The guy's dead, he kept saying, which seemed profound—the guy's dead. I mean really.

SOURCE: Tim O'Brien, "The Things They Carried" (Boston: Houghton Mifflin, 1990).

---

for France brought Soviet and Chinese aid for nationalist leader Ho Chi Minh, and Marxist ideology came to dominate the independence movement. After 1954, the Communists controlled the North, and an American-supported government was established in South Vietnam. Faced with a Communist insurgency supported from North Vietnam, and concerned that failure would lead to the further spread of communism—the *domino theory*—the Americans committed troops, with numbers reaching a peak of 541,000 in January 1969. (See the Sources box "The Things They Carried" for a harrowing account of what these troops potentially faced.) American strategy, however, was wrongly based on the assumption that unacceptable losses could be inflicted on the North Vietnamese. But the North Vietnamese coercive political system gave individuals no choice in the matter, and the United States probably underestimated Vietnamese commitment to their cause. Instead, the Americans cracked first, after an inability to secure victory had resulted in an attrition that led to apparent stalemate.

Looked at differently, the Americans came to appreciate the consequences of limited war, namely that it could lead to failure. Subsequent debate as to whether total war, which with the technology of the period might have extended from unlimited bombing to the use of nuclear weapons, would have led to American victory, can only go so far. The intention was not to fight such a war, especially due to concern that it might lead the Chinese and Soviets to move from the provision of aid to the North Vietnamese to full-scale participation.

Furthermore, in the wider strategic sense, the concerns that had helped lead to American intervention had been assuaged. Far from the fall of South Vietnam leading to the collapse of the pro-Western position throughout Southeast Asia, it had only extended to Cambodia and Laos, both of which had been drawn into the Vietnam War as the result of the North Vietnamese use of their territory in order to support the war in the South, and American interventions in response. In contrast, Thailand, an important American ally, had not fallen. Instead, the overthrow in 1965–66, by the local military with CIA encouragement, of the anti-Western Indonesian leader Sukarno and the defeat of the Communist movement there, gave key strategic depth to containment. Furthermore, in the early-1970s, President Nixon exploited growing rivalry between China and the Soviet Union. This led not only to closer relations between the United States and China, which was a major strategic advantage, but also, by 1978–79, to conflict between China and North Vietnam, which was pro-Soviet.

The Cold War Meets the Guerrilla Age: Rebels and Proxies

Alongside large-scale conflict involving the regular forces of Western powers, there was also warfare at the interface of the Cold War and guerrilla struggles in which the role of the major powers was more indirect. In part, this was a matter of the use of proxies, as with the Soviet Union's deployment from the 1970s of Cuban forces in anti-Western causes in Africa, and the American use in the 1980s of Contras to destabilize the left-wing Sandinista government of Nicaragua. Far from being marginal, success in Africa in the 1970s gave many Soviets a renewed sense of pride in their own achievements and a conviction that the USSR could contribute decisively to breakthroughs for communism. In part, there was an atomization of the Cold War, with confused struggles that encompassed, for example, rivalry between Chinese-backed and Soviet-backed guerrilla forces in southern Africa.

The military analysis of these struggles, which became important in the 1970s and 1980s, especially in Africa and in Latin America, is complex, not least because of the limited amount of detailed research on the conflicts and the related difficulty of assessing effectiveness. The most important conclusion relates to the absence of any separate civilian and military

spheres. This ensured not only a high level of antisocietal violence, as with terrorism and massacres, but also the difficulty of grounding any "military" verdict in terms of the consent of the defeated. As a consequence, the continued supply of arms, money, and support by outside powers proved important. Thus, in Sudan, the government received Soviet weapons and advisors, as well as support from Egypt, in its conflict with black, non-Islamic southern separatists who, in the 1960s, were supported by Israel. When the flow of outside supplies ended, these struggles often became less bitter. This was noticeable in Central America and Angola with the end of the Cold War, although this cessation did not necessarily mean the coming of peace. Earlier, the struggle had reflected the changing chronology of the Cold War. From the mid-1960s, for example, it was clear to both Moscow and Washington that the focus for Cold War competition in Africa was shifting from North and Central to Southern Africa, in part because of the Marxist slant of many of that region's liberation movements.

Bad Neighbors: Regional Conventional Conflicts

Although the Cold War and decolonization serve as the two central narratives and explanations of conflict in this period, they certainly do not exhaust it, nor, more generally, the use of force. Instead, there was warfare between and within states, in some cases as a quasi-normal aspect of international relations and politics.

Wars Between States   As colonial rule receded, a series of conflicts erupted between states. Whether peaceful or not, decolonization immediately led to new international frontiers (where hitherto borders had often separated territories of the same colonial power) and to disputes. In South Asia, for example, the end of British rule led to wars between India and Pakistan in 1947, 1965, and 1971. Pakistan's defeat in the last ensured success for the rebellion in East Pakistan, which became independent as Bangladesh. Decolonization also ensured that earlier disputes that would have been limited by the strength and influence of the imperial powers, whether as participants or as arbiters, became more urgent. This led, for example, to war between Britain and Argentina over the Falkland Islands in 1982, with an Argentine invasion eventually totally defeated, while in 1974, a Turkish invasion led to the creation of the Turkish Republic of North Cyprus.

The Middle East, meanwhile, witnessed a series of wars between Israel and its Arab neighbors. The Arabs proved unwilling to accept the culmination of the Zionist movement in the form of an independent Israel, and this ensured a high level of tension in the region. Israel was able to establish its independence in the face of attacks by neighboring Arab states in 1948–49. In 1956, Israel attacked Egypt in concert with Britain and France, overrunning the Sinai Peninsula, but withdrew in the face of American and Soviet pressure. In 1967, rising regional tension led to a preemptive Israeli attack on Egypt and, as the war spread, to the conquest not only of the Sinai but also of the West Bank section of Jordan and the Golan Heights in Syria.

In 1973, in the Yom Kippur War, Egypt and Syria could neither inflict defeats on Israel in a surprise attack nor establish strong defensive positions that would lead to superpower mediation (see the Highlights box "High-Tempo War in the Cold War: The Yom Kippur War of 1973"). The United States tried to ease regional tensions and helped arrange a peace settlement between Egypt and Israel in 1979. However, Israel's determination to act as a regional power and its concern about instability on its borders led to its invasion of southern Lebanon in 1978; Syria had occupied much of the country in 1976. In 1982, the Israelis occupied southern Lebanon, advancing as far as Beirut, but it proved impossible to stabilize the situation there in Israel's interests, and the Israelis had to withdraw from the bulk of Lebanon in 1985.

The Iran-Iraq War of 1980–88 involved more combatants (probably over 2.5 million by 1988) and casualties (reportedly up to 1 million killed) than other conflicts of the period. Seeking to exploit the chaos following the overthrow of the shah and to gain both a favorable settlement of border disputes and regional hegemony, Saddam Hussein, the dictator of Iraq, who had used oil money to build up his military, attacked in 1980. However, his war aims were misconceived, in part because the nature of Iranian politics had been misread: Far from collapsing, the Iranian forces fought back, helped by an upsurge in patriotism. As with the Israelis in fighting Egypt in 1973, the Iraqis suffered from the extent to which their opponents' missiles destroyed planes and tanks. The opening mobile phase of the conflict was rapidly replaced by position warfare in which artillery was important to the struggle over front lines. This repeated the pattern of the Korean War and indicated the need to understand the persistence of tactical and operational stereotypes whatever the desire for movement and speed.

Sub-Saharan Africa, which has seen the most conflict over the past decade (surpassing the Middle East, which tends to excite most attention), was also the setting of much warfare over the previous half-century. For example, the Tanzanian invasion of neighboring Uganda in 1979 led to the overthrow of its murderous dictator Idi Amin. This campaign was typical of many in Africa. The fighting quality of the Ugandan army varied greatly, with elite units mounting a resistance that most of the demoralized army was unwilling to offer. Infantry played a significant role in the conflict, slowing the rate of the Tanzanian advance on Entebbe, the Ugandan capital, to around ten miles a day. Tactical mobility was crucial in clashes, helping ensure that light antitank weapons were used to destroy armored personnel carriers, which were largely road-bound. Libyan military intervention on behalf of Amin could not sway the struggle but, again, helped to locate it, at least in part, in terms of Cold War rivalries.

War Within States   Force was also used to maintain the cohesion of new states, suppressing regional separatism. For example, in Burma, a series of challenges led to a serious civil war in 1948–55; in 1959, the Moroccan army crushed a revolt by the Berbers in the Rif mountains; and in 1967–70, in one of the largest-scale conflicts of the decade, Nigeria defeated an attempt by the Ibo minority to create the state of Biafra.

This was the first major war in sub-Saharan Africa fought to a resolution with modern weapons in which all the commanders were African. The Biafrans, who fought a conventional war with front lines, had no answer to the airpower of their opponents and little response to their armored vehicles. After the initial stages of the conflict, they were also heavily outnumbered. Unlike the pro-Communist Viet Cong in South Vietnam during the Vietnam War, the Biafrans were rapidly cut off from foreign land links. The contrast was more widely important as the degree and effectiveness of foreign support were key elements in the success of insurgency movements and, more generally, of regional conflicts. The loss of foreign land links exacerbated the Biafran lack of food and military supplies. And anticipating later conflicts in Africa, the Nigerian government felt no hesitation in using starvation to help destroy the Ibos.

In many states, force became the norm in politics, and this was linked to the absence of stable democracy. Postcolonial states frequently lacked any practice of

HIGHLIGHTS

High-Tempo War in the Cold War: The Yom Kippur War of 1973

Tanks on the Golan Heights   Tank battles on the Golan Heights in 1973 took a heavy toll on both sides, affecting the postwar development of doctrine, especially on the Israeli side.

Suffering from an over-confidence similar to that which had affected the Arabs in 1967 and from a failure to appreciate intelligence of Arab preparations, the Israelis were unprepared for the attack launched on October 6. The weakly defended Israeli Bar Lev line on the east bank of the Suez Canal rapidly fell, while the Syrians broke the Israeli line on the Golan Heights. Furthermore, in responding to the Egyptian attack, the Israelis found it difficult to penetrate the integrated air defense missile system that the Egyptians had received from the Soviets. Meanwhile, east of the Suez Canal, the Egyptians repelled a series of Israeli counterattacks, inflicting serious damage on Israeli armor, which suffered from a doctrine that, based on the experience of 1967, exaggerated the effectiveness of tank attack and failed to provide adequate combined-arms capability, especially sufficient artillery support and mobile infantry. Israeli aircraft and tanks proved vulnerable to mobile ground-to-air and air-to-ground missiles and to Sagger antitank guided missiles.

The Israelis, nevertheless, were able to drive the Syrians back, advancing into Syria and repelling counterattacks. In response to Syrian pressure for help, the Egyptians changed their strategy and moved their armored reserve forward, attacking on October 14. This was a mistake, because the Israelis were strong in defense, especially as the Egyptians advanced beyond their anti-aircraft cover. In an attack that highlighted the deficiencies of Egyptian tactics, the Egyptians lost heavily. In turn, benefiting from this destruction of the Egyptian reserve, the Israelis attacked, exploiting the Egyptian failure to cover their entire front and, more generally, their limitations at maneuver warfare that resulted from an overly rigid command structure and a culture of command that inhibited initiative by local commanders. The Israelis managed a daring crossing of the Suez Canal where the Egyptians were weakest, encircling Egyptian forces before a ceasefire ended the war on October 24.

In the 1973 war, command skills were particularly tested by the need to adapt to the large-scale use of tanks. More seriously, Arab militaries lacked effective practices, especially information acquisition and management, unit cohesion, and command skills, while Israeli forces were more effective in using the initiative.

tolerance toward groups and regions that were outside the state hierarchy. In Syria, where the Baath Party seized power in a coup in 1963, the military was used to suppress revolts in the late 1970s and early 1980s. In turn, the use of state power in Syria and elsewhere encouraged a violent response. In Pakistan, the military, under General Ayub Khan, seized power in 1958, only to be replaced by another coup in 1969. Defeat by India in 1971 led to the return to civilian rule, but in 1977, another coup put General Zia ul-Haw in control. He retained it until killed in 1988 in an air crash, probably caused by a bomb. The army seized power again in 1999 under General Pervez Musharraf. This was not the sum total of military intervention in Pakistan, as army support for "constitutional coups" was also crucial. In Africa and Latin America, the list of military-backed coups and attempted coups is too lengthy to detail.

The role of politics, domestic and international, was generally central to the use of force, but the nature of the fighting varied, in large part depending on the interaction of the nature of the combatants with the geography in the war zone. Internal conflicts often deteriorated into brigandage, drug smuggling, and protection rackets, all of which were used by insurgent groups to fund their activities.

CONCLUSION

The Cold War is generally contrasted with World War II and discussed in terms of limited warfare, often with an emphasis on the brinkmanship seen in the Cuban Missile Crisis of 1962. However, this is a less-than-accurate account of the widespread nature of conflict, much of which deserves attention in light of the nature of warfare after the end of the Cold War. The variety of conflicts discussed in this chapter defy easy categorization or generalization about strategy, tactics, and political lessons. But any military history of the period needs to devote due weight to such struggles, which for those involved were often anything but limited. It is crucial, in these and other cases, to locate the fighting in its political contexts, domestic and international, as shifts in these helped explain much of the dynamic of conflict.

The end of the Cold War in 1989 brought the promise of a more peaceful world, expressed in peculiarly self-centered form in the United States as the potential for a "New World Order." But such hopes were rapidly dashed, and a welter of new conflicts continued to disturb the globe's peace. It is to these conflicts that we turn in Chapter 30.

SUGGESTED READINGS

Beckett, Ian. *Modern Insurgencies and Counter-Insurgencies.* London: Routledge, 2001. A wide-ranging and interesting look at the techniques of nonconventional warfare.

Black, Jeremy. *War Since 1945.* London: Reaktion, 2004. A clear introduction that looks not only at Cold War but also at non–Cold War topics.

Bregman, Ahron. *Israel's Wars, 1947–93.* London: Routledge, 2000. An excellent account, by a former Israeli army officer, that offers a first-rate introduction to conflicts and contexts.

Clayton, Anthony. *Frontiersmen: Warfare in Africa Since 1950.* London: Routledge, 1998. Effective, not least in explaining trends in the nature of conflict.

Lawrence, Mark Atwood. *Assuming the Burden: Europe and the American Commitment to War in Vietnam.* Berkeley: University of California Press, 2005. An insightful account of the diplomacy and elite decision making that moved the United States into a major role in a French colonial conflict.

Millett, Allan R. *Their War for Korea: American, Asian and European Combatants and Civilians, 1945–53.* Washington, DC: Brassey, 2002. A fascinating examination of the personal impact of the Korean War on the lives of individuals on all sides of the conflict.

Suri, Jeremi. *Power and Protest: Global Revolution and the Rise of Détente.* Cambridge: Harvard University Press, 2003. Complements Lawrence's book in examining the role of popular protest in shifting elite diplomatic priorities in the late 1960s.

Tucker, Spencer. *Vietnam.* Lexington: University Press of Kentocky, 1999. A reliable introduction by a former American army officer.

Westad, Odd. *The Global Cold War.* Cambridge: Cambridge University Press, 2005. An excellent recent synthesis on the global impact of the Cold War.

CHAPTER 30

Conflict and Culture: Warfare Since 1989

The end of the Cold War led to a moment of optimism about the end of war and the triumph of Western values. There was also talk of a peace dividend in the shape of major savings on military expenditure and a hope that these could be diverted into other fields. This optimism, however, proved short-lived. Indeed, confrontation and war were to be major themes of international relations in the 1990s and 2000s—in some respects, as much as, if not more so than, in the 1970s and 1980s.

The end of the Cold War did, however, bring changes to the patterns of conflict, or perhaps even more to the perception of what sorts of conflict mattered. This needs to be discussed within the interacting contexts of the changing world of modern warfare and the problems of assessment arising from the movement from history to current affairs. If we entered in Chapter 29 into the world of wars that took place within the living memory of many people, we enter now into the world of wars currently taking place and of potential future conflicts. This complicates the task of the historian in several ways. First, it is impossible to gain any historical perspective on current events. Second, the policy implications of historical analysis and judgment are immediate and likely to be much more hotly contested. In other words, the politics of historical interpretation—always an issue, but usually a fairly muted one in the study of the distant past—is unavoidable in discussion of contemporary affairs, and the importance of warfare in politics further highlights this problem.

Another way of saying this is that both contemporary warfare and its history are shaped by and help shape the cultures of the modern world, a theme that will run throughout this chapter.

CHANGING CONTEXTS

Warfare since 1989 has been conditioned by the changing political, economic, and cultural structures of global society (Figure 30.1). The contexts for conflict these structures have created show some continuities from the Cold War era, but they have also introduced significant differences as globalization in various forms has advanced. This, in turn, has spawned new forms of resistance to the distribution of gains and losses fostered by globalization. The complexity of conflict since 1989, involving more sorts of actors than just the states that dominated warfare in the previous century, reflects these changing contexts.

Political Contexts

Postcolonial Coloniality From one perspective, some conflicts can be seen as another stage of the wars of decolonization. In this case, however, the colonialism and the resistance it engendered was more complex than that of the Western imperial empires of the mid-twentieth century. The spread of nationalism, especially in conjunction with the growth of ethnically based identity politics (see "Cultural Contexts," below), led to attempts to challenge the smaller-scale empires that had developed from the midcentury, if not earlier. This could be seen most prominently in the Slovene and Croat challenge to the Serbian imperialism that underlay the state of Yugoslavia. It was also the case with the challenge to Ethiopian rule over Eritrea, which had followed the collapse of Italian influence in World War II.

Often, as a result, the new wars of decolonization entailed challenges to the territorial configuration of states inherited from 1945 or earlier. In essence, decolonization did not destroy imperial boundaries, which subsequently were maintained as the frontiers of newly independent states. This challenge to the existing boundaries was pronounced in the Balkans and the Horn of Africa but was also seen elsewhere. Thus, in the far-flung Indonesian archipelago, there were demands for independence from both East Timor and Aceh (in Sumatra),

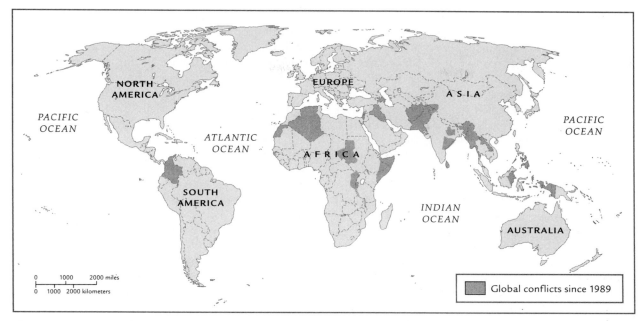

Figure 30.1 Global Conflicts Since 1989

demands that were resisted by the military and linked militia groups. This challenge was also seen in the habit of interventionism in other states, as with the dispatch of the forces of Rwanda and Uganda into Congo in the late 1990s, which helped ensure that the war there from 1998 to 2003 became the bloodiest single conflict since World War II. State borders inherited from old imperial boundaries that cut across perceived ethnic and tribal configurations contributed significantly to such interventions. This interventionism also reflected an overlap between international and domestic conflict. In some cases, it can be seen as an aspect of warfare; in some cases, of large-scale feuding; and in some cases, of politics.

Disputes between local peoples and states had often interacted with, first, the spread of Western imperialism and, subsequently, the Cold War, as the protagonists in the latter sought local allies. This pattern continued after the Cold War ended, with both sides in disputes seeking powerful supporters that could, in particular, offer political backing and provide arms, free or at a reasonable cost.

The End of the Cold War   A key political context, whatever the level of conflict, was provided by the end of the Cold War. The collapse of the Soviet Union destroyed the balancing element seen during the Cold War, because China's growing economic strength did not lead it to seek to balance the United States other than in South Asia where, for example, America's closer relations with India in the mid-2000s were countered by Chinese links with Pakistan—just as, in the 1970s, Soviet links with India had been countered by Chinese links with Pakistan, including the supply of arms. In the 2000s, growing Chinese interest in resources, in order to fuel and supply its economic growth, also led China into greater commitments in Africa, and it is possible that a more far-flung geopolitics of confrontation will develop. The end of the Cold War also led, on the other hand, to a major reduction in the strategic arsenals of the two leading nuclear powers, the United States and Russia. By 2010, they are each due to have only 1700–2000 deployed strategic warheads. Nevertheless, nuclear proliferation remains a pressing problem.

The end of the Cold War ensured that powers that had earlier looked to the Soviet Union to counter the United States and its allies found themselves newly vulnerable. This was true of Iraq under Saddam Hussein and of the Serbs. Without the Soviet collapse, it would have been difficult to ensure the outcomes of either of the Gulf Wars or of the eventual Serbian failure in the Bosnian (1995) and Kosovo (1999) crises. And this is a reminder of the need to put wars in their context. It is insufficient to compare, for example, American success against Iraq in 1991 and, initially, 2003 with earlier failure in Vietnam unless the very different opportunities created by Soviet collapse are considered as an aspect of the contrast. In 1991 and 2003, the context of Russian weakness was such that Russian backing for Saddam was insufficient to deter the Americans from attacking. These opportunities, however, were by no means the sole factor that was different from Vietnam nor, necessarily, the most important one.

The appearance of American hegemony encouraged a more assertive American position in regional conflicts. This was particularly marked in the Middle East, understood in the widest sense, for example, to include Somalia, but was also the case more generally. In Latin America, the United States continued the assertive stance it had displayed in Central America and the Caribbean in the 1980s, with a large force sent to Haiti in 1994. American assertiveness raises questions about multilateralism, the role of international political institutions such as the UN, and the possible speed with which the unilateral reach of U.S. power will exceed its grasp. For the U.S., economic dominance after 1989 was much less clear than it had been after 1945.

Economic Contexts

Global Inequalities and Resources The economic context was a matter, not simply of the wide range wealth levels created and sustained by global capitalism, but also the sense of grievance to which apparently different levels of opportunity and the uneven spread of economic development could give rise. The dominance in the post–Cold War world of Western, American-centered global economic institutions such as the International Monetary Fund and the World Bank sometimes exacerbated tensions. At the least, the wealth distributed as aid by these institutions and directly by rich countries to many developing countries often became a contested commodity within those countries, with the potential of heightening conflict over the state mechanisms that controlled distribution of the aid. That much aid ended up in the pockets of powerful political supporters of current regimes is neither surprising nor unproblematic. Developing country indebtedness also contributed to economic disparities and structural inequality.

One consequence of economic inequalities and tensions was migration, legal and illegal, from poor countries to rich ones by workers in search of jobs and other opportunities. This created or accentuated both concerns about social and cultural changes and a more general sense of flux that many found disorienting. Pressure on resources was massively increased by population growth. This continued to be a marked factor, especially in the Third World, and contributed strongly to environmental degradation, not least in the shape of pressures on water supplies and on land use. At the local level, much conflict resulted—for example, from disputes between new immigrant settlers who cleared land and created farms, and longer-established peoples who used the land less intensively.

Drug Economies Civil order is also under challenge in states threatened by large-scale criminality, especially when the latter is linked to violent political movements. A good example is Colombia where the radical guerrilla FARC movement partly funds itself by links to the large-scale drug trade. Concern about both drugs and radicalism has led the United States to provide aid to Colombia—over $4 billion in 2000–6, much to the army, with an annual level in 2006 of $600 million. As an instance, however, of the problems posed by drug wealth, some of the army units intended to fight drug trafficking were, in turn, linked to that drug traffic and its massive profits. There were similar problems elsewhere—for example, in Myanmar (Burma) and Afghanistan, where the War on Terror intersects uncomfortably with heroin trafficking, religion, and warlordism. It is important to recognize that the problem of drug-financed armed force depends not just on supply in poor countries but on demand in rich ones. Another "war," the long-standing American "War on Drugs," contributes to the profits of the drug trade by forcing drugs outside of government regulation into the hands of criminal gangs and the black market, much as Prohibition did with alcohol.

The Global Arms Trade The end of the Cold War from one perspective promised an era of reduced conflict and a "peace dividend." From the perspective of arms manufacturers (or, in Cold War terms, various military-industrial complexes), this was a threat rather than a promise. Unfortunately for the interests of peace, aggressive marketing on the part of manufacturers and militarized responses to new threats, both real and invented, on the part of many governments have kept the global arms trade booming, with

A Somali Fighter   Civil wars and other identerest conflicts, combined with the massive scale of the global arms trade, usually result in high levels of militarization of entire populations in areas of persistent conflict, blurring the line between armies and civilian society.

the United States stretching its lead as the world's top supplier of weaponry in the wake of the decline of Soviet/Russian arms manufacturing in terms of both quality and quantity. Ready access to weapons has stimulated and exacerbated the resort to force as a way of resolving many conflicts, a trend reinforced by developments in world political culture.

Cultural Contexts

The Warfare Paradigm   The semi-metaphorical application of the term "war" to government policy concerning drug trafficking and use—the War on Drugs noted above—highlights one aspect of the cultural context of conflict, the influence of the cultural emphasis on warfare as a model for dealing with problems. The *warfare paradigm* often overshadows alternate cultural lenses through which problems might be viewed—for instance, more cooperative notions of economic development, education, negotiation, and so forth. It thus contributes to the militarization of cultural perceptions of history, religion, ethnicity, and other contestable markers of cultural identity that form potential but not inevitable sources of armed conflict.

The influence of the warfare paradigm can be seen in the framing of long-standing political disputes. For example, in the Horn of Africa, there was a centuries-old rivalry between the Ethiopians who lived in the mountainous interior and the Eritreans and Somalis who lived on the coast, fueled by contrasting religious and ethnic constructions. In November 2006, the prime minister of Ethiopia called Islamists in Somalia a "clear and present danger" to Ethiopia, claiming they were being armed by Ethiopia's enemy Eritrea. In turn, the Somali Islamists met at Mogadishu and declared that they would defend Somalia against a "reckless and war-thirsty" Ethiopia. Both Eritrea and Ethiopia sent troops into Somalia. The warfare paradigm shaped foreign intervention in struggles such as this one: Possibly ten states had by November 2006 breached the UN arms embargo and sent munitions into the country, illustrating the intersection of the warfare paradigm with the global arms trade.

The problems created by the warfare paradigm have became more acute from 2001 as the United States' so-called War on Terror has led to an inter-pretation of local struggles in terms of alleged wider alignments and indeed with reference to what the American political scientist Samuel Huntington termed a "clash of civilizations" (see the Issues box "The 'Clash of Civilizations'"), which encouraged intervention elsewhere. For example, in Somalia in 2006, warlords' resistance to the Islamist attempt to capture Mogadishu was

ISSUES

The "Clash of Civilizations"

A clear example of the application of the warfare paradigm to current global policy analysis is Samuel Huntington's "Clash of Civilizations" thesis, which he first expounded in the influential journal *Foreign Affairs* and later expanded into a book. In it, he posits that there are five (or perhaps six or seven) major *civilizations*—areas united by common cultural characteristics. These include an East Asian "Confucian" civilization, a South Asian "Hindu" civilization, an Islamic civilization, and a liberal, democratic, modern "Western" civilization. He then posits that these civilizations, especially the latter two, are on an inevitable collision course based in an unbridgeable incompatibility of values, and that "the West" must be prepared to fight for its civilization by force.

The problems with this thesis are numerous and fundamental, and it would almost not be worth critiquing it were it not for the influence it has had on recent American policy making. As already noted, it falls into the trap of the warfare paradigm, in which differences must be settled by force, downplaying or ignoring possibilities for negotiation, accommodation, and compromise. The resort to force in this argument is justified by an essentialization of culture in the form of the hand-picked ideological features that supposedly characterize each civilization. This ignores the evidence that cultural identities are in fact multivalent, malleable, and constantly both constructed and contested, within as well as between what might be seen as large cultural areas. Such multiplicity of voices is

illustrated by, and the idea of a supposed rivalry between Islam and the West undermined by, the extent to which the victims of fundamentalist Islamic violence were principally other Muslims, as was made abundantly clear in the sectarian killings in Iraq after the overthrow of the Saddam Hussein regime in 2003. The essentialization of culture is further undermined if world history is read in an informed way, which shows again that cultural boundaries are permeable, negotiable, and often nonconfrontational.

The problem of relating all conflicts to a supposed clash of civilizations is demonstrated in the far south of Thailand where Muslim separatists are seen as resisting a pro-Western government. There are certainly cultural elements involved in a conflict that has been ongoing since 2004, with over 1700 people killed, but other elements are involved as well. Not only are the cultural factors more complex than the thesis allows, including the problems of absorbing a largely Malay-speaking Muslim people annexed in 1902 by a Thai-speaking Buddhist state, but the "cultural" issues are often actualized by issues of military brutality, which played a major role in the upsurge of tension in late 2004 when troops fired on demonstrators, as well as exploitation of potential conflicts by politicians and drug barons seeking their own local advantages. Ultimately, the "clash of civilizations" is an idea that seems designed not to analyze conflict but to foster it, which leads to the question, conflict for whose benefit?

---

covertly supported by the United States although, in the event, the capital fell that June. The warfare paradigm also shaped policies relating to preparation for war: The key example is that the Bush administration used the idea of a War on Terror to justify a major increase in American military expenditure. It rose from $276 billion in 1998, to $295 billion in 2000, to $310 billion in 2001. In February 2006, Bush proposed a defense budget of $439.3 billion.

Identerest Conflict   A second and vitally important cultural context for warfare since 1989 has been conceptions of ethnic identity. Indeed, so-called ethnic conflict has been at the heart of many armed struggles and has led to episodes of ethnic cleansing and genocide in the Balkans, Africa, and elsewhere. Understanding such episodes, however (and so having a better chance of preventing them), requires that ethnicity not be essentialized or taken as a primary and natural category of human identity that has always and inevitably led to armed strife. Groups certainly share cultures, but the fields of language, material culture, historical consciousness, and other markers of ethnicity never overlap perfectly and also intersect with other vital elements of personal identity including class, gender, and age (see the Sources box "Gender and Identity in Occupied Iraq"). Each category can create for individuals different political and social interests that are subject to manipulation by various leaders who have their own competing interests. And one of the constants in the world history of warfare, going back to the formation of hierarchical societies and the invention of warfare (see Chapter 1) is that warfare is potentially advantageous for leaders who wish to strengthen their position (and the elites who support strong leaders), even (or especially) when it is disadvantageous to the broader society.

Anthropologist Brian Ferguson thus proposes the category *identerest conflict*—that is, conflict brought about by the cultivation of particular forms of "ethnicized identity" by particular leaders and elite groups seeking to gain or increase their power—as a way of marking the constructed and nonessential nature of the cultural categories in such warfare. Identerest conflict can gain a momentum of its own and become an entrenched feature of local conflicts that transcends the influence of any particular leader. However, identerest conflict is always subject to deconstruction by counternarratives that stress different identities, interests, and histories. In fact, the global history of warfare also shows that conflict is by no means the norm between different cultures, peoples, or ethnicities, however the last is constructed. Understanding ethnic, or more properly identerest, conflict thus requires close attention to local cultural, economic and political dynamics.

PATTERNS OF CONFLICT

Types of Warfare

Types of warfare in this period appear to have shifted greatly because of the reconfiguration of American concerns after the Cold War and, in particular, as part of the War on Terror. The shift is probably greater in terms of expectations and focus than in practice, but it is real nonetheless.

Categories and Characteristics   We may identify five categories of the use of armed force in this period.

Most prominent from the perspective of the United States have been wars between strong states and weaker states, such as the two Iraq wars. Less noticed but somewhat more common have been wars between weaker, non-Western states on both sides. Wars in these two categories tend to conform most closely to Western expectations of conventional warfare that dominated pre-1989 thinking about military affairs. More common than either of these categories, however, have been intrastate conflicts, including civil wars, separatist movements, and other forms of internal strife. This sort of fighting has sometimes led to humanitarian/liberal interventionism and peacekeeping, which have been particularly prominent in European thought, although not only there. Finally, terrorism and antiterror operations have gained new prominence since September 2001.

Across all these categories, warfare since 1989 has shown several general characteristics. First, violence has tended to become more decentralized and diffuse, escaping somewhat from the confines of state control. While this has sometimes meant the restriction of violence to limited geographic areas, it has also created, in terrorism, the possibility for widely diffused but connected violence. This decentralization of violence represents a significant departure from the trend (at least in most state-level societies) toward state monopolization of violence and the means of coercion, a trend that has steadily differentiated war from a less-violent civilian world. This trend has created expectations that heighten the psychological impact of terrorism. In general, the decentralization of violence has blurred the lines between warfare, civil strife, and interpersonal violence; treating all of these manifestations of coercive force as warfare may reflect a problematic extension of the warfare paradigm discussed above, but it is difficult to avoid.

Second, warfare has tended, except in the case of some conventional wars between non-Western powers, toward some sort of asymmetry. That is, one side will often have a significant advantage in terms of technology and weaponry, numbers, organization, or some other attribute considered important in Western conceptions of conventional warfare. But the asymmetry almost always extends to goals and conceptions of war, so that the material asymmetry, or asymmetry of output, does not always lead to a favorable outcome for the apparently dominant power.

The third characteristic, the use of armed force since 1989, has tended to unconventionality, as measured by Western conceptions of "normal,"

SOURCES

Gender and Identity in Occupied Iraq

The following passages are from "Baghdad Burning," a "Girl blog from Iraq . . . let's talk war, politics and occupation."

■ ■ ■

Residents of Baghdad are systematically being pushed out of the city. Some families are waking up to find a Kalashnikov bullet and a letter in an envelope with the words "Leave your area or else." The culprits behind these attacks and threats are Sadr's followers—Mahdi Army. It's general knowledge, although no one dares say it out loud. In the last month we've had two different families staying with us in our house, after having to leave their neighborhoods due to death threats and attacks. It's not just Sunnis—it's Shia, Arabs, Kurds—most of the middle-class areas are being targeted by militias.

Other areas are being overrun by armed Islamists. The Americans have absolutely no control in these areas. Or maybe they simply don't want to control the areas because when there's a clash between Sadr's militia and another militia in a residential neighborhood, they surround the area and watch things happen.

Since the beginning of July, the men in our area have been patrolling the streets. Some of them patrol the rooftops and others sit quietly by the homemade road blocks we have on the major roads leading into the area. You cannot in any way rely on Americans or the government. You can only hope your family and friends will remain alive—not safe, not secure—just alive. That's good enough.

For me, June marked the first month I don't dare leave the house without a hijab, or headscarf. I don't wear a hijab usually, but it's no longer possible to drive around Baghdad without one. It's just not a good idea. (Take note that when I say "drive" I actually mean "sit in the back seat of the car"—I haven't driven for the longest time.)

Going around bare-headed in a car or in the street also puts the family members with you in danger. You risk hearing something you don't want to hear and then the father or the brother or cousin or uncle can't just sit by and let it happen. I haven't driven for the longest time. If you're a female, you risk being attacked.

---

state-to-state warfare. Opponents, tactics, strategic goals, and even funding sources have all periodically defied expectations, leading to major disappointments in the outcomes of the use of force by conventional forces. The insurgency in Iraq after the success of the Americans in the conventional phase of the second Iraq war is a prominent example of this. Unconventional and decentered warfare affected the nature of combatants, who were not usually regular troops or who were only regular insofar as the state had been annexed by some identerest group. But unconventional need not mean limited: The totality of war was underlined by the large-scale use of child soldiers—for example, by insurrectionary movements in Nepal (the Maoists) and Uganda, and by warlords in Liberia.

In practice, of course, these categories and characteristics of warfare overlap and intersect in a messy reality that is best appreciated by a survey of examples.

Varieties of Asymmetry   The dispatch of Western forces on humanitarian interventions and peacekeeping missions under NATO, European Union (EU), or UN auspices to a host of countries—including Afghanistan, Kosovo, Macedonia, Congo, and, in 2006, Lebanon—has been one factor leading to the emphasis in much discussion on asymmetrical warfare between technically advanced Western professional forces and less technically advanced non-Western forces who do not seek engagement in battle. This asymmetry includes not just this type of conflict but instead a range involving considerable variety in combatants, goals, and methods.

I look at my older clothes—the jeans and t-shirts and colorful skirts—and it's like I'm studying a wardrobe from another country, another lifetime. There was a time, a couple of years ago, when you could more or less wear what you wanted if you weren't going to a public place. If you were going to a friend's or relative's house, you could wear trousers and a shirt, or jeans, something you wouldn't ordinarily wear. We don't do that anymore because there's always that risk of getting stopped in the car and checked by one militia or another.

There are no laws that say we have to wear a hijab (yet), but there are the men in head-to-toe black and the turbans, the extremists and fanatics who were liberated by the occupation, and at some point, you tire of the defiance. You no longer want to be seen. I feel like the black or white scarf I fling haphazardly on my head as I walk out the door makes me invisible to a certain degree—it's easier to blend in with the masses shrouded in black. If you're a female, you don't want the attention—you don't want it from Iraqi police, you don't want it from the black-clad militia man, you don't want it from the American soldier. You don't want to be noticed or seen.

I have nothing against the hijab, of course, as long as it is being worn by choice. Many of my relatives and friends wear a headscarf. Most of them began wearing it after the war. It started out as a way to avoid trouble and undue attention, and now they just keep it on because it makes no sense to take it off. What is happening to the country?

I realized how common it had become only in mid-July when M., a childhood friend, came to say goodbye before leaving the country. She walked into the house, complaining of the heat and the roads, her brother following closely behind. It took me to the end of the visit for the peculiarity of the situation to hit me. She was getting ready to leave before the sun set, and she picked up the beige headscarf folded neatly by her side. As she told me about one of her neighbors being shot, she opened up the scarf with a flourish, set it on her head like a pro, and pinned it snuggly under her chin with the precision of a seasoned hijab-wearer. All this without a mirror—like she had done it a hundred times over . . . which would be fine, except that M. is Christian. If M. can wear one quietly—so can I.

SOURCE: Retrieved from *http://riverbendblog.blogspot.com/*

State forces facing insurrectionary movements and guerrilla operations—for example, the Naxalite resistance in India in the 2000s, or the Gam separatist movement in Aceh in Sumatra in 2003—found themselves facing an asymmetry every bit as difficult as the Israelis coping with the first Palestinian *intifada,* or rebellion, (1987–94) and its more violent sequel (2000–5) or the American and allied forces operating in Iraq and Afghanistan since 2003.

Furthermore, the variety in asymmetrical warfare is changing in response both to political developments and to those in military capability. For example, the challenge posed by the weaker side in such warfare is considerably enhanced when it can gain access to rocketry—relatively inexpensive missiles were used by Arab opponents in Lebanon and Gaza to threaten and attack Israel in the 2000s. This ensured that Israeli hopes of using fixed defenses, such as walls, to provide protection appeared otiose, although they were largely designed to provide checkpoints that would limit vulnerability to suicide bombers. Some asymmetries reflect older patterns of political conflict. For example, Operation Murambatsvina, launched in 2005 by Zimbabwe's dictator Robert Mugabe, involved the destruction of the homes or businesses of about 700,000 people. This is interest conflict, but by a state so controlling the means of force that the combat was one-sided. The same is true of the situation in Myanmar (Burma) where the army-ruled state uses force against minority peoples such as the Karens who defy its power.

Soldiers in Mosul
Soldiers of the Army's
101st Airborne Division
(Air Assault) fire a TOW
missile at a building in
Mosul, Iraq, in July 2003.
Urban warfare against
irregular forces proved
as hard for high-tech
U.S. forces as it has
throughout history.

Intra- and Substate Violence   On a different scale, although again indicating the role of ethnic or interest division as part of the reasons for internal conflict, it is pertinent to consider a part of the world that is generally omitted from military history—Oceania, the islands of the Pacific. They play a major role in discussions of conflict between Japan and the United States, in World War II, but are subsequently ignored. The situation in the region has become more unstable, however, as imperial presences have receded. Internal disputes over employment and other opportunities were exacerbated by economic problems, and the resulting disagreements led to a high level of tension in which violence became common and sapped any sense of security. The result was endemic strife, as in Papua New Guinea, where armed gangs of unemployed civilians challenged the social order. In the Soloman Islands, serious ethnic conflicts led to a coup in 2000, the year in which there was also an attempted coup in Fiji that included a bloody but unsuccessful army mutiny. In 2006, rioting and conflict between police and army led to a collapse of security in East Timor, while a coup occurred in Fiji. Paradoxically, this disorder led former imperial powers to send troops and police back into the region. In 2006, Australian and New Zealand troops and police were sent into East Timor, the Soloman Islands, and Tonga to try to preserve civil order.

This illustrates the overlap between politics, disorder, and civil conflict, an overlap also seen elsewhere. Thus, in Bangladesh, the two main political parties, the Bangladesh Nationalist Party and the Awami League, compete violently as well as electorally, with mob violence, strikes, targeted assassinations, and politicized judicial decisions all part of the process. This leads to the distribution of weapons, especially staves, which are used in street battles, while politicians wear bulletproof vests. This level of violence threatens to move from politics by other means to a subversion of politics, as in 2004 when the leader of the Bangladesh opposition was nearly killed by a grenade attack at an election rally.

Tactical, Strategic, and Logistical Implications   Tactics and strategy in this context could be genocidal, or at least linked to the destruction of the rival society by, for example, forced migration. A prime instance was that of the conflict in the Darfur region of Sudan from 2004 in which the Janjaweed, an Arab militia with, at the very least, the connivance of the government, attacked the black population, killing large numbers, destroying their settlements, seizing their livestock, and encouraging a flight of refugees into neighboring Chad, into which the conflict then spread. Large-scale rape was an integral part of the violent attack on the local society, as was the mutilation of women.

Conflict of this type, if small-scale, could, in part, be supported by looting and expropriation, but larger-scale sustained conflict posed supply problems, not least due to the logistical limitations of the combatant forces and the poverty of much of the land being contested. As a consequence, key funding was frequently supplied by the sale of raw materials that had international value. To that extent, these wars were an aspect of the global economy, as conflict so frequently was. Thus, in Angola in the 1990s, the civil war was largely supported on the government side by the sale of oil and on that of the rebel UNITA movement by the sale of diamonds. The latter was also important in the conflicts in Liberia and Sierra Leone in West Africa in the 2000s. There, the overlap between violence and criminality was readily apparent.

Issues

Ethnicity and Identerest Conflict   Seeing ethnically focused identerest division as one of the biggest causes of conflict provides a way to consider both the international relations and the warfare of the period. Again, it is important to bear in mind the malleability of constructions of ethnicity, which can include elements of religious sectarianism, language, and material and moral culture. Often, these elements are synthesized in accounts of the putatively shared history of a group. In other words, history continues to be a vital subject, since shared perceptions of the past shape the options a group will consider for its future, and manipulation of history is a central tool of those who foster particular identities for particular (often material) interests.

Much identerest conflict was at the substate level. In Indonesia, the 1990s brought a strengthening of ethnic tension and regional consciousness, with widespread violence. Thus, in Kalimantan (Indonesian Borneo), from 1997, native Dayaks fought Madurans who had immigrated beginning in the 1950s, in part with government encouragement: Thinking of Indonesia as a unit, the government sought to move people from areas of overcrowding without the consent of the population in the receiving areas. Adding to the horror of this conflict, beheading played a major role in the violence: It was important in traditional Dayak culture, seen as the way to win favorable magic. Its persistence was encouraged by culturally framed conflict, but in Indonesia, as in many other states, ethnic rivalry was linked to tension over material resources, particularly land and jobs. Across much of the world, similar conflicts over power and economics were shaped and expressed in local terms of ethnicity and religion.

Ethnic Rivalry and the Great Powers   Ethnic tensions were sometimes treated as an instance of the allegedly primitive nature of Third World politics, but it is important to note that the Great Powers were sometimes complicit in fostering identerest conflict. This was particularly true of France and the genocide in Rwanda in 1994, in which about 937,000 Tutsis were slaughtered—the figure may have been over 1 million, one in seven of the population. French policy reflected the misplaced conviction that the Anglo-Saxons represented a threat to Françafrique, a zone seen by the French as including former Belgian colonies including Rwanda and Congo. Indeed, France and Belgium had intervened in Congo in 1978 in support of the brutal and authoritarian Mobutu government.

Rwanda was divided, with the Hutu-dominated government close to France while many Tutsis took refuge in Uganda. There, in an example of the interrelationship of struggles in different states, the Tutsi Rwandan Patriotic Front (RPF) fought with Ugandans under Yoweri Museveni against the dictators Idi Amin and Milton Obote. After Museveni won, the RPF had his support when they invaded Rwanda in 1990. When they did well against the Rwandan army (FAR), the French saw the RPF as an Anglo-Saxon-backed Ugandan army and sent troops to help the Hutu regime. Large amounts of arms were sent to the FAR, which was put under effective French control. The French proved willing to encourage the Hutus to slaughter the Tutsis, including direct assistance in the genocide launched in 1994, as well as in earlier killings. This genocide was a response to the killing of the Rwandan president, which led to a renewal of the conflict between the RPF and the government that had been ended by an agreement in 1993, as well as the genocide, which the UN did little to stop.

The ably commanded and well-disciplined RPF was subsequently able to overthrow the Hutu regime, but the French government then sent their military to help their allies take refuge in camps at Goma in Congo. Their presence there helped accelerate the crisis in Congo. Yet again, it proved impossible to

The Second Iraq War

In the case of Iraq, U.S. concern about prolifera-tion to the benefit of a hostile regime provided the pretext for war in 2003, though misperceptions or even apparently deliberate exaggeration and de-ception on the part of the Bush administration make it difficult to assess their true motivations for the invasion. Cultural misperception seems to have dominated on both sides. The Iraqi dictator Saddam Hussein appears to have believed that the United States would not invade and that, even if they did, the problems of urban warfare would lessen American technological advantages and lead to casualties that would oblige the American government to change policy—an analysis that certainly was mistaken in the short term. In any event, Saddam could not prevent conquest by a well-organized, high-tempo, American-dominated invasion force. Similarly, Saddam's hope that inter-national pressure, particularly from France and Russia via the United Nations, would prevent the Americans from acting proved an inaccurate read-ing of the dynamics of contemporary international relations.

The coherence of Saddam's regime, its ability to intimidate the population, and the possibility of exploiting American vulnerability along their long lines of advance and supply were all undermined by the tempo of American attacks. This accentu-ated weaknesses in the regime, including its fear of the Iraqi military and concern about the possibility of its mounting a coup. Much of the Republican Guard ran away in the face of American firepower; U.S. airpower proved particularly effective. Units that redeployed or that stood and fought were pul-verized, with particular U.S. effort being devoted to destroying Iraqi armor. Once they had closed on Baghdad, the Americans launched "thunder runs," armored thrusts into the city demonstrating that their opponents could not prevent these ad-vances and therefore undermining their position. The Americans thus demonstrated that maneuver warfare could work in an urban context. Having captured Baghdad, the Americans pressed on to overrun the rest of Iraq. British forces played an important supporting role in the conquest of southern Iraq.

There were, however, indications in the con-quest that the military situation would be less pro-pitious in the long term. The Iraqi attacks on supply lines—for example, at the Euphrates bridge-town

isolate conflict, and Rwandan and Ugandan inter-vention against the Hutus in Congo led to the over-throw of the Mobutu government there in 1997. Thus, the cultural perceptions of French and African actors in this conflict interacted in disastrous ways.

Proliferation and WMDs Many non-Western states sought to develop an advanced military capabil-ity in the shape of weapons of mass destruction and related delivery systems. Although the regular forces of states such as North Korea and Iran probably lack the capability in defense to defeat the conventional forces of stronger powers, which in this case means the United States, and certainly could not stage an effective offen-sive war, such weapons would enable them to threaten these forces, including the American troops in South Korea, and, perhaps even eventually, home territory.

In the aftermath of the September 11 attacks, allowing this capability seemed particularly undesirable to U.S. policy makers. The National Security Strategy (NSS) issued in September 2002 pressed the need for preemptive strikes in response to what were seen as the dual threats of terrorism and rogue states possessing or developing weapons of mass destruction. Thus, it sought to transform the global political order so as to lessen the chance of these threats developing. The end of the Cold War was linked to the new challenge, and the NSS proposed the global extension of American values as the answer:

The great struggles of the twentieth century between liberty and totalitarianism ended with a decisive victory for the forces of freedom. . . . These values of freedom are right and true for every person, in every society—

of Nasiriya—attracted considerable media attention, but the forces available for such attacks were a local irritant that could be bypassed on the drive to Baghdad, rather than being operationally significant. The use of Fedayeen irregulars, some of whom fought vigorously, led, however, to somewhat naïve complaints about such tactics as disguised or faked surrenders. Both tactically and operationally, this resistance prefigured the problems that were to become more acute after it proved impossible to stabilize Iraq. Far, therefore, from proving inconsequential, as it seemed in the short term, the resistance indicated the mistake in assuming a top-down approach to the situation in which the "decapitation" of the Iraqi leadership (and overrunning of the capital) would ensure that the tempo of success could be sustained.

Instead, ham-handed American policy at the local level and a critically insufficient number of troops to secure order in the immediate aftermath of the invasion exacerbated and inflamed identerest divides in Iraq, including Shia-Sunni rivalry and Arab-Kurdish hostility, which helped wreck chances of a peaceful transition after the overthrow of Saddam Hussein. The forces at the disposal of sectarian groups challenged the divided and poorly disciplined Iraqi army. This was particularly true of the Mahdi forces of the radical Shia cleric Muqtada al-Sadr. Bush administration failure to understand the culture of Iraqi politics thus played a crucial role in turning apparent success into a serious, ongoing problem.

Rapid initial American success in Iraq in 2003 at first led to talk of pressing on to attack other states that harbored terrorists and possibly were developing weapons of mass destruction, particularly Iran and Syria. However, it is more likely that the American failure to restore order in Iraq and the costs of that commitment—which by March 2007 had gone over $500 billion, at a rate of $275 million per day, not to mention almost 4000 U.S. dead, over 60,000 U.S. wounded, at least 700,000 Iraqi dead, and another 4 million displaced as refugees—will foster a measure of caution and lead to a reaction against interventionism, at least insofar as the use of land forces is concerned. Indeed, talk in 2006 about possible action against Iran, which owed much to concern about Iran's nuclear ambitions, focused on air strikes.

and the duty of protecting these values against their enemies is the common calling of freedom-loving people across the globe and across the ages. . . . We will extend the peace by encouraging free and open societies on every continent.

Concern about proliferation, however, proved selective, as the West was more worried about Iraq (see the Highlights box "The Second Iraq War"), Iran, and North Korea than India and Pakistan, both of which have developed nuclear weaponry and missile delivery systems. India first tested the atomic bomb in 1974, and Pakistan followed suit in 1998. America's willingness to breach the Nuclear Non-Proliferation Treaty by agreeing in 2006 to support India's nuclear activities was directed by expediency—the search for allies, concern about China, and the desire for contracts—but it represented a fundamental breach in the practice of international cooperation against proliferation.

Varieties of Strategic Culture   It is important to see military capability and action not solely in terms of the United States, rogue states, ethnic groups, and terrorists. It is also appropriate to consider other major powers, albeit those that lacked the hegemonic position of the United States. A number of other states displayed, developed, or claimed force projection capabilities. For instance, the chief of the Russian General Staff declared in September 2004 that Russia could deliver preventive strikes on terrorist bases anywhere in the world. Britain played a major role in projecting force into Sierra Leone in 2000, Iraq in 2003, and Afghanistan in 2006; while France did likewise in Ivory Coast in 2002, continuing their postcolonial practice of intervening in former colonies in Africa.

China, in contrast, benefited greatly from economic growth in the 1990s and 2000s but did not seek distant force projection. Instead, China concentrated on enhancing its short-range projection capability, thus matching the military consequences of Japan's economic growth in the 1970s and 1980s. Indeed, the contrast between, on the one hand, the force structures and doctrines of China and, on the other, those of Britain and France indicates the role of politics and strategic culture in shaping military capability and tasks.

War and State Power   The large majority of states in the world are neither leading military powers nor rogue states. In many—especially, but not only, in postindependence Latin America, sub-Saharan Africa, and Oceania—the prime purpose of the military is internal control, with the army in particular serving as the arm of the state. However, force as a tool of internal control is an uncertain weapon, as likely to inflame resistance as to suppress it. The connection between war and state power need not be so overt, however. The War on Terror, as practiced by the Bush administration, has entailed not just the extension or the distortion of U.S. policy in favor of military-industrial complexes that now extend their reach into military contracting and postwar reconstruction, exemplified most infamously by the role of Halliburton in Iraq; arguably, it also includes the threat to constitutional government and the rule of law, justified by "wartime necessity," posed by extensions of state power into the lives of its citizens. Curtailed civil liberties, domestic spying, close control (and even manufacturing) of news about war, and claims that the presidency is in key respects above the law have been the consistent results of a culture of wartime emergency that, in a war against as nebulous a foe as terrorism, has the potential to be never-ending. Here the warfare paradigm extends ominously into the heart of democratic culture.

PRACTICES OF WARFARE

The Revolution in Military Affairs

By underlining the variety of states involved in military activity, it is easier to understand why recent conventional warfare has been far from uniform. In particular, it is clear that the notion of a Revolution in Military Affairs (RMA), which was much pushed by American commentators in the 1990s and early 2000s, is of limited validity.

The RMA had its origins in earlier military issues and developments. It owed much to the doctrine of mobile battle and the related weaponry that developed in American thinking from the late 1970s in response both to the Soviet doctrine of deep battle and to the need to be able to fight a conventional war in Europe. The RMA can indeed be seen as an alternative to Armageddon: an attempt to create a winnable option for nonnuclear or subnuclear war. The roots of the RMA are therefore in the late Cold War. In particular, from the American concept of AirLand Battle and the Soviet idea of a military-technological revolution, thinkers on both sides were considering ways to change radically the way main battles are fought, and so to gain an edge. They interpreted their own thinking as meaning that a revolution was happening (or could be forced) and that, by adjusting to this revolution, they could improve their relative position.

That this doctrine and weaponry were, in the event, to be used most prominently in the Iraq Wars of 1991 and 2003 creates a post–Cold War impression for the timing and tasking of this warfare. But the reality, instead, is of a delayed application of Cold War military ideas. This is also true, for example, of guided aerial munitions, which, in fact, were used from the Vietnam War, and of cruise missiles, which were deployed in Europe from 1983.

Thus, the RMA, as conventionally understood, actually describes the improvement, or modernization in terms of technological possibilities, of World War II/early–Cold War systems, within a tasking driven by competitive pressures, both those of the late Cold War and those subsequent to it. In particular, for the United States, this entailed a response to the enhancement offered by electronics for weapon's and systems' characteristics, in order to confront the scenarios posed by successive challenges from the Communist powers, and within the context of a willingness, and in the 1980s even an eagerness, to spend the money to face the challenge. This indeed was crucial to the Reaganite claim to be resolute against communism and to be winning the Cold War.

The resulting capability was shaped by commentators into an RMA in the very different context of post–Cold War pressures and priorities, especially the need to provide for power projection as well as the call for "transformation" so as to move from a Cold War military to a more varied successor. Requirements and possibilities put the emphasis on a multipurpose and joint, or integrated, military, while leaving specific tasks less clear. As a consequence, the capabilities of weapons and organizations seemed key to success, as both means and goal, and thus the RMA could be proclaimed both process and result.

Broader requirements were also served by this creation of a belief that total victory can be ensured through a specific type of high-intensity conflict, the type allegedly made possible by the RMA or, looked at differently, the type that had to occur were the RMA to be practicable. These tasks and assumptions can be discussed, without any suggestion of prioritization, in terms of liberal internationalism, the particular requirements of American foreign policy, and the growing disjuncture between highly ambitious Western goals and a widespread reluctance to risk casualties. Liberal internationalism became part of the new world order that followed the collapse of the Soviet Union with the argument, fed in particular by the atrocities in Rwanda in 1994 and Bosnia in 1995, that there was a duty to intervene in order to prevent humanitarian disasters. Such intervention, however, presupposed that success could be readily obtained, and belief in this intervention relied on the notion of a clear capability gap between the two sides. Indeed, from the humanitarian perspective, the forces of good had to be swiftly successful in order to avoid the suffering that would result from a difficult conquest. This concept helped explain the difficulties faced by Anglo-American representatives when they discussed massive Iraqi civilian casualties during and after the war of 2003.

From the perspective of American foreign policy, the RMA also explained how policy goals could be fulfilled, as this policy rested in part on a military underpinning, and in particular on how best to forestall threats. The need to be able to respond to more than one threat simultaneously was regarded as especially important by American strategists, and the force multiplication apparently offered by the RMA was especially important in this context. In short, the RMA made American foreign policy possible: It contributed not only to strategic concerns but also to foreign policy interests around the world. Looked at more critically, the RMA aided in a militarization of this policy in which, furthermore, the views of allies were of limited significance. The same approach could be adopted to the policies of Israel, or indeed to the radical Islamic opponents of the United States and Israel, with the RMA in this case seen as residing in varied combinations of weapons of mass destruction and terrorist tactics.

It is also necessary to consider the extent to which the American RMA was the necessary product of the RAM (Revolution in Attitudes to the Military), in the shape of the greater reluctance to take casualties. This was true both in specifics and in generalities. In specific terms, for example, American concern about the impact on morale of having aircrew shot down and taken prisoner in the Vietnam War helped encourage an interest in standoff weaponry: guided missiles and bombs fired from a distance.

The RMA linked developments in weapon systems with a doctrine that meshed with theories of modernization that rest on the adoption of technological systems. The cause of American belief in the RMA is instructive. The RMA met the need to believe in the possibility of high-intensity conflict and of total victory, appeared to counter the threats posed by the spread among rivals of earlier technologies and their development of new ones, and seemed to give substance to the possibility of reordering the world by overthrowing or intimidating rogue states and by spreading democracy.

Integral to the RMA was a number of concepts with a common focus on "smart" doctrine and on operational planning and practice designed to take advantage of a new generation of weapons and the possibilities posed by advances in information technology. The emphasis on precise information as a tool of conflict related to being able to locate forces accurately, thus overcoming the friction of war, and then destroy enemy units with semi-automated weapons. Accurate targeting is required if precision weaponry is to be effective, and this led to the goal of information dominance in order to deny the capability for accurate targeting to opponents. The RMA also called for network-centric warfare. This entailed a highly integrated and digitally linked information system stemming from a realization of the new capability of information systems, rather than the traditional, platform-centric practices and structures of command and control. In the language of the RMA, weaponry was designed to ensure what were termed dominant-maneuver, precision engagements, full-dimensional protection, focused logistics, and information warfare. All of these were seen as desirable goals and methods of future military structures and particular organizational forms. Joint operations were seen as crucial to the war of maneuver that was advocated and as stemming from the interest of all services in deep battle.

A Harpoon Missile Launched from Shipboard   Cruise missile technology offers flexibility in terms of launch platforms.

Belief in the RMA played a major role in American attitudes during the Gulf War of 2003. Iraq offered a definite and defiant target with regular armed forces, rather than more intangible terrorist opponents. The American attack indeed indicated the technological proficiency of its military and its skill in regular warfare. Particular use was made in 2003 of Joint Direct Attack Munitions, which used Global Positioning Systems (GPS) to make conventional bombs act as satellite-guided weapons. Effective use was also made of unmanned aerial weapons.

A prime element of debate before the campaign related to the number of troops required for a successful invasion. The secretary of defense, Donald Rumsfeld, and other nonmilitary commentators, had been encouraged by the rapid overthrow of the Taliban regime in Afghanistan in 2001 to argue that airpower and special forces were the prime requirements, and that the large number of troops pressed for by the army leadership, both for the invasion and for subsequent occupation, was excessive. In the event, too few troops were dispatched, in large part because the difficulty of securing support within Iraq had been underrated, and there was totally inadequate preparation for postwar disorder.

The subsequent crisis in Iraq cast serious doubts on the RMA and, in doing so, underlined the limits of technology. Furthermore, the situation exemplified the degree to which technological output should not be equated with political outcome. Output had been enhanced by military developments, not least those in airpower, ensuring that individual weapons could achieve far more destruction, and more precisely so, than their predecessors. This was exemplified in the case of the cruise missile. But enhanced output did not guarantee a favorable outcome, and indeed, by distancing military American personnel from both their battlefield opponents and, inevitably, the civilian population, probably contributed to policy failure.

Modern Weaponry

Cruise Missiles   Cruise missiles represented a key gain in military capability from the 1980s and were important to military planning both in the final stage of the Cold War and in post–Cold War warfare. These missiles were valuable because they could deliver precise firepower without the risks and limitations associated with airpower. In their planning for conflict with the Soviet Union in the 1980s, the United States intended to respond to any attack by using cruise missiles to inflict heavy damage on advancing Soviet armor. These missiles can carry conventional warheads or use tactical nuclear weaponry. And they can be fired in all weathers and can be launched from a variety of platforms.

The Soviet Union also developed such weaponry, but the arms race reflected the advantage the West enjoyed in electronic engineering, as well as higher growth rates and more flexible economic processes than those in the Soviet Union. However, for some time, the Soviet belief in the apparently inevitably insoluble contradictions of Western capitalism ensured that they failed to appreciate the mounting crises their own economy, society, and political system were facing.

In the Gulf War of 1991, both cruise missiles and precision-guided bombs were employed by the United States, although tactical nuclear warheads were not employed. At that stage, cruise weaponry had a crucial advantage over airpower due to the minimal extent to which the United States used precision-guided munitions. Some 9300 precision-guided munitions were dropped in that war, but most American aircraft were not equipped, or their pilots trained, for their use and, instead, employed unguided munitions, which made up 90 percent of the aerial munitions used. This was despite the extensive and effective use of precision-guided munitions in the Linebacker I and II campaigns in Vietnam in 1972. The flexibility of cruise missiles was such that they could be launched from land, sea, and air. Thus, in 1991, the battleship USS *Wisconsin* was converted to ensure that it could launch missiles as well as fire guns.

Subsequently, the United States fired seventy-nine sea-launched cruise missiles at terrorist targets in Afghanistan and Sudan in 1998, an impressive display of force, but not one that stopped the terrorists. Indeed, Osama bin Laden was able to raise funds by selling missiles that did not detonate to the Chinese, who were interested in cutting-edge American military technology.

Cruise missiles were also used against Serbia in 1999 as part of a combined NATO air and missile assault designed to ensure that Serb forces withdrew from Kosovo. In 1998, the submarine HMS *Splendid* achieved Britain's first firing of a cruise missile, which had been bought from the United States. The following year, the *Splendid* fired cruise missiles at Serb targets in Kosovo as part of NATO operations there. During the attack on the Taliban regime in Afghanistan

in 2001, cruise missiles were fired from warships in the Arabian Sea. By then, air attack capabilities had improved as the availability of dual-mode, laser, and GPS guidance for bombs increased the degree of precision available.

Other states also developed cruise missile capacity. In 2004, Australia announced that it would spend up to $450 million on air-launched cruise missiles with a range of at least 250 kilometers. The same year, there was speculation that a Chinese invasion of Taiwan would be countered by a Taiwanese cruise missile attack on the Three Gorges Dam in the Yangzi Valley, exploiting a key point of economic and environmental vulnerability.

Targeting Information in the form of precise positioning was key to the effectiveness of the missiles. They made use of the precise prior mapping of target and traverse by satellites using GPS, so that the missiles could follow predetermined courses to targets that were actualized for the weapons as grid references. The digital terrain models of the intended flight path facilitated precise long-distance firepower, while the TERCOM guidance system enabled in-flight course corrections. But limitations of information thus inevitably limited the weapons' effectiveness. In the attack on Iraq in 2003, the precision of the cruise missiles and their attacks on Baghdad were presented as the cutting edge of a shock-and-awe campaign that ushered in a new age of warfare. This was overstated, however, and it proved necessary to defeat Iraqi forces on the ground, as in fact ground forces had proved necessary to ensure a favorable outcome in Serbia and a lack of sufficient ground forces spelled failure for cruise missile attacks against terrorist bases in Afghanistan.

Manpower and Platforms Cruise missile guidance systems reflected the importance of complex automatic systems in advanced modern weaponry. The force multiplier characteristics of weaponry had been greatly enhanced and had become more varied. Industrial age mass production was replaced by technological superiority as a key factor in weaponry, not least because of the transformation of operational and tactical horizons by computers.

Skilled personnel using computer systems can direct UAVs (unmanned aerial vehicles) and RPVs (remotely piloted vehicles). These platforms are designed to take further advantage of the missiles by providing mobile platforms from which they can be fired or from which bombs can be dropped. Such platforms do not require on-site crews and thus can be used without risk to the life or liberty of personnel. As a consequence, they can be low-flying, as the risk of losses of pilots to anti-aircraft fire has been removed. This is important in part given the extent to which the fate of captured pilots has, since the Vietnam War, become a major propaganda issue. In addition, at least in theory, the logistical burden of airpower is reduced. So too is the cost, as unmanned platforms are less expensive than manned counterparts, and there are big savings on pilot training. Unmanned platforms are also more compact and "stealthy"—that is, less easy to detect—while the acceleration and maneuverability of such platforms are no longer limited by G-forces that would render a pilot unconscious.

In 1999, unarmed American drones were used extensively for surveillance over Kosovo in order to send information on bomb damage and refugee columns; and, in Afghanistan in 2001 and Iraq in 2003, armed American drones were used as firing platforms. The 26-foot American Predator, with its operating radius of 500 miles, flight duration of up to 40 hours, cruising speed of 80 mph, and normal operating altitude of 15,000 feet, is designed to destroy air defense batteries and command centers. It can be used in areas contaminated by chemical or germ warfare. In the clash between Israel and Hezbollah in Lebanon in 2006, both sides used drones, with the Israelis making particularly marked use of them as an aspect of their aerial dominance and attack capacity. Hezbollah's drones had been provided by Iran, which uses its oil wealth to fund the movement, supplying it via Syria.

Personnel

This emphasis on high-tech weaponry put a premium on skilled personnel, which led to greater military concern about the quality of both troops and training. This encouraged military support for a professional volunteer force, rather than conscripts, a preference that dovetailed with the growing unpopularity of conscription in advanced countries. But volunteer forces raise their own issues. Since military recruitment takes place in a competitive employment market, recruits tend to come disproportionately from disadvantaged groups in the population: the poor, the less educated, and minorities. Maintenance of standards thus becomes crucial if the recruits are to supply the skills the military needs, one reason why the lowering of standards in the face of shortfalls created by the unpopu-

larity of the Iraq War has been so problematic for the U.S. Army since 2006. All-volunteer forces also face size limits, another factor in the force multiplier rationale of the RMA. Faced with a major commitment, the U.S. military has had to make much more prolonged and combat-intensive use of the National Guard, a supposedly part-time militia force, than expected.

The twin pressures of personnel shortages and the need for skilled specialists has led not just the United States but other combatants to contract out some functions, especially logistical and support services, to private sector firms, often with unhappy results. Though the United States, strictly speaking, does not employ mercenary troops, the difficulty of separating combat and noncombat duty in a theater defined by guerrilla operations and unconventional tactics has meant that, in practice, private security firms have effectively assumed some combat roles in occupied Iraq. And professional mercenaries have been open participants in other wars, especially in Africa.

A final personnel issue that intersects in part with the emphasis on technical skill as opposed to sheer brute force is the growing role of women in the militaries of many advanced countries. Formerly restricted to support roles, women are increasingly becoming part of combat units. Although this trend is still hotly debated, it seems irreversible, given both the developments already discussed in terms of weaponry and the need for skilled personnel, and the general cultural movement of Western (and many other) societies toward gender equality as a fundamental principle of human rights. Much the same could be said about the presence of gays in the military.

Technology, Doctrine, Politics

Proliferation and Politics   There was a major expansion in the advanced weaponry held by a number of states in the late 1990s and early 2000s. This was particularly acute in South India. First India and then Pakistan tested nuclear weapons in 1998. That year, Pakistan also test-fired its new Ghauri intermediate-range missile. And the following year; India fired its new long-range Agni 2 missile; its range is 2000–3000 kilometers (1200–1800 miles), extending to Tehran, and covering most of China and Southeast Asia. In March 2003, both states test-fired short-range surface-to-surface missiles that could have been used to carry nuclear warheads. Pakistan, in turn, sold weapons technology to other states, including North Korea, Iraq, Iran, Libya, and, probably, Egypt and Syria. Saudi Arabia likely funded the Pakistani nuclear weapons program and in the late 1980s purchased long-range Chinese missiles. In 2003, Iran conducted what it termed the final test of the Shahabz missile, first tested in 1998. With a range of 1300 kilometers (812 miles), it is able to reach both Israel and U.S. forces located in the region.

These weapon programs were designed to provide regimes with the ability to counter the military superiority or plans of other states. Thus, North Korea saw atomic weaponry as a counter to American power, while Syria sought to develop chemical and biological weapons in response to Israeli conventional superiority. Japan, in turn, felt threatened by North Korea's rocketry, leading, in response, to Japanese interest in antimissile defenses and in satellite surveillance, while the Israelis built up a substantial stockpile of nuclear bombs in response to the chemical weapons of its Arab neighbors. In 2003, Libya abandoned its nuclear program, but Iran proved unwilling to follow suit even after its violations of nuclear safeguards were exposed. Since 2006, this has caused a serious crisis in relations between Iran and the West, with Iran unwilling to back down in the face of international pressure. Were Iran to gain an atomic capability, then other regional powers would probably want one. Indeed, if Egypt, Saudi Arabia, Syria, and Turkey joined Israel, Iran, Pakistan, and India in having such a capability, then the possibility of avoiding nuclear confrontations might be remote.

The RMA Revisited   A continual process of innovation was an aspect of the procurement process, and the cruise missile was far from alone. In 2006, for example, the U.S. Air Force conducted tests in which aircraft used synthetic fuel as part of their jet fuel. Outcome, however, in terms of the desired consequence of action, continued to prove elusive. This indicated that investment in high-tech weaponry could achieve only so much. This represented not only a serious military frustration but also a major political one. The RMA could not suppress risk.

Picking apart the RMA is not some parlor game, but instead is crucial to an assessment of Western capability. As recent years have shown, this is important if appropriate policies are to be followed. As a result, there has been a revival of earlier concepts, such as hearts and minds, with related concerns about training—for example, in operating in built-up areas in the Third World. Technology should therefore be seen as an adjunct to doctrine, rather than as a substitute for it.

A contrast is also readily apparent between sea/airpower and land capability. Superiority in forms of military technology and military-industrial complexes are more important in the former, where their effect is fundamental; but precisely the same forms of superiority in technology and industry have a far smaller impact so far as land power goes. A general theoretical conclusion that emerges is that factors that help provide a capability advantage or cause success (the two are not synonymous) in one context are not necessarily relevant in others. The RMA as an ideology, indeed, is in many respects an airpower ideology.

Far from assuming that the world is an isotropic surface, made knowable, pliable, and controllable by new technology, it is necessary to understand not simply the limitations of the latter but also the limitations of a technology-driven account of capability and change. The alternative is the illusion that fresh technologies can, and thus will, bring new powers, and therefore that problems can be readily banished. That is not the appropriate military analysis and tasking for the twenty-first century.

CONCLUSION

Claims made both in the shadow of atomic weaponry and in the immediate aftermath of the Cold War about the obsolescence of warfare now seem curious and naïve. On the one hand, the transformation of the invasion of Iraq into an imbroglio that defies ready resolution encouraged skepticism in the United States and Britain about the effectiveness of interventionism. On the other, however, the continued extent of conflict in Africa in the 2000s underlines the extent to which reliance on force remains habitual.

At a different level, the military buildup of the major East and South Asian powers—China, Japan, and India—a buildup that also encouraged active procurement by other regional powers, such as Malaya, Pakistan, and Taiwan, reflected a sense that force was a key deterrent and conflict an ever-present possibility.

Alien Ships Outside Roswell   Visions of space-age technology and even battles with beings from other planets often dominate popular images of the future of warfare, as in this "photograph" of alien ships over Roswell, New Mexico. The real future of warfare is likely to be much more mundane (literally, earthly), and to be decided as much, if not more, by social, cultural, and political dynamics as by technological advances.

As far as these and other regional states were concerned, there was an emphasis not on numbers of troops but on advanced weaponry. If the problems facing coalition forces in Iraq after the invasion of 2003 indicated the limitations of the military for regime sustaining and peacekeeping, the investment in East and South Asia reflected a confidence in the value of, or at least need for, such investment for state protection against potential attack by conventional forces.

However, some historians and political scientists point to trends that may make major conventional wars less likely in the future. Two stand out, one material and one cultural. First, the growing interconnectedness of the world economy raises the stakes of potential conflicts and therefore encourages peaceful solutions to disputes so as not to damage valuable trade links. Especially for a growing economy such as China's, which is dependent on foreign investment and markets, such calculations may prove crucial in policy decisions. Second, there is the so-called democracy effect, whose claim is that truly democratic polities have never gone to war with each other. While one can quibble about definitions and qualifications (do the USA and the Confederacy count as separate democratic states? was Germany before World War I democratic?), there does seem to be a tendency here, even if not a "law" of historical development. The slow but steady spread of democratic institutions, governments, and related cultural assumptions (not unconnected to the spread of market mechanisms in the global economy) in the 1990s and early 2000s is thus, perhaps, a hopeful sign for the decreased frequency of state-to-state war, at the least.

Neither trend, however, addresses directly the many and varied causes of substate and nonstate violence, whose cultural complexities resist simple, formulaic solutions. Nor is either trend immune to possible reversals if the contexts that have encouraged them—above all, the spread of economic development and a concomitant rise in personal standards of living—disappear. A worldwide environmental crisis brought on by catastrophic consequences of global warming could create just such a changed context, raising competition for suddenly scarce resources above cooperation in the table of global cultural values. Already, naval expenditures in East and South Asia owe much to confrontations over offshore oil reserves.

Thus, an understanding of the variety of military activities today and the complex contexts in which conflict occurs underlines the need, when looking at the past, to avoid the oversimplifications of a monocausal or monocultural approach to military developments and effectiveness. The absence of such an approach may make military history more complex, but a more complex military history that pays due attention to society and culture better captures the reality of a subject that interacts with so many other aspects of human experience and development.

SUGGESTED READINGS

Barnett, Thomas. *The Pentagon's New Map: War and Peace in the Twenty-First Century*. New York and London: Penguin Books, 2004. An interesting exposition, from a policy-making perspective, of global challenges facing the United States and the force structures necessary to meet them; contributes to the RMA debate.

Black, Jeremy. *War and the New Disorder in the 21st Century*. New York: Continuum, 2004. The future of war analyzed from a global perspective.

Cordesman, Anthony. *The Lessons of Afghanistan*. Washington, DC: CSIS Press, 2002. A rapidly produced but worthwhile work on the 2001 war.

Corera, Gordon. *Shopping for Bombs: Nuclear Proliferation, Global Insecurity, and the Rise and Fall of the A. Q. Khan Network*. Oxford: Oxford University Press, 2006. A well-informed account of a recent and important episode in the global arms trade.

Ferguson, Brian, ed. *The State, Identity, and Violence: Political Disintegration in the Post-Cold War World*. London: Routledge, 2003. An excellent collection of articles, including Ferguson's own, "Violent Conflict and Control of the State," analyzing modern war from an anthropological perspective.

Murray, Williamson, and Robert H. Scales Jr. *The Iraq War: A Military History*. Cambridge: Belknap Press of Harvard University, 2003. A clear account of the conventional military portion of the second Iraq war.

Ovendale, Ritchie. *The Origins of the Arab-Israeli Wars*, 4th ed., London: Longman, 2004. Analyzes the complexity of causation in these wars; includes analysis of the second intifada.

Ricks, Thomas E. *Fiasco: The American Military Adventure in Iraq*. New York: Penguin Books, 2006. A devastating analysis of the Iraq War, from planning through insurgency, by a veteran Pentagon correspondent.

Woodward, Bob. *Plan of Attack*. New York: Simon & Schuster, 2004. An account of the invasion of Iraq in 2003 that focuses on American policy making.

COMMENTARY: PART 6, 1914–PRESENT

Summing up the military history of the twentieth and early twenty-first centuries in a 2000-word Commentary presents special challenges. It is a contradictory and ongoing period—an age of global wars and intensely local conflicts, of wars between the most massive states in world history and wars involving no states at all. And we are so close to it (indeed, are still living it) that we can gain little historical perspective on it, yet at the same time, that closeness heightens the demand for historical lessons drawn from it that might be applicable to the near future. What are we to make of the past century of warfare? How does the perspective of global military history since the dawn of history contribute to this task?

TECHNOLOGY, INDUSTRY, "PROGRESS"

On one level, the character of modern warfare seems obvious. The forces set in motion in the nineteenth century came to fruition, as the industrialization of warfare accelerated and expanded. One face of this, the face most visible in popular presentations of war in venues such as the History Channel, was technological. War became mechanized: For the first time in human history, the tactical speed of armies could exceed the pace of marching men and horses, while the strategic range and rapidity of deployment of modern military forces is unparalleled, as troops move not just overland by rail and truck and by sea but, in massive numbers, by air. Entire weapons systems—tanks, air forces, submarines, ballistic missiles—were conjured up out of the fertile intersection of science and mass production. The destructive power and range of weaponry grew so vast that the entire earth came into the line of fire. Yet at the same time, military medicine improved drastically, though reducing deaths from disease and infection in some ways only heightened the emphasis on wounds and deaths inflicted by weaponry.

Industrialization meant that in the major wars of the twentieth century—World Wars I and II and the Cold War—industrial productivity became the chief multiplier of sheer population numbers in determining great-power status. It also proved to be the grand strategic key to winning conflicts between the Great Powers, whether through the total wars in which entire societies and their economies engaged in the World Wars or through the extended economic competition that eventually decided the Cold War. The necessity of mobilizing entire societies for extended conflicts contributed significantly to the intensely ideological character of much modern warfare, even when the ideologies themselves were not necessarily military in origin. Propaganda, the mass production of ideology, became in the twentieth century a necessary component of major war efforts.

As a result of industrialization and its effects, warfare in the twentieth century partook of a general characteristic of the age: profligacy. Production and resource usage soared, dwarfing the consumption levels and global environmental impact of all previous human history combined, growth that both allowed and was spurred by unprecedented population explosion. But the costs of warfare in material production and destruction and, above all, in human lives, also soared, though the success of humanity (so far) in avoiding falling over the precipice of massive nuclear exchanges has meant that profligacy in production has far outpaced the stunning profligacy of destruction of the past century.

In the writing of military history, this story has most often been cast in the mold of "progress" (though the scale of destruction has sometimes blunted the triumphalism of that concept as it had been conceived of in the nineteenth century). Progress, in technological advancement, in the dominance of great powers, and often in the values for which wars were fought, was often associated in this sort of historiography with the "Western" world: Western technology and science, Western powers, Western ideologies (whether democratic, capitalist, or communist). The rest of the world from this perspective was the recipient, via diffusion, of Western inventions. In its most polemical and inaccurate form, this became an argument about the superiority of a "Western way of war." Even in more nuanced forms, it involved assumptions about who the players in conflicts were and would be and about how wars were and would be fought. By the beginning of the twenty-first century, many of these assumptions had been exposed as, at best, incomplete.

Culture and Politics: Diffusion to Confusion

The events of September 11, 2001, did little to change the realities of modern warfare, but they did much to change perceptions, especially in the advanced industrial democracies. The major terrorist attack within the borders of the United States exposed to Western view complexities in the patterns of warfare that had been obscured by the dominant "great power–diffusionist–progress" paradigm, though in many other parts of the world and many other eras in the past, the complexities of reality had already been readily apparent and successfully exploited by some.

The view of war as an activity conducted lawfully between states—war as "politics with an admixture of other means," as Clausewitz put it—had now to accommodate the obvious reality that much war in the present involved intrastate, substate, and non-state actors who did not always, or even reliably, play by "the rules." Attempts to understand such conflict led historians and anthropologists to new (or rediscovered) understandings of the many forms of warfare in the past that did not conform to the state-centered assumptions of the progress paradigm. The prevalence of decentralized conflicts in the late twentieth and early twenty-first centuries, and the role of warfare in fragmenting some modern states and turning others into failed states, served as a reminder that, as the history of warfare can show since the beginnings of organized communal violence, there is no straightforward or necessary correlation between warfare and state power. The complexities of this relationship have been one of the foci of the history of war presented in this book.

Nor is there a simple correlation between superior technology and military success, as the victories of guerrilla fighters in conflicts ranging from decolonization struggles to insurgencies, as well as the low-tech means deployed by many terrorists, attest all too abundantly. Here, too, we find affirmed one of the recurring themes of this work: that technology is essentially a dependent variable in the equation of warfare. In other words, the uses to which particular technologies are put vary significantly depending on the social and cultural contexts in which they are deployed. In terms more directly relevant to conditions of modern warfare, there is often a significant difference between output and outcome, between the sheer productive capacity of a state's military-industrial infrastructure, qualitatively and quantitatively, and the ability of that state to achieve its grand strategic and political goals, as the problems the United States has encountered in Iraq tragically illustrate. Conversely, the use of certain technologies does not necessarily lead to certain forms of military, never mind social, organization. Technological determinism is a historiographical nonstarter.

While one set of the determinants of how technology is used for warfare can be fit comfortably into materially based social science analysis of social and economic structures, much recent conflict has highlighted the role of cultural perceptions in the causes and conduct of war. This is especially true of the construction, often by self-interested parties, especially leaders or would-be leaders, of identity and interest groups around cultural factors including ethnicity and religion. Here, too, historical precedents are many, and another consistent theme of this book has been the influence of culture on how societies organize and conduct war. But the evidence of history also cautions against oversimplified and essentialized notions of culture: Claims for "clashes of civilizations" are as polemical as claims for "Western ways of war" and fail to capture the complexity of cultural reality. Cultures are never monolithic. They are composites of different subgroups (themselves constructed or perceived in different ways) with different interests and perspectives. Thus, identity is always multiple and contested, as much at the level of civilizations or nation-states as at the individual and small-group level. Dominant constructions are subject to counternarratives and reinterpretation, and so the connection between culture and war, like that between war and state formation, or war and technology, is complicated and contingent. But one thing that this view of culture and its impact on war highlights is the role of the writing of history—official, academic, popular, and polemical—in constructing the contexts for conflict or, conversely, in constructing contexts that militate against conflict.

THE FUTURE IN THE PAST

Such a conclusion inevitably leads, at the end of a book such as this, to the question of where the world is headed with respect to conflict and warfare. Historians have generally proven no better than anyone else at predicting the future, and any detailed prediction would look foolish even more quickly than a general one will. But we can make some general points based on a broad reading of military history and the themes contained in this book.

Logically, one might predict three broad paths for the future of warfare. Things could continue much as they are now in terms of the amount of warfare; the amount of warfare could decrease; or the amount of warfare could increase. Of course, sheer number of wars is not the sole question here: One war that featured a general exchange of nuclear weaponry would be more than sufficient to exceed the current level of military destructiveness. And the difficulty of encompassing all the different levels of warfare from great-power confrontations to substate and nonstate actions in one analytical framework is significant. But, on the assumption that stasis is, in fact, the least likely path for the future of warfare, let us examine briefly the optimistic and pessimistic views of the future of war.

There is a not uncommon view that the continuing effects of globalization in tying states and regions together into interdependent economic spheres and in broadening and deepening cultural communications and understanding will tend to decrease the incidence of warfare, at least at the state level. The same forces of economic globalization, to the extent that they enrich everyone who participates, will, in this view, ease tensions within states and thus militate against civil and indenterest conflict. The spread of democracy and the political scientists' observation that democracies do not go to war with each other add to the optimists' forecast.

On the other hand, critics of globalization point to the vast inequalities between and within nations that capitalism tends to create and that by many measures have worsened recently. Such inequalities, in this view, will remain a powerful incentive toward armed conflict. But the more compelling pessimist case rests on critical examination of the assumed context for the optimists' case. Above all, they question whether continued economic growth on the current model is environmentally sustainable. Given the reality of global warming, the question becomes one of managing the consequences. Should the consequences become extreme in terms of coastal flooding, drastic shifts in climate and thus agricultural production, and breakdowns of communications and trade networks, many more parties might find it rationally conceivable to defend their share of a shrinking pie by force.

The frightening parallel here is to the conditions that, in the view adopted by this book, gave rise to warfare in human history in the first place, raised to a global scale. Hierarchy and inequality exist; exacerbated, they provide ready ammunition for the use of demagogic leaders interested in aggrandizing their power (war makes leaders, and leaders make war). Add a sudden resource crisis brought about by a significant environmental change, and the conditions that led to the invention of warfare more than 12,000 years ago could lead to its reinvention (an apt word especially if the optimist case proves more correct up to the crisis point) at a global scale whose consequences are unimaginable.

Should this come to pass, warfare will have become the failure of politics with an admixture of other means, and democratic culture—perhaps human culture—will be the victim.

Credits

Index